Sunbelt Revolution

Florida A&M University, Tallahassee
Florida Atlantic University, Boca Raton
Florida Gulf Coast University, Ft. Myers
Florida International University, Miami
Florida State University, Tallahassee
University of Central Florida, Orlando
University of Florida, Gainesville
University of North Florida, Jacksonville
University of South Florida, Tampa
University of West Florida, Pensacola

Sunbelt Revolution

The Historical Progression of the Civil Rights Struggle in the Gulf South, 1866–2000

Edited by Samuel C. Hyde Jr.

University Press of Florida

Gainesville · Tallahassee · Tampa · Boca Raton
Pensacola · Orlando · Miami · Jacksonville · Ft. Myers

08 07 06 05 04 03   6 5 4 3 2 1

Library of Congress Cataloging-in-Publication Data
Sunbelt revolution: the historical progression of the civil rights
struggle in the Gulf South, 1866-2000 / edited by Samuel C. Hyde, Jr.
p. cm.
Includes bibliographical references and index.
ISBN 0-8130-2577-X (cloth: alk. paper)
1. African Americans—Civil rights—Gulf States—History. 2. Civil rights
movements—Gulf States—History. 3. Gulf States—Race relations.
I. Hyde, Samuel C., 1958–
E185.92 .S87 2003
323'.0976'09034—dc21   2002035880

The University Press of Florida is the scholarly publishing agency
for the State University System of Florida, comprising Florida A&M
University, Florida Atlantic University, Florida Gulf Coast University,
Florida International University, Florida State University, University
of Central Florida, University of Florida, University of North Florida,
University of South Florida, and University of West Florida.

University Press of Florida
15 Northwest 15th Street
Gainesville, FL 32611-2079
http://www.upf.com

Contents

Part III. Forward toward an Elusive Goal

Figures

Acknowledgments

Those who have embraced the challenge of coordinating the evolution of a diverse set of ideas forward to the development of a cohesive compilation well understand the difficulties involved. There are also many rewards, not the least of which is the opportunity such a project affords for highlighting the significance of cutting-edge research as well as coming to know scholars maintaining similar interests. In the final regard, I was particularly fortunate. Each of the contributors worked diligently in the face of pressing time constraints while committed to the vision inherent in the purpose of this volume.

Even the best intentions can result in unexpected demands upon many. This project could not have been completed without abundant assistance from many individuals. The staff of the Center for Southeast Louisiana Studies at Southeastern Louisiana University stoically endured the endless deadlines and frequent disruptions in their own routines through the course of the project. A special word of thanks is due Lois Wagner for her clerical support as well as Victoria Mocsary and Anna Clark for their efforts in the photo lab. Brad Bond, Charles Elliott, and Randy Sanders each provided constructive criticism of portions of the manuscript. Randall Miller and Stan Harrold kindly provided critical commentary that enhanced both the quality and the purpose of the project. Larry Powell and Ray Arsenault furnished crucial insight and facilitated the acquisition of key elements of the volume. I am deeply grateful for their contributions.

This venture marked my first with the University Press of Florida. Meredith Morris-Babb and her staff exhibited the highest degree of professionalism, maintaining a kind and considerate demeanor despite my regular diversions from their normal expectations. Their courteous consideration and commitment to scholarship sustained the project through times of stress.

For those who do not understand, this final word may seem bizarre. During the course of this project, Joey Ramone succumbed to a long illness. Those who found release in the manic beats and mindless chants central to any Ramones tune readily acknowledge the sad denouement our world experienced through the loss of this musical pioneer. No matter what collar we may wear today, once a punk always a punk. In his last days Joey remarked that, despite what is said by others, the Ramones truly enjoyed the greatest fans because they liked *only* the Ramones. It is in the spirit of the positivism his music evoked and his ability to judge people by their love of life, not by their skin color or political persuasion, that Joey is herein remembered.

Introduction

The Challenges and Expectations of Social Change
in the Gulf South, 1866–2000

SAMUEL C. HYDE JR.

"Sun and sin—that is what makes this region the best place to live," a party-loving friend once boldly declared. The eight or nine months of summer common to the states bordering the Gulf of Mexico no doubt command the envy of many Americans residing in cooler regions. Indeed, few areas of the Gulf South have escaped the implications of steady migration to a region once ridiculed, now increasingly regarded as a haven from the cold, expensive North. As for sin, one need only consider the overt sexuality evident along the vast beaches of Florida, the centrality of vice along the Mississippi coast, or the multifaceted decadence of Bourbon Street in New Orleans to acknowledge the power of its appeal. While certainly attractive to many, the regional allure has nonetheless never been unanimously perceived. The blistering heat of the sun and its concomitant oppressive humidity can often prove as shocking to those paying air-conditioning bills as to those unaccustomed to the sultry climate. Likewise, the playful sinfulness has repulsed the deeply religious nearly as much as the excesses, such as the extralegal violence of the Ku Klux Klan, have incensed African Americans.

Paradise amid hell—an appropriate adage that may describe the enviable paradox that is the Gulf South. The contradictions of the region have long been acknowledged, but often remain buried within larger studies of the South. It may seem surprising to some that the territory comprising the core of what is now known as the "Sunbelt" long remained a decided backwater in the annals of southern history. Despite the increasing allure of long summers, mild winters, and miles of sandy beaches that attract ever growing numbers of visitors, most historical accounts continued to emphasize the eastern seaboard and upper South. Writing in 1995, John B. Boles alluded to the institutional neglect of the region, declaring, "The South's history after 1607 is often thought of as the progress of English settlement across a grand sweep of a continent occupied only by decreasing numbers of Indians, and the presence of French and Spanish settlers is only incidentally noted as background to the Louisiana Purchase and later to the controversy over the annexation of Texas. Yet the cultures of Spain and France left a deeper impress on the region from Florida to Texas than the short shrift given them in most histories suggests."[1]

More recently, numerous studies have done much to correct the imbalance in southern history by highlighting development in the states of the Gulf South.[2] Yet the proverbial surface has barely been scratched, particularly so regarding the scores of issues and events that characterized the progression toward human dignity across the region. Seemingly countless studies highlight the course and development of the civil rights struggle across the nation, yet it remains difficult to identify a reliable source devoted to explaining the historical emergence and evolution of the movement in the states bordering the Gulf of Mexico. The Gulf South offers exceptionally rich resources for identifying less publicized struggles that contributed mightily to the overall progress of the movement. Advancing understanding of the smaller issues that characterized the distinctive pattern of development in the Gulf South, as well as our awareness of how events there shaped the course of national identity, remains a primary purpose of this volume.[3]

The collection of essays included in this book serve to highlight how events centered in the Gulf South contributed to the course and progression of the civil rights movement nationwide. Moreover, the essays encourage scholarly reconsideration of the region suggesting that the states of the Gulf South should more appropriately be regarded as pioneering in relation to the movement for civil rights rather than merely as champions of the resistance to change. Such a perspective demands a subtle variation in terminology. For generations historians and other observers have spoken of the Deep South rather than the Gulf South; some regard the expressions as synonymous. The two terms nonetheless connote subtly distinctive regions as well as identities.

Deep South traditionally serves as a pseudonym for describing all of the states bordering the Gulf of Mexico with the addition of Georgia and South Carolina. While it is often used to distinguish the region from the upper South and the border states, during the course of the civil rights struggle the term was frequently associated with the hardest resistance to social change. Many observers embrace the perspective presented by journalist Robert Sherrill, who in 1968 proclaimed that the Deep South's "resistance to integration has left the region thoroughly discredited. In social matters, in humanistic affairs of the nation, its motives are properly suspect and its word is generally viewed as worthless." In short, in the minds of some, Deep South assumed a decidedly negative imagery. Gulf South by contrast involves exclusively the states bordering the Gulf of Mexico, or more specifically those regions whose development was shaped largely by proximity to the Gulf. While it may have once referred exclusively to an alluvial plain, Gulf South now serves as a standard expression commonly found in tourist guides and other popular descriptive accounts of the region. Far from suffering from a negative stereotype, Gulf South suggests the future, opportunity, and potential for a higher quality of life—attributes that seem most appropriate in a volume dedicated to celebrating the struggle for equality among those less fortunate and ones that remain in sharp contrast with the antebellum connotations of Deep South. Students of the region enjoy the opportunity of viewing civil rights era events from one of two distinct perspectives, that of the hardened opposition to change consistent with attitudes in much of the Deep South, or from those who pioneered the reform efforts, many of which this volume will demonstrate first emerged in the states bordering the Gulf of Mexico. The optimism apparent in a volume primarily highlighting those who fought for civil rights, rather than one emphasizing individuals and groups resistant to change, suggests that Gulf South is the more appropriate descriptive term for the studies included here.[4]

The survey area precisely includes Florida, Alabama, Mississippi, Louisiana, and the region of east Texas influenced more by contact with the Gulf than by environs to the west. The specific geographic focus of the volume may cause some readers to question the inclusion of studies concentrating on, say, Montgomery, Alabama. While obviously not located on the Gulf Coast, Montgomery clearly remains part of the Gulf South, subject to the cultural and demographic shifts associated with the progressive migration to the warmer, more humid environs of the region. Montgomery also witnessed a civil rights struggle that in many regards pioneered an optimism the nonviolent movement embraced for ultimate success—a virtue consistent with the vision presented here of Gulf South and one that remains in sharp contrast with standard pessimistic notions of the Deep South. A survey of recent scholarship reveals the emergence of Gulf South as an appropriate appellation to describe all of the territory encompassing the states bordering the Gulf of Mexico. Studies by James Dormon, Loren Schweninger, and others include discussion of diverse areas such as Natchitoches, Louisiana, in the northern portion of that state and St. Augustine, Florida, along the Atlantic coast, within their surveys of Gulf South ethnic groups.[5]

Regionalism remains a theme central to any study of a subsection. Students of southern history typically acknowledge that social and political development in the Gulf South remains as curious as the region is distinctive. Initially fashioned during a colonial period characterized by the permeating influences of Spain and France that rivaled the force of the British contribution evident in the eastern seaboard states, the Gulf South enjoys a rich cultural heritage. Separate from the northeast and upper South, which looked to the Atlantic and beyond for contributions to development, the states of the Far West who shared many aspects of identity with the Pacific and Central America, or even the midwestern states who lay claim as "America's heartland," the Gulf South has been subject to a combination of influences that cultivated a colorful pattern of development.

In the years preceding the 1954 *Brown v. Board of Education* decision, many of the same circumstances that contributed to the region's distinctive identity provided a basis for hope among those who demanded the extension of basic rights to black southerners. Much of the encouragement centered on the obvious influences occasioned by regional proximity to the Caribbean. Despite enduring a harsh slaveholding period of its own, by the mid-twentieth century the islands of the Caribbean were popularly regarded as relaxed tourist destinations boasting a carefree carnival atmosphere that seemed to transcend any lingering racial animosities. The Creole tradition evident in Tampa, Mobile, New Orleans, and Galveston, among other areas of the Gulf South, caused some observers to speculate that the drastic social restructuring desegregation would occasion might best be received in those areas long accustomed to a close proximity, if not blending, among the races. Historians such as Gwendolyn Midlo Hall and Kimberly Hanger have argued that a "frontier fluidity" characterized much of the region, a multicultural milieu in which white, black, and Creole created functioning networks among themselves. Some even speculated that the economic bonanza, evident yet undeveloped, along the sandy beaches of the Gulf South could contribute to collective advancement that would mitigate the pain of desegregation. Still others looked to the pervasive influence of Catholicism along the Gulf Coast as an important determinant of events to come. Most of the region endured at least temporary Spanish overlordship during the course of colonial development where adherence to Roman Catholicism was actively encouraged. The Catholic Church's more moderate position regarding slavery, in comparison to many Protestant perspectives, as well as its long tradition of incorporating peoples of all races and classes into individual parishes provided a potential basis for reconciliation of the races on an equal footing that remained virtually absent in most regions of the upper South. In his analysis of the connection between the humane treatment of slaves and favorable race relations, Frank Tannenbaum ranked Spanish holdings among the best and British territories worst, noting that both the Catholic Church and the Spanish legal system accentuated the slaves' humanity in contrast to the Anglo Protestant emphasis on individualism and the preeminence of property rights.[6]

History has shown that optimism proved premature. Some of the most violent events characterizing the civil rights struggle nationally occurred in the Gulf South. Enumerating that history, or more specifically the historical progression of the civil rights process, serves as the second distinctive feature evident in this collection. Often erroneously identified as a movement that originated in the aftermath of World War II, the essays demonstrate that the struggle to overcome oppression, and advance the standing of the newly freed slaves, emerged during Reconstruction and developed with increasing force through the late nineteenth century and into the early twentieth. Rather than examining the twentieth century exclusively, or simply events directly connected to the 1954 *Brown* decision, the essays demonstrate that the struggle for equality has remained an ongoing process that continues today. Moreover, the included essays further reveal that development in the Gulf South did not occur in a vacuum. Far from being a backwater to the earlier settled eastern seaboard, in terms of the civil rights struggle, the states of the Gulf South contributed massively to defining the means for challenging oppression as well as to shaping the most ferocious resistance to minority advancement. This volume in no way seeks to claim that events associated with the struggle for equality in other areas remained secondary to those in the Gulf South. The brutal acts of violence practiced against black Americans in other regions of the South, like the calls for massive resistance in Virginia and the courage evident in the Greensboro, North Carolina, lunch counter sit-ins, among other milestones, burn brightly in the annals of the civil rights struggle.

Nonetheless, whether one thinks of Reconstruction, Jim Crow, the sheer numbers of extralegal murders and intimidation, or freedom rides and marches, events in the Gulf South always remain at the forefront of casting a national identity.

The Gulf South can arguably be considered the region most essential to determining the course of the civil rights struggle from its inception. Unlike the North, where slavery had ceased to exist by the early nineteenth century, and many states of the eastern seaboard and upper South, where slavery proved in decline, by the late antebellum period the states bordering the Gulf of Mexico served as home to an expanding and hardening slave system. On the eve of the Civil War, life for African Americans may very well have remained at its worst in the Gulf South and immediate surrounding environs. Likewise, Gulf South residents applied some of the most aggressive means identifiable for inhibiting black assertiveness. It is the magnitude of the challenge confronting Gulf South minorities that initially attracted the interest of many of the contributors to this volume. The authors included here represent diverse interests and perspectives. Some of the essays provide new perspectives on well-known events. Others highlight inherent contradictions in the movement while some seek to recast our understanding of the meaning and relevance of certain issues and events. A couple challenge the traditional focus and/or method for interpreting specific incidents; others remind us that there was more than one oppressed group in the Gulf South. Despite a certain eclecticism, their research remains faithful to a common theme, the critical role played by people, places, and events in the Gulf South to determine the course of the civil rights struggle.[7]

The first section of the book, entitled "Regional Initiatives, National Implications," includes essays that may be among the volume's most controversial. The two selections suggest that many of the initial elements necessary to forge a determined civil rights movement first appeared in the Gulf South. Just when that movement began to take form serves as the focus of the first contribution.

The destruction of the slave system facilitated the inception of a civil rights movement that was furthered by the passage of the Fourteenth and Fifteenth Amendments. As the struggle progressed, a powerful weapon of change developed in the form of the civil rights march or demonstration. In an effort to identify the origin of demonstrations in support of civil rights, Jim Hollandsworth builds upon his earlier analysis of the Louisiana Native Guards to suggest that the first such march occurred in imme-

diate postwar New Orleans. According to Hollandsworth, the Union occupation of New Orleans in April 1862 permitted the emergence of black
assertiveness years earlier than that found in other areas of the South. His
study indicates that as early as the fall of 1863, blacks initiated limited
demonstrations to secure constitutional rights. Building upon a developing base and emboldened by the defeat of Confederate arms, in the summer of 1866 Crescent City blacks embarked upon what Hollandsworth
argues may have been the first coordinated civil rights march in American
history. Seemingly prophetic of how such events would be received in the
future, the sheer ferocity of the white reaction to the demonstration has
assigned it to history as the 1866 New Orleans Race Riot.[8]

The riot served notice that whites remained uncompromising in their
determination to maintain the racial status quo. Through a difficult period of Reconstruction, and for the remainder of the nineteenth century,
Louisiana joined many of her sister states of the Gulf South at the forefront of violent resistance to black advancement. As they had in the antebellum period, events in the Gulf South, and specifically Louisiana, would
continue to shape the course of race relations for the country as a whole.[9]

The year 1896 proved one of dramatic consequence. The Populist Revolt pitted desperate farmers and laborers in an unprecedented struggle to
determine the course of national identity. The combination of impoverished black and white laborers that characterized the Populist movement
across the South provoked a determined reaction from the ruling Bourbon elite. In their effort to smash an emerging class consciousness that
transcended racial barriers, the governing elite extended limited rights to
poorer whites in order to further the notion of racial superiority. The
most dramatic example of the effort to divide and rule emerged in the
1896 *Plessy v. Ferguson* decision, which ultimately gave legal sanction to
the very pillar of segregation, the "separate but equal" clause. Despite the
devastating implications the decision maintained for black advancement,
as well as the legal standing it afforded intensifying racial oppression, it
did not dissuade continuing assertiveness on the part of individual African
Americans.

Shortly before his untimely death in 1999, Joseph Logsdon completed
a study that dramatically demonstrated black efforts to challenge the racial injustice overtly manifest in the *Plessy* decision. Enhanced through
some posthumous editing by his friend and colleague Lawrence Powell,
the Logsdon essay furthers the line of argumentation raised by Jim Hollandsworth that identifies New Orleans, or more specifically the black

Creole community residing there, as crucial to sustaining African American defiance in the face of ever hardening racial attitudes and laws. While much of the nation applauded the racially accommodating rhetoric of Booker T. Washington, in New Orleans Rodolphe Lucien Desdunes directed a principled stand against the increasing restrictions of segregation. Far from a movement that merely responded to events, Logsdon argues that Desdunes and his followers remained at the forefront of a relentless challenge to racial oppression from the close of the Civil War into the early twentieth century. Even more significant, their efforts produced a legacy of resistance, providing a blueprint for the coordination of boycotts and legal challenges that inspired a new generation of activists including such noted reformers as A. P. Tureaud. In short, Logsdon's essay suggests the centrality of events in the Gulf South to the emergence of the national civil rights movement as well as in sustaining the effort through its darkest days.

Essays complexifying our understanding of those who suffered under segregation, the curious mechanisms employed to sustain an unjust society, and venues where determined individuals gathered to coordinate the challenge to racial oppression during the darkest days of Jim Crow constitute Part II of the collection, entitled "Black, Brown, and White: Confronting and Accommodating Jim Crow." Scholars have long acknowledged the central role black churches played in advancing African American demands for justice. The formidable power traditionally wielded by black ministers in their respective communities made them among the most effective of civil rights advocates. Among the most identifiable churches associated with the movement was Dexter Avenue Baptist Church in Montgomery, Alabama. Serving as the initial pulpit for Dr. Martin Luther King Jr. as well as ground zero for the Montgomery bus boycott, this church continues to attract considerable scholarly attention. In a refreshing new approach to analyzing the relevance of black churches in the civil rights struggle, Houston Roberson examines life at the Dexter Avenue Baptist Church between 1883 and 1920 with emphasis on the ministry of Robert Chapman Judkins.

Roberson's study reveals the complex fusion of accommodation and activism that characterized the cautious move toward justice at the turn of the twentieth century. Ever conscious of working within the parameters assigned to blacks by white society, the congregants of Dexter Avenue considered the building itself, looming prominently in the heart of the original capital of the southern Confederacy, to be an important statement of the spiritual righteousness inherent in their struggle. Although the reality of their condition demanded caution, it did not prevent the emergence of subtle yet significant activism. Like Joe Logsdon, Roberson concludes that during the transitional years marking the close of the nineteenth century and continuing into the early twentieth century, significant traditions of black protest were established that defined the pathway to eventual success.

The civil rights struggle is often regarded as almost exclusively an African American issue. While blacks may have emerged as the primary beneficiaries of civil rights legislation, they were not the only oppressed group residing in the Gulf South. Nowhere was the racial complexity that characterized certain regions of the Gulf South more obvious than in Texas. Although Mexican Americans avoided the enslavement central to defining black identity, they endured equally callous discrimination if not persecution. In an essay that forces an expanded approach to analysis of the civil rights struggle, Rebecca Montes argues that during the painful years of the Great Depression Texas longshoremen created a racial hierarchy that assigned the bottom rung to brown laborers.

The potential of the International Longshoremen's Association to challenge racial discrimination in the early twentieth century foundered on the racial ideology common to Texas and the wider South. Black workers, strictly segregated into separate locals, used their second-class status within the union to dramatize the detrimental effects segregation maintained for society in general. Mexican American laborers, attached to white locals, encountered more intense challenges to advancement. Montes argues that while both black and brown laborers, as well as the union itself, suffered as a result of white racism, their inability to overcome the additional stigmatization assigned to foreign immigrants ensured that the Mexican Americans struggled more. Not exactly white under the prevailing code of racial categories, and maintaining a distinctive culture made obvious by their foreign language and intense devotion to Catholicism, the Mexican Americans remained suspect citizens. The ultimate losers of such racial categorization were the longshoremen collectively whose inability to overcome division within their own ranks ensured their own continuing exploitation.

As the nation moved out of the economic depression that characterized the 1930s and initiated the first substantive steps to curtail the overt racial violence common to the Bourbon period in the South, new methods emerged to sustain white supremacy. White efforts to inhibit African

American advancement would largely be responsive to enhanced initiatives from the black community. Improving economic conditions, as well
as the return of servicemen from Europe after World War II, encouraged
a newfound assertiveness among black Americans. The large minority
population in every state of the Gulf South encouraged black leaders to
explore their undiscovered power at the ballot box. Equally aware of the
unrealized implications an empowered black electorate posed to their
very way of life, members of the existing political establishment sought
mechanisms to replace terror tactics that had facilitated white supremacy
so effectively since the close of the Civil War. One of the most effective
weapons emerged in the form of the white political primary.[10]

In his survey of the curious history of Florida's white primary, Gary
Mormino reveals the strategic considerations that produced this new
method of racial oppression. In Mormino's analysis, the white primary
provided a flexible mechanism to prevent African Americans from voting.
By vesting the power to determine voting qualifications in the hands of
local and state party committees, white political leaders skillfully circum-
vented the legal demands inherent in the Fifteenth Amendment. The
white primary also facilitated the emergence of powerful deterrents to
voting such as the poll tax and at-large elections designed to dilute black
voting strength. The destruction of the white primary ultimately served as
a sign of black advancement. Critical court rulings in the 1940s, including
the *Smith v. Allwright* decision, undermined this form of white resistance
to black political participation. With the demise of the exclusive primary,
its white supporters lashed out in a tragic spasm of violence that left key
figures in the primary's destruction dead in its wake. Events in Florida
demonstrated that even though federal courts could mandate change,
they could not ensure white acceptance of reform.

The historic *Brown* decision provided an unstoppable impetus for social change. With the legal weapons in place to facilitate reform, many
residents of the Gulf South courageously tested their newfound power
despite the danger of challenging the status quo. Just how severe the challenge would be, and how sweeping the social transformation should go,
serves as the focus of the final section, entitled "Forward toward an Elusive Goal." White resistance emerged as only one of the challenges confronting black leaders as they continued to demand change. As the call for
civil rights secured increasing legitimacy after World War II, the movement began to experience some growing pains. One of the newly emerging concerns centered on the need to accommodate the desire of some

activists to sustain a homegrown movement of and for southern blacks with the increasing expectations of the national civil rights movement. Again, Gulf South developments emerged at the forefront in defining the course of events.

In 1956 attention turned to Montgomery, Alabama, where an ill-defined bus boycott was shaping into a major test of wills. What began as a local demand for equitable treatment soon emerged as one of the more significant dramas following the 1954 *Brown* decision. Ray Arsenault maintains that the Montgomery bus boycott provided a learning ground from which a successful formula for challenging racial oppression in the South was first debated and then institutionalized.

Arsenault's study emphasizes the contributions of two outsiders who came to Alabama in the midst of the boycott, Bayard Rustin and Glenn Smiley. He argues that each played a critical role in developing a successful strategy and advancing the movement in general. According to Arsenault, Montgomery became a testing ground for resolving competing theories of racial adjustment. At Montgomery, where even most moderate whites seemed unable to compromise, national civil rights advocates came to appreciate the courage and determination of southern blacks as well as the emotional power of African American religious beliefs. Meanwhile, local civil rights leaders had to acknowledge their financial dependence on national organizations and embrace the compelling benefits of the nonviolent direct action advocated by Rustin and others. What emerged from the fusion of Gulf South grassroots activism and the international appeal of nonviolence was a movement culture that provided a common language, a common perspective, and a unified vision to advance the cause.

Boycotts of public transportation in defiance of the demeaning race-based seating assignments that characterized such services across the South became one of the most visible and energizing methods of challenging segregation. While the Montgomery bus boycott captivated the popular imagination, it remained only one of numerous such actions. Some have argued that Montgomery activists capitalized on the pioneering accomplishments of those who participated in the brief 1953 bus boycott at Baton Rouge, Louisiana.[11] Regardless of the origins, the Montgomery action immediately inspired similar boycotts across the Gulf South.

One of the most convoluted series of events occurred in Tallahassee, Florida. In his essay, Greg Padgett demonstrates that events in Tallahassee reveal the challenges presented by the factional disputes prevailing

Figure I.1. Blacks in Baton Rouge congregate to secure free rides from supporters during the 1953 bus boycott. Photo courtesy Ernest Ritchie, Rembrandt Studio Collection, Plaquemine, Louisiana.

within the ranks of civil rights activists. At Tallahassee the fierce divisions separating activists and accommodationists within the movement emerged in full force. Padgett describes the bitter mistrust prevailing between moderates and radicals, the use of force by activists to enforce participation in the boycott, and the mechanisms of intimidation employed by white racists to overcome the boycott. Although influenced by events at Montgomery, the peculiar circumstances at Tallahassee encouraged black leaders to avoid a media circus and instead concentrate on securing their goal through education and enhanced political participation. In the end, Padgett challenges those who believe that the Tallahassee activists achieved less than a clear victory. He argues instead that the Tallahassee boycott marked the emergence of a sophisticated ability to adapt to local circumstances within the movement in the Gulf South.[12]

Few dispute that national civil rights organizations played a critical role in securing continued success for the movement. The extent of the contribution provided by national organizations and the proverbial "outside agitator" does, nonetheless, remain a subject for debate. Events in

Tallahassee and other cities across the Gulf South suggest that despite encouragement and support from outside, the movement could not sustain itself, much less succeed, without an exceptional level of commitment from local activists. Some of the most intense resistance to change emerged in Mississippi. Along with thousands of facilities, parks, and recreational areas across the state, Mississippi's coastal beaches remained the exclusive domain of whites. Moreover, the beaches served as a high profile reminder of the absence of egalitarianism afforded black Mississippians. In an essay certain to impact the debate concerning local activists' ability to coordinate independently initiated action to a successful conclusion, Pat Smith examines the desegregation of the beaches and the forces that contributed to success.[13]

When considering events in Mississippi, the popular imagination is typically drawn to the fierce resistance to the voter registration drives, the murder of three young civil rights workers in Neshoba County, and the widespread violence associated with the desegregation of the University of Mississippi. Non-Mississippians played prominent roles in each of these episodes. But several years earlier—preceding even the Greensboro, North Carolina, lunch counter sit-ins that first provided a national audience for nonviolent direct action protests—several citizens along the Mississippi Gulf Coast initiated a homegrown direct assault on segregation independent of the national organizations. Smith argues that resistance to the wade-ins, as the actions to desegregate the beaches were known, provoked a ferocious, equally homegrown reaction that included apparent official complicity in the bloodiest race riot in Mississippi history. Despite the expected resistance, local leaders' exemplary courage in the face of repeated reprisals for the wade-ins eventually inspired their supporters with an unflinching determination to carry on. According to Smith, emboldened by their eventual success on the beaches, the local wade-in leaders initiated Mississippi's first successful modern black voter registration drive, filed the state's first school desegregation suit, and played a major role in revitalizing the Mississippi conference of the NAACP. Local leaders' understanding of, and personal familiarity with, many of their adversaries as well as their ability to work with, rather than simply direct, the local black population proved central to their pioneering success along the Gulf Coast.

In Mississippi, black leaders frequently regarded local police as a major obstacle to their advancement. During the wade-ins, many believed that police complicity had facilitated white resistance to the activists. As the

1960s progressed, images of police violence against civil rights demonstrators became a regular feature of national news broadcasts. Their outright assaults on activists, as well as their alleged sympathy with reactionary forces embodied in such organizations as the Ku Klux Klan, rendered law enforcement personnel in the states of the Gulf South highly suspect. The final selection in this volume discusses the uses and implications of state police power as white southerners confronted increasing social change. Through comparative analysis of the highly publicized incidents of police abuse that characterized the movement in Alabama, Mississippi, and other areas, Roman Heleniak reveals the peculiar pattern of state police involvement that emerged in Louisiana.

Heleniak's essay centers on the pivotal role played by Louisiana governor John McKeithen. Like other governors in the Gulf South, McKeithen secured election as a segregationist, albeit a moderate one. Yet unlike Mississippi's Ross Barnett, or Alabama's George Wallace, McKeithen refused to employ his state police in an effort to sustain segregation. Although McKeithen secured widespread acclaim for his stand from the national media, Heleniak cautions against viewing McKeithen as a true progressive, suggesting the practical considerations of Louisiana politics assumed ultimate responsibility for the governor's decision. By 1964 Louisiana boasted the largest voting bloc of blacks anywhere in the Gulf South, numbers that were certain to dramatically increase with the passage of the Voting Rights Act of 1965. Running what some have called the "three hat campaign," in which he advocated a different perspective before each respective constituency, McKeithen secured election as the lesser of evils to both white extremists and black activists.[14]

Even though McKeithen's well-known national political aspirations would be advanced by a progressive stand, Heleniak argues that the true character of the man emerged in his direction of the state police. In contrast to the governors of neighboring states, McKeithen used the Louisiana state police to protect black activists and to facilitate the progression toward racial equality. Even more significant, McKeithen permitted the integration of the state police at a time when other states regarded their troopers as a bulwark in defense of segregation. In the 1960s, McKeithen opened the door to black participation in a respected state agency, yet the troubled history of the Louisiana state police through the course of the late twentieth century demonstrates the continuing elusiveness of equality. Indeed, the subtitle of Heleniak's essay, "A Work in Progress," may aptly summarize the continuing struggle for equality in the Gulf South.

*   *   *

Years ago, one of my first graduate projects dramatically influenced my understanding of southern history. The assignment required students from the South to conduct a survey of desegregation in their home parish/county. My home region, Tangipahoa, Louisiana, maintained the dubious distinction of enduring one of the most violent patterns of development evident in rural America. The white-on-white violence contributing to the reputation of "Bloody Tangipahoa" captivated the popular imagination; little media or scholarly interest centered on the black struggle. During the course of numerous oral history interviews with influential black residents in my hometown, I was shocked to learn that the conditions they had faced were not merely the stuff of Hollywood and distant places but instead the reality of life for my own neighbors. Struggling to overcome the traditional preconceptions and prejudices common to those reared in small southern towns, I determined to embrace a sympathetic understanding for conditions I had previously underappreciated. When I uncomfortably asked a prominent black minister if he believed things had truly changed, his response seemed designed both to enlighten and to reassure. "Son, the fact that you are here with me now demonstrates just how far we have come."[15]

Like my hometown, the Gulf South has come a long way. A civil rights movement initiated in the immediate aftermath of the Civil War and continuing into the present has contributed to the emergence of a higher quality of life for all residents. As in the rest of the nation, problems continue, but to those aware of the vast advances in sympathetic understanding and human compassion that have characterized the transformation of the Gulf South from the close of the antebellum period to the present, the change has simply been remarkable. A new era of dialogue and accommodation prevails in a region that once championed racial violence to sustain white supremacy. For black Americans the process has been slow and painful; for many whites the change has been far less traumatic than expected. Healthier race relations have contributed to the emergence of an emotional security that comes when one is at peace—and peace remains a quality long absent in the Gulf South that the residents are unlikely to relinquish willingly.

Notes

1. John B. Boles, *The South Through Time: A History of an American Region* (Englewood Cliffs, N.J.: Prentice Hall, 1995), 45.

2. For some examples of this trend, see Bradley G. Bond, *Political Culture in the Nineteenth-Century South: Mississippi, 1830–1860* (Baton Rouge: Louisiana State University Press, 1995); Nadine Cohodas, *The Band Played Dixie: Race and the Liberal Conscience at Ole Miss* (New York: Free Press, 1997); Samuel C. Hyde Jr., *Pistols and Politics: The Dilemma of Democracy in Louisiana's Florida Parishes, 1810–1899* (Baton Rouge: Louisiana State University Press, 1996); Christopher Olsen, *Political Culture and Secession in Mississippi: Masculinity, Honor, and the Antiparty Tradition, 1830–1860* (New York: Oxford University Press, 2000); J. Mills Thornton, *Politics and Power in a Slaveholding Society: Alabama, 1800–1860* (Baton Rouge: Louisiana State University Press, 1978); Ralph Wooster, *Civil War Texas: A History and a Guide* (Austin: Texas State Historical Association, 1999).

3. Immense volumes of research highlighting the civil rights movement continue to appear. Among the most useful studies are Taylor Branch's *Parting the Waters: America in the King Years, 1954–1963* (New York: Simon and Schuster, 1988) and *Pillar of Fire: America in the King Years, 1963–1965* (New York: Simon and Schuster, 1998); Clayborne Carson, *In Struggle: SNCC and the Black Awakening of the 1960s* (Cambridge: Harvard University Press, 1981); Manning Marable, *Race, Reform, and Rebellion: The Second Reconstruction in Black America, 1945–1982* (Jackson: University of Mississippi Press, 1991); Aldon Morris, *The Origins of the Civil Rights Movement: Black Communities Organizing for Change* (New York: Free Press, 1984). For more recent treatments highlighting aspects of the civil rights struggle in the individual states of the Gulf South, see Thomas Cole, *No Color Is My Kind: The Life of Eldrewey Stearns and the Integration of Houston* (Austin: University of Texas Press, 1997); Charles Eagles, *Outside Agitator: Jon Daniels and the Civil Rights Movement in Alabama* (Chapel Hill: University of North Carolina Press, 1993); Glen Eskew, *But for Birmingham: The Local and National Movements in the Civil Rights Struggle* (Chapel Hill: University of North Carolina Press, 1997); Adam Fairclough, *Race and Democracy: The Civil Rights Struggle in Louisiana, 1915–1972* (Athens: University of Georgia Press, 1995); John Dittmer, *Local People: The Struggle for Civil Rights in Mississippi* (Urbana: University of Illinois Press, 1994); Charles Payne, *I've Got the Light of Freedom: The Organizing Tradition and the Mississippi Freedom Struggle* (Berkeley: University of California Press, 1995); Glenda Rabby, *The Pain and the Promise: The Struggle for Civil Rights in Tallahassee, Florida* (Athens: University of Georgia Press, 1999).

4. Robert Sherrill, *Gothic Politics in the Deep South: Stars of the New Confederacy* (New York: Grossman, 1968), 2. For an upbeat discussion of society and culture in the Gulf South, see James H. Dormon, *Creoles of Color of the Gulf South* (Knoxville: University of Tennessee Press, 1996). Less positive discussions of the Deep South can be found in Allison Davis, Burleigh Gardner, and Mary Gardner, *Deep South: A Social Anthropological Study of Caste and Class* (Los Angeles: Center for Afro-American Studies, Univer-

sity of California, 1988); John B. Martin, *The Deep South Says Never* (New York: Ballantine Books, 1957); Cecil Williams, *Freedom and Justice: Four Decades of the Civil Rights Struggle as Seen by a Black Photographer of the Deep South* (Macon, Ga.: Mercer University Press, 1995). In his recollections of the challenges that confronted civil rights workers, Howell Raines expanded the definition to include North Carolina. See Raines, *My Soul Is Rested: Movement Days in the Deep South Remembered* (New York: Putnam, 1977).

5. See James Dormon's preface and Loren Schweninger, "Socioeconomic Dynamics among the Gulf Creole Populations: The Antebellum and Civil War Years," both in *Creoles of Color*, ed. Dormon, ix–xiv, 51–63.

6. Gwendolyn Midlo Hall, *Africans in Colonial Louisiana: The Development of Afro-Creole Culture in the Eighteenth Century* (Baton Rouge: Louisiana State University Press, 1992), xiii–xiv; Kimberly Hanger, *Bounded Lives, Bounded Places: Free Black Society in Colonial New Orleans, 1769–1803* (Durham: Duke University Press, 1997), 2–3; Daniel H. Usner Jr., *Indians, Settlers, and Slaves in a Frontier Exchange Economy: The Lower Mississippi Valley before 1783* (Chapel Hill: Institute of Early American History and Culture by the University of North Carolina Press, 1992). While these studies concentrate primarily on Louisiana, they suggest a similar pattern prevailed across much of the Gulf South. For discussion of similar circumstances in other regions of the Gulf South, see Virginia Gould, "The Free Creoles of Color of the Antebellum Gulf Ports of Mobile and Pensacola: A Struggle for the Middle Ground," in *Creoles of Color*, ed. Dormon, 28–50; Frank Tannenbaum, *Slave and Citizen: The Negro in the Americas* (New York: Knopf, 1947).

7. For recent descriptions of the slave system in the Gulf South and surrounding environs, see Bradley Bond, *Political Culture in the Nineteenth-Century South;* Randolph Campbell, *An Empire for Slavery: The Peculiar Institution in Texas, 1821–1865* (Baton Rouge: Louisiana State University Press, 1991); Hyde, *Pistols and Politics;* Clarence Mohr, *On the Threshold of Freedom: Masters and Slaves in Civil War Georgia* (Athens: University of Georgia Press, 1986); Larry Rivers, *Slavery in Florida: Territorial Days to Emancipation* (Gainesville: University Press of Florida, 2000).

8. James G. Hollandsworth, *The Louisiana Native Guards: The Black Military Experience during the Civil War* (Baton Rouge: Louisiana State University Press, 1995).

9. For descriptions of post–Civil War violence in Louisiana, see Hyde, *Pistols and Politics,* 139–212; Ted Tunnell, *Crucible of Reconstruction: War, Radicalism, and Race in Louisiana, 1862–1877* (Baton Rouge: Louisiana State University Press, 1984); Joe Gray Taylor, *Louisiana Reconstructed, 1863–1877* (Baton Rouge: Louisiana State University Press, 1974); Gilles Vandal, *Rethinking Southern Violence: Homicides in Post–Civil War Louisiana, 1866–1884* (Columbus: Ohio State University Press, 2000).

10. For a sample of studies detailing violence against blacks in the late nineteenth and early twentieth centuries, see Horace Mann Bond, *The Star Creek Papers* (Athens: University of Georgia Press, 1997); W. Fitzhugh Brundage, *Lynching in the New South: Georgia and Virginia, 1880–1930* (Urbana: University of Illinois Press, 1993); Fairclough, *Race and Democracy;* Hyde, *Pistols and Politics;* James R. McGovern, *Anatomy of*

a Lynching: The Killing of Claude Neal (Baton Rouge: Louisiana State University Press, 1982); George Rable, *But There Was No Peace: Violence and Reconstruction Politics* (Baton Rouge: Louisiana State University Press, 1978); George C. Wright, *Racial Violence in Kentucky, 1865–1940: Lynchings, Mob Rule, and Legal Lynchings* (Baton Rouge: Louisiana State University Press, 1996).

11. *The Baton Rouge Bus Boycott* (Baton Rouge: McKinley High School Summer Oral History Project, 1998).

12. Adam Fairclough, *To Redeem the Soul of America* (Athens: University of Georgia Press, 1987), 43.

13. For a discussion of the debate concerning the relationship between national organizations and local activists, see Morris, *Origins of the Civil Rights Movement,* 12–16, 40–50, 128–34.

14. The late professor of history at LSU and longtime Louisiana historian Mark T. Carlton is credited with developing the term "three hat campaign" to describe Mc-Keithen's tactics in the 1964 election. Fairclough, *Race and Democracy,* 378–88.

15. For references to Bloody Tangipahoa, see New Orleans *Times Democrat,* July 4, 1897; New Orleans *Daily Picayune,* June 15, July 4, 12, 1897; Hodding Carter, "Not Much of a Man If He Hadn't," *Southern Legacy* (Baton Rouge: Louisiana State University Press, 1966), 48–63; Hyde, *Pistols and Politics,* 199–262; interview of Reverend Willard Vernon, Amite, Louisiana, October 15, 1982.

I

Regional Initiatives, National Implications

"Damned Sons of Bitches"

The First Demonstrations for Black Civil Rights in the Gulf South

James G. Hollandsworth

It is easy to forget that the civil rights movement in the United States began in the nineteenth, not the twentieth, century. Histories of the movement tend to reinforce this oversight when they fail to acknowledge the contributions of civil rights activists more than a hundred years ago. For example, the chronology in Ralph E. Luker's *Historical Dictionary of the Civil Rights Movement* starts in 1941. In *Weary Feet, Rested Souls: A Guided History of the Civil Rights Movement*, Townsend Davis begins his survey in 1954. Although it is understandable that sixty years of Jim Crow may have obscured the memory of early activists, there was a civil rights movement in the nineteenth century, and its accomplishments, such as this country's first civil rights legislation, should not be forgotten.[1]

Activists in the nineteenth century were interested in the same civil rights that their counterparts wanted a century later—equal accommodation on public transportation, access to public schools, parks, and libraries, and the right to vote. The issue of black suffrage was particularly important, for participation in the electoral process was necessary to complete the successful transition of the South from a slave to a free society.

Civil rights for black Americans were hardly an issue before the Civil War when slavery was the law of the land. It was not until the Fourteenth Amendment in 1866 that the prospect of black civil rights became a reality. Nevertheless, a large community of free blacks in New Orleans did not wait for Congress to act before expressing their demand for civil rights.

In late September 1862, Paul Trévigne, a prominent free man of color who had taught in a Catholic school for black children before the war, began editing *L'Union*, a biweekly French-language newspaper that advocated civil rights for free blacks. "We inaugurate today a new era in the South," Trévigne wrote in *L'Union*'s salutatory editorial. "We proclaim the Declaration of Independence as the basis of our platform.... You who aspire to establish true republicanism, democracy without shackles, gather around us and contribute your grain of sand to the construction of the Temple of Liberty!" Trévigne continued to promote civil rights for free blacks in *L'Union* throughout 1862 and into 1863.[2]

What might be considered to be the first public demonstration for black civil rights in the Gulf South occurred on November 5, 1863, when an enthusiastic crowd converged on the Economy Hall to demand that free men of color be enfranchised. Some of the speakers were white men, Unionists who sought to establish a common cause with their free black neighbors. But free black leaders set the tone. "They did not ask for social equality, and did not expect it," P. B. S. Pinchback, a former captain in the Louisiana Native Guards, told the audience, "but they [free blacks in New Orleans] demanded political rights—they wanted to become men."[3]

In January 1864, free blacks in New Orleans circulated a petition for black suffrage and selected two delegates to represent their interests in Washington. The two men they selected, Jean Baptiste Roudanez (an engineer) and Arnold Bertonneau (a wine merchant), were well educated, prominent businessmen. Bertonneau had also served as an officer in the Louisiana Native Guards. Leaving New Orleans in mid-February, they met with President Abraham Lincoln in his office on March 12, 1863, and delivered a petition signed by a thousand of their black compatriots. The president remained noncommittal during the interview, but apparently he had been impressed by the black emissaries, for the next day Lincoln composed a confidential letter to the Union governor of Louisiana, Michael Hahn. "I barely suggest, for your private consideration," Lincoln wrote, "whether some of the colored people may not be let in [i.e., enfranchised], as, for instance, the very intelligent, and especially those who have fought gallantly in our ranks." Although Hahn waited to release the contents of the letter until after Lincoln's death more than two years later, the notion of black suffrage had been endorsed at the highest level more than a year before the war ended.[4]

Back in New Orleans, Trévigne did not wait for Roudanez and Bertonneau to return before taking the quest for civil rights a step further by demanding suffrage for all black males, regardless of their status as free men or freedmen. The qualification to vote should be based on "the rightful capacity of all native and free born Americans by virtue of their nativity in the country, irrespective of national descent, wealth or intelligence," Trévigne argued in *L'Union*, "and that all not free, within the state, be immediately enfranchised by the abolition of slavery in the state forever, and by a statute or constitutional provision declaring the absolute equality of all free men as to their governmental rights."[5]

Although some free men of color believed that limited suffrage based on strict qualifications was still the best way to gain political equality with whites, the majority decided to join forces with freedmen and present a united black front. The result of this decision was the formation of the Equal Rights League in January 1865, an early civil rights organization committed to black suffrage regardless of whether the voter owned property or had an education.

The Equal Rights League's hopes were dashed, however, when thousands of former Confederates returned home at the end of the war and attempted to regain political and social dominance. President Andrew Johnson's amnesty proclamation in May 1865 and the wholesale distribution of pardons in the months that followed enfranchised all but a handful of these rebels, allowing them to elect Confederate veterans and secessionists to office. By the end of the year, most southern states were under the control of the same men who had led these states out of the Union four years earlier.[6]

The return of former Confederates to power meant the ouster of Union loyalists in Louisiana who had been elected to political offices during the war. These were the men Abraham Lincoln had encouraged to set up a "Free State" government while secessionists were off fighting in the Confederate Army or living as refugees beyond federal lines. But Lincoln's death created a void that no one, least of all the new president, could fill. Lacking strong support or direction from Washington, Unionists in Louisiana were powerless to halt the erosion of what they had gained during the war. The weakness of their position was highlighted in the fall of 1865 when a newly elected state legislature passed a series of laws that reinstated the oppressive Black Code used before the war to control Louisiana's slave population.

Louisiana Unionists had failed to heed the call for black suffrage during their brief tenure in office. Even whites who had remained loyal to the Union were reluctant to offer the ballot to citizens of African descent. But with the success of former Confederates in seizing the reins of government after the war, some Unionists realized that black suffrage was the only tool they had to stem the conservative tide.

The Unionist plan for enfranchising black males was notable for its simplicity. In April 1864, the military commander of the Department of the Gulf, Nathaniel P. Banks, had convened a convention to draft a new constitution for Louisiana. The document it produced abolished slavery but left the question of black suffrage to the legislature. The Free State legislature that assembled under the provisions of the new constitution had failed to give black males the vote, and the conservative legislature that convened after the war was unwilling to consider the issue. Nevertheless, members of the constitutional convention who favored black suffrage had refused to give up.

The convention had adjourned in 1864 with a proviso that allowed it to reconvene at a later date. Seizing on this parliamentary loophole, a handful of former delegates decided to bypass the conservative legislature by reconvening the convention and amending the constitution to disfranchise former Confederates and enfranchise blacks.

Most whites in Louisiana believed that reconvening the constitutional convention was illegal and that this blatant bid for power would surely fail in the courts. Some white leaders thought that it would be best to ignore these proceedings, but many whites did not like the idea of black suffrage being promoted at all, regardless of its chances for success.[7]

On Friday night, July 27, 1866, supporters of the constitutional convention gathered at the Mechanics' Institute. The meeting actually consisted of two rallies that went on simultaneously. Speakers in the main hall told the audience about their plans to reconvene the convention and presented a set of resolutions in support of the venture. The former Union governor of Louisiana, Michael Hahn, was there, as were other white supporters of the convention. The audience was composed mostly of professionals and small businessmen. The speakers endorsed black suffrage but urged restraint. Be patient, keep calm, one of them told the audience. Do not force the issue too strongly, for doing so might jeopardize their success.[8]

The meeting outside the Mechanics' Institute on Dryades Street (now University Place) was very different than the one inside. A crowd of three to five hundred men, black and white, had gathered in front of a wooden stage erected especially for the occasion. Coal oil lamps were placed on the stage to illuminate the speakers. Boys with torches stood on the pavement to provide more light.[9]

The temper of the speeches outside was more militant than those inside. "We have got you your freedom; we have fought for your freedom," Dr. A. P. Dostie, a white dentist with radical views, shouted. "Now will you fight for your votes?" he asked. "We will, we will," came a response from the crowd, followed by a chant: "Fight to vote! Fight to vote!" again and again. Dostie then invited members of the audience to come to the Institute on Monday to show their support for the convention. It was like an old-time political rally with cheers and shouts. This time, however, the cries were from black men who had been excluded from the political process but who now saw the prospect of suffrage within their grasp.[10]

By ten-thirty the speeches were over, and two or three hundred men started off on a torchlight procession from the Institute, down Canal Street and along St. Charles Avenue to City Hall. Dostie led the way with a United States flag by his side. The mood in the procession was defiant. As the marchers passed whites standing on the banquette, they cheered and jeered, waved their hats, and gestured.[11]

Arriving at City Hall, Dostie climbed the steps and gave an impromptu speech. His speech was not long, but it was passionate. Referring to the black marchers as his brothers, Dostie exhorted them to stand firm in the face of opposition to their cause. "Now friends, go home peaceably, quietly; make no noise; disturb no person; but . . . I learn . . . that there are prowling bands of armed men out to waylay you," he warned. "If you are insulted by any of these bands of men, pay no attention to them. Go home right by them without saying a word to them, but if they strike you, kill them."[12]

Reports of the Friday night rally were in all of the papers Saturday morning. "The Radical Mob . . . Threatens and Thunders" read a headline in the New Orleans *Times*. The article portrayed the assembly as "a large crowd of those who aspire to become American citizens without distinction of color." The leaders were described as "the most uncharitable set of white men it has been our ill fortune to look upon for many a day," and the various speeches were characterized as "embittered elaboration," "a tirade of abuse," or "drivellings." The New Orleans *Daily Picayune* described the participants as "extreme fanatics" and condemned A. P. Dostie especially for his remarks on the steps of City Hall.[13]

Although the reference in the *Daily Picayune* to Dostie's remarks was accurate, the newspaper reported erroneously that speakers at the rally had urged blacks to arm themselves to defend the convention. In reality, some of the speakers had asked the crowd to stay away, not wanting to give the police an excuse to intervene.[14]

Despite these warnings, a large crowd gathered in front of the Institute on Monday morning, July 30. The group included black men, women, and children dressed in their Sunday best. For them, it was a special occasion, a time to celebrate, and their eager anticipation showed. Supporters of the convention inside the building, however, were concerned that the large gathering would provide an excuse for the police to break up the meeting.[15]

Down the street, a large crowd of white men had gathered at the corner of Canal and Dryades. A few policemen were on duty there, but not enough to control things should they get out of hand. The day was exceedingly hot, "as hot as any day [that] summer," a physician recalled. By noon the mercury had risen to ninety-two degrees.[16]

Unbeknownst to the people inside the Institute, a procession of black men that had formed in the Third District marched through the French Quarter on their way to the Institute to voice their support for black suffrage. The nucleus of the procession was made up of Union army veterans. They had seen action under fire—Port Hudson, Mansura, and Fort Blakely. Unafraid of a fight, they were armed with pistols, broomsticks, and weighted canes. At their head were three drummers, a man with a fife, and a man with a tattered American flag—the battle standard, some said, of the Louisiana Native Guards.[17]

The procession marched down Dauphine to Conti, where it turned right for one block to Burgundy and then left toward Canal. It gained recruits along the way—black men who left their work to join the demonstration. One had a carpenter's saw, another a cotton hook. The procession grew until it filled the street. Its members were determined, unafraid, and vocal, but they conducted themselves with orderly restraint. On they marched, a compact group of seventy to a hundred men, all headed toward an inevitable collision with the volatile throng on Canal.[18]

At noon, just as the convention's president pro tem called the meeting to order, the head of the procession reached the intersection of Canal and Dryades. Three young white men standing on the banquette jeered the flag bearer. The black man waved his flag defiantly in response. Two of the men leaped from the banquette and attempted to seize the colors. Several blacks in the procession responded, and the two men went down, crawling back on their hands and knees.[19]

At the rear of the procession, a group of white men traded insults with the black marchers. A white boy of twelve or thirteen who worked on a city streetcar shoved one of the marchers to the pavement with an oath: "Go away, you black son of a bitch." Whites on the banquette urged the boy on. The black marcher got up and hit the boy. J. A. Elmore, a Confederate veteran and now a special officer for the City Railroad Company, intervened. Pulling back the lapel of his coat to display a badge, Elmore told the black man to stop hitting the boy. "God damn police officer," the marcher swore when he turned toward Elmore. Elmore pulled his revolver. "I'll shoot the first man that strikes me," he warned. At that instant, someone hit Elmore with a heavy stick on the right side of the face. Legs numb, Elmore felt pins and needles. Instinctively, he fired his pistol and missed. Edward Crevon, an aid to the chief of police, was on the scene and saw who had hit the detective. Crevon dragged the assailant out of the procession and hurried him down Canal Street toward the lockup.[20]

Suddenly, someone fired a shot at the procession from a coffeehouse on the corner of Burgundy and Canal. Several members of the procession returned fire, six shots or more, scattering people in every direction. The three drummers beat the "long roll," just as they had during the war to rally the troops on the field of battle. "Fall in boys," they cried, "rally, boys." The procession pushed across Canal and down Dryades. The two groups traded insults as the last of the marchers cleared the street, but for the time being the potential for an explosive outburst was held in check.[21]

The crowd of convention supporters greeted the procession excitedly when it reached the front of the Institute. The black veterans gave three cheers, and the crowd cheered in return. The flag bearer stood on the steps of the Institute, waving his banner defiantly at the whites on Canal.[22]

Several members of the procession went inside and up the stairs to the hall, taking the flag with them. Most of the procession stayed in the street and mingled with the crowd sitting on the banquette in front of the building. New Orleans chief of police Thomas Adams, who had been at the Common Street end of Dryades when the procession arrived, walked past them on his way toward Canal. "All those people up the street are rebels and should be cleaned out," a black man in front of the Institute remarked as the chief walked by. Adams let the comment pass, not wanting to provoke a confrontation. For the moment, the situation remained calm, and Adams decided to return to his office.[23]

The atmosphere among the black supporters continued to be festive. Some of the men had been drinking, and a few of them began to show the effects of alcohol. Concerned that the celebration was getting out of hand, some members of the convention inside the Institute sent a black man into the street to ask the crowd to disperse. This was not a public meeting, the man told them; go away and be quiet. But they would not go and cheered even louder. Another black man, older than the first, also addressed the crowd, asking them to go home. He, too, was unsuccessful.[24]

Shortly before one o'clock, the trouble started again. The white boy who had tangled with the procession when it crossed Canal Street ventured up Dryades and began taunting the convention supporters. "Damned sons of bitches!" he yelled. Several black men with sticks separated themselves from the crowd and began moving toward the boy. The boy retreated toward Canal Street until he came to a pile of bricks, building material for a house under construction. There he made a stand, a brick in each hand, and dared the men to touch him. One of the police officers on duty at the corner of Canal and Dryades saw what was happening and rushed up from behind. Grabbing the boy by the collar, the officer ordered the black men with sticks to stay back. "Take him away and kill him," one of the black men yelled as the officer dragged the boy down the street. "No, no; let him go," shouted the crowd of whites on Canal. Several of the black men followed as far as the pile of bricks. Stopping there, they began throwing bricks at whites on the corner. And then it happened. One of the black men pulled out a revolver and fired.[25]

The whites on Canal rushed up the street toward the Institute, firing their pistols as they came. The black men behind the pile of bricks retaliated with shots of their own. The two sides clashed briefly and then fell back. Two black men were left lying on the pavement, one dead and the other dying. A third lay close by, badly injured. Several whites wounded during the skirmish were carried off by their friends.[26]

The white mob rallied in Canal Street. Many of the men were armed with revolvers; some carried bricks, clubs, and stones. A young man held a bloody slug shot with black hair stuck to it. "What is that," Rush Plumly, a former superintendent of education for the Freedmen's Bureau, asked the young man. "I have just killed a nigger with that," he boasted.[27]

Some of the police and a few citizens attempted to restore order. Charles Beyer, a second lieutenant in the 81st Infantry, United States

Figure 1.1. A white mob attacks black demonstrators during the New Orleans race riot, July 30, 1866. *Harper's Weekly.*

Colored Troops, was in Ricketson's Confectionery when he heard the firing. Someone in the store wondered aloud whether something could be done to prevent bloodshed. Beyer said he would try. Running out into the street, he accosted a policeman and asked him to help. "You go to hell," the officer replied. Refusing to give up, Beyer placed himself in front of the whites on Canal Street and tried to keep them back. A few policemen joined him in the attempt. One man with a brick in each hand refused to obey. Beyer knocked the bricks out of his hands, and the man pulled a knife out of his boot. "You Yankee son of a bitch," he sneered as he made a sweeping cut at Beyer. A policeman came to Beyer's aid and smashed the man across the head with his nightstick. For a few minutes, the commotion died down. Someone suggested bringing up one or two fire engines to drench the crowd with water, but no one paid attention.[28]

Chief Adams was sitting in his office at the main police station on Lafayette Square when a young clerk came running through the door. "It has started," he blurted. "The negroes are shooting at people on the sidewalk." Adams decided that it was time to order the police to the Mechanics' Institute. Adams knew that he could depend on his men to keep rowdy blacks under control, for they had been Confederate soldiers. Mayor John T. Monroe had seen to that as soon as he had assumed office in May by dismissing officers who had served in the Union Army and replacing them with Confederate veterans. Although a handful of former Yankees whose special skills made them difficult to replace had been retained, about two-thirds of the 499-man force had served in either the Confederate Army or the Louisiana Militia during the war.[29]

Adams sent word to his men by the fire-police telegraph. The system consisted of the thirteen large alarm bells located strategically throughout the city, usually on the steeples of prominent churches. The signal for the police was twelve taps on the alarm bells. Since the city was divided into nine fire districts, the twelve-tap signal would not be confused with a real fire alarm. Nor would the twelve-tap signal be confused with the fire department's general alarm, which was twenty taps. Adams gave the word to the telegraph operator in charge of the system, and he sent out the twelve-tap signal from his desk. It was one o'clock.[30]

The police in Lafayette Square formed into ranks and started up St. Charles as soon as they heard the alarm bell. They turned left at Poydras and then right on Carondolet. From Carondolet they went up Common until they reached Baronne, where a detachment split off to cover the rear of the Institute. The remainder continued up Common toward Dryades.[31]

When Police Sergeant Lucien Adams heard the alarm bell, he called for his men to assemble outside the First District substation on the corner of Pecanier and Terpsichore. "I want you to make yourselves very active," he told them as they filed out the door. "Make yourselves lively; see what you can do." Almost two miles from the Institute, they would have to hustle to get there in time.[32]

The fifty-four men fell into line on the banquette. They were veterans of many battles and certainly not afraid of a fight. They started off at a trot with Adams and his two corporals in the lead. The band turned right on Camp and continued until they came to Lafayette Square as the first prisoners were coming in. Some of Adams's men wanted to tear into them. Adams motioned them off; there was more important work to do.[33]

Police from the Second District converged on the Institute from two

Figure 1.2. New Orleans Mechanics' Institute, scene of the worst fighting during the race riot, July 30, 1866. *Harper's Weekly.*

stations, one at Tremé Market and the other in the arsenal behind the Cabildo on Jackson Square. "Gentlemen," Lieutenant William H. Manning told his men when he heard the alarm, "I want you all to do your duty." At the Tremé station a corporal went into the yard at the sound of the twelve taps and asked for ten volunteers. Ten men stepped forward and followed the corporal up Dauphine to Canal. The two detachments of police from the Second District reached the intersection of Canal and

Dryades about ten minutes after the alarm sounded. "Boys, keep quiet and cool," Lieutenant Manning ordered. "No one move before I give you orders." One of the blacks in the street near the Institute fired a shot at the crowd. "Clear the street," Manning ordered. Twenty policemen advanced in a skirmish line, just as they had done during the war. About fifty members of the white mob tagged along behind.[34]

A single black man stood at the pile of bricks as Manning's men advanced. When the police were almost on him, he took off down the street. Several black men hid in doorways along Dryades and fired at the police as they swept up the street. The police returned fire as these men raced from one doorway to the next. Thomas Cooney, who had once served as General Banks's bodyguard, jumped up on the pile of bricks. "Come on," he urged the police. "Don't stand back and be cowards." Some blacks rushed inside the Institute, but many of them continued up Dryades across Common to escape.[35]

Manning's men caught up with a few blacks here and there. One police officer prodded a tall black man with a full beard by hitting him repeatedly over the head with the butt of his revolver. The black man did not strike back but shielded his head and face with his hands, protesting each blow. Satisfied that he had taught the man a lesson, the officer turned his attention to two black men headed toward Common on the opposite side of the street. One of the men was Charles Gibbons, the former captain in the Louisiana Native Guards, who had joined the procession on its way to the Institute. The policeman recognized him. "There goes one damned nigger captain, the son of a bitch," he cried. "Kill him." Gibbons and his comrade, a veteran of the same regiment, began to run. "Let's turn around, and we may have a chance to dodge the balls," Gibbons yelled to his companion. They had used this trick during the war. He had gone about ten steps backward when his friend let out a groan and put his hand to his side. "I am shot," the friend cried. "I am killed." Gibbons turned and ran as fast as he could. He made it as far as the corner of Common and Baronne before he ran into the police from Lafayette Square on their way to the Institute. The street was now sealed, and blacks who had not made it across Common before the police arrived were trapped inside the Institute.[36]

Dryades itself was empty, except for three black bodies. The police kept the large crowd of whites back on Canal. For the moment, order had been restored. The police spread out, surrounding the Institute, and prepared to deal with the convention itself. Two delegates to the convention,

Cyrus W. Stauffer and James Duane, watched from the entrance of the building as the police took up their positions. "Jim," Stauffer remarked, "they look as if they are going to come for us."[37]

And come they did. Members of the white mob followed close behind the police and joined in the fray. Attacking supporters of the convention who had sought refuge on the ground floor of the Institute, the police dragged them out into the street, where they were beaten and arrested. Once the ground floor was clear, the police turned their attention to the people in the meeting hall upstairs. Although they repelled three attempts by the police to force their way into the room, supporters of the convention finally surrendered, only to be assaulted as they were herded outside.

There was an absolute crush of people at both ends of Dryades at Common and Canal. These were mostly civilians. In front of the Institute there was a smaller but more aggressive force made up mostly of police but with a number of civilians mixed in. Together, they outnumbered the convention delegates and spectators five to one.[38]

Supporters of the convention coming out of the Institute had no choice other than to make a run for it. When one appeared, the mob would "run for him like dogs after rats coming out from a wharf," as one observer put it. The mob fired indiscriminately as the blacks emerged. "Here come those black sons of bitches," one cried as he opened fire. A black man attempted to beat his way through the crowd with the back of a chair. He made it as far as Common Street before he went down with several pistol balls in his body. The scenario was repeated over and over. Whites at both ends of Dryades intercepted blacks who made it through the mob in front of the Institute. First, they would shoot until the man was brought down. Then the mob would close in and pound the victim with bricks and clubs until he was dead.[39]

When Michael Hahn came out, the crowd went wild. "There's old Hahn!" they cried. "Kill him! Hang him!" Two policemen held him on each side. Hahn had a club foot, and his long crutch stuck out in front. When they reached the edge of the banquette, someone fired a shot. Hahn drew himself up to his full height, as if to challenge the would-be assassin. Then someone threw a brick, which struck Hahn on the back of the head, and his feet went out from under him. The policemen called for Chief Adams, who was on the other side of the street. Adams helped push the crowd back, knocking down several citizens in the process. The crowd closed in again, and the police protecting Hahn had to beat them back. The police retrieved Hahn's crutch and carried him along toward Common. Adams commandeered a carriage on Carondolet and started back to Dryades. "My life is in danger," Hahn cried out to Adams as he turned to go. "I insist upon your going with me." Adams assented and climbed aboard with one of his officers. Even then the crowd closed in, and the policeman pulled out his revolver and dared anyone to interfere. "The man is dying," he cried. "Leave him alone." The carriage started off down the street with Adams and his colleague guarding their prisoner all the way to the lockup.[40]

Dr. Dostie's appearance sent the crowd into a frenzy. "There's Dostie," they yelled. "Kill him! Kill him!" The police escorted Dostie up Dryades toward Canal. They had gone only a short distance when the mob closed in. The police released Dostie and backed away. A small boy picked up a brick and threw it at Dostie, and several of the crowd moved in with their revolvers drawn. "You assassins," Dostie muttered as a man in shirt sleeves and white pants fired. Dostie staggered, and the policemen again took his arms. "Protect me, protect me," he implored. A man in a grey linen coat behind Dostie fired a shot into the Doctor's back. The ball severed his spinal column. Dostie fell forward on his face. Using his arms, he rolled over on his back and put his hands over his eyes. Still, the mob would not let him be. A group of men with white handkerchiefs tied around their necks grabbed Dostie by his legs and started dragging him down Dryades. The Doctor's head bounced on the pavement. When they reached Canal, the men stopped in front of a cake shop and gave a cheer for Jeff Davis.[41]

On Dryades the scene was wild. The shrill sound of police whistles filled the air, and there was much yelling. "Hurrah for hell!" a drunken rowdy waving a pistol yelled. "Hurrah for Louisiana!" Another man stood in the street, with clenched fists and tears in his eyes. "It's a shame! It's a shame," was all he could say.[42]

The police had lost control. Men were running everywhere. Vagrant boys joined in the fun. They had been too young to fight in the war; now it was their turn to do battle. "Now they are going to get it!" they cried with glee.[43]

As the riot progressed, the mob was strengthened by the arrival of unemployed whites and low-life types who were naturally attracted to trouble. Many of these men were drunk. A large man of about thirty on a brown horse with crutches tied to the saddle rode amongst them, urging them on. When each time a member of the convention was brought out, he would yell, "Kill those damned convention sons of bitches." A Confederate veteran who had lost both arms during the war shouldered his way

Figure 1.3. White New Orleanians collecting the bodies of black victims of the 1866 race riot. The massacre was arguably precipitated by the first civil rights march in American history. *Harper's Weekly.*

through the crowd urging them on. "Kill all the damned sons of bitches in the building," he yelled. "Don't let any escape."[44]

More and more civilians were swept away in the ebb tide of fury. Mary Ann Larkin, an Irish prostitute, chased several black men as they fled. Hair flying and clothes disheveled by her pursuit, she screamed, "Kill the black sons of bitches, kill the black sons of bitches." Finally she caught up with one who had been slowed by the stroke of a club in the hands of one of the mob. The two fell together. Larkin had a broken sword-cane about six inches long and cut him across the face and chest and once in the arm, which stuck out stiff like a mannequin. Satisfied, Larkin jumped up and ran after some other blacks she spied down the street, although by then she was too breathless to catch them.[45]

The violence continued throughout the afternoon until the streets in the vicinity of the Institute had been cleared. Belatedly, the U.S. Army arrived at four o'clock to assume control, but by then it was too late. The number of dead and wounded will never be known with certainty. The surgeon at Sedwick Military Hospital, Dr. Albert Hartsuff, counted "thirty-seven certainly, and ten more probably, killed on the side of the convention, against a single citizen on the side of the city authorities." Hartsuff also noted that although forty-eight men siding with the convention had been severely wounded, there was "not a single man in that category upon the other side."[46]

Coming as it did on the heels of similar eruptions in Memphis and Charleston, the New Orleans riot increased the perception in the North that white southerners were determined to unleash a reign of terror on recently emancipated slaves. The barrage of self-congratulatory editorials in southern newspapers, which praised whites in New Orleans for giving a "salutary warning" that the South would never submit to Yankee rule, strengthened this belief and convinced northern voters that the South had refused to accept the verdict arrived at by four years of a bloody war.[47]

The riot in New Orleans also discredited Andrew Johnson's policy regarding Reconstruction. Hoping to diminish his presidential powers further, Congress passed the Tenure of Office Act in March 1867. This required the president to obtain the Senate's consent for removals or appointments to any federal office, including his cabinet. This restriction presented a particular problem for Johnson in regard to Edwin Stanton, the secretary of war.[48]

Some of Johnson's supporters urged the president to remove Stanton and declare the Tenure of Office Act null and void. But Johnson wanted to avoid a showdown and decided to take advantage of a provision in the act that would allow him to suspend Stanton while Congress was out of session. Johnson waited until the summer recess in 1867 and then dismissed Stanton, replacing him with Ulysses S. Grant. When the House reconvened in November, the Judiciary Committee voted to impeach the president, but the motion failed on the floor. Vindicated, or so he thought, Johnson delivered a message on Stanton's suspension five days later. Of the many complaints Johnson could have voiced to justify Stanton's removal, the president chose to emphasize the secretary of war's failure to use the army to keep things from getting out of hand in New Orleans on July 30, 1866. Johnson felt that he had been blamed, unfairly, for the violence in New Orleans and wanted to use this opportunity to set the record straight.[49]

Then the unexpected happened. Grant resigned his appointment as secretary of war and returned to his duties as commanding general of the Army, which put Stanton back at work in his old office. After considering his options for several weeks, Johnson decided on February 21, 1868, to remove Stanton once again. The Senate quickly passed a resolution stating that the president did not have the authority to dismiss Stanton, and the House voted three days later to impeach Johnson.[50]

The trial began in the Senate on March 23 and lasted more than seven weeks. Finally, on May 16, the chief justice called for a vote on the strongest of the charges in the bills of indictment. Needing a two-thirds majority, the Senate failed to convict by one vote, thirty-five to nineteen. Seven

Republican senators sacrificed their political careers by voting not guilty.[51] Although Johnson survived impeachment, his political future had been ruined. Six months later, Ulysses S. Grant was elected president of the United States.

With the president's plan for Reconstruction in disarray, the Radicals passed a series of bills that gave Congress control of the process. Among other things, these laws mandated that every southern state had to accept universal male suffrage as a condition for readmission to the Union. Louisiana dutifully convened another constitutional convention and adopted a new constitution giving blacks the right to vote and hold office. The document was ratified in April 1868, and Louisiana rejoined her sister states in the Union shortly thereafter.[52]

Ironically, the violent reaction of whites in New Orleans allowed members of the convention to accomplish what they had wanted all along. But their victory was short-lived. By 1877, former Confederates had reestablished themselves as a political force in Louisiana. In the decade that followed, white Louisianians tightened their control over the state's black citizens. "For the first time since the war," a white New Orleanian boasted in 1888, "we've got the nigger where we want him." By 1898, when the state adopted another constitution, blacks in Louisiana had lost all the civil rights they had achieved, including the right to vote. This time, however, the North turned its back. Administrative inefficiency on the part of the federal government, the constitutional conservatism of Americans in general, and racism in the North and South doomed the attempt to establish a new social order based on the principle that all men are equal before the law.[53]

It has been said that the South lost the war but won the peace.[54] That statement applied only to white southerners, however, for blacks in the South were the real losers. Disfranchised, terrorized, and marginalized, black Americans had to wait for more than a century to accomplish what the first demonstrations for black civil rights in New Orleans had set in motion.[55]

Notes

Much of the material for this chapter comes from James G. Hollandsworth, *An Absolute Massacre: The New Orleans Race Riot of July 30, 1866* (Baton Rouge: Louisiana State University Press, 2001).

1. Townsend Davis, *Weary Feet, Rested Souls: A Guided History of the Civil Rights*

Movement (New York: W. W. Norton, 1998), 381; Ralph E. Luker, *Historical Dictionary of the Civil Rights Movement* (Lanham, Md.: Scarecrow Press, 1997), xi.

2. Joseph Logsdon and Caryn Cossé Bell, "The Americanization of Black New Orleans, 1850–1900," in *Creole New Orleans: Race and Americanization,* ed. Arnold R. Hirsch and Joseph Logsdon (Baton Rouge: Louisiana State University Press, 1992), 222–25; Caryn Cossé Bell, *Revolution, Romanticism, and the Afro-Creole Protest Tradition in Louisiana, 1718–1868* (Baton Rouge: Louisiana State University Press, 1997), 226–27; Ted Tunnell, *Crucible of Reconstruction: War, Radicalism, and Race in Louisiana, 1862–1877* (Baton Rouge: Louisiana State University Press, 1984), 75; *L'Union,* September 27, 1862, as translated in James McPherson, *The Negro's Civil War: How American Blacks Felt and Acted during the War for the Union* (New York: Pantheon Books, 1965; reprint, New York: Ballantine Books, 1991), 280.

3. "A Meeting of Free Colored Citizens at Economy Hall," New Orleans *Times,* November 6, 1863.

4. "President Lincoln's Letter to Gov. Hahn," New Orleans *Daily Picayune,* July 6, 1865; James G. Hollandsworth, *The Louisiana Native Guards: The Black Military Experience during the Civil War* (Baton Rouge: Louisiana State University Press, 1995), 3, 73, 94–95; Logsdon and Bell, "The Americanization of Black New Orleans," 224–26; C. Peter Ripley, *Slaves and Freedmen in Civil War Louisiana* (Baton Rouge: Louisiana State University Press, 1976), 173; Tunnell, *Crucible of Reconstruction,* 39, 78–79.

5. Quotation from the *L'Union* taken from Logsdon and Bell, "The Americanization of Black New Orleans," 228.

6. Ripley, *Slaves and Freedmen,* 178–80; Eric Foner, *Reconstruction: America's Unfinished Revolution, 1863–1877* (New York: Harper and Row, 1988), 185–216.

7. George C. Rable, *But There Was No Peace: The Role of Violence in the Politics of Reconstruction* (Athens: University of Georgia Press, 1984), 46–49.

8. Gilles Vandal, "The Origins of the New Orleans Riot of 1866, Revisited," *Louisiana History* 22 (spring 1981): 148–49; Congress, House, Select Committee, *House Report No. 16: Report of the Select Committee on New Orleans Riots,* 39th Cong., 2d sess. (Washington, D.C.: Government Printing Office, 1867; reprint, Freeport, N.Y.: Books for Libraries Press, 1971), 15–16, 23, 39, 44, 476 (hereafter cited as *House Report*).

9. Congress, House, *Executive Documents No. 68: New Orleans Riots,* 39th Cong., 2d sess. (Washington: Government Printing Office, 1866), 194 (hereafter cited as *Military Commission Report*); *House Report,* 482.

10. Orleans Parish, Louisiana, *Grand Jury Report, and the Evidence Taken by Them in Reference to the Great Riot in New Orleans, Louisiana, July 30, 1866* (New Orleans: Daily Crescent Office, [1866?]), 8 (hereafter cited as *Grand Jury Report*); *House Report,* 312, 476, 478; *Military Commission Report,* 194, 226, 279–80.

11. *House Report,* 1, 32, 291–92.

12. Ibid., 38–39, 66. Dostie's remarks were reported independently by two witnesses, William Henry Hire and Stephen F. Fish, both of whom were supporters of the convention. Hire and Fish's uncle, W. R. Fish, were members. The quotation in the text is from

Stephen Fish's testimony. Hire's account was more succinct. "Now, friends, go peaceably home; go orderly; do not disturb anybody; but if anybody disturbs you, kill him!"

13. New Orleans *Times,* July 28, 1866; New Orleans *Daily Picayune,* July 28, 1866.

14. *House Report,* 350, 376, 478.

15. *Grand Jury Report,* 6; *Military Commission Report,* 159, 177–78, 252; New Orleans *Daily Crescent,* August 1, 1866.

16. *House Report,* 164, 353. The temperature comes from the New Orleans *Bee,* July 31, 1866.

17. *Grand Jury Report,* 5; *House Report,* 77, 125; *Military Commission Report,* 44, 49, 112, 188, 232, 264; John Gibbons to N. P. Banks, July 30, 1866, Banks Collection, Library of Congress.

18. *Grand Jury Report,* 3, 10, 13; *House Report,* 125, 289; *Military Commission Report,* 126, 141, 156. Estimates of the size of the procession ranged from 50 to 150 men.

19. *Grand Jury Report,* 3; *Military Commission Report,* 142–43, 231.

20. *Grand Jury Report,* 4–5, 11–12; *House Report,* 188, 204, 401; *Military Commission Report,* 112, 255–56, 264; New Orleans *Times,* July 31, 1866.

21. *Grand Jury Report,* 4, 6, 8, 11–12; *Military Commission Report,* 44–45, 49, 121, 188, 196. Several witnesses claimed that the first shot came from the procession. However, the preponderance of testimony suggests that the first shot was fired at the procession (e.g., *Grand Jury Report,* 12).

22. *Grand Jury Report,* 4; *House Report,* 72, 104; *Military Commission Report,* 182, 196, 250.

23. *Grand Jury Report,* 13; *House Report,* 77; *Military Commission Report,* 144.

24. *Grand Jury Report,* 4, 10; *Military Commission Report,* 116, 195, 250, 254, 282.

25. *Grand Jury Report,* 4, 7, 10, 17; *House Report,* 77, 251–53, 334; *Military Commission Report,* 116, 120, 193, 216, 221, 251, 255, 264; New Orleans *Times,* July 31, 1866. For the time the riot started, see *Military Commission Report,* 119, 158, 268 and *House Report,* 55.

26. *Grand Jury Report,* 4; *Military Commission Report,* 96, 143, 179.

27. *House Report,* 353; *Military Commission Report,* 143.

28. *Grand Jury Report,* 5, 8, 10, 15; *Military Commission Report,* 44, 173, 217, 282.

29. *House Report,* 5, 67, 238, 394, 529; *Military Commission Report,* 277, 287; see also "Police Reorganization" [in German], New Orleans *Deutsche Zeitung,* May 29, 1866, and Vandal, "Origins of the New Orleans Riot," 254–55.

30. *Grand Jury Report,* 13; *House Report,* 309; *Military Commission Report,* 114; New Orleans *Daily True Delta,* March 27, 1860; New Orleans *Daily Crescent,* March 29, 1860; New Orleans *Times,* February 24, 1866; *The American Fire Alarm and Police Telegraph* (New Orleans: Clark and Brisbin, 1859), 6; George H. Allen to Alderman Bosworth, January 3, 1867, Superintendent to the Board of Assistant Aldermen, March 29, 1867, both in City Council Reports of City Departments to the Board of Aldermen, 1866–1869, City Archives, Louisiana Division, New Orleans Public Library.

31. *Military Commission Report,* 109–10, 138.

32. *House Report,* 203.

33. Ibid., 70, 213.

34. *Grand Jury Report,* 5–6; *House Report,* 40; *Military Commission Report,* 152, 157, 169, 196, 207.

35. *Grand Jury Report,* 6, 9; *Military Commission Report,* 121, 148, 154, 156, 196, 214, 222, 251.

36. *House Report,* 125; *Military Commission Report,* 81, 193. Gibbons was arrested and taken to jail.

37. *Grand Jury Report,* 15; *House Report,* 18; *Military Commission Report,* 226–27, 237, 239.

38. *Military Commission Report,* 178.

39. *House Report,* 110, 180, 186; *Military Commission Report,* 120–21, 163, 233, 253.

40. *Grand Jury Report,* 7, 11; *House Report,* 172–73, 199, 286, 293, 354; *Military Commission Report,* 56, 114, 140, 220, 258. Later that night, Hahn sought out Chief Adams and thanked him for saving his life (*House Report,* 286).

41. *Grand Jury Report,* 13; *House Report,* 119, 205; *Military Commission Report,* 108, 124, 143–44, 147, 236, 245–46.

42. *Grand Jury Report,* 15, 17; *House Report,* 16; report from the Cincinnati *Commercial* reprinted in *The New Orleans Riot: "My Policy" in Louisiana* (Washington, D.C.: Daily Morning Chronicle, 1866), 7.

43. *Grand Jury Report,* 7; *Military Commission Report,* 134, 220, 261.

44. *House Report,* 281, 461; *Military Commission Report,* 135, 238, 286; New Orleans *Times,* July 31, 1866. With an ironic twist, the armless veteran was later appointed to the post of sergeant-at-arms at the State House.

45. *Military Commission Report,* 232–33, 254, 267.

46. Ibid., 93.

47. W. R. Brock, *An American Crisis: Congress and Reconstruction, 1865–1867* (New York: Harper Torchbooks, 1963), 158–59; Dan T. Carter, *When the War Was Over: The Failure of Self-Reconstruction in the South, 1865–1867* (Baton Rouge: Louisiana State University Press, 1985), 249–53.

48. Foner, *Reconstruction,* 333–34; James E. Sefton, *Andrew Johnson and the Uses of Constitutional Power* (Boston: Little, Brown, 1980), 159.

49. Sefton, *Andrew Johnson,* 160–61, 167–68; *Message of the President of the United States and the Report of the Committee on Military Affairs, Etc., in Regard to the Suspension of Hon. E. M. Stanton* (Washington: Government Printing Office, 1868).

50. Sefton, *Andrew Johnson,* 172–73.

51. Ibid., 179–80.

52. Philip D. Uzee, "The Beginnings of the Louisiana Republican Party," *Louisiana History* 12 (summer 1971): 209–11; Vandal, "Origins of the New Orleans Riot," 135.

53. R. C. Hitchcock to George Washington Cable, September 1, 1888, quoted in Dale A. Somers, "Black and White in New Orleans: A Study in Urban Race Relations, 1865–1900," *Journal of Southern History* 40 (February 1974): 42; Foner, *Reconstruction,* 590–

litical struggle that Du Bois recommended and instead to make the best of racial isolation and subordination in the United States. The speech of Du Bois in New York, entitled "Negro Ideals," exhibited to the audience what one of his biographers called "a new form of protest . . . more strident and waspish, indifferent to the resentment he might create in white opinion."[3] Du Bois also showed some discouragement with black southerners by looking elsewhere for suitable examples of Negro achievement, particularly to the Haitian revolutionary, Toussaint L'Ouverture.

Reports of Du Bois's speech caused a less well known black leader, Rodolphe Lucien Desdunes, to take unusual exception to the observations of Du Bois. Unlike most of Du Bois's black critics, Desdunes did not disparage Du Bois by defending the sage of Tuskegee. Instead, he urged Du Bois to take note of a very accomplished and assertive group of black southerners in New Orleans. He also questioned the praise that Du Bois had lavished upon L'Ouverture by asserting that the Caribbean leader was no hero to Haitians or to other French-speaking black people like himself who considered L'Ouverture, "the Booker T. Washington of San Domingo."[4]

What Desdunes attempted to highlight for Du Bois was one of the most remarkable and influential traditions of social protest in the United States. Well before Du Bois had arrived in violence-torn Atlanta, the black community in New Orleans had done more than produce some of the most noteworthy artists and writers in North America; it had also sustained the most successful campaign for racial equality in the South. Most of those black leaders in New Orleans, like Desdunes, called themselves Creoles. They came from a different background and tradition in North America—a peculiar and almost forgotten human remnant of the French and Spanish empires in the United States.

Desdunes noted for Du Bois this "Creole" tradition of New Orleans and contrasted it with the dominant "American" mentality. He spoke of the different outlooks as "two distinct schools of politics among the Negroes." The "Latin Negro," he insisted, differed radically from the "Anglo-Saxon Negro" in aspiration and in method. Treating the Creole or "Latin Negro" first, Desdunes went on with his parallel profile:

> One hopes, the other doubts. Thus we often perceive that one makes every effort to aspire to equality, the other to identity.
> One will forget that he is a Negro in order to think that he is a man; the other will forget that he is a man to think that he is a Negro.[5]

Desdunes brought his unusual political view to bear on key points of Du Bois's recent speech. He clearly admired the young professor, but he questioned the racialism that Du Bois had displayed in scorning his white tormentors. For Desdunes, both "over-maning" as well as "under-maning the Negro" was wrong. And when it came to "dealing with fundamental ideals," Desdunes thought it was "a most erroneous doctrine . . . to be Negroes at all." Instead, he thought that "Negroes, in treating all essential principles, should cease to be Negroes, in order to live, think, feel and act as true Americans, just as Brown, Garrison, Lovejoy, Phillips, Lincoln and Longworth, ceased to be whites, that they might become the instruments of loving humanity."[6] In taking such a view, Desdunes did not endorse any policy that called for black Americans to give up their identity or ancestral memory. Indeed, he pointedly rejected "the amalgamated 'candied tongue licks the lip of pomp,' hoping to thrive on his apostasy." He waxed in anger at anyone who sought whiteness as a solution to the racial oppression of his day:

He is a fool in his own house and esteems nothing so much as the fairness of his skin, and the souple [*sic*] strains of his hair. These two convenient accessories are his most precious possessions with which to fix himself in the sphere of tolerated consideration.

He hides the place of his birth, tries to die unknown so as not to be confounded; he often turns his back upon his mother, and will despise his children in obedience to his delusions. He is cruel, unnatural and vile, and has sacrificed so absolutely to his ideal that his heart is forever closed to the appeals of reason, love, or duty.[7]

What Desdunes wanted was neither racial chauvinism nor self-denial. Instead, he harkened to black and white models within the world of the Franco-Africans of New Orleans who had espoused an interracial brotherhood that went beyond the usual conceptions of social thought in the United States. Desdunes and his band of black radicals in New Orleans had built upon the revolutionary traditions of France that called for Liberty, Equality, and Fraternity. It was the last appeal of this revolutionary slogan—fraternity—that Desdunes felt had eluded the thinking of almost all Americans, both black and white. He wanted to make the three inseparable—a concept beyond simple homogeneity or segmented pluralism.[8]

It is not clear from his surviving personal papers whether Du Bois ever received the pamphlet that Desdunes had entitled *A Few Words to Dr. Du*

Bois with Malice towards None. Nor is it clear whether Desdunes ever saw more than the excerpt of Du Bois's speech that left out the New Englander's insistence that "human brotherhood" was one of the "three great ends of Negro ambition."[9] Only much later would Du Bois discover the special contributions made by black New Orleanians in shaping the constitutional rights of all black people in the United States.

In 1934, Du Bois came to New Orleans in order to look at old files of black newspapers and add some finishing touches to his massive study of the Civil War and Reconstruction era in the United States. He noted in this work, *Black Reconstruction*, that the drive for equal national citizenship for black Americans had begun in New Orleans during the Civil War. Earlier in his monthly journal, *Crisis*, he had also described the Creoles of that city as a distinct group and praised them as having "the longest history in modern culture of any group of Negro descent in the United States."[10]

Despite his important discoveries, Du Bois never fully understood the Creole leaders of the late nineteenth century, particularly the source and evolution of their peculiar ideology. He made no reference to the history of the group published by Desdunes in 1911 beyond citing it in his bibliography for *Black Reconstruction*. True, Du Bois read the Reconstruction newspapers of the Creole radicals, but ascribed their advanced appeals for equal citizenship to their remarkable wealth and education. Not until the important work of Caryn Cossé Bell have historians gone beyond this general conclusion, and some have even dismissed the black Creole assertions as little more than the elitist expressions of their narrow self-interest.[11]

The black community of New Orleans has never fit very neatly into the general history of black Americans in the United States. Perhaps only a small coterie of music historians has seen the city's peculiar black community as more than a provincial curiosity. The international interest in jazz has, no doubt, led to the special work of the musicologists who have tried to uncover the origins of that artistic tradition in New Orleans. Their curiosity has led them to explain how this unique American art form emerged from the least American of the cities in the United States. The groundbreaking work in this field by the anthropologist Alan Lomax pointed to the same insight that Desdunes had much earlier noted for Du Bois: the duality of cultural tradition in the New Orleans black community between Francophone Creoles and Anglophone Americans. Lomax recognized that jazz drew heavily upon the cultural traditions of black American migrants who came to New Orleans, but he concluded that the Creoles provided the special element lacking in other areas of the United States that brought jazz into existence.

Ever since the appearance in 1935 of the revisionist work of W.E.B. Du Bois, historians have recognized that New Orleans served as a key laboratory for black citizenship. Few have noticed, however, that the role of events in the city resulted from more than the privileged status of the free black leadership or the mere coincidence of early Union occupation of the state during the Civil War. In fact, the radical ideas about civil equality that sprang up in New Orleans depended upon the same duality of culture between black Creoles and Americans that later produced the musical expression of jazz. Again the Creoles acted as the catalyst.

Desdunes tried to keep the memory of the Creole role in Reconstruction politics alive by writing a history of his Creole compatriots called *Nos hommes et notre histoire*. But because his account was written in French and published in Canada, the 1911 work reached very few readers. It took more than six decades for it to find a wider audience with an English translation published in the United States. But, even then, few scholars probed the roots of Creole radicalism or realized that Desdunes was more than a mere chronicler of that intellectual tradition.[12]

Desdunes was a modest man. He did not celebrate his own accomplishments or leadership, but the treatise that he directed to Du Bois in 1907 demonstrated the profundity of his thought. As an activist who came of age during the late Reconstruction period, Desdunes saw himself as a protégé of older leaders and teachers who often joined him in militant protest against the violent overthrow of Reconstruction and the disfranchisement of black southerners. He was also the chief proponent of a series of legal battles, including *Plessy v. Ferguson*, that reflected the unusual strain of Franco-African ideology in New Orleans.[13]

Born in New Orleans on November 14, 1849, Desdunes entered a new world for Franco-Africans in the Western Hemisphere. The revolution of 1848 in France had brought a radical departure in the history of New World slavery. The French government not only abolished slavery in their colonial possessions but also enfranchised everyone of African descent. Freedom and equal citizenship for black people in the Americas existed nowhere except in the independent black republic of Haiti. True, British authorities had ended slavery in 1834, but they refused to grant equal citizenship to black people in their colonies. In 1848, the same am-bivalence marked all other white-dominated jurisdictions in the Americas, even in the strongholds of the New England abolitionists.

For New Orleanians, such as Desdunes and his family, freedom in the French Antilles inspired both hope and despair. On one hand, they could celebrate the breakthrough in French policy. But as inhabitants of the slave state of Louisiana in the United States, French sovereignty no longer determined their lives and careers. Indeed, their new republican rulers responded to the international upsurge of emancipation by drafting laws that made life even more restrictive for all free blacks and slaves in Louisiana.

As the possibilities of life grew more limited, some of the Francophone black Creoles fled to French territory. There, some became soldiers and statesmen; others became prominent musicians and writers. Some turned to Haiti. A few like Emile Desdunes, probably a relative of Rodolphe's family, sought more than individual escape. He obtained financial and political support from Haitian authorities in order to organize a mass emigration from New Orleans to Haiti. Rodolphe Desdunes may well have grown up as a Haitian citizen, but events altered Emile Desdunes's plans when a change of government in Haiti ended his official support. For Rodolphe, personal tragedy compounded the growing repression when his father, Jeremie, died.[14]

Although stranded and impoverished in New Orleans along with five brothers and one sister, Rodolphe Desdunes did not lose contact with the tradition of hope and aspiration aroused by French and Haitian policies. Creole leaders in New Orleans provided him solace in an orphanage school founded by an African woman, Madame Couvent, where several free black teachers, particularly Armand Lanusse and Joani Questy, taught French literature and history. More important, in 1862, just as Desdunes came of age to comprehend the world of politics and power around him, Union forces captured New Orleans and undermined the slavocracy of Louisiana.

Within several months of the Union capture, one of Desdunes's former teachers, Paul Trévigne, began a newspaper, *L'Union*, which boldly evoked the revolutionary outlook of a key group of Franco-African leaders in New Orleans. Trévigne's newspaper columns announced objectives which showed the French roots of a radicalism that had already moved well beyond the cautious policies of the Republican president, Abraham Lincoln, who was trying to promote the emigration of black Americans as the best solution for the nation's racial dilemma. The black Creole columnist, François Boisdoré, wrote:

> Brothers! the hour strikes for us: a new sun, like the one of 89, must soon appear on our horizon: let the cry which electrified France in the taking of the Bastille, resound today in our ears. . . . Cast a backward glance to the Chamber of 48, when France was a Republic: we see . . . celebrated Negroes and mulattoes, also representing their native country. . . . Ah! France, in proclaiming liberty for blacks, has not sought to expatriate them, to colonize them in Chiriqui: it has wanted to make them men, and fellow citizens. . . . Nations of America! Whatever may be your systems of government, in the name of Christianity, copy your fundamental principles from those of France, and like it, you will arrive at the heights of civilization![15]

When Lincoln's generals rejected such demands in setting up a new government in occupied New Orleans, the black Creoles refused to back down. They knew that the Civil War had revolutionized the Louisiana political and social order. To gain allies, they turned to radical and socialist whites as well as courageous black Protestant leaders who lived in other neighborhoods of the city with their own churches and associations.[16] To counter the reluctant Union generals, this coalition decided to take their demands for black citizenship directly to Lincoln in Washington. But before they could dispatch such a delegation, Lincoln made clear his own opposition to any suffrage for black Louisiana. The Creoles refused to abandon their campaign. Very reluctantly, however, they accepted the advice of their white supporters to limit their demand for suffrage just to free blacks in order to find some legal argument that might persuade the cautious president to move toward their more radical position.

They based their limited legal demand on the French-American treaty of 1803, which transferred Louisiana to the United States. In doing so, they resurrected a plea of their free black ancestors who had tried to convince the Jefferson administration in 1804 to include them in the equal citizenship that was promised to the free inhabitants of the former French colony. When the black Creole delegates E. Arnold Bertonneau and Jean Baptiste Roudanez reached Washington and discovered Republican radicals, such as Senator Charles Sumner, who shared their original objec-

tives, they amended their petition to request freedom and enfranchise-
ment for all black Louisiana.[17]

Although Lincoln politely rejected their demands, he was the first
president to meet black Americans in the White House. Unbeknownst to
the black Creoles who remained critical of Lincoln until his death, their
visit in March 1864 caused him to begin a quiet reversal of his policies on
black citizenship by urging his Louisiana subordinates to consider granting suffrage to black Louisianians who fought in the war or who possessed
substantial education and property.[18]

The Creoles did not wait for Lincoln or his more conservative subordinates to act. The delegates went on to rally New England abolitionists to
their cause at a dinner in Boston, where they boldly revealed objectives
that went beyond liberty and suffrage to equality and brotherhood. In the
words of E. Arnold Bertonneau, they wanted to "enjoy every civil, political and religious right that white citizens enjoy; in a word, that every man
shall stand equal before the law." Their ultimate goal was to change "the
character of the whole people" by sending their children to racially integrated schools "to learn the great truth that God 'created of one blood all
nations of men to dwell on the face of the earth'—so will caste, founded
on prejudice against color, disappear."[19]

When William Lloyd Garrison balked at endorsing this startling
agenda and instead backed the Lincoln government in granting emancipation without black suffrage—explicitly favoring the British model in
Jamaica—the New Orleans Creoles widened an existing fissure in the
abolitionist movement by demanding abolitionist support for equal citizenship and universal male suffrage. They embraced Wendell Phillips as a
new ally and relentlessly condemned Garrison for his seeming reluctance
to support their full equality. When Garrison countered that the British
had not granted the franchise to the slaves whom they had emancipated in
the British West Indies, the new daily newspaper of the black Creoles, the
Tribune, vented the editors' Gallic rage:

> From the outset in England there could be no question of univer-
> sal suffrage, in a monarchical country where restrictions are imposed
> on whites themselves. But that which was denied after the general
> emancipation in the English colonies, is precisely that which we de-
> mand for our liberated brothers, equality before the law. In French
> colonies it is the same: at the moment that liberty was proclaimed,

legal equality was immediately a fact; everyone can read at the top of the glorious French constitution the lines: "All French men without distinction of class or color are equal before the law." The proud Anglo-Saxon, he alone, hesitates to fulfill an act of justice.[20]

The battle was not easy for the black radical leadership in New Orleans. Before they were able to translate their ideology into the new state constitution of 1868, they faced terrible violence and bitter denunciation. But their unswerving principles enabled them to shape the most democratic constitution in the United States. More than freedom and political equality found its way into that document: They mandated the complete desegregation of government facilities including the public schools and also required complete equality in all private businesses that served the public.

In almost every instance, the advanced ideas that became embodied in the fundamental laws of Louisiana came from the minds and leadership of the Franco-Africans. Their names attest to their ethnic backgrounds. Paul Trévigne was the first to proclaim their demands in his newspaper, *L'Union*. Arnold Bertonneau and Jean Baptiste Roudanez were the delegates who took their demands to the Republican leadership in Washington and to the black and white abolitionists of New York and Boston. Louis Charles Roudanez, a medical graduate of the University of Paris and a veteran of the Paris barricades in 1848, sponsored the daily newspaper, the *Tribune*, which gave their ideas a national audience. Aristide Mary, another returning exile from Paris, helped to imbed the ideas of equality and fraternity into the Louisiana constitution of 1868. And Francis Dumas, the candidate who narrowly lost the vote to be nominated as the first black Republican governor in 1868, also had returned from exile in Paris to become the first black captain in the Union army.

The black Creoles were not able to sustain their remarkable constitutional achievements. First, they lost control of the Louisiana Republican Party to a coalition of out-of-state white leaders led by Henry Warmoth. With the help of P.B.S. Pinchback, an American black migrant to the state, Warmoth gathered the support of just enough black delegates to secure his party's nomination for governor of Louisiana. After his election, Warmoth refused to enforce integration of the schools or public accommodations in order to court white voters and fashion a more conservative Republican party in Louisiana. The divisions led finally to the defeat of the Republicans in 1876 when the federal government refused any longer to suppress the violence of white Democrats that kept black voters from exercising their voting rights.[21] Before they abandoned the experiment of integrated public education, Paul Trévigne and E. Arnold Bertonneau each filed suits to reverse the Bourbon Democrats' immediate implementation of segregated schools in 1877.[22]

It was during the subsequent overthrow of Reconstruction and the gradual elimination of citizenship rights from black southerners that Rodolphe Desdunes emerged to lead his fellow Creoles. He entered the field as a protégé of the Civil War generation of black Creole radicals, since he not only studied the tomes of French literature and history as their student but also modeled his life after their examples. He wrote in both French and English, but most elegantly in French.[23] And throughout his life he turned to the radicalism and ideals of France in 1848 that gave lasting national citizenship to black people, "because all Frenchmen were equal before the law."[24]

Although too young to play a major role in the events of the 1860s in New Orleans, Desdunes emerged in the public eye during the mid-1870s and went on to become the primary strategist for the Creole resistance. Seriously wounded while serving as a Metropolitan policeman in 1874, he refused to surrender to the violent counterrevolution in Louisiana. He felt certain that the virtual lack of organized protest and resistance among blacks only encouraged the growing number of lynchings of rural blacks in the northern part of the state.[25]

Already in 1875, he had come forward to challenge the corruption and conservatism that had infiltrated the Republican Party in Louisiana and to call for renewed militancy and idealism among younger black leaders. By 1878, he had helped organize a key group of militants into the Young Men's Progressive Association. "If we are citizens of this great and free country," they declared, "we demand our rights as such." Desdunes openly labeled himself as a "radical" and allied himself with the Creole faction of the party against the cautious approach of Pinchback's American faction.[26]

While attending the integrated law school of Straight University from which he received a law degree in 1882, Desdunes became convinced that the federal courts offered black southerners the best opportunity to reverse their declining status. By 1881, he began to agitate for an Association of Equal Rights to support a counterattack in the courts to protect black voting rights and win enforcement of the Civil Rights Act of 1875, which guaranteed black Americans access to public accommodations. He exhibited remarkable bravado. "It is time," he wrote, "that some of these 'unregenerates' should know that we mean to test their legal right to humiliate us. . . . It is the duty of colored men to fight for an equal chance in the race of life and not depend upon the generosity of others to do so for them." And then he added, "I do not see any reason why we should adopt the doctrine of nonresistance, when experience and manliness argue that 'eternal vigilance is the price of liberty.' . . . Let us stand together, and crowd our enemies to the wall."[27]

More and more Desdunes reached back into his French and Creole heritage for a radical ideology and militant tradition. He not only drew upon his knowledge of French history and literature, but he also nurtured his outlook inside several anticlerical organizations, groups of like-minded French-speaking radicals in the city, particularly a black spiritualist society and an integrated Scottish rite Masonic lodge headquartered in Paris.[28] Discouraged by the methods of other black leaders in the South, Desdunes urged his fellow black Creoles to return to their proven methods during Reconstruction. Without the centrality of a black Protestant church or the leadership of black clergymen in the Creole communities, he knew that they needed an ideological organization and a newspaper—their own bold, militant newspaper to unify and lead them. In 1887, with the support of Paul Trévigne, he helped form L'Union Louisianaise, and then circulated their prospectus for a revolutionary paper with French columns:

> Our efforts [are] to create here a republican organ in the language that is still spoken with pride by a class of men who have drawn their republicanism from reading the great *philosophes* of the 18th century. . . . Those to whom it [L'Union Louisianaise] has entrusted the editing will put all their efforts . . . into continuing its progressive work. They will endeavor to graft, so to speak, the truth onto the side of error, in order to produce a result, which . . . assures to each the plenitude of his civil and political rights. [translation by Caryn Cossé Bell][29]

This call eventually resulted, instead, in a community corporation to support the New Orleans *Crusader*, a weekly newspaper just recently begun by another young black Creole, Louis A. Martinet.[30] With both French and English columns, it created an aggressive vehicle for racial protest in New Orleans. Martinet had once been an ally of Pinchback and had even joined him in support of the Constitution of 1879, which overturned many of the key features of the 1868 Reconstruction Constitution, but Martinet later abandoned the narrow patronage politics of his former mentor and closed ranks with his fellow Creoles.[31] The newspaper obviously struck a chord in the black community and helped to encourage a new assertive spirit in the city as its founders had hoped. By 1894, the editors received enough support from black New Orleanians to become the only black newspaper in the United States during the 1890s.

That the *Crusader* resounded with the same spirit of the earlier *Tribune* and *L'Union* from the Reconstruction era was not accidental, because one of its regular contributors, Paul Trévigne, then an old man, helped in its founding and reminded its readers how he and an earlier generation had originally won the rights that the *Crusader* now proposed to regain three decades later. The new paper rallied the community to protest an upsurge of political violence in the sugar parishes of south Louisiana and condemned police brutality in New Orleans. Calling itself a "Labor and Republican" paper, it also supported labor unions, including the Knights of Labor, and any other movement in the South such as the early Populist Party that seemed to offer protection for the rights of black citizens.[32]

But above all, the *Crusader* served as the organ of the assertive civil rights effort in the courts that Desdunes had envisioned at the beginning of the 1880s. Louis Martinet, who had also graduated from Straight Law School, agreed with Desdunes that well-chosen legal suits offered more hope than the fraudulent policies of the state to recapture basic constitutional rights under the Fourteenth and Fifteenth Amendments. It was clear that they anticipated a national movement. Early in 1890, the editors helped to gather other leaders throughout the South in Washington, D.C., to form a new national civil rights group, the American Citizens Equal Rights Association (ACERA). At that conference, both Desdunes and Martinet insisted upon a name that would open the group to all sympathizers irrespective of race, setting it at odds with all those—black or white—who were then touting racial exclusivity.[33] Within a few weeks of the group's formation, a cause emerged for the Louisiana branch of the association: The state legislature passed laws forbidding interracial marriage and mandating segregation of blacks on all railroads operating within Louisiana.

Initially both American and Creole leaders participated in the local chapters of the ACERA to protest the Jim Crow laws in Louisiana. In fact, after returning from the ACERA convention in Washington, Desdunes began to exert his skills as an organizer, ideologue, and publicist. First, he issued the call for the formation of local chapters in New Orleans. Then he drafted a protest of May 24, 1890, against the separate car law and organized a delegation of the ACERA leaders to present it to the state legislature. It was at that very moment that Desdunes and others formed a new corporation to help supply the *Crusader* with a new press and office facilities.

Some American leaders joined the board of the *Crusader*, and even Pinchback, the national president of ACERA, helped at the beginning.[34] However, ethnic divisions quickly developed. Assuring Desdunes and others that they had struck a logrolling agreement with lobbyists for the infamous Louisiana Lottery to support the gambling company's rechartering in exchange for the lottery faction's opposition to the enactment of Jim Crow laws, black legislators, mostly from the Protestant community, had successfully demanded that the ACERA protest be toned down. The deal boomeranged against the black lawmakers. Outfoxing their black allies, the lobbyists had their rechartering bill passed first. In retaliation, white opponents of the Lottery Company supported the antilottery governor, Francis T. Nicholls, in helping pass the separate car act on July 10, 1890, which the angry governor, true to his threats, quickly signed into law.

Paul Trévigne lashed out in the *Crusader* against the Jim Crow measure, Desdunes called for a boycott of the railroads, and Martinet called for the leaders of the ACERA to raise funds to bring a test case "before the Federal Courts."[35] But black Creoles soon had to maintain the burden of the struggle, as other leaders, particularly the black Protestant ministers, backed away from the dangerous challenge to the white supremacists. A few were forced out. At the outset, Rev. A.E.P. Albert, the first president of the state branch of ACERA, aligned his Methodist newspaper with the *Crusader*. But as he gathered support for the campaign and called upon Methodist churches to pledge opposition to the state laws, national church officials removed Albert from the editorship of the *Southwestern Christian Advocate* and left him without any comparable base of leadership in Louisiana. The Catholic Creole activists probably made matters worse by railing stridently against politicians and preachers, including Albert himself.[36]

After the quarreling led to the collapse of the ACERA, local appeals to raise funds foundered. More discouraging, no one stepped forward to mount a legal challenge to the Jim Crow law. It was at this critical juncture that Desdunes decided to visit the old, wealthy Reconstruction radical,

Aristide Mary. Clearly Desdunes's personal appeal, bolstered by his well-earned reputation as a true protégé of Mary's convictions as a "free-thinker and spiritualist," had their desired effect.[37] Mary's support permitted Desdunes and seventeen other activists to establish the Citizens' Committee on September 1, 1891. Their experiences with the ACERA convinced them to form a relatively small, tightly organized group who possessed what they called courage and "manhood" to maintain a struggle with the state's conservative white leadership. Four days later, they announced their existence and appealed "to the citizens of New Orleans, of Louisiana, and of the whole Union to give us their moral sanction and financial aid in our endeavors to have that oppressive law annulled by the courts."[38]

Shortly after this appeal, Albion Tourgée, a nationally syndicated columnist for the Chicago *Inter-Ocean*, took notice of the *Crusader*'s new resolve and offered his legal services free of charge to shape the Citizens' Committee's suit. He had been waiting for some group of black leaders to take up such an initiative. One of the most outspoken white defenders of African American rights alive at that time, Tourgée had won the respect of black southerners for his denunciations not only of conservative southern Democrats but also of northern Republicans who were retreating from any defense of black Americans. The Citizens' Committee promptly voted to accept his generous offer. They also concurred with his suggestion to help form a national organization to shape public opinion against the drift of the Republican Party and the federal courts away from the enforcement of the constitutional rights guaranteed African Americans.[39]

Again Desdunes took the lead for such efforts in Louisiana. A larger interracial organization had been his dream since his law school days in the 1880s. Even before Tourgée had decided finally on the name of the proposed group, the National Citizens Rights Association, Desdunes had put his organizing skills into operation. He tried always to recruit "friends" who were "young, honest and faithful and entirely removed from the field of practical politics." They, in turn, made him president. More than any of the leaders in New Orleans, Desdunes shared Tourgée's buoyant faith in interracial democracy: "I believe," he wrote Tourgée, "that in the course of a few years, you shall have changed the current of ideas in the Negro race. The colored people will learn from you the value of systematic agencies. They will think, reason and act according to principles, and in this lies the secret of their future happiness."[40]

Desdunes also took the lead in raising money for the proposed suit against the separate car law. Before the end of 1891, his energetic fund-raising brought in more than enough to hire local counsel and to pay the expenses necessary to carry out a lengthy court case. Although much of the money came from a few large contributors, Desdunes made sure to make participation as broad as possible. He gained support from more than sixty community groups and from almost fifty organizations outside of New Orleans, primarily from Louisiana and Mississippi but also from a few northern cities.[41] When Tourgée sought several black men from the South to serve on the NCRA's executive committee, or "Council of Administration," Martinet suggested Desdunes because of the latter's contribution to the cause and his organizing abilities. He assured Tourgée that there was "no better selection" and that Desdunes had the "peculiar fitness required for this purpose in a higher degree."[42]

Desdunes also personally recruited both volunteers for the test cases. He and other New Orleans organizers usually tried to follow the guidelines set down by Tourgée, who requested that persons of noticeably mixed racial ancestry serve in the test cases. For the first suit Tourgée wanted a woman light enough to pass for white, but Martinet and others on the Citizens' Committee balked at that advice. Instead, Desdunes recruited his own son, Daniel, because they thought that they needed someone dark enough to be refused admission to a "white" car. In March the young volunteer was arrested in the test case, and by May federal courts had declared Louisiana's Jim Crow railroad car law unconstitutional in any application to interstate passengers such as the young Desdunes.[43]

Jubilation greeted the victory. At first, the Citizens' Committee leaders failed to understand the desire of their attorneys to file yet another suit to challenge segregation on railroads running *just inside* Louisiana as well. But Tourgée, determined to attack the power of a state to segregate by race, insisted on pushing ahead.[44] And thus, even before the Daniel Desdunes verdict was handed down, the organizers, led by the elder Desdunes himself, set out to find another test case volunteer. This time they complied with Tourgée's insistence that they recruit a very light-skinned defendant. This issue of color definition never seemed an important question for the Citizens' Committee, as some later historians would muse without much investigation of the origins of that legal argument and strategy. The strategy sprang either from a minor expedient to ensure that the test case defendant would gain entry to a white car, or from a reasoned decision to illustrate the arbitrariness of racial categories in a state like Louisiana, where swarthy whites and light-skinned blacks seemed to blend imperceptibly one into the other. In either event, the question grew in importance as Tourgée and his local counsel searched for ways to circumvent the case law then building up in federal courts, which was steadily rejecting their argument with a different interpretation of the Fourteenth Amendment. Desdunes dutifully located a nearly white friend, Homére Adolphe Plessy, one of his anticlerical and Scottish rite Masonic friends who had been well known as a black community activist for more than a decade. Seven-eighths Caucasian and one-eighth black, Plessy boarded the East Louisiana Railroad bound for Covington, Louisiana, across the lake from New Orleans, and took a seat in the white coach, stating he was colored when queried by the conductor and refusing to move to the Jim Crow car. He was arrested on June 7, 1892.[45]

Desdunes, who by then was a regular columnist for the *Crusader*, had confidently pronounced Jim Crow "dead as a door nail" following his son's legal victory in the first test case, and he hammered away at the white supremacists while the lawyers continued the long process of legal maneuvers and appeals that brought their second, more significant *Plessy v. Ferguson* suit to the Supreme Court. "No theory of white supremacy," Desdunes reminded the fainthearted, "no method of lynching, no class legislation, no undue disqualification of citizenship, no system of enforced ignorance, no privileged classes at the expenses of others can be tolerated, and much less, openly encouraged by any citizen who loves justice, law and right."[46]

The group scarcely confined their activism to assaults against segregated railroads. They pursued several other legal cases, especially one against the denial of black citizens to sit on criminal juries. Between 1892 and 1896, Desdunes even tried to rally opposition against the efforts of southern legislatures to disfranchise black voters by literacy and property requirements. In 1895, after the *Crusader* became the only daily black newspaper in the nation, he assumed the role of associate editor and brought a greater class appeal to the newspaper: "This question of qualified suffrage," he warned, "is one in which all the common people, whether colored or white, are virtually interested." He rued the day "when once the wealthy classes get the laws as they want them. The elect of creation, as they believe themselves to be, aim to kill the right [of universal suffrage] as a short cut to assured and permanent ascendancy."[47]

After 1893, however, in the bleaker racial repressiveness following the inauguration of Democratic president Grover Cleveland, it became harder to sustain the mood of optimism that reigned following the first test case victory, and some of the *Plessy* activists began to lose heart. That fall, Tourgée confided his concerns to Martinet that the increasing number of conservative appointees to the Supreme Court seemed to be stacking the deck against their case, and he warned that the Court had "never reversed itself on a constitutional question." Martinet's own confidence had already broken down. In the face of the mounting number of lynchings and other outrages, he had written an editorial that exclaimed, "Let us get out of this hell of the United States" and urged his readers to start an exodus to Mexico. Desdunes alone seemed to keep the Citizens' Committee on track. By 1894, despite the recent suicide of Aristide Mary, their major benefactor, the Desdunes-led group even raised enough money and volunteers to make the *Crusader* the only daily, black-edited newspaper in the United States. When the *Crusader* became a daily, Desdunes assumed the position of associate editor, bringing greater assertiveness to the paper.

In 1896, however, the paper's bravado ended when the Supreme Court ruled against Plessy and explicitly sanctioned segregation. It must have seemed that the total weight of American power suddenly arrayed itself against the long struggle of the black New Orleans leaders. Even most of the stalwarts who had steadfastly pursued the case were too discouraged or fearful to continue any further protest. With the numbing efficiency of undertakers, they dismantled the Citizens' Committee and distributed a published accounting of their fund-raising before they called a large public meeting to announce their formal disbandment. Desdunes recalled that pessimism and fear had finally taken their toll. The Creole leaders, he said, "believed that the continuation of the *Crusader* would not only be fruitless but decidedly dangerous." They believed that "it was better to suffer in silence than to attract attention to their misfortune and weakness."[48]

As Desdunes had warned, the end to organized resistance did not lessen the violent determination of the white supremacists to subordinate black Louisianians. Within the next few years, black New Orleanians lost the right to vote and were deprived of almost all access to public education. Even the prelates of the Catholic Church in the New Orleans diocese finally imposed the color line.

For a while the storm of black Creole protest in 1895 led by Desdunes and Martinet in the *Crusader* had confined the creation of exclusively black "national" parishes to two small churches. In that battle, Desdunes had urged the Church to maintain its universal principles and to uphold "justice, equality and fraternity" within its ranks. He repeated his constant refrain: "Whether we be citizens or Christians, we never cease to be the children of God and the brothers of other men." But here, too, he could only delay the inevitable. By the end of World War I, the prelates of the city had segregated all of the city's Catholic churches.[49]

Church leaders praised these and other developments as part of the Americanization of their church. As in other private organizations in the city, almost all of the foreign white leaders, particularly the foreign French, had died off by the early twentieth century, and hardly any new French immigrants took their place. Other integrated institutions, like the Scottish rite Masonic lodges, either became all black as older white members died or, like the French Opera House, simply disappeared from the city. Increasingly, in its race relations, New Orleans became very similar to other American cities in the South.

In fact, even from afar, France itself had lost much of its glow as a beacon of liberation for black New Orleanians. Most of the younger Creoles either lost the ability to speak French or failed to gain the training to read French literature and history. And even those who retained such interests and abilities could only wonder about the commitment of France to its nineteenth-century ideals. When, in 1896, one of the younger activist writers for the *Crusader*, Numa S. Mansion, heard that French authorities had dismissed a black general during their ruthless subjugation of the Indo-Chinese, he wrote to a black member of the French Assembly to ask whether it was true. The legislator from Guadaloupe, E. Gerville-Reache, expressed his own disbelief, but the new French empire no longer could offer the alternative vision and policy that French republicanism had once nurtured for the black Creoles in New Orleans.[50]

From the perspective of the early twentieth century, the promise that Radical Republicans and abolitionists once held out for black New Orleanians of freedom, opportunity, and equal citizenship had turned into a nightmare of peonage, segregation, and disfranchisement. In the face of such reality, even the black Creoles of the city turned inward. By 1915, a new generation of their leaders greeted Booker T. Washington with almost the same enthusiasm as other black southerners. If Creoles and Americans still maintained their own distinctive churches and benevolent societies in different neighborhoods, both groups had conformed, it seemed, to the American color line.[51]

The often futile nineteenth-century resistance led by black Creoles to erosion of citizenship rights of African Americans had not been a pro-

longed fool's errand. The complex traditions that had produced their peculiar militant resistance had left a proud legacy not only for themselves
but for the whole nation, because they played a major role in embedding a
policy of racial justice into the Reconstruction amendments of the U.S.
Constitution. Indeed, even the *Plessy* case had not been a total failure, for
it generated a powerful dissent that would be used to rescue those amendments in later Supreme Court decisions.[52]

And, finally, the peculiar traditions of black New Orleanians survived
within their own communities, for they have preserved their own memories and written history. Even after the defeat of the *Plessy* suit, not all the
leaders accommodated to the new racial order. Many maintained a militant interracial labor organization in the city; hundreds boycotted segregated streetcars; and before the end of the 1920s, black leaders returned to
the federal courts to reopen their old battles. None of these recalcitrants
was more defiant than Rodolphe Desdunes. He decried any sort of accommodation to the prevailing American racial order. From the beginning of the struggle against the state laws that segregated railroad cars,
Desdunes recognized that he was fighting against all odds in resisting racial segregation in the American South.

Early in that battle, when a subscriber to the *Crusader* wrote that
Desdunes was calling the black community to a "battle which is forlorn,"
Desdunes refused to be shaken from his faith that "liberty is won by continued resistance to tyranny." What is more, he would not succumb to the
seemingly fixed outcome of the federal judiciary's decision that "colored
men ought to be satisfied with the enjoyment of the three first natural
rights" of the Declaration of Independence. He insisted that there must
be more than life, liberty, and the pursuit of freedom. He argued that
equal rights could not be divided among separated groups of humanity
within the same society. Fraternity and equal rights were inseparable. His
reading of history told him that "forlorn hopes like utopias have been the
cause of beginnings of all the great principles which now bless . . . the free
and progressive nations of the earth." In his mind, a "forlorn hope" should
not be "a disconcerting element to a true lover of the good and the just,
and that his devotion to principle must be above perturbation from the
most threatening prospects of temporary disappointment."

In this response, Desdunes quite frankly warned his compatriots that
they should be prepared to "show a noble despair" and be ready to "face
any disappointment that might await them at the bar of American justice."
He knew, it seems, that he was fighting not just for them but for a genera-

tion yet unborn. He proudly admitted on a later occasion that he fought in the tradition of Hugo, Lamartine, and John Brown as a "champion of impossible doctrines, or as a debater of dreams, just fallen from the skies."[53] It was in this spirit that he also wrote to W.E.B. Du Bois when that younger leader seemed to be at his wits' end in 1907.

Before an accident blinded him at the turn of the century, Desdunes managed to complete a history in French of his people so that their achievements and struggles would be remembered and used by its readers to continue the fight against racial prejudice in America. He wanted the accomplishments of the Creoles to be absorbed by all blacks, whether American or Creole. But, above all, Desdunes wanted any reader to learn from the story of the Creole radicals that "it is more noble and dignified to fight, no matter what, than to show a passive attitude of resignation. Absolute submission augments the oppressor's power and creates doubt about the feeling of the oppressed." Desdunes went to his grave on August 14, 1928, without any apparent change of mind.[54]

His efforts were not in vain, although he would not live to see their fruition. His example as well as his writings ensured that the peculiar traditions of the city's black Creole militants survived within their own communities, for others nurtured their memories and wrote down their history. And others, even after the *Plessy* setback, refused to accommodate the new racial order. Many maintained a militant interracial labor organization in the city; hundreds boycotted segregated streetcars; and before the end of the 1920s, black leaders such as A. P. Tureaud returned to the federal courts to reopen their ancestors' old battles.[55] None of these steadfast forebears was more defiant than Rodolphe Desdunes. He decried any sort of acquiescence to the prevailing racial arrangements of the fin de siècle America.

It was a remarkable life. Tourgée was right when he stood back to look at the Citizens' Committee's stubborn refusal to acquiesce in racial reaction. In January 1896, he confessed to one of the few remaining sympathetic U.S. senators:

> The effort of the men who have run the *Crusader*, to establish a daily Republican newspaper in New Orleans, is the bravest thing I have ever known and the most heroic endeavor ever made by individuals of the colored race in the United States. I have been familiar with the enterprise, in a sense, ever since its initiation and I must say I have never seen such dogged resolution and such cheerful self-sacrifice

displayed by any group of men as a mere matter of principle and for the benefit of others. . . . It was not wise, they admitted at this time, but said that if something was not done the colored people would lose all pride and hope and be content to sell themselves politically, for any mess of pottage that might be offered to any one of them.

At that moment, Tourgée was quite discouraged about his prospects of success in the *Plessy* case, but he still hoped "in spite of the previous rulings of the court, we are going to knock this sort of legislation out or at least give it a very black eye."[56] That the *Plessy* decision did become a "black eye" on the American past was due to the principled stand by men such as Rodolphe Lucien Desdunes and the black Creole tradition that sustained him.

Notes

1. Edwin R. A. Seligman to W.E.B. Du Bois, October 28, 1906, in *The Correspondence of W.E.B. Du Bois,* ed. Herbert Aptheker (Amherst: University of Massachusetts Press, 1973), 1:123.

2. W.E.B. Du Bois, "A Litany of Atlanta," in the *Independent,* October 11, 1906.

3. Francis Broderick, *W.E.B. Du Bois: Negro Leader in a Time of Crisis* (Stanford: Stanford University Press, 1959), 80.

4. Rodolphe Lucien Desdunes, *A Few Words to Dr. Du Bois with Malice Towards None* (New Orleans, 1907), 6.

5. Ibid., 13.

6. Ibid., 4–5.

7. Ibid., 10–11.

8. For one of the rare discussions of the difficulties that Americans face in trying "to understand the revolutionary slogan of France, 'liberty, equality, fraternity,'" see the essay by Nathan Glazer in *Ethnic Dilemmas, 1964–1982* (Cambridge: Harvard University Press, 1983), 209–29.

9. The bulk of Du Bois's speech appeared in the New York *Evening Post,* February 18, 1907. Desdunes, it seems, saw only a portion of it in the New Orleans *Item,* February 24, 1907.

10. W.E.B. Du Bois, *Black Reconstruction* (New York: Harcourt Brace, 1935) and Du Bois, "A Journey to Texas and New Orleans," *Crisis,* April 1934.

11. Caryn Cossé Bell, *Revolution, Romanticism, and the Afro-Creole Protest Tradition in Louisiana, 1718–1868* (Baton Rouge: Louisiana State University Press, 1997); and Joseph Logsdon and Caryn Cossé Bell, "The Americanization of Black New Orleans, 1850–1900," in *Creole New Orleans: Race and Americanization,* ed. Arnold Hirsch and Joseph Logsdon (Baton Rouge: Louisiana State University Press, 1992), 201–61. See also David C. Rankin, "The Politics of Caste: Free Colored Leadership in New Orleans dur-

ing the Civil War," in *Louisiana's Black Heritage,* ed. Robert R. Macdonald, John R. Kemp, and Edward F. Haas (New Orleans: Louisiana State Museum, 1979), 107–46.

12. Rodolphe Lucien Desdunes, *Our People and Our History,* trans. and ed. Sister Dorothea Olga McCants (Baton Rouge: Louisiana State University Press, 1973). This edition has a good sketch of Desdunes in the foreword by Charles E. O'Neil.

13. In setting out Desdunes's role, let me emphasize that I do not wish to ignore or denigrate the leadership of his close associate, Louis A. Martinet, the editor of the *Crusader.* Until recently the paucity of records had not permitted scholars of the *Plessy* case to uncover Desdunes's key role in the famous litigation. Although Martinet had preserved a complete file of the *Crusader*'s publisher's files, his widow had sold them to a junk dealer for scrap, as A. P. Tureaud discovered when he tried to retrieve them in the 1920s. Consequently, only a few intact issues of the paper have survived, and Desdunes had modestly erased his own activities in his published history of the nineteenth-century black Creoles of New Orleans. The story of the *Plessy* case in the rich and well-preserved correspondence of Albion Tourgée also turns primarily around the correspondence between Tourgée and Martinet. As a result, even the meticulous scholarship of Otto Olsen was unable to discern very much about Desdunes's leadership. Recently, however, new records have begun to reveal the roots of Desdunes's ideology and to demonstrate his importance in the struggle that produced the *Plessy* case, as the rest of this essay tries to make clear. The major new collections bearing on this subject include the Charles Rousséve Papers and the A. P. Tureaud Papers at the Amistad Research Center, Tulane University, both of which contain clippings from the *Crusader* as well as rare pamphlets by Desdunes and other Creole activists. Not to be overlooked at the University of New Orleans are the papers of René Grandjean, a white Frenchman who married into the black Creole family of Antoine Dubuclet, assisted Desdunes in writing his 1911 history, corresponded with Desdunes in Omaha, and preserved the voluminous transcriptions of nineteenth-century séances of a Creole spiritualist circle that had its roots in the antebellum period. Lastly, there is Desdunes's *Crusader* scrapbook, recently uncovered in forgotten storage at Xavier University of Louisiana. For Otto Olsen's important work on Tourgée and the Citizens' Committee of New Orleans, see his *Carpetbagger's Crusade: The Life of Albion Winegar Tourgée* (Baltimore: Johns Hopkins University Press, 1965); *The Thin Disguise: Turning Points in Negro History,* Plessy v. Ferguson, *a Documentary Presentation, 1864–1896* (New York: Humanities Press for the American Institute for Marxist Studies, 1967); and "Reflections on the *Plessy v. Ferguson* Decision of 1896," in *Louisiana's Legal Heritage,* ed. Edward F. Haas (Pensacola, Fla.: Perdido Press for the Louisiana State Museum, 1983).

14. R. L. Desdunes to René Grandjean, February 3, 1919, in the Grandjean Collection at the University of New Orleans; undated obituary of Desdunes's mother, Henrietta Guillard Desdunes, in the *Crusader* scrapbook, p. 93, at Xavier University of Louisiana.

15. *L'Union,* September 27, October 18, 1862. For an elaboration of the roots of this Franco-African radical tradition, see Bell, *Revolution, Romanticism.*

16. For studies of two key white allies, Thomas Jefferson Durant, an American

Fourierist, and Jean-Charles Houzeau, a Belgian exile who was active in the revolution of 1848, see Joseph G. Tregle Jr., "Thomas J. Durant, Utopian Socialism and the Failure of Presidential Reconstruction in Louisiana," *Journal of Southern History* 45 (November 1979): 485–512; and Jean-Charles Houzeau, *My Passage at the New Orleans Tribune*, ed. David C. Rankin (Baton Rouge: Louisiana State University Press, 1984).

17. See Logsdon and Bell, "The Americanization of Black New Orleans," esp. 221–32. For an earlier interpretation of these black Creole leaders and their outlook, see David Rankin, "The Impact of the Civil War on the Free Colored Community of New Orleans," *Perspectives in American History* 11 (1977–78): 379–416; Rankin, "The Politics of Caste."

18. Although Lincoln and the recipient of his letter, Louisiana governor Michael Hahn, showed the letter to several people, black leaders in New Orleans did not learn its contents until after Lincoln's death. The release of the letter following his assassination helped change the radical Creoles' view of him. See New Orleans *Tribune*, July 7, 1865.

19. *Liberator,* April 15, 1864.

20. New Orleans *Tribune*, January 28, 1865.

21. For a summary of Reconstruction in Louisiana, see Ted Tunnel, *Crucible of Reconstruction: War, Radicalism, and Race in Louisiana, 1862–1877* (Baton Rouge: Louisiana State University Press, 1984).

22. Donald E. DeVore and Joseph Logsdon, *Crescent City Schools: Public Education in New Orleans, 1841–1991* (Lafayette: University of Southwest Louisiana Press, 1991), 88–89. See also Roger A. Fischer, *The Segregation Struggle in Louisiana, 1862–1877* (Urbana: University of Illinois Press, 1974), 140–41.

23. For a keen study of Desdunes's language abilities, see the long review of the translation of Desdunes's 1911 history by J. John Perret in *Louisiana Studies* 13 (summer 1974): 187–92.

24. See the *Crusader,* undated clipping from 1892 signed by Desdunes, in *Crusader* scrapbook, p. 7.

25. Desdunes discussed his 1874 injuries late in his life; see R. L. Desdunes to René Grandjean, February 3, 1919, in the Grandjean Collection.

26. *Louisianian,* October 30, December 4, 1875; December 28, 1878.

27. *Louisianian,* July 2, 1881. For similar views see July 9, 16, 23, 30, August 6, 13, 1881. A call for a meeting to form such an organization appeared in French expressing a need to "la résistance légal," noting that the objective of the gathering was to organize "une Association pour la défense des droits de l'homme." *Louisianian,* August 6, 1881. For a notice of his graduation from the Straight Law School, see *Louisianian,* May 6, 1882.

28. The spiritualist society which began in the 1850s had contact with French spiritualists. The Scottish rite Masonic order was desegregated in 1867 at the order of French authorities in Paris. The records of the spiritualist society have survived in the Grandjean Collection at the University of New Orleans and the records of one of the Masonic lodges can be found in the George Longe Papers at the Amistad Research Center, Tulane University. For an example of Desdunes's attention to radical works in

the Franco-African world of his day, see the New Orleans *Pelican,* July 9, 1887, which speaks of Desdunes's familiarity with the work of A. Firmin, a Haitian who published a book in Paris in 1885 entitled *Of the Equality of Races.* In 1879, Desdunes also organized a French-speaking unit of the Odd Fellows, La Creole Lodge, designed in part to keep its members abreast of their distinctive Creole past and of French literature. See *Louisianian,* July 19, September 20, 1879, as well as the pamphlet *Discours de M. R. L. Desdunes . . . 14 févrie 1882,* which is located in the A. P. Tureaud Papers, box 77, folder 19, Amistad Research Center, Tulane University.

29. See Editorial Committee, *Prospectus,* September 15, 1887, in the A. P. Tureaud Papers, box 77, folder 21, Amistad Research Center, Tulane University. The editorial staff was not listed in the document, except for *Rodolphe L. Desdunes,* its secretary. The persons listed as taking subscriptions indicates it was a Creole initiative: L. N. Deguercy, Paul Trévigne, *Alcée Labat, M. J. Piron,* H. Galleaud, M. O. Bart, and *P. A. Desdunes.*

30. Martinet had begun the *Crusader* in early March 1889. The directors of the Crusader Publishing Company assumed control with the issue of March 29, 1890, as noted in that issue. They bought a new electric-powered press, rented an office on Exchange Alley in the heart of the French Quarter, and promised to open a French page "for the benefit of our large number of readers who have retained the love of their mother tongue." They also added a more militant tone to the paper's objectives: "We shall pay much attention to industrial and economic questions . . . and particularly shall we devote space to questions of labor. Our special aim, in fact, shall be to make a great Republican-Labor organ through which the working classes can at all times be heard and have their grievances made known and their wrongs righted." The board of directors included the core of what would become the Citizens' Committee: *Eugene Luscy* (president), R. D. Wilde (vice president), Joseph Jacques (treasurer), *L. J. Joubert* (secretary). Other members of the board were *Rev. A.E.P. Albert,* G. Chalaire, Rev. I. H. Hall, M. Jackson, *Arthur Estéves, Alcée Labat,* Joseph Garidelle, Dr. William H. Harrison, A. St. Amant, and *L. A. Martinet.* Those whose names were italicized in notes 29 and 30 later served on the Citizens' Committee.

31. Martinet had even flirted with membership in the state Democratic Party. See the long letter of Martinet to Albion W. Tourgée, October 5, 1891, item 5760 in the microfilm copy of the Albion W. Tourgée Papers at the Chautauqua Historical Museum in Westfield, New York (hereinafter cited as Tourgée Papers). A good portion of this long letter was published in Olsen, *Thin Disguise,* 55–60. For Martinet's close association with Pinchback after the Compromise of 1877, see *Louisianian,* September 24, 1881 (note letter of W. Posey to editor, September 18), April 15, 29, 1882. Martinet and his wife also accepted teaching posts at Southern University, the all-black college created by the Constitutional Convention of 1879 to gain Pinchback's support for the elimination of the desegregation mandates of the earlier 1868 state constitution. For many of the militant Creoles, particularly Aristide Mary, the creation of Southern University and the tacit acceptance of the color line by black leaders that its establishment betokened was an especial outrage. Mary "thundered with indignation against the scheming of men of color who took part in the Convention of 1879. Ex-Governor

Pinchback was the leader, and it was he who presented the article seeking the establishment of a University for persons of color in the State of Louisiana. It is this clause that Mary characterized as a 'black stain' in the Constitution of the State, and in that, he has had the support and sympathy of the population called Creole. . . . I believe that Mary never spoke a word to Pinchback from that time until his death. They would say that his repugnance had grown out of the contempt for the man who had said that 'this government is a government of whites,' in order to justify his conduct on this occasion." See Rodolphe Lucien Desdunes, *Hommage rendu à la mémoire de Alexandre Aristide Mary décédé à la Nouvelle-Orleans, le 15 mai 1893, à l'âge de 70 ans* (New Orleans, 1893), 9–10 [translation by Caryn C. Bell], a copy of which can be found in the A. P. Tureaud Papers. For Pinchback's view of that crisis, see the report that appeared in his newspaper, the *Louisianian,* July 12, 19, 26, 1879. One of Pinchback's supporters, T. T. Allain, defended Pinchback's cooperation with the Bourbon Democrats: "What Gov. Pinchback did in connection with Nicholls' Government, he was but carrying the Southern policy of the National Administration at the time, from the very fact that President Hayes appointed him as Special Agent of the Internal Revenue." See *Louisianian,* September 17, 1881.

32. *Crusader,* March 29, 1890, in the Charles Rousseve Collection.

33. Unsuccessfully, they also challenged the effort of northern black leaders, under the guidance of T. Thomas Fortune, to name their group the Afro-American League. See L. A. Martinet to Albion W. Tourgée, October 5, 1891, item 5760 in the Tourgée Papers. Desdunes and Martinet did not oppose racial solidarity and organization but did not wish to create any color line that might act to exclude like-minded white supporters. They wished to be consistent, moreover, in their attacks on color lines imposed by white leaders. They applied their views against segregation to both private groups as well as public agencies and organizations. It was often difficult for black Americans to understand this thinking when it was directed at private agencies like churches and other voluntary organizations. A fuller explanation of their thinking comes through in the attack launched by Martinet and Desdunes against Catholic Church leaders who were segregating congregations and other church facilities. When fellow black Catholics tried to form a Catholic orphanage and added a racial designation to the institution, Martinet and Desdunes attacked both the name and the fund-raising effort that had been mounted on its behalf. When the Catholic officials agreed to change the name, the *Crusader* led a successful fund-raising drive to support the orphanage. See L. A. Martinet to Albion W. Tourgée, July 4, 1892, item 6377, in the Tourgée Papers.

34. See the *Crusader,* March 22, 29, 1890. For a copy of the petition to the legislature, see "Protest of the American Citizens Equal Rights Association of Louisiana against Class Legislation," item 4752 in the Tourgée Papers. It is also reprinted in Olsen, *The Thin Disguise,* 47–50.

35. *Crusader,* July 19, 1890.

36. A bilingual Creole but also a bitterly anti-Catholic Methodist minister, Albert had commented in his weekly newspaper, the *Southwestern Christian Advocate,* that the defeat of the Lodge Bill in the U.S. Senate was probably for the best, because "rivers of blood" might have swept over black southerners if the federal government had tried to

enforce their right to vote. In fairness to Albert, it should be noted that he had tried to maintain his militancy in the face of fierce pressure to moderate his views. For the initial efforts of Albert in his church during 1891, see *Journal of the Louisiana Conference of the Methodist Episcopal Church,* 1892, 296. For the subsequent reprisals he suffered, see *Southwestern Christian Advocate,* March 3, 1892.

37. About two years later, Desdunes publicly recalled that Mary promised his financial assistance and gave him names of others to approach for funds. "You will not be abandoned," Mary vowed. "The population cannot remain silent when prejudice provokes it with such boldness and such inhumanity." Desdunes, *Hommage rendu à la mémoire de Alexandre Aristide Mary,* 12. This account in French, privately published and circulated in May 1893, is perhaps the best inside account of the politics and planning that led to the formation of the Citizens' Committee. Desdunes admitted that he, Martinet, and their friend Laurent Auguste had previously failed, after the collapse of the ACERA, to form another group to take up their now long threatened suit. In his funeral oration for Mary, Desdunes not only underscored their close ideological bonds rooted in French anticlerical thought and organization but he also proudly pointed to other Creole radicals of the Civil War and Reconstruction generation: "If the cause of right has lost a great deal through weakness and treason, it must be admitted that it would not have existed at all without champions like Mary, Roudanez, Auguste, Bertonneau, and an entire legion of others, whose memory is worth retaining forever." Desdunes, *Hommage rendu à la mémoire de Alexandre Aristide Mary,* 3, 16.

38. Citizens' Committee, *Report of Proceedings for the Annulment of Act No. 111 of 1890* (New Orleans, ca. 1897), 2. As can be seen, all but three of the committee had non–Anglo-American names: Arthur Estèves (president), C. C. Antoine (vice president), Firmin Christophe (secretary), G. G. Johnson (assistant secretary), Paul Bonseigneur (treasurer), Laurent Auguste, R. L. Desdunes, Alcée Labat, Pierre Chevalier, N. E. Mansion, A. B. Kennedy, R. B. Baquie, A. J. Giuranovich, E. A. Williams, L. A. Martinet, L. J. Joubert, M. J. Piron, and Eugene Luscy. The membership of the Committee fluctuated, although it kept to about the same number of members. At its end in 1897, Johnson, Mansion, Williams, and Piron were no longer on the board, but others were serving in their place: Junius Hall, Frank Hall, Noel Bachus, George Geddes, and A.E.P. Albert. In 1897, the officers were still the same except for Luscy, who had taken Johnson's place as assistant secretary.

39. L. A. Martinet to Albion W. Tourgée, October 5, 11, 1891, items respectively 5760 and 5763 in the Tourgée Papers. Martinet may have already proffered this offer to the ACERA more than a year before his exchanges with Martinet in the fall of 1891. Well before the Citizens' Committee had been formed, Eli C. Freeman, a young member of the ACERA in Louisiana, had dashed off a letter to Tourgée, asking only for a few lines of advice about testing the Jim Crow law in Louisiana. Without much hesitation, Tourgée responded and apparently offered not just his advice but announced his willingness to act as the group's attorney free of charge. It is unclear, however, whether the two offers were connected in Martinet's mind. See Eli C. Freeman to Albion W. Tourgée, August 4, 1890, item 4872 in the Tourgée Papers; a second letter from Freeman, August

26, 1890, item 4895, notes that Tourgée's letter with his "advices relative the best case of the separate car law" was published in part in one of the several black-edited newspapers then being published in New Orleans. In a subsequent letter to Tourgée (October 14, 1891, item 5766 in the Tourgée Papers), Freeman noted that he was in personal contact with Martinet: "Mr. Martinet of New Orleans informs that the Citizens' Committee has employed you as the principle [sic] attorney in the separate car suit."

Tourgée's first published call, in his "Bystander's Notes," for a national "voluntary organization for the enforcement of legal rights" appeared in his column dated October 2, 1891, which appeared the next day in the *Inter-Ocean*. See the copy of that article, item 8897, also in the Tourgée Papers. In fact, it was clear that Tourgée's call for a national organization was in response to the Citizens' Committee public appeal of September 5. By the time of his column of October 16 (item 8897 in the Tourgée Papers), he was referring to it as both the Liberty League and the Citizens' Equal Rights Association and included a tear-off application form at the end of his column. Because his column began to be printed regularly about this time in the *Crusader*, Tourgée's ideas were reaching black New Orleans even faster than his correspondence. The new organization gained the name of National Citizens' Right Association in his column of December 4, 1891 (item 8897 in the Tourgée Papers).

Both Tourgée and the Citizens' Committee recognized that their assault on the Jim Crow railroad car law was also an indirect attack on the drive toward disfranchisement which had begun in Mississippi in 1890. Martinet wrote with remarkable awareness about the larger struggle: "You desire to abolish the 'Jim Crow' car & to paralyze the Mississippi ballot restriction. We are going to do what we can against the 'Jim Crow' car now, and when we get the case well underway, we must turn our attention to the suffrage restriction. The signs are also ominous in Louisiana. There is a row going on now among the Democrats over the Lottery question—they are fairly split. . . . Both sides want him [the black man] disfranchised, and . . . I see looming up the ominous figure of a constitutional convention to qualify suffrage after the Mississippi plan. . . . The National Citizens' Equal Rights Ass'n. might then be able to pull us out." L. A. Martinet to Albion W. Tourgée, October 25, 1891, items 5768 in the Tourgée Papers.

40. R. L. Desdunes to Albion W. Tourgée, December 1, 1891, February 5, 1892 (quotation), both items marked 7614 (the NCRA file) in the Tourgée Papers.

41. Citizens' Committee, *Report* (1897), 9–12. Contributions averaged between five and ten dollars from community groups (perhaps about one hundred to two hundred dollars in today's inflated currency). Most of the participating groups seemed to be benevolent societies, but trade unions, Protestant churches, and lodges also took part. Once the movement got beyond the infighting of 1890, non-Creole black New Orleanians pitched in their support. If men dominated almost every leadership position in the movement's organizations, women played a significant role in fund-raising. More than a quarter of the contributing groups were women's societies in New Orleans. In northern cities, women like Ida Wells-Barnett, Charlotte Grimke, and Florence A. Lewis took up active leadership in the NCRA. But in the very patriarchal culture of New Orleans, especially in the downtown Creole world of Rodolphe Desdunes, women sel-

dom if ever occupied decision-making positions in the activist groups. For the role of women in the NCRA, see Florence A. Lewis to Tourgée, December 2, 1891, February 5, 1892, items 5816, 7614 (NCRA file); Charlotte L. Grimke to Tourgée, May 27, June 7, 1892, both item 7614 (NCRA file); Ida B. Wells to Tourgée, November 3, 1892, item 7614 (NCRA), all in the Tourgée Papers.

42. Tourgée never came to New Orleans to meet with his clients and finally settled on Martinet—through whom he carried on most of the negotiations with the Citizens' Committee—as the black southern member of the Administrative Council. L. A. Martinet to Tourgée, December 7, 1891 (quotation), December 28, 1891, February 3, 1892, items 5837, 5877, and 6007, respectively, in the Tourgée Papers.

43. Martinet to Tourgée, October 5, 1891, item 5760 in the Tourgée Papers. Daniel Desdunes was arrested on February 24, 1892, after buying a ticket to Mobile on the Louisville and Nashville Railroad. In an arrangement worked out with railroad officials, he was released on bail after less than two hours in jail. He was scheduled for trial on May 14. James C. Walker to Tourgée, February 25, March 14, 1892, items 6058 and 6109 in the Tourgée Papers. He never went to trial because another case concerning Pullman cars in Shreveport had declared the Jim Crow law unconstitutional when applied to interstate passengers. Under that decision, the Desdunes case was dismissed on July 11 and the defendant was released.

44. Apparently Martinet was one of the least supportive of the *Plessy* case among the members of the Citizens' Committee, perhaps because he was also the group's only practicing lawyer. See Martinet to Tourgée, July 4, 1892 [but not completed and sent until August 29], item 6377 in the Tourgée Papers. In that letter (a portion of which was written after Daniel Desdunes's formal release from charges on July 11), Martinet admitted that he did not expect as favorable a result in the *Plessy* case (which was launched on June 7, the day Plessy had been arrested): "Of course I do not entertain the same favorable result as hopefully as in the Desdunes [case]. But perhaps it is best that the battle be fought. I rely, however, more on the fact that the Negro's right to travel interstate being recognized, & if maintained by him, it will throw the 'Jim Crow' car into disuse as you say." Although he was designated by the Citizens' Committee as a member of the legal team, he never submitted a brief as did the other three lawyers.

45. Tourgée to James A. Walker, undated but about March 16 [it begins: "Yours of the 14th just rec'd."], item 6101 in the Tourgée Papers. The initial objective was to show the difficulty of enforcing the color line in Louisiana, or as Tourgée put it in his letter, "It is a question we may as well take up, if nothing else, to let the court sharpen its wits over." For the most up-to-date treatment of Plessy and the famous case that bears his name, see Keith Medley, "The Sad Story of How Separate but Equal Was Born," *Smithsonian Magazine*, February 1994, 105–17. For evidence of Plessy's role in organized activism, see DeVore and Logsdon, *Crescent City Schools*, 115.

46. R. L. Desdunes, "Judge Ferguson and Allies," *Crusader*, [n.d. 1893], in the *Crusader* scrapbook, p. 19.

47. *Crusader*, June 12, 1895, in the *Crusader* scrapbook, p. 53.

48. Desdunes, *Our People and Our History*, 147. Citizens' Committee, *Report of the*

Proceedings for the Annulment of Act 111 of 1890 (New Orleans, ca. 1897). This publication and an earlier publication, L. A. Martinet, ed., *The Violation of a Constitutional Right* (New Orleans, 1893), demonstrate the large following that the committee gathered at various meetings to protest discrimination and support various legal cases.

49. See Dolores Egger Labbe, *Jim Crow Comes to Church: The Establishment of Segregated Parishes in South Louisiana* (Lafayette: University of Southwest Louisiana Press, 1971).

50. E. Gerville-Reache to N. S. Mansion, postmarked October 5, 1896, in the Charles Rousséve Papers.

51. New Orleans *States,* February 29, 1915; New Orleans *Times-Picayune,* April 13, 14, 1915.

52. Charles A. Lofgren, *The* Plessy *Case: A Legal-Historical Interpretation* (New York: Oxford University Press, 1987), 204–7.

53. *Crusader,* August 15, 1891, in the Charles Rousseve Collection; and May 14, 1895, in the *Crusader* scrapbook, p. 45.

54. Desdunes, *Our History and Our People,* 147. Desdunes died in Omaha at the home of one of his five children. They had his body shipped for burial in New Orleans. His outlook in his last years is revealed in his correspondence with René Grandjean. See this correspondence in the Grandjean Collection.

55. Two works that relate the direct connection between the struggle of the Citizens' Committee and the twentieth-century civil rights movement in Louisiana are Donald E. DeVore, "Rise from the Nadir: Black New Orleans Between the Wars, 1920–1940," master's thesis, University of New Orleans, 1983, and Adam Fairclough, *Race and Democracy: The Civil Rights Struggle in Louisiana, 1915–1972* (Athens: University of Georgia Press, 1995).

56. Tourgée to William E. Chandler, January 30, 1896, item 8958 in the Tourgée Papers.

II

Black, Brown, and White

Confronting and Accommodating Jim Crow

3

Accommodating Activism

Dexter Avenue Baptist Church and Robert Chapman Judkins, Workers That Needeth Not Be Ashamed, 1883–1920

HOUSTON B. ROBERSON

Study to show thyself approved unto God,
a workman that needeth not be shamed.
2 Timothy 2:15 RSV

On October 26, 1907, in the Montgomery *Colored Alabamian*, a widely circulated black newspaper, Lincoln Laconia Burwell, a Spanish-American War veteran, prominent Alabama physician, and druggist, issued a clarion call to African Americans throughout the state of Alabama: "We as a race must make our own history . . . so act that no excuse can be rendered why we may not enjoy the rights and privileges of Americans." Similarly, in a December 14, 1912, editorial announcing the upcoming observance of the fiftieth anniversary of emancipation, Dexter Avenue Baptist Church pastor Robert Chapman Judkins, also the activist editor of the *Colored Alabamian*, reminded his church and community that "the eyes of the world will be turned upon the race with a deep and anxious inquiry: has the Negro manifested in this period sufficient evidence of his capability to be a full-fledged citizen of America?"

Heeding these words, African Americans at Dexter Avenue Baptist Church in Montgomery, as in other parts of the Gulf South, became more convinced than ever that their freedom depended upon the efficacy of the institutions, primarily religious and educational, that they controlled. At the turn of the twenty-first century, such statements are open to criticism, riddled, as they are, with the insignias of traditional accommodationism— the racially conciliatory practice of postponing the demand for immediate recognition of African Americans' political rights and social equality.

Booker T. Washington captured the essence of this approach to race relations in his "Atlanta Exposition" speech when he stated, "The wisest among my race understand that the agitation of questions of social equality is the extremist folly, and that progress in the enjoyment of all privileges that will come to us must be the result of severe and constant struggle rather than artificial forcing."[1] The kind of accommodation practiced by churches like Dexter Avenue deserves a deeper analysis. My study of this church shows that such efforts were more vibrant and effective than historians have previously considered. Between 1883, when church members embarked upon a program to build a permanent edifice across from the Alabama state capitol, and 1920, just after congregants joined with the local NAACP to protest lynching in the state, Dexter Avenue members and pastors created important traditions of protest and activism. These efforts, despite seemingly insurmountable obstacles, nurtured a fragile but steadily emerging sense of self-empowerment—an accommodating activism—that helped lay the groundwork for the more direct, confrontational activism that characterized civil rights protest in the mid-twentieth century. In their fight to secure basic rights and freedoms, members of the congregation studied to show themselves approved—workers that needeth not be ashamed.

Despite a large literature examining the black church at the turn of the twentieth century, less has been written about local churches in the lives of their communities.[2] Investigating the function of a single congregation in its local milieu over time helps to render visible ambiguities and complexities and leads to fresh insights into previously held notions. In its exploration of life at Dexter Avenue between 1883 and 1920, particularly the ministry of Robert Chapman Judkins, this article considers some of the complexities and ambiguities of the activism of accommodationism.

White racism in the early twentieth century Gulf South was especially oppressive and unyielding. While we have long recognized that racism, only recently have we begun to understand the range of attitudes, behavior, and resistance that characterized black life in the area during this time. Many African Americans actively challenged the racial status quo in ways that most whites construed as audacious effronteries to the southern caste system. Blacks often discovered ideas of equality through their churches. Congregations like Dexter Avenue and people like Judkins contested racism more strongly than they accommodated white fears. They saw such challenges as rightful and necessary expressions of their status as citizens. Further, their beliefs and actions took on even greater significance in light of the considerably meager effort on the part of the federal government to protect black freedom and civil rights.

To secure spiritual, intellectual, and civil freedom, African Americans developed effective self-help strategies. Dexter Avenue's first pastor, Charles Octavius Boothe, captured the essence of blacks' thinking when he wrote, "We had to look to our own heads for light, to our own hearts for courage, and to our own consciences for moral dictation."[3] In this struggle, black institutions worked to prepare a generation of African Americans to challenge the almost universally held white belief in black inferiority and prove themselves worthy of basic freedoms guaranteed all Americans by virtue of citizenship.[4]

In many ways, the Dexter Avenue Baptist Church community might seem to epitomize traditional notions of the activism historians call accommodationism: its overwhelmingly middle-class congregation; its disapproval of emotional displays during Sunday services; and members' strict adherence to the Victorian values of self-restraint and propriety. And yet life at Dexter Avenue between 1883 and the 1920s suggests that accommodation was more nuanced than has been previously acknowledged.[5] The kind of accommodation practiced by this church was not simple, inactive, or quiescent. Still, accommodating activism was a difficult balancing act. As Kevin Gaines has persuasively argued, the traditional racial accommodation practiced by the black middle class [representing roughly 2 percent of the black population] was fraught with problems, limitations, and contradictions. In fact, some historians have argued that early twentieth-century black activism and notions of race progress sometimes unwittingly aided white supremacists.[6]

We cannot ignore or underestimate the degree to which these efforts immediately broadened black freedoms. Accommodating activism significantly improved the quality of life within local communities, kept hope alive, and helped provide a corpus of leadership and traditions of protests that aided in bringing about the successes in the midcentury assault on de jure racial discrimination. Against the backdrop of persistent racial hostility and oppression, this strategy recognized and tried to allay white fears of black efforts to become equal citizens, all the while resisting, contesting, and challenging the circumscribed niche into which white society placed African Americans. Through accommodating activism, African Americans sought power and opportunity, organized and galvanized resources, and steadily pushed to enlarge black freedom with the ultimate goal of achieving an optimum measure of self-expression and empowerment. This essay, then, is a portion of a story about an institution, a congregation, and a minister who sometimes placated extant white beliefs about blacks but more often confronted and battled white estimations of black potential and character.

Three episodes in the early history of Dexter Avenue Baptist Church particularly exemplify accommodating activism protest: the church's resolve to build a permanent edifice in a white neighborhood across from the state capitol; the rituals of affirmation and political protests exemplified in the dynamic ministry of Robert Chapman Judkins; and the efforts on the part of church women to establish programs to improve the quality of day-to-day life for African Americans in the community. While these incidents did not swell into a national movement for civil rights, they do illustrate the importance of this church in the life of its community during the era of heightened and turbulent race relations that characterized the post-Reconstruction Gulf South.

Founded in 1877 on a former slave trader's pen, Dexter Avenue Baptist Church almost literally rose out of the ashes of slavery as a phoenix of freedom and as a symbol of black Alabamians' tenacity in exacting some measure of control over their lives.[7] Members of the church transcended the legacy of slavery to set out on their own walk of Christian faith. They established a prophetic appropriation of Christianity that shunned racism, advocated a radical equality, and insisted upon the kinship of all people. Initially, it is easy to be drawn to Dexter Avenue because of its renown. The church's national and international celebrity date back to the 1950s, when its pastor, Dr. Martin Luther King Jr., led a peaceful and successful struggle against the second-class citizenship status of a significant portion of America's population. In the basement of this church, King, along with other local ministers and community leaders, including Jo Ann Robinson and E. D. Nixon, organized the Montgomery Improvement Association. This community organization operated the successful 1955 Montgomery bus boycott, which lasted some 380 days and resulted in the desegregation of public conveyances.[8] The celebrity of this religious institution is only a small part of its story, however. Almost unknown is the story of this church as an independent black community of faith which provided a place of fellowship and an affirming space that helped to institutionalize the early twentieth-century struggle for the recognition of African American equality decades before it became a national icon.

In the wake of phenomenally successful institution building within the black community during the early days of Reconstruction, the late nineteenth and early twentieth centuries ushered in a period of fermented political enervation, economic deprivation, and social segregation for African Americans in Alabama—a nadir of postbellum race relations.[9] Though far from adequate in number, by the 1880s, Montgomery could boast of a few black educational institutions in the area, a health infirmary, and a host of black churches.[10] Nevertheless, black political disfranchisement and the subsequent social segregation of this era forced upon African Americans a harness of racial inequity. The acute nature of these political and social proscriptions and the use of violence, including lynching, to enforce them created a hostile environment in which the physical oppression of slavery met its twentieth-century incarnation—the psychological and emotional oppression of second-class citizenship.[11] Ratifying a new state constitution in 1901, Alabama Democrats, who had wrested control of state politics from the hands of Republicans, managed to overthrow state constitutional protections granted African Americans just after the Civil War.[12] The passage of this new state constitution successfully nullified any remnants of federal protection of black freedoms in the state, and it laid the foundation for "decades of reaction, injustice, recurring violence and sectional stagnation" for all Alabamians and indeed the rest of the Gulf South.[13] Addressing a session of the American Bankers' Association in Atlantic City, New Jersey, in 1907, Virginia governor Claude Augustus Swanson stated that the "disfranchisement of the Negro and his consequent elimination from politics . . . had been one of the greatest factors in the advancement of the South." Swanson continued, "With God's help and our own good right arm, we will hold [the Negro] where he is for his own good and our own salvation."[14]

This was the political climate in which postbellum black churches like Dexter Avenue found themselves. Perhaps at no other time was having both a symbolic and concrete space more critical for black churches' efforts to not only address spiritual needs but also to respond to circumstances created by white racism. In its resolve to construct a permanent facility on the corner of Decatur Street and Dexter Avenue—a prominent white Montgomery neighborhood just across from the state capitol and the first White House of the Confederacy—church members established an undeniable sanctuary of protest that challenged the gleaming white power structures that surround it. Having a safe space in which to explore strategies to challenge the hostile society took on, arguably, even greater significance than it had during the earlier years of emancipation.

In 1877, when church members, led by trustee H. A. Loveless, purchased for $270 a former slave trader's pen located directly across from the state capitol, it raised no controversy. Most of the business sections and the heart of the city of Montgomery were located away from the capitol. This development had been an intentional move on the part of the city fathers; they built the capitol away from the heart of the city so as not to suggest that Montgomery would receive any kind of special benefit as the capital city.[15] By the early 1880s, however, the business community of Montgomery extended up Dexter Avenue to the capitol. Equally important, this locality had become populated mostly by state government employees.

In 1883, congregants at Dexter Avenue began to solidify its place in the neighborhood. Along with their pastor, A. N. McEwen, they began a program to construct a new facility. Using their dray wagons, members collected bricks discarded by city workers paving the streets and in two years had enough bricks to build a one-story structure. Their activities did not go unnoticed by some of Montgomery's white community. When it became clear that this black congregation intended to build a permanent worship facility one block from the state capitol, some white citizens objected. One resident pleaded in a May 6, 1885, editorial directed at white and black readers of the Montgomery *Daily Advertiser*, "This street will in the near future be one of the best improved streets in the city of Montgomery . . . and nothing should be allowed that would deter citizens from building on Dexter Avenue." The editorialist went on to claim he had "no race prejudice that would cause him to do any injustice to 'our brother in black,'" but admonished his fellow white citizens to "refuse to contribute a nickel until he finds out where the church is to be located." He concluded, "Fair minded and thinking ones among the colored people can see the justice of the foregoing remarks and the propriety of choosing some other place for a house of worship." Rumors persisted, as late as 1972, that state government officials and other prominent Montgomery citizens were plotting to force the congregation to sell this property, but members refused to be deterred.[16]

The first worship service was held in the basement of the new church in July 1885. Architect Pelham J. Anderson had designed a red brick Gothic revival structure with white Victorian bracketing.[17] William Watkins, Dexter Avenue deacon and the contractor in charge of the project, was able to have the upstairs sanctuary ready for Thanksgiving services in 1889.[18] For the members of Dexter Avenue, their new facility was an object of pride. Many in the Montgomery community agreed, and even the

Montgomery *Daily Advertiser* noted in 1885 that "the Colored Baptists" have erected "a handsome brick church."[19]

Church members believed it was their responsibility to prove to Montgomery's white community that Dexter Avenue members were worthy to build their church in the heart of the city. Charles Octavius Boothe explained that white objections centered around their misunderstanding of the kind of people who made up Dexter Avenue's congregation. Boothe explained that in sharp contrast to the time "when colored people like dumb driven cattle before hound and lash, were wending their way through the streets of Montgomery—that those who worship at Dexter Avenue are people of money and refinement." After all, Holland Thompson, a church founder, had served on the city council for three terms and in the state legislature for three terms. Then there was H. A. Loveless. Born enslaved in Union Springs, Alabama, in 1854, he had come to Montgomery in 1870, worked odd jobs, saved his money, and established a butcher's shop. Soon his business expanded to include a coal yard, a funeral home, and a horse and carriage taxi service.[20] William Watkins was a successful contractor. From this evidence Boothe claimed that "the colored people of this city own many hundreds of thousands of dollars in real estate." He concluded that church members care about propriety and that it was entirely proper for them to build in town.[21]

Here we see the accommodationist effort to demonstrate to the white community that black people are worthy and capable of negotiating shared public space. Moreover, Boothe's comments betrayed one of the internal struggles of this church from its inception and accommodationism in general—its inability to provide the same level of support and affirmation for Montgomery's working-class African Americans.[22] Still, the persistent refusal to back down from members' plans permanently to locate their religious facility across from the capital building was a real and symbolic action that contested whites' Jim Crow efforts to relegate African Americans to particular areas of the city. Over the years, being located in so conspicuous a place induced a routine ebb and flow of threats to force relocation.[23] Church members' determination becomes even more significant when one considers that this building would become the site for planning the 1955 Montgomery bus boycott and an important meeting space in 1919 when Montgomery's branch of the National Association for the Advancement of Colored People met to demand that the state take some action against lynching and improve the condition of black schools.[24]

Dexter Avenue's founding, then, was a dramatic act of resistance and of self-determination.[25] Opening in a structure formerly used as a slave trader's pen transformed a profane facility of enslavement and bondage into a hallowed shrine from which to exercise self-expression and to fight for African American freedom.[26] On the very space where blacks had been held awaiting a life of enslavement and illiteracy, the founders of Dexter Avenue established a religious institution that promoted education as indispensable to good Christian character, good citizenship, and personal liberation. Also, permanently locating the church two blocks from the state capitol, where just sixteen years earlier Jefferson Davis had taken the oath of office as president of the Confederacy, was a dramatic symbol of resistance. In the era of Jim Crow segregation practices and in defiance to those who complained, "It is not right for them [African Americans] to build nor for us [whites] to assist them to build in every place," church members were successful in their efforts to build a permanent edifice on the corner of Dexter Avenue and Decatur Streets.[27]

By 1900, Dexter Avenue had erected a physical structure, established a stable congregation, selected several pastors, and participated in domestic and foreign missions. Leading the work of the church during the second generation of Dexter Avenue's existence was a passionate and dynamic young pastor, Robert Chapman Judkins.[28] In June 1905, Judkins completed his divinity studies at Virginia Union University in Richmond, married schoolteacher Virginia Harper, and accepted a call to the pastorate at Dexter Avenue.[29] Enthusiastic about this new venture, Judkins returned to his home state full of ideas and with a vision for every part of church life, from improving the physical structure to creating a series of religious and intellectual programs to broaden the ministry and mission of the church. Judkins enlisted the aid of a relatively privileged black congregation to help him establish his ministry of social justice and racial uplift. His earnest belief that churches must not only provide salvation for the soul but also serve as God's vehicle for political and social justice guided him in cultivating church members' emerging sense of self-empowerment.[30]

Judkins structured a ministry, sought out leadership and workers and established community programs in the hope of achieving what he believed to be the earthly mission of a church. To these ends, he founded and published out of his home on 105 Tatum Street a weekly newspaper, the *Colored Alabamian*, which served the black community in Montgomery and beyond. This newspaper aided Judkins in his efforts to give vitality to

Above: Figure 3.1. The Dexter Avenue Baptist Church, circa 1900. Site of early organizational efforts to confront white supremacy. The church served as a visible symbol of black defiance during the darkest days of segregation. Note the proximity of the Alabama state capitol. Alabama State Archives.

Left: Figure 3.2. Robert Chapman Judkins, charismatic pastor of the Dexter Avenue Baptist Church, Montgomery, Alabama, 1905–16. Alabama State Archives.

the church's growing sense of self-determination and to promote justice. Judkins and his congregation regarded the newspaper as "an organ of the church." The newspaper's motto, "Equal justice for all, special privileges to none," clearly signified Judkins's determination to inform and try to marshal the community in a fight for fairness and for African Americans to determine their own destinies.[31]

In an editorial written in May 1908, Judkins expressed his visceral motivation and belief concerning the relationship between justice and the work of the church. He began his editorial by quoting Matthew 7:12: "In all things whatsoever ye would that men should do to you do you even so to them." He called this statement the "Christ rock that constitutes the foundation stone of the temple of justice." Therefore, he concluded, the "inculcation of this principle [justice] is the one concern of the earthward mission of religion."[32]

Judkins's pursuit of justice centered, in part, on his outrage over disfranchisement. He editorialized, "Ten million Negroes of the United States live in a land that knew them in times past as slaves, now scornfully proclaim them to be of . . . unacceptable blood . . . [and] denied representation in law making. . . . This decision is not a crime against man but a sin against man's maker." He explained that "Negro religious organizations have thus felt it their responsibility to point out the golden rule to the politicians of society."[33] Later he stated that "deprived of the protection of the very law we are called upon to obey and respect . . . Negroes in this community have . . . borne it all with patience." He appealed to state lawmakers, stating that "every spirit of justice and fair play demands that the law be upheld."[34]

Often pictured in his newspaper in a stiff-bosom, high-collared shirt with a bow tie, dark vest, and jacket, Judkins appeared the epitome of erudition, the embodiment of the Victorian values of restraint and propriety that characterized his proper education at the hands of northern missionaries. Yet his fervent indignation at the injustices experienced by African Americans sometimes drove him to exchange his usually proper and measured demeanor for sarcasm. In yet another editorial decrying the injustice of social segregation, he queried, "When President [Theodore] Roosevelt and his fellow Negro hunters were away in the swamp hunting bears, what became of the colored brethren when they stopped for lunch? . . . How far apart did they have to sit before it was settled that there was no social equality?"[35] Judkins reveals here that in the same way Roosevelt worked alongside African Americans in his hunting ventures, that white and black Montgomerians encountered and worked with one another in their daily lives in ways that probably transgressed the rigid boundaries of racial etiquette observed in public. Conscious that racial segregation was more concerned with conferring a badge of inferiority on African Americans than it was with literally keeping black people and white people separate in all avenues of life, here Judkins contests social segregation by highlighting its illogicality and impracticality.

In 1908, Judkins combined the voice of his church with those of other community leaders when he aired the concerns of a group of local black ministers responding to a series of attacks on local African Americans. Along with Judkins, W. C. Branton, N. N. Nealy, J. B. Branam, W. A. Blackwell, and E. E. Scott wrote a letter of protest to the city council. The ministers laid out several complaints. First, they condemned the assault on an honored and highly respected Negro woman by a strong white man because she boarded the streetcar ahead of him. The man was ordered to pay a minor fine, and the Negro woman apparently was charged with breaking segregation laws. They denounced an incident in which a white man who killed a Negro man, for no stated reason, was released without a trial. Next, they condemned the killing of a Negro man by a policeman because the man failed to drive as far to one side of the road as the white officer felt he should. Finally, they protested the brutal treatment suffered by African Americans while in the custody of the police.

The group "viewed with grave concern the widespread spirit of lawlessness and violence which has manifested itself . . . within the past few weeks." The ministers vowed "to do all in their power to suppress evil and lawbreaking committed by Negroes." For this accommodation, however, they demanded "that Negroes charged with misdemeanors or minor crimes have a fair and impartial trial." Fair treatment, they pointed out, was essential to ensure that African Americans would not soon believe "that laws are not made for their protection but their punishment."[36]

Clearly what these ministers were doing was confrontational beyond our traditional notions of accommodation. They were insisting that the community recognize and honor the equal protection clause of the Fourteenth Amendment. We must keep in mind that the accommodation and the activism that we see here are products of a particular historical moment. Jim Crow laws and the racial etiquette that they demanded were just in the process of being solidified. Many African Americans, though it might seem naïve from the vantage point of the twenty-first century, still believed that their ability to embrace and espouse Victorian bourgeois values demonstrated their inner worthiness to the white community and their potential to be productive citizens.[37] Modeling such behavior, blacks hoped, would gnaw away white prejudice and crumble the walls of segregation. But as Glenda Gilmore points out, "White men reordered southern society through segregation and disfranchisement in the 1890s because they realized that African American success not only meant competition in the market place and the sharing of political influence but also entailed a challenge to fundamental social hierarchies."[38] Many black activists did not believe that the system of racial oppression would become even more entrenched after World War I.

Judkins structured his ministry at Dexter Avenue in a way that nurtured members' sense of self-worth and empowerment. He sought to create a cadre of faithful Christian leaders and workers, in all areas of church life, who combined intellectual ability with a strong sense of morality, spirituality, and commitment to racial uplift.[39] We see this illustrated especially in his focus on education and programming for church youth. Judkins appointed J. W. Beverly as superintendent of Sunday school programming. Since the 1890s, Dexter Avenue's Sunday school had provided not only Bible study but also general instruction in reading and writing to supplement the inadequate public schools for African Americans.[40] Beverly was particularly interested in training children, and he published two pamphlets, "Practical Ethics for Children" and "A Guide to English Oration," which he provided for the youth at Dexter Avenue and distributed to community children who for various reasons could not attend public school.[41] Beverly was just the kind of man Judkins was looking for, both capable and willing to help lead in the "spiritual and intellectual uplift of the race."[42]

As a further means of vesting adults in the responsibility of helping train church youth, Judkins created what he called the Youth Musical and Literary Program, which was led by Agnes Jenkins, Elizabeth Brown De Ramus, and Edna Doak King. In addition to a yearly Youth Day program where church youth were in charge of the regular service, the Musical and Literary Program gave children the opportunity to recite short poems and excerpts from pieces of literature as a prelude to the seasonal revivals and lecture series that Judkins inaugurated.[43] These pieces included works by African American authors like Paul Laurance Dunbar.[44] In a society offering fewer and fewer opportunities for African Americans to exercise leadership, such church work afforded opportunities to lead and affirmed African Americans' sense of themselves as capable and thus contributed to their sense of self-empowerment.

Judkins's ministry included a tenacious effort to expose his congregation to contemporary ideas about political equality and social justice for African Americans. As part of his commitment to education and racial uplift, he inaugurated a seasonal lecture series at the church. He used this opportunity to bring in some of the most famous and influential African Americans in the country to speak on race relations. United in their belief that race relations were in crisis, these lecturers represented a variety of professions and exemplified the rich and varied points of view on this complex issue.

Sutton Elbert Griggs presented one of the first lectures. When he addressed the audience at Dexter Avenue on November 18, 1907, Griggs was pastor of First Baptist Church of East Nashville, Tennessee. He had written five novels, the most famous of which was *Imperium in Imperio*, a tale about a group of African Americans who created a secret, separate country within the United States whose purpose was to protect African Americans from injustice when the federal government refused to do so.[45]

He spoke at Dexter Avenue to "a large assemblage of Montgomery's cultured, educated and progressive Negroes."[46] After church youth performed a musical and literary program, Griggs presented his speech on "The Race Problem." In many ways, his talk embodied accommodating activism—it contested black disfranchisement even as it tried to accommodate white fears. He began by stating that "the problem of the races will be solved when the Negro is granted every right guaranteed him by state and federal constitutions." He called for intensified self-help beginning with as many Negroes as possible qualifying themselves to vote. Yet he cautioned that those who vote must always vote "in the interest of their community."[47] This was his way of responding to whites' justification for denying African Americans the franchise by claiming that blacks always vote Republican.

Also, parts of Griggs's speech attempted to reason away virulent white racism. He told the crowd "the Southern white man has a heart and Negroes must strive to find it. . . . If a white man mistreats you, in a straightforward, non abusive way, tell him of it—chances are he will hear you." Even so, his concluding comments, which he began by reciting a litany of black achievements in scholarship, the arts, the military, science, and sports—asserted a faith in African American potential and equality. "The

Negro," he contended, "has demonstrated by every test that prejudice and incredulity has [*sic*] set up that he is a man in the fullest, broadest application of the term." Judkins observed in his newspaper that Griggs's well-received speech was neither bitter nor abusive but impassioned, and he went far in trying to "mould [*sic*] correct and just public sentiment to lift up the race."[48]

Over the course of the next few years, lecture series speakers included minister and humorist D. Webster Davis, who spoke on "Jim Crow's Search for the Promised Land." Lecturers also included Kelley Miller, the celebrated intellectual and dean of Howard University, and John Milton Waldron, a Baptist minister who was a member of the 1912 Woodrow Wilson Presidential Inauguration Committee. Waldron had attended the 1909 Niagara Conference, become a charter member of the NAACP, and opposed Booker T. Washington's ideas about gradualism improving race relations. Each of these speakers expounded upon the importance of African Americans getting their due political rights, and they complained of how social segregation placed a badge of inferiority on African Americans. These speakers also strongly advocated the immediate recognition of black equality and of the important contributions African Americans had made to the health of the nation.[49]

In February 1913, Booker T. Washington, president of Tuskegee Institute, spoke at Dexter Avenue's lecture series on what blacks and whites could do to help one another. Not only did Washington address an interracial audience; he was introduced to the audience by Alabama governor Emmet O'Neal, who claimed that "an officer of the state should be willing . . . to work harder for Negroes than for members of his own race" and promised that the state would do more to support black education.

Washington began, "I am anxious that here in Alabama each white man do all he can to contribute to the happiness and usefulness of the colored race, and that each colored man do all he can to make himself of value to the white race so that . . . both are helping each other forward toward a happier life." He spoke of the enormous contributions African Americans made to the state of Alabama though their productivity in the industrial arts. The many prizes African Americans won at state fairs, Washington suggested, brought pride to the state and were evidence of their thrift and ability to contribute to the community. Continuing to work even harder in these areas was what black Montgomerians could do to help their city. Whites, he stated, could help by providing more schools and funds to lengthen the school terms in black schools to equal the length of white school terms. And finally, there was a need for better teacher training and better teaching salaries in black schools. Washington stated, "There is exceptional opportunity in a city like Montgomery to show the world how two races different in color and separate in their social affairs, still can live side by side in peace and harmony, and each race in its own separate way contribute toward the prosperity of the city." Washington's speech was true to his notions of traditional accommodationism. Unlike any of the other lecture series speakers, he openly embraced the practice of social segregation, and he made no mention of political rights for African Americans.

Though a strong advocate of immediate recognition of African Americans' political rights as was typical of accommodating activists, Judkins nevertheless greatly admired Washington. In particular, he respected Washington's encouraging African Americans to be productive and independent by doing things like growing their own gardens. In editorializing Washington's lecture, Judkins reported that the main auditorium of Dexter Avenue was filled to overflowing with the "best blood of both races. Hopes were high that the meeting would give impulse to a new understanding."[50] In inviting Washington to address the Dexter Avenue congregation, we see Judkins's pragmatic strain. As pastor, newspaper editor, and avid gardener himself, Judkins modeled Washington's notion of the black productive citizen.

The only woman to speak at the lecture series was Nannie Helen Burroughs. Born in Virginia, Burroughs attended high school in Washington, D.C. Upon graduation, she became a bookkeeper and an editorial secretary for the Foreign Mission Board of the National Baptist Convention. At the age of thirty she realized her dream of opening a school in Washington, D.C., the National Training School for Women and Girls. When Burroughs lectured at Dexter Avenue, she was president of this school and traveling on the lecture circuit in Europe and the United States. While she was in Montgomery, she gave a special address to the women of the community on the issue of suffrage. She also spoke on race. She acknowledged the power of institutional racism but asserted that an individual's determination and will were more powerful and more important to a person's success. Burroughs "paid high tribute to the progress already made" by African Americans and encouraged her audience to keep faith that progress would continue.[51]

These educational programs in conjunction with editorials in the *Colored Alabamian* and Sunday sermons were part of Judkins's activist ministry. Such presentations and writings always focused on the issue of race—sometimes to lament and bitterly complain of injustices—other times to create a milieu to encourage black agency and optimism. It seemed important to Judkins to expose the congregation to various opinions within the black community concerning the best way to cope with and address the problem of race in America. Lecturers provided a rhythmic succession of spiritual and intellectual affirmation for the congregation and the community, encouraging them to contest the current state of affairs. Also, these speakers were "success" stories, helping to counter extant perceptions of African Americans as incompetent and unworthy of sharing the rights and privileges of American citizenship. These speakers, in many ways, embodied the hopes and dreams of the congregation. Each found a way to remind the audience of the work that was yet to be done. And all offered a solution in which church membership was essential.

Judkins's newspaper and ministry at once affirmed and informed African Americans in Montgomery and helped spur them into action. This is best illustrated by the quotidian activism of the women of Dexter Avenue. As with many other religious institutions during the early twentieth century, women's presence and contributions were essential to the day-to-day functioning of the church in service to its members. Moreover, as Evelyn Brooks Higginbotham argues in her analysis of black Baptist women's undertakings, women's work was critical to churches' effective service to the community at large.[52] Much of the effort of the women at Dexter Avenue was expressed through the ladies' missionary society. Like other church activities, women's missionary work also illustrates accommodating activism. Even though they accepted that African Americans should have to prove their worthiness through adhering to certain Victorian bourgeois standards, they were even more determined to broaden black freedoms and opportunities and improve the quality of life through their daily activism.

Early in its establishment in the late nineteenth century, the ladies' missionary society concerned itself with fostering certain standards and attitudes among the women in the church that illustrate its embracing traditional ideas of accommodationism. One of their special meetings for women focused on "What I Can Do to Make Myself More Attractive." At this meeting, women discussed beauty tips of the day as well as what was available in the area of hair care and cosmetics.[53] At another such meeting a speech was given entitled "Has My Tongue Been a Blessing to the Community?" The speaker began by reading James 3:2–10, which warned that while no one can tame the tongue, it can be used as either a blessing or a curse. Following the talk, a discussion was held. Edna King, who was 104 years old at the time of our July 1993 interview, recalled that between the rules at Alabama State from which she graduated in 1910 and the behavioral and attitudinal expectations promoted by the missionary society, she lived within the confines of very strict rules. She told me, "We had to watch every aspect of our behavior and attitude, including where we went and with whom we associated." She claimed that church people were all expected to be very dignified. "We had to watch how loudly we walked or talked. . . . We just didn't have that old kind of Negro talk. . . . No kind of smoking and drinking and no kind of loudness." As Higginbotham argues in her work on black Baptist women, standards for such discussions on attitudes, styles, and fashions, like most ethical and moral values, were examples not just of Christian but also of Victorian and accommodationist insignias on church life.[54] Even though the society advocated this kind of strict behavior, they still labored unrelentingly to improve the quality of life for African Americans at the church and in the Montgomery community.

Examples of accommodating activist missionary society work at Dexter Avenue date back to the very beginnings of the church's history with its commitment to help newly emancipated slaves. The church's decision to officially incorporate as Dexter Avenue Missionary Baptist Church meant that it would participate in both domestic and foreign outreach programs. The missionary society was defined at Dexter Avenue as "a place for showing love through obedience . . . with God's plan [to give] . . . each disciple a part in saving the world."[55]

Missionary society activities during these years were quite varied. In the area of home missions, the society created programs to help the poor in the community. Each year, usually on December 27, the missionary society prepared and served a traditional Christmas dinner for the poor. The society would sponsor a service of prayer and singing, Judkins would give a short sermon, and then all would sit down together for a meal in the basement of the church.[56] Also part of the missionary society's holiday ministry was to prepare and serve a Christmas dinner at the county poorhouse and to donate groceries to Hale infirmary so that workers there might prepare a holiday meal.[57]

Concerns with beauty standards and preparing Thanksgiving and Christmas dinners for the poor fall within our notions of traditional accommodation, but three other instances of Dexter Avenue women's missionary society work illustrate ways in which the organization sought to empower the black community and contest white racist notions: helping to raise money to build a school to train black Baptist preachers, sponsoring the church's Health Week Program, and supporting universal suffrage.

Sallie W. Wright, one of the charter members of the missionary society at Dexter Avenue, led the society in its first recorded work, helping to raise much needed funds to build Selma University in Selma, Alabama.[58] In the late nineteenth century, black ministers wanted those capable among them to write and disseminate Sunday school literature and pamphlets explicating parts of Christian theology. They could rely on, at best, tepid support from white ministers and conventions that often claimed that black ministers had inadequate understandings of essential Christian theology to write Sunday school literature.[59] Wright and the ladies' missionary society's efforts, in combination with many others, led to the creation of a training and instructional space where black ministers were educated and then could appropriate a Christianity that proliferated a race consciousness of affirmation and self-respect. Such institutions aided black ministers, as Reginald Hildebrand has demonstrated in his work, in preaching a "gospel of freedom"—that being a good Christian meant opposing any obstacle that might interfere with one's pursuit of the divine or a person's ability to answer God's call.[60] Such fund-raising ventures should be understood as important examples of black resistance. Two Dexter Avenue pastors, Robert Thomas Pollard and J. C. Curry, graduated from Selma University. A. F. Owens, who was both a Dexter Avenue pastor and professor at the theological division of Selma, submitted petitions to the Alabama legislature challenging the morality of disfranchising black men and demanding "some humble share in choosing those who [would] rule over them."[61] Owens's example suggests that some black ministers encouraged their students to directly confront political injustice. Additionally significant, we should not lose sight that Dexter Avenue missionary society efforts, in helping create an educational institution, was promoting literacy among African Americans and shoring up one of Dexter Avenue's founding principles that "there can be little revelation of God where there is arrested mental development."[62]

The ladies' missionary society, in fact, sought to educate community members on various issues. Disease and death disproportionately affected persons living in the Gulf South. Among African Americans, the infant mortality rate was 27 percent, and the four leading causes of death were tuberculosis, pneumonia, heart disease, and Bright's disease.[63] In late March 1915, the ladies' missionary society invited health officials in the community, most of them members of the congregation, to speak at the church on various ways to improve health and hygiene. Dr. R. T. Adair spoke on "Dissipation as Cause of Disease," Dr. James De Ramus explained the importance of proper home ventilation, Dr. F. W. Watkins discussed ways to maintain healthy oral hygiene, Dr. Daisy Norcross spoke on the problems of infant mortality in the state, and Dr. D.H.C. Scott discussed proper nourishment.[64] A question-and-answer session followed each presentation, giving the audience an opportunity to engage in a discussion of what the *Colored Alabamian* described as "vital questions" about health. This program contrasted sharply with the stereotypes that abounded in academic and popular discourse about African Americans' physical and intellectual inferiority. From Edgar Rice Burroughs's creation of the idealized white male body in *Tarzan*, to the ideas propagated in D. W. Griffith's *Birth of a Nation*, to the degradation of black bodies through lynching, African Americans in the early twentieth century faced an image of the black body as inferior and the transmitter of disease, especially tuberculosis.[65] In the Health Week program, then, we have another example of missionary society action that helped empower African Americans to contest extant notions and rumors which suggested they were inherently weaker physically.

Activities sponsored by the ladies' missionary society sometimes provided an opportunity for more women's voices to be heard at the church. In 1914, the society brought in Cornelia Bowen, Judkins's teacher at Mt. Meigs and president of the State Federation of Colored Women's Clubs in Alabama, to speak. Bowen had a close association with another member of the Dexter Avenue family. She and Henrietta Gibbs had worked to establish the State Boys' Industrial Center Reform School at Mt. Meigs.[66] Such ventures were common among black women during the first quarter of the twentieth century. Most black women believed that "to be fully participating members of American society" they needed to work to "establish long lasting educational and social service programs for poor and uneducated blacks."[67]

In a presentation entitled "The True Test," Bowen reminded the packed audience at Dexter Avenue that the success of African Americans' integration into society was the "true test" of democracy.[68] Bowen's visit also included a special address on the issue of women's suffrage. Dexter Avenue women organized information sessions to raise awareness and support in the community, and they sponsored a community debate on women's suffrage as a way to raise money for the cause locally.

Judkins strongly supported the efforts of all advocates of women's suffrage with regular editorials. He wrote, "The universal suffrage movement, like the movement against slavery, will not go down until it has accomplished its full purpose. We [in the black community] are glad to see this movement take root and begin such a healthy growth right here in the South." He further contended that the "white men of Alabama met . . . and greatly restricted the electoral privileges." "Their actions," he explained, "placed many citizens in the position of bearing the burden of taxation without representation," and furthermore, "when Negroes are taxed for everything white men are taxed for but deprived of public institutions that are kept up by taxes, it is robbery." And yet it was Judkins's hope and belief that "this narrow, ignorant and short-sighted statesmanship on the part of Alabama will be overcome and finally overruled by the spirit of universal suffrage."[69]

As has been suggested by Rosalyn Terborg-Penn, black women were indeed anxious to get the ballot. Missionary society member Henrietta Gibbs was the first black woman in Alabama to vote in the 1920 election.[70]

We can see that even though the ladies' missionary society accommodated some white racists' notions, they more often challenged them. For the most part they seemed to accommodate some white beauty standards and embrace the strict Victorian moral code of whites. However, we must not lose sight of how the society sought to enlarge the autonomy of black clergymen by helping to create and sustain independent educational institutions. Of equal import, missionary society members rejected the idea that African Americans were weaker or more susceptible to disease, and they advocated universal suffrage.

In 1916, perhaps feeling that his work in Montgomery was done or maybe believing that another place needed him more, Judkins tendered his resignation to accept a position at Salem Baptist Church in Jersey City, New Jersey.[71] Judkins and the congregation at Dexter Avenue had a remarkably productive working relationship in the eleven years of his pastorate. He saw to it that noteworthy ministers, intellectuals, literary figures, and politicians regularly graced the pulpit as speakers. He carefully and consistently—through his newspaper and church ministry—encouraged members' sense of themselves as competent, worthwhile people entitled to the same rights and privileges enjoyed by white Americans.

The Judkins ministry to fight for political and social justice was at once religious and political. As Alexis de Tocqueville noted of religious expression in America, "Every religion has some political opinion linked to it."[72] Nevertheless, it is important to understand that Judkins regarded his work as profoundly spiritual. When he spoke of equality and justice, he did so out of what he believed was divine imperative. As he stated, he considered injustices directed toward African Americans "not a crime against man but a sin against man's maker."[73] It must also be considered, however, that in the *Colored Alabamian*, which Judkins considered an extension of his ministry, he stated that the newspaper was a "race journal and race defender with the object . . . to strenuously contend for the Negro's political and civil rights."[74]

The newspaper's advocacy of black civil rights was something Judkins considered an essential part of his divine calling. When some members of the congregation, perhaps believing that their adherence to middle-class sensibilities or their status in the community at large was somehow compromised by having their names on the roll as paid subscribers to the *Colored Alabamian*, Judkins protested. He editorialized, "Negroes who feel it a disgrace to have their names on subscription rolls of Negro newspapers should ask white editors to publish their social news."[75] Some church members' reticence to openly support the newspaper, brought on by their belief that the white community somehow felt threatened by its existence, attests to the power of this publication and the courage of its editor to confront and denounce the racism of the day. Judkins's newspaper and his work at Dexter Avenue were typical of "two major tendencies characteristic of the turn-of-the-century black church: an outward secular involvement in community activism and universalistic principles, and an inward spiritualistic and localized withdrawal from the wider society."[76] As Carter G. Woodson has explained concerning black churches and the social gospel, "Negro churches gradually realized the necessity for connecting the church more closely with the things of the world to make it [the world] a decent place to live in." Woodson is quick to add, however, that these same churches did not go "as far as the white man in divesting Christian duty of spiritual ministration and reducing it to mere service for social uplift."[77]

The foremost evidence of the congregation's emerging sense of self-determination and empowerment by Judkins's ministry was the church's continued community activism after his 1916 departure. City officials put Dexter Avenue in charge of the January 1, 1918, Emancipation Day ceremony to be held in Montgomery. Meeting in the Dexter Avenue sanctuary, the Emancipation Association Committee planned what it hoped would be "the greatest celebration ever."[78] The committee planned a parade with floats to represent all phases of "Negro development and activity" since emancipation.[79] There would be special reason to celebrate in 1918 because the compulsory education law for which many African Americans had worked so hard for well over twenty years was scheduled to go into effect on Emancipation Day. Black leaders hailed this regulation as "the greatest blessing to ever come to the commonwealth of Alabama."[80]

Members of Dexter Avenue were part of a group of sixty people who met at the Congregational Church at the intersection of High and Union Streets to establish a local chapter of the NAACP in August 1918. Along with the Minister's Alliance and the Negro Betterment League, the NAACP convened a group of black leaders from across the state. Meeting at Dexter Avenue, they petitioned the state legislature to do more for public education. Specifically, they asked that the compulsory education law be enforced and that the legislature agree to pay more than two dollars each year for the education of each black child. Equally important, this group expressed its grave concern over the escalation of lynchings. Using NAACP statistics, they reported to the legislature that 3,785 persons had been lynched in the United States between 1885 and 1918, and that 95 percent of the victims had been black. They also suggested that the following penalties be adopted to deter further lynchings: immediately to fire the sheriff of the county and his assistants, to pay $10,000 to the lynched victim's family, and to provide sure and certain punishment for all perpetrators. This group also endorsed the prohibition amendment and requested impartial enforcement of the constitutional provision for enfranchisement.[81]

Judkins's successor, Peter Callahan, later led a discussion at Dexter Avenue on how to get the vote to more African Americans. Ultimately, the NAACP created a brief pamphlet that clearly laid out the requirements for voting. They distributed five thousand copies throughout the state. Callahan, whose son Andrew had died in World War I, said he wanted "to remind men, especially the returned soldier, of his duty and his opportunity" to vote.[82] These actions suggest that congregants at Dexter Avenue were continuing to participate in efforts to enlarge black political and social freedoms.

In August 1919, members learned that R. C. Judkins had died. While it had been three years since Judkins led Dexter Avenue, he had stayed in close communication. Members felt a deep sense of loss. In many ways Judkins's leadership had helped to provide stability and direction for the church.[83] H. A. Loveless, one of the church's most active pioneers, died at his home on August 8, 1921. Loveless had attended the 1877 organizational and founding meeting of the church on 630 High Street, in the home of Samuel Phillips. He was one of the church's first trustees, and he helped to purchase the land on which the church was built. Loveless was committed to Dexter Avenue, and he had served the church in various capacities, including as a deacon. Often he was a spokesman for the congregation. Loveless had risen from enslavement to business success, receiving appointments from the governor and serving on the trustee boards of Swayne School and Alabama State University.[84] These losses seemed to symbolize the close of an age—the passing of those who lived through the first two generations in the life of this important Baptist church.

Still, in the early 1920s Gulf South where white racism was particularly virulent and violent, Dexter Avenue Baptist Church stood as a vital force in the community with firmly established organizational structures to sustain an effective ministry of salvation, political activism, and racial uplift. Leaders and workers were trained, capable, and affirmed in their sense of self-empowerment. It is true that in their activism they accommodated white fears of black equality and that they struggled within the church with the notion that they should have to prove themselves worthy. Yet this accommodation was accompanied by an activism that helped enlarge black opportunities within the Montgomery community as exemplified by some church members' efforts in successfully pressing for the state to pass a compulsory education law. Members and pastors, through seasonal lecture series, brought in speakers who challenged extant white beliefs and public perceptions about black character, ability, and potential. Between 1883 and 1920, we clearly see important traditions of protest being established, for example, in church members' insistence on constructing a sanctuary of black affirmation and resistance to white racism in so prominent a place in the community. Further, congregants' participation in the NAACP's initiative to force the state to acknowledge the problem of lynching suggests a level of activism similar to that practiced by the church during the 1955 Montgomery bus boycott. Armed with a measure of confidence in their abilities and faith in their power to improve the spiritual, intellectual, and civil lives of African Americans, church members stood ready—as workers that need not be ashamed—to face the challenges of the third generation of life as an independent, effective religious organization.

Notes

1. "Booker T. Washington's Platform of Accommodation: The Atlanta Exposition Speech, 1895," in *Negro Protest Thought in the Twentieth Century,* ed. Francis Broderick and August Meier (Indianapolis: Bobbs-Merrill, 1965), 7. For a brief survey of the dissemination of Washington's speech in the southern press, see Rayford W. Logan, *The Betrayal of the Negro from Rutherford B. Hayes to Woodrow Wilson* (New York: Da Capo Press, 1997), 275–313.

2. See Carter G. Woodson, *The History of the Negro Church,* 3d ed. (1921; reprint, Washington, D.C.: Associated Press, 1945), 103, 224–303; Sydney Ahlstrom, *A Religious History of the American People* (New Haven: Yale University Press, 1972), 698–714, 785–804; Robert T. Handy, *A Christian America: Protestant Hopes and Historical Realities* (New York: Oxford University Press, 1971), 70–72, 106–10, 174–83; E. Franklin Frazier, *The Negro Church in America* (1963; reprint, New York: Schocken Press, 1974), 23–25, 35–90; C. Eric Lincoln, *The Church since Frazier* (New York: Schocken Press, 1974), 101–34; Benjamin Mays and Joseph Nicholson, *The Negro Church* (1933; reprint, New York: Russell and Russell Press, 1969), 273; Aldon Morris, *The Origins of the Civil Rights Movement* (New York: Free Press, 1984), 4–16; Hart M. Nelson, Royth L Yokley, and Anne K. Nelson, eds., *The Black Church in America* (New York: Basic Books, 1971), 299–315; C. Eric Lincoln and Lawrence Mamiya, *The Black Church in the African American Experience* (Durham: Duke University Press, 1990), 20–46; James Melvin Washington, *Frustrated Fellowship: The Baptist Quest for Social Power* (Macon: Mercer University Press, 1986), 135–207; Paul Harvey, *Redeeming the South: Religious Cultures and Racial Identities among Southern Baptists, 1865–1925* (Chapel Hill: University of North Carolina Press, 1997), 45–74.

3. Charles Octavius Boothe, *The Cyclopedia of the Colored Baptists of Alabama* (Birmingham: Alabama Publishing, 1895), 239.

4. For a discussion of the black church as "the first black freedom movement," see Gayruad Wilmore, *Black Religion and Black Radicalism: An Interpretation of the Religious History of Afro-American People* (Maryknoll: Orbis Books, 1983), 78; Washington, *Frustrated Fellowship,* 83–89; William L. Andrews, "The Politics of African American Ministerial Autobiography from Reconstruction to the 1920s," in *African American Christianity: Essays in History,* ed. Paul E. Johnson (Berkeley: University of California Press, 1994), 111–12.

5. For a discussion of accommodationism and African American religion at the turn of the century, see Hans Baer and Merrill Singer, *African American Religion in the Twentieth Century: Varieties of Protest and Accommodation* (Knoxville: University of Tennessee Press, 1992), ix–xxxi.

6. Glenda Gilmore, *Gender and Jim Crow: Women and the Politics of White Su-*

premacy in North Carolina, 1896–1920 (Chapel Hill: University of North Carolina Press, 1996), 3; Kevin Gaines, *Uplifting the Race: Black Leadership, Politics, and Culture in the Twentieth Century* (Chapel Hill: University of North Carolina Press, 1996), xiv. Also see the discussion of "the politics of respectability" in Evelyn Brooks Higginbotham, *Righteous Discontent: The Women's Movement in the Black Baptist Church, 1880–1920* (Cambridge: Harvard University Press, 1993), 185–229.

7. The congregation of Dexter Avenue Baptist Church dates back to 1842, when it was founded as an enslaved congregation within Montgomery's white First Baptist Church. In 1867, the black congregation separated from First Baptist to form Montgomery's first African American independent Baptist church [also named First Baptist Church]. Dexter Avenue was born ten years later in a second exodus of disgruntled church members.

8. See journalist Taylor Branch's Pulitzer prize-winning history, *Parting the Waters: America during the King Years, 1954–1963* (New York: Simon and Schuster, 1988).

9. Logan, *The Betrayal of the Negro*, 343.

10. In addition to a few small schools run by missionaries, there were a few pre-college educational facilities of note for African Americans in Montgomery: Swayne School (established by the Freedman's Bureau) and the laboratory school at Alabama State University. There was also Langridge Academy and the Montgomery Industrial School. These institutions graduated many successful students, but there were many more black children who needed training than could be served by these institutions. See Robert Glen Sherer, *Subordination or Liberation: The Development and Conflicting Theories of Black Education in Nineteenth-Century Alabama* (Tuscaloosa: University of Alabama Press, 1977).

11. See Joel Williamson, *A Rage for Order: Black-White Relations in the American South since Emancipation* (New York: Oxford University Press, 1986), 117–51.

12. Joseph M. Brittain, "Negro Suffrage and Politics in Alabama since 1870," Ph.D. diss., Indiana University, 1958, 132; Virginia Van Deer Ver Hamilton, *Alabama: A Bicentennial History* (New York: W. W. Norton, 1977), 93. Though not a single African American was elected as a delegate to the convention, twelve black men, among them former Dexter Avenue Baptist pastor A. F. Owens, requested that blacks be permitted some say in who would rule over them.

13. William W. Rogers, Robert D. Ward, Leah Rawls Atkins, and Wayne Flynt, *Alabama: The History of a Deep South State* (Tuscaloosa: University of Alabama Press, 1994), 343.

14. *Colored Alabamian,* October 8, 1907.

15. Rogers et al., *Alabama,* 147–49; Edith Higgins, ed., *From Civil War to Civil Rights* (Tuscaloosa: University of Alabama Press, 1987), 410–63.

16. *Alabama Journal,* 3 July 1974; interview with Robert Doak Nesbitt, May 4, 1994; interview with Thelma Austin Rice, May 16, 1996.

17. Montgomery *Advertiser,* August 20, 1980.

18. Zelia S. Evans and James T. Alexander, *Dexter Avenue Baptist Church, 1877–1977* (Montgomery: Dexter Avenue Baptist Church, 1978), 13.

19. "Life in the Capital, Gossip from the Street and Sidewalk," Montgomery *Daily Advertiser,* July 16, 1885.

20. Boothe, *Cyclopedia of the Colored Baptists of Alabama,* 266.

21. Ibid., 13. Most likely Boothe's estimate of black-owned property was exaggerated. But the church population was mostly middle class. Peter Kolchin in *First Freedom: The Responses of Alabama's Blacks to Emancipation and Reconstruction* (Westport, Conn.: Greenwood Press, 1972), 131, estimates that 10 percent of blacks would have fit into a middle class by 1870, which he defines as possessing worth equal to $500 for a rural dweller and $750 for an urban dweller. W.E.B. Du Bois, *Black Reconstruction* (1953; reprint, New York: Macmillan, 1992), 487–526.

22. Class at Dexter Avenue was a persistent and problematic issue from the founding of the church to its current struggles in attempting to remain a vital congregation.

23. *Alabama Journal,* July 3, 1974; interview with Robert Doak Nesbitt, May 4, 1994; interview with Thelma Austin Rice, May 16, 1996; interview with Zelia Evans, March 24, 1994.

24. "NAACP Holds Interesting Meeting at Dexter Avenue Baptist Church," *Emancipator,* June 21, 1919.

25. For a discussion of the significance of self-determination in establishing independent black churches, see V. P. Franklin, *Black Self-Determination: A Cultural History of African American Resistance* (Brooklyn: Lawrence Hill Books, 1992), 48–54, 67, 87, 193–94. See Sara Evans and Harry Boyte, *Free Spaces: The Sources of Democratic Change* (New York: Harper and Row, 1986), especially the chapter entitled "Crossing the Jordan," for a discussion of the significance of oppressed groups carving out a physical space to buffer themselves from a hostile society; Gilmore, *Gender and Jim Crow,* 1–30.

26. Franklin, *Black Self-Determination,* 27–69; Reginald Hildebrand, *The Times Were Strange and Stirring: Methodist Preachers and the Crisis of Emancipation* (Durham: Duke University Press, 1995), 50–75.

27. Editorial, Montgomery *Daily Advertiser,* May 6, 1885.

28. Born in 1868 on the Carter Plantation in Waugh, Alabama, R. C. Judkins was the oldest child of Julius and Isabelle Judkins and possessed an unshakable determination to get a formal education. In the 1890s, returning to school as an adult, he first enrolled at Mt. Meigs Institute and eventually went to Talladega College in Talladega, Alabama, and then completed a divinity degree at Virginia Union College in Richmond, Virginia.

29. In keeping with the burgeoning social gospel movement of the day, one of the major emphases of the divinity school was to train ministers to believe in the "divinity of the gospel, its power in solving the problems of the world and the importance of living in such a way as to bring the world up to the gospel standard." See Virginia Union University, *University Journal* 3, no. 8 (May 1903): 7; 4, no. 7 (May 1904): 97.

30. "Question of Justice," *Colored Alabamian,* May 16, 1908.

31. "Last Sunday at Dexter Avenue Baptist Church," *Colored Alabamian,* September 3, 1910; *Colored Alabamian,* October 17, 1907.

32. "Question of Justice," *Colored Alabamian,* May 16, 1908.

33. *Colored Alabamian,* December 14, 1907.

34. *Colored Alabamian*, August 22, 1908.

35. *Colored Alabamian*, October 26, 1907.

36. "Colored Ministers and Leaders Make Protest against Cruel and Inhuman Treatment of Their Race: They Condemn Crime and Plead for the Protection of the Law," *Colored Alabamian*, August 22, 1908.

37. Washington, *Frustrated Fellowship*, 196.

38. Gilmore, *Gender and Jim Crow*, 3.

39. "The Call and Equipment of a Disciple," a sermon preached by R. C. Judkins at Dexter Avenue Baptist Church on June 15, 1913; "Last Sunday at Dexter Avenue," *Colored Alabamian*, June 21, 1913.

40. Interview with Edna Doak King, July 14, 1993; Dexter Avenue Sunday School Program, 1892.

41. J. W. Beverly was an 1890 graduate of Brown University in Providence, Rhode Island. He served as the first African American president of Alabama State, succeeding William Paterson.

42. *Colored Alabamian*, August 22, 1908.

43. Interview with Edna Doak King, July 23, 1993.

44. Judkins distributed a memorial anthology, *Life and Works of Paul Lawrence Dunbar*. See *Colored Alabamian*, October 26, 1907.

45. *Dictionary of Negro Biography*, ed. Rayford W. Logan and Michael R. Winston (New York: W. W. Norton, 1982), 271.

46. "The Great Mass Meeting at Dexter Avenue Baptist Church," *Colored Alabamian*, November 23, 1907.

47. "Reverend Sutton E. Griggs of Nashville, Tennessee Gives Speech on Race Problem," *Colored Alabamian*, November 16, 1907.

48. "The Great Mass Meeting at Dexter Avenue Baptist Church," *Colored Alabamian*, November 23, 1907.

49. "Literary and Social Circles Enlivened by Coming of Webster Davis," *Colored Alabamian*, August 15, 1908; "Kelly Miller Appears in the Great Lecture Course at Dexter Avenue Baptist Church," *Colored Alabamian*, February 27, 1909; "Fifth Anniversary of the Pastorate of Rev. R. C. Judkins," *Colored Alabamian*, June 18, 1910.

50. "A Notable Gathering at Dexter Avenue Baptist Church," *Colored Alabamian*, February 22, 1913.

51. "Miss N. H. Burroughs in Montgomery," *Colored Alabamian*, March 29, 1913. For a discussion of the work of Nannie Helen Burroughs, see Evelyn Brooks Higginbotham, "Religion, Politics, and Gender: The Leadership of Nannie Helen Burroughs," in *This Far by Faith*, ed. Judith Weisenfeld and Richard Newman (New York: Routledge Press, 1996), 140–54.

52. Higginbotham, *Righteous Discontent*, 1.

53. "Woman's Missionary Society at Dexter Avenue Met Last Tuesday," *Colored Alabamian*, April 23, 1910. Based on a listing of membership in the *Colored Alabamian*, dated October 19, 1907, approximately 68 percent of the congregation were women.

54. Higginbotham, *Righteous Discontent*, 200.

55. "Articles of Incorporation," July 25, 1887, as recorded in Evans and Alexander, *Dexter Avenue Baptist Church*, 204–7.

56. "Christmas Dinner for the Poor," *Colored Alabamian*, December 25, 1909.

57. "Xmas Dinner," *Colored Alabamian*, January 4, 1913.

58. Obituary of Sallie W. Wright, "Ladies Missionary Society Passes Resolutions," *Colored Alabamian*, March 1, 1913.

59. Washington, *Frustrated Fellowship*, 137–57.

60. Hildebrand, *The Times Were Strange*, 50–72.

61. Brittain, "Negro Suffrage and Politics in Alabama since 1870," 132.

62. Woodson, *History of the Negro Church*, 227.

63. "Health Week Program at Dexter Avenue Baptist Church," *Colored Alabamian*, March 27, 1915.

64. "Health Week Comes to Brilliant Close at Dexter Avenue Baptist Church," *Colored Alabamian*, April 3, 1915.

65. See Tara Hunter, *To 'Joy My Freedom: Southern Black Women's Lives and Labors after the Civil War* (Cambridge: Harvard University Press, 1997), especially "Tuberculosis as the 'Negro Servant Disease,'" 187–219. For a discussion of how endemic and epidemic illnesses become infused with cultural meanings, see Susan Sontag, *Illness as Metaphor* (New York: Farrar, Straus and Giroux, 1977). For a discussion of disease and social thought during the late nineteenth and early twentieth centuries, see Charles E. Rosenberg, *No Other Gods: On Science and American Social Thought* (Baltimore: Johns Hopkins University Press, 1997), 25–54.

66. Obituary for Henrietta M. Gibbs, December 1, 1960.

67. Cynthia Neverdon-Morton, "The Black Woman's Struggle for Equality in the South, 1895–1925," in *The Afro-American Woman: Struggles and Images* (Port Washington: Kennikat Press, 1978), 43.

68. "Miss Cornelia Bowen's Appearance at Dexter Avenue Baptist Church," *Colored Alabamian*, May 9, 1914.

69. *Colored Alabamian*, September 28, 1912.

70. Gibbs obituary. For a discussion of African American women and suffrage, see Rosalyn Terborg-Penn, "Discontented Black Feminists: Preludes and Postscript to the Passage of the Nineteenth Amendment," in *We Specialize in the Wholly Impossible: A Reader in Black Women's History*, ed. Darlene Clark Hine, Wilma King, and Linda Reed (New York: New York University Press, 1995), 487–505.

71. "Negro Preacher Resigns Charge of Local Church—Pastor of Dexter Avenue Baptist Congregation Quits after 11 Years of Continuous Service," Montgomery *Advertiser*, 1916.

72. Alexis de Tocqueville, *Democracy in America* (New York: Doubleday, 1969), 287.

73. *Colored Alabamian*, December 14, 1907.

74. *Colored Alabamian*, February 8, 1908.

75. *Colored Alabamian*, January 7, 1911.

76. John Brown Childs, *The Political Black Minister: A Study in Afro-American Politics and Religion* (Boston: G. K. Hall, 1980), 1.

77. Woodson, *History of the Negro Church,* 248.

78. *Emancipator,* December 8, 1917.

79. *Emancipator,* November 17, 1917.

80. *Emancipator,* October 6, 1917. It should be noted here that the bill that was finally passed was significantly weaker than the original bill, which would have guaranteed free public education for all Alabama children. The bill that passed included several exceptions. For example, people in rural areas were exempt if there was no school nearby, and communities were not compelled to build a public school. Families who could demonstrate hardship so that they needed their children to work could keep their children at home.

81. "National Association for the Advancement of Colored People Holds Interesting Meeting," *Emancipator,* August 31, 1918; "Memorial to Alabama Legislature Aroused Keen Interest," *Emancipator,* February 8, 1919. The state paid $5 per child for each white child's education. J. H. Fagan was president of the local chapter of the NAACP, and the annual membership fee was $1.

82. "NAACP Holds Interesting Meeting at Dexter Avenue Baptist Church," *Emancipator,* June 21, 1919.

83. "Death Claims Prominent Preacher: R. C. Judkins, Former Resident of Montgomery Dies in New Jersey," *Emancipator,* August 16, 1919; "Memorial Held in Honor of Late Reverend R. C. Judkins Tuesday Evening," *Emancipator,* November 11, 1919.

84. Clement Richardson, *The National Cyclopedia of the Colored Race* (Montgomery: National, 1919), 47; estate of Henry A. Loveless, 1921.

4

Working for American Rights

Black, White, and Mexican American Dockworkers in Texas during the Great Depression

REBECCA MONTES

In the fall of 1935, the members of the International Longshoremen's Association (ILA) in Texas, emboldened by the Wagner Act to fight for their American right to a better standard of living, engaged in a dramatic ten-week strike. Their immediate goals included expanding current contracts to other ports in the Gulf South, increasing wages, and gaining recognition from Houston employers of warehousemen's locals. In sharp contrast to the segregation that plagued Texas society, black, white, and Mexican American union members worked together to try to make the strike a success. Together they manned picket lines, fought with scabs, strikebreakers, and police, and endured serious financial hardship.[1]

However, this front of solidarity could not hide the serious racial divisions and prejudices embedded within the union. Off the picket lines, the three groups spent little time together. Mexican Americans, feeling unwelcome, avoided the union-sponsored kitchen that provided food during the strike.[2] Members disagreed over how long to keep up the strike: Black longshoremen, who had more to lose from a prolonged strike, pushed for an early end, while white longshoremen prioritized meeting more goals over a quick return to work. Mexican Americans, who had the least influence in the union, would have benefited the most from accomplishing the third goal, the recognition of warehousemen's locals. But when black and white longshoremen came to an agreement about ending the strike, they sacrificed that goal in their contract negotiations.[3] Whites, blacks, and Mexican Americans brought different and sometimes conflicting assumptions and goals to the ILA. The struggles of the multiracial ILA to survive in a segregationist culture provide an opportunity to examine the complex and often ambiguous relationships of race, class, and citizenship in the western Gulf South.

To reach their union goals and bridge racial divides, longshoremen tried to create a common identity around what they understood to be the characteristics of good union men: shared citizenship, manliness, and Christianity. Longshoremen found the most strength in identifying as good American male citizens. They used this identity to legitimize their demands for a better standard of living and more control over work conditions. Emphasizing an American identity provided an avenue for the ILA to combat public opinion, formed in the 1910s and 1920s, that unions were radical, Communistic, and dangerous. But longshoremen also found empowerment to work for greater access to the rights that good union men, good Christian American working men, deserved. Longshoremen understood these values in racial terms, and as a result, though they struggled to cohere around them, they largely failed.[4] I argue that while white longshoremen never saw nonwhite ILA members as equally deserving of the benefits of union membership and worked to reserve the greatest of these benefits for themselves, blacks and Mexican Americans tried to fashion the ILA into an organization that would meet both their labor and civil rights goals. Ultimately, black longshoremen used the union more successfully. Mexican Americans reaped fewer benefits, as they were too closely associated with foreign immigrants in the minds of their ILA brothers and therefore less able to take advantage of their identity as citizens.

Even though pragmatism drove the union to include multiple racial groups, this multiracial cooperation challenged the strict segregation of the Gulf South in the first half of the twentieth century and the virulent racism of many other unions affiliated with the American Federation of Labor (AFL). The ILA dominated longshore organizing throughout the Gulf South for most of the twentieth century. While the ILA organized throughout the country, only in the Gulf South did blacks historically constitute the majority of longshoremen, which necessitated that the union be biracial. Whites could not afford to exclude blacks who dominated the industry, and blacks would have been hard pressed to exclude whites without facing serious repercussions from white supremacists.[5] The situation in Texas varied from the rest of the Gulf South in its incorporation of Mexican Americans. But the union could not escape from the racial ideologies of the society in which it lived, and racial ideologies influenced both the structure of the union, seen most clearly in its separate locals, and the behavior of its members.

The ILA began organizing in Texas in 1913 with the chartering of one black local in Houston. Several years later, a white local formed, and the two locals agreed to divide work equally, per the standard arrangement in the Gulf South. These locals later became a part of the South Atlantic and Gulf Coast district of the ILA. Black and white locals in the Gulf Coast district negotiated contracts together and earned the same wage, which made longshoring an unusually equitable industry. An executive council of elected longshoremen oversaw policy for the Gulf South. This council always included black members, though never as president of the district. Throughout the 1930s, Texans dominated the district with more locals and hence more representatives sent to annual district meetings, or conventions, at which they set the union agenda for the coming year. More important, Texas longshoremen composed over half the executive board for much of the 1930s. The district was the most important leadership body for longshoremen in Texas, having more interaction with them than the all-white, Northeast-based ILA leadership.

In the 1910s and 1920s, the ILA succeeded in securing high wages of 70–80 cents an hour, spread to ports throughout Texas, and secured small improvements in job safety and security.[6] The Great Depression seriously challenged the strides the ILA had made in Texas and throughout the Gulf South. Longshoremen in the 1930s faced many problems: threats from potential scab labor, declining wages, hostile ship owners, and insufficient work on which to support their families.[7] These significant problems led the Texas ILA to include Mexican Americans in the 1930s. In so doing, Texas ILA members assumed a challenge that the rest of the Gulf South would not face for many years: the formation of a multiracial union. Mexican Americans generally worked as cotton compressmen, fruit handlers, and warehousemen, but not as longshoremen. ILA leaders offered ILA membership to these men as part of a plan to gain control over all aspects of dock work and limit the number of available scabs.[8] Mexican Americans who chose to join the ILA under these circumstances must have seen, in ILA membership, the chance to improve their working conditions and become more accepted by their fellow workers. More important, they saw the opportunity to claim their rights as Americans by associating with an organization that loudly proclaimed its dedication to the values of American citizens. The ILA also hoped to combat the encroachment of more left-leaning unions that were taking advantage of this time of weakness to organize in their territory. In the late 1930s, the Congress of Industrial Organizations (CIO) became active in the Gulf South. In the face of this competition, it became more important for the ILA to have a strong hold on labor on the docks and also to maintain the loyalty of its nonwhite members.

District leaders envisioned blacks, whites, and Mexican Americans coming together to solidify their rights as workers, which they also considered their rights as Americans. However, union leaders failed to consider the effects of race on the experience of work, the goals of workers, and the individual longshoremen's understandings of who deserved the rights of American citizenship. Rather than a cohesive unit, the ILA comprised three distinct racial groups trying to work together as "Americans" and "brothers" to improve their working conditions, while concurrently each group pursued its own pragmatic goals. Union leaders also failed to understand that the union values they espoused did not have the same meaning for all members because of the ways in which race affected longshoremen's experience as workers and their understanding of these values.

ILA members experienced their position as workers differently by race, creating subtly different work-related goals for each racial group. For example, black longshoremen maintained a position of prestige within the black working class due to their relatively high wages and the amount of power they commanded within the union. Black longshoremen were less willing to engage in risky strikes, since they had relatively more to lose.[9] White longshoremen felt stigmatized by working in a predominately black profession.[10] For them, longshoring was not a prestigious occupation but rather one which placed them at the lower end of white society.[11]

ILA leaders tried to bring these disparate groups together around shared beliefs in America, God, and fraternal brotherhood. But these ideas, and the relationships the ILA tried to form around them, were shaped by the complex racial landscape of Texas. The racial assumptions of Texans in the 1930s derived from the histories of both slavery and the coercive incorporation of Mexican territory and Mexican citizens. As Neil Foley has argued, Texas is a "border Province" between the South and the West and incorporates "two sets of race and class relations," those of "blacks and whites in the South and Mexican and Anglos in the Southwest." As a result, both blacks and Mexican Americans faced well-developed systems of racial oppression. Jim Crow segregation, inferior education, restriction on voting rights, and strictly limited employment opportunities marred the Gulf South.[12]

White Texans considered blacks and Mexican Americans to be racially inferior to whites but in distinct ways. Whites saw blacks as unfit for social equality but still granted them a limited status as citizens. However, they perceived Mexican Americans as more foreign than American, as being "outside of American civilization."[13] Texans not only considered Mexican Americans racially inferior but associated them with Mexican immigrants and therefore viewed them as noncitizens. Mexican Americans' continued use of Spanish distanced them from English-speaking white Texans. Mexican Americans' Catholicism also made them seem strange and inferior to Texans. Black and white longshoremen were most likely Protestants who would have considered Catholicism "foreign," even heathenish. Many Texans considered Catholicism distinct from and inferior to the Christian values that union members associated with true Americans.[14] So while blacks were considered second-class citizens, Mexican Americans were perceived as not quite citizens, as more Mexican than American.

In Texas, the ILA followed the Gulf South organization standard and had separate black and white locals. Mexican Americans fit into this schema awkwardly. In terms of membership in locals, the union considered Mexican Americans somewhat white. Mexican Americans often formed their own locals, which they and their ILA brothers referred to as locals of Latin Americans. But sometimes the situation called for Mexican Americans and whites to work and unionize together. In these situations, Mexican Americans joined white unions. But rather than an indication that Mexican Americans were seen as equals, this often meant that the whites in these locals had fallen on hard times and had been pushed into a low-paying, undesirable job. Longshoremen rarely allowed Mexican Americans into their locals, limiting them to less remunerative and less prestigious related jobs. White longshoremen's locals were reserved for white men, not Mexican Americans. In this way, the structure of the ILA in Texas reflects the racial assumptions of Texas: racially unclear but still exclusive. For example, some cities in Texas allowed Mexican Americans to vote in the all-white primary, while others excluded them.[15]

Blacks in Houston objected when federal relief agencies put Mexicans and Mexican Americans in the colored line for relief during the Great Depression.[16] Some organizations, such as the League of United Latin American Citizens (LULAC), fought to have Mexican Americans recognized as whites without qualification, emphasizing their European heritage.[17] Overall, Mexican Americans continued to occupy an ambiguous racial position in Texas. In the words of a sociologist, "American society has no social technique for handling partly colored races. We have a place for the Negro and a place for the white man: the Mexican is not a Negro, and the white man refuses him an equal status."[18]

These racist ideas did not go uncontested. Mexican Americans and blacks in the union fought the prejudice of white longshoremen as well as social structures of inequality. Though threats of white violence and the financial problems of the Depression made fighting for social equality difficult, the National Association for the Advancement of Colored People (NAACP) and LULAC were both active in Texas. The Depression seriously limited the activity of the Houston NAACP branch in the early 1930s, but a few years later black longshoremen worked with and through that organization to demand equality from white longshoremen and from Texans in general.[19] Unlike the NAACP, LULAC did not intervene directly with ILA members. However, LULAC did support working-class endeavors and provided a strategic model for Mexican Americans to pursue civil rights by emphasizing their American identity.[20] For Mexican Americans and blacks, the ILA was an additional organization that should be used to pursue social equality. These efforts both challenged and were made more difficult by white longshoremen's cultural assumptions about race.

Texas's culture of racism made it difficult for longshoremen to cohere around common values. But the union ideals had the potential to cross some of these boundaries and also give meaning and legitimacy to varying union goals. In order to understand how blacks, whites, and Mexican Americans developed their particular relationship to the ILA, it is essential to understand the ideal of union membership, the good union man, promoted by the ILA. This ideal hinged on members being good American citizens, good Christians, and good union brothers. Union minutes, propaganda, and even the comments of longshoremen in oral histories use this language.

In the early 1930s a group of longshoremen drafted an official funeral service that reveals the ways in which religion, citizenship, and masculinity intersected in the ILA's ideology. While there is no way to know how often they used the service, delegates from both white and black locals approved the service and decided to read a portion of it to all new members when they joined. Designed to be read at the graveside, it praised the departed for being "true to God and the Brotherhood of Man, as he defended the Rights of Man and was loyal to truth, as he performed his allotted task [labor] as a free man . . . so shall he be rewarded." His eternal reward is predicated on his having labored diligently and defended the Rights of Man—"the right to organize for our own protection and the liberty of the press and free speech. These rights are stated in the American Constitution." The Rights of Man, then, are the rights given by God and guaranteed by the union, the "organized brotherhood" which in "this uncertain age [is] the strongest tie on which we may depend to maintain a freeman's standard of living and to keep our civilization from drifting back to slavery."[21]

"Spiritual values" were essential to maintaining civilization. The tendency to "ignore God" makes society "almost unfit for self-government and responsible citizenship." But unions help people to "perform their duties to God and man more unselfishly. History acknowledges that these organizations have made the normal life the proper standard of living and have placed that standard within the reach of the working man and his family. Democracy finds home in the Union, which offers a moral standard in an age of physical science."[22] The drafters of the funeral service saw the rights of laborers/citizens as contingent upon performing one's duties to God. Catholic Mexican Americans then would be less able to execute the duties of citizens and less deserving of the benefits.

The drafters of this document captured the mixture of both high ideals and pragmatic interest in living standards that marked the ILA. By defending democracy and the Constitution, they earned their rights as citizens/laborers, which they believed included their right to a proper standard of living. But they also included their hope that "there be realized the Brotherhood of Man with his just rights and a world at peace with itself forever. Make Thou the Labor Movement Thy means to this Thine end and purpose for our troubled world and lives."[23] That the union failed to move beyond racism does not mean that these higher ideals were insincere. Black, white, and Mexican Americans in the ILA may all have sincerely wanted a "brotherhood of Man" and "world at peace" even as each group understood these ideas differently.

ILA members saw support for the union and belief in God as distinctly American—defending democracy and demanding their constitutionally guaranteed and "sacred" rights. In their use of strong American language, ideas, and imagery, the ILA was part of a nationwide trend in which labor unions made use of an Americanist language to emphasize the legitimacy of their claims. As Gary Gerstle has described, this language of Americanism, though ambiguous in its multiple applications, could be used as a powerful political language. It tied its users to a set of common symbols and history and was malleable enough to be invoked to legitimize radically different claims.[24]

For a multiracial union, this approach could be especially useful; their claims would not have the same legitimacy as those of an all-white union in the racial milieu of the Gulf South. The Americanist, mainstream language could counter the non-normative aspect of the union while stressing their genuine rights as citizens. By emphasizing their American values, they could de-emphasize the ways in which they had gone against socially accepted practices. This rhetoric appealed to different union members for different reasons. For nonwhites it emphasized their legal standing as citizens, whereas for whites who valued their white privilege, it de-emphasized their relationship with nonwhites and any radical sentiment this seemed to imply, by highlighting their dedication to American values that included white dominance.

The Americanist rhetoric of the ILA also had the potential to bring together white and nonwhite longshoremen. The ILA in the Gulf Coast had always been a racially diverse if segregated organization. While unionized workers of the nineteenth century may have called on their rights as "free white men," the ILA of the twentieth century could not. Common citizenship hypothetically provided a more appropriate rallying cry. All members of the ILA regardless of race or ethnicity were citizens of the United States and as such had claim to the Rights of Man. In Texas this would have had added meaning. ILA members wanted the rights that were theirs by virtue of citizenship and that did not belong to the immigrants, currently the target of repatriation programs, with whom they and their families competed for livelihood (though not all Mexican American members shared these sentiments).

During the Great Depression, many men's perceptions of their rights as citizens changed. New Deal programs, which targeted men as family heads to be recipients of government programs, legitimized longshoremen's view that they were entitled to a fair standard of living as citizens of the United States. New Deal labor legislation also legitimized the connection between workers' rights and citizens' rights by bringing work issues under the purview of the federal government.[25] First the National Industrial Recovery Act's Section 7a and later the Wagner Act legitimized labor unions' rights to organize and to call on the federal government to intervene on their behalf. While all male citizens may have felt a greater sense of entitlement as citizens, New Deal propaganda and programs favored white males, thereby reinforcing the idea that they were entitled to more than nonwhite males.[26] Through actions like trying to secure more work for themselves, thereby reducing the work of their black sister local, as well as maintaining leadership control, white longshoremen indicated that they also believed they were entitled to more than their nonwhite brothers.[27]

While the emphasis in the ILA remained on issues of wages and working conditions, this growing sense of entitlement and responsibility, based on membership in an American citizenry, manifested itself in the development of a civil rights consciousness on the part of union members. Blacks, whites, and Mexican American union members shared a sense of entitlement that brought them together around significant issues beyond their immediate concerns of wages and working conditions, most notably their voting rights. But more often their different interpretations of this entitlement separated them. So, while a civil rights consciousness developed in the union around the ideas of Americanism, it was not a cohesive vision. In the minds of white members, their rights included the right to be superior, whereas in the minds of blacks and Mexican Americans, being an American citizen meant social equality. All three groups felt a growing sense of entitlement to rights which propelled them to fight together to give laborers a greater voice in politics. But different interpretations of the boundaries of these rights put limits on multiracial cooperation in these civil rights arenas.

The ILA's voter registration campaign highlights these conflicts. Workers in the ILA knew that their position as workers was intimately tied to their status as citizens. As members of the working class, their limited access to political power constrained their political influence. Some aspects of voting restriction affected whites as well as nonwhites. The poll tax effectively inhibited poor working people of all races from voting and thereby limited the voice of the working class in Texas politics. As a result, the working class had difficulty preventing the government from enacting antilabor legislation. Blacks, whites, and Mexican Americans were all vulnerable to antilabor government actions because of the limited voice of laborers in Texas politics. Members of the ILA were aware of this connection. They joined the State Federation of Labor in passing resolutions urging the government to abolish the poll tax.[28] In the 1930s, the Ladies' Auxiliary of the ILA carried on a registration/poll tax drive urging people to exercise their right to vote.[29] The antilabor legislation enacted and threatened by the conservative governor and state legislature in the 1930s made the connection between citizens' rights and workers' rights painfully clear. Of particular concern to workers at this time was the proposed O'Daniel antistrike law, which criminalized violence that occurred during strikes. Laborers in Texas felt that the governor had written the law in such a way as to outlaw virtually any strike. This would limit their ability to fight for their rights. ILA men, working with other laborers through the Port Arthur Trades and Labor Council, wrote their legislators protesting this law.[30] Such laws made clear that rights guaranteed to workers could be impinged upon because those workers' access to their citizenship rights was limited by the poll tax.

Many ILA men and their families made the sacrifice to pay the poll tax in order to exercise their right to vote. According to a Mr. Nelson of the colored deep sea Local 872, "All the members pay their poll taxes and almost always vote together. The majority at this time are for Roosevelt." Nelson went on to say that he believed the purpose of the ILA was to "uphold the wages and condition of the longshoremen."[31] This could not be done, their rights as workers could not be defended, if they could not exercise their rights as citizens.[32] However, blacks in Texas faced a further limitation: The Democratic Party would not let them vote in primary elections. Some counties also prevented Mexican Americans from voting in these all-white primaries, which in Texas held much more weight than the final election. But the ILA did not cohere around this issue. Mexican Americans fought the all-white primary in their own way—by asserting their whiteness and thereby their qualification to vote. Many white longshoremen did not want to extend this right, another step toward social equality with blacks, even to their longshore brothers.

Black longshoremen, however, did see the all-white primary as a violation of their American rights and protested it in a variety of ways. Several Gulf South states prohibited blacks from voting in primary elections, and blacks, often working with the NAACP, struggled throughout the 1930s and the early 1940s to change this situation through legal campaigns and public protest.[33] In Houston, longshoremen participated in acts of protest both as individuals and as union members. To protest their unconstitutional exclusion from the official all-white primary, black Houstonians held their own unofficial primaries, known as the Bronze elections, in which local blacks "ran" for office.[34] John Fowlkes, the president of black Local 1409 of Houston, ran for "Bronze mayor" of Houston in 1937. The *Negro Labor News* published a front-page editorial on December 4, 1937, endorsing his candidacy. It described him as "a man who toils . . . a high class Christian gentleman, and is qualified to represent the Negro citizens." This description indicates a harmony of values between the black community in which Fowlkes was involved and those around which the longshoremen galvanized. Fowlkes's involvement in this act of protest and its coverage in the *Negro Labor News* demonstrates the interest of working people, including longshoremen, in civil rights activities. Though the union at large did not participate in protests such as this one, Fowlkes's connection to the union certainly played a role in giving him the community standing that allowed him to participate on this level. Additionally, longshoremen like Fowlkes brought their concerns about the conditions blacks faced to the union and tried to use the union's power to make change. Although white longshoremen did not work to end the white primary, black longshoremen would be able to push them to support other civil rights issues.

Six months before Fowlkes ran for Bronze mayor, he and several other representatives of black locals in Texas attended the 1937 convention of the South Atlantic and Gulf Coast district of the ILA. Several of the representatives were active members of the Houston branch of the NAACP, including Freeman Everett and C. W. Rice, who held leadership positions in their longshore locals and shared the labor-industry chair position in the late 1930s. A longshoremen from a black Port Arthur, Texas, local made a motion that the assembled representatives send a telegram to senators and representatives in all of the states in the South Atlantic and Gulf South district requesting that they support the Wagner–Van Nuys–Gavagan antilynching bill pending in Congress. A longshoreman from Mobile, Alabama, seconded the motion. The motion carried, and the district secretary, also a black Texas longshoreman, sent telegrams to Gulf South legislators. The telegram notes that the assembled body represented fifteen thousand members in the South Atlantic and Gulf South ports.[35] Blacks saw the union as a legitimate American organization whose large membership body could be used to further their political goals. Black longshoremen from Texas had the support of black longshoremen in other Gulf South states who shared their concerns and supported their motions to use the ILA to pursue black political issues. Mexican Americans, their membership limited to Texas ports, did not have supporters throughout the Gulf South to draw upon for strength and would not be able to push their political agenda onto the district agenda in a similar fashion.

Black Texans, especially Houstonians, had had recent experiences with lynching in their community, which helps explain their particular interest in acting on this issue. In the early 1920s, white supremacists castrated a black dentist and tarred and feathered a doctor. These crimes went unpunished. In 1928, Robert Powell was lynched. A jury acquitted two suspects, and in 1931, the Houston district attorney's office dismissed the case against the remaining suspects. This miscarriage of justice outraged black Houstonians.[36] The Wagner–Van Nuys–Gavagan bill would have made lynching a federal offense, thereby taking the investigation and conviction for these crimes out of the hands of corrupt local law enforcement. The NAACP proposed the antilynching bill (through allies in Congress) and organized campaigns in its support. In fact, the Washington office of the NAACP thought it would be beneficial if legislators heard from Texans urging passage of the bill.[37] The Houston branch, once recovered from its early Great Depression paralysis, had a closer relationship with working-class people than the NAACP in other areas of the Gulf South, and many black ILA men were also members of the Houston branch.[38] Black longshoremen, however, felt that this matter was an appropriate issue for the union to address and used the district convention as a power base to do so. The ILA's willingness to support the bill and risk accusations of working for blacks' rights is remarkable. Clearly, black longshoremen influenced ILA policy.

Clearly blacks had the ability to take advantage of union membership. They identified with ILA values, and membership in the union became a useful way to fight for a better standard of living and for their civil rights. The ILA's multiracial cooperation was an important defiance of segregation in the Gulf South; however, it did not exist in a vacuum. White supremacy intruded into the ILA experience. Both ILA leaders and rank-and-file white members treated blacks and Mexican Americans unfairly and unequally. White members who benefited from white supremacy wanted to see this maintained within the union. Their hostility and feelings of superiority toward black members undermined the alleged brotherhood of the union. It also put blacks in the position of having to fight for the very rights which the union guaranteed them.

Unionized blacks reaped many, though not all, of the benefits of ILA membership. Contracts guaranteed them the same hourly wage as their sister white local, which resulted in higher wages for black longshoremen than for most other working-class blacks. They also sent delegates to the district conventions, the Texas State Federation of Labor conventions, and the monthly Dock and Marine Council meetings. They exercised power in the union, using their strength in numbers to influence union activity. In fact, national white ILA leaders praised the Gulf Coast district for "intelligently handling the race question" and the "harmony that existed between the races."[39]

However, tensions within the ILA reveal the ways in which white members often failed to treat black members in the true spirit of brotherhood. On one occasion, Gilbert Mers, a white longshoreman, accompanied a group of black longshoremen to a meeting with a shipping line representative. These black longshoremen took advantage of their alliance with white longshoremen to improve their relationship with the shipping line. Mers thought that his informal assistance would deter the shipping line representatives from treating the black members with condescension. His white brothers thoroughly disapproved of this behavior. In their eyes, Mers had "crossed the color line and demeaned them."[40] The racial hierarchy of the Gulf South tainted ideals of ILA brotherhood.

The mandate to divide work equally between black and white locals created the most outright hostility between black and white longshoremen. Often the black locals had many more members than their white counterpart, or sister local. According to W. G. Bell, a black longshoreman, the ILA expected black locals to incorporate as many of the black scabs as possible after major strikes to strengthen the union. But these locals' share of work did not always increase proportionately.[41] In fact, white locals frequently controlled contracts for more than 50 percent of the work even when they had fewer members than their black counterpart. In ports where blacks did control more of the work, it often provoked the anger of their white brothers even when the amount of work was in proportion to the ratio of black and white members.[42]

In Houston, the issue of division of work dramatically polarized black and white longshoremen and made strange allies of white longshoremen and the city council. Throughout the 1930s the ILA often was at odds with the city council, which usually sided with big business in labor disputes and which the longshoremen held responsible for what they considered the excessive force they faced at the hands of city police during strikes. But at one point, white longshoremen turned to the city council to intervene in an internal ILA dispute. White longshoremen felt that black longshoremen held contracts to an unfair amount of the work in Houston and that this prevented whites from having adequate work. In an interview in 1936, F. N. Hunter, a white Houston longshoreman, said that he thought "the government would do something about it as a matter of constitutional rights if they knew how the situation was."[43] Hunter interpreted the competition for work between blacks and whites as a matter of "constitutional rights." Viewing his rights as a citizen through the lens of Jim Crow, he believed that losing work to a black man violated his rights. Black men should not have access to a higher standard of living than white men. In this situation, whites' understanding of their civil rights came into direct conflict with the rights of their black brothers.

Hunter turned out to be right about the government, at least on the local level. In 1939 the city council issued a resolution urging ship owners and stevedores to give white men at least half the work in the port. R. J. Landgrebe, president of white Local 1273, spoke on behalf of the resolution and claimed that blacks had at least 75 percent of the work.[44] The city council justified its decision on the grounds that this division would be more reflective of the population of Houston (though not of union membership) and would ensure that white longshoremen had a sufficient amount of work. It upheld the superiority of whites by defending their right to a higher standard of living. They upheld the social structures of Jim Crow. While this episode reveals a deep tension within the union, it also shows that black longshoremen in the Gulf South had a strong grip on work. They had a certain amount of power within the union that made it difficult for whites to take work from them without outside intervention.

While these dramatic confrontations make it difficult to imagine the ILA coming to the defense of its black members, the union did fight for the civil rights of its black members in some instances, and blacks were often able to wrest benefits from the union. Though many union members may not have personally supported blacks' rights, in order to function as a multiracial union in the Gulf South, the union had to take a stand on racial discrimination. For example, in the early 1930s the cities of Brownsville and Port Isabel refused to allow any blacks to work in their ports.[45] The union responded by drafting a resolution calling on the Justice Department, the attorney general, and the Commerce Department to investigate this blatant prejudice. While this may not seem like vigorous action, the union as a whole did make a public stand and did not see it as solely a black problem.

WHEREAS, This most unfair, un-American, and prejudicial ruling has resulted in a deprivation of their American rights and as well as [sic] the sacred right to work; and

WHEREAS, These citizens are members of the International Longshoremen's Association, affiliated with the American Federa-

tion of Labor, which said organizations are organized for the purpose of improving the social and economic status of wage earners
regardless of race, creed or color.[46]

Despite the segregation and tension within the ILA, the language used
in this resolution indicates that the union considered citizenship fruitful
ground on which to fight for equal treatment for blacks. They used powerful language to demand intervention from federal government agencies
responsible for defending the rights of worker citizens. They wrote of
their black members as citizens being denied their rights and portrayed
the AFL as an organization that would fight for them. Blacks were considered "American" in ways that the Mexican American members were not.
The district convention attendees deemed it appropriate to fight for the
American rights of black union members. In this case, defending the
rights of blacks helped the union to meet its goals of controlling work in
the Gulf South. But even when injustices did not threaten the work of
white longshoremen, they often acted slowly or less vigorously than necessary to combat the prejudice that black longshoremen faced.

Several years after this resolution passed, black longshoremen in Har-
lingen, Texas, who were supposed to work these ports, reported that the
problem continued. According to them, their white brothers, who had no
problem securing work, refused to aid them in gaining access to their fair
share of the work. This black local found that the ILA, local or international, did not make their problems in this situation a priority and simply
claimed that "they cannot be of assistance . . . at this time."[47] To add insult
to injury, the ILA insisted that they keep up with their dues payments
despite not having work.[48] Faced with this denial of their right to work on
the basis of race and the additional frustration of a slow-acting union,
blacks put pressure on the ILA to pressure their erstwhile employers. To
do so they, like the white longshoremen of Houston, turned to an outside
organization for assistance—in this case, the NAACP.

The NAACP initiated correspondence with the ILA international
president, insisting that this matter be investigated and acted on.[49] This
strategy succeeded in getting the attention of the ILA president. Credit
for this success does not belong solely to the NAACP. The letters exchanged make it clear that these longshoremen contacted the NAACP
and had been struggling with this issue for quite some time. That these
men turned to the NAACP indicates that they saw both the problems they
faced from the Port Authority and the indifference of ILA leaders as civil
rights issues. Their right to work and the obligation of union leaders to

protect that right were abrogated by racial prejudice. Their rights as workers were intimately connected to their civil rights. This issue sparked an increase in civil rights activism among these men. A significant number joined the NAACP, indicating a commitment to support future civil rights activity.[50]

Black longshoremen, though obviously concerned about their rights as workers and improving their situation, could not always take a straightforward approach in demanding their rights or equal treatment within the union. As a speech made by W. G. Bell, of the Beaumont colored local, to the Texas State Federation of Labor indicates, the reality of Jim Crow also shaped the approach that blacks took within the union. Black longshoremen had to exercise caution to be able to claim worker and civil rights in a hostile environment. Bell implored the ILA/AFL to fund a colored organizer to help solidify the ILA's hold in Beaumont. Much of his speech mimicked the power relations of the Jim Crow South. As a delegate to a convention, Bell would have been selected by the rank-and-file members of his local to represent their views. After apologizing for black workers who steal white jobs and assuring his audience that he and his brothers were not after social equality, though much of their other activities belie this claim, Bell concluded:

> We depend upon you white people. . . . You set the example for us, whether it be for good or bad, because you are the dominant power and we know that. . . . Why not live peaceably and happily in our own spheres? . . . We know you have been very good to us; you furnish us with good schools, we turn out of these schools men with knowledge and training and we want them to work according to rules; we want them to make union men. . . . Help us let them get better acquainted with our purposes and our principles and the good work we are doing, and to become a part of the organized body of Texas. I thank you.[51]

Only W. G. Bell can know the degree of sincerity intended by these words. Certainly they reflect the fact that whites led the union and most opposed social equality. Bell's words, presented in front of a white audience whom he knew supported racial segregation, elide blacks' intentions to further challenge their social inequality through the union. Bell actively fought the white-only primary, going so far as to be the plaintiff in an unsuccessful lawsuit. When interviewed about race problems in the ILA, he said that he blamed "ignorant hillbilly whites who poison the organization." These insights into Bell's beliefs reveal his speech as a clever attempt to gain strength while appearing unthreatening.[52] Ultimately, Bell's speech is pro-union. It indicates that blacks believed in the union and benefited from it. They were willing to "follow" the lead of whites, in exchange for the benefits of unionism. Black longshoremen found it beneficial to play to white longshoremen's feelings of superiority in order to avoid conflict and maintain their support. By appearing as less of a threat to their fellow longshoremen's white privilege under the Jim Crow system, black longshoremen could continue to use the union as a vehicle to pursue not only better working conditions but also their political interests as demonstrated by the antilynching movement example. In some situations, playing by the rules of the dominant racial ideology seemed to be the only realistic approach to achieving their goals.[53]

Black ILA members chose to remain loyal to the ILA despite being repeatedly approached by other organizations eager to recruit them. Many of these organizations actively promoted social equality, and yet black locals seemed to be least willing of all ILA members to entertain these more leftist ideas; they consistently refused even to grant an audience with touring lecturers representing these groups.[54] One local condemned the Maritime Federation of the Gulf, an intertrade union movement, as "radical and bolshevik . . . because [national ILA president Joseph P.] Ryan wrote them a letter condemning . . . the federation."[55] The *Negro Labor News* of Houston also condemned the CIO as a branch of Leninism in which the workers would "become only a pawn."[56] Some white longshoremen have hypothesized that it was because of the loyalty of the black members of the ILA that Texas longshoremen remained predominately AFL affiliated and did not follow the more radical leanings of West Coast longshoremen. A union that promoted Americanism better met their needs. In the words of ILA president Joseph Ryan, "When you are true to your organization you will be true to your country."[57] Loyalty to the ILA provided one way that black longshoremen could prove their worthiness as citizens.

Longshoremen of the time and scholars since have hypothesized that black longshoremen resisted other options because they did not want to risk their standing in society.[58] Some considered black longshoremen "the aristocracy of the southern black labor."[59] While the ILA presented problems, they were not unfamiliar ones. Within the context of a racist society and economic depression, the ILA held some promise for black longshoremen. Not only had the ILA secured black longshoremen decent contracts, but black members also knew they had influence within the union and, within limits, could use that influence to meet their interests. They renounced communism and presented themselves as good Christians and Americans who deserved the full rights of citizenship.

Unlike blacks, Mexican Americans did not have a strong history of unionizing in longshoring, nor did they have strength in numbers to use as leverage. Whites, already threatened by the power of blacks in the union, and blacks, struggling to achieve equality, did not see benefits in improving the status of Mexican Americans. The ILA organized Mexican Americans in longshore-related work during the Great Depression to strengthen the union movement, but the ILA did not make their welfare a priority. Mexican Americans would have to fight for the benefits of unionism.

The Great Depression exacerbated racial tensions in Texas, intensifying animosity toward Mexican American and Mexican immigrant laborers and making multiracial unionism more difficult. Popular discussion developed of a "Mexican problem," the threats Texas laborers faced from Mexican immigrants. As David Montejano has argued, the popular conception of Mexican Americans in Texas changed. Though previously racialized as docile and therefore a good source of cheap labor, Mexican Americans were now viewed as a threat to American jobs.[60] During the Depression, numerous states enacted Repatriation programs, designed to alleviate fears about Mexican immigrants stealing American jobs, which arranged paid passage back to Mexico for Mexican immigrants on a volunteer basis. However, many immigrants were coerced, or they volunteered because they feared that otherwise they would be deported. Many of those who returned, especially children, were U.S. citizens.[61] These programs contributed to the idea that Mexican Americans were not really Americans.[62] Associated with Mexican immigrants, Mexican Americans suffered from increased hostility, and their fellow Texans saw them as "singularly un-American."[63] Clearly, this alienness, though inaccurate, was incompatible with the ILA ideology. Unable to meet the more ambiguous definition of citizenship, that of "belonging," of "patriotism," white Texans saw Mexican Americans as not deserving the rights of citizenship.[64]

Houston locals unequivocally excluded Mexican Americans from longshoring.[65] There are records of a few Mexican American men longshoring in Galveston and Corpus Christi. From an analysis of the Galveston white Local 307's roll books, it seems that during the most difficult years of the Great Depression, those members with Spanish surnames worked least,

Figure 4.1. Unionized black stevedores packing the hold of a cotton freighter, Galveston, circa 1939. Library of Congress.

although as conditions improved their activity matches that of the white members.[66] Except for these rare cases, white and black longshoremen limited Mexican Americans to the less remunerative longshoring-related occupations of warehousing, fruit handling, and cotton compressing. Even as late as the 1940s, Bill Follett, a white Texas longshoreman, "got the hell beat out of him" by his local brothers for hiring Mexican Americans during a labor shortage.[67]

Figure 4.2. Mexican American laborers loading a cotton freighter, Galveston, circa 1939. Library of Congress.

Figure 4.3. Black and white stevedores stacking cotton to be loaded for shipment, Galveston, circa 1939. Though both groups were unionized, they proved unable to overcome the racial divisions that frequently qualified the power of southern labor movements. Library of Congress.

The ILA organized Mexican Americans in large numbers in warehouse locals, compressmen's locals, and the fruit handlers' local, all of which had serious problems with the ILA mainstream. The ILA organized these men beginning in 1934, as part of their strategy to regain control of Texas ports.[68] Given that they were only organized for the benefit of black and white longshoremen, who excluded them from the most desirable jobs, and that since the ILA only organized citizens they would have to separate themselves from the noncitizens with whom they had been working, why did Mexican Americans choose to join the ILA? The obvious reason is economics: Nonunionized cotton compressmen and warehousemen made horribly low wages—about 25 cents an hour at a time when longshoremen made about 85 cents an hour.[69] They also knew about changes occurring in the cotton compressing business. More companies chose to compress their cotton where it was harvested and save on shipping costs to the port. Previously, companies had more of their cotton compressed on the docks. As a result, job competition was increasing, making an already tenuous situation potentially worse.

However, joining the union presented opportunities to improve not just their economic situation but also their social standing. In the face of segregation and discrimination, organizations emerged within the Mexican American community to demand their full citizenship rights. LULAC was one such organization that emerged in San Antonio in the late 1920s and spread to Houston during the 1930s. Their strategy, shared by other Mexican American groups, was to work for full inclusion in society by emphasizing their Americanness—a logical response to the specific prejudices Mexican Americans faced. They also limited their membership to American citizens. Mexican American working-class people, like the men who joined the ILA, rarely became members of LULAC, a predominately middle-class organization.[70] However, in the small Mexican and Mexican American communities in Galveston and Houston, working-class people knew members and witnessed their efforts and tactics.[71]

For Mexican American compressmen and warehousemen, joining the ILA and affiliating with the AFL provided a means to assert their American identity. By joining the ILA, Mexican Americans had the legitimacy of the AFL—an organization that only organized Americans—behind their assertions to the rights of citizenship. Just as laborers sought to use the language of Americanism to remove the stigma of radicalism and communism from their demands, Mexican Americans could use it to remove the stigma of foreignness.

First among those they would need to convince of their Americanness would be their fellow workers. Unfortunately, black and white longshoremen benefited from not seeing Mexican Americans as their equals and thereby maintained their hierarchy of positions. They limited their job competition by excluding the least American from the best jobs. Despite the potential benefits, Mexican Americans would have to struggle for access to the benefits of unionism. Over time, some grew frustrated with the prejudice they faced in the ILA and turned to other options. However, some stayed with the union despite the problems, determined to reap the benefits of membership.

Mexican American ILA members actively rejected the third-class treatment they received. They demanded treatment as equal members. The way they did so reflects the problems they faced in the union. Local 1581, a Mexican American local of compressmen, warehousemen, and cotton yard workers, reported having problems with their ILA brothers who consistently went against ILA regulation by refusing to hire them for extra work. According to ILA rules, when a local has a job too large for its membership, it is their "imperative duty" when hiring "to give preference to any union man whose Local is affiliated with the ILA." Houston locals consistently hired nonunionized men in these situations instead of hiring the men of Local 1581. Local 1581 needed this work because their employers, in an attempt to break the union, had laid off workers and hired scab labor. They needed these opportunities for work in order to feed their families, and they needed the support of the other ILA locals to keep their local alive.[72]

To demand the support they needed, they wrote an unusually straightforward and powerful letter of complaint to the 1939 district convention asking for intervention. The way in which they expressed their anger demonstrates the distance between them and the union mainstream. Their letter made no use of the usual union language. The compressmen did not identify themselves as citizens, Americans, or union men but rather as "Latin Americans." They did not invoke the spirit of union brotherhood or demand their sacred right to work. They simply listed rules and regulations that the other Houston locals had violated. The union bond between the "Latin American" compressmen and the ILA mainstream was one of rules and regulations, not shared ideals and values. They chose the argument they felt would have the most force with their ILA brethren. In their minds, longshoremen would not be moved by the usual language of Americanism, fraternal brotherhood, and denial of citizenship rights. Additionally, through the use of the term *Latin American* they attempted to distance themselves from the negative stereotypes associated with Mexicans in Texas and to distance themselves from Mexican immigrants and emphasize their whiteness.[73] The use of *Latin American* then was a response to the racism of white longshoremen.

The ILA had organized 1581 to replace a failed local. Their letter notes that lack of support from the other Houston locals and the district leadership contributed to the first local's failure and continued to make their situation difficult: "It was very hard to organize our workers, due mainly to the fact that a similar organization (I.L.A Local 1309) existed here in the past which resulted in a complete failure after having two ineffective and poorly supported strikes in which many of our best men lost their jobs."[74]

Local 1309 had participated in the 1935 strike, but union negotiators had not made their goal of union recognition a priority, and eventually 1309 had dissolved. The men of 1581 then joined the ILA knowing they would face serious difficulties. Still they chose to join and take advantage of union membership. They appealed to the district to force the other Houston locals to obey the regulations and to include their contract demands with all others in the next round of negotiations.[75] Local 1581 had to work with other locals in the district in order to survive. Their so-called brothers made it very difficult for them. But the men of 1581 felt ILA membership still offered them advantages that were worthwhile. They fought for their rights and demanded the fair treatment that they needed to realize the benefits of union membership.

Over time, some Mexican Americans found it impossible to pursue their right to a fair standard of living and equal opportunity within the ILA. Their actions speak louder than their choice of words to indicate the distance between Mexican Americans and white and black longshoremen. The experience of Mexican American fruit handlers in Galveston exemplifies many of the problems they faced in the ILA. The banana handlers local, composed of an almost equal number of Mexican Americans and whites, received their charter, 1350, in 1934.[76] Fruit handling, like compressing and warehousing, paid significantly less than longshoring. In 1935, the local applied to the Dock and Marine Council (composed of representatives from the Galveston longshore locals) requesting that their charter be expanded to include longshore work, which would allow them to earn a decent wage. They argued, "Since Galveston has two black locals, there ought to be two white locals [in longshoring]."[77] Local 1350 was chartered as a white local or "so-called white local," as one white longshoremen referred to locals with Mexican American members.[78]

The Council refused to expand their charter to include longshoring. It is possible that the three existing locals did not want to further divide the available longshoring work. But the union was growing in strength at this time and was generally willing to add new members. The longshoremen of the already established locals did not want to work side by side with such a large number of Mexican Americans. They did not consider the fruit handlers quite white enough to be a white local in mainstream longshoring. While 1350 may have been called a white local, others within the ILA considered its members racially inferior. Introducing such a large number of Mexican Americans into longshoring would disturb the hierarchy of jobs that privileged white and black longshoremen.

The members of 1350 did not passively accept this decision. Over the next few years they developed a strained relationship with the Dock and Marine Council and became involved with the Maritime Federation of the Gulf. Finally, in 1938, unable to get what they wanted within the ILA, they broke with ILA/AFL and joined the CIO-affiliated union, which was vigorously competing with the AFL unions for control of labor unions in the Gulf South and which had been vocal in its stand against segregation.[79] In leaving the ILA, they declared their refusal to be treated as inferior members of the union, and in joining a union accused of Communist leanings, they abandoned the Americanist approach to claiming their rights. Local ILA leaders tried to delegitimize their leaving the union by blaming Communist infiltrators for the decision.[80] They also quickly formed a replacement local to fight for control of the ship contracts they had had while affiliated with the ILA. In an attempt to put pressure on the ship owner to allow them to keep their contracts, the new CIO members called upon Mexican longshoremen to refuse to load banana ships bound for Galveston until the contracts were given to them.[81] Perhaps a common Mexican identity could be used to stifle the work of the ILA, who had failed to fully recognize their American identity.

Significantly fewer Mexican Americans worked in the longshoring industry than blacks. They did not have the strength in numbers or the long union history necessary to fight their way into the better paying, more highly esteemed longshore jobs. The ILA organized Mexican Americans for pragmatic reasons and never welcomed them into the union brotherhood. Although their locals were technically "white," they were fairly well segregated from both blacks and whites. The ILA clearly did not consider them equals, and black and white union members made little effort to treat them as "brothers." As a result, there seems to have been little investment on their part in the ILA identity during this time.

The ILA largely failed Mexican Americans. It was in the best work-related interests of ILA members to affiliate with one another to secure influence over the ports of Texas, but white longshoremen, especially in their dealings with Mexican Americans, often put their investment in a white identity before their worker interest. And since no other Gulf South locals had a significant number of Mexican Americans, the particular problems of the Mexican Americans in Texas ports received little attention.

The ILA did not exist outside of Jim Crow or Anglos beliefs about the inferiority of Mexican Americans. In fact, its members were at times quite vocal in denying their interest in social equality. Separate locals suggest that the union accepted many of the tenets of Jim Crow segregation either sincerely or to accommodate the social norm and therefore avoid more violent repression. However, some scholars have argued that nonwhites may have preferred separate locals because it allowed them to manage their own affairs.[82]

Though in many ways the dominant racial thinking of Texas shaped the ILA, they did not live in easy harmony. The ILA, like other multiracial unions, challenged the Jim Crow norm. The ILA acknowledged similarity of interest among the races. It put blacks and whites on the same wage scale. It forced ship owners to work with nonwhites. Even though they did not set out to challenge the racial ideologies of the Gulf South in the interest of social equality, union members found themselves at times taking a stand on civil rights in order to increase the power of the union. Blacks and Mexican Americans tried to take advantage of this reality to pursue their own goals.[83]

The ILA had a complicated and tense relationship with the racial ideologies of 1930s Texas, just as its members had complicated and tense relationships with one another. Ironically, though Mexican Americans were organized into "white" locals, they fared worst in the union, unable to meet the characteristics of good union men. Blacks, clearly segregated into their own locals, used the union as a vehicle for civil rights action despite the firm racist beliefs of many of its white members.

The ILA vision of the good union man (American, Christian, Brother) had the potential to unite ILA members across racial boundaries. But longshoremen's understanding of these concepts had been shaped by the racial ideology of Texas. Instead of a basis for unity, these concepts determined to what degree nonwhite longshoremen would benefit from the union. In this way, racial boundaries prevented the union from exercising its full potential as an organizing body on the waterfront and as a means for nonwhites to counter the limits of the Jim Crow Gulf South.

Notes

1. James L. Reeves, "Gunfire along the Gulf: The International Longshoremen's Strike of 1935," 3–7. Unpublished article in the Gilbert Mers Collection, box 1, folder 8, Houston Metropolitan Research Center, Houston Public Library.

2. Gilbert Mers, *Working the Waterfront: The Ups and Downs of a Rebel Longshoreman* (Austin: University of Texas Press, 1988), 106.

3. Reeves, "Gunfire along the Gulf," 7, 11.

4. In "Gaining a Hearing for Black-White Unity: Covington Hall and the Complexities of Race, Gender, and Class," in *Towards the Abolition of Whiteness* (London: Verso, 1994), David Roediger examines how an IWW attempt to unify across racial division by emphasizing common gender and class issues failed because race ideologies could not be separated from class and gender ideologies. Similarly, I am arguing here that racial ideologies could not be separated from longshoremen's understanding of citizenship and brotherhood or worker's rights.

5. James C. Maroney, "The International Longshoremen's Association in the Gulf States during the Progressive Era," *Southern Studies,* summer 1977, 225.

6. Charles J. Hill, a brief history of Local 872, T331.8809764 In8, Center for American History, University of Texas at Austin, 1–8.

7. Dock and Marine Council notes, as well as convention proceedings, chronicle at great length the work shortages that made it impossible for many longshoremen to support themselves and their families and that also undermined their control over the Texas ports. At the convention in 1931, Local 814 reported having had no work in six months. Proceedings of the 21st annual convention, 1931, T331.88 In8, Center for American History, University of Texas at Austin, 7.

8. This tactic was confirmed in a resolution. Proceedings of the 24th annual convention of the South Atlantic and Gulf Coast district International Longshoremen's Association, 1934, 68.

9. One contemporary longshoreman commented that blacks were "willing to settle strikes for a smaller gain than what the white man wanted." If so, it would seem that even in strikes, which brought blacks and whites into close cooperation, they did not have the same goals. Bill Follett, interview by George Green, August 29, 1985, Oral History Collection, University of Texas at Arlington, Special Collections, 49.

10. Lester Rubin, *The Negro in the Longshore Industry* (Philadelphia: Wharton School, Industrial Research Unit, University of Pennsylvania, 1974), 41. According to Rubin, Texas longshoremen were 69.8 percent black in 1930 and 63.5 percent black in

1940. Perhaps like the Irish workers described in David Roediger's *Wages of Whiteness: Race and the Making of the American Working Class* (London: Verso, 1991), 150, the white longshoremen would rather have assumed the "degradation" of blacks by assuming their "avocation."

11. Jacqueline Jones, commenting on Alabama coal miners, suggests that black and white workers would perceive their positions differently in relation to their relative job opportunities in the community as well as their prospects for advancement into supervisory positions within the mine. White miners could aspire to supervisory positions and therefore may have had more investment in the mine, while black workers could not. "Interracialism Above Ground, Jim Crow Below," *Labor History* 41, no. 1 (2000): 72.

12. Neil Foley, *The White Scourge: Mexicans, Blacks, and Poor Whites in Texas Cotton Culture* (Berkeley: University of California, 1997), 3–4.

13. Ibid., 40.

14. George Sánchez, *Becoming Mexican American: Ethnicity, Culture, and Identity in Chicano Los Angeles, 1900–1945* (New York: Oxford University Press, 1993), 157.

15. Despite the ruling of the attorney general of Texas that Mexican Americans should be considered legally white, some counties refused to allow them to vote in the all-white primary. Travis County, Texas, prohibited Mexican Americans from voting in 1934, according to "Bars Voting by Mexicans," *New York Times,* July 27, 1934, from the NAACP Branch Papers—Houston, microfilm edition. Reproduced from the NAACP Papers, Manuscript Division, Library of Congress.

16. "Relief in Houston Goes 'Jim Crow': Mexicans Put with Negroes in Bread Line Apart from Whites," *Houston Informer and Texas Freeman,* March 31, 1934, 1.

17. The LULAC members who strove to be seen as white were predominately middle class. One of their tactics was to segregate themselves from blacks, particularly not joining in any organizations with blacks. This was not a possibility for Mexican Americans who wanted to work in longshoring. Foley, *The White Scourge,* 209.

18. David Montejano, *Anglos and Mexicans in the Making of Texas, 1836–1986* (Austin: University of Texas Press, 1987), 159.

19. Merline Pitre, *In Struggle against Jim Crow: Lulu B. White and the NAACP, 1900–1957* (College Station: Texas A&M University Press), 27. Pitre specifically addresses the Houston local of the NAACP, which was dormant for much of the early 1930s.

20. See Mario T. Garcia, *Mexican Americans: Leadership, Ideology, and Identity, 1930–1960* (New Haven: Yale University Press, 1989), esp. 33–53, for a brief history of LULAC beliefs and activities in Texas.

21. Proceedings of the 29th annual convention, 1939, 101–3.

22. Ibid., 103.

23. Ibid., 105.

24. Gary Gerstle, *Working-Class Americanism: The Politics of Labor in a Textile City, 1914–1960* (Cambridge: Cambridge University Press, 1989).

25. Melvyn Dubofsky, *The State and Labor in Modern America* (Chapel Hill: University of North Carolina Press, 1994), 127.

26. In *Making a New Deal: Industrial Workers in Chicago, 1919–1939* (New York: Cambridge University Press, 1990), 252–89, Lizabeth Cohen argues that one result of New Deal programs was workers having a greater sense of entitlement from the government. In *Dividing Citizens: Gender and Federalism in New Deal Public Policy* (Ithaca, N.Y.: Cornell University Press, 1998), Suzanne Mettler argues that white men were privileged in the administration of New Deal programs and therefore were endowed with a nationalized, more expansive citizenship than nonwhite men and women.

27. T. H. Marshall has outlined how the meaning of citizenship in a liberal state evolves or rather builds over time, largely through the acts of government and how they are interpreted over time. In his theory, the rights of citizens began as civil rights, expanded to include political rights, and in the twentieth century expanded to include a set of basic social rights to a certain status and standard of living. I argue that longshoremen were caught between fighting for political rights and social rights, with white longshoremen particularly feeling entitled to the right to a standard of living enjoyed by middle-class whites. For a greater explication of Marshall's theory as well as other theories about the meanings of citizenship, see *The Citizenship Debates: A Reader,* ed. Gershon Shafir (Minneapolis: University of Minnesota Press, 1998).

28. Report of Harry Acreman on the 42d convention of the State Federation of Labor, Sabine Area Trades and Labor Council, Beaumont Texas Collection, AR 62, box 3, folder 9, University of Texas at Arlington, Special Collections.

29. Reeves, "Gunfire along the Gulf," 12.

30. The council wrote numerous letters to various legislators. The Council was composed of representatives from various AFL-related unions in the Port Arthur area and several longshore locals. Sabine Area Trades, box 3, folder 11.

31. Interview with Nelson and Curtis, July 1, 1936, Labor Movement in Texas Collection, box 2e306, folder 7, Center for American History, University of Texas at Austin.

32. According to a standard of living survey done by Ruth Allen in the 1930s in which longshoremen listed their expenses, it appears that they were in fact paying the poll tax despite the economic difficulty of so doing. However, it appears that only one poll tax was being paid and that, despite the fact that the ladies' auxiliary was so involved in the movement to get workers to vote, only one member of the household voted. Labor Movement in Texas Collection, box 2e306, folders 8 and 9.

33. Finally in 1944, the Supreme Court declared this practice unconstitutional in the *Smith v. Allwright* decision.

34. Patricia Sullivan, *Days of Hope: Race and Democracy in the New Deal Era* (Chapel Hill: University of North Carolina Press, 1996), 91.

35. Proceedings of the 27th annual convention, 1937, 90–91.

36. James M. SoRelle, "Race Relations in Heavenly Houston, 1919–45," in *Black Dixie: Afro-Texan History and Culture in Houston,* ed. Howard Beeth and Cary D. Wintz (College Station: Texas A&M University Press, 1992), 178, 179.

37. Letter to J. H. Harmon Jr., secretary of the Houston branch, May 11, 1937, NAACP Branch Papers—Houston.

38. The membership rolls of the Houston branch of the NAACP made special note

of longshoremen who joined the union. They also enrolled with the union hall listed as their address rather than their home, perhaps indicating that they joined as a group or their NAACP activities were an extension of their union life. NAACP Branch Papers—Houston.

39. Proceedings of the 25th annual convention, 4, 38.

40. Mers, *Working the Waterfront,* 68.

41. W. G. Bell, interview, Labor Movement in Texas Collection, box 2e306, folder 5.

42. Convention proceedings throughout the 1930s are filled with complaints from both black and white longshoremen about the disproportionate division of work. For a particularly hostile exchange, see proceedings of the 26th annual convention, 54–55.

43. Interview with F. N. Hunter, Local 1273, ILA, Houston on July 4, 1936, Labor Movement in Texas Collection, box 2e306, folder 7.

44. Clipping from the Houston *Chronicle,* April 25, 1939, Labor Movement in Texas Collection, box 2e306, folder 2.

45. Proceedings of the 26th annual convention, 48.

46. Ibid., 67.

47. John R. Owens, secretary-treasurer of the ILA, to Archie Anderson, secretary of Locals 1368, 1370, and 1371, January 24, 1939, NAACP Subject Files—Labor Disputes—Longshoremen.

48. Owens to Anderson, December 15, 1938, NAACP Subject Files—Labor Disputes—Longshoremen.

49. Thurgood Marshall, assistant special counsel, to Joseph P. Ryan, president of the International Longshoremen's Association, January 23 and March 8, 1939, NAACP Subject Files—Labor Disputes—Longshoremen.

50. William Pickens, director of branches, to O. L. Archer regarding membership applications, April 28, 1939, NAACP Subject Files—Labor Disputes—Longshoremen.

51. Ruth Allen, *Chapters in the History of Organized Labor in Texas* (Austin: University of Texas Publications, 1941), 217.

52. *W. G. Bell et al. v. Fred G. Hill, county clerk of Jefferson County, Texas, et al.,* Supreme Court of Texas, motion no. 11,520, July 20, 1934; interview with W. G. Bell of Local 325, Beaumont, Labor Movement in Texas Collection, box 2e306, folder 5.

53. James Scott argues that the "powerless are often obliged to adopt a strategic pose in the presence of the powerful." However, if we take these interactions at face value, we will miss the ideological insubordination visible in actions and private words. Scott, *Domination and the Arts of Resistance: Hidden Transcripts* (New Haven: Yale University Press, 1990), xii.

54. Mers, *Working the Waterfront,* 117, 147.

55. Follett interview, 72–73.

56. "Leninist Theories and Tactics Are Behind John L. Lewis' CIO, Communist Heads Swell Its Ranks; Movement Is Political according to National Magazine," *Negro Labor News,* no. 18 (July 31, 1937): 1.

57. Proceedings of the 29th annual convention, 1939, 10.

58. F. Ray Marshall, *Labor in the South* (Cambridge: Harvard University Press, 1967), 207.

59. Mers, *Working the Waterfront,* 148.

60. David Montejano discusses this change in racial ideology in *Anglos and Mexicans,* 162–96.

61. In *Decade of Betrayal: Mexican Repatriation in the 1930s* (Albuquerque: University of New Mexico Press, 1995), Francisco Balderrama and Raymond Rodriguez discuss the repatriation process, what it said about racial attitudes toward Mexicans and Mexican Americans, and the effect on those who left and the community at large.

62. Ian Haney-López, *White by Law: The Legal Construction of Race* (New York: New York University Press, 1996), 117. Haney-López posits that U.S. immigration policies construct an idea of citizenship in which full citizenship is reserved for whites.

63. David Gutiérrez, *Walls and Mirrors: Mexican Americans, Mexican Immigrants, and the Politics of Ethnicity* (Berkeley: University of California Press, 1995), 72.

64. Toby Miller, *The Well-Tempered Self: Citizenship, Culture, and the Postmodern Subject* (Baltimore: Johns Hopkins University Press, 1993), 3.

65. Gilbert Mers, interview by George Green, June 5, 1985, Oral History Collection, University of Texas at Arlington, Special Collections, 51.

66. Roll book, AR 268, University of Texas at Arlington, Special Collections.

67. Mers interview, 51.

68. Proceedings of the 24th annual convention, 68.

69. Dock and Marine Council minute book, AR 269, Labor Collection, University of Texas at Arlington, Special Collections, 143.

70. Garcia, *Mexican Americans,* 33–55.

71. In Houston, most Mexicans and Mexican Americans lived in a small part of the city near the ship channel known as Magnolia Park.

72. Proceedings of the 29th annual convention, 51–52.

73. Foley, *The White Scourge,* 209.

74. Proceedings of the 29th annual convention, 51.

75. Ibid., 52.

76. Dock and Marine Council minute book, 79.

77. Ibid., 100.

78. Mers interview, 56

79. Dock and Marine Council minute book, 142. Additionally, 1350 was not the first group of Mexican Americans to abandon the ILA. A group of compressmen in Corpus Christi left the union in 1935, claiming that they had been discriminated against, although the accused denied this was true. Proceedings of the 25th annual convention, 1935, 39.

80. "Phoney CIO's Defeated Again: Injunction Denied, Judge Rules I.L.A. Shall Work Ships," *Longshoremen's News,* August 4, 1938, 1.

81. "Maritime Labor Board Asked to Act Here: Mexican Labor Group Asked to Refuse to Load Ships Bound for Galveston," Galveston *News,* July 21, 1938, clipping in Labor Movement in Texas Collection, box 2e306, folder 10.

82. In *The Challenge of Interracial Unionism: Alabama Coal Miners, 1878–1921* (Chapel Hill: University of North Carolina Press, 1998), Daniel Letwin argues that an interracial union of Alabama coal miners was in several ways shaped by Jim Crow society. Alex Lichtenstein suggests that blacks may have had their own interests in separate locals; see Lichtenstein, "Exploring the Local World of Interracialism," *Labor History* 41, no. 1 (2000): 67.

83. There has been considerable debate on whether and how multiracial unions challenged Jim Crow society. See "Symposium on Daniel Letwin: The Challenge of Interracial Unionism," *Labor History* 41, no. 1 (2000): 63–90; Letwin, *The Challenge of Interracial Unionism;* Michael Honey, *Southern Labor and Black Civil Rights: Organizing Memphis Workers* (Urbana: University of Illinois Press, 1993).

5

A History of Florida's White Primary

GARY R. MORMINO

Just where *does* Florida belong? Is it the southernmost American state, or is it the northernmost colony of the Caribbean? The question of Florida's rightful place in the American South is a debate of long standing, inviting a spirited argument as to the protean meanings of regionalism, the Old South, the New South, and the Gulf South. A history of slavery, secession, Civil War and Reconstruction, Bourbon restoration, Jim Crow legisla-tion, a large African American population, violence and lynchings, one-party rule, and resistance to integration all seem to place Florida firmly within the traditions and experiences of the American South. Not every-one has agreed. In 1928, historian Ulrich B. Phillips wrote that "Miami Beach, Palm Beach, and Coral Gables are southern only in latitude."[1] Yet historians of the modern South have exhibited more indifference than interest in Florida. Impressive scholarship by Woodward, Tindall, Terrill, Wright, Ayers, Daniel, and Bartley provide scant details or analysis of modern Florida.[2] Such oversight is understandable, if regrettable. Florida did not create a state archives until 1967. Our understanding of Florida, until recently, rested upon a thin foundation of published histories.

Florida's role in the civil rights movement also receives short shrift from scholars. Taylor Branch opens his magisterial study, *Pillar of Fire*, in St. Augustine, but most studies largely ignore the struggle for justice in Pensacola, Tallahassee, Tampa, St. Petersburg, Orlando, Miami, and other communities.[3] Times may be changing. Recently, Harvard Sitkoff noted, "While every U.S. history textbook and every work on African American history highlights the story of the Montgomery bus boycott, few even mention in passing that less than six months later another city-wide boycott began in Tallahassee, Florida, in May 1956.[4] The 1999 biog-raphy of Harry T. Moore contained a fascinating subtitle: *America's First Civil Rights Martyr*. While books amply and justifiably document the role of Medgar Evers and Emmett Till, who remembers Harry T. Moore?

Historians would be wise to look southward at the unfolding scholarship on Florida's civil rights movement.[5]

This essay represents an effort to explore one chapter of Florida's past: the evolution and demise of Florida's white primary, from its germination in the late nineteenth century to its court-ordered abolishment in the 1940s. The crusade to invalidate the white primary and secure a meaningful vote united black civic and political leaders and served as a bridge to the modern civil rights movement and Second Reconstruction. How and why did the white primary evolve in Florida? How did Florida's white primary fit into the state's political culture? What were the consequences of Florida's white primary? When the U.S. Supreme Court ruled in *Smith v. Allwright* (1944) that the white primary was unconstitutional, how did white leaders react? What was the role of black Floridians in this struggle?

The history of Florida election law reflects a consistent and systematic pattern of discrimination and racism. Efforts to bar and dilute African American political participation followed the Civil War and Reconstruction. Florida's state constitutions through 1865 limited the elective franchise to "free white males." White Floridians had adopted the 1865 constitution to seek readmission to the Union, but Congress denied Florida's request. In particular, the inclusion of the onerous Black Codes in the document angered congressional Republicans. Historian Theodore B. Wilson has called Florida's 1865 constitution with its Black Codes "the most bigoted and short-sighted of all the southern legislatures of 1865 and 1866." Neither Radical Republicans nor African American freedmen ever dominated Reconstruction Florida; rather, a coalition of conservative Democrats and Republicans (white and black) seized power. Fearful that freedmen might gain power in Florida's Black Belt, the cotton lands between the Apalachicola and Suwannee Rivers, politicians maximized the appointive power of the governor in the state constitution of 1868.[6]

In 1880, African Americans constituted nearly half of Florida's population. Moreover, Florida's black population was growing at a faster rate than whites. The solution to the threat (perceived and real) of black rule was to change the structure of the political system and the rules of voting. White Democrats had ended Reconstruction with victories in the 1876 elections. Republicans, however, posed a serious threat. Convinced of their political power, Democrats called for a constitutional convention in 1884. The convention gathered in June 1885.[7]

Floridians ratified the 1885 constitution, called by one historian "a white supremacy document."[8] Haunted by the spectre of Reconstruction

Republican governors, the new state constitution greatly reduced the powers of the governor. The constitution authorized a poll tax as a voting requirement, a provision adopted by the 1889 legislature. Additional legislation, intended to confuse and dissuade ignorant black voters, appeared in Bourbon Florida. An 1889 law introduced the "Eight Box" requirement, forcing voters to place each ballot in the correct box, an impediment that proved an insurmountable challenge for most poorly educated blacks. In 1890, fully 45 percent of Florida's adult male blacks were illiterate.[9]

The political consequences and designs of the 1885 state constitution were swift and dramatic. "Markedly democratic during the 1880s," writes historian J. Morgan Kousser, "Florida became solidly Democratic by the 1890s." Black voter turnout fell precipitously. In 1884, 87 percent of the eligible black electorate participated in the gubernatorial election; by 1896, an estimated 5 percent did so. White turnout also fell significantly, from an estimated 96 percent in 1880 to 57 percent in 1896. The $2 poll tax also deterred poor whites.[10]

Jim Crow legislation, racial violence, and political disfranchisement converged during the 1890s. The Florida constitution of 1885 decreed only that "white and colored children shall not be taught in the same school." Subsequent legislatures enacted harsher language. An 1895 law mandated, "It shall be a penal offense for any official . . . to conduct within this state any school of any grade, public, private or parochial wherein white persons and negroes shall be instructed or boarded within the same building, or taught in the same class." Racial violence escalated during the 1890s and persisted for decades thereafter. Shockingly, Florida recorded 244 lynchings between 1889 and 1930, a rate double that of Alabama.[11]

In 1897 the Florida legislature began regulating county primary elections, adopting the first statutorily authorized white primaries. Primaries were not required, but if the county party chose to have a primary, it was to be held consistent with the general election law of the state, except as modified by this act. Section 2 of this act required the enforcement of the poll tax as a prerequisite to voting. Section 3 sanctioned state authorization to exclude blacks, giving the county party officials the power to "declare the terms and conditions on which legal electors offering to vote at such election shall be regarded and taken as proper members of the party."[12]

Democrats had been holding primaries since at least 1892. The Democratic Party platform of 1892 barred those whose admission would violate "the purity and integrity of the party," meaning blacks. The 1900 Democratic platform endorsed "the nomination of all candidates for office, both state and county . . . by a majority in white Democratic primary election."[13] The white primary had become de facto and de jure the custom and law of the state.

The Florida statutes of 1901 regulated primaries held by any state or local party. Primaries were still optional, but if the state, congressional district, or county executive of any party held a primary, it was to be in conformity with the general election law. The statute gave to party committees—thus navigating the Fifteenth Amendment of the U.S. Constitution—the power to "declare the terms and conditions on which legal electors offering to vote at such election shall be regarded and taken as proper members of the party." The 1901 statute was later amended to include municipal primaries.[14]

The white primary combined with other devices accomplished the virtual elimination of African Americans in Florida as meaningful voters and officeholders. In 1909, *Tampa Morning Tribune* plainly asserted the meaning of the white primary in an editorial.

In Florida, the negro has no voice whatever in the selection of United States Senators, Representatives in Congress, Governor, statehouse officers, members of the legislature, county officers. In only one municipality of the State—Tampa—does he have any voice in the election of city officers. He has had, by the way, his last voice in this particular city. His vote has ceased to be either an asset of citizenship or valuable commercial commodity. His right of suffrage is only a name.[15]

In 1915 the Florida legislature attempted to enact a literacy test, a move designed to further dampen the black voting threat. Between 1883 and 1913, seven other southern states adopted a literacy test as a requirement for voting. In this case, the legislature voted to adopt a literacy test, along with a $500 property qualification for voting. To mollify poor whites, the bill included a grandfather clause, asserting "that no person or lineal descendent of any such person who was on January 1, 1867, or prior thereto, entitled to vote under the Constitution and law of any of the States or Territories, or entitled to vote under any form of government, or any naturalized citizen or his descendants, shall be denied the right to register and vote because he shall not be able to read, write and interpret any section of the Constitution of the State of Florida." Following debate, the Senate approved the disfranchisement bill unanimously, while the House passed the measure 53–6. Because the measure was designed to amend the state constitution, Florida voters were required to approve the changes in November 1916.[16]

The debate over this amendment occurred during a terrifying upsurge of lynching and violence in Florida. In 1915, white Floridians lynched five blacks, and nine more were lynched the following year. Headlines such as "Mob Lynched a Vicious Black at Forrest City" and "Five Blacks Hanged to Oak Tree by Mob" were commonplace.[17] Reflective of this milieu, the *Tallahassee Daily Democrat* editorialized, "While the white primary in our state has largely improved conditions, it does not prevent the illiterate negro vote from being a factor in city politics."[18]

In November 1916, Florida voters rejected the proposed constitutional amendment 19,688 to 10,518. The referendum was held *after* the Supreme Court decision, *Guinn v. United States*, 238 U.S. 347 (1915), which invalidated Oklahoma's provision to exempt from the literacy test persons who were entitled to vote in 1866. Why did Floridians reject the amendment? Floridians were in no mood to defy the U.S. Supreme Court. Moreover, the referendum coincided with a bitter gubernatorial election, whereby Florida's poor whites elected Sidney Johnston Catts, "the Cracker Messiah." Catts won the election in an extraordinary upset, running on the Prohibition ticket. Catts told Floridians in his victory statement, "I have frowned upon, and would not tolerate, a negro vote coming in to settle a Democratic fuss."[19]

Southern progressivism—"for whites only" in the words of C. Vann Woodward—embraced the white primary as a tool of reform and control. Rationalizing that political disfranchisement of African Americans was a noble reform—allowing white leaders the freedom of debate absent the issue of race—southern politicians applauded the white primary. In Florida, scores of municipalities followed the example set in Tallahassee, establishing nonpartisan white primaries. Acting upon the principle of political reform, the notion that a "controlled" black vote tainted elections, Tampa leaders organized the White Municipal Party in 1908. "For the first time in the history of Tampa," editorialized the *Tampa Morning Tribune* on April 5, 1910, "candidates have not found it necessary to go down into the dives of the 'Scrub' [a black neighborhood] to hobnob with the festive colored brother on his own ground." The white primary helped blacks know their place.[20]

The white primary served the interests of Florida's white ruling classes.

By delegating the responsibility for establishing voting qualifications to local and state party committees, the white party cleverly danced around the Fifteenth Amendment's language that "no state shall . . ." Moreover, the white primary satisfied the concerns of politicians that there were never too many hurdles to prevent African Americans from voting. The white primary, reinforced by the poll tax and custom, served as a powerful deterrent. Other measures were being introduced to dilute the black vote. Not coincidentally, a movement to implement at-large elections at the city and county level—a plan undermining and/or diluting the black or immigrant vote—gained momentum in the early twentieth century.[21]

Florida's color line stood unbending and unbent during the early twentieth century. One could well understand Florida's adherence to white supremacy and strict segregation in Jefferson, Leon, and Gadsden Counties, where blacks outnumbered whites and where whites were overwhelmingly native and southern born. But how did rapid demographic, social, and economic change affect race relations in south Florida? Pinellas County served as a bellwether of Florida race relations. Created in 1911, the result of a secession movement from Hillsborough County (Tampa), Pinellas soon became the first county in Florida to be populated by a majority of whites born outside the South. Yet St. Petersburg residents—even Populist transplants from the upper Midwest—accommodated to the South's color line. Writes historian Raymond Arsenault, "In St. Petersburg . . . interaction between blacks and whites was ruthlessly and systematically controlled by a combination of custom and law . . . whites who questioned the Jim Crow system were excluded from polite society, and blacks who challenged the system were often subjected to physical violence or death." Indeed, Arsenault notes, "[I]t was sometimes the Northerners who pushed the hardest for segregation."[22]

St. Petersburg also adopted the white primary as a reform measure. Alarmed at the numbers of black registered voters, Lew B. Brown, editor of the *St. Petersburg Independent*, endorsed the white primary in 1913 as "a voluntary expression of the white voters to maintain control of city affairs in the hands of white people."[23]

During the 1920s, Florida became ingrained in American popular culture. The Florida Boom was synonymous with prosperity and visions of Mediterranean paradise in America: Coral Gables, bathing beauty pageants, the Dixie Highway, and newfound leisure lured Americans to the Sunshine State. The Florida Boom, however, thinly disguised a deeply stratified Jim Crow state.

For African Americans, the gaiety of Florida's Roaring Twenties was a facade, a mask for a bitter reality. The white primary became a secondary concern. African Americans had emerged from World War I with optimism and hope that their participation ensured racial peace and prosperity. Such illusions were soon shattered. In Ocoee, an agricultural hamlet near Orlando, a savage race riot occurred in November 1920 when returning black servicemen attempted to register to vote. The *Tampa Tribune* editorialized after the event, "There will always be some things [voting] reserved exclusively for the white men and women of this state." Whites burned Ocoee's black section to the ground, killing several residents. In 1923, Rosewood, a lumber village near Cedar Key, erupted in a now infamous (but for decades undiscussed) race riot. At least eight deaths have been verified, but many more may have occurred. The 1920s also reintroduced the Ku Klux Klan. A recent study of the Rosewood massacre commented on the role of the Klan: "Often allied with local police and sheriff's departments—the Klan sought to intimidate blacks into quietly accepting segregation."[24]

The white primary survived the 1920s and 1930s, but powerful forces within and outside the South began to challenge the legal and political foundations of the doctrine. Most important, World War II sowed the seeds of the modern civil rights movement. Deeply moved by President Roosevelt's enunciation of the "Four Freedoms," but also keenly aware of the political calculations of the chief executive, African Americans vowed a "Double V" campaign, fully supporting the war against totalitarianism but also championing the fight against racism at home.[25]

Florida became both racial battleground and cauldron for the homefront war. The Sunshine State became home to 172 military establishments during the war. The presence of black servicemen, especially those reared in the North, challenged Jim Crow traditions and notions of white supremacy. A series of serious racial incidents disrupted the peace and shattered the peace of mind of many Floridians. Fearing the worst, the State Defense Council and Army Service Forces prepared secret plans to declare martial law in the event of racial disturbances in Jacksonville, Tallahassee, Orlando, Tampa, St. Petersburg, and Miami.[26]

If World War II crystallized the civil rights movement, an assault against Jim Crow had already begun on a series of fronts. Before Pearl Harbor, civil rights lawyers and activists identified two critical salients: the appalling inequities in education and the white primary. The issues and participants frequently intersected, principally because of the ubiquitous presence of the NAACP chief legal counsel, Thurgood Marshall, and a Florida school teacher, Harry T. Moore.

Marshall's energies and tenacity dazzled everyone around him, including his most recent biographer. Carl Rowan asks the reader to try to understand and appreciate Marshall in the late 1930s and early 1940s by asking, "How can one lawyer simultaneously defend a man accused of rape in Connecticut, try to rescue a young black accused of triple murder in Oklahoma, and struggle in the courts to win equal pay for black teachers and wipe out Jim Crow at law schools in Maryland and Missouri at the same time that he pursues what till then was the biggest prize of all: the right of blacks to vote?"[27]

In 1937, a letter came across Marshall's desk. He recognized neither the author nor the postmark, but over the next decade and a half, he would come to know Harry Moore and Mims, Florida, intimately. In 1937, Moore was principal of the Mims Colored Elementary School and head of the Brevard County branch of the NAACP. He was beseeching the NAACP to help prepare a lawsuit addressing the salary disparity between white and black teachers. The idea clicked with Marshall. That 1937 letter linked Marshall and Moore into a fateful alliance that brought both men national notoriety and helped launch Florida's civil rights movement. Two issues dominated their relationship: educational equality and the right to the ballot.

Born in Suwannee County, Florida, in 1905, Moore settled in Brevard County in 1925, accepting a teaching position at Titusville. A dedicated teacher, he instilled in his students lessons of pride and hope, bringing to class issues of the *Pittsburgh Courier* and sample ballots. In 1934, he helped organize the local NAACP chapter. He fought against racial injustice, railing against police brutality and the plight of grove workers. He became a marked man for his activism, especially his agitation for educational and voting equality.[28]

In 1940, Marshall and the Florida State Teachers Association (representing black instructors) launched a series of lawsuits against Dade, Palm Beach, Brevard, Hillsborough, Pinellas, Escambia, and Duval Counties (representing the state's urban centers). Remarkably, Marshall won many of these cases, which guaranteed equal pay for black teachers. Lamentably, most of the original litigants (including Moore) were fired from their jobs.[29]

Since the 1920s, the U.S. Supreme Court had ruled on state contraventions of the Fifteenth Amendment: *Nixon v. Herndon* (1927), *Nixon v.*

Condon (1932), and *Nixon v. Townsend* (1935). In 1941, in *U.S. v. Classic*, the Court ruled that even if the state delegated to political parties the power to set voting qualifications, the primary was such an integral part of the electoral choice that it was subject to the same constitutional provisions as the general election. Throughout the early 1940s, the indefatigable Marshall probed for weaknesses in the white primary doctrine. The files of the NAACP amply document the struggle for political equality in Florida and the South.[30]

In April 1944, the Supreme Court issued its landmark ruling, *Smith v. Allwright*, holding that political primaries were so enmeshed with the state that parties could not discriminate in their membership. The implication for other southern states was obvious: The ruse of "private parties" defining the electorate and running private primaries was unconstitutional. White Floridians recoiled at the decision. Gubernatorial candidate Millard Caldwell called the case a "menace to the independence of the state and party and must be resisted with well directed energy."[31] Senator Claude Pepper, a leading southern liberal, exhorted, "Southerners will not allow matters peculiar to us to be determined by those who do not know and understand our problem. The South will allow nothing to impair white supremacy."[32] Tom Conely, chairman of Florida's Democratic Party, stated, "We'll certainly resist if possible any attempt to have Negroes vote in our primaries."[33]

African Americans sought justice. In the May 1944 Democratic primaries, blacks attempted to register and vote. In Jacksonville, a prominent black minister was told by two white men, "You won't go to jail [for voting], but you will be killed. This is Florida. We don't allow niggers to vote here in the Democratic primaries." Florida, along with its southern neighbors, defied the Supreme Court.[34]

African American leaders pressed the attack. Decades later, Justice Marshall attempted to put the *Smith* decision in perspective. "I don't know whether the voting case or the school desegregation case was more important," he told biographer Carl Rowan. "Without the ballot you've got no goddamned citizenship, no status, no power, in this country. But without the chance to get an education you have no capacity to use the ballot effectively. Hell, I don't know which case I'm proudest of."[35] He realized the ballot transcended politics. Until African Americans registered and voted in all elections and in large numbers, the battle would not be over. A two-front war now ensued, to engage individual southern states, counties, and municipalities for the right to register as Democrats and vote in primaries, but more important to engage black southerners in realizing that without a meaningful vote, there can be no dignity as citizens. Voting, as much as homeownership and schools, defined citizenship and class.

Fierce resistance followed. Across Florida, state and local Democratic Party officials routinely ignored the *Smith* decision. In Jacksonville, Dallas J. Graham attempted to register for the April 1945 primary, but was denied by Fleming H. Bowden, supervisor of registration for the city of Jacksonville. Graham won the right to register as a Democrat in the Circuit Court, *State of Florida et rel Graham v. Bowden* (1945). In Tampa, Perry Harvey Sr., head of the Longshoremen's Union, sued the Tampa City Council in July 1945 in protest of "White Municipal Rule."[36]

In Florida, blacks' likelihood of registering as Democrats or switching registration from Republican to Democrat depended in large part on the willingness of election supervisors. Voter registration was largely a local matter. In Brevard County, an African American remembered the supervisor of elections pledging, "Before I register any niggers as Democrats, I will get out of politics altogether." In Arcadia, DeSoto County, a delegation of African Americans asked to register as Democrats in July 1945. The city recorder informed them that the city primary was "for whites only." The city attorney counseled the Arcadia City Council, "It is therefore my opinion that no person of the COLORED RACE should be allowed to register to vote or participate in same [municipal election].[37]

In Tampa, Orlando, Miami, St. Petersburg, and Pensacola, African Americans sought to accomplish what the Supreme Court had ruled. "In point of fact," wrote one scholar, "the legal right of Negroes to vote in Florida's Democratic primaries was not definitely established until three years after the *Smith* decision."[38]

The Florida Supreme Court's decision in July 1945, *Davis v. State et rel Cromwell* reaffirmed the rights of blacks to register as Democrats. Escambia County's supervisor of elections had refused to register R. A. Cromwell, a Pensacolian, because he was black. Still, state and local officials disregarded the court's rulings. Before his death in April 1945, President Roosevelt—"the lion and the fox"—was reluctant to force the issue, fearful that white southerners might defect, a harbinger of 1948. Marshall pressured Attorney General Francis Biddle to enforce the decision, but understood that inaction was the result of political, not legal, decisions.[39] In Florida, legislators contemplated measures intended to deter and detract black voting. In the 1945 legislature, a white primary bill, modeled after a South Carolina measure, was introduced but tabled. The bill would have repealed all state statutes relating to primary elections and given Florida's political parties control over the primaries. Many legislators feared widespread fraud in the event of privately monitored primaries. The *Tampa Morning Tribune* called the plan "the most obnoxious proposition made to a Florida legislature in many years. It would produce and promote a crop of Florida Bilbos." (Theodore Bilbo was a very prominent racist governor of Mississippi.) Governor Caldwell told Floridians that the South Carolina Plan, whereby the state sponsored a "private primary," might work in Florida.[40]

The Florida Democratic Party attempted to turn the tide by recommending that county commissioners provide separate voting booths for blacks and whites. Florida's attorney general, Tom Watson, opined that whites might "reduce the evils" of black voting through segregated facilities. Black leaders feared that such action would imperil voters and discount votes, as well as lead to fraud.[41]

While white solons debated a political Lost Cause, African Americans organized at the state and local levels to push for justice. Harry Moore emerged as Florida's most visible and effective activist. A whirling dervish, he was seemingly everywhere between 1944 and 1951, writing endless letters and manifestos, speaking at church socials and political caucuses. In August 1944, Moore and other state leaders organized the Progressive Voters' League (PVL), a political action arm of the NAACP. Moore became the PVL's most visible spokesman. By the 1946 Democratic primaries, the PVL helped register thirty-two thousand African Americans as Democrats. Most of them voted in the May 1946 primaries. In general, African Americans registered freely in most urban locales, but met resistance when attempting to vote in north and west Florida. Eight counties still refused to register any African Americans as Democrats in 1946.[42]

Undaunted, Moore organized at a furious pace. He energized a moribund state NAACP. In 1941, Florida had organized only nine NAACP branches with a few hundred members. By the end of 1945, the PVL pointed to 53 branches with nearly ten thousand members. The NAACP boasted large chapters in Jacksonville, Tampa, and Brevard County, but Moore was proudest of branches in Florida's Black Belt, Taylor, Dixie, and Bay Counties. His agitation brought increasing notice from Florida's white establishment. Governor Caldwell, a caustic critic of the *Smith* decision, directed his executive secretary to gather information about Moore. A prominent Brevard County citizen replied that Moore "is a trouble maker and negro organizer." Action followed. In the spring of 1946, Moore was fired from his longtime job as school principal. Florida's black citizens rallied around him, urging NAACP chapters and members to support Moore. Donations and letters poured in. In the summer of 1946, Moore became a paid field officer of the NAACP.[43]

In 1947, the Florida legislature tilted at the windmills of the white primary one last time. Legislators resoundingly defeated the measure. A number of factors explain the demise of the white primary. The failure to defy the courts should not be mistaken for a sudden mellowing of race relations in the state. Rather, Democratic leaders, exhausted by the battle to preserve the white primary, shifted to higher ground where battles would be fought over new issues: schools and integration. In more subtle ways, a shift to at-large elections, such as the 1947 law that now required county school board members to run at large, rather than in member districts, ensured white control.

"Florida Negro citizens now face a bright political future," wrote Moore in November 1947.[44] That year, an estimated 13–15 percent of eligible African Americans in Florida had registered, a remarkable jump considering only 3–6 percent of such Floridians were registered in 1940.[45] Between the landmark decision to outlaw the white primary in 1944 and the *Brown* decision in 1954, the number of black voters registered in Florida rose from 20,000 to 128,000. No other southern state matched Florida's record.[46]

Moore had little time to savor victory. In November 1949, he protested to Governor Fuller Warren that in four Florida counties (Madison, Liberty, Lafayette, and Hendry), not a single African American was registered to vote. He also became involved in a cause célèbre known as the Groveland Case. In July 1949, four black youths were arrested for allegedly raping a seventeen-year-old farm wife in Lake County. The facts of the case indicated that the charges of "ravishing white womanhood" were outrageous. But Moore's protest met the resistance of his longtime nemesis, Lake County sheriff Willis McCall. National criticism of the handling of the case only strengthened McCall's resolve. In November 1951, McCall shot to death one of the handcuffed "Groveland boys," claiming he had attacked him while attempting to escape. A month later, Moore and his wife were killed when a dynamite blast leveled their Mims home. No one was ever convicted of the crime. When the NAACP's Walter White criticized the governor's handling of the affair, Warren labeled

White a mulatto "who combines in his being few of the attractive qualities of either race and the repulsive qualities of both."[47]

The battle over the white primary signaled an end as well as a beginning. The white primary's demise culminated the work of dedicated civil rights lawyers, leaders, and courageous citizens willing to take a stand. By the late 1940s, Florida's white political establishment accepted, albeit reluctantly, the ruling of *Smith v. Allwright*. In this respect, Florida more resembled the attitudes and reactions of leaders in Virginia and Tennessee than in Alabama or Georgia. To be sure, it was not a total victory. Resistance was greatest in Florida's Black Belt, the old plantation belt between the Suwannee and Apalachicola Rivers. In 1950, only two counties, Jefferson and Gadsden, still retained majority black populations. White officials fiercely opposed any black voting threat to white rule. Edward D. Davis, an AME minister, school principal, and associate of Moore, observed the struggle in Liberty County. An impoverished area bordering the Apalachicola River, Liberty County was an especially hostile place for African Americans. When blacks attempted to register to vote in the late 1940s, Davis recalled, "All hell broke loose. Culprits would shoot at their homes." The Liberty County sheriff informed the black residents that "if they would go down and take their names off the [registration] books, everything would be normal again." In fact, Liberty County residents voted with their feet. In 1920, Liberty County had 2,242 black inhabitants; by 1970, the number had fallen to 485. In 1963, Liberty County had *no* black registered voters.[48]

The death of Harry T. Moore, coinciding with the last gasp of the white primary, signaled an end as well as a beginning. If Florida's racial policies and attitudes mirrored the Gulf South before 1950, it soon portrayed a state deeply divided and ambivalent about race and place.

Conventional wisdom suggests that Florida deviated dramatically from its Gulf South neighbors in the 1950s and 1960s. Most telling, the 1950s signaled Florida's Big Bang, an extraordinary population explosion that transformed Florida from America's twentieth most populous state in 1950 to the ninth most populous state in 1970 to the fourth largest today. In 1940, a population of 1.9 million placed Florida last in the South (behind South Carolina); by 2000, Florida's population approached 16 million. More significant than the sheer numbers have been the changes in origin and composition. In 1950, African Americans comprised 22 percent of the population. By 1970, that figure had dropped to 16 percent.

Florida has not been losing black residents; rather, overwhelming numbers of white migrants (especially retirees) have established new lives in Florida. The great majority of the new residents were midwesterners and northeasterners. During the 1950s, for instance, Florida's white population increased by 1.2 million, while Florida's black population grew by only 80,000. In contrast, Virginia's black population declined by almost 70,000. New Yorkers and Ohioans changed Florida's social climate. Race was not an obsession. Governor LeRoy Collins symbolized Florida's racial moderation. Collins, a deeply moral man, was more interested in education and growth than racial confrontation. He helped defuse a number of racial crises. When sit-ins threatened Florida in the early 1960s, businessmen almost always accepted peaceful integration to protracted conflict. Florida was largely spared the intense, paralyzing racial conflict of the Gulf South. The reasons may have had more to do with growth and image than with sentiment. The location of Walt Disney World in Orlando symbolized the New Florida. It is inconceivable that an image-minded corporation would have located Disney World in Alabama or Mississippi in 1971.

But the New Florida of the 1950s and 1960s resembled the New South in many ways. For all of the hype about tourism and growth, Floridians also resisted racial change. When Collins left office in 1960, the state of Florida had not desegregated a single public school. In 1956, the Florida legislature voted unanimously for "interposition," a move to block the U.S. Supreme Court's efforts to integrate schools. The leader of the interposition movement was Farris Bryant. In 1960, Floridians rejected Collins's urgings and elected Bryant, a segregationist. He, too, was succeeded by a staunch segregationist. Yet Bryant and Haydon Burns, for all of their rhetoric, would not take Florida into a racial abyss for personal aggrandizement. It was Haydon Burns who negotiated with Walt Disney about Florida's virtues.

Ironically, the last bastion of the white primary fell in Orlando in 1950. There, city leaders officially disbanded the White Voters Executive Committee. Orlando had once been so attached to the Old Florida. Today, Orlando may be the most un-southern spot in the South; indeed, the city has few attachments to Florida. Fewer and fewer Floridians have memories of an era when the Democratic Party was "for whites only." Vestiges of the white primary gather dust in archives and supervisor of election offices. But for more than fifty years, the white primary served as a touchstone, a beleaguered symbol of white unity, and a powerful emblem of black dreams.

Notes

1. Ulrich B. Phillips, "The Central Theme of Southern History," *American Historical Review* 34 (October 1928): 30.

2. C. Vann Woodward, *Origins of the New South, 1877–1913* (Baton Rouge: Louisiana State University Press, 1951); George B. Tindall, *The Emergence of the New South, 1915–1945* (Baton Rouge: Louisiana State University Press, 1967); William J. Cooper and Tom Terrill, *The American South: A History* (New York: Knopf, 1990); Gavin Wright, *Old South, New South: Revolutions in the Southern Economy since the Civil War* (New York: Basic Books, 1986); Edward L. Ayers, *The Promise of the New South: Life after Reconstruction* (New York: Oxford University Press, 1992); Pete Daniel, *Standing at the Crossroads: Southern Life since 1900* (New York: Hill and Wang, 1986); Numan V. Bartley, *The New South, 1945–1980* (Baton Rouge: Louisiana State University Press, 1995).

3. Taylor Branch, *Pillar of Fire: America in the King Years, 1963–1965* (New York: Simon and Schuster, 1998); Branch, *Parting the Waters: America in the King Years, 1954–1963* (New York: Simon and Schuster, 1988); David J. Garrow, *Bearing the Cross* (New York: William Morrow, 1986).

4. Harvard Sitkoff, review of *The Pain and the Promise,* in *Florida Historical Quarterly* 79 (summer 2000): 110.

5. Ben Green, *Before His Time: The Untold Story of Harry T. Moore, America's First Civil Rights Martyr* (New York: Free Press, 1999); David R. Colburn, *Racial Change and Community Crisis: St. Augustine, Florida, 1877–1980* (Gainesville: University Press of Florida, 1985); Glenda Alice Rabby, *The Pain and the Promise: The Struggle for Civil Rights in Tallahassee, Florida* (Athens: University of Georgia Press, 1999); Marvin Dunn, *Black Miami in the Twentieth Century* (Gainesville: University Press of Florida, 1997); Robert W. Saunders Sr., *Bridging the Gap: Continuing the Florida NAACP Legacy of Harry T. Moore* (Tampa: University of Tampa Press, 2000); Stacy Braukman, "Women and the Civil Rights Movement in Tampa," *Tampa Bay History* 14 (fall/winter 1992): 62–69; Stephen F. Lawson, "From Sit-In to Race Riot: Businessmen, Blacks, and the Pursuit of Moderation in Tampa, 1960–1967," in *Southern Businessmen and Desegregation,* ed. Elizabeth Jacoway and David Colburn (Baton Rouge: Louisiana State University Press, 1982), 257–81; "Civil Rights Protests in Tampa: Oral Memoirs of Conflicts and Accommodation," *Tampa Bay History* 1 (spring/summer 1979): 37–54; Darryl Paulson and Milly St. Julien, "Desegregating Public Schools in Manatee and Pinellas Counties, 1954–1971," *Tampa Bay History* 7 (spring/summer 1985): 30–41; Darryl Paulson, "Stay Out, the Water's Fine: Desegregation Municipal Swimming in St. Petersburg, Florida," *Tampa Bay History* 4 (fall/winter 1982): 6–19; Kermit Hall, "Civil Rights:

The Florida Version," *Forum: The Magazine of Florida Humanities Council* (winter/ 1994–95): 10–13; Steven Lawson, David Colburn, and Darryl Paulson, "Groveland: Florida's Little Scottsboro," *Florida Historical Quarterly* 65 (July 1986): 1–26; Patricia Dillon, "Civil Rights and School Desegregation in Sanford," *Florida Historical Quarterly* 76 (winter 1998): 310–25; James C. Clark, "Civil Rights Leader Harry T. Moore and the Ku Klux Klan in Florida," *Florida Historical Quarterly* 73 (October 1994): 166–83; Raymond A. Mohl, "Miami: The Ethnic Cauldron," in *Sunbelt Cities,* ed. Richard Bernard and Bradley Rice (Austin: University of Texas Press, 1983): 58–99; Mohl, "Race and Housing in Miami during the New Deal," *Prologue* 19 (spring 1987): 7–21; Mohl, "'South of the South?' Jews, Blacks, and the Civil Rights Movement in Miami, 1945– 1960," *Journal of American Ethnic History* 18 (spring 1999): 3–36; Mohl, "Making the Second Ghetto in Metropolitan Miami, 1940–1960," *Journal of Urban History* 21 (March 1995): 395–427.

6. Florida Constitution (1838), art. 6, sec. 1.; Florida Constitution (1861), art. 6, sec. 1; Florida Constitution (1865), art. 6, sec. 1; Theodore B. Wilson, *The Black Codes of the South* (Tuscaloosa: University of Alabama Press, 1965), 143; Jerrell H. Shofner, *Nor Is It Over Yet: Florida in the Era of Reconstruction* (Gainesville: University Press of Florida, 1974); William Cash, *History of the Democratic Party in Florida* (n.p., 1936), 79.

7. Wilson, *The Black Codes of the South,* 142.

8. Edward Williamson, *Florida Politics in the Gilded Age* (Gainesville: University Press of Florida, 1976), 137–50.

9. *Report on the Population of the United States at the Eleventh Census: 1890,* pt. 2 (Washington, 1892), 22, 197, 203, 206, 216; James Knauss, "The Growth of Florida's Election Laws," *Florida Historical Quarterly* 5 (July 1926): 10.

10. J. Morgan Kousser, *Shaping the Southern Politics: Suffrage Restriction and the Establishment of the One-Party South, 1880–1900* (New Haven: Yale University Press, 1974).

11. Florida Constitution (1885), art. 12, sec. 12; Florida Laws, 1895, ch. 4335; Charles Johnson, *Statistical Atlas of Southern Counties* (Chapel Hill: University of North Carolina Press, 1941), 73; NAACP, *Thirty Years of Lynching in the United States* (New York, 1919), 53–56; Arthur F. Raper, *The Tragedy of Lynching in the United States* (Chapel Hill: University of North Carolina Press, 1933), 28.

12. Florida Laws, 1897, ch. 4335.

13. Cash, *History of the Democratic Party,* 171, 178.

14. Florida Laws, 1901, ch. 5014, § 1; Florida Laws, 1905, ch. 5471, § 1.

15. *Tampa Morning Tribune,* May 4, 1909.

16. *Florida Journal of the House of Representatives of the Session of 1915* (Tallahassee, 1915), 2428–31; *Journal of the State Senate of Florida of the Session of 1915* (Tallahassee, 1915), 1685; Kousser, *Shaping the Southern Politics,* 57; Tracy E. Danese, "Disfranchisement: Women's Suffrage and the Failure of Florida's Grandfather Clause," *Florida Historical Quarterly* 74 (fall 1995): 117–31.

17. *St. Petersburg Times,* August 20, 1916; *Tampa Daily Times,* February 24, 1915.

18. *Tallahassee Daily Democrat,* May 5, 1915; NAACP, *Thirty Years of Lynching,* 56.

19. Wayne Flynt, *The Cracker Messiah* (Baton Rouge: Louisiana State University Press, 1971), 93; Stephen Kerber, "Park Trammell of Florida: A Political Biography," Ph.D. diss., University of Florida, 1979, 162.

20. Woodward, *Origins of the New South*, 369; Pam Iorio, "Colorless Primaries: Tampa's White Municipal Party," *Florida Historical Quarterly* 79 (winter 2001): 297–318.

21. Bradley Rice, *Progressive Cities* (Austin: University of Texas Press, 1977), 5; Gary R. Mormino and George E. Pozzetta, *The Immigrant World of Ybor City* (Urbana: University of Illinois Press, 1987), 58–59; V. O. Key, *Southern Politics and the Nation* (New York, 1949), 620.

22. Raymond O. Arsenault, *St. Petersburg and the Florida Dream* (Norfolk, Va., 1988), 123, 134.

23. *St. Petersburg Evening Independent*, June 24, 1913; see also Jon L. Wilson, "Days of Fear: A Lynching in St. Petersburg," *Tampa Bay History* 5 (fall 1983): 11.

24. Jerrell H. Shofner, "Custom, Law, and History: The Enduring Influence of Florida's 'Black Code,'" *Florida Historical Quarterly* 55 (winter 1977): 277–98; *Tampa Morning Tribune*, November 5, 1920; Maxine Jones, David Colburn, and William Rogers, *A Documented History of the Incident Which Occurred at Rosewood, Florida, in January 1923* (Tallahassee, 1993), 9–10; David Chalmers, *Hooded Americanism* (Garden City, N.Y.: Doubleday, 1965), 225–26.

25. Harvard Sitkoff, "Racial Militancy and Interracial Violence in the Second World War," *Journal of American History* 57 (December 1971): 661–81.

26. Gary R. Mormino, "GI Joe Meets Jim Crow: Racial Violence and Reform in World War II Florida," *Florida Historical Quarterly* 73 (July 1994): 23–42. See Papers of the NAACP, pt. 9, sec. B, "Discrimination in the U.S. Armed Forces, Armed Forces Legal Files, reel 9, 700–793; Alan Osur, *Blacks in the Army Air Forces during WWII* (Washington, 1977), 90; "Racial Disturbance Plan," District no. 5, Fourth Service Command, State Defense Council, box 57, R6 191, Florida State Archives, Tallahassee.

27. Carl T. Rowan, *Dream Makers, Dream Breakers: The World of Justice Thurgood Marshall* (Boston: Little, Brown, 1993), 124.

28. Green, *Before His Time*, 16–42.

29. Edward D. Davis, *A Half Century of Struggle for Freedom in Florida* (Orlando, 1981); Gilbert L. Porter and Leedell W. Neyland, *A History of the Florida State Teachers Association* (Washington, 1977); J. Irving E. Scott, *The Education of Black People in Florida* (Philadelphia: Dorrance, 1974), 64–80; Papers of the NAACP, pt. 3, sec. A, "The Campaign for Educational Equality, 1913–1950," 24 reels, see esp. reels 6 and 22.

30. Hugh Price, *The Negro and Southern Politics* (New York: New York University Press, 1957), 24–29; Papers of the NAACP, "The Voting Rights Campaign," pt. 4, reels 6 and 7.

31. *Tampa Morning Tribune*, April 4, 1944.

32. *Tampa Morning Tribune*, April 5, 1944; *Miami Herald*, April 5, 1944.

33. *Tampa Morning Tribune*, April 5, 1944; For reaction to the *Smith* decision, see Rowan, *Dream Makers*, 126–27.

34. *Atlanta Daily World,* May 6, 1944.

35. Rowan, *Dream Makers,* 129.

36. Papers of the NAACP, pt. 4, The Voting Rights Campaign, 1916–1950, reels 7, 4–15; *Tampa Morning Tribune,* July 10, 1945.

37. Green, *Before His Time,* 54; Arcadia City Council minutes, July 20, 1945, DeSoto County Courthouse, Arcadia, copies to be found in University of South Florida Library, Special Collections, Tampa.

38. Charles D. Farris, "The Re-Enfranchisement of Negroes in Florida," *Journal of Negro History* 39 (January 1954): 271.

39. Steven Lawson, *Black Ballots* (New York: Columbia University Press, 1976), 47–49.

40. Price, *The Negro and Southern Politics,* 29; *Miami Herald,* April 13, 1945; Farris, "Re-Enfranchisement," 273–75; *Tampa Morning Tribune,* November 8, 1946, April 12, 1947.

41. *Pittsburgh Courier,* March 3, 1945; "So They Tell Me," Tampa *Sentinel,* January 26 and February 16, 1946. The *Sentinel* is one of the few black papers whose back issues survived. See also Arcadia City Council minutes, August 9, 1947.

42. Papers of the NAACP, Voting Rights Campaign, pt. 4, reel 6, 776–81, 789–800, 849, 923, 928, 941–43; Caroline Emmons Poore, "Striking the First Blow: Harry T. Moore and the Fight for Black Equality in Florida," master's thesis, Florida State University, 1992, 36–61; Green, *Before His Time,* 58–59.

43. Green, *Before His Time,* 59–63.

44. Moore, "Negroes Urged to Organize Voters," Tampa *Sentinel,* November 1, 1947.

45. The data is inconsistent. See Harold W. Stanley, *Voter Mobilization and the Politics of Race* (New York: Praeger, 1987), 97; and Donald R. Matthews and James W. Protho, *Negroes and the New Southern Politics* (New York: Harcourt Brace and World, 1966), 148.

46. Hugh Price, "The Negro and Florida Politics, 1944– 1954," *Journal of Politics* 17 (1954): 200; Lawson, *Black Ballots,* 139.

47. *Tampa Morning Tribune,* November 8, 1949; Green, *Before His Time,* 81–153; Lawson, Colburn, and Paulson, "Groveland"; Warren quoted in Poore, "Striking the First Blow," 7.

48. *Tampa Tribune,* November 3, 1963; Davis, *A Half Century of Struggle,* 145–46.

III

Forward toward an Elusive Goal

6

One Brick at a Time

The Montgomery Bus Boycott, Nonviolent Direct Action, and the Development of a National Civil Rights Movement

RAYMOND ARSENAULT

The Montgomery bus boycott—the protest movement that made Rosa Parks a folk hero, launched the remarkable civil rights career of the Reverend Martin Luther King Jr., and introduced the use of nonviolent direct action in the Gulf South—was one of the major news stories of 1956. By the time it was over, journalists and pundits had probed and dissected its meaning to the point where nearly everyone knew, or thought they knew, what had happened in Montgomery. This collective demystification was so complete that it is now easy to forget that in the early going no one had a clear sense of what was transpiring. In Montgomery itself, confusion about the character and scope of the protest was rampant, especially in the white community where segregationists were not sure what they were up against: the entering wedge of an international conspiracy to destroy the southern way of life, an ad hoc local movement led by misguided black preachers, or something in between. The early press reports were hopelessly confusing on this point. At times, local editors and reporters characterized the boycott as part of a powerful and malevolent national movement. But more commonly they stressed the boycotters' isolation and vulnerability. In early January, for example, a *Montgomery Advertiser* editorial warned that sooner or later the Montgomery Improvement Association (MIA), the local black organization responsible for the boycott, would have to "reckon with two realities: The white man's economic artillery is far superior, better emplaced, and commanded by more experienced gunners. Second, the white man holds all the offices of government machinery. There will be white rule as far as the eye can see."[1]

At the time, the MIA was in no position to ignore the *Advertiser*'s intimidating words. Everyone in the city knew that the boycotters' local resources were extremely limited and that to sustain the protest indefinitely the MIA would require a substantial amount of aid from allies outside of Montgomery. MIA leaders were reluctant to acknowledge this fact publicly, but privately they agonized over the problem of local limitations. If it became necessary to extend the boycott into the spring, they would need a great deal of help. Yet no one could be sure that such help was forthcoming. The resources of the nation's leading civil rights organizations were already stretched to the breaking point, and earlier efforts to funnel aid to black communities in the Gulf South had produced meager results. Perhaps this time it would be different, but there were moments in December and January when the boycotters felt they were waging a solitary struggle, when it seemed that no one in the wider world knew or cared what was happening in the streets of Montgomery.

In the end, of course, the boycott was anything but a solitary struggle. During the third month of the boycott, the Montgomery protest became a subject of national and international interest. Reporters and columnists had a lot to do with this transformation. But they did not do it alone. As the boycott dragged on far longer than anyone had expected and as white supremacist resistance hardened, the beleaguered leaders of the MIA reached out to regional and national civil rights organizations for help. The responses to the MIA's call for help varied from organization to organization, and the assistance offered did not always meet the MIA's actual needs. But the overall response exceeded nearly everyone's expectations.

Following the mass indictment of boycott leaders in late February, and in some cases even earlier, national civil rights leaders began to realize that more than local bus desegregation was at stake in Montgomery. By the time the boycott entered its fourth month, the MIA was drawing upon the resources of scores of organizations, including the National Association for the Advancement of Colored People, the Fellowship of Reconciliation, the War Resisters League, the Congress of Racial Equality, the Brotherhood of Sleeping Car Porters, the National Urban League, and the Southern Conference Education Fund. This external support, which continued for the remainder of the year, became a critical factor in the boycotters' success and magnified the boycott's impact on black and white America. By donating funds, dispensing advice, or simply passing resolutions of support, these organizations ensured and broadened vicarious participation in the Montgomery movement. Blacks and whites who lived far from Montgomery, some of whom had no direct experience with the indignities of Jim Crow, were drawn into a social protest that directly challenged the myth of American equality.

Equally important, as far as the future of the civil rights movement was concerned, the organizations themselves underwent important changes once they became involved with the boycott. Confronting an unexpected mass movement in the Gulf South forced civil rights advocates to reconsider their assumptions about the nature of the struggle for racial equality. To many observers, the traditional reliance on northern-directed legal challenges suddenly seemed unnecessarily restrictive. This was especially true among impatient social activists like A. Philip Randolph and Bayard Rustin who came to regard the Montgomery protest as proof that southern blacks could be enlisted in their own liberation. In effect, Montgomery became a testing ground for theories of racial adjustment and social change. What civil rights advocates observed there—the economic and moral vulnerability of segregation, the inability of even moderate white segregationists to compromise, the resolute courage of southern blacks, the emotional power of African American religious belief, and the viability of nonviolent direct action—ultimately reshaped the organizational and philosophical contours of the entire American freedom struggle.

This considerable legacy tends to obscure the fact that these broad patterns of interaction and influence caught almost everyone by surprise. As already noted, during the first two months of the Montgomery protest there was no reason to believe that the boycotters could depend on outside help. Nor was there any hint that the boycott would have a significant impact on the national civil rights community. The local-national symbiosis that developed was unprecedented, and initially both sides had limited expectations of the other. For a time they weren't even sure that they shared common goals. Searching for common ground is a necessity for any social movement trying to combine local and national perspectives, but in this case the process was complicated by a lack of experience and by the fragmented nature of the emerging civil rights movement. As yet, there was no movement culture—nothing to provide a common language or a common perspective. That kind of solidarity would come later, in the wake of Montgomery, Greensboro, and a dozen other mass protests. In the early years of the struggle, efforts at cooperation often foundered in a sea of personal and organizational rivalries, real and imagined conflicts of interest, arcane ideological disagreements, and deeply held regional stereotypes. In this context, as boycott leaders would ultimately discover, establishing a mutually beneficial link between a local movement and the rest of the civil rights community was no mean feat.[2]

Of the many factors inhibiting the development of such a relationship, the sharp cultural divide between North and South was probably the most difficult to overcome. The conspiratorial theories of white segregationists notwithstanding, the MIA was unmistakably a product of the Deep South. By contrast, the national civil rights movement, insofar as it existed in 1955, was essentially a product of the North. Representing a coalition dominated by middle-class northern blacks and liberal and radical northern whites, the leadership of the national movement maintained only a tenuous connection to the South. Most white civil rights activists lived and worked in the North, and many of the nation's most prominent black leaders—including Roy Wilkins and Adam Clayton Powell Jr.—were northern-born. Some, like A. Philip Randolph and Lester Granger, were southern transplants, and others, most notably Thurgood Marshall and Ralph Bunche, were from the border states. But whatever their background, the leaders of the movement spent most of their time in northern communities, primarily in the Northeast. Most black leaders had family connections south of the Mason-Dixon line, and during the boycott some made a good-faith effort to rediscover their southern roots. But ties of blood were often a poor substitute for direct experience.[3]

In the early weeks of the boycott, then, national civil rights leaders had little to go on but secondhand impressions and stereotypic images. Despite the promising reports coming out of Montgomery, preconceived notions died hard, particularly the assumption that southern blacks were too timid to challenge the Jim Crow system. By the same token, most black Montgomerians had little or no experience with life outside the South. In many cases, they did not know what to expect from people who lived beyond the borders of de jure segregation, other than condescension and a modulated dialect. As the boycott progressed, contact with the outside world lowered the potential for interregional mistrust and misunderstanding. Indeed, the deep emotional bond between the boycotters and their allies became one of the hallmarks of the Montgomery movement, leading to the creation of the Southern Christian Leadership Conference in 1957. Nevertheless, it is important to remember that the creation of this historic partnership was neither simple nor preordained. Like Montgomery's renowned First Baptist Church (Colored), a sprawling structure built in the early twentieth century by parishioners who faithfully an-

swered their preacher's call to bring "a brick every Sunday," the partnership that became a movement had to be assembled one brick at a time.[4]

* * *

Since the relationship between the bus boycott and the national civil
rights community varied from organization to organization, a full understanding of this relationship would require a careful and pointed examination of each element of the Montgomery coalition. This essay—which
focuses on the Congress of Racial Equality (CORE) and the Fellowship of
Reconciliation (FOR) and the activities of two behind-the-scenes activists, Bayard Rustin and Glenn Smiley—represents a modest first step in
the process of reevaluating the bus boycott's impact on the development
of the modern civil rights movement.

To the nonviolent activists of CORE, the bus boycotters' willingness to
take the southern civil rights struggle into the streets of Montgomery was
both surprising and exhilarating. A mass movement that enlisted the talents and aspirations of ordinary people was just what CORE had been
calling for since its founding in 1942. Long before the emergence of King
and the MIA, CORE had championed nonviolent direct action as a means
of resolving America's racial dilemma. At the time of the boycott, CORE
was the only national organization with broad experience in the area of
transit desegregation, having sponsored the Journey of Reconciliation,
the nation's first freedom ride, in 1947. For a variety of reasons, however,
CORE was destined to play an inconsequential role in Montgomery. Despite its pioneering contributions to the civil rights movement, CORE
was a fragile organization in 1955. Plagued by factionalism, antiradical
repression, and an uncertain relationship with its parent organization, the
Fellowship of Reconciliation, CORE had suffered several years of steady
decline. Many of the organization's early stalwarts, including Bayard
Rustin and James Farmer, had redirected their energies elsewhere, and
outside of the celebrated Baltimore and St. Louis chapters there was little
activity or enthusiasm. To make matters worse, the Fellowship of Reconciliation had withdrawn most of its financial support in 1953, forcing the
resignation of executive director George Houser, who was technically an
FOR staff member on loan to CORE.[5]

Following Houser's departure in early 1954, the burden of leadership
fell upon the shoulders of James Peck, the editor of the organization's
newsletter, *CORE-lator*, and Billie Ames, a talented and energetic St.

Louis woman who served as CORE's national group coordinator. In the summer of 1954, Ames tried to revive CORE's flagging spirit by proposing a "Ride for Freedom," a second Journey of Reconciliation that would recapture the momentum of the organization's glory days. Ames planned to challenge segregated railway coaches and terminals as far south as Birmingham, but the project collapsed when the NAACP, which had provided financial and legal support for the original 1947 freedom ride, refused to cooperate. Arguing that an impending Interstate Commerce Commission ruling made the "Ride for Freedom" unnecessary, NAACP leaders advised CORE to devote its attention "to some other purpose." This disappointment, combined with continuing factionalism and dissension, brought CORE to the verge of dissolution. After personal problems forced Billie Ames to leave CORE in March 1955, some wondered if the organization would last the year. In desperation, the delegates to the 1955 national convention voted to hire a national field organizer for the expressed purpose of extending CORE's influence into the South. Encouraged by the formation of a small student chapter in Nashville earlier in the year, many CORE activists regarded the South as the organization's last best hope. Even though the potential for successful nonviolent direct action in the region was unproven, the organization had few options at this point.[6]

In early December 1955, within days of Rosa Parks's arrest, LeRoy Carter became CORE's first national field organizer. A former NAACP field secretary with twenty years of experience in the civil rights struggle, Carter seemed well suited to the task of spreading the CORE philosophy to the South. Soft-spoken and deliberate, yet full of determination, he could have been an important resource for the MIA during the early weeks of the boycott—if the leadership of CORE had seen fit to send him to Montgomery. Unfortunately, CORE was slow to react to the unexpected events that coincided with its southward thrust. Although Carter and other CORE leaders monitored the boycott's progress from the beginning, they did not rush to embrace the Montgomery movement. Despite its obvious affinity with what was happening in Montgomery, CORE made no attempt to associate itself publicly with the MIA during the first three months of the boycott. Convinced that the Montgomery protest would soon collapse, CORE activists worried that the boycotters' untutored efforts would do more harm than good by seemingly demonstrating the futility of direct action. Accordingly, when James Robinson, CORE's finance secretary, composed a fund-raising letter in early February highlighting the potential for direct action in the South, he made no mention of the controversial bus boycott in Montgomery.[7]

Predictably, such disdain all but disappeared in late February when the mass arrest of boycott leaders, including King and several dozen other black ministers, turned the Montgomery protest into front-page news and a national cause célèbre. Realizing that they had misjudged the situation, embarrassed CORE leaders scurried to make up for lost time. On February 22, a group of local CORE enthusiasts organized a Montgomery chapter, and in late March the national council of CORE adopted a resolution commending the boycotters "for their vision, courage, and steadfastness of purpose in sustaining a significant struggle against a great evil, and at the same time pioneering in the mass use in this country of a technique and spirit which holds unlimited promise for use elsewhere against oppression." The council also voted to send LeRoy Carter to Montgomery. Carter subsequently spent several days conferring with King and other boycott leaders, but he arrived too late to have any measurable influence on the character of the Montgomery movement. Although MIA leaders welcomed CORE's support, they were understandably wary of an organization that presumed to teach them the "rules" of nonviolent protest. Even King, who knew something about CORE's long-standing commitment to nonviolent direct action, had mixed feelings about what appeared to be a belated and opportunistic attempt to capitalize on the boycotters' struggle. To his surprise, when the spring 1956 issue of *CORE-lator* ran a picture of MIA officials standing on the steps of the Holt Street Baptist, it identified them as the "leaders of the CORE-type protest in Montgomery." In the accompanying story, editor Jim Peck proclaimed that "the CORE technique of non-violence has been spotlighted to the entire world through the effective protest action which the Montgomery Improvement Association has been conducting since December 5." And in an adjoining column, Peck proudly quoted a *New York Post* article that reminded the world that CORE had employed Gandhian techniques "long before Montgomery joined the passive resistance movement."[8]

For Peck, as for most CORE veterans, the "miracle in Montgomery" was a bittersweet development. Having suffered through the lean years of the early 1950s, when nonviolent resistance was routinely dismissed as an irrelevant pipe dream, they could not help viewing the boycott with a mixture of pride and jealousy. "I had labored a decade and a half in the vineyards of nonviolence," James Farmer explained in his 1985 memoir. "Now, out of nowhere, someone comes and harvests the grapes and drinks the wine." Farmer and his colleagues eventually overcame such feelings, acknowledging that the MIA's success gave nonviolent resistance a new legitimacy and probably saved CORE from extinction. As he put it, "No longer did we have to explain nonviolence to people. Thanks to Martin Luther King, it was a household word." But this graciousness was the product of years of reflection and common struggle. In the uncertain atmosphere of the mid-1950s, charity did not come so easily, even among men and women who had dedicated their lives to social justice.[9]

*　　*　　*

CORE's formal involvement in the boycott never amounted to much, but this did not prevent the boycotters from drawing upon the organization's philosophical traditions and tactical experiences. In the beginning, the MIA's connection with earlier manifestations of direct action and nonviolent activism was tenuous and largely unconscious. But this spirit of innocence and intellectual isolation did not last. By the end of February, the leaders of the boycott had learned a great deal about their historical antecedents and the wider world of radical politics. While some of this education came from the media and other public sources, the MIA also had the benefit of private tutelage. During the course of the boycott, a number of veteran activists journeyed to Montgomery to offer support and advice. Although most stayed only a few days and were soon forgotten, several had a lasting impact on the local movement.

The MIA's most influential tutor was clearly Bayard Rustin, the peripatetic CORE veteran who was serving as executive secretary of the War Resisters' League at the time of the boycott. A free-wheeling intellectual who put little stock in organizational discipline or orthodoxy—Nat Hentoff once called him "the Socrates of the civil rights movement"—Rustin was perhaps the first civil rights leader to grasp the significance of what was happening in Montgomery. Impulsive and irrepressible, he thrust himself into the center of the struggle, eventually emerging as one of the MIA's major intellectual resources. Acting as a self-appointed Gandhian sage, he sought to sharpen the boycotters' historical vision and to broaden their philosophical horizons. He wanted them to feel the pride and responsibility of being part of a worldwide movement for human rights, and in a spirit of well-intended condescension he became convinced that he was the one person who could show them how to make the most of an extraordinary opportunity. Together, he and the boycotters would point the way to the promised land.

Rustin had good reason to feel that he had a special calling. Born in 1912, in West Chester, Pennsylvania, to an unwed mother (his absent father was Archie Hopkins, a West Indian immigrant) he was raised by an extended family of grandparents (who adopted him), aunts, and uncles who collectively eked out a living by cooking and catering for the local Quaker gentry. His grandmother and adoptive mother, Julia Rustin, was a member of the local Quaker meeting before joining her husband's African Methodist Episcopal (AME) church following their marriage in 1891. And she remained a Quaker "at heart," naming her grandson for Bayard Taylor, a celebrated mid-nineteenth-century Quaker leader. A woman of substance and deep moral conviction, Julia was the most important influence in young Bayard's upbringing and the primary source of the pacifist doctrines that would anchor his lifelong commitment to nonviolence. Indulged as the favorite child of the Rustin clan, he gained a reputation as a brilliant student and gifted singer and musician, first as one of a handful of black students at West Chester High School, where he excelled as a track and football star, and later at all-black Wilberforce University, where he studied history and toured as the lead soloist of the Wilberforce Quartet. Expelled from Wilberforce in December 1933 following a homosexual incident (Rustin reportedly fell in love with the son of the university president), he enrolled at Cheyney State Teachers College in early 1934. At Cheyney, he continued to distinguish himself as a singer, but in the winter of 1934 a second scandalous "incident" forced him to leave college.

Cast adrift and facing the vagaries of the Great Depression, Rustin soon accepted a position as a "peace volunteer" with the Emergency Peace Campaign (EPC) of the pacifist American Friends Service Committee (AFSC). Already primed for a career in social action by his family and religious background, he received new inspiration from Muriel Lester, a noted British pacifist and Gandhi protégé, who addressed the EPC volunteers during a training session. With Lester's encouragement, he threw himself into the peace campaign with the uncommon zeal that would later become his trademark. Along with three other volunteers—including Carl Rachlin, who would later serve as a CORE and Freedom Rider attorney—he spent the summer of 1937 in the upstate New York town of Auburn honing his skills as a lecturer and organizer. At the end of the summer, he returned to West Chester, but the lack of radical political ferment and social action in his hometown and in nearby Philadelphia soon drove him northward to Harlem, where he embarked on a remarkable odyssey of survival and discovery that propelled him through a labyrinth of radical politics and bohemian culture. Along the way, he became a professional singer, a dedicated Communist, and a practicing homosexual. During the late 1930s, he sang backup for Josh White and Huddie "Leadbelly" Ledbetter, worked as a recruiter for the Young Communist League, preached revolution and brotherhood on countless street corners, and even squeezed in a few classes at City College, all the while gaining a reputation as one of Harlem's most colorful characters.

In early 1941, the Young Communist League asked Rustin to organize a campaign against segregation in the American armed forces, but later in the year, following the unexpected German attack on the Soviet Union, League leaders ordered him to cancel the campaign in the interests of Allied military solidarity. With this apparent shift away from racial and social justice agitation, Rustin became deeply disillusioned with the Communist Party. "You can all go to hell," he told his New York comrades. "I see that the Communist movement is only interested in what happens in Russia. You don't give a damn about Negroes." In June 1941, he left the Communist fold for good and transferred his allegiance to A. Philip Randolph, the legendary black socialist and labor leader who was then planning a mass march on Washington to protest the Roosevelt administration's refusal to guarantee equal employment opportunities for black and white defense workers. Randolph appointed Rustin youth organizer for the march, but the two men soon had a serious falling-out. After Franklin Roosevelt responded to Randolph's threatened march with an executive order creating a Fair Employment Practices Committee (FEPC), Randolph agreed to call off the march. But many of his young supporters, including Rustin, thought the protest march should continue as planned. Later in the war Rustin and Randolph resumed their friendship and collaboration, but their temporary break in 1941 prompted the young activist to look elsewhere for a political and spiritual home. Thus, in the fall of 1941, he accepted a staff position with A. J. Muste's Fellowship of Reconciliation.

As FOR youth secretary, Rustin returned to the pacifist track that he had followed as an EPC volunteer, immersing himself in the writings and teachings of Gandhi and pledging his loyalty to nonviolence, not just as a strategy for change but as a way of life. Muste, the radical pacifist who presided over FOR, encouraged and nurtured Rustin's determination to apply Gandhian precepts to the African American struggle for racial equality, and in the spring of 1942 the two men joined forces with other FOR activists to help found the Committee (later "Congress") of Racial

Equality (CORE). "Certainly the Negro possesses qualities essential for nonviolent direct action," Rustin wrote prophetically in October 1942. "He has long since learned to endure suffering. He can admit his own share of guilt and has to be pushed hard to become bitter. . . . He is creative and has learned to adjust himself to conditions easily. But above all he possesses a rich religious heritage and today finds the church the center of his life."[10]

As a CORE stalwart, Rustin participated in a number of nonviolent protests, including an impromptu refusal to move to the back of a bus during a trip from Louisville to Nashville in the summer of 1942. This particular episode earned him a roadside beating at the hands of the Nashville police, but, fortunately, the timely intervention of several sympathetic white bystanders saved him from permanent injury, reinforcing his suspicion that even the white South could be redeemed through nonviolent struggle.

Soon after his narrow escape in Nashville, Rustin became a friend and devoted follower of Krishnalal Shridharani, a leading Gandhian scholar and the author of *War without Violence*. This discipleship deepened his commitment to nonviolent resistance and noncooperation with evil, and in 1943 he rejected the traditional Quaker compromise of alternative service in an army hospital. Convicted of draft evasion, he spent the next twenty-eight months in federal prison. For nearly two years he was imprisoned at the Ashland, Ohio, penitentiary, where he waged spirited but futile campaigns against everything from the censorship of reading materials to racial segregation. In August 1945, a final effort to desegregate the prison dining hall led to solitary confinement, but soon thereafter he and several other pacifist malcontents were transferred to a federal facility in Lewisburg, Pennsylvania.

Following his release from Lewisburg in June 1946, Rustin returned to New York to accept an appointment as secretary of FOR's Race and Industrial Department, a position that he promptly turned into a roving ambassadorship of Gandhian nonviolence. Though physically weak and emaciated, he took to the road, preaching the gospel of nonviolent direct action to anyone who would listen. As FOR's race relations secretary, he organized a Free India Committee, which picketed the British embassy in Washington, directed Randolph's Committee against Discrimination in the Armed Forces, and masterminded CORE's 1947 Journey of Reconciliation, an audacious two-week test of interstate transit facilities in Virginia, North Carolina, and Tennessee. For Rustin and several of his fellow travelers, the Journey ended in arrest and a series of show trials, but this experience only served to reinforce his belief in Gandhian activism. In 1948, following Gandhi's assassination, he spent six months in India as a guest of the slain leader's Congress Party, and on the way home he stopped off in Africa, where he spent several weeks consulting with Kwame Nkrumah and other anticolonialist leaders. After his return, there was a new round of arrests and jailings—including a harrowing twenty-two days in a North Carolina prison camp—but he never once lost his pacifist composure.[11]

Though virtually unknown to the general public, by 1950 Rustin had become a revered figure in the international subculture of Gandhian intellectuals. No one who met him could fail to be impressed by the quality of his mind and the depth of his commitment to nonviolence, not to mention his boundless energy. However, those who knew him well were painfully aware of another side of his life. In an age when homosexuality was associated with social and political subversion, his personal life was a source of concern and embarrassment for the FOR, a fragile organization that could ill afford a major public scandal. After several encounters with the vice squad and a stern reprimand from the normally placid Muste, Rustin promised to behave. But in June 1953, an arrest for lewd and lascivious behavior in Pasadena, California, led to a thirty-day jail term and resignation from the FOR staff. By the time he returned to New York to pick up the pieces of his life, even some of his closest friends had concluded that the nonviolent movement might be better off without him. Although he soon found a temporary haven at the War Resisters League, which offered him a position as executive secretary, Rustin's career as an influential activist appeared to be over. He, of course, felt otherwise. Despite his personal problems and the increasing intolerance engendered by McCarthyism and the cold war, he remained convinced that he was destined to play an important role in the continuing struggle for human rights. All he needed was a chance to redeem himself, an opportunity to use his hard-earned wisdom to demonstrate the liberating power of nonviolence. Amazingly, he would soon find what he was looking for—not in New York or Chicago or any of the other cities that had witnessed the courage of FOR and CORE activists—but rather in the faraway streets of Montgomery.[12]

*　　*　　*

Soon after the boycott began, the radical white southern novelist Lillian Smith, who had once served on the national board of FOR, wired Rustin and urged him to offer his assistance to King and the MIA. If someone with experience in Gandhian tactics could bring his knowledge to bear on the situation, she suggested, the boycotters might have a real chance to sustain their movement. Rustin had never been to Alabama, but as he pondered Smith's suggestion and mulled over the early news reports on the boycott, a bold plan began to take shape. If he could find a sponsor, he would "fly to Montgomery with the idea of getting the bus boycott temporarily called off." Then, with the help of FOR, he would organize "a workshop or school for non-violence with a goal of 100 young Negro men who will then promote it not only in Montgomery but elsewhere in the South." In early January, he shared his thoughts with several friends at FOR but found little enthusiasm for his plan. Charles Lawrence, FOR's national chairman, not only questioned the wisdom of suspending an ongoing protest but also worried "that it would be easy for the police to frame him [Rustin] with his record in L.A. and New York, and set back the whole cause there." FOR executive director John Swomley shared Lawrence's concern, as did the socialist leader Norman Thomas, who thought Rustin was "entirely too vulnerable on his record." "This young King is doing well. Bayard is considered a homosexual, a Communist and a draft dodger. Why do you put such a burden on King?" Thomas asked.[13]

Eventually Rustin found a more sympathetic audience in A. Philip Randolph and James Farmer, but even they had strong misgivings about dispatching a gay ex-Communist to a conservative Deep South city. Though he admired Rustin's bravado, Randolph agreed to fund the trip only after it became clear that his old friend was prepared to hitchhike to Montgomery if necessary. After a telephone call to King confirmed that the MIA would welcome Rustin's visit, only the details needed to be worked out. Rustin wanted Bob Gilmore of the American Friends Service Committee to accompany him and to act as a liaison with the white community in Montgomery. But Randolph and Farmer, fearing that an interracial team would be too conspicuous, turned instead to Bill Worthy, a thirty-four-year-old black reporter for the *Baltimore Afro-American*. Worthy was a seasoned activist who had participated in a number of FOR and CORE campaigns, including the 1947 Journey of Reconciliation. Nevertheless, the decision to send him to Montgomery as Rustin's unofficial chaperon was one that Randolph and Farmer would later regret. In 1954 Worthy had raised the hackles of the State Department with a series of sympathetic stories on the Soviet Union, and his presence in Montgomery only served to exacerbate the fear that Communists had infiltrated the MIA.[14]

As fate would have it, Rustin and Worthy arrived in Montgomery on Tuesday, February 21, the day of the mass indictments. The MIA office was in chaos. Rustin asked to speak to King but was told that the MIA president was in Nashville, preaching at Fisk University. At this point, no one in the MIA, other than King, had the faintest idea who Rustin was. But he soon talked his way into the office of Ralph Abernathy, who after a brief conversation warned his visitor that Montgomery was a dangerous place for an unarmed black activist. Undaunted, Rustin found his way to E. D. Nixon, who became an instant ally after Rustin produced a letter of introduction from Randolph. For more than an hour, Nixon briefed Rustin on the boycotters' situation, which was obviously growing more perilous by the day. "They can bomb us out and they can kill us," he vowed, "but we are not going to give in." For a time Rustin simply listened, but when Nixon confessed that he was not sure how the boycotters should respond to the mass indictments, the veteran activist promptly suggested the Gandhian option of voluntarily filling the jails. As Rustin laid out the rationale for nonviolent martyrdom, Nixon became intrigued, and the next morning he became the first boycott leader to turn himself in. "Are you looking for me?" he asked a stunned sheriff's deputy. "Well, here I am." Once the news of Nixon's arrest got out, there was a virtual stampede at the county courthouse, as scores of black leaders joined in the ritual of self-sacrifice. Through it all Rustin was on the scene, dispensing advice and encouragement and basking in the knowledge that, even though he had been in Montgomery for less than a day, he had already made a difference. Even Worthy, who had seen his friend in action many times before, was impressed, though he worried that this early triumph would feed Rustin's reckless spirit and ultimately lead to trouble.[15]

Such trouble was not long in coming. On Wednesday evening, after attending a rousing prayer meeting at Dexter Avenue Baptist Church, Rustin decided to pay a visit to Jeanette Reece, who a week earlier had been frightened into dropping her legal challenge to segregated buses. To Rustin's surprise, Reece's home was under police surveillance, and as he approached the front door he was immediately accosted by gun-waving white policemen who demanded to know who he was. Rustin assured them that he just wanted to talk to Reece and that he meant her no harm. But the officers continued to press him for some identification. On the verge of being arrested, he blurted out: "I am Bayard Rustin; I am here as a journalist working for *Le Figaro* and the *Manchester Guardian.*" This seemed to satisfy the policemen, who granted him a brief interview with Reece. But this impromptu cover story would later come back to haunt him.

Having narrowly escaped arrest, a somewhat chastened Rustin finally met Dr. King on Thursday morning, following the boycott leader's booking at the county courthouse. Surrounded by dozens of reporters and a throng of cheering supporters, King had little time to greet visitors. But at Nixon's urging, he invited Rustin to a late morning strategy session of the MIA executive committee. At the session, Rustin was impressed by King's intelligent, forthright leadership, and he was thrilled when the committee voted to turn the MIA's traditional mass meetings into prayer meetings. After King and his colleagues agreed that all future meetings would center around five prayers, including "A prayer for those who oppose us," he knew that he had underestimated his southern hosts. In their own untutored way, he now realized, the boycotters had already begun to master the art of moral warfare. Although he still had doubts about the depth of the MIA's commitment to nonviolence, his original plan for a temporary suspension of the boycott no longer seemed realistic. As he told King later that afternoon, in all his travels, even in India and Africa, he had never witnessed anything comparable to the Montgomery movement. The boycotters' accomplishments were already remarkable. With a little help from the outside—with the proper publicity, with a disciplined and carefully constructed long-range strategy, and with enough funds to hold out against the die-hard segregationists—the Montgomery story could become a beacon for nonviolent activists everywhere. To this end, he and his friends at FOR were ready to help in any way they could. Though still a bit puzzled by this strange visitor from New York, King thanked Rustin for his gracious offer and invited him to the MIA's Thursday evening prayer meeting at the First Baptist Church.

What Rustin saw that evening confirmed his growing optimism. The meeting at First Baptist was the first mass gathering since the arrests, and the spirit that poured out of the overflow crowd was like nothing Rustin had ever seen. When the ninety indicted leaders gathered around the pulpit to open the meeting, the sanctuary exploded with emotion. As Rustin later described the scene:

Overnight these leaders had become symbols of courage. Women held their babies to touch them. The people stood in ovation. Television cameras ground away, as King was finally able to open the meeting. He began: "We are not struggling merely for the right of Negroes but for all the people of Montgomery, black and white. We are determined to make America a better place for all people. Ours is a non-violent protest. We pray God that no man shall use arms."

Near the close of the meeting, one of the speakers seized the moment to declare that Friday would be a "Double-P Day," a time for prayer and pilgrimage. The car pools would be suspended, private cars would be left at home, and everyone would walk. This gesture was almost too much for Rustin, who after years of lonely struggle could hardly believe what he was witnessing. Later that evening, he called John Swomley in New York and breathlessly related what he had seen. The Montgomery movement had unlimited potential, he reported, but the boycotters were in desperate need of assistance—not only money for legal fees but also veteran activists who could teach them the finer points of nonviolence. In the short run, he would do what he could, but he urged Swomley to alert Muste and Randolph that a full mobilization of resources was in order.

True to his word, Rustin cut a wide swath through the MIA in the days that followed. On Friday and Saturday, he discussed strategy with the executive committee, sat in on a meeting of the car pool committee, survived an awkward interview with Robert Hughes, the executive director of the Alabama Council on Human Relations, and even helped a group of volunteers design a new logo for the MIA. But the climax of his whirlwind tour came when he spent most of Sunday with King. The day began with morning services at Dexter, where the young minister preached a moving sermon on the philosophy of nonviolence. "We are concerned not merely to win justice in the buses," King explained, "but rather to behave in a new and different way—to be non-violent so that we may remove injustice itself, both from society and from ourselves." Later, during a private dinner at the parsonage, King briefed Rustin on the boycott. Rustin listened attentively, but as the evening progressed he began to regale his hosts with tales of Harlem and the northern underground. Coretta, who suddenly recalled that she had heard Rustin speak at Antioch in the early 1950s, was utterly charmed, and her husband was captivated by his guest's sweeping vision of social justice. For several hours Rustin and the Kings discussed religion, pacifism, nonviolent resistance, and other moral imperatives, and by the end of the evening a deep philosophical and personal bond had been sealed. Despite periodic disagreements over strategy, they would remain close friends until King's assassination in 1968.[16]

Not everyone in the MIA was so enamored with the strange visitor from New York. Within hours of Rustin's arrival, there were complaints about "outside agitators" and rumors that subversives were trying to take over the Montgomery movement. Even those who dismissed these fears as groundless worried about the MIA's credibility and public image. Despite the recent eclipse of Senator Joseph McCarthy, fear of Communist infiltration was still rife in the United States, even among black Americans. No popular movement could afford the taint of communism, especially in a state where the Scottsboro case was a relatively recent memory. In Deep South communities like Montgomery, smooth-talking outsiders like Rustin were always a little suspect, but any chance he had of gaining broad acceptance ended when he posed as a European correspondent. When word got around that the editors of *Le Figaro* and the *Manchester Guardian* had never heard of him, Rustin's situation in Montgomery became precarious. Several of the national reporters covering the mass indictment story knew the true identity and background of both Rustin and Bill Worthy, and the inevitable murmurings soon alerted the local press and police. Rustin was having the time of his life and was determined to hang on as long as he could. But by the end of his first week in town, there were enough cold stares and wary handshakes to convince him that his days in Montgomery were numbered. Reluctantly, he informed Swomley and the FOR staff that sooner or later he would need a replacement. Swomley, who had opposed Rustin's venture from the outset, needed no prodding to send a replacement. Indeed, Glenn Smiley, FOR's national field secretary, was already on his way to Montgomery.[17]

Smiley and Rustin were old friends and compatriots, but they were strikingly different in style and temperament. Though he was born the same year as Rustin and ultimately shared his Quaker colleague's pacifist faith, Smiley came from a radically different world. A soft-spoken Texan with a wry smile, he grew up in the cattle country west of Fort Worth, attended an all-white Methodist college in Abilene, and entered the ministry in his early twenties. A strong belief in pacifism and a commitment to the social gospel led him to the FOR in 1942, and for the next twelve years he worked as FOR's southwestern field secretary, operating mostly in southern California and Arizona. Like Rustin, he served a federal prison term for draft evasion during World War II, emerging from the ordeal with a renewed faith in nonviolent resistance. After the war, he worked with pacifists, labor organizers, and civil libertarians all across the Southwest, lectured for FOR in Mexico and Europe, and barely survived the ravages of cold war inquisition. Named FOR's national field secretary in 1954, he redirected his attention to the East Coast. His first foray into the Deep South came in November 1955, when he went to Orangeburg, South Carolina, to aid a black boycott of local white businesses. Unfortunately, his experience in Orangeburg, where a counterboycott by the White Citizens' Council threatened blacks with unemployment and starvation, was a sobering introduction to the repressive atmosphere of the post-*Brown* South and a preview of what he would encounter in Montgomery.[18]

By the time Smiley arrived in Montgomery, on February 27, Rustin's situation had become untenable. The FBI, the local police, and several suspicious reporters were following his every move, and there were rumors that he would soon be arrested for inciting to riot. *Le Figaro* had offered a reward to anyone who could identify the impostor posing as its correspondent, and there was increasing pressure from Emory Jackson, an editor of the black *Birmingham World*, who knew about Rustin's—and Worthy's—background. Appalled by King's apparent lack of concern about left-wing infiltration, Jackson threatened to publish an exposé if MIA leaders failed to expel the northern intruders. All of this alarmed E. D. Nixon, who phoned Randolph for an explanation. He assured Nixon that Rustin was a trusted associate and an asset to the movement, but he was deeply troubled by Nixon's call. The following morning a hastily assembled group of twenty civil rights leaders met in Randolph's office to decide what to do about Rustin's maverick crusade. Thomas, Swomley, Farmer, and nearly everyone else present concluded that Rustin had outlived his usefulness in Montgomery. The crisis-born meeting also forced the leaders to reevaluate their potential role in the Montgomery protest. As Swomley wrote to Smiley on February 29, "It was the conviction yesterday that we should not try from the North to train or otherwise run the non-violent campaign in Montgomery, as Bayard had hoped to do, but rather to expect them to indicate ways in which we could be of help. Only Bayard's roommate argued for his staying in the South. Phil Randolph indicated that the Montgomery leaders had managed thus far more successfully than any 'of our so-called non-violence experts' a mass resistance campaign and we should learn from them rather than assume we knew it all."

Smiley had strict instructions to avoid public association—or even private contact—with Rustin while he was in Montgomery; no one—not even the leadership of the MIA—was to know that they were colleagues. But on Wednesday morning Smiley ran into Rustin and Worthy at MIA headquarters. This chance encounter gave Rustin the opportunity to brief Smiley on his activities. To Smiley's relief, King was the only MIA leader to witness the meeting. Nevertheless, when FOR officials learned of the encounter later in the day, the pressure to get Rustin and Worthy out of Montgomery took on a new urgency. Randolph immediately phoned Rustin and begged him to leave. At first Rustin pleaded for a few more days in Montgomery, but in the end, realizing that he had pushed his patron to the limit and confident that Smiley would carry on in his absence, he relented. After a round of bittersweet good-byes, he and Worthy set out for Birmingham, where the trial of Autherine Lucy, a young black woman seeking admission to the University of Alabama, was about to begin. Rustin's role in the boycott was far from over, as he continued to advise King and the MIA, both by phone and in periodic meetings in Birmingham. But it would be several weeks before he returned to Montgomery. With King's blessing, he spent most of the spring and summer of 1956 in New York publicizing the boycott and trying to raise funds for the MIA.[19]

*　　*　　*

Following Rustin's departure, Smiley worked tirelessly to expand FOR's role in the boycott. During the remainder of the boycott, he shuttled in and out of Montgomery, sometimes staying for weeks at a time. At first, some boycott leaders were understandably suspicious of the inquisitive white stranger with the Texas twang, but it did not take him long to endear himself to the MIA staff. He grew especially close to King and Abernathy, with whom he engaged in lengthy discussions of movement strategy and moral philosophy. Smiley's wry humor and gentle prodding on behalf of nonviolence eventually disarmed even his toughest critics.[20]

Smiley, in turn, came to respect and admire his MIA hosts, though he often fretted about their ideological naïveté. Soon after his arrival in Montgomery, he informed the FOR office in New York that King was "a grand guy" who "had Gandhi in mind when this thing started." But he warned his superiors that King and the boycotters had a lot to learn about the moral strictures of nonviolence: "[King] is aware of the dangers to him inwardly, wants to do it right, but is too young and some of his close help is violent. King accepts, as an example, a body guard, and asks for permits for them to carry guns. This was denied by the police, but nevertheless, the place is an arsenal. King sees the inconsistency, but not enough. He believes and yet he doesn't believe. The whole movement is armed in a sense, and this is what I must convince him to see as the greatest evil. At first King was merely asked to be the spokesman of the movement, but as sometimes happens, he has really become the real leader and symbol of growing magnitude. If he can *really* be won to a faith in non-violence there is no end to what he can do." Despite this caveat, Smiley communicated an almost breathless enthusiasm for the boycott, which, thanks to his and Rustin's influence, was now officially known as a "non-violent protest" among MIA leaders. "The story is not a clear one, not nearly as clear as we would like," he admitted, "but potentially it is the most exciting thing I have ever touched."[21]

The more Smiley saw of King and the boycotters, the more he was impressed, even awed, by their raw courage and spiritual strength. On March 2, he wrote Swomley, "Strange—Whites are scared stiff and Negroes are calm as cucumbers. It is an experience I shall never forget. The mass meeting last night was like another world. 2500 people, laughing, crying, moaning, shouting, singing. . . . Not once was there an expression of hatred towards whites, and the ovation I received when I talked of Gandhi, his campaign, and then of the cross, was tremendous. They want to do the will of God, and they are sure this is the will of God."

Even so, he continued to insist that the boycott could not succeed without increased support and counsel from movement leaders in the North. The brief involvement of FOR had already made a difference; in the short span of ten days he and Rustin had helped to give the Montgomery protest a new image and a renewed sense of purpose. Now that he was on the scene, he was convinced that Randolph, who had been arguing for several weeks that the boycotters needed little help or advice from the outside, was "wrong in several respects." As he told Swomley:

> Montgomery leaders have managed a mass resistance campaign, but it was petering out until (1) the indictments & arrests, (2) King suddenly remembered Gandhi and what he had heard from Chalmers and others. Although the protest had been going on for 9 weeks little help, if any of consequence, had come from the outside until the announcement of the non-violent features, and the quotation of King's magnificent address. When that hit the press, simultaneous with the arrests, handled with a non-violent response, help began to

pour in. Hundreds of telegrams, letters, checks, etc. poured in. . . . The non-violent method has caught the imagination of people, especially negroes everywhere. No one will know how much pacifism through the FOR has had to do with this. All I can say is that we have had a lot, and can have more. Secondly, we can learn from their courage and plain earthy devices for building morale, etc., but they can learn more from us, for being so new at this. King runs out of ideas quickly and does the old things again and again. He wants help, and we can give it to him without attempting to run the movement or pretend we know it all.[22]

Smiley's skills as an interracial organizer and his ability to lend a helping hand without being condescending or controlling proved invaluable to the MIA during the spring and summer of 1956. He was seemingly everywhere: addressing the weekly mass meetings on the relevance of nonviolence to the southern freedom struggle, organizing workshops on the tactics of direct action and passive resistance, distributing pacifist literature, encouraging white ministers to take a public stand against segregation, and overseeing the production of a fifteen-minute documentary film entitled *Walk to Freedom*. On occasion, he even served as an intelligence agent: Posing as a segregationist sympathizer, he attended several White Citizens' Council meetings and one Klan rally. These periodic forays into the segregationist camp provided the MIA with important information. But Smiley spent most of his time, and made his greatest contributions, either cultivating local white liberals or strengthening the bond between the MIA and movement leaders in the North.

At his suggestion, in early March the national office of FOR drew up a statement of support for the boycott and mailed it to sixteen hundred clergymen around the country. The statement, which began with the words "As Christian ministers we rejoice in the leadership our brother pastors in Montgomery are giving in the nonviolent campaign for racial brotherhood," received the endorsement of several hundred ministers, more than two hundred of which expressed "their own willingness to go personally to Montgomery to supply the pulpits of any of the defending ministers who were jailed." To Smiley's dismay, none of the signees lived in Alabama. But he refused to abandon his efforts to awaken the Christian conscience of white Alabama.

On March 10, just prior to the mass mailing, he had convened a secret meeting of ten white Alabama ministers, who agreed to hold a larger meeting of sixty-five ministers on April 6. The second gathering, held at a

YMCA camp ten miles outside of Montgomery, included religious leaders from seven denominations, and even though the participants did not feel comfortable enough to publicize the meeting, Smiley was heartened by what transpired. He informed Swomley:

> It was the first meeting of this sort that has been held in Alabama since the crisis began, and the men were tremendously encouraged to learn that there were this many standing out, and it could very easily be the starting of something most exciting. Since the meeting was to be held without publicity, there were no statements issued. . . . But they did set up another meeting in a month, at which time they planned to make a general announcement inviting men to attend and would issue a public statement. This is the thing that we need, for if we could get 100 men who would issue a statement, it is inconceivable to me that the 100 men could be fired, even in Alabama.

Although the plans for a public mass meeting of liberal white ministers never materialized, Smiley continued to search for potential supporters in the white community. With the help of Abernathy and Wilson Riles, a black FOR field secretary and former head of the Arizona NAACP who spent most of April in Montgomery, he organized a series of interracial prayer meetings which strengthened the lines of communication between the city's black and white ministers. The vast majority of the white ministers remained cautious in their dealings with the MIA, but the resolute courage of a small group of FOR converts who met periodically at Bob Graetz's church gave Smiley some hope for the future.[23]

*   *   *

During the spring of 1956, Smiley and Riles constituted the official FOR presence in Montgomery. However, throughout this pivotal period their efforts were reinforced by Rustin's increasingly close relationship with King. Although operating out of Birmingham and New York, Rustin was in frequent contact with the MIA president, who had come to regard him as a trusted advisor and who did not seem to be troubled by his radical past or maverick ways. In a series of meetings held in Birmingham in early March, the two men continued their ongoing philosophical discussion of nonviolence and also addressed practical matters such as fund-raising, publicity, and coalition building. Most important, they tackled the difficult problem of determining how movement leaders in the North could help the MIA without exacerbating fears of meddling and outside agitation. Since even some MIA leaders were extremely wary of outside interference, King and Rustin agreed that all "communications, ideas, and programs" should be funneled through King or E. D. Nixon, and that publicly the MIA "must give the appearance of developing all of the ideas and strategies used in the struggle." Whatever the real source, the MIA was to be given credit. In this spirit, Rustin asked Randolph and other movement leaders to provide "ghostwriters for King, who cannot find time at present to write articles, speeches, etc., himself." Rustin himself soon wrote an article under King's byline that appeared in the April 1956 issue of *Liberation*. Entitled "Our Struggle," it was King's first published work.[24]

The MIA's growing dependence on Rustin, Smiley, and the FOR represented an important turning point in the history of the boycott and perhaps in the history of the civil rights movement as well. Despite its haphazard beginnings, this historic alliance established a pattern of collaboration and interdependence that would be repeated and expanded upon in the months and years that followed. No one can be sure what would have happened if these nonviolent missionaries had not become actively involved in the boycott during the crucial months of February and March. But it is highly unlikely that either the movement-building process or the evolution of the perceived meaning of Montgomery would have proceeded as rapidly, or as creatively, without them. Thanks in large part to the FOR's influence, the leaders of the MIA adopted an increasingly self-conscious identification with Gandhian nonviolence, an identification that magnified and deepened the national and international impact of the boycott.

Several factors contributed to this fortunate turn of events, but none was more important than King's leadership. To some degree, the MIA's receptiveness to outside help was born of necessity. During the tense days of late February and early March, the boycotters' resources were pressed to the limit, and the MIA was in no position to refuse any reasonable offer of assistance. With or without King, the MIA eventually would have forged some kind of relationship with national civil rights organizations. However, it was by no means inevitable that this relationship would involve anything more than a one-way pipeline propelling funds and advice into the benighted South. Fortunately for the future of the movement, King's presence encouraged a true collaboration between local and national leaders. Among the leaders of the MIA, he alone possessed enough intellectual sophistication to deal with Rustin and Smiley on a more or less equal plane. While he lacked their experience, his broad educational background, especially his years at Crozer and Boston University, gave him the self-confidence to advance his own ideas about the strategic and moral implications of nonviolence. From the outset, he was able to mediate between Gandhianism and African American evangelism—and between the protest traditions of North and South—because, unlike most Southern Baptist ministers, he was already familiar with the language and political culture of northern intellectuals and activists. Although his deliberative style and intellectual stubbornness did not always sit well with his older and more experienced northern allies, King's ability to grasp the subtleties of both movement politics and nonviolent philosophy inspired confidence and loyalty, convincing Rustin, Smiley, and many others that this young Alabama preacher had the potential to become an American Gandhi. With King's help, they were able to look beyond the traditional stereotypes of the black South and to appreciate the largely untapped intellectual resources of a people long burdened by condescension and neglect.

Of course, even King had his limitations. Contrary to hagiographic mythology, King's advanced understanding of nonviolent philosophy did not spring forth full blown; rather, it emerged from months of careful nurturing and reflective deliberation. Even his basic commitment to nonviolence came later than myth now suggests. "Quite contrary to what many people think," Rustin recalled in a 1976 interview, "Dr. King was not a confirmed believer in nonviolence, totally, at the time that the boycott began." To prove his point, Rustin related a troubling incident during an early visit to the Dexter parsonage. When Bill Worthy "went to sit down in the King living room," he encountered a loaded gun resting on the seat of a chair. Later in the evening, Rustin pressed King for an explanation: How could the leader of a nonviolent movement be so casual about firearms? King explained that he and his colleagues had no intention of using their weapons except in cases of self-defense, a response that hardly assuaged Rustin's fears. For several hours that night, and in the weeks that followed, Rustin tried to persuade King that any association with weapons negated the spirit of nonviolence. At first, King rejected Rustin's argument as impractical, but "within six weeks, he had demanded that there be no armed guards" in the MIA.

Smiley's recollections offer a similar picture of King's conversion to nonviolence. "He didn't even use the word at first. He used 'passive resistance' almost entirely," Smiley recalled. During their first meeting, Smiley presented King with a pile of books on Gandhianism, hoping to engage the young minister in a discussion of the finer points of nonviolent theory. But after an awkward silence King sheepishly confessed that, although he admired Gandhi, he knew "very little about the man." Undaunted, Smiley pledged to do what he could to remedy the situation, an offer which King gratefully accepted and which Smiley more than made good on in the weeks that followed. "The role that I played," he told Aldon Morris in 1978, ". . . was one in which I literally lived with him hours and hours and hours at a time, and he pumped me about what nonviolence was." Blessed with a talented and willing student, Smiley had a profound influence on King's "pilgrimage to nonviolence." When King took the first integrated bus ride following the boycott's successful conclusion in December 1956, he fittingly gave Smiley the honor of sitting by his side, though then and later the always gracious Texan insisted that Rustin deserved most of the credit for nurturing the MIA leader's maturation as a proponent of nonviolent resistance.[25]

Whatever its sources, by late spring King's pilgrimage had progressed to the point where Rustin and Smiley were eager to show off their protégé's progress. To this end, Smiley invited King and Abernathy to Atlanta to meet with Muste, Swomley, Lawrence, and a handful of FOR activists from across the South. In late March, following a speaking engagement in New York City, King had met briefly with an FOR-sponsored group known as the Committee for Nonviolent Integration. But the Atlanta meeting represented the first real opportunity for the nation's leading pacifists to engage the MIA president in a face-to-face dialogue. Held at Morehouse College on May 12, the daylong meeting focused on the racial crises in Alabama, South Carolina, and Mississippi and on "the future of nonviolence in the South." Specifically, the FOR leaders wanted to know how other potential centers of nonviolent resistance could "achieve the unity of Montgomery." After listening to depressing reports on Orangeburg, South Carolina, where white segregationists were on the offensive and where black leaders were squabbling among themselves, and on the situation in Mississippi, where the FOR movement had been driven underground, the leaders looked to King for a measure of solace.

He did not disappoint them. Flanked by Abernathy and Martin Luther King Sr., the young minister presented a moving account of how thousands of seemingly ordinary citizens had become infused with the extraordinary power of nonviolent direct action. As Muste and his colleagues listened with rapt attention, King insisted that a successful nonviolent movement required both personal resistance, which was "a day-by-day affair," and collective passive resistance, which "must be used with care in a controlled situation." To Smiley's relief, the eloquence and thoughtfulness of King's words dispelled the gloom of the earlier reports, and at the close of the meeting the participants endorsed a proposal for two subregional conferences to be held in mid-July. Under the proposal each southern city would send two representatives to compare notes and exchange ideas, with the expectation that a coordinated network of protest would emerge.

Despite its brevity and bittersweet quality, the Morehouse conference represented a major step forward in FOR's fledgling southern campaign. Muste, in particular, left the meeting with renewed hope. This was his first encounter with the young Alabama preacher, though King had been in the audience when Muste had given a speech at Crozer Seminary in 1949. As Muste later told his friends in New York, King was even more impressive than he had been led to believe, and the idea that the boycott leader could become an American Gandhi no longer seemed far-fetched. For more than half a century, Muste had dreamed of spreading the FOR message to the American masses. Now it appeared he had found an ideal messenger, one who could not only prick the conscience of white Americans but who could also demonstrate the transformative power of nonviolence. From Muste's perspective, the boycotters had to do more than win the struggle in Montgomery; they also had to win it in the right way, creating a model of nonviolent resistance that others could follow. One false step, one act of violence, he feared, could sully the MIA's image and halt the nonviolent movement's newfound momentum. With this in mind, he urged Smiley and Rustin to stay close to King and to redouble their efforts to mold the MIA president in the Gandhian image.[26]

*　　*　　*

Other movement leaders, including Muste's old friends Norman Thomas and A. Philip Randolph, saw things somewhat differently. In late March, Thomas warned King that "the intrusion of Northerners in Montgomery will do more harm than good." As a socialist who had barely survived the ravages of McCarthyism, he was sensitive to the realities of the cold war and did not want the MIA to take any unnecessary chances. To him, collaborating with individuals who might taint the Montgomery movement with the appearance of left-wing infiltration or, as in the case of Rustin, with personal scandal was not worth the risk. Randolph shared Thomas's fears, but he also had concerns of a broader nature: white infringement on an indigenous black movement, elite manipulation of a grassroots protest, the likelihood of organizational squabbling, and an unhealthy preoccupation with ideology. In his calculation, allowing outsiders to set unrealistic goals—to measure the boycotters' moral progress with an absolutist ideological or philosophical yardstick that made sense in New York or New Delhi but not necessarily in Montgomery—would almost certainly doom the boycott to failure. Although he had great respect for Muste, whom he had known and admired for nearly twenty years, Randolph questioned the wisdom of subjecting local leaders to indoctrination and extended debate on the finer points of nonviolent theory.[27]

Despite his misgivings about the FOR campaign, Randolph never wavered in his support of the boycott. More than any other nationally prominent black leader, he welcomed the appearance of nonviolent direct action in the Deep South. A longtime critic of the NAACP's legalistic approach to social change, he had been one of the first African American leaders to advocate direct action on a mass scale. Although Franklin Roosevelt's executive order creating the FEPC rendered the planned 1941 March on Washington unnecessary, Randolph continued to press for nonviolent resistance during and after World War II. In 1942 he called for "a fusion of Gandhi's Satyagraha with the sit-down strike of the industrial union movement" and later lent his support to Rustin, Farmer, and other CORE activists who staged sit-ins in Chicago and other northern cities. None of this activity drew much enthusiasm from the black masses, and unsympathetic observers chided him for presuming to be "a kind of Gandhi of the Negroes." But Randolph never lost his conviction that "nonviolent mass activity" was destined to be "an important part of the future strategy and technique of the Negro."[28]

The Montgomery movement thus brought a measure of redemption to Randolph, who was especially proud of the role that his old friend E. D. Nixon had played in the creation of the boycott. From the beginning of the protest, Nixon's frequent phone calls and letters kept his mentor abreast of what was happening in Montgomery, and Randolph responded with increasing enthusiasm as the boycotters sustained and extended their defiance of Jim Crow. Although he needed little prodding, the old socialist's interest in the boycott took on a new urgency in early February after white supremacists bombed Nixon's home. When the Eisenhower administration all but ignored his telegrams demanding federal protection for MIA leaders, an angry but determined Randolph stepped up his efforts to aid and encourage the boycotters. This new determination led to the funding of Rustin's pilgrimage to Montgomery and to renewed co-operation with the FOR, but Randolph devoted most of his energy to the difficult task of raising money for the MIA.[29]

Since early January 1956, he had been a leading supporter of In Friend-ship, a new relief organization dedicated to "aiding those who are suffer-ing economic reprisals because of their fight against segregation." Origi-nally conceived as a response to "race terror" in Mississippi and South Carolina, In Friendship was the brainchild of Rustin and two remarkable behind-the-scenes activists, Stanley Levison, a socialist gadfly and profes-sional fund-raiser for the liberal American Jewish Congress, and Ella Baker, a transplanted black Virginian who had lived in New York since 1927. During the 1940s, Baker had worked as an NAACP field secretary and as national director of branches for the NAACP, and since 1954 she had served as president of the New York City branch of the NAACP. Known in movement circles as a courageous truth-teller, this "tiny woman with a booming voice" had long been a vocal inside critic of the NAACP's preoccupation with legal and organizational matters. Thus, no one was surprised when, with Levison's help, she brought together a num-ber of New York City's most prominent religious leaders, labor organiz-ers, and liberal and radical activists for In Friendship's founding meeting on January 5, or when she later persuaded Randolph to serve as the organization's first chairman.[30]

In a February 17 letter inviting sympathetic leaders to In Friendship's first "Action Conference," Randolph emphasized the plight of black Mis-sissippi farmers who were being squeezed by the White Citizens' Coun-cils, which had "succeeded in choking off loans and other credits on which farmers depend." But, following the mass indictments in Montgomery, he wasted no time in redirecting In Friendship's activities toward the struggle in Alabama. The organization began raising funds for the MIA.[31]

In early March, in an effort to depoliticize In Friendship's image, Ran-dolph resigned as chairman and was replaced by three distinguished reli-gious cochairmen, Rabbi Edward Klein, Monsignor Cornelius Drew, and Dr. Harry Emerson Fosdick. But Randolph continued to serve as the organization's principal sponsor. When In Friendship held a mass rally and fund-raiser in Madison Square Garden on May 24, Randolph's in-volvement was a key element of the event's success. In large part, it was his stature which enabled Baker and Levison to enlist a star-studded array of celebrities, including Eleanor Roosevelt, Tallulah Bankhead, Sammy Davis Jr., Pearl Bailey, Cab Calloway, and Josh White, who brought down the house with a throbbing rendition of "Free and Equal Blues." King, Rosa Parks, and Autherine Lucy were also on hand, but Bankhead, the daughter of a former senator from Alabama, stole the show when she kissed Parks and Lucy on stage. "Prejudice is so stupid," the actress told the crowd in her best Alabama drawl. "I'm a Bankhead and there have been generations of Bankheads in Alabama, but I'm not proud of what's happening there today." To Randolph's delight, the rally drew sixteen thousand participants and, despite Adam Clayton Powell's financial she-nanigans, raised more than $8,000, half of which went to the MIA.[32]

Unfortunately, the May rally proved to be the high water mark of In Friendship's fund-raising activities. With Randolph's blessing, Baker and Levison continued to work feverishly through the summer and fall. But their efforts were hampered by stiff competition from political fund-rais-ers—particularly after the presidential contest between Dwight Eisen-hower and Adlai Stevenson took shape—and by lukewarm support from the national leadership of the AFL-CIO and the NAACP. Even though In Friendship's publications repeatedly pledged that the organization would "limit itself to programs of economic aid and will not attempt to duplicate the legal, legislative, and other phases of civil rights which are now being carried on by other appropriate organizations," George Meany, Roy Wil-kins, and others remained wary of the new organization's intentions. For this reason, In Friendship's activities were essentially limited to the New York area and never became national in scope. On December 5, the orga-nization celebrated the boycott's first anniversary with a benefit concert at Manhattan Center that featured Harry Belafonte, a vocal solo by Coretta King, and jazz accompaniment by Duke Ellington. But the $1,863 that the concert raised for the MIA represented only a small fraction of what might have been raised if Baker and Levison had enjoyed the backing of a unified civil rights movement.[33]

Randolph had worked long and hard to foster such a movement. But in 1956 not even he could overcome the organizational rivalries and ideo-logical divisions that had plagued civil rights advocates for decades. Al-though Randolph, Wilkins, and other civil rights leaders developed close personal friendships, were in frequent communication with one another, and sometimes even shared resources, true cooperation eluded them. Ironically, the situation had gotten worse in the wake of the NAACP's victory in the 1954 *Brown* decision, which simultaneously reinforced and undermined a legalistic approach. The victory elevated the NAACP's status, but it also unleashed expectations and feelings that inevitably led to impatience, dissatisfaction, and experimentation with direct action. An event like the bus boycott, which ideally should have served as a rallying point for the movement, actually complicated the task of organizational cooperation. In the long run, the boycott helped to create a unifying movement culture, but in the short run it probably created more confusion than solidarity.

This unfortunate reality became apparent when Randolph convened a "private" conference on "The State of the Race" in Washington on April 24. Originally conceived as a counterpoint to the pro-segregation "Dixie Manifesto" signed by southern congressmen in February, the conference attracted scores of black leaders representing religious, civic, business, and labor organizations from across the nation. It was Randolph's hope that in framing a response to the segregationists' manifesto, the gathering would move toward the creation of an omnibus organization that could coordinate the civil rights movement on a national level. But it was not to be, even though the discussions among the black leaders were generally civil. At the end of the day the participants approved a statement calling for an end to segregation, the strengthening of the NAACP's legal and educational programs, the passage of federal legislation ensuring voting rights and fair employment, and an immediate meeting with President Eisenhower to discuss the dangerous state of race relations in the South. Yet the conference took no stand on the need for an omnibus organization or the advisability of direct action. Worst of all, following adjournment the leaders went their separate ways as if nothing had happened. As one biographer put it, whatever unity the conference inspired soon "dissolve[d] into competition for funds, membership, and publicity," leaving Randolph "deeply discouraged by his inability to unite black leadership."[34]

Randolph's frustrations serve as a reminder that the creation of the modern civil rights movement was neither simple nor preordained. Montgomery provided a focal point for the emerging movement in the critical year of 1956, but it did not eliminate the difficulties of bridging long-standing ideological, regional, organizational, and personal divisions. Years of negotiation, compromise, sacrifice, and struggle lay ahead. The bus boycott forced the issue, accelerating the evolution of the idea—and to some extent the reality—of a national civil rights movement that acknowledged the viability of nonviolent direct action in the Jim Crow

South. As King declared in his memoir of the boycott, the lessons learned on the streets of Montgomery represented a significant "stride toward freedom," encouraging African Americans everywhere to quicken their steps on the road to racial justice. But as King and other movement leaders would discover during a tumultuous decade of sit-ins, freedom rides, and protest marches, the road itself remained long and hard.[35]

Notes

1. *Montgomery Advertiser,* January 8, 1956 (quotation). For information on Rosa Parks, the forty-three-year-old black seamstress and NAACP leader who triggered the bus boycott by refusing to give up her seat on December 1, 1955, see Rosa Parks, *My Story* (New York: Dial, 1992); Jo Ann Robinson, *The Montgomery Bus Boycott and the Women Who Started It* (Knoxville: University of Tennessee Press, 1987); Douglas Brinkley, *Rosa Parks* (New York: Viking Penguin, 2000); and Lynne Olson, *Freedom's Daughters: The Unsung Heroines of the Civil Rights Movement from 1830 to 1970* (New York: Scribner, 2001), 87–131. On King and the bus boycott, see Martin Luther King Jr., *Stride toward Freedom* (New York: Harper and Row, 1958); David Garrow, *Bearing the Cross: Martin Luther King Jr. and the Southern Christian Leadership Conference* (New York: William Morrow, 1986), 11–125; Taylor Branch, *Parting the Waters: America in the King Years, 1954–1963* (New York: Simon and Schuster, 1988), 1–205; Adam Fairclough, *To Redeem the Soul of America: The Southern Christian Leadership Conference and Martin Luther King Jr.* (Athens: University of Georgia Press, 1987), 11–35; and Stewart Burns, ed., *Daybreak of Freedom: The Montgomery Bus Boycott* (Chapel Hill: University of North Carolina Press, 1997).

2. For an extensive discussion of the organizational aspects of the civil rights movement in the 1950s, see Aldon D. Morris, *The Origins of the Civil Rights Movement: Black Communities Organizing for Change* (New York: Free Press, 1984).

3. Ibid., 46.

4. Founded by ex-slaves in 1867, the First Baptist Church (Colored) of Montgomery boasted the largest black congregation in the United States during the 1910s. Following a devastating fire in 1910, the church building was rebuilt in 1910 under the leadership of the Reverend Andrew Jackson Stokes, who asked parishioners who could not afford to contribute to the rebuilding fund to contribute a brick every Sunday. Known locally as the "Brick-a-Day Church," First Baptist was the Reverend Ralph Abernathy's church from 1950 to 1961. See Barbara Carter, "A Brick Every Sunday," *Reporter,* September 20, 1961, 39–40; Branch, *Parting the Waters,* 1–4; and Ralph David Abernathy, *And the Walls Came Tumbling Down: An Autobiography* (New York: Harper and Row, 1989), 82–83, 101–2, 118–19, 185–88.

5. August Meier and Elliott Rudwick, *CORE: A Study in the Civil Rights Movement* (Urbana: University of Illinois Press, 1973), 3–69; James Farmer, *Lay Bare the Heart: The Autobiography of the Civil Rights Movement* (New York: New American Library, 1985),

101–84; Jo Ann Ooiman Robinson, *Abraham Went Out: A Biography of A. J. Muste* (Philadelphia: Temple University Press, 1981), 112–17; Paula F. Pfeffer, *A. Philip Randolph: Pioneer of the Civil Rights Movement* (Baton Rouge: Louisiana State University Press, 1990), 61–63, 149–53; Milton Viorst, *Fire in the Streets: America in the 1960s* (New York: Simon and Schuster, 1979), 133–40; "Discrimination in Interstate Transportation, April 1947–May 1955," folder 40, reel 10, series 3, Congress of Racial Equality (CORE) Papers, microfilm edition of collection at the State Historical Society of Wisconsin, Library of Congress, Washington, D.C.; *CORE-lator,* October 1947–November 1954, reel 49, series 6, CORE Papers. On the Journey of Reconciliation, see Bayard Rustin, *Down the Line: The Collected Writings of Bayard Rustin* (Chicago: Quadrangle, 1971), 13–25; James Peck, *Freedom Ride* (New York: Simon and Schuster, 1962), 14–27; Meier and Rudwick, *CORE,* 33–40; Jervis Anderson, *Bayard Rustin: Troubles I've Seen* (New York: HarperCollins, 1997), 114–24; Daniel Levine, *Bayard Rustin and the Civil Rights Movement* (New Brunswick, N.J.: Rutgers University Press, 2000), 51–56; Catherine A. Barnes, *Journey from Jim Crow: The Desegregation of Southern Transit* (New York: Columbia University Press, 1982), 58–60, 157–58, 196; Branch, *Parting the Waters,* 171–72; Viorst, *Fire in the Streets,* 137–40; and Farmer, *Lay Bare the Heart,* 165–66.

6. Meier and Rudwick, *CORE,* 69–75; Morris, *Origins,* 128–30; George M. Houser to Thurgood Marshall, March 10, 1954; James Peck to Maurice McCrackin, n.d.; Robert L. Carter to Billie Ames, October 22, 1954 (quotation); Ames to Carter, October 26, 1954, all in folder 40, reel 10, series 3, CORE Papers; *CORE-lator,* October/November 1954, February 1955, spring 1955, fall 1955, reel 49, series 6, CORE Papers.

7. Meier and Rudwick, *CORE,* 75–76; Farmer, *Lay Bare the Heart,* 185–87; typescript by James R. Robinson, February 8, 1956, folder 183, reel 30, series 5, CORE Papers. For a brief biographical sketch of Carter, see John McCormally, "Profile of a Man with a Job," Hutchinson (Kansas) *News-Herald,* July 29, 1956, clipping in folder 31, reel 31, series 5, CORE Papers.

8. Meier and Rudwick, *CORE,* 76; Morris, *Origins,* 135; *CORE-lator,* spring 1956, reel 49, series 6 (quotations); typescript by James R. Robinson, August 20, 1956, folder 183, reel 30, series 5; James Peck to Martin Luther King Jr., March 9, 1956 (first quotation), King to Peck, May 10, 1956, folder 313, reel 39, series 5, all in CORE Papers.

9. Glenn Smiley, "The Miracle in Montgomery," typescript, 1956, box 16, Fellowship of Reconciliation (FOR) Papers, Swarthmore College, Swarthmore, Pennsylvania; Farmer, *Lay Bare the Heart,* 186–88 (quotations); Morris, *Origins,* 128–38; Barnes, *Journey from Jim Crow,* 161; Meier and Rudwick, *CORE,* 76, 78; *CORE-lator,* February 1957, spring 1958, fall 1958, February 1959, reel 49, series 6, CORE Papers.

10. Charles Moritz, ed., *Current Biography Yearbook 1967* (New York: H. W. Wilson, 1967), 360; Anderson, *Rustin,* 6–95, 23 (first quotation); Levine, *Rustin,* 7–29; Branch, *Parting the Waters,* 168–71; Fairclough, *Redeem,* 23–24; Robinson, *Abraham Went Out,* 111; Jervis Anderson, *A. Philip Randolph: A Biographical Portrait* (New York: Harcourt Brace Jovanovich, 1973), 249–74, 275 (second quotation), 280–81, 378–80; Pfeffer, *Randolph,* 51–90; Viorst, *Fire in the Streets,* 200–208; Bayard Rustin, "The Negro and

Non-Violence," *Fellowship* 8 (October 1942), 166–67 (third quotation); Rustin, *Down the Line,* ix–xv, 11. On Carl Rachlin, see Anderson, *Rustin,* 41–44, 157, 271; Meier and Rudwick, *CORE,* 143, 151, 168, 173, 180, 226, 271, 277, 283, 412; and *New York Times,* January 4, 2000 (obituary).

11. Anderson, *Rustin,* 96–110, 111 (quotation); Levine, *Rustin,* 27–28, 34–51; Moritz, ed., *Current Biography Yearbook 1967,* 360–61; Rustin, *Down the Line,* ix–x, 5–52; Branch, *Parting the Waters,* 171–72; Fairclough, *Redeem,* 24; Robinson, *Abraham Went Out,* 111–17; Viorst, *Fire in the Streets,* 208–10; Pfeffer, *Randolph,* 62, 142, 150–68; Meier and Rudwick, *CORE,* 12–20, 34–50, 57, 64.

12. John Swomley, interviewed by Raymond Arsenault, November 8, 1985; Anderson, *Rustin,* 140–79; Levine, *Rustin,* 70–75; Viorst, *Fire in the Streets,* 210; Branch, *Parting the Waters,* 168, 172–73; Garrow, *Bearing the Cross,* 66

13. Howell Raines, *My Soul Is Rested: Movement Days in the Deep South Remembered* (New York: Putnam, 1977), 53; Swomley interview; John M. Swomley Jr. to Wilson Riles, February 21, 1956, FOR Papers (first three quotations); Garrow, *Bearing the Cross,* 66, 642 n. 46; Norman Thomas to Homer Jack, February 12, 1956, box 62, Norman Thomas Papers, New York Public Library (fourth quotation); Viorst, *Fire in the Streets,* 210–11 (fifth quotation); Anderson, *Rustin,* 183–86. Levine, *Rustin,* 78–82, 263–65 nn. 5–13, offers an alternative chronology and explanation of Rustin's mission to Montgomery. Based largely on an interview with James Farmer, Levine argues that the idea for the trip came from Randolph, that Farmer suggested that Rustin would be the best person for the mission, and that Rustin may have visited Montgomery as early as December 1955. While some of the details related to Rustin's trip to Montgomery are open to speculation, at this point Levine's account does not appear to rest on solid evidence.

14. Swomley interview; John Swomley to Glenn Smiley, February 29, 1956, FOR Papers; Raines, *My Soul Is Rested,* 53–54; Anderson, *Rustin,* 187; Viorst, *Fire in the Streets,* 210–11; Farmer, *Lay Bare the Heart,* 186–87; Garrow, *Bearing the Cross,* 66–67; Robinson, *Abraham Went Out,* 117; Pfeffer, *Randolph,* 173–74; Bayard Rustin, "Report on Montgomery, Alabama" (New York: War Resisters League, March 21, 1956), copy in Bayard Rustin Files, FOR Papers; Fairclough, *Redeem,* 24; William Worthy, interviewed by Raymond Arsenault, May 10, 2001. On Worthy, see Meier and Rudwick, *CORE,* 35, 40, 45–46; Pfeffer, *Randolph,* 149–50, 155–56, 161, 166–67; Raines, *My Soul Is Rested,* 53; and *Who's Who among Black Americans, 1990–91* (Detroit: Gale Research, 1991), 1408.

15. Bayard Rustin, "Montgomery Diary," *Liberation* 1 (April 1956): 7; Branch, *Parting the Waters,* 173–77; Garrow, *Bearing the Cross,* 67; Anderson, *Rustin,* 186.

16. Rustin, "Montgomery Diary," 7–10 (quotations); Rustin, "Report on Montgomery, Alabama"; Swomley interview; Glenn Smiley to John Swomley and Al Hassler, February 29, 1956, box 16, FOR Papers; Branch, *Parting the Waters,* 177–80; Garrow, *Bearing the Cross,* 67–68; Raines, *My Soul Is Rested,* 52–57; Farmer, *Lay Bare the Heart,* 187; Fairclough, *Redeem,* 23–24; David L. Lewis, *King: A Critical Biography* (New York: Praeger, 1970), 41–42, 72; and Anderson, *Rustin,* 187. On the long-term relationship between Rustin and King, see Anderson, *Bayard Rustin,* 197–308; and Viorst, *Fire in the Streets,* 211–31.

17. Rustin, "Montgomery Diary," 10; Swomley interview; Swomley to Riles, February 21, 1956; Smiley to Swomley and Hassler, February 29, 1956, both in box 16, FOR Papers; Branch, *Parting the Waters*, 179–80; Farmer, *Lay Bare the Heart*, 187; Fairclough, *Redeem*, 24; Garrow, *Bearing the Cross*, 68–69; Raines, *My Soul Is Rested*, 55; Robinson, *Abraham Went Out*, 117; Anderson, *Rustin*, 189–93. In a letter written in Birmingham, Rustin explained the *Le Figaro* and *Manchester Guardian* statement to King: "For the record, at no time did I say that I was a correspondent for either of these papers. I did say that I was writing articles which were to be submitted to them, and this is now in the process of being done." Rustin to King, March 8, 1956, box 5, Martin Luther King Jr. Papers, Boston University.

18. Swomley interview; Glenn Smiley, interviewed by Katherine M. Shannon, September 12, 1967, transcript at the Ralph J. Bunche Oral History Collection, Moorland-Spingarn Research Center, Howard University, Washington, D.C.; Frank Wilkinson, interviewed by Raymond Arsenault, March 23, 1993; "Data Sheet: Rev. Glenn E. Smiley," 1958 typescript; "Proposal for Race Relations Work in the South," typescript, February 13, 1956; Smiley, "Report from the South, Number 1," February 29, 1956; Hassler to Smiley, November 4, 1955; Smiley to "Dear Friend," December 5, 1955; Swomley to whom it may concern, February 8, 1956, all in box 16, FOR Papers; Branch, *Parting the Waters*, 180; Garrow, *Bearing the Cross*, 68; Morris, *Origins*, 62, 157, 159–60; David L. Chappell, *Inside Agitators: White Southerners in the Civil Rights Movement* (Baltimore: Johns Hopkins University Press, 1994), 58–59; Anderson, *Rustin*, 191.

19. Swomley interview; Smiley interview; Swomley to Smiley February 29, 1956 (quotation), and March 1, 1956; Smiley to Swomley, March 2, 1956, all in box 16, FOR Papers; Branch, *Parting the Waters*, 179–80; Garrow, *Bearing the Cross*, 69, 642 n. 45; Farmer, *Lay Bare the Heart*, 187; Fairclough, *Redeem*, 24; Robinson, *Abraham Went Out*, 117; Raines, *My Soul Is Rested*, 55. Chappell, *Inside Agitators*, 59, incorrectly states that Smiley arrived in Montgomery on February 14. During his interview with Katherine Shannon in 1967, Smiley himself incorrectly recalled his arrival date as February 14. See also Levine, *Rustin*, 84, 264 n. 9.

20. Smiley, "Report from the South, Number 1"; Smiley interview; Swomley interview; Morris, *Origins*, 157–62; Garrow, *Bearing the Cross*, 69–70, 72, 79; Branch, *Parting the Waters*, 180; Fairclough, *Redeem*, 24–25; Chappell, *Inside Agitators*, 59–60; Anderson, *Rustin*, 191–92.

21. Smiley to Swomley and Hassler, February 29, 1956, box 16, FOR Papers.

22. Smiley to Swomley, March 2, 1956, box 16, FOR Papers.

23. Smiley interview; Morris, *Origins*, 159–62, 166; Branch, *Parting the Waters*, 180; Garrow, *Bearing the Cross*, 70, 72; Chappell, *Inside Agitators*, 59–60, 240–41 n. 24; Miller, *Martin Luther King Jr.*, 57–58, 60, 63; *Washington Afro-American*, March 20, 1956; "Four Hundred Clergymen Express Support for Montgomery Pastors," typescript press release, March 18, 1956, reel 39, series 5, CORE Papers (first and second quotations); Smiley, "Report from the South, Number 1"; Smiley, "Report from the South, Number 2," August 15, 1956; Smiley to the editor of the Lungerville (Arizona) *News*, March 9, 1956; Smiley to George C. Hardin, April 6, 1956; Smiley, memorandum to Paul Macy et

al., April 7, 1956; Smiley to John Swomley, April 7, 1956 (third quotation); Smiley to Swomley (2 letters), April 10, 1956; Smiley to Rev. Matthew M. McCollum, n.d.; Smiley to Swomley, April 12, 1956; "Proposal for Race Relations Work in the South"; Smiley, "The Miracle of Montgomery," typescript, 1956; Smiley to King, April 13, 1956; King to Smiley, July 5, 1956; Robert Graetz to Hassler, May 15, 1957, all in box 16, FOR Papers; Smiley to King, June 1, 1956, box 5, King Papers, Boston University. On Graetz's role in the boycott, see Robert S. Graetz, *A White Preacher's Memoir: The Montgomery Bus Boycott* (Montgomery: Black Belt Press, 1998).

24. Bayard Rustin, "Notes on a Conference," reel 3, Bayard Rustin Papers, microfilm edition of collection at A. Philip Randolph Institute, New York; Garrow, *Bearing the Cross,* 72–73; Robinson, *Abraham Went Out,* 117; Raines, *My Soul Is Rested,* 54–57; Viorst, *Fire in the Streets,* 211; Fairclough, *Redeem,* 25–26; Martin Luther King Jr., "Our Struggle," *Liberation* 1 (April 1956): 3–6; Anderson, *Rustin,* 193–94.

25. Raines, *My Soul Is Rested,* 53 (Rustin quotations); Garrow, *Bearing the Cross,* 72–73 (first Smiley quotation); Fairclough, *Redeem,* 25–26; Morris, *Origins,* 159–60 (second Smiley quotation); Robinson, *Abraham Went Out,* 117; Anderson, *Rustin,* 187–88. See Keith D. Miller, *Voice of Deliverance: The Language of Martin Luther King Jr. and Its Sources* (New York: Free Press, 1992), chap. 5, for a perceptive discussion of the origins and evolution of King's ideas on nonviolence. See also Harris Wofford, *Of Kennedys and Kings: Making Sense of the Sixties* (Pittsburgh: University of Pittsburgh Press, 1992), 103ff.; Lewis, *King,* 29–40, 72, 85–111; and William R. Miller, *Martin Luther King Jr.* (New York: Weybright and Talley, 1968), 29–31, 63, 82, 90, 298–99. King's own account of his "Pilgrimage to Nonviolence" in *Stride toward Freedom,* 66–88, raises more questions than it answers and must be used with caution. On the desegregation of Montgomery's buses and the integrated bus ride of December 21, 1956, see King, *Stride toward Freedom,* 147–51.

26. Minutes of the Atlanta Conference, May 12, 1956 (quotations); Smiley, "Report from the South, Number 2," 3, both in box 16, FOR Papers; Robinson, *Abraham Went Out,* 109–18; King, *Stride toward Freedom,* 77; Fairclough, *Redeem,* 29; Garrow, *Bearing the Cross,* 75, 643 n. 50; Anderson, *Rustin,* 194.

27. Norman Thomas to King, March 23, 1956 (quotation); Thomas to Homer Jack, March 12, 1956, both in box 62, Norman Thomas Papers; Garrow, *Bearing the Cross,* 69–70, 642 n. 45; Viorst, *Fire in the Streets,* 210–11; Fairclough, *Redeem,* 32; Morris Milgrim to Daniel James, January 1, March 19, 1949; Thomas to A. Philip Randolph, January 19, 1956; Randolph to Thomas, January 23, 1956, all in Correspondence box, A. Philip Randolph Papers, Library of Congress; Robinson, *Abraham Went Out,* 111–17, 131; Pfeffer, *Randolph,* 66, 142, 150–52, 165–66, 203–5. Harris Wofford expressed similar concerns after he became involved with King in 1957: "If King had asked me to join him full-time I suspect I would have gone, but already he was being plagued by offers of assistance from people all over the world. Even the shrewd and intelligent help of Bayard Rustin verged on a kind of manipulation I disliked. Steeped in Gandhian lore, with extraordinary personal experience in nonviolent action, Rustin seemed ever-present with advice, and sometimes acted as if King were a precious puppet whose

symbolic actions were to be planned by a Gandhian high command." Wofford, *Of Kennedys and Kings*, 115.

28. A. Philip Randolph to Martin Luther King Jr., November 19, 1958, Correspondence box, Randolph Papers; Pfeffer, *Randolph*, 58 (first quotation), 62 (third quotation), 169–205; Thomas Sancton, "Something's Happened to the Negro," *New Republic* (February 8, 1943): 177, quoted in Pfeffer, *Randolph*, 64; Anderson, *Randolph*, 90, 105, 231, 250, 265–66, 279; Robinson, *Abraham Went Out*, 111–12; Branch, *Parting the Waters*, 170–71; Randolph to Nathaniel Cooper, February 13, 1953; Cooper to Randolph, January 30, 1953, February 14, 1953, all in Correspondence box, Randolph Papers. On the March on Washington Movement, see Pfeffer, *Randolph*, 45–132; and Anderson, *Randolph*, 249–61.

29. Pfeffer, *Randolph*, 23, 88, 172–74; Anderson, *Randolph*, 177; Branch, *Parting the Waters*, 121; Morris, *Origins*, 158; Viorst, *Fire in the Streets*, 21–25, 30; Randolph to Dr. George D. Cannon, June 21, 1956, Correspondence box, Randolph Papers; Randolph to Dwight D. Eisenhower, February 2, 1956, telegram, box 3, Randolph Papers; Warren Olney III to Randolph, February 8, 1956, box 15; Randolph to George Meany, March 3, 1956, box 19, both in Brotherhood of Sleeping Car Porters Papers (BSCP), Library of Congress.

30. "Memo on In Friendship," February 17, 1956 (first quotation); Walter Petersen, "Proceedings of Conference on Aid to Race Terror Victims," January 5, 1956; Madison S. Jones to Roy Wilkins, January 9, 1956, both in box B-186, series 3, NAACP Papers, Library of Congress; Randolph to Eleanor Roosevelt, January 31, 1956, box 24, BSCP Papers; Norman Thomas to Wilkins, Randolph, et al., January 12, 1956, Correspondence box; Thomas to Randolph, March 8, 1956, box 2, both in Randolph Papers; Fairclough, *Redeem*, 29–32; Branch, *Parting the Waters*, 208–9, 231, 233, 330; Anderson, *Rustin*, 195; Garrow, *Bearing the Cross*, 84, 102–3; David J. Garrow, *The FBI and Martin Luther King Jr.: From "Solo" to Memphis* (New York: W. W. Norton, 1981), 26, 40–44; Morris, *Origins*, 83. For a discussion of Baker's remarkable career, see Joanne Grant, *Ella Baker: Freedom Bound* (New York: Wiley, 1998); Olson, *Freedom's Daughters*, 132–50; Sharon Harley, "Ella Jo Baker," in Charles Reagan Wilson and William Ferris, eds., *The Encyclopedia of Southern Culture* (Chapel Hill: University of North Carolina Press, 1989), 1570–71; Belinda Robnett, *How Long? How Long? African American Women in the Struggle for Civil Rights* (New York: Oxford University Press, 1997); Peggy Peterman, "A Leader in the Struggle," St. Petersburg *Times*, February 11, 1992 (second quotation); Viorst, *Fire in the Streets*, 119–24; Clayborne Carson, *In Struggle: SNCC and the Black Awakening of the 1960s* (Cambridge: Harvard University Press, 1981), 19–31, 41–42, 70–71; and Gerda Lerner, "Developing Community Leadership: Ella Baker," in *Black Women in White America: A Documentary History*, ed. Lerner (New York: Vintage Books, 1973), 352. See also the transcript of a June 19, 1968, interview with Baker, in The Civil Rights Documentation Project, Ralph J. Bunche Oral History Collection, Moorland-Spingarn Research Center, Howard University, Washington, D.C. There is no general history of In Friendship, but see Eugene P. Walker, "A History of the Southern Christian Leadership Conference, 1955–1965: The Evolution of a Southern Strategy

for Social Change," Ph.D. diss., Duke University, 1978; and "A Brief Digest of the Activities of 'In Friendship,'" March 6, 1957, box 2, Randolph Papers.

31. Randolph to "Dear Friend," February 17, 1956, box B-186, series 3, NAACP Papers (quotation); "A Brief Digest."

32. Randolph to Ella Baker, March 7, 1956; Randolph to Rabbi Edward E. Klein, March 15, 1956; "A Brief Digest," all in box 2, Randolph Papers; Chicago *Defender,* June 2, 9, 1956 (quotation); Fairclough, *Redeem,* 31–32; Garrow, *The FBI,* 26; Anderson, *Rustin,* 195–96; Roy Wilkins, with Tom Mathews, *Standing Fast: The Autobiography of Roy Wilkins* (New York: Penguin, 1984), 235–36.

33. "A Brief Digest"; Baker to Randolph, August 29, 1956; In Friendship, minutes of executive committee, June 20 and July 19, 1956; Baker to Cornelius J. Drew, October 9, 1956; Baker to Randolph, memorandum, January 1, 1957, all in box 2, Randolph Papers; Norman Thomas to Randolph, August 26, 1956, Correspondence box, Randolph Papers; Baker to "Dear Friend," June 2, 1956; In Friendship, "We Believe," broadside, c. 1956, both in box B-186, series 3, NAACP Papers; Garrow, *The FBI,* 42; Garrow, *Bearing the Cross,* 103; Morris, *Origins,* 116; Branch, *Parting the Waters,* 209, 216, 227, 231. The NAACP did provide strong support for the December 5 concert. See Drew et al. to Mrs. Roy Wilkins, telegram, October 14, 1956; Ella Baker to Roy Wilkins, November 10, 1956; Wilkins to "Dear NAACP Member," November 23, 1956; Stanley Levison to Wilkins, December 12, 1956, all in box B-186, series 3, NAACP Papers; and Fairclough, *Redeem,* 32, which probably overstates the degree of cooperation between the two organizations.

34. Wilkins, *Standing Fast,* 237–38; Pfeffer, *Randolph,* 174–76 (quotation); "Map, 'State of Race' Confab for D.C.," *Jet,* April 19, 1956, 3; "73 Negro Leaders in D.C. Session Seek Immediate Meeting with Ike," *Jet,* May 10, 1956, 4–5; Randolph to Eisenhower, May 8, 1956, box 3, Randolph Papers. On Randolph's complicated and often frustrating relationship with Wilkins, see Randolph to Wilkins, March 16, 1956, Wilkins to Randolph, September 22, 1958, Randolph to Wilkins, October 6, 1958, all in box 30, BSCP Papers; Anderson, *Randolph,* 319–24, 348; Pfeffer, *Randolph,* 190–205; and Wilkins, *Standing Fast.* On the Dixie Manifesto, also known as the "Southern Manifesto" or "Declaration of Constitutional Principles," see Numan V. Bartley, *The Rise of Massive Resistance: Race and Politics in the South during the 1950s* (Baton Rouge: Louisiana State University Press, 1969), 116–17; *Congressional Record,* 84th Cong., 2d sess., March 12, 1956, 3948, 4004; and Brooks Hays, *A Southern Moderate Speaks* (Chapel Hill: University of North Carolina Press, 1959), 89.

35. King, *Stride toward Freedom,* 158–201.

7

The Tallahassee Bus Boycott

GREGORY B. PADGETT

It has been well documented that the Montgomery bus boycott was the primary catalyst of the modern civil rights movement that occurred between 1954 and 1974. The success of the Montgomery protest and the emergence of the Reverend Martin Luther King as a national figure in the ensuing civil rights struggle has eclipsed other desegregation campaigns of the same era. In *The Origins of the Civil Rights Movement*, sociologist Aldon Morris writes that "Montgomery, Alabama, was one of several movement centers characterized by blacks organizing and taking proactive measures to resist segregation and racial discrimination." Many of these movement centers were located in the Gulf South states. Tallahassee, Florida, has received less scholarly attention, despite its impact on the embryonic stages of the civil rights movement.[1]

The thesis of this narrative is that the Tallahassee bus boycott's unique characteristics deserve further study. Unlike Montgomery, this boycott began as a protest by college students. C. U. Smith contends that the role of black students in the Tallahassee bus protest provided a model for later student involvement in the civil rights movement.[2] The desegregation campaign in Tallahassee is also unique because of its rapid development and effectiveness. It permanently transformed social, political, and economic institutions in the city.

Tallahassee, like Montgomery, also produced a charismatic leader, the Reverend Charles Kenzie Steele. He made a significant contribution to the national civil rights effort as one of the founders of the Southern Christian Leadership Conference in 1957.[3] Martin Luther King was the SCLC's founding president, and Steele served as its first executive vice president. He held that post for the rest of his life. SCLC spearheaded many of the major desegregation campaigns in the Gulf South states.[4]

In the first half of the twentieth century, African Americans living in the Gulf South were subjected to what Aldon Morris calls the tripartite system of racial domination. They were controlled economically, politically, and personally under this system. Race relations were peaceful on the surface before the boycott in Florida's capital, although all of the elements of the tripartite system were certainly present. A study by C. U. Smith and Lewis Killian indicates that African Americans in Tallahassee were unusually well received within the framework of segregation. Still, the laws of segregation affected every aspect of a black Tallahassean's life.[5]

In 1952, Tallahassee had a population of 27,237. African Americans composed 39.5 percent of the population. Whites had a median annual salary that was more than double that of blacks. In 1950, the annual median income of whites was $2,952 compared with $1,141 for blacks. Most Tallahassee blacks lived in poverty.[6]

This economic subordination was aided by the fact that whites held most supervisory and managerial positions.[7] Hiring, promotions, and retention were under their control. Economic control facilitated political and personal control. Economically vulnerable African Americans had few resources with which to resist political and personal oppression.

A significant number of black women in Tallahassee worked as domestics.[8] They were employed in white households in the city's suburban areas. The city bus line was the maid's chief mode of transportation.

Tallahassee's black community also had a small, closely knit middle class. There were physicians and attorneys, but most were public school teachers or employees of the all-black Florida Agricultural and Mechanical University (FAMU). The university's band and football team were a source of pride for the entire city. The head football coach, Jake Gaither, was a popular, influential figure. FAMU added a vital dimension to the social structure of the city's black community. The various civic and social clubs provided a distinct identity. The Tallahassee Ministerial Alliance linked the various black denominations. Its newest member, C. K. Steele, had assumed the pastorship of Bethel Baptist Church in 1952. He was a small, energetic man with a well-earned reputation as a charismatic preacher.[9]

Although FAMU's campus was only a mile from all-white Florida State University, the state board of control expressly forbade any social contact between the two schools. There was, however, a double standard. FSU students could visit FAMU's campus with parental supervision. No FAMU student could visit FSU's campus as an individual under any circumstances. On rare occasions, groups from FAMU like the choir or glee club were invited to perform at FSU.[10]

Despite this constrained environment, or because of it, African Americans in Tallahassee formed a strong, viable community. Segregation made cooperation necessary for survival. Regardless of income, education, or social background, all were bound by the color line.

Black Tallahasseans could boast of some significant signs of progress. The Tallahassee Police Department had two uniformed patrol officers, but their jurisdiction was confined to black neighborhoods.[11] Even with representation on the police force, no black resident could be assured of equal protection before the law in a segregated society.

The church provided continuity for every level of Tallahassee's black community. Educated professionals worked in concert with common wage earners for the benefit of all. Black churches would be vehicles for change and provide organizational structure and leadership for the mass civil rights protests that swept across the Gulf South. Tallahassee's 10,622 African Americans would be in the vanguard of the movement, which challenged the manifestations of segregation that permeated every aspect of their lives.

The movement began as a personal protest. On May 27, 1956, two FAMU students, twenty-six-year-old Wilhemina Jakes of West Palm Beach and twenty-one-year-old Carrie Patterson of Lakeland, went shopping in downtown Tallahassee. On their return home, the pair boarded a crowded city bus. All of the seats in the "colored section" were occupied. The two students sat in a pair of vacant seats in the "whites-only" area. Max Coggins, the bus driver, demanded they move to the "colored section" in the rear of the bus. The women refused but offered to get off the bus if their fares were refunded. Coggins could have defused the situation at that point. Instead, he flatly refused their request. He drove to a gas station and telephoned the police. The two women were arrested and charged with "inciting a riot."[12] They were later released on $25 bonds, and the case was remanded to FAMU officials. Eventually the charges were dropped. When they were questioned later, Jakes and Patterson claimed fatigue was the only motivation for their actions.[13] The example of the Montgomery bus boycott then in progress should not be discounted. The local newspaper, the *Tallahassee Democrat*, treated this violation of segregation laws as a minor incident worthy of only a brief paragraph. The newspaper article did, however, report the women's home address at West Jennings Street.[14] This action put the women at risk. On the night of their arrest, a cross was burned in front of their residence. FAMU officials moved the two women into a dormitory on campus for their protection.[15]

The cross burning did not have the desired effect. Instead of inspiring fear, the incident galvanized FAMU students and the city's black community into action. Thus, with a few nearly accidental twists of circumstance, the momentum for a mass protest was developing.

The following day at noon, FAMU students held a mass meeting on campus. The student government association, led by president Broadus Hartley, called for a boycott of city buses. It was essentially a symbolic protest, since only two weeks remained in the school term. Students organized themselves into teams that boarded buses passing through FAMU's campus. The students urged all black passengers to disembark. Most people complied without objection, but one minister, Reverend R. N. Webb, refused and students removed him by force. This incident and pressure from the State Board of Control prompted FAMU's administrators to prohibit students from boarding city buses to enforce the boycott. They wanted to lessen the very real possibility of violence and ensure student safety.[16]

The rest of the black community became involved on the third day of the protest. On May 29, Dr. James Hudson, president of the Tallahassee Ministerial Alliance, and C. K. Steele, acting president of the Tallahassee chapter of the NAACP, called a joint meeting. A committee was appointed to contact city officials and bus company managers. It was decided that a citywide meeting of the black community should be held at Bethel African Methodist Episcopal Church.[17]

Approximately 450 people attended the meeting, an indication of the black community's interest. The meeting had two significant results: The Tallahassee Inter-Civic Council (ICC) was organized, and Steele was elected its president. Privately, Steele stated he would have preferred the NAACP conduct the boycott, but he recognized the need of having a locally based organization. This prevented boycott opponents from charging that the protest was a result of outside agitation. Such allegations were commonplace during the civil rights era.

The Inter-Civic Council's stated objectives were "to plan and execute civic, religious, scientific, educational and recreational programs for the benefit, enjoyment, general improvement and welfare of its members; to stimulate the attainment of high ideals and intellectual growth to occupy a progressive and constructive place in the community; to develop friendship, peace and goodwill among men; and to advance the idea of the eternal fatherhood of God and the universal brotherhood of men."

The ICC's methods were to be nonviolent, direct confrontation. The organization's immediate goal was the desegregation of the city bus service. The ICC formulated three demands to be conveyed to the management of the bus company: (1) seating was to be on a first come, first served basis; (2) white drivers were to treat Negro passengers with courtesy, and (3) black drivers were to be hired for routes through the black community. The ICC vowed to impose the boycott until all conditions were met, and to form a car pool system to provide transportation for black maids, who formed the majority of the city bus lines' clientele.[18]

The members of the Tallahassee city commission ignored the ICC's three demands, published in the *Tallahassee Democrat* on May 30, 1956. Several members of the commission stated publicly that "they were unaware of the desires of the Negro community."

The commission attempted to settle matters on its own terms. On May 29, 1956, commission members met privately after regular business hours at Leon Federal Savings and Loan with some prominent members of the black community: Father David Brooks, coach Jake Gaither, and businessmen George W. Conoly and Dan Speed. This meeting precipitated the first test of C. K. Steele's leadership of the bus boycott. Unaware of the clandestine meeting, Steele chose Judas's betrayal of Jesus as a topic of his Sunday sermon.

Those individuals who had attended the secret meeting, not surprisingly, thought the sermon was a veiled attack on them. Steele had unwittingly created a rift in Tallahassee's black community that would take years to heal. Indeed, some of the dissension that arose in Steele's own congregation at Bethel Baptist Church never abated, and that lingering resentment plagued Steele's ministry until his death. Some of Steele's personal relationships were also severely strained. Father Brooks was a longtime friend and confidant, and as a result Coach Gaither was convinced he had disclosed the details of the meeting to Steele. Steele's attempts to ease the tension were unsuccessful. A phone call to Gaither only served to fan the flames. Gaither threatened to kill Brooks "with his bare hands." Afraid that the situation was spinning out of control, Steele went to Gaither's home. He recalled, "I jumped in the car and rushed over to him to try to point out to him that one of the most subtle things the city could do to me and to us was to get us to attack him, the most popular black man in Florida." Steele's pleas fell on deaf ears. Gaither remained convinced that Father Brooks had betrayed his trust. It would be twenty years before the rift between Gaither and Brooks healed.[19]

This controversy so early in the protest could have destroyed the desegregation campaign. Steele worked hard to foster a spirit of unity and cooperation. Despite his best efforts, people active in the boycott displayed resentment toward those who had attended the secret meeting. Conoly lost so much patronage that he was forced to close his gas station at the corner of St. Augustine and McComb Streets. Few in the black community remembered that Conoly had been active in the civil rights movement since the 1930s. After a lynching in Tallahassee, African Americans led by Conoly had established a civic league to combat racism. As president of the league, Conoly had organized the petition drive that resulted in the hiring of Tallahassee's first black police officers. Years later, Steele declared that had he known about the secret meeting, he never would have preached that particular sermon.[20]

Steele's personal life was also profoundly affected by his participation in the protest. After he was identified as president of the ICC, Steele was subjected to threats and constant harassment. By phone, mail, and overt violence, there were attempts to intimidate him. One of his sons, the Reverend Henry Marion Steele, recalled that rocks and sometimes gunfire were directed at the parsonage on the corner of Boulevard and Tennessee Streets. Bullet holes were still visible in the walls almost twenty years later when the house was torn down.

Despite personal distractions, C. K. Steele prudently focused on maintaining the momentum of the boycott. The biweekly mass meeting was the means of sustaining the community interest and support. All of the churches in the black community were responsible for hosting these meetings on a rotating basis. The meetings were used to bolster morale and raise funds. Mass meetings were conducted as religious observances with hymns and sermons.

Similar to the campaign in Montgomery, the car pool was critical to the success of the boycott. Dan Speed served as chairman of the ICC transportation committee. Speed and his assistant, Elbert Jones, established a network of pickup points in the black community for people requiring a ride to work. The similarity between operations in Montgomery and Tallahassee was not coincidental. Henry Steele recounts that Martin Luther King visited their home on several occasions in the summer of 1956 to confer with his father. It was possible for King to travel to Tallahassee without exciting notice since he had not yet attained national prominence.

Steele and King's friendship and collaboration would continue in 1957 with the establishment of the Southern Christian Leadership Conference.[21]

The opponents of the boycott also recognized the importance of the car pool. The city commission employed a two-prong attack on the car pool: external opposition and internal dissension. David Brooks led the group of dissidents who actively opposed the car pool. Most of this group had attended the May 29 meeting.

On June 1, 1956, ICC attorney J. Theries Lindsey met with city commissioners James Messer and Ben Willis and bus company attorney Charles Ausley. Lindsey formally presented the ICC's three demands. In its published response in the *Tallahassee Democrat* on June 2, the commission attempted to bypass the issue of segregated seating by proposing that no race give up seating for another. Seating based upon race was not addressed. The commission promised to give immediate attention to the hiring of black drivers. The ICC membership rejected the commission proposal at its June 3 mass meeting. In a press release published in the *Tallahassee Democrat* on June 5, Steele said, "Since the present bus seating arrangement is economically unsound, humiliating, arbitrary, inequitable, inconvenient and morally unjustifiable, all bus passengers shall have the right to sit where ever they choose. . . . Since all races by their patronage contribute to the support of the bus company, all races should have the opportunity to work for the company in various capacities." The demand for courtesy from white drivers was reemphasized. One of the ugliest aspects of segregated public transportation was the degrading verbal abuse that some drivers directed toward black passengers.[22]

The city commission stepped up its harassment of car pool participants after Steele's press release. Steele was among the first arrested on May 30, 1956. In early June, the police intimidation intensified. As president of the ICC, Steele was considered a high profile target and was arrested three times in one day.[23] The bus company's management responded by declaring that bus routes in black neighborhoods were economically unstable and requesting that those routes be suspended. Charles Carter, bus company manager, told the Ministerial Alliance on May 29 that "he did not care if Negroes ever rode the buses." Carter's comment was ironic, since statistical studies indicated that a significant portion of bus company revenue was derived from black patronage.[24] On June 5, 1956, the city commission authorized the route suspensions and rejected the ICC's three demands.

The city commission had a setback the next day. On June 6, a three-judge panel ruled that Montgomery's segregated seating laws were unconstitutional.[25] This ruling placed Tallahassee's segregation ordinances in serious question. It was welcome news to the ICC membership, but they had no illusions that change would be quick and painless. It was understood that the city commission would continue its efforts to end the boycott. The mass meeting that evening confirmed that belief. Father Brooks issued a statement opposing the boycott and urging cooperation with the city commission. The statement was met with hostility from the ICC membership. As a result Brooks lost considerable credibility in the black community.

The bus company's tactics quickly backfired. The city commission granted the bus company's request for a fare increase on June 10, to compensate for the revenue lost when routes were suspended. The commission also reduced the bus company's city franchise tax from 3 percent to 0.5 percent. The city sacrificed $5,000 in annual tax revenue to preserve segregation. Tallahassee's blacks were undeterred and gaining a sense of their collective economic power. A critical element of the tripartite system, economic control, was being undermined.[26]

On June 15, the *Tallahassee Democrat* announced a total suspension of bus service effective July 1, 1956. The ICC bus boycott had deprived the bus company of 60 percent of its revenue. The Montgomery bus boycott, begun six months before the campaign in Tallahassee, did not produce such dramatic results.[27] The city commission persisted in its efforts to bypass the ICC as the sole bargaining agent in the bus protest by continuing its negotiations with the group led by Father Brooks. Steele reacted with characteristic calm to this challenge to his leadership. He thought the Brooks faction was sincere but clearly out of touch with the mood of Tallahassee's black community. In each mass meeting, Steele counseled the ICC membership against bitterness or reprisals toward these individuals. He was determined to thwart the commission's strategy of divide and conquer. He vigorously advocated unity and harmony. At Steele's urging, rumors of special favors being granted by city officials to boycott opponents were generally ignored.[28] Steele urged members not to be influenced by rumors of favoritism by city officials toward boycott opponents.

The city commission's next move was an attack on Steele's leadership. An editorial in the July 1 issue of the *Tallahassee Democrat* asserted, "Negro leaders who have been in Tallahassee only a few years and who allegedly speak for the boycott have turned down all proposals . . . they have left no room for the moderate." The *Democrat* also quoted Governor Leroy Collins criticizing the protest leadership for "pushing too far, too fast." Collins's motives for issuing this statement have never been firmly established. Perhaps he felt the need to take a firm stand in response to criticism from diehard segregationists. These comments are a stark contrast to Collins's later role as a moderate champion of civil rights. Steele later theorized that the governor's statements encouraged continued city commission opposition. Steele responded to the governor's statement in the July 4 mass meeting. He said, "We cannot sit quietly by and wait for freedom to come to us on a silver platter. For us there must be no adherence to gradualism. . . . No Negro worth his salt can afford to stand for anything other than the complete liberation of our people."[29]

Steele's uncompromising stance earned him the wrath of both whites and blacks fearful of change. Father Brooks continued his efforts to slow the pace of events. At the July 8 mass meeting, Brooks tried to convince the ICC membership that segregated seating should be tested in the courts. Steele countered with the opinion that the three-judge panel's ruling made such an action unnecessary.[30]

The city commission found another legal justification for attacking the car pool. The commission declared that the ICC car pool violated the state's "for hire" tag law. On July 18, city officials announced an "all out crack down."[31] All commercial transportation providers were required to have these tags. In the midst of this development, the ICC leadership began to formulate future strategy.

Steele created considerable alarm in the city's white business community when he suggested extending the boycott to stores in downtown Tallahassee.[32] Dr. Edward D. Irons suggested that the ICC conduct voter registration drives. With increased voting strength, African Americans could hold white politicians accountable for their actions. Both strategies would be applied with telling effect later in the desegregation campaign.

The Florida state legislature began to plot its own strategy to stall desegregation. Governor Collins appointed a committee chaired by Judge L. L. Fabisniski to research how that could be accomplished. As a result, the House committee adopted five bills and three resolutions in a special session held between July 23 to August 1, 1956. House bill 24XX prohibited forced integration of public schools. House bill 25XX authorized the state attorney general to assist local school boards in resisting integration. Local school boards were authorized to close schools in the "public interest." Local school boards could also assign students, thereby preempting the attempted registration of black students in all-white districts.[33]

One bill was specifically intended to limit support for the bus boycott. It prohibited the participation of state, county, and municipal employees in boycotts.[34] This measure put considerable pressure on FAMU employees. An individual's sense of economic stability determined their level of participation in the boycott. Administrators and untenured faculty seemed less inclined to support the protest than career service staff and students.

It was rumored that FAMU president George Gore had directed university employees to refrain from protest activity or risk loss of employment.[35] The *Tallahassee Democrat* fueled the rumor by printing such in a series of articles. Acutely cognizant of the divisive potential of the rumor, Steele publicly defended Gore. He worked to keep the ICC membership's attention focused on the boycott. Gore was caught between white conservatives in the legislature and black activists. He managed to deflect legislators' hostility from FAMU. An individual with less diplomatic skill might have made a bad situation worse.

On August 1, 1956, the city commission officially recognized the ICC as the sole bargaining agent of the black community. Bus service resumed the next day, and black patrons on buses gave boycott opponents false hope. The bus company conducted an intense public relations campaign to persuade African Americans to ride the buses. Lapel buttons were distributed with the slogan "I am riding the bus are you?" Free coffee was served on buses, and full-page ads in the *Democrat* were also part of the campaign.[36]

The bus company's tactics did not have the anticipated outcome. Blacks rode only on the routes with black drivers. Many rode the bus for the simple pleasure of seeing fellow blacks function in unfamiliar roles. FAMU students continued to boycott all bus service.[37] Despite this, the bus company declared its "Ride the Bus" campaign a success.[38] Florida attorney general Richard Ervin publicly supported the city commission's contention that the ICC car pool violated the "for hire" tag law. City officials believed that destruction of the car pool would force African Americans to resume riding the buses. Instead, blacks used the campaign to strengthen their sense of community. Arrests for violation of the "for hire" tag law replaced the premeditated traffic stops employed by the police at the start of the boycott. In a letter published September 1 in the *Tallahassee Democrat*, Jean Sue Brubaker pointed out that state government and FSU employees carpooled without hindrance. Didn't the Ervin ruling apply to everyone? The car pool trials in the fall of 1956 provided an answer.

Steele wrote to Governor Collins requesting his intervention in the car pool trials. Steele told Collins that the car pool defendants would be tried on the basis of their race, not the merits of the case.[39] Collins declined to intervene. In a September 23, 1956, telegram to Steele, he wrote: "The only prosecutions I know anything about are pending in the courts upon the alleged failure of car pool operators to obtain the proper license to carry on a business of this kind. The issues involved are questions of law and fact and the court is the proper forum in which such be settled. So far as I know, no one questions the rights of our Negro citizens to ride the buses or not as they wish. Certainly I do not."

After Collins rejected his appeal, Steele solicited the aid of the national branch of the NAACP. Executive Secretary Roy Wilkins responded with funds and a staff lawyer, Francisco Rodriquez. Although J. Theries Lindsey, the ICC's lawyer, was capable, he was just out of law school and relatively inexperienced. There was considerable concern about the case being tried in the court of Judge John Rudd. Rudd's views on race were common knowledge. Few of the ICC car pool defendants had any illusions about receiving a fair trial. In an interview in 1978, Rudd revealed that two decades had not altered his perspective. He told Professor Jackson Lee, "You know the older blacks weren't that unhappy. Because just like you and I, we were raised in an environment, in an atmosphere that this is my right place, this is where I am happy. You take a semi-intelligent person and put him in a responsible position, he's lost. You put him on a bulldozer or something that was right even with his mentality then he is delighted, he's happy, he's reached his peak."[40]

Southern conservatives like John Rudd were completely out of touch with the changes occurring in American society. Stereotypes and time-worn rationalizations were inadequate explanations. Blinded by bigotry, many white Southerners could not understand the new militancy of African Americans or the conditions that created it.

In September 1956, efforts to intimidate Tallahassee's black community intensified. Four hundred Klansmen marched through the city. Their line of march went past Bethel Baptist Church. The march ended at a Klan rally west of the city. "They marched hooded by our church," Steele noted, "which gave rise to one of the biggest prayer meetings in this town, because when they came by we were praying with the church packed with people." The black community's response to the Klan demonstrated how much their attitudes had changed. They were learning how to resist various aspects of systematic racial domination. In the past, a Klan march might have discouraged participation in the boycott. Instead, there was an unprecedented surge in African American voter registration in Leon County.

The harassment of C. K. Steele began to take a bizarre turn. On two occasions, undertakers in Steele's congregation answered summons to the parsonage to pick up Steele's corpse. In each instance, they were told their pastor had been murdered. Both times Steele greeted them at the door. Steele took the pranks in stride, but his family was horrified. His attention was focused on the pending car pool trial.[41]

The car pool trial began on October 17, 1956. Steele had done his best to prepare the ICC membership for a negative outcome. He was uncertain whether the bus boycott could be maintained without the car pool. At the October 8 mass meeting, Steele repeated the ICC's pledge to continue the boycott, regardless of the outcome of the trial. He told the ICC membership, "We are still walking, praying and trusting God that the final outcome and consequences of our passive protest will end injustice, unfairness and segregation on city coaches. Ladies and gentlemen, the battle is not over, the race is not completed. We must not give up, not let up for a second, instead we must fight this vicious monster called segregation until he is dead, buried, embalmed and sent to hell." Steele's sermon had the desired effect. The ICC membership maintained its resolve, despite the almost certain knowledge that the car pool defendants would be convicted.

At the start of the trial, attorneys for the city claimed that the ICC was an illegal business rival of the City Transit Company. Steele and the other twenty-one defendants were charged with this offense. The city had seventy-five witnesses scheduled to testify on its behalf. Charles Carter, bus company manager, testified that bus company profits had declined from $15,000 to $9,000 per month since the inception of the ICC car pool. Lindsey stated that since the car pool patrons rode for free, it was a nonprofit operation. Unfortunately, some car pool participants' testimony contradicted Lindsey's claims.[42]

The ICC defense team could not refute the fact that some car pool drivers had accepted "donations" from passengers. After three days of testimony, the court decided that those "donations" constituted profit-making by the ICC. All twenty-two defendants were found guilty and sentenced to sixty days in jail and a fine of $500. The jail sentences were suspended, but the defendants were liable for the fines, totaling $11,000.[43] This was an obvious attempt to bankrupt the ICC and end the boycott.

The car pool trial got national media attention. Much of the news coverage was negative. Don Meickle John, a reporter for the *Democrat*, wrote an October 20 article minimizing the importance of the bus boycott. Two days later, Henry Gitano, editor of a socialist newspaper, the *Militant*, pointed out the hypocrisy of the city paying $4,000 to nationally famous lawyer Mark R. Hawe to assist city attorney Edward Hill while city officials and the local press complained bitterly about the NAACP's interference when it made its attorney, Francisco Rodriquez, available to the ICC's defense team. In his editorial, Gitano wrote,

> The twenty-one Negroes were victimized in the car pool trial. . . . City Judge John Rudd tossed out as irrelevant a motion by defense attorney Francisco Rodriquez, a Tampa NAACP lawyer, which stated that boycotters were not engaged in a business activity, but a protest movement. That the right of free speech cannot be licensed by public authority, that the requirement of racial segregation on the city buses is a bill of attainder, that the action of the city denies equal protection of the law.

To the dismay of city officials, the ICC abandoned the car pool but continued the boycott and intensified its voter registration drive. Steele was emphatic about the ICC's position. He told the press, "The war is not over, we are still walking."[44] The city's court victory did not end the legal battles over the bus boycott. ICC lawyers filed an appeal immediately following the trial. The appeals process took six years. Steele decided to pay the $11,000 fine himself rather than burden his fellow defendants. To raise funds, Steele booked speaking engagements whenever possible. The long absences drew criticism from boycott opponents in Steele's congregation. Their resentment festered for over a decade, but in the fall of 1956, Steele's immediate concern was the maintenance of the boycott as the opposition intensified.

The city commission increased its efforts to intimidate boycott participants. A notable example was the case of businessmen, Riley Haywood and Robert Landers, owners of the Economy Cab Company. City officials informed the men that their franchise license would be revoked because Landers had served as the ICC's transportation coordinator.[45] The members of the city commission clearly misjudged the mood of Tallahassee's black community. Despite the outcome of the car pool trial, morale and resolve among bus protestors remained high. When the news of the commission's punitive action was made public, the black community responded by accelerating the pace of its voter registration drive.

A sustained voter registration drive was possible because the Ministerial Alliance and various civic organizations gave Tallahassee's black community the necessary infrastructure. At the center of these various organizations was the black community's most viable, stable institution, the church. The black community was already in the habit of attending biweekly mass meetings, so it was not difficult to direct that organizational discipline to new endeavors. This was helpful to the ICC leadership's diversified attack on segregation. If one approach was thwarted, it did not impede the whole desegregation campaign; hence the loss of the car pool could not end the boycott. The ICC's campaign systematically attacked each of the dimensions of the tripartite system of racial domination.

The ICC leadership also became adept at utilizing the media. In December 1956, C. K. Steele and the ICC executive board decided some dramatic demonstration was needed to sustain the membership's morale. On Christmas Eve, Steele, A. C. Reed, and H. McNeal Harris rode in the "whites only" section of a city bus with local news media present. Steele told local reporters, "Before I will be a slave, I will be in my grave."[46]

This act of defiance got an immediate response from city officials. The city commission revoked the company's franchise for allowing this "integrated ride." The bus company manager and nine drivers were arrested. They were each required to pay $100 bond, then released. They were charged with violating section 4 of the company's franchise agreement, which stated, "The bus company shall make and enforce reasonable rules and regulations providing for the segregation of the human races when more than one race is present on the same bus." Company officials contended that since three ministers were the only passengers on the bus, no violation had occurred. Charles Ausley, the bus company attorney, asserted that revocation of a franchise license required thirty days' notice.

The relationship between the bus company and the city commission changed profoundly. Concern about lost profits overruled the cooperative effort to stop integration. The bus company filed suit to test the legal validity of the city's segregation ordinance in an effort to protect the franchise agreement. The three ministers repeated their "integrated ride" for the benefit of *Life* magazine photographers. The involvement of the national media added fuel to the controversy. In its struggle to survive, the

Figure 7.1. C. K. Steele and a colleague ride in the "whites-only" section during the struggle to desegregate the Tallahassee bus system, January 1957. Florida State Archives.

bus company became the unwitting ally of the black community. The bus company obtained a temporary restraining order prohibiting commission interference in its business operations.[47]

After his photo appeared in *Life* magazine, Reverend Steele suffered more personal attacks. Bricks, bottles, and bullets were directed against the parsonage almost daily. In an effort to ease the tension, Governor Leroy Collins suspended all bus service pending a decision by the courts. Reverend Steele publicly opposed the governor's decision because it slowed the desegregation process. This statement apparently inspired more acts of personal intimidation. On the night of January 13, 1957, a cross was burned in front of Steele's home. He was attending a mass meeting at Fountain Chapel AME Church when he learned of the incident. A neighbor, Mrs. Maude Lomars, told Steele that she had seen uniformed policemen ignite the cross and leave in a marked patrol car. The cross burning had an unanticipated effect. Concern for the safety of the Steele family eased some of the dissension in the congregation over the boycott. Men in the congregation including boycott opponents began guarding the parsonage at night. Steele decided to move his family out of the parsonage to ensure their safety. The family moved in with two church members, Primus and Bonnie Harris. They stayed with the couple for one year.[48]

To its credit, the *Democrat* condemned such acts of racist violence in its January 15, 1957, editorial:

> However much we regret the provocative zealousness and disagree with the tactics and judgement of some of Tallahassee's Negro leaders we hold nothing but revulsion in our hearts for those who would creep up to one's house and burn a cross on the lawn . . . it is strange that a symbol of Christian tolerance and forbearance can be twisted into a symbol of hatred, terror and intolerance.

Other boycott leaders were also targets of violence. Dan Speed's grocery store windows were blown out by shotgun blasts on the night of January 15. Governor Leroy Collins was so concerned about the acts of violence that he issued a statement that he would intervene if violence persisted.[49] Collins was emphatic in his opposition to the terrorist tactics employed against boycott leaders despite his personal reservations about

Figure 7.2. The Reverend C. K. Steele, principal organizer of the Tallahassee, Florida, bus boycott, stands before his church holding a cross that was burned on the parsonage lawn the previous evening, January 1957. Florida State Archives.

the bus protest. It was a significant step for him to take, because violence went unchecked in other regions of the Gulf South where government leaders gave tacit support to segregationists.

A case in point: Four black churches were bombed in Montgomery, Alabama, on January 10, 1957. State government officials in Alabama had been adamant in their opposition to integration. Governor Collins's firm stand against violence probably helped to curtail more destructive behavior in Tallahassee.

Meanwhile, the bus company actively sought some means of getting the governor's suspension rescinded. The city commission approved a reserved seating policy on January 16, 1957. Bus drivers were authorized to assign numbered seats. The penalty for noncompliance by the passengers was a $500 fine and a sixty-day jail term. In an obvious attempt to avoid the scenario that started the boycott, dissatisfied passengers would have their fares returned and be allowed to vacate the bus. Steele was attending a meeting in Atlanta, which led to the founding of the Southern Christian Leadership Conference, when the new seating policy was announced. He returned in time to draft the ICC's response to the bus company's new proposal. The ICC rejected the reserved seating arrangement. Nothing but complete integration was acceptable.

The boycott entered a new phase when white students from FSU became active participants. Joe Spragna and John Herndon of FSU and Leonard Speed of FAMU deliberately defied the new seating policy on January 20, 1957. The trio was duly arrested. Court officials accused Reverend Speed of encouraging his son Leonard to violate the seating policy. The young men were tried and swiftly convicted in Judge Rudd's court. They received the maximum sentence for noncompliance. The three students bailed out of jail pending the outcome of their appeal. When the appeal was denied, they were ordered rearrested. Speed and Herndon surrendered to police, but Spragna jumped bail and never returned.[50]

The State Board of Control forbade all student participation in civil rights activity. Students at both state universities violated this rule sometimes at great personal cost. FSU graduate student John Boardman was expelled for taking two FAMU students to a party on FSU's campus. This violated the long-standing prohibition against social contact between FSU and FAMU students. Boardman told *Democrat* reporters that FSU administrators had offered to readmit him if he abandoned his public support of integration.[51] University officials denied Boardman's allegations, and his expulsion was upheld.[52] The collaboration of white and black students was a harbinger of the SNCC and Congress of Racial Equality (CORE) campaigns of the 1960s.

The ICC voter registration campaign reached its climax in February 1957. Reverend King Solomon Dupont was the first African American to run for the Tallahassee city commission in the twentieth century. Dupont was subjected to the same pattern of harassment encountered by other civil rights activists. The election was significant because Dupont received some support from FSU students.[53] In the February election, Reverend Dupont failed to unseat segregationist Davis Atkinson, but the election had a record black voter turnout. Atkinson received 6,804 votes and Dupont received 2,405 votes.[54] It was an excellent showing for a first-time candidate with limited resources. The political climate in Tallahassee had changed profoundly.

Steele and the ICC faced another challenge. The Florida legislature had established the Johns Committee to monitor alleged "subversive" activities.[55] Steele was summoned to testify before the Johns Committee in February 1957. He was concerned that the ICC's membership roll might be subpoenaed and used to harass boycott participants. As a precaution, most of the ICC's records were destroyed before Steele testified.[56] He testified on February 19, with NAACP attorney Francisco Rodriquez at his side.

The committee's questions did not focus on the ICC and bus boycott. Members were more concerned about the activities of the NAACP in Florida. This contradicts an article printed in the August 22, 1993, edition of the *Democrat*, which claimed the committee was established to destroy the boycott.[57] Articles published July 2, 1993, in the *St. Petersburg Times* confirm that the committee had a broader mission to curb "subversive" activity throughout the state.[58]

Ironically the bus boycott, which had begun in an atmosphere of tension and drama, ended in anticlimactic calm. The City Commission rescinded the segregated seating clause, which greatly cooled tensions. The final process of bus integration in 1957 was evolutionary rather than revolutionary. Perhaps this is why historians have not accorded the Tallahassee bus boycott the attention it deserves. By contrast, the Montgomery bus boycott culminated with national media attention. Some observers even incorrectly concluded that Tallahassee's boycott failed to achieve a clear victory as a result of the absence of a media circus.

The boycott was the first in a long sequence of related desegregation campaigns. The ICC continued to support civil rights activity throughout the 1960s. Between 1958 and 1963, the ICC provided administrative and financial support to CORE desegregation campaigns of stores, housing, theaters, and schools in Leon County. Because of the courage of FAMU students and C. K. Steele's inspired leadership, the Tallahassee bus boycott served as an impetus to substantive social change and improved race relations in the early period of the modern civil rights movement.

Notes

1. See Taylor Branch, *Parting the Waters: America in the King Years, 1954–63* (New York: Simon and Schuster, 1988); Aldon Morris, *The Origins of the Civil Rights Movement: Black Communities Organizing for Change* (New York: Free Press, 1984), 1–5; Marvin P. Dawkins and Gregory Padgett, "Tallahassee's Bus Protest: The Other Boycott That Sparked the Civil Rights Movement," *Negro Educational Review* 49 (July–October 1998): 101.

2. See C. U. Smith, *Migration, Education and Race Relations* (Silver Spring, Md.: n.p., 1996).

3. Morris, *Origins*, 86.

4. C. K. Steele, interview with author, Tallahassee, Florida, April 17, 1976.

5. Morris, *Origins*, 1–5; C. U. Smith and Lewis M. Killian, "The Tallahassee Bus Protest," *Field Reports on Desegregation in the South* (New York, 1958), 5.

6. Florida Bureau of the Census, *1960 Census Population* (Washington, D.C.: GPO, 1963), 11, table 9.

7. Morris, *Origins*, 2.

8. Florida Bureau of the Census, *1960*, 8.

9. Rev. A. L. Lowry, interview with author, Tampa, 1990.

10. Smith and Killian, "The Tallahassee Bus Protest," 5.

11. C. K. Steele, interview with author, November 12, 1975.

12. *Tallahassee Democrat*, May 27, 1956.

13. Steele interview, November 12, 1975.

14. *Tallahassee Democrat*, May 28, 1956. The house belonged to Mrs. Eloise Kendrick.

15. Mrs. Lara Dixie, interview with author, May 15, 1991.

16. Daisey Young, ICC secretary, interview with author, November 11, 1975.

17. The committee was composed of Elbert Jones, Tallahassee Civic League; Reverend Dan Speed, Tallahassee Business League; Reverend C. P. Allen, George W. Conoly, Reverend J. Metz Rollins, Dr. James Hudson, Reverend C. K. Steele, James Mobley, and J. H. Hobbs, president of the Community Defense Club.

18. C. K. Steele, interview with author, November 14, 1975; Morris, *Origins*, 1–5.

19. C. K. Steele, interview with author, October 3, 1975.

20. C. K. Steele, interview with author, November 1, 1975.

21. Henry Marion Steele, interview with author, December 11, 1990; C. K. Steele, interview with author, October 3, 1975.

22. Young, Christine Knowles, telephone interview with author, April 10, 1991, and Lara Dixie interview.

23. C. K. Steele, interview with author, April 28, 1976.

24. See Killian and Smith, "*The Tallahassee Bus Protest.*"

25. *Tallahassee Democrat,* June 6, 1956.

26. Steele interview, April 28, 1976.

27. See Adam Fairclough, *To Redeem the Soul of America: The Southern Christian Leadership Conference and Martin Luther King Jr.* (Athens: University of Georgia Press, 1987).

28. Steele interview, November 1, 1975.

29. Ibid.

30. Ibid.

31. *Tallahassee Democrat,* July 20, 1956.

32. *Tallahassee Democrat,* July 4, 1956.

33. *Journal of the House of Representatives Special Session,* July 23–August 1, 1956, 7, 23.

34. House Bill 76xx, *Journal of the House of Representatives,* July 27, 1956, 82–83.

35. Young interview.

36. *Tallahassee Democrat,* September 20, 1956.

37. Young interview.

38. *Tallahassee Democrat,* August 3, 1956.

39. Steele interview, November 1, 1975.

40. Judge John A. Rudd, interview with Jackson Ice, July 18, 1978, p. 16, Florida State University, Special Collections.

41. Steele interview, November 1, 1975.

42. Young interview; Steele interview, November 1, 1975.

43. *Tallahassee Democrat,* October 19, 1956.

44. *Tallahassee Democrat,* October 22, 1956.

45. *Tallahassee Democrat,* October 24, 1956.

46. *Tallahassee Democrat,* December 24, 1956.

47. *Tallahassee Democrat,* December 27, 1956; "*Cities Transit Company Inc. v. City of Tallahassee,*" *Race Relations Law Reporter* 2 (1957): 135, 137.

48. C. K. Steele, interview with author, October 14, 1976.

49. *Tallahassee Democrat,* January 17, 1957.

50. Steele interview, October 14, 1976; *Tallahassee Democrat,* January 20, 1957.

51. *Tallahassee Democrat,* January 23, 1957.

52. *Tallahassee Democrat,* January 24, 1957.

53. Steele interview, November 1, 1975.

54. *Tallahassee Democrat,* February 28, 1957.

55. *Laws of Florida Extraordinary Sessions, 1955–56, Chapters 31378–31498,* 396–97.

56. Steele interview, November 1, 1975.

57. *Tallahassee Democrat,* August 22, 1956.

58. *St. Petersburg Times,* July 2, 1993.

8

Local Leadership, the Biloxi Beach Riot, and the Origins of the Civil Rights Movement on the Mississippi Gulf Coast, 1959–1964

JAMES PATTERSON SMITH

In May 1959, several months before the Greensboro lunch counter sit-ins made nonviolent direct action protests a trademark of the 1960s civil rights movement, nine black citizens of the Gulf Coast resort town of Biloxi stepped onto a whites-only public beach in deliberate defiance of Mississippi's Jim Crow laws and practices. Without support or sanction from any civil rights organization, this "wade-in" marked the beginning of a new, public, and confrontational phase for the civil rights struggle in Mississippi. The black swimmers were forcefully removed from the beach with little fanfare. However, the leaders of this pioneering wade-in became the prime movers in a sustained mobilization of the black community on the Mississippi Gulf Coast for voter registration, repeated acts of civil disobedience, and a series of legal challenges to state-sanctioned segregation of public facilities. In the process, Biloxi exploded in the bloodiest race riot in the history of Mississippi.

Biloxi has been neglected in recent scholarly works on the civil rights movement. Scholars have focused on Mississippi's northwest Delta plantation region, the rural southwest, or the state capital at Jackson where the activities of the Student Nonviolent Coordinating Committee were concentrated in 1963 and during Freedom Summer in 1964.[1] However, the recent opening of the State Sovereignty Commission (SSC) files, completion of new civil rights–related Gulf Coast oral history interviews, and a major memoir by Dr. Gilbert Mason[2] make clear the precedent-setting significance of the Biloxi struggle. After withstanding arrest and violent reprisals for their repeated wade-in activities, the leaders of these protests created the first successful modern black voter registration drives in Mississippi. The movement's early success in voter registration dramatically changed Biloxi politics. The activists behind these Gulf Coast successes went on to file the first Mississippi public school desegregation suit, and they played a major role in revitalizing the Mississippi Conference of the NAACP in the early 1960s.

The ultimate success of the civil rights movement on the Mississippi Gulf Coast required courageous local leaders who were willing to risk their lives to initiate challenges to an entrenched, state-backed racial caste system. Constrained by political concerns and by legal doctrines that made responsibility for law and order a local matter, federal authorities were reluctant to intervene to protect civil rights activists from hostile state and city officials.[3] From 1959 until 1964, federal civil rights enforcement on the Mississippi Gulf Coast was always cautious, slow, and, at certain critical junctures, passive. No president could afford to ignore the sensitivities of segregationist James O. Eastland of Mississippi, chairman of the Senate Judiciary Committee from 1956 to 1979. The presence of Mississippi senator John Stennis as a high-ranking member of the Appropriations and Armed Services Committees created additional executive branch caution where Mississippi civil rights issues were involved.[4]

Although a steady stream of federal court decisions in the 1940s and 1950s built hope that change was possible, available federal legal remedies required much of plaintiffs whose lives and economic security were placed in immediate danger the moment their names appeared on a complaint. Thus, Charles M. Payne argues that in Mississippi civil rights history, the period before 1964 was particularly significant and dangerous. Mississippi activists had to work alone without federal protection, without outside civil rights workers, and without predictable coverage from the national news media. For these reasons national civil rights groups focused their attentions and resources elsewhere.[5]

Nonetheless, locally organized NAACP activity on the Mississippi Gulf Coast dates from immediately after World War II. In 1946, Vernando R. Collier, a war veteran and the president of the new Gulfport branch of the NAACP, voluntarily gave statements before the Senate committee investigating Theodore G. Bilbo's infamous 1946 race-baiting reelection campaign. Collier testified that on election day he was beaten in Gulfport and physically prevented from voting in the white Democratic primary. In other areas of the state, a few hardy souls persevered to create local NAACP branches in the late 1940s and early 1950s. In 1954, when the Supreme Court handed down its school desegregation decision in *Brown v. Board of Education*, NAACP membership in Mississippi stood at twenty-seven hundred. Surprisingly, in the summer of 1955, parents in five Mississippi school districts had mustered the courage to file petitions with their local school boards asking for school desegregation under the provisions of *Brown*.[6]

A wave of threats and economic reprisals sponsored by the White Citizens' Council immediately fell down upon the heads of petitioners whose names were routinely published in local newspapers. Petitioners were bombarded with hostile telephone calls and mail. They lost their jobs and business licenses or were forced to leave the area. The NAACP petition campaign thus died on the vine as harried parents withdrew their names.

Under duress, black leadership across the state became divided and paralyzed. The unexpected meanness of the White Citizens' Council's campaign coincided with a new wave of unsolved white-on-black murders. Just fifty miles from Biloxi, in the town of Poplarville, the last lynching in Mississippi history occurred in 1959. One month before the first Biloxi wade-in, a white mob dragged Mack Charles Parker, a Negro accused of raping a pregnant white woman, from his Poplarville jail cell. They killed Parker and mutilated his body.[7]

In February 1959, Sheriff J. J. Whitman reported to an SSC investigator, Van Landingham, that "he was sure that there was an active NAACP operating in Gulfport," but they "kept their movements and activities secret." Police Chief Herbert McDonnell reported that there was no NAACP chapter in neighboring Biloxi and that there were only two suspected members of the NAACP in that town, Dr. Gilbert Mason and mortician W. B. McDaniel. Chief McDonnell therefore reported confidently that he "did not expect any racial problems" in Biloxi. On the Mississippi Gulf Coast in 1959 as elsewhere in the state, the NAACP had dropped out of sight. With large numbers of their leaders facing economic reprisals and boycotts from the white power structure in Mississippi, most black citizens sought to avoid public linkage with anything the white community might label as NAACP-inspired.[8]

Mason, a native of Jackson, set up a medical practice in Biloxi in 1955. He had attended traditionally black Tennessee State University in Nashville and Howard University College of Medicine in Washington. During the spring of 1954, the Supreme Court handed down its landmark decision in the *Brown* case. James Nabrit III, the dean of Howard Law School, had helped argue the *Brown* case. Mason had heard Nabrit speak at Howard.[9]

With the promise of desegregation and equal rights on the national horizon, Mason found Mississippi in 1955 to be just as segregated as it had been ten years earlier when he left home to enter college. In Biloxi, the hospital was segregated, with African American patients confined to two open wardrooms in a somewhat dilapidated frame building called the colored annex, located just behind the main facility. There were separate white and black USOs to serve the thousands of airmen in training at Keesler Air Force Base. Movie theaters and even courtrooms were segregated. White bus drivers routinely ordered Natalie Mason, a master's degree social worker, to the back of the bus when she and her one-year-old son, Gilbert Jr., used public transportation for shopping or other business in Biloxi. The schools were segregated, and the city's all-black Nichols High School offered vocational courses but none of the heavy math, science, and foreign languages available in the college preparatory curriculum at the all-white Biloxi High School. Most glaringly, police and sheriff's deputies routinely removed black sunbathers and swimmers from the Mississippi Coast's greatest recreational asset, the twenty-six-mile-long county-maintained beach.

Upon arriving in Biloxi, the Masons paid a courtesy call on the community's retired black physician, W. P. Kyle. Mason told Kyle he intended to desegregate the local schools within seven years. He would file suit the moment his son entered school and gave the family the proper legal standing to do so. For Dr. Kyle, who had practiced medicine in Biloxi since 1919, this seemed impossible. "You might as well leave now," Kyle told Mason. Although they were to suffer greatly for the stand they took, and although they became very much aware of the economic reprisals and acts of violence perpetrated against known NAACP activists elsewhere in Mississippi, the Masons did not leave. They registered to vote and, just as the Biloxi police suspected, they joined the "secretive" Gulfport branch of the NAACP. Another young black physician, Felix Dunn, had just assumed the presidency of the Gulfport branch. An enduring friendship and political collaboration quickly developed between these two young men.[10]

Geographically and culturally, white Biloxians believed that they shared more in common with nearby New Orleans than with the small towns of the piney woods, northeast hills, or the plantation-dominated delta and river regions of Mississippi. In 1699, Biloxi became the first French settlement in the Gulf South and for a short time served as capital for the Louisiana Colony. As a testament of this heritage, Biloxi in 1959 remained a distinctively Catholic city within a state otherwise stereotyped as a Protestant-fundamentalist bastion. Moreover, plantation agriculture never established itself in southeast Mississippi. Isolated from the rest of the state, Biloxi developed a maritime orientation with fishing, seafood canning, and the production of forest products supplementing small farming. The coming of rail connections in the 1890s created the foundations of a modern beachfront tourist industry, while the labor needs of the seafood industry drew significant immigrant populations from southern Europe. World War II brought major naval and air corps installations to the Mississippi Gulf Coast, including Keesler Air Force Base.[11] All these developments added to a community image of itself as somehow more cosmopolitan than the rest of Mississippi.[12]

Some aspects of life in Biloxi and on the Mississippi Gulf Coast tended to support this congratulatory self-image in the white community. For example, almost everywhere in the United States in 1959, black physicians had difficulty getting hospital privileges. In Biloxi, Mason found that the hospital administrator, Emma Lou Ford, was willing to grant him hospital privileges, at least on a courtesy basis, but not voting privileges in medical staff meetings.[13]

Adding to the notion that the Coast was somehow different from the rest of Mississippi, Sheriff Whitman reported to SSC agents that there was no White Citizens' Council operating in Harrison County in February 1959. Moreover, the behavior of the circuit clerks who controlled voter registration in all three Mississippi Gulf Coast counties was far more liberal than that of clerks elsewhere in the state. Facing fewer clerk-imposed impediments, black citizens were able to register to vote in comparatively large numbers along the coast once the impetus to registration gained momentum and effective organization. The struggle to desegregate the beach provided that impetus from 1959 onward.[14] Despite the comparatively progressive treatment accorded its black doctor, the brutal racial confrontations that were to transpire on the Biloxi beaches from 1959 to 1963 greatly challenged the community's complacent self-image of tolerance and sophistication.[15]

The legal conflict came to center on the question of whether the Harrison County beach was privately or publicly owned. From the 1920s, the natural beaches lining the shore of the Mississippi Sound in Harrison County were subjected to a number of publicly financed improvement projects. In the 1920s, a seawall was constructed across the length of the county to protect the improved modern road that became U.S. Highway 90. The improved road and seawall separated beachfront property owners from the water to which their riparian rights guaranteed access and use. In 1947, a major hurricane caused serious new erosion that threatened to undermine the seawall and the adjacent highway it protected. Thus, the Harrison County board of supervisors requested federal and state funds to reconstruct the eroded beach as a barrier to protect the seawall. The federal funds came to the county with the stipulation that the reclaimed beach would be open to the public in perpetuity.

Despite these facts, police in the 1950s and 1960s routinely removed black swimmers from the beach whenever property owners on the north side of U.S. Highway 90 complained. In doing so, local officials acted on the theory that beachfront property owners continued to exercise undiluted riparian rights. This theory obviously ignored the federal mandate that the beach reconstructed with public money be open to *all* members of the public.[16]

As early as 1955, when he joined the Gulfport branch of the NAACP, Gilbert Mason had urged the branch to become active in securing free access to the Mississippi Gulf Coast beaches for all citizens. However, members showed little interest in challenging the whites-only practice. In view of the reprisals that had come down upon the heads of NAACP activists in other parts of the state in the wake of the *Brown* decision, the New York headquarters staff of the NAACP was also reluctant to endorse direct action in Mississippi. Moreover, state NAACP conference leaders such as C. R. Darden and C. C. Bryant counseled against sit-ins and public demonstrations out of concern that direct action would bring more violent white reaction.[17]

Notwithstanding the lack of commitment coming from the Gulfport branch, for several years Mason talked up the idea of direct action. From the network of friends that he had built in Biloxi through his medical practice, through his work as a Boy Scout leader, and through his active memberships in the Elks and Masonic lodges, First Missionary Baptist Church, and several local black fraternal societies, Mason found sympathetic spirits who pledged to go to the beach with him whenever he was ready.

On Thursday, May 14, 1959, without the sanction of any national or local civil rights organization, Mason announced his intention to swim. Murray Saucier, James Hoze, and Hoze's children, Jimmie, Gloria, and Jackie, joined Mason, his son, and two teenage Boy Scouts, Otha Lee Floyd and Adell Lott, for a drive to the beach. Along Highway 90, just south of the Old Biloxi Cemetery, they launched Biloxi's first wade-in.

A Biloxi police officer working a nearby traffic accident noticed them and yelled, "You know that you can't swim here." Mason demanded to know why he could not swim on a beach maintained with public money. The officer asserted that the beach was private property and ordered the black waders to get into their vehicles and follow him to Biloxi police headquarters. At police headquarters Mason continued to insist on knowing exactly why he was forbidden to use the beach. Apparently at a loss as to how to handle a highly educated and insistent black male, and with the police chief and mayor out of the office, the arresting officer and assistant police chief decided to let Mason go without entering a formal arrest. They admonished Mason that if he wanted to know about the legal status of the beach he would have to return when the police chief or mayor could explain things.

No doubt to their surprise, Mason returned the next morning. The police presented him to Biloxi mayor Laz Quave, a former sheriff of Harrison County. Quave could produce nothing to satisfy Mason's repeated demands to "see the book with this statute on it" denying black citizens use of the beach. Instead, Quave resorted to intimidation tactics, accusing Mason of "trying to get that NAACP down here" and "start trouble." In the face of Mason's admission of membership in the NAACP and his refusal to abandon his insistence on seeing "the book," Quave warned that if Mason went back to the beach, the police would "leave you down there."

Undaunted, Mason left the mayor's office and contacted Felix Dunn. Out of their own pockets, they retained a white Gulfport lawyer, Knox Walker, and paid him to research the legal basis of the authorities' claim that the beach was somehow private property. Walker's association with Mason and Dunn eventually brought threats on his life and lost him many white clients.

Walker's legal research demonstrated the substantial public investments in the seawall and beach going back over four decades. Most important, it revealed that federal funds had come to the beach project on condition that the beach be open to the public in perpetuity. Mason and Dunn presented Walker's research to the Gulfport branch of the NAACP, but branch members had no desire to act.

At this critical juncture in 1959, at a time when the vast majority of African Americans along the Mississippi Coast feared they would lose their jobs if they became in any way associated with the NAACP, and with the majority of the members of the "secretive" Gulfport NAACP branch refusing to seize upon the beach as an organizing issue, the civil rights movement on the Mississippi Gulf Coast might have been stillborn. Such an impasse might have defeated less energetic, less determined, or less creative leaders. Instead, Mason and Dunn went to work building an alternative countywide umbrella organization to carry on the struggle, and they began raising funds outside of NAACP sources.[18]

Their organization became known as the Harrison County Civic Action Committee, with Dunn serving as president. Its affiliate in Biloxi was known as the Biloxi Civic League, with Mason as its president. A similar organization sprang up, the North Gulfport Civic League, with Robert Cook as its president. The new coast umbrella groups harkened back to an earlier era of black activism in the late 1940s when the Mississippi Progressive Voters League claimed five thousand members and had a much easier time selling memberships than the NAACP.[19] While Mason and Dunn were NAACP activists, several of their fellow officers in the new coast civic leagues had never joined the NAACP. No one seemed to lose jobs after joining a local civic club.[20]

Between May 1959 and April 1960, as Mason recalled, the Civic Action Committee and civic leagues engineered a series of mass meetings aimed at galvanizing the black community for the struggle over the beach. Mason and Dunn quickly recognized that mass meetings to discuss the beach could be used to embolden people to register to vote. Organized voter registration drives became a part of rallying support for desegregating the beach. Vigor in African American voter registration in Harrison County, even at this early date, made SSC agents report to Governor Ross Barnett their suspicions that at least one successful white candidate for countywide office had pandered to gain the black vote in the 1959 Democratic primary.[21]

Mason and Dunn spoke wherever they could find an audience. Mason's diary shows that on September 3, 1959, he and Dunn met with Gulfport's Negro recreation director, Joseph Austin, and home repairman Eulice White to draw up a beach petition to be presented to the Harrison County board of supervisors.[22] The petition noted that the beach was "maintained and operated by and through Public Funds, and for Public use." It asserted that "Certain Citizens have been denied the public use" of the beach "as manifested by intimidations, molestations and frustrations by some of the police of the Municipalities located in Harrison County" and requested that the supervisors "STOP such impediments and guarantee the unrestrained use of the beach." On September 7, at a mass rally in an open field in the Soria City neighborhood of Gulfport, the Civic League endorsed the beach petition. Mason, Dunn, White, and Austin then signed the document and agreed to present it in person.[23]

At the October 5 meeting of the board of supervisors, Mason spoke for the group. His simple presentation of the petition provoked a hostile retort from board president Dewey Lawrence Sr. "If you go back down there again," Lawrence warned, "there's going to be bloodshed." Mason replied that blood flowed "in white folks' veins as well as in black folks' veins, . . . but we didn't come here to talk about blood, we're talking about the beach." Lawrence then pointed to the possibility that county officials might be willing to designate an improved beach area for "blacks only," and he asked Mason, "How much of the beach do you want?" Mason answered, "All twenty-six miles, every damn inch of it."[24]

In public, the board of supervisors declined to act but took the petition "under advisement."[25] In private, however, Stanford Morse, the board's attorney, contacted the SSC office in Jackson to request an immediate investigation of Mason and strongly hinted that he was looking for information to discredit him. Morris believed that he had "considerable information already" on Dunn that could be presented to "some grievance committee of the Medical Association," and he believed that local authorities could "handle" Joseph N. Austin and Eulice White.[26]

Within twenty-four hours of the presentation of the petition, the meaning of the word *handle* became clear. Austin and White were fired from their jobs, a cross was burned in front of Austin's residence, and a second cross was burned on the beach three nights later. Threatening telephone calls poured into the homes and offices of all four petitioners. Within forty-eight hours Eulice White asked the board to remove his name from the petition on grounds that he "did not want anything to come to breach the good relations between the races."[27]

Anonymous threats and harassments against Mason and Dunn intensified, and according to Mason, their attorney reported that the two men had made a Ku Klux Klan hit list in late 1959, along with NAACP field director Medgar Evers and several other known NAACP leaders across Mississippi.

Refusing to be defeated, an expanding circle of black leaders rose to meet the challenge. A group in Biloxi, who took to calling themselves BAM for "Black Angry Men," organized a guard detail for Mason. Local black leaders also created a special fund to provide relief to the families of Joseph Austin and Eulice White.[28]

The Harrison County Civic Action Committee and the Biloxi Civic League also began planning a major public protest to challenge segregation along the beach if the recalcitrant county board should refuse to act on the October 1959 petition. Operation Surf called for a mass wade-in across the entire county.[29]

Buoyed by their legal research and by growing encouragement in the black community, Mason and Dunn renewed their determination to raise the necessary funds for an independent legal battle to carry the issue to the Supreme Court. The mass protest, they reasoned, would lead to arrests that could be appealed through the courts. The officers of the Harrison County Civic Action Committee and the Biloxi Civic League appealed for donations nationwide from black lodges, fraternities, church groups, and professional associations.[30] However, according to Mason, most of the money accumulated to cover the anticipated legal fees and bail for Operation Surf came from the pockets of the local leaders themselves.

By January 1960, it was clear that the Harrison County board of supervisors had no intention of acting on the October beach petition. The Biloxi Civic League and the Harrison County Civic Action Committee intensified their preparations pointing toward a mass wade-in for Easter. As Mason remembered it, from January through April 1960, he and Dunn spoke in lodge halls and churches in Gulfport and Biloxi to keep the issue before the public. Always making clear their intention to integrate or desegregate the entire beach, it appeared to Mason that most people supported that goal and the idea of a countywide wade-in. Moreover, the beach issue became a teaching and organizing issue for new and intense voter registration, since it was easy to demonstrate that an increased black vote potential in the county might force the board of supervisors to reconsider its stand.[31]

After dozens of speeches in lodge halls and churches, Mason believed that a solid foundation had been laid for an effective mass protest. At the last public meeting promoting the mass wade-in, as Mason recalls it, everybody seemed enthusiastic. On Easter morning, April 17, 1960, Mason attended services at First Missionary Baptist Church in Biloxi and made a final appeal for members of the congregation to join him on the beach that afternoon. At the appointed hour, Mason drove into a beachfront parking bay a few yards east of the Biloxi lighthouse. To his surprise, after months of effort, he was all alone. Several miles to his west, Felix Dunn and his family deployed themselves on the beach at Gulfport and, like Mason, discovered that no one else was willing to defy Jim Crow practices. In due time, police officers confronted both men. Dunn was ordered to police headquarters, where Gulfport mayor R. B. Meadows gave him a lecture and released Dunn without making a formal arrest.[32] As these men understood their situation, they needed an arrest in order to bring the case to trial and begin the march toward the Supreme Court. Gulfport officials would not take the bait. The Biloxi police department did, and the Biloxi response unwittingly created the dynamic that birthed a genuine grassroots civil rights movement.

As Mason swam, a Biloxi motorcycle policeman appeared on the scene and called him out of the water, placed him under arrest, and took him to police headquarters. There Natalie Mason heard Chief Herbert McDonnell curse her husband and threaten to have him beaten up if he ever put his "ass on that goddamn beach again." Mrs. Mason signed a sworn affidavit in witness to the police chief's dire threat. Mason was charged with disorderly conduct and disturbing the peace. His trial was set for the next evening in Biloxi Municipal Court. Mason was determined to take the case all the way to the Supreme Court, alone if necessary.[33]

Going it alone turned out to be unnecessary. Mason's arrest and trial brought to his support what seemed to him to be the entire black community in Biloxi. Many young people volunteered for a new wade-in the following Sunday. One man's arrest produced a moment of action that required only coordination and encouragement. Mason supplied these ingredients. An indigenous civil rights movement was coming to life without outside help or support. No national civil rights organization presented itself to midwife this movement.[34]

From the Biloxi mayor's office to the Mississippi governor's office, the white establishment decided to counteract this sudden new civil rights interest. Judge Jules Schwan heard the testimony before a packed courtroom on April 18, but he declined to issue a public ruling. Instead, he announced that he would take the case "under advisement." SSC files show that this tactic was part of a plan formed by Mayor Quave and Governor Barnett. If they could delay things indefinitely, the white authorities believed that they could wear Mason out.

These obstructionist maneuvers did not take into account the response to Mason's risky challenge. Biloxi's black community embraced a new champion. Formerly apathetic and fearful citizens were energized. A mass meeting two evenings following Mason's trial produced more volunteers for a true mass wade-in. Under Mason's guidance, they agreed on a plan. According to SSC reports, on Friday, April 22, a delegation representing the Harrison County Civic Action Committee met with Sheriff Curtis Dedeaux to ask for security precautions for a nonviolent demonstration to take to the beach at three points in Biloxi on the following Sunday. Since the county maintained the beaches, these men believed that the safety of the demonstrators demanded that the sheriff's office be informed of the intended protest.

News spread quickly through state and county political establishments. State Representative Tommy Brooks asked SSC investigator Bob Thomas to make an immediate trip to Gulfport. By Friday afternoon, when Thomas arrived, Biloxi police officials had already developed an ominous plan to set loose a white mob on the protestors. Assistant Police Chief Walter Williams had told agents that the only way to take care of the problem was to "go out and beat the hell out of any Negro found on the beach." Now Chief McDonnell complained to Thomas that since there was no White Citizens' Council in Biloxi, there was no one "besides the police who could coordinate the activities of the citizens against this particular type of trouble." This being the case, McDonnell stated that the police intended to thin their ranks to "a sort of skeleton crew" on Sunday and that neither the chief nor his assistant would be on duty. McDonnell further stated that "a lot of people" had told him that "they would be around the beach in case Mason showed up, and they [the police] felt like the public could take care of this situation." In this spirit, the Biloxi police department planned to withdraw its units from the scene of the demonstration and let white hooligans take care of business. The white establishment in Biloxi thus reacted to its first major civil rights challenge with the same brutal intimidation tactics that many other supposedly less cosmopolitan Mississippi white establishments were to use over the next decade.[35]

On Sunday, April 24, 125 black protesters, including many women, children, and teenagers, assembled outside Mason's office several blocks from the Biloxi beach. As protesters organized into groups, they noticed whites with handheld radios reporting on their activities. Near the three predetermined protest sites, Biloxi police officers were observed talking to large groups of whites who were milling around just north of the beach. At each of the protest points, whites outnumbered black demonstrators by three or four to one. Still, when the black protesters ventured onto the beach, the Biloxi police cruisers quickly drove away. Mississippi Highway Patrol cars and units of the Harrison County sheriff's department also appeared in large numbers on U.S. Highway 90 near each of the protest locations. However, in the absence of Biloxi police units, the other police agencies refrained from interfering with the melee that soon developed on the sands just south of the highway. Ominously, the SSC agent reported Sheriff Dedeaux's radio command to his deputies to make no arrests.[36]

Once the black protesters established themselves on the beach, violence quickly erupted. Large gangs of white men and youths armed with pipes, chains, baseball bats, and cue sticks ran onto the sand. Fights broke out, and unarmed men, women, and children panicked and ran in all directions. Injured and bleeding, they fell to the ground. A black airman was beaten unconscious on the lawn of a house across the highway from the beach while the sheriff and several deputies stood at the edge of the seawall and watched. Thus began one of the worst race riots in Mississippi history.[37]

When Mason arrived at one of the points under attack, he abandoned his automobile and ran to the neutral ground in the middle of the highway where five white men with sawed-off cue sticks were beating two black youths. Mason waded into this fray, seized one of the cue sticks and began beating the white assailants. According to Mason, the nearby deputy who had refrained from intervening when the black youths were being beaten now jumped in and quickly placed Mason under arrest. Pointing to wounded demonstrators lying on the beach, the doctor insisted on delivering first aid and walked into the white crowd, cue stick still in hand, to help several of the injured into cars and on to the hospital. At the hospital emergency room, the admissions nurse dutifully labeled each demonstrator's injuries as "integrational" and recorded the names of their employers. This information made its way into the SSC files.[38]

As black demonstrators ran from the beach, white thugs pursued them north into the black neighborhoods. Violence spread over the entire downtown part of the city. White gangs stopped traffic, sometimes rocking cars, sometimes pulling black drivers out and beating them. Carloads of armed whites began racing through the black neighborhoods. A crowd of several hundred blacks gathered at Mason's Division Street office, and Mrs. Mason recalled that large crowds also gathered outside the Masons' apartment on Nixon Street vowing to protect the doctor and his family. Biloxi police cruisers that were nowhere to be seen earlier at the beach now roamed up and down the street near Mason's residence blaring warnings that Mason would be held responsible for any further trouble.[39]

As afternoon gave way to evening, cars loaded with white men and boys attempted to run down blacks in the streets. Shots rang out from some of these speeding vehicles, wounding innocent bystanders and shattering windows in black-owned businesses, clubs, and cafes. Newspapers reported that eight blacks and two whites made their way to the hospital with gunshot wounds. As the mayhem in the streets continued, nearly two dozen riot-related injuries were reported. At 10:00 P.M. Mayor Quave finally declared a curfew. Still, sporadic shooting continued into the early morning hours. Over the next several evenings, black service workers employed in the white neighborhoods of East Biloxi were unable to leave work without armed escort for fear of white gangs surrounding establishments known to employ them.[40]

Now, for the first time, after a solid year of sustained organizing, public petitioning, and protest, Mason and Dunn decided to call the NAACP for assistance and advice. Top national NAACP officials Roy Wilkins and Clarence Mitchell were visiting Meridian. From Mason's office the two local leaders explained developments in Biloxi to Wilkins and Mitchell. Wilkins pledged to send Medgar Evers to investigate.[41]

On Monday morning, two firebombs were tossed into Mason's office as sporadic acts of white violence continued. Providentially, one bomb burned itself out, and nearby residents doused the other before it could do serious damage.[42] When businesses opened, harried black residents made a run on hardware stores, purchasing guns and ammunition to protect themselves. Hearing that blacks were arming themselves, whites also rushed to purchase arms in such numbers that the sheriff of Harrison County issued a decree demanding registration of all firearms at his office. Few people complied.[43]

The gravest white-on-black reprisals came over the next two or three days as two black teenagers were murdered. Malcomb Jackson was arrested and released on the day of the riot for carrying a concealed weapon.[44] A short time later, the Pascagoula Police, fifteen miles down the coast to the east of Biloxi, arrested Jackson again. Jackson was then beaten to death in the Pascagoula jail. No witnesses came forward. Even more tragically, someone picked up Bud Strong, a mentally retarded youth, cut his throat, and dumped the body out in the Highway 90 median in front of historic Beauvoir mansion. Beauvoir, a shrine owned by the Sons of Confederate Veterans, was the post–Civil War home of Jefferson Davis. The symbolism of this murder was not lost on the black community. They pooled their resources to hire an investigator, but neither crime was ever solved.[45]

Elsewhere in Mississippi, similar violence and intimidation tactics had all but destroyed the NAACP. However, in the wake of the 1960 riot and killings, the Biloxi movement proved to be far more resilient than anyone could have expected. In the African American community in back of town in Biloxi, an aroused group, not affiliated with the NAACP or any other national civil rights organization, had followed an idealistic young leader onto the beach. Months of local organizing activity, mass meetings, voter registration, and issue education had preceded the wade-ins. Rather than breaking the movement, white violence and intimidation tactics solidified the black community in Biloxi behind its homegrown organizers, heroes, and martyrs.[46]

When Evers arrived in Biloxi on the morning following the riot, he found scores of people ready to form a new branch of the NAACP. He began taking sworn statements from people beaten or shot in the riot. On April 17, no one in Biloxi had been willing to face arrest on the beach with Mason. However, the events of April 24–25 were transforming. By the end of the week following the bloody wade-in, ninety-two Biloxians had signed up as charter members of the new Biloxi branch of the NAACP. Mason became its president. Perhaps more significant as a signal of a newfound black courage and determination, seventy-two people signed sworn affidavits announcing their willingness to testify about the brutality they had suffered and seen on the beach.[47]

Still further, the black community stepped in behind its leader to execute a successful targeted boycott of two white-owned businesses. The prime boycott target was Claude Trahan, the owner of a grocery and general hardware store who led one of the white gangs on the beach and supplied pipes and chains to those attacking the black waders. Faced with a drastic drop in trade, this man went out of business within the week. Likewise, a milk distributor, who fired black employees rumored to have gone to the beach, was also driven out of business in Biloxi. Both of these enterprises had done a large part of their trade in the black section of town.[48]

Mason and four other Negro demonstrators were tried, convicted, and fined for disturbing the peace—this time behind closed doors in the private office of a county justice of the peace. No whites were charged or tried.[49] Still, fearing more demonstrations the next weekend, the Mississippi legislature acted within seventy-two hours of the Biloxi riot to suppress any further beach protests. Breach of peace was declared a felony punishable by up to ten years in prison if anyone was injured or killed in a riot arising from a breach of peace. Moreover, breach of peace "on a coastal beach" became a crime punishable with a four-month prison term, whether or not injury or death resulted. Back in Harrison County, the board of supervisors appointed an all-white nine-man committee to recommend a compromise solution involving possible new designated all-black beach access areas in each of the coastal municipalities. Notwithstanding the fact that Mason announced his intention to appeal the issue to the Supreme Court, local officials believed that they had the instruments needed to regain control of the situation.[50]

However, unknown to the white leadership elite in Biloxi, the sworn affidavits that Evers had taken in the black community made their way up through the NAACP hierarchy and on to the Justice Department Civil Rights Division.[51] The 1957 Civil Rights Act gave the Justice Department power to bring suits on behalf of Negroes denied rights protected under the Constitution or under Reconstruction-era federal civil rights statutes. Federal intervention under the 1957 Civil Rights Act could potentially save plaintiffs time and money spent in state courts and administrative proceedings that were previously required when seeking enforcement of their rights under the old civil rights laws. Nonetheless, local officials in Biloxi in 1960 were little concerned that their actions might wind up in federal court. In fact, during the three years after the 1957 federal civil rights legislation passed, the Eisenhower administration had filed only ten suits across the entire South.[52]

Nonetheless, this sluggish federal enforcement record belied a changing attitude in the Justice Department that Mississippi officials failed to calculate. On November 17, 1959, Attorney General William P. Rogers publicly criticized the failure of a Mississippi grand jury to indict ten white men known to have lynched Mack Charles Parker in Poplarville, a town just fifty miles inland from Biloxi. Rogers asserted that the Justice Department would intervene in such cases under Reconstruction-era laws to prosecute local officials who act "under color of law" to deny citizens their federally guaranteed rights. In January 1960, the Justice Department had followed up by filing four civil suits against local officials in Alabama, Georgia, and Louisiana in a new move to deliberately test the scope of federal authority to initiate such cases under the 1957 act. On February 29, 1960, just seven weeks before the Biloxi riot, the Supreme Court upheld the constitutionality of the Civil Rights Act of 1957.[53] A new mood of confidence thus reigned in the Civil Rights Division of the Justice Department when the Biloxi beach riot affidavits arrived.

To the chagrin of the white establishment in Mississippi, on May 17,

1960, the anniversary of the *Brown* decision, the Justice Department filed suit on behalf of the black complainants in the bloody April 24 wade-in. The mayor of Biloxi, the police chief, the sheriff of Harrison County, and the county board of supervisors were accused in federal court of permitting or promoting mob violence to deny African Americans their rights to use the beach. This Justice Department intervention in Biloxi constituted the first federal legal assault on Jim Crow practices in the state of Mississippi.[54]

Hopes ran high in black Biloxi that the federal court might declare the Mississippi beaches open to all citizens before the end of the summer. Unfortunately, state officials, under the leadership of Governor Barnett, employed an array of delaying tactics before the sympathetic ears of segregationist Federal District judge Sidney Mize. The state frustrated all hope for rapid resolution of the beach dispute.[55]

The struggle for the beach, however, channeled the hitherto untapped energies of the black community into an unprecedented array of other civic activities carried out through the newly formed Biloxi branch of the NAACP. With municipal elections slated for the spring of 1961, black leaders in Biloxi focused more and more keenly on voter registration aimed at using the increasing leverage of the black vote to defeat Mayor Quave and his henchmen, who had unleashed the brutal mob violence on April 24.[56] Still further, in the fall of 1960, Mason and several members of the Biloxi branch began petitioning the local school board for desegregation as required under the guidelines for implementation of the *Brown* decision. Both actions were locally initiated and executed. In fact, the decision of the Biloxi branch to move forward with school desegregation efforts inspired Medgar Evers to ask permission of the New York office to join in filing a similar desegregation suit on behalf of his own children in Jackson.[57]

In the larger world of NAACP politics, historian John Dittmer found that the 1960 Biloxi wade-in challenged the more conservative leaders on the state NAACP board who argued vigorously against direct action tactics in Mississippi. On May 8, 1960, in an Atlanta speech, NAACP executive secretary Roy Wilkins made clear the national organization's support for the Mississippi Gulf Coast activists when he called for a national "wade-in" campaign.[58] In the fall of 1960, C. R. Darden stepped down as state NAACP president, and a new generation of more militant NAACP leaders came to the fore. Aaron Henry was elected president of the Mississippi Conference of the NAACP. Gilbert Mason and Felix Dunn were elected state vice presidents. The 1960 Biloxi wade-in also forced the national NAACP to reevaluate its position on direct action. In 1961, it endorsed Operation Mississippi, a strategy for desegregating the state's public facilities through civil disobedience.[59] Thus, determined local action, conceived, planned, and carried out without national support, created a strategic ripple effect which the Gulf Coast organizers could not have anticipated when they first ventured onto the forbidden Biloxi beach in May 1959.

In the spring of 1961, black Biloxi realized the first fruits of the vigorous and ongoing voter registration campaigns growing out of the struggle for the beach. In alliance with white moderate voters in the city, the black vote was strong enough to defeat the recalcitrant Biloxi mayor and elect a moderate Tulane-educated lawyer, Daniel Guice. Guice owed his 74-vote margin of victory to his solid support in the black community. Thus, in a true about-face in Biloxi politics, the Guice administration became the first in Biloxi's history to appoint black citizens to policymaking boards and commissions.[60] Moreover, black voter registration on the Mississippi Gulf Coast continued to succeed beyond all expectation. In 1961, when the Civil Rights Commission estimated that there were only 22,000 registered Negro voters in all of Mississippi, SSC agents believed that between 2,500 and 4,000 Negroes were voting in Harrison County. This meant that the home of less than 2 percent of the state's Negro citizens was home to between 11 and 18 percent of Mississippi's Negro voters.[61] Biloxi and Harrison County politics moderated greatly once it became clear that black voters held the balance in city and county elections. The beach had furnished the organizing impetus, and the ballot furnished the necessary power.

The last of the Mississippi Gulf Coast wade-ins occurred in June 1963. Frustrated with the interminable delays that Judge Mize allowed the state in the beach case, the Biloxi complainants petitioned Attorney General Robert Kennedy, urging him to "*act* to secure the rights of Negroes in use of the . . . beach by whatever maneuver as may be appropriate, including requesting the Court of Appeals to order Judge Mize to hold an early hearing on the merits of this case."[62] Consistent with his policy elsewhere in Mississippi and the South, Kennedy refrained from answering this petition and left the beach case in the unfriendly hands of Judge Mize. Any other course of action would have created serious difficulties with Mississippi's senior senator, James Eastland, chairman of the Senate Judiciary Committee and the patron of Judge Mize.[63]

Thus, by early 1963, civil rights activists in Biloxi reluctantly came to see the Justice Department as an unsatisfactory legal agent in their struggle for rights to use the beach. Once again, acting on their own initiative, the Biloxi activists conceived a plan to open a second beach lawsuit. They planned a new wade-in, hoping that it would bring mass arrests which would generate a separate court case under their own control. The new strategy was designed to move a case through the Mississippi courts, expecting defeat at every level, but with the intent of appealing directly from the state supreme court to the U.S. Supreme Court in order to bypass Mize's delaying tactics.

In light of the bloody episodes of the 1960 wade-ins and the 1962 Ole Miss riots, a new wade-in was understood to be very risky.[64] Still, the Biloxi activists determined to proceed. The change in the mayor's office in Biloxi created an opportunity for the Biloxi NAACP branch to actually negotiate the details of the safety guarantees for the 1963 wade-in. According to Mason, at Mayor Guice's request, the wade-in organizers agreed to adjust the date of the proposed 1963 demonstration to avoid a conflict with a major Biloxi tourist event, the blessing of the fishing fleet. Determined to avoid a repeat of the 1960 violence, Biloxi city officials promised protection for peaceful demonstrators, but warned that if property owners swore out complaints, they would have no choice but to make arrests. For their part, demonstration organizers hoped for white complaints and arrests as a means of launching the new legal challenge through the state courts.[65]

As fate would have it, in June 1963, a wave of demonstrations in Jackson ended with the assassination of the beloved Medgar Evers. Evers's funeral delayed the planned 1963 wade-in by one week. With a renewed sense of the potential dangers before them, seventy-five black demonstrators drove to the beach on Sunday afternoon, June 23, and deployed themselves near the Biloxi lighthouse where some of the worst violence had occurred in 1960. Once again, a large white mob gathered, numbering perhaps two thousand. This time, however, the Biloxi police, reinforced by officers from other coastal Mississippi towns, threw a protective line between the black demonstrators and the white crowds. About forty minutes passed before a complaint was filed. During that time white ruffians overturned an automobile and set the interior of Mason's car on fire. The police moved quickly to douse the flames. With the complaint formalized, police peacefully escorted the demonstrators off the beach and placed them in a hot moving van for transport to city hall and on to the county jail to await bail.[66]

The 1963 wade-in produced a new court case and a great and memorable spectacle but no violence. Police units quickly set up road blocks to prevent white troublemakers from driving into the black neighborhood.[67] That there was no repeat of the chaos of April 24, 1960, is a testament to the success of the massive, locally directed voter registration projects undertaken continually on the Mississippi Gulf Coast from 1959 onward. The black vote had changed the quality and character of Biloxi city government.

The direct action phase of the civil rights movement in Mississippi began on the Gulf Coast in 1959 without the benefit of outside organizers or the outside resources of any national civil rights organization. In this, the Mississippi Gulf Coast was unique. Elsewhere in Mississippi, organizers from the Student Nonviolent Coordinating Committee (SNCC) moved into communities from McComb in the south to Greenwood and Cleveland in the north with the objective of teaching local people how to challenge entrenched systems of racial oppression. The massive deployment of white and black students from outside the South to Mississippi during the Freedom Summer of 1964 reflected the SNCC model. Freedom summer drew unparalleled national attention to the plight of Mississippi blacks and mobilized national support for the Civil Rights Act of 1964 and the Voting Rights Act of 1965. However, when outside leadership withdrew and the freedom schools ended, the local organizations that SNCC had spawned tended to collapse.

This was not true of the wholly indigenous civil rights movement that came to life on the Mississippi Gulf Coast in 1959 and 1960. At a time when major national civil rights groups had given up on Mississippi, strong local organizations grew up around persevering leaders such as Gilbert Mason and Felix Dunn. As the movement on the Mississippi Gulf Coast matured, national civil rights organizations, especially the NAACP, became a tool to enhance the effectiveness of the local struggle, but the national organizations never called the shots, never set the agenda, and never supplied the leadership. These enterprising and enduring locally grown organizers and organizations pushed both the Justice Department and the state and national NAACP toward more vigorous stances. Biloxi activists filed Mississippi's first public school desegregation suit. These same activists went on to secure funding for one of the earliest Headstart grants in Mississippi, and they provided leadership to transform public housing initiatives on the Mississippi Gulf Coast in the 1960s.[68]

The more liberal attitudes toward black voter registration that characterized county circuit clerks on the Mississippi Gulf Coast enabled homegrown leadership to achieve influence more quickly than comparable black leaders in other Mississippi communities. Beyond this, the organizers of the Biloxi wade-ins endured years of threats and harassment and still stayed in the communities they had called to action. The power of that example of strength in adversity cannot be underestimated. In 1968, the Fifth Circuit Court of Appeals overturned lower court rulings and finally established the freedom of black citizens to use the Mississippi Gulf Coast beaches. The staying power of local leadership brought out untold strengths in others and thereby multiplied the power of the minority community.

The Biloxi branch of the NAACP is now more than forty years old. For thirty-three years Gilbert Mason was its president. Mason's advocacy record eventually brought him appointments to an array of local, state, and federal boards and committees, including the Mississippi Advisory Committee to the Civil Rights Commission and President Nixon's Mississippi Advisory Committee to the Cabinet Committee on Education.[69] Because indigenous leadership created and sustained the civil rights movement on the Mississippi Gulf Coast, a firm local base was established which proved capable of sustaining strong and continuous civil rights advocacy. The moderating influence of this self-sustaining force in the local politics of the Mississippi Gulf Coast in the 1960s, 1970s, and 1980s can scarcely be overestimated.

Notes

1. John Dittmer, *Local People: The Struggle for Civil Rights in Mississippi* (Urbana: University of Illinois Press, 1994), 86–87; Charles M. Payne, *I've Got the Light of Freedom: The Organizing Tradition and the Mississippi Freedom Struggle* (Berkeley: University of California Press, 1995), 4, 61–62. Like these secondary studies, Myrlie Evers's 1967 memoir also neglects Gulf Coast events in which her martyred husband, Medgar Evers, was deeply involved from 1960 to 1963 as NAACP Mississippi field director. See Myrlie Evers with William Peters, *For Us the Living* (New York: Doubleday, 1967; Jackson: University Press of Mississippi, 1996).

2. Gilbert R. Mason, M.D., with James Patterson Smith, *Beaches, Blood, and Ballots: A Black Doctor's Civil Rights Struggle* (Jackson: University Press of Mississippi, 2000). Mason, the principal organizer of the Biloxi struggle, refused all civil rights interview requests for more than thirty years. This refusal to talk ended only when his friend and

civil rights comrade Aaron Henry died without leaving an up-to-date memoir. Mason finally agreed to sit with me for several dozen hours of recorded interviews in the spring and summer of 1998. Without these interviews, the episode might well have been lost to the memory of the civil rights movement of the 1960s. This essay represents my own interpretation based upon recently released SSC files, newspaper accounts, and the wealth of insight gained in the interviews with Mason in 1998.

3. Mark Stern, "Eisenhower and Kennedy: A Comparison of Confrontations at Little Rock and Ole Miss," *Policy Studies Journal* 21, no. 3 (1993): 575–88.

4. Richard Kluger, *Simple Justice: The History of* Brown v. *Board of Education and Black America's Struggle for Equality* (New York: Random House, 1997), 753–55; and Dittmer, *Local People,* 153–54, 223, 372.

5. Payne, *Light of Freedom,* 4, 55–56; Dittmer, *Local People,* 52, 75–76.

6. Dittmer, *Local People,* 2–5, 50–51; Payne, *Light of Freedom,* 21–25.

7. Payne, *Light of Freedom,* 34, 56.

8. Gilbert R. Mason, interview by James P. Smith (Mason, USM interview), March 17, 1998, University of Southern Mississippi Oral History Collection, McCain Archive, Hattiesburg; Van Landingham to Director, February 16, 1959, SSC files, Victim Classification, ID 2-56-1-6-1-1-1, Mississippi Department of Archives and History, Jackson.

9. Mason, USM interviews, March 12, 17, April 7, 14, 1998.

10. Mason, *Beaches, Blood, and Ballots,* 36, 54–64, 71–73, 101–6.

11. Charles L. Sullivan and Murella Herbert Powell, *The Mississippi Gulf Coast: Portrait of a People* (Sun Valley, Calif.: American Historical Press, 1999), 43–69, 99–149.

12. Fairfax to Guild and Moffett, April 15, 1954, American Friends Service Committee, Mississippi Series, no. 1, p. 4.

13. Mason, USM interview, March 17, 1998.

14. Mason, USM interview, April 14, 1998; Van Landingham to Director, February 16, 1959, and Scarbrough memo, Harrison County, January 16, 1961, SSC files, Victim ID 2-56-1-6-1-1-1 and ID 2-56-1-77-3-1-1. See also Payne, *Light of Freedom,* 26.

15. Fairfax to Guild and Moffett, April 15, 1954, American Friends Service Committee, Mississippi Series, no. 1, p. 5.

16. Gulfport *Daily Herald,* May 9, 17, 18, 19, 1960.

17. Dittmer, *Local People,* 84–86; Payne, *Light of Freedom,* 32–33, 61–62.

18. Mason, USM interview, March 17, 31, 1998.

19. Dittmer, *Local People,* 25–35.

20. Mason, USM interviews, March 31, July 9, 1998.

21. Mason, USM interview, July 30, 1998; Van Landingham to Governor Ross Barnett, February 4, 1960, SSC files, Victim ID 2-56-1-21-1-1-1.

22. Gilbert R. Mason, diary for 1959, Mason Papers, in the possession of Dr. Gilbert R. Mason, Biloxi.

23. Copies of the petition made their way into Mason's SSC file, Victim ID 5-4-0-2-1-1-1. The substance of the petition was reported in the Gulfport *Daily Herald,* October 5, 1959, Jackson *Clarion Ledger,* October 6, 1959, and Memphis *Commercial Appeal,* October 7, 1959.

24. Mason, USM interview, March 17, 1998.

25. Jackson *Clarion Ledger,* October 6, 1959.

26. Van Landingham to Director, October 14, 1959, SSC files, Victim ID 5-4-0-1-1-1-1.

27. Gulfport *Daily Herald,* October 10, 1959.

28. Mason, USM interview, April 7, 1998.

29. Mason, diary, October 22, 1959.

30. Mason, diary, January 24, 1960.

31. Mason, USM interview, March 31, 1998.

32. Van Landingham, memo to file 5–4, May 4, 1960, SSC files, Victim ID 2-56-1-33-5-1-1.

33. Natalie L. Mason, sworn affidavit, April 17, 1960, Mason Papers; Mason, USM interviews, March 17, 31, and July 9, 1998; Mason, *Beaches, Blood, and Ballots,* 63–64.

34. Mason, USM interviews, March 17, July 9, 1998.

35. Bob Thomas, investigative report, "Beach Disturbances, Biloxi, Harrison Co., Mississippi, 4/22/60 to 5/2/60," in Thomas to Governor Ross Barnett, May 2, 1960, SSC files, Victim ID 5-4-0-50-1-1-1 and 5-4-0-50-12-1-1; Van Landingham to Director, October 20, 1959, SSC files, Victim ID 2-56-1-17-5-1-1.

36. Thomas to Barnett, "Beach Disturbances," May 2, 1960.

37. Biloxi *Daily Herald,* April 25 and 26, 1960; New Orleans *Times-Picayune,* April 25 and 26, 1960; Jackson *Clarion Ledger,* April 25 and 26, 1960; and New York *Amsterdam News,* April 30, 1960.

38. Mason, USM interviews, March 17, 31, April 7, July 9, 30, 1998; Thomas to Barnett, "Beach Disturbances," May 2, 1960.

39. Natalie Mason, interview by author, March 11, 1999; Biloxi *Daily Herald,* April 25 and 26, 1960; New Orleans *Times-Picayune,* April 25 and 26, 1960; Jackson *Clarion Ledger,* April 25 and 26, 1960; and New York *Amsterdam News,* April 30, 1960.

40. Biloxi *Daily Herald,* April 25 and 26, 1960; New Orleans *Times-Picayune,* April 25 and 26, 1960; Jackson *Clarion Ledger,* April 25 and 26, 1960; New York *Amsterdam News,* April 30, 1960; and Mason, USM interviews, March 17, 31, April 7, July 9, 30, 1998.

41. Mason, USM interview, March 31, 1998.

42. Mason, USM interview, April 7, 1998.

43. Biloxi *Daily Herald,* April 25 and 26, 1960; New Orleans *Times-Picayune,* April 25 and 26, 1960; Jackson *Clarion Ledger,* April 25 and 26, 1960; New York *Amsterdam News,* April 30, 1960.

44. Thomas to Barnett, "Beach Disturbances," May 2, 1960.

45. Mason, USM interview, April 7, 1998.

46. Mason, *Beaches, Blood and Ballots,* 65–87.

47. Mason, USM interview, March 17, 1998.

48. Alex Poinsett, "Biloxi Racial Flare-Up Causes $1 Million-Plus Business Loss," *Jet Magazine,* May 2, 1960, 14–17; Mason, USM interview, March 31, 1998.

49. Biloxi *Daily Herald,* April 26, 1960.

50. Biloxi *Daily Herald,* April 27–30, May 3, 1960; Jackson *Daily News,* May 2, 1960;

and Van Landingham, memo to file 5-4, May 5, 1960, SSC files Victim ID 5-4-0-55-1-1-1 and 9-22-0-9-2-1- 1.

51. Mason, USM interview, March 17, 1998.

52. "The Civil Rights Bill, What It Is and Where It Stands," *Time,* May 6, 1957, 26; "A New Law on Civil Rights . . . What Happens Now," *U.S. News and World Report,* September 6, 1957, 43; Kluger, *Simple Justice,* 753–54; Dittmer, *Local People,* 128.

53. "New Crackdown on the South: Laws of Reconstruction Era Dusted Off for Mississippi," *U.S. News and World Report,* November 30, 1959; "Fact Sheet on Civil Rights Outlook," *Congressional Quarterly Weekly Report,* January 1, 1960, 28; "What Congress Plans to Do about Negro Rights," *U.S. News and World Report,* March 14, 1960, 46.

54. Biloxi *Daily Herald,* May 17, 1960; Mason, USM interview, March 31, 1998.

55. Biloxi *Daily Herald,* May 18–21, 25, 27, June 6, 9, July 18, August 9, 11, 16, 18, September 6, 7, 20, 21, 23, 1960; Greenville *Delta Democrat Times,* August 18, 1960; Jackson *Advocate,* May 21, 1960; Memphis *Commercial Appeal,* August 10, 19, 1960; Jackson *Clarion Ledger,* May 8, 1962; and Mason, USM interview, March 31, 1998.

56. Biloxi *Daily Herald,* May 10, 16, 17, 1961; and Mason, *Beaches, Blood, and Ballots,* 115, 121–23.

57. Evers to Mason, October 18, 1960, and Evers to Carter, October 11, 1960, Mason Papers. See also Mason, USM interviews, April 7, 14, May 21, and July 30, 1998.

58. Biloxi *Daily Herald,* May 9, 1960.

59. Dittmer, *Local People,* 84–88.

60. Mason, USM interview, April 14, 1998; Biloxi *Daily Herald,* May 10, 16, 17, 1961; and Mason, *Beaches, Blood, and Ballots,* 115, 121–23.

61. *U.S. News and World Report,* March 28, 1960, 40; Tom Scarborough memo, Harrison County, January 16, 1961, SSC files, Victim ID 2-56-1-77-1-1-1.

62. Petition to Hon. Robert Kennedy, undated copy, Mason Papers.

63. Dittmer, *Local People,* 153–54, 194–97.

64. Ibid., 140–41.

65. Mason, USM interviews, March 17, 31, 1998, and July 16, 1998.

66. Mason, USM interviews, March 17, 31, 1998, April 7, 1998, and July 16, 1998.

67. Biloxi *Daily Herald,* June 12, 24, 25, 1963.

68. Mason, *Beaches, Blood, and Ballots,* 168–74.

69. Ibid., 184–91.

9

John McKeithen, Integration, and the Louisiana State Police

A Work in Progress

Roman J. Heleniak

The major battles of the civil rights struggle were fought in the states on the Gulf of Mexico. The critical period began in 1961 when John F. Kennedy took the oath of office, and for the most part the issue was not decided until African Americans gained some degree of legal equality following passage of the Civil Rights Acts of 1964 and 1965. After horrendous violence and bloodshed rocked Mississippi and Alabama, Louisiana managed to avoid major racial strife because its governor at this time, John McKeithen, chose not to replicate the fire-spouting defiance of Mississippi's governor, Ross Barnett, and two Alabama governors, John Patterson and George C. Wallace.

McKeithen safely led his state through three of the most tumultuous years of the civil rights struggle. First, he used state troopers to protect the lives of all of the state's citizens, including civil rights demonstrators. Second, in 1967, he directed the Louisiana state police to recruit African Americans for troopers at a time when many southern whites bristled at the thought of black policemen. To be sure, one can credit McKeithen with too much courage for integrating the state police. His action came after he received pressure from the state's black leaders, but he deserves credit for not playing the race card with a "stand in the schoolhouse door" performance.

Less than thirty-seven years after McKeithen's wise decision to integrate the state police, another governor, Murphy "Mike" Foster, appointed the first black superintendent of the state police. This occurred on July 12, 2000, when the state police went through one of those periodic upheavals that are a fact of life in most state bureaucracies. Col. W. R. "Rut" Whittington, abruptly resigned his position a few days after he sent a letter to his troopers informing them, "Despite the rumors that you may have heard, I intend to serve out my tenure as your superintendent of the Louisiana State Police."[1]

Foster immediately replaced Whittington with the department's highest ranking deputy superintendent, Col. Terry C. Landry. A twenty-two-year veteran of the state police, the 6'6" Landry was an obvious choice. He had the record, the experience, and the support of Whittington and most of the troopers.[2] Foster, a recent convert to conservative Republican politics, did not hesitate in naming a black to head the troopers, even though, in one of his first actions as governor, he had terminated the state's affirmative action and "set aside" programs.

Journalists Jack Wardlaw and Ed Anderson saw Foster's affirmative action stance as symbolism, a bone tossed to the conservatives. They pointed out that Foster's elimination of affirmative action only applied to the top appointees in state agencies. The remaining positions were civil service positions and/or subject to the 1964 Civil Rights Act.[3]

Louisiana was not the first state in the central Gulf South to name an African American to head its state police. Earlier in 2000, the new Democratic administration in Mississippi appointed L. M. Claiborne chief of the highway patrol. This was no small matter. Only four decades earlier, troopers in the region battled southern blacks and their white supporters with truncheons, tear gas, and even bullwhips when they challenged the South's segregation laws. In the central Gulf region, only Louisiana escaped the bloodletting.

The most serious confrontations between civil rights demonstrators and state authorities occurred after Kennedy's inauguration, even though the new president did not relish using federal forces to desegregate schools and facilities. In fact, Kennedy had employed President Dwight D. Eisenhower's use of federal troops in Little Rock as a campaign issue.[4]

Kennedy knew that he owed his close win over Nixon to black voters, and he tried to placate them with a go-slow approach using the Justice Department to back black voter registration drives in the South and appointing African Americans to administration positions.

Kennedy's cautious approach could not hold back the momentum of the civil rights movement. Now that African Americans had a president willing to champion their cause, they wasted no opportunity to challenging segregation in Alabama, Mississippi, and Louisiana.

How the authorities in these states reacted to more militant civil rights confrontations is an important element in this chapter. Alabama and Mississippi used state troopers to block demonstrators, and at times this meant using brute force. Louisiana, in contrast, used the state police to preserve the peace, even if it meant protecting the protesters. Therefore, a brief review of the events in Alabama and Mississippi will be essential to grasp the importance of what was done in the Pelican State.

When civil rights leaders chose to take more aggressive action than the administration's voter registration drives, they selected as their first course of action the testing of southern compliance with the Supreme Court decision banning segregation at facilities serving interstate travelers. Boarding two buses, black and white "Freedom Riders" left Washington on May 1, 1961, on a trip to New Orleans that would take them through much of the South, including Virginia, North Carolina, South Carolina, Georgia, Alabama, and Mississippi. The Reverend Martin Luther King Jr. warned the riders, "You will never make it through Alabama."[5]

King's prophecy came close to fulfillment. "The Heart of Dixie" would be the battleground of some of the bloodiest civil rights battles of the 1960s, primarily because two of its governors, Patterson and Wallace, used the police to defend segregation and to block civil rights demonstrators.

Patterson did little to protect the Freedom Riders. He could have used the highway patrol to provide a safe passage through Alabama and at bus stations along the route, but he entrusted those responsibilities to local law enforcement agencies. He had legal cover: According to Alabama law, the troopers could not enter one of the larger cities in the state without permission.[6]

As a result, when the bus pulled into the first stop in Alabama, the bus station in Anniston, a crowd of angry whites attacked the travelers with fists, baseball bats, and lead pipes. The local police had vanished. Eventually, members of the highway patrol arrived, but not in time to prevent the crowd from turning the bus over and putting it to the torch.[7]

The Freedom Riders encountered more violence at the bus station in Birmingham, where the safety commissioner, Eugene "Bull" Connor, gave Klansmen and other white extremists fifteen minutes to assault the riders before he sent in the local police.[8]

Following the Birmingham riot, Patterson ordered the Alabama troopers to escort the bus to the outskirts of Montgomery. After a helicopter sighted Montgomery policemen in the depot, the troopers left the caravan, ending the escort. The Montgomery police, however, disappeared moments before the bus pulled into the station. Another white mob savagely attacked the passengers, setting off a general riot in the state's capital.[9]

The Montgomery riot marked the end of the violence of the Freedom Rider episode. Patterson belatedly used the Alabama National Guard and some troopers to escort and protect the Freedom Riders when they headed for Jackson, Mississippi. At the state line, a large contingent of Mississippi guardsmen and state police took over and accompanied the Riders to the bus depot in Jackson, where authorities arrested the activists for violating the state's "whites-only" waiting room laws.

The National Guard/state police escorts and the arrests of the Freedom Riders in Jackson were part of an intricate deal worked out between Robert Kennedy, John Patterson, and Ross Barnett. They agreed to do what they could to prevent violence, thus eliminating the need to send in federal forces. In return, authorities in Alabama and Mississippi were allowed to arrest the Freedom Riders for violating state laws, putting the dispute in the courts and not the streets.[10]

Slightly more than fifteen months later, Barnett faced another desegregation showdown between his state and the federal government. In September 1962, after more than a year of court battles, the University of Mississippi was ordered to admit James Meredith as a student. In public, Barnett vowed that Mississippi would never "surrender to the evil and illegal forces of tyranny."[11]

Privately, for their own ends, Barnett and Robert Kennedy had a string of telephone conversations seeking some way to avoid violence and for Barnett to save face. Kennedy wanted Barnett's assurances that Mississippi law enforcement personnel would prevent mob violence.

Kennedy decided that Barnett could not guarantee Meredith's safety. Therefore, on Sunday, September 30, 1962, he ordered federal marshals to sneak Meredith on campus so that he could begin classes the next day. When the white mob surrounding the university got wind of the scheme, a massive riot erupted. Backed by some members of the highway patrol, marshals did their best to protect Meredith from an angry mob that grew larger by the hour.[12] At 7:25 P.M., as the violence escalated, the FBI intercepted a telephone call, supposedly from Barnett, ordering the troopers to pull out. Fifteen minutes later, most of them were gone; the rest remained on duty, only to get dosed with tear gas fired by the marshals. Kennedy had no choice but to send troops to Oxford. Before the first troops arrived the next morning, the marshals had suffered 160 casualties, 28 by gun-fire.[13]

John Patterson and Ross Barnett, at best, followed a policy of "malig-nant neglect" in their use of state troopers to maintain the peace, fearing that using the state police to protect demonstrators would be difficult to explain to angry white voters.

Greater violence occurred in the late spring and summer of 1963. Alabama's new governor, George Wallace, who warned in his inaugural address that his policy was "segregation forever," never entertained the thought of using Alabama troopers to protect civil rights demonstrators. In one of his first actions, Wallace appointed Albert J. Lingo, a racist busi-nessman with minimal law enforcement experience, to head the Alabama highway patrol. Given free rein, Lingo changed the name of the highway patrol to the Alabama state troopers and beefed up the intelligence gath-ering duties of the agency.[14]

Wallace also used the troopers to crack down on demonstrators. In Birmingham in the spring of 1963, they outdid that city's police in "main-taining order" and making arrests. In only a few weeks, Jamie Moore, chief of the Birmingham police force, would observe that local blacks hated "Colonel Lingo's head-beaters" more than they despised Bull Connor's Birmingham police.[15]

Wallace's troopers, however, would gain their greatest infamy in cen-tral Alabama's Dallas County, fifty miles due west of Montgomery. In 1964, local African Americans launched a voter registration drive, com-plete with parades and protest demonstrations. The actions of the state police in the small town of Marion caused the Montgomery *Journal* to describe Lingo's tactics as a "nightmare of State Police stupidity and bru-tality." In plain view of photographers, journalists, and television crews, his troopers bloodied a television newsman.[16] Worse would come at the Edmund Pettus Bridge in Selma, the county's largest town.

On March 7, 1965, about 525 demonstrators began what was adver-tised as a march to Montgomery on U.S. Highway 80. The march would take them over the Pettus Bridge east of town. On the western end of the bridge, they found the road blocked by fifty troopers and several dozen of the local sheriff's mounted volunteers.[17] A *Life* photographer captured the violence as troopers and Jim Clark's posse gassed, clubbed, and lashed the marchers with bullwhips.[18] That night, millions of viewers watched the carnage on television.[19] Selma became a synonym for police brutality.

John J. McKeithen understood full well the damage Selma did to Alabama's image and did not want a "Selma" in Louisiana. Although McKeithen won election as a segregationist, he did not adopt Barnett and Wallace as role models. Instead, he used the Louisiana state police to protect civil rights workers, even if it meant cracking skulls of segregationists. The contrast between McKeithen the candidate and McKeithen the governor caused the *New York Times* to praise him as a moderate shortly after he took office. McKeithen's conversion to moderation may have owed as much to political reality as it did to a genuine change of heart.[20] Although it is difficult to find any aversion to segregation in McKeithen's past, in his race for the governor's mansion in 1963 he did not open the campaign as a rigid segregationist.

On July 15, 1963, McKeithen, a public service commissioner for north Louisiana, formally entered the crowded gubernatorial race and released a fourteen-point platform.[21] He did not call for an all-out defense of segregation. Instead, he promised to work for the "improvement of Louisiana's national image by putting the needs of all the people before the needs of a selfish few." With nine others in the race, several of them major players, McKeithen had to carve out a segment of the vote large enough to earn him second place in the December Democratic primary.

Most observers gave the top spot to Delesseps "Chep" Morrison, former mayor of New Orleans, who ran as a "moderate" even though he described himself as a segregationist. Nevertheless, he had the small but important black vote in his pocket. He also had the backing of the state's most important paper, the New Orleans *Times-Picayune*.[22]

McKeithen's task was formidable. Morrison had the moderate vote. Shelby Jackson, state superintendent of education, owned the lion's share of the hard-core segregationist vote. But since Jackson was not considered a strong candidate, McKeithen had to move slightly to the left of Jackson and to the right of Morrison to finish second. U.S. Representative Gillis Long and former governor Robert Kennon were his major competitors for second place.

Of the two, Gillis Long represented the greatest threat. First, because he came from Alexandria, he would compete with McKeithen in the state's central and northern parishes, which McKeithen needed to carry. Second, Gillis had some claim to the Long voters because of his last name and kinship to "Uncle" Earl Long. McKeithen also had strong ties to the

Long legacy, having been Governor Earl Long's floor leader in the Louisiana House and a friend to the family. He was so close a friend, in fact, that Long's widow served as his state campaign manager.[23]

McKeithen did run as a segregationist, but a paternalistic one. Speaking in Lafayette, the candidate advised blacks that "neither marches on our nation's capital or legislation are the solutions to our racial problems" and that "colored people" must guard against being used by outside interests. "Nowhere in the world do colored people enjoy freedoms, privileges and prosperity more than in this country."[24]

McKeithen did attack outside interests, a favorite segregationist ploy. In Jena, Louisiana, he played to white xenophobia by promising to "keep this state out of the grips of the Washington powers," and no outsiders were better targets than the Kennedys.[25] In Clinton, McKeithen laid the blame for the racial violence on the Kennedy administration, and he went after Gillis Long for voting to expand the House Rules Committee, allowing the civil rights bill to clear committee and go to the floor for debate and a vote.[26]

Fortunately for McKeithen, his attacks on the president did not match in vitriol those of Robert Kennon, whose chances faded after Kennedy's assassination in November. McKeithen got lucky. Ten days before the assassination, the Shreveport *Times* criticized McKeithen for voting for Kennedy in 1960.[27]

McKeithen's tactics gained him a second-place finish in the December primary, but Chep Morrison's lead seemed insurmountable. Morrison had 295,000 votes, and McKeithen had 154,000, less than 20,000 more than Long. McKeithen seemed undaunted and boasted that he would win the runoff by 200,000 votes.[28] In truth, he knew that he faced an awesome task.

Since both candidates ran as segregationists, McKeithen had to move to Morrison's right. A little over a week before the January 11 runoff, the candidates debated one another, and several of the questions dealt with race, in particular the civil rights bill before the Congress. Morrison said, if elected, he would work with the congressional delegation from Louisiana "to do everything possible to defeat it," a bloodless response.[29]

McKeithen's answer provided angry whites with some raw meat. His delivery fooled people, and those who heard him for the first time were reminded of other race-baiting southern segregationists. He had a rapid-fire style, delivered with a heavy southern accent, and he knew which code words and phrases to use: He would utilize "massive but dignified resistance"; he would "not surrender or compromise or give up."[30] At worst, McKeithen only toyed with the Wallace style, but this hint of standing in the schoolhouse door appealed to many of the state's white voters.

To the surprise of some, McKeithen won the January election by beating Morrison, 493,400 to 452,390. One Baton Rouge paper did not regard it as an upset. Its reporter observed that McKeithen's victory followed a familiar pattern, the rural segregationist beating the "big city's 'reasonable' candidate." He added that being described as "suave" in the newspapers did not help Morrison.[31]

With a May inauguration, McKeithen had ample time to plan his administration. In early March he met with Governors Orval Faubus of Arkansas and Paul Johnson of Mississippi to "consolidate forces to restrict encroachment from Washington." The governor-elect offered no specifics. The Lake Charles *American Press* took issue with McKeithen and warned that if he planned to resist the federal government as Mississippi did at Ole Miss and as Arkansas did at Little Rock, he had better find some new advisors. The Lake Charles paper underestimated Johnson, who ran for governor as a staunch segregationist and, like McKeithen, embraced a more moderate position on integration after he entered office.[32]

Financial matters, not defiance, shaped McKeithen's approach to Washington. Louisiana and the federal government had conflicting claims on offshore oil revenues, a dispute that began in the Truman presidency, and a favorable agreement between the state and federal government on the exact location of the state's coastline could mean hundreds of millions of dollars for Louisiana. Sitting in the White House was Lyndon B. Johnson, who had a reputation for being a wheeler-dealer, a man who got things done, a politician who understood the meaning of quid pro quo.

In early April, McKeithen went to Washington, met with the president, and upon his return expressed enthusiasm about LBJ's chances in Louisiana in the November election: "Democrats have always done well in Louisiana." He also said that he had discussed the Tidelands dispute with White House officials.[33] He spent six months dropping hints about what he would do in the election. The Republican candidate, Senator Barry Goldwater, voted against the 1964 Civil Rights Act and enjoyed enormous popularity in the South.[34] On September 4, he hinted that he might be neutral.[35]

Political reporter F. E. Shepherd wrote in the Baton Rouge *State Times* that McKeithen's stance of neutrality cloaked his great respect for LBJ and his desire to maintain his long ties to the National Democratic Party. Endorsing the Johnson/Humphrey ticket would not have helped the president and would have destroyed McKeithen's political career.[36]

Shepherd read McKeithen correctly, for the truth of the matter is that McKeithen did admire the president. In a 1980 interview, McKeithen described Lyndon Johnson as a "great leader, a strong leader," and a better man than John Kennedy. He proudly noted that Johnson, a southerner, pushed the civil rights laws through to passage. In this same interview, McKeithen expressed little surprise that blacks had made great progress in the South since the 1960s. He felt that gaining the right to vote gave blacks justice and equal opportunity.[37]

In 1964, he kept such thoughts to himself. That is why McKeithen shadowboxed with the press about whether he would be in New Orleans to greet the president and Lady Bird Johnson.[38] Lindy Boggs, then the wife of U.S. Representative Hale Boggs and his successor following his fatal airplane crash, never doubted that McKeithen would be there to greet the president of the United States. Lady Bird would never have come without an invitation, she maintained. Both she and McKeithen told the president that since he had no chance of carrying the state, New Orleans would be a good place to give his only civil rights speech of the campaign.[39]

Historian and Johnson aide Eric Goldman believes that New Orleans was Lyndon Johnson's finest hour. Johnson spoke about how the South had been divided over race. After finishing his prepared speech, the president continued without notes. Looking at his audience, he discussed the 1964 Civil Rights Act: "I signed it, and I am going to enforce it, and I am going to observe it."[40]

McKeithen got the message. Not long after the election, he spoke out against racial violence following the death and possible murder of a civil rights worker in a fire near the north Louisiana town of Ferriday.[41]

Nonetheless, McKeithen observed with satisfaction that Louisiana had escaped major racial violence. He almost spoke too soon. Emboldened by the passage of the Civil Rights Act of 1964, southern blacks launched an all-out challenge to Jim Crow and did so with the backing of the federal judiciary. While McKeithen might complain about federal laws and judges, he did not openly defy Washington, and federal troops would not be sent to Louisiana while he was governor. Unlike Barnett and Wallace, McKeithen would use his state police to protect African Americans demonstrating for equal rights.

In March 1965, James Farmer, director of the Congress of Racial Equality (CORE), announced that his group had targeted two Louisiana towns, Jonesboro and Bogalusa, to test the 1964 Civil Rights Act, and he called for a federal "presence" in Louisiana. Farmer anticipated that Louisiana would use force to oppose integration.[42]

CORE struck first in Jonesboro in the northern part of the state where the black community launched a protest movement on two fronts. Blacks demonstrated against restaurants, cafes, and other public places for violating the public accommodations provisions of the Civil Rights Act of 1964. They also wanted improvements in the black schools. Until those problems were addressed, students would boycott the schools.[43] They were also angry because a popular coach, an active civil rights worker, had been fired.[44]

While it did not get extensive coverage in the national press, the Jonesboro movement marked a turning point in the civil rights movement. In this small Louisiana town, the black community abandoned Martin Luther King's tactics of passive resistance and nonviolence. Jonesboro's blacks saw what happened in Mississippi and Alabama; consequently, they had no confidence in the ability or the desire of state and local law enforcement bodies to protect them from violent whites. They decided to provide for their own protection by organizing a Deacons for Defense and Justice chapter. Instead of Bibles, these Deacons carried guns. If attacked, they would not turn the other cheek; if shot at, they would shoot back.[45]

With the aid of state troopers, Jonesboro's police erected temporary barricades to prevent anyone from entering or leaving the black section of town. With the state police working to maintain order, the governor decided to go to Jonesboro and speak to the demonstrators. An aide warned him, "If you go up there and talk to those niggers, you never will be elected to a thing in Louisiana." But the governor intervened, and the tense situation cooled off. By the end of the month, after McKeithen promised them that "various actions would be taken," all the students were back in school.[46]

McKeithen did not take a major political risk going to Jonesboro. The 1964 Civil Rights Act gave blacks a legal right to challenge segregation laws, and any southern governor who ignored such protests risked intervention by the federal government. Second, a voting rights bill was before Congress. If it passed, Louisiana's black vote, already over 163,000, stood to double. Furthermore, by the time McKeithen decided to go to Jonesboro, the brutal events in Selma all but ensured passage of the Voting Rights Act.[47]

McKeithen's determination to avoid a bloody confrontation met its severest test in CORE's other Louisiana target, the small city of Bogalusa in Washington Parish (county), home of a large paper mill owned by Crown Zellerbach. In 1965, the mill employed twenty-nine hundred local people, six hundred fewer jobs since the company began modernizing the plant five years earlier. On top of all other issues, black and white competition for a declining number of jobs exacerbated the racial tension in the town.[48] The clouded employment picture in the mill remained another reason why blacks demanded more city jobs, including the hiring of blacks by the police department.[49]

There were those in the state who did not see Bogalusa as a likely spot for major civil rights demonstrations. One journalist, Kenneth Englade, noted that blacks formed 40 percent of the population and almost a third of the registered voters. When the demonstrations began in January, local blacks sidestepped the emotionally charged issue of school integration to focus their concerns on public accommodations and employment opportunities with the city and downtown businesses.[50] Furthermore, the president of the Bogalusa Negro Voters League (BNVL), Andrew Moses, agreed with Bogalusa's mildly segregationist mayor, Jesse Cutrer, that outsiders should not come to Bogalusa. And while Moses spoke for much of the league membership, some of the younger blacks dismissed him as an "Uncle Tom."[51] Many of those who disagreed with the Moses approach helped organize a local chapter of the Deacons for Defense and Justice to protect the demonstrators and the black community. When they patrolled black neighborhoods, they rode around with their guns openly, and legally, displayed on the front seat.[52]

Whites also drove around town with guns in view: This was Klan country. The *Washington Post* reported that the Ku Klux Klan claimed a membership of eight hundred, probably an accurate figure, since Klan rallies usually attracted crowds of fifteen hundred or more.[53] A strong Klan presence caused John Doar, who headed the Justice Department's Civil Rights Division, to obtain a federal injunction prohibiting the Invisible Empire from interfering with equal rights demonstrations.[54]

The demonstrations staged by CORE and the BNVL began in January. This, in turn, caused the Klan to respond with threats and violence. Many in Bogalusa became Klan targets: black and white civil rights workers, white politicians who seemed unwilling to defy Washington, and white businessmen who refused to follow the Klan line. Klan victims endured physical assaults, political reappraisals, economic boycotts, arson, and drive-by shootings. In early February two white CORE workers claimed that a mob of whites chased and beat them. Although the local police and some of the city's leaders doubted the story, Col. Tom Burbank, superintendent of the state police, sent forty troopers under the command of Maj. Tom Bradley to Bogalusa to assist the city police.[55]

Much of the burden for maintaining peace in Bogalusa fell to the troopers because neither the chief of police, Claxton Knight, nor the commissioner of public safety, Arnold Spiers, had any enthusiasm for protecting civil rights demonstrators. Eventually, on July 10, Federal Judge Herbert Christenberry enjoined the pair from using violence or threats of violence against civil rights demonstrators.[56] Until that court action, the Ku Klux Klan had nothing to fear from the local police, and the Klan preyed on racial moderates with impunity.

The local radio station, WBOX, owned by Ralph Blumberg, a non-Louisianian, supported compromise. The Klan retaliated by urging local businesses to withdraw all advertising. When that did not silence Blumberg, night riders fired bullets into his building.[57] Another Klan foe, Lou Majors, the editor of the Bogalusa *Daily News*, attracted the same kind of treatment. He found burning crosses on his lawn several times. Like many others in Bogalusa, Majors drove around town with a gun beside him.[58]

Eventually McKeithen decided to send more troopers to Bogalusa. On April 21, three hundred state police were dispatched to the besieged city with orders to prevent serious violence by keeping the Deacons and the segregationists apart. This proved easier said than done, since the Klan and the Deacons continued to glare and shout at one another from opposite sides of the city's main street.[59]

When the antagonists were not reviling one another, they directed their venom at the troopers. This angered the Louisiana troopers because white policemen in the South had little experience being jeered and taunted by African Americans. The prospect caused some units of the state police from the northern part of the state to beg off going to Bogalusa. Maj. Morton "Moe" Kavanaugh from Ruston, for one, persuaded the superintendent to send troopers from another part of the state. "You'll have the goddamndest scuffle you ever heard of in your life," he told Tom Burbank. He feared that the blacks would spit in the faces of his men or make sexually explicit comments about the troopers' wives.[60]

Of course, the catcalling and shouting went in both directions, to Bradley's embarrassment. When he told a federal judge that he never heard policemen or others curse the demonstrators, the incredulous Christenberry asked him, "You hear all right?"[61]

Keeping angry locals from going at one another's throats was made more difficult by controversial visitors. A speech by black activist Dick Gregory was followed three days later by a major rally sponsored by the Klan-friendly United Conservatives of Bogalusa.[62]

Bogalusa survived both events, but the situation remained a tinderbox as armed blacks and whites continued to patrol their sides of town. On May 23, Mayor Jesse Cutrer moved boldly to defuse the crisis by presenting the city's five-step plan to the black community:

1. Immediate repeal of all ordinances giving segregation legal status.
2. Open all public facilities to all citizens.
3. Impartial enforcement of all the laws.
4. Employment of a Negro policeman in the "near future."
5. Giving qualified blacks consideration for city jobs.[63]

The five points did not appease Bogalusa's African Americans, and the demonstrations continued, as did the violence. Three hundred troopers could not patrol all the streets, nor could they prevent whites and blacks from taunting each other and throwing punches whenever a trooper looked the other way.

Hard-pressed city officials asked Judge Christenberry to issue a restraining order against the demonstrators, but he refused. He informed them that the city already had the authority to cancel any parade that posed a threat to public order. Christenberry did show a willingness to look at both sides by chastising black leaders for continuing the demonstrations after the mayor had promised to meet some of their original demands.[64]

On July 9, the governor increased the number of troopers to 325 following an altercation involving two Deacons for Defense and Justice. They shot a white man when he tried to prevent them from rushing a young black woman to the hospital who had been hit in the head by another white man.[65]

A timely move, for on July 11 the additional troopers may have prevented a disastrous racial clash when both blacks and whites staged major demonstrations. The pro-segregation march had the potential for serious trouble. The notorious J. B. Stoner, an Atlanta attorney with many Klan affiliations and a major suspect in a long list of bombings, led the parade.[66] Five hundred whites, many of them Klansmen, followed him, waving Confederate battle flags and practicing rebel yells. More Klansmen had been expected, but the state police blocked all roads coming into the city and turned away Klansmen from other parts of Louisiana and Mississippi. In the sky above the city, a state police helicopter carrying armed troopers searched for trouble spots. For all practical purposes, the state police had imposed a state of martial law in Bogalusa.[67]

For the next two days, the governor tried to convince the BNVL to declare a moratorium on the demonstrations. He even flew into Bogalusa to confer with BNVL leaders. They gave him a difficult time and refused to halt the demonstrations.[68] McKeithen returned to Baton Rouge and began work on establishing a state biracial commission made up of moderates of both races. McKeithen hoped that his Commission on Human Relations, Rights, and Responsibilities would help to defuse future racial crises.[69]

With the collapse of the governor's mediation try, the city, the BNVL, and the editors of the Baton Rouge *Morning Advocate* appealed to President Johnson to send federal marshals to Bogalusa. Instead, Johnson sent United States assistant attorney general John Doar.[70]

At this time, McKeithen tried to force the BNVL to compromise by recalling all but ninety of the troopers.[71] Many of the troopers breathed a sigh of relief. Since the troopers got little help from the Bogalusa police, the state police bore the responsibility of protecting the demonstrators by standing between them and the segregationists. Some local whites deeply resented the troopers, and "Louisiana's finest" had orders to stay out of roadhouses near Bogalusa and to travel in pairs when going to restaurants.[72]

After Doar arrived in Bogalusa, he spent several days watching the local police look the other way while white thugs and hooded Klansmen attacked marchers. On July 19, Doar asked Judge Christenberry to hold Spiers and Knight in contempt and to declare area businesses in violation of the 1964 Civil Rights Act. Christenberry complied.[73]

Doar's action marked the beginning of the end of the Bogalusa crisis, for on the following day, African Americans successfully integrated all but one of the restaurants. The sole holdout became a "private" club. In all others, blacks entered and were served with politeness, if not genuine friendliness. Proprietors had responded to the pleas of a large group of business, religious, and civic leaders who asked whites to act with moderation, if for no other reason than to spare Knight and Spiers from additional trouble. By this time, Farmer had left Bogalusa for New York and announced that CORE would cut back on some of its activities because of a shortage of funds.[74]

Bogalusa did return to "normal," and the city escaped the notoriety of being "another Selma." The Louisiana state police deserve much of the credit for preventing major violence, but the margin of victory was paper-thin. The ingredients for a new racial crisis remained. The Ku Klux Klan continued to be a strong force in Bogalusa and the surrounding region, and they seemed determined to fight integration every step of the way. But Klan intimidation had little effect on the militant young blacks in Bogalusa. For them and much of black America, things would never be the same. The Deacons pushed the struggle of African Americans for freedom in a new and more dangerous direction. The black writer James Baldwin saw it coming and, borrowing from an old spiritual, warned white America of "Fire the next time."[75]

The "next time" began with the Los Angeles race riot in August 1965. A routine traffic arrest by the Los Angeles police set off the spark. Six days of rioting resulted in thirty-four deaths, almost nine hundred people injured, four thousand rioters arrested, and property damage of $45 million. Most chilling were the news tapes showing American soldiers in tanks firing away at snipers on top of buildings.[76] Los Angeles marked the start of the nation's string of "long hot summers." Black Power and "Burn, Baby, Burn" became the new slogans of African Americans.

In Louisiana, Governor McKeithen expressed sorrow, "a sad and tragic thing," but something that could not happen in Louisiana. "Thank God that here in Louisiana we don't have citizens like that."[77]

Perhaps, but the potential for racial strife in Louisiana remained, especially in Bogalusa. Two years after the demonstrations in that city sputtered to an end, a new sense of frustration and disappointment fueled a new expression of black rage. In 1967 A. Z. Young and Robert Hicks of the Bogalusa Civic and Voters League (the new name of the Bogalusa Negro Voters League) expressed dissatisfaction with the lack of progress since 1965 and announced that the BCVL would hit the streets to publicize black grievances. The timing could not have been worse.

In the summer of 1967, urban rioting in the United States reached a zenith with major riots in Newark and Plainfield, New Jersey, Milwaukee, Detroit, and Cambridge, Maryland. Johnson appointed Illinois governor Otto Kerner to head a commission to study urban violence. Understandably, the burning of American cities contributed to a wave of "white backlash."[78]

On July 21, A. Z. Young announced that he and Lincoln Lynch of CORE would lead a march from Bogalusa to the parish seat, Franklinton, to protest Klan violence and the refusal of white juries to convict whites of crimes against blacks.[79] Word of the march perturbed McKeithen, especially if Lynch was participating. Lynch raised eyebrows when he objected to whites using the word *riot*. He much preferred *insurrection* or *rebellion*. He also said that Louisiana's blacks should be "willing to kill" for freedom. Lynch's remarks also outraged the black members of the governor's biracial commission, established in 1965. However, while he differed with Young's tactics, McKeithen ordered the state police to escort the eighty-six marchers.[80]

When this march ended without incident, Young launched a more ambitious project. On August 10, he would begin a ten-day, 105-mile march from Bogalusa to Baton Rouge. Major Bradley of the state police assigned twenty mounted state troopers to escort the marchers. Bradley did not think more would be needed, since most of the march would pass through the sparsely populated southeastern region of the state.[81]

Young did not give reasons for the protest, but said he would provide a list of grievances at a Sunday rally at the state capitol at the conclusion of the march. H. "Rap" Brown, a Louisiana native, chairman of SNCC, and a controversial if not incendiary black militant, would address the crowd. Earlier that summer, Brown told an audience in Cambridge, Maryland, that "violence is as American as cherry pie." Following his speech, African Americans went on a rampage and set fire to a dozen buildings.[82] Fortunately for Baton Rouge, Brown ran afoul of authorities in New York, who arrested him on a weapons charge several days before his scheduled Baton Rouge appearance.[83]

The march provided the evening news with plenty of action footage. Bradley miscalculated when he assigned a small number of troopers to escort the marchers. The 105 miles from Bogalusa to Baton Rouge ran through the heart of Ku Klux Klan territory. The combination of militant blacks and the Klan resulted in three outbursts of violence along the route. Had it not been for the state police and the National Guard, a tense situation in the small city of Denham Springs could have escalated into a major riot.

The Klan did not precipitate the first violence, although it is likely that some members of the organization took part. On the fourth day of the

Figure 9.1. Louisiana state troopers, deployed on orders from Governor John McKeithen, form a human cordon to protect black marchers between Bogalusa and Baton Rouge, August 1967. Louisiana State Police Archives.

march, a group of African Americans pulled up to a combination bar/ service station east of the town of Hammond in Tangipahoa Parish to buy some beer. After a brief conversation between the blacks and white patrons, shots rang out. One of the African Americans fired a shotgun into the crowd of whites, wounding five. Later that day, the sheriff of adjoining St. Tammany Parish arrested ten blacks who had been involved in the shooting, and four more were booked the next day. Several of those arrested had been with the march when it left Bogalusa.[84]

West of Hammond the marchers entered Livingston Parish, which a Baton Rouge newspaper warned was "Klan Land." Near the small village of Holden, a gang of whites suddenly appeared and attacked the marchers. Caught off guard, the troopers quickly recovered and restored order, arresting two white men in the process. As a precaution, the state police increased the number of troopers to one hundred.[85]

The following day, August 16, saw the most spectacular violence. As the marchers neared the small town of Satsuma, a column of white men, one hundred strong, approached them. When the two groups came abreast of one another, the whites attacked. Troopers quickly waded in and beat the segregationists with clubs and fists, sending four of them to the hospital. State police arrested nine more white men following the "Battle of Satsuma."[86]

A thoroughly irritated John McKeithen carped that the march was costing the state $2,500 a day and producing nothing but trouble. He also knew he had to provide more security for the last leg of the march and the Baton Rouge rallies. The latter had a real potential for violence in the governor's mind, although he had no idea that Rap Brown would be arrested in New York, preventing him from appearing in Baton Rouge. McKeithen did know, however, that the Klan planned to stage counter-rallies elsewhere in Baton Rouge at the same time as the CORE events. As a precaution, he beefed up the contingent of troopers to 175 and brought in 650 National Guard troops. The National Guard had no ammunition, but the sharp bayonets affixed to the ends of their rifles had a chilling effect on white hecklers.[87]

The show of force may have prevented a major riot in Denham Springs. There was a big turnout of the town's citizens, including women and children, who lined the streets and harassed the marchers and the state police escort, peppering them with eggs, cherry bombs, and empty beer bottles. Troopers arrested ten more whites in Denham Springs.[88]

Figure 9.2. Louisiana state troopers armed with automatic rifles, pistols, and batons attack white counterdemonstrators during the march from Bogalusa to Baton Rouge, August 1967. Louisiana State Police Archives.

Figure 9.3. Ku Klux Klansmen and supporters stage a counterdemonstration on the steps of the Louisiana state capitol during the closing hours of the August 1967 march. Louisiana State Police Archives.

With Rap Brown in custody in New York, the Baton Rouge rally participants had to be satisfied with intemperate, but not inflammatory, rhetoric from those who did speak. One orator exhorted the audience to be "boldly aggressive" and to go after the object "no holds barred"—fairly tame stuff to American ears when compared with the rhetoric of Rap Brown and other black militants.[89] Baton Rouge had dodged a race riot thanks to the absence of Brown and the presence of the troopers and fifteen hundred guardsmen. Other American cities that summer were not so fortunate.

The urban violence moved President Johnson to appoint the Kerner Commission to determine the root causes of black discontent, but Americans who kept up with the news did not have to wait for the commission to issue its final report. They knew that police action preceded almost every riot. Urban blacks hated the police, who were known as "pigs" in the inner city. White domination of state and local police forces added fuel to the fire. Common sense dictated that the best way to break down the wall of distrust between African Americans and the police would be to hire black policemen.

The message of the Kerner Report was not lost on Governor Mc-Keithen, who was also being moved forward by internal pressures from within the state to integrate the state police. His statewide biracial commission had been after him to recruit blacks for the force but had a difficult time getting him to move on the question until A. Z. Young threatened to lead more marches on Baton Rouge. The issue acquired increased urgency when the state police added another 150 white troopers. Mc-Keithen decided that the time was right to hire black troopers, and he asked people in his administration to recruit qualified blacks for the force.[90]

Given the racial climate in 1967, McKeithen's decision to recruit African Americans for the state police carried some political risk because many white southerners had qualms about black policemen.[91]

No one could play to these fears better than George Wallace, as shown in his 1970 campaign for governor, three years after the Louisiana state police integrated. One of his opponents, the "moderate" incumbent Albert Brewer, was asked by another candidate, a black man, to endorse a proposal to hire at least fifty black state troopers. Wallace knew a soft underbelly when he saw one, and he played to white fears with an outrageous radio spot. The sound of a wailing siren supplied the backdrop of the following narration: "Suppose your wife is driving home at eleven o'clock at night. She's stopped by a highway patrolman. He turns out to be black. Think about it."[92]

Three years earlier McKeithen did think about it, and in late August 1967 he asked the director of civil service, W. W. McDougall, to hire African Americans for the state police. Although a McKeithen appointee, McDougall demurred and claimed he could not break state law to hire a black. He noted that to become eligible for a trooper's position, the prospect had to pass a state civil service exam, and although fourteen blacks had passed the exam, none ranked higher than ninth on the test score. State law stipulated that civil service send only the names of the top three candidates to the hiring agency, and the department could pick from those. If two positions opened up, the names of the top five candidates would be sent to the hiring agency. Unfortunately, the black with the highest rank was ninth on the list.[93]

The governor, a persistent man, got his way. Later in the year, Mc-Dougall found some flexibility in the civil service rules and two blacks entered the state police academy.[94] Ernest Marcelle has the distinction of being the first to complete the training course and become a trooper. This was "heralded" as a step forward in race relations. Almost unnoticed, Anthony Sylvester, another black, was hired shortly after Marcelle and attended the same academy class. Marcelle said that he did experience some hostility during training but got along with the other troopers. Both began their service as troopers at the detective bureau in New Orleans on January 20, 1968.

Six months after it began, Marcelle ended his career as a trooper. When he first reported for duty, Marcelle got on the wrong side of his supervisor, Capt. Joe McDonald, and did not get the assignment he sought, narcotics. The captain told Marcelle that because of the publicity surrounding his employment he had to use him elsewhere. Six months later, he suspended Marcelle and took him off a case.[95]

Did racism bring to an end Marcelle's career as a trooper? It does not appear likely that McDonald targeted Marcelle for dismissal. First, McKeithen had made a commitment to integrate the state police, and in Louisiana it is not wise to antagonize the governor. Second, a city the size of New Orleans needed more black policemen, including troopers, because of the growth of the illicit narcotics trade and the ever present threat of urban violence.

In 1974, superintendent Donald Thibodeaux made a public plea for more black investigators because "whites find it difficult and dangerous to do undercover work in black areas."[96]

Thibodeaux's request illustrates that the state police remained serious about integration but were not enthusiastic about affirmative action. The troopers welcomed blacks who passed the written test and made it through training. Even Marcelle said that while he faced some resentment at the academy, once he reported for duty in New Orleans, he had no complaints about the way his fellow troopers treated him.[97]

It would be incorrect to label Marcelle and Sylvester as tokens, but their employment did not presage a great flux of black state troopers. The number joining the state police remained low, because blacks had trouble passing the written examination. Consequently, the percentage remained low and exposed the state police to charges of discrimination.

In 1975, the department did use "affirmative action" to attract new recruits, but the efforts were directed more at women than blacks. A 1975 recruiting brochure, which promised that the department was an "equal opportunity employer," for all practical purposes did away with height and weight requirements in order to attract women. The brochure stressed that the recruit's weight must be proportional with height. For example, someone 5' tall could weigh 100–140 pounds. Someone 6'10" could weigh 180–270 pounds.[98] In contrast, when Louisiana established the state police in 1936, all prospective troopers had to be at least 5'10" and had to weigh at least 160 pounds.[99] The new physical requirements did not shield the LSP from accusations of discrimination.

In 1991, Albert Bell Jr. filed suit against the state police for violating the 1964 Civil Rights Act. Bell said that he tried to join the force but could not pass the written exam because it discriminated against blacks. In September 1994, the Justice Department began investigating complaints that state troopers were making "derogatory racist and sexist comments" and that blacks and women faced a "pattern of discrimination." Justice Department officials provided the press with statistics that it alleged were proof of discrimination. Three will suffice. Of the force of 732 troopers, only 10 were women. In the previous five years, blacks constituted 30 percent of applicants but only 19 percent of those who became troopers. Finally, 32 percent of the population of Louisiana was black, but only 14 percent of the troopers were black.[100]

The numbers speak for themselves. What is more difficult to verify is the degree of racist and sexist remarks that women and African Americans had to endure. Surely there were some. The Louisiana state police has always had its share of racists and misogynists, and it is reasonable to assume that on occasion these white officers allowed their feelings to become known. The consent decree between the state police and the Justice Department, signed on August 11, 1996, does not include any specific examples of racist or sexist language, but it does provide that "any State Police Cadet or any applicant for that position, who believes that he or she has been discriminated against, treated unfavorably or harassed by an employee or agent of the LSP based on race or sex may complain."[101] While it is safe to assume that some troopers made derogatory remarks to black and female co-workers, can it be asserted that racism and sexism represented the views of a majority of the force?

The official journal of the Louisiana State Troopers Association, *Louisiana Trooper*, can be a useful source in determining the attitude of white troopers toward black and female coworkers, provided it is used with care. The journal's major purpose is to make the troopers look good. Established in 1974, the *Louisiana Trooper* is independent of state control and remains the voice of the troopers who exercise editorial control and monitor the magazine's content. It is fair to say the publication reflects the thinking of the membership.[102] The journal has always printed items about the affairs of the membership, articles of interest to troopers, editorials by the staff and guest writers, and "relevant" news items from outside Louisiana. Photographs accompany most articles.

A thorough examination of all the issues illustrates that the commitment of white troopers to a fully integrated state police is somewhat soft. For example, in the November 1975 issue of *Louisiana State Trooper*, there is a complimentary article about Senator James L. Buckley of New York, the conservative younger brother of William F. Buckley. Senator Buckley opposed "federally imposed racial and ethnic quotas" for policemen. The journal's editors did not comment, but their inclusion of this item in *Louisiana State Trooper* reveals their support of the Buckley position.

The November 1974 issue carried an item about a federal court ordering the Mississippi highway patrol to institute an affirmative action program "to overcome past discrimination" in hiring. Again, the editors made no comment about the case. The spring 1989 issue ran a short history of the Mississippi highway patrol but made no mention of its integration. The histories of other state police forces became regular features. The autumn 1988 issue spotlighted South Carolina's troopers but made no mention of black troopers. These brief histories, however, did mention other states hiring their first female troopers.

Yet the publication also promoted racial harmony. It included retirement announcements, death notices, news of awards won by troopers, and the affairs of the association. The last is important because it provides some information about the relationships between whites and blacks, especially at association-sponsored affairs such as basketball tournaments and other sports events. From the beginning, African Americans played on local troop teams. Winning teams rated a photograph in the publication, and the number of blacks in the pictures reflected the number in the association. In a 1975 issue, only one African American played on the team that finished third; the other teams had none. By 1982, the winning troop had two blacks on the starting five, Mike "Motion Lotion" Simon and Homer "Slow Motion Lotion" O'Neal.[103]

The *Louisiana State Trooper* allocates many of its pages to promotion announcements, including those of blacks. For example, in 1975 Joseph

H. Guillory of Troop K in Opelousas became the first black to win promotion to sergeant. A three-year veteran of the force, he was assigned to Motor Vehicle Inspection. Guillory discounted race. "I believe I was the best man for the position."[104]

Some issues carried news of troopers honored by the department or by community organizations. Black troopers have won their fair share of awards. The January 1982 edition carried two items, with photographs, of black troopers winning accolades. Trooper First Class Toxie Turner was shown with the superintendent, Col. Grover "Bo" Garrison, who presented him with the Life Saving Award. Garrison was also shown giving Trooper First Class Otis Blanson his second Ace Award; an Ace was awarded when a trooper arrested five drivers of stolen vehicles.[105]

Local communities gave some of the awards, indicating public acceptance of black troopers. In 1985 American Legion Post 175 in Metairie, near New Orleans, presented its Americanism Award to four troopers, three of them African American. American Legion Post 187 gave Sgt. Randy F. Johnson its Law Enforcement Officer of the Year Award. Johnson wrote the "Local Color" column for *Louisiana Trooper* (the name of the journal at that time). In 1990, the "Trooper of the Year" award went to an African American, Senior Trooper Edgar Clay. Clay once worked for the Kenner police department but left to become a trooper. "I wanted to be one of the best and I considered being a Louisiana Trooper to be best."[106]

Blatant racism is difficult to find in the publication, for every issue includes news of black troopers winning awards or participating in association affairs with their families. What is rare, however, is much open discussion of racial problems in the state police, especially the underrepresentation of African Americans on the force.

The *Louisiana Trooper* seldom dealt with the integration question. In the spring 1990 issue, Col. Marlin A. Flores discussed the complaints of the Louisiana legislature's Black Caucus that a disproportionately low number of African Americans had been admitted to the recent session of the state police academy, the first class in years. Flores met with the legislators to reassure them that "we are headed in the right direction," but he could not violate civil service regulations by creating another list and lower standards. Apparently nine blacks passed the exam but were not high enough on the list to be hired as cadets. Flores said that he showed the files of the nine applicants to two black troopers and they advised him not to hire any of them. The civil service regulations mentioned by Flores were a source of constant controversy, not necessarily because those regulations hurt black applicants.[107]

The Louisiana State Troopers Association (LSTA) had long complained about the unfairness of recruits having to take a civil service exam, as well as troopers having to take civil service tests for promotion. The troopers argued, with logic, that police work had little in common with most civil service jobs. The state police even had their own retirement system, and the LSTA lobbied to change the civil service status of troopers.

In the fall election of 1990, Louisiana voters had fifteen proposed constitutional amendments to consider. One of them, Proposition Six, if passed, would take the state police out of civil service and establish the Louisiana state police commission. The troopers knew they would have a tough fight on their hands winning voter approval, so the association hired one of the state's best political operatives, Gus Weill, to handle the campaign. Weill had to counter the opposition of some of the "good government" organizations who argued that approval of Proposition Six would cause a proliferation of similar systems for other state employees. Proponents countered that the state police were different from other workers and needed their own system. The troopers persuaded 51 percent to vote for Proposition Six.[108] Ultimately, this victory produced unintended consequences.

In 1991 Jane Orr, a veteran of the state civil service system, became director of the state police merit system. She had the task of developing a new set of tests for hiring and promoting that would be relevant to police work and would be administered by the Assessment Center. Orr indicated that the state police would move away from total reliance on written tests, because she believed oral examinations were equally good as an assessment tool.[109]

Part of Orr's job included the responsibility of recruiting African Americans and women. She acknowledged that neither would be easy to hire. For one thing, the state police had to compete with other law enforcement agencies, such as the Baton Rouge police department, which paid higher salaries and eagerly recruited women and blacks.

Somehow the state police would have to make law enforcement work more attractive. Blacks in particular have always been suspicious of the police. Orr commented, "I think a lot of blacks think of police as their enemy, and certainly what happened in Los Angeles [the Rodney King beating] hasn't helped the matter at all." She brought in as her assistant a young black woman, Debra Johnson, "a real ball of fire," thinking Johnson could be of great help in recruiting.[110]

Contrary to expectations, the new tests administered by the Assessment Center did not result in more African Americans or women being hired. The Justice Department charged that from 1990 to 1995, blacks continued to fail the written part of the entry-level examination at a higher rate than did white applicants. Blacks constituted 30 percent of applicants but only 19 percent of those who became troopers. Women fared somewhat better, as 25 percent of those who applied were hired.[111]

The state police, while not admitting that they were in the wrong, nevertheless signed a consent agreement with the Justice Department on August 29, 1996. The forty-six-page document required the state police to deposit with the clerk of the District Court of the Middle District of Louisiana the sum of $1 million to pay damages to those who failed to pass the entry-level examination. Claimants had to follow the court's procedure to file a claim and had to do so within forty-five days. The state police had plans to employ one hundred new troopers, and the consent decree stipulated that eighteen had to be black. Furthermore, new examinations that did not discriminate against African Americans and women had to be used.[112]

The consent decree resulted in some progress.[113]

Table 9.1. Diversity Hiring Statistics in the Louisiana State Police, 1996–2000

Year	Black Male	Female	Total
6/30/96	139	20	159
6/30/97	149	18	167
6/30/98	153	26	179
6/30/99	159	26	185
6/30/00	149	24	173

However, an examination of the data shows that ten of the twenty African Americans hired by June 30, 1996, left the state police between June 30, 1999, and June 30, 2000. The employment figures for women are only marginally better. This suggests that the problem of employing a sufficient number of blacks and women may not be totally attributable to racism and sexism.

The observations made above, however, do not obscure the fact that a racial divide persists in the state police. The white/black friction surfaced in the early summer of 2000 and swirls around Debra Johnson, who became the director of the state police merit system when Jane Orr retired in 1993. She incurred the wrath of LSTA president Charles Dupuy, who demanded that she be fired because of her testing procedures. He claimed that the tests "are not applicable to our job." She countered that the high scores of some black applicants caused the controversy. Dupuy replied somewhat disingenuously, "I don't think race was ever brought up." Dupuy knew better. Johnson has been under fire since 1996 for allegedly showing favoritism to black troopers who were taking tests for promotion. The controversy took an uglier turn when the soon-to-be-retired superintendent, Rut Whittington, chimed in and noted that the test results produced "odd variances" in scores compared with previous years. Specifically, white troopers claimed that some black troopers made dramatic improvements on their test scores from one year to the next.[114]

The summer of 2000 ended with no resolution of the dispute between the LSTA and Debra Johnson. One side or the other will probably take the issue to court; therefore, it is impossible at this time to pass judgment on the legitimacy of the LSTA's charges. However, whether the association is ultimately vindicated or not, there is evidence that the testing controversy has created friction between white and black troopers.

Trooper First Class Charron Leachman of the state police EEOC/recruiting office, an African American, believes the dispute is driving a wedge between the black troopers and the LSTA. Several have dropped their LSTA membership. Some have kept their membership but have affiliated with a new organization, the Central States Troopers Association, a group made up of black troopers from Louisiana, Mississippi, and Arkansas.[115] The existence of two separate trooper associations, one white, the other black, is not necessarily an indication that the integration of the Louisiana state police is a failed effort. On the contrary, if a free and equal society means choice, the black troopers are exercising their birthright.

Another positive point is that the testing controversy came to light just days before Col. Terry Landry became the first black superintendent of police, and his appointment is evidence that what John McKeithen began in 1968 has come a long way. Landry's visible presence has the opportunity to greatly reduce the importance of race in the Louisiana state police. However, the testing controversy and the rise of the Central States

Troopers Association are indications that a state police free of racial divisions remains a work in progress.

Notes

1. Baton Rouge *Advocate,* July 13, 2000.
2. Baton Rouge *Advocate,* July 23, 2000.
3. Jack Wardlaw and Ed Anderson, "Foster Orders La. Agencies to End Affirmative Action," New Orleans *Times-Picayune,* January 12, 1996.
4. Taylor Branch, *Parting of the Waters: America in the King Years, 1954–1963* (New York: Simon and Schuster, 1989), 434.
5. Ibid., 417.
6. Ibid., 444.
7. Ibid., 417.
8. Ibid., 421–22.
9. Ibid., 445.
10. Ibid., 469.
11. William Manchester, *The Glory and the Dream: A Narrative History of America, 1932–1972* (New York: Bantam Books, 1975), 944–45.
12. Ibid., 949–50.
13. Branch, *Parting of the Waters,* 665, 670.
14. Dan T. Carter, *The Politics of Rage: George C. Wallace, the Origins of the New Conservatism, and the Transformation of American Politics* (New York: Simon and Schuster, 1995), 108–9, 123–25.
15. Ibid., 170.
16. Ibid., 242.
17. Ibid.
18. *Life,* March 19, 1965.
19. Carter, *Politics of Rage,* 249–50.
20. *New York Times,* April 26, 1965.
21. Baton Rouge *State Times,* July 16, 1963.
22. New Orleans *Times-Picayune,* December 1, 1963.
23. Baton Rouge *Morning Advocate,* October 13, 1963.
24. New Orleans *Times-Picayune,* August 29, 1963.
25. Jena *Times,* July 18, 1963.
26. New Orleans *Times-Picayune,* September 22, 1963.
27. Shreveport *Times,* November 13, 1963.
28. New Orleans *Times-Picayune,* December 9, 1963.
29. New Orleans *Times-Picayune,* January 2, 1964.
30. Ibid.; Baton Rouge *State Times,* January 13, 1964.
31. Baton Rouge *State Times,* January 13, 1964.

32. Lake Charles *American Press,* March 15, 1964; Reid Stoner Derr, "The Triumph of Progressivism: Governor Paul B. Johnson Jr. and Mississippi in the 1960s," Ph.D. diss., University of Southern Mississippi, 1994.

33. Baton Rouge *State Times,* April 9, 1964.

34. Carter, *Politics of Rage,* 218.

35. New Orleans *Times-Picayune,* September 5, 1964.

36. F. E. Shepherd, "Just Plain Politics," Baton Rouge *State Times,* September 17, 1964.

37. John McKeithen, interview by author, January 15, 1980, Columbia, Louisiana, tape recording, Oral History Collection at the Center for South East Louisiana Studies at Southeastern Louisiana University, Hammond.

38. M. Hargroder, "McKeithen Not Sure He Will Be in N.O. to Greet LBJ," New Orleans *Times-Picayune,* September 24, 1964.

39. Lindy Boggs, interviewed by author, March 29, 1978, New Orleans, typed transcript, Oral History Collection at the Center for South East Louisiana Studies, Hammond.

40. Eric Goldman, *Tragedy of Lyndon Johnson* (New York: Knopf, 1969), 292–93.

41. Baton Rouge *Morning Advocate,* December 19, 1964.

42. Baton Rouge *Morning Advocate,* March 10, 1965.

43. Bogalusa *Daily News,* March 23, 1965.

44. Baton Rouge, *Morning Advocate,* March 10, 1965.

45. *New York Times,* March 12, 1965.

46. *New York Times,* March 29, 1965.

47. *New York Times,* April 26, 1965; Goldman, *The Tragedy of Lyndon Johnson,* 377.

48. Roman Heleniak, *Soldiers of the Law: Louisiana State Police* (Topeka: Josten's Publications, 1980), 92.

49. Baton Rouge *Morning Advocate,* May 24, 1965.

50. Shreveport *Times,* February 7, 1965.

51. Tupelo, Mississippi, *Daily Journal,* February 6, 1965.

52. Heleniak, *Soldiers of the Law,* 93.

53. *Washington Post,* January 11, 1965.

54. *New York Times,* July 19, 1965.

55. Baton Rouge, *Morning Advocate,* February 4, 1965.

56. *New York Times,* July 11, 1965.

57. New Orleans *Times-Picayune,* March 23, 1965.

58. *Washington Post,* January 11, 1965.

59. New Orleans *States-Item,* April 22, 1965.

60. Morton Kavanaugh, interviewed by the author, March 19, 1980, Ruston, Louisiana, typed manuscript, Oral History Collection at the Center for South East Louisiana Studies, Hammond.

61. Adam Fairclough, *Race and Democracy: The Civil Rights Struggle in Louisiana, 1915–1972* (Athens: University of Georgia Press, 1999), 368.

62. Baton Rouge *Sunday Advocate,* May 2, 1965; Baton Rouge *Morning Advocate,* May 5, 1965.

63. Baton Rouge, *Morning Advocate,* May 24, 1965.

64. *New York Times,* July 11, 1965.

65. *New York Times,* July 9, 1965.

66. Carter, *Politics of Rage,* 164–65.

67. Roy Reed, "Troopers Avert a Racial Clash," *New York Times,* July 12, 1965.

68. *New York Times,* July 13 and 14, 1965.

69. Fairclough, *Race and Democracy,* 378–79.

70. *New York Times,* July 15, 1965.

71. Baton Rouge, *Morning Advocate,* July 17, 1965.

72. Heleniak, *Soldiers of the Law,* 94.

73. Baton Rouge *Morning Advocate,* July 18 and 19, 1965.

74. Baton Rouge *Morning Advocate,* July 20 and 21, 1965.

75. Manchester, *Glory and the Dream,* 983.

76. Ibid., 1062.

77. Baton Rouge *State Times,* August 18, 1967.

78. Baton Rouge *Morning Advocate,* July 28, 1967; Carter, *Politics of Rage,* 349.

79. Baton Rouge *Morning Advocate,* July 22, 1967.

80. Ibid., July 24, 1967.

81. Ibid., August 11, 1967.

82. Ibid., July 26, 1967; Manchester, *Glory and the Dream,* 1081.

83. Baton Rouge *Morning Advocate,* August 19, 1967.

84. Baton Rouge *Morning Advocate,* August 14 and 15, 1967.

85. Baton Rouge *Morning Advocate,* August 16, 1967.

86. Baton Rouge *Morning Advocate,* August 17, 1967.

87. Heleniak, *Soldiers of the Law,* 101.

88. Baton Rouge, *Morning Advocate,* August 19, 1967.

89. Heleniak, *Soldiers of the Law,* 101.

90. Fairclough, *Race and Democracy,* 414; V. David De Villier, interviewed by the author, July 6, 2000, Baton Rouge, written notes, Oral History Collection at the Center for South East Louisiana Studies, Hammond.

91. Baton Rouge *Advocate,* September 30, 2000. James Benoit, in 1953, was the first black policeman hired in Lafayette, Louisiana. He could not carry a gun, nor could he give a ticket to a white.

92. Carter, *Politics of Rage,* 393.

93. Baton Rouge *State Times,* August 25, 1967.

94. Fairclough, *Race and Democracy,* 368.

95. Baton Rouge *State Times,* July 13, 1965.

96. New Orleans *Times-Picayune,* February 8, 1974.

97. Baton Rouge *State Times,* July 13, 1968.

98. Louisiana State Police vertical file, Louisiana State University Library.

99. *First Annual Report of the Department of State Police, State of Louisiana* (Baton Rouge: Department of Archives, 1936), 8.

100. Baton Rouge *Advocate,* January 18, 1995.

101. Ibid., August 30, 1996.

102. Over the years this journal has changed titles four times. The endnotes will reflect the title being used at the time of the citation. The author has discarded volume numbers because the troopers changed the "system" every time a new printer got the contract to publish the journal. A complete collection of the *Louisiana Trooper* and its antecedents is located at the LSTA headquarters, 8120 Jefferson Highway, Baton Rouge.

103. *Louisiana State Trooper,* March 1975, 8; spring 1982, 25.

104. *Louisiana State Trooper,* January 1975, 9.

105. *Louisiana State Trooper,* January 1982, 33, 37.

106. *Louisiana State Trooper,* spring 1985, 33; *Louisiana Trooper,* summer 1987; fall 1990, 53.

107. *Louisiana Trooper,* spring 1990, 35–36.

108. *Louisiana Trooper,* summer 1991, 56; Jack Wardlaw, "Louisiana Politics," New Orleans *Times-Picayune,* October 2, 1990.

109. *Louisiana Trooper,* summer 1991, 56, 64. Cindy Bell became the first female trooper in 1975. The issue of the *Louisiana State Trooper* that carried this news introduced a new feature: "Trooper of the Month." The "trooper" was a pretty girl posing for a cheesecake photo wearing a trooper shirt. *Louisiana Trooper,* October 1974, 11, 23.

110. *Louisiana Trooper,* summer 1991, 56, 64.

111. Peter Nicholas, "Capital Bureau," New Orleans *Times-Picayune,* January 18, 1995.

112. *United States of America v. the State of Louisiana, The Department of Public Safety and Corrections, and the Louisiana State Police Commission.* A copy of this document is housed in the Center for South East Louisiana Studies, Hammond.

113. Sgt. Lawrence McLeary, "Minority Statistics." Copy is in the Center for South East Louisiana Studies, Hammond.

114. Baton Rouge *Advocate,* June 28, 2000.

115. Charron Leachman, interviewed by author, Baton Rouge, Louisiana, July 21, 2000, written notes, Oral History Collection at the Center for South East Louisiana Studies, Hammond.

Contributors

Raymond Arsenault is John Hope Franklin Professor of History at the University of South Florida, St. Petersburg. Among his many publications are *Crucible of Liberty: Two Hundred Years of the Bill of Rights* and *The Wild Ass of the Ozarks: Jeff Davis and the Social Bases of Southern Politics*.

Roman J. Heleniak is professor emeritus at Southeastern Louisiana University. He is the author of *Soldiers of the Law: The Louisiana State Police*.

James G. Hollandsworth is associate provost at the University of Southern Mississippi. He is the author of *The Louisiana Native Guards: The Black Military Experience during the Civil War* and *An Absolute Massacre: The New Orleans Race Riot of July 30, 1866*.

Samuel C. Hyde Jr. is Leon Ford Associate Professor of History at Southeastern Louisiana University. He is the author of *Pistols and Politics: The Dilemma of Democracy in Louisiana's Florida Parishes, 1810–1899* and editor of *Plain Folk of the South Revisited*.

Joseph Logsdon was a professor of history at the University of New Orleans. He is perhaps best known for his editing of *Twelve Years a Slave* and *Creole New Orleans: Race and Americanization*.

Rebecca Montes is a Ph.D. candidate holding the dissertation fellowship in Texas and southwestern history at the University of Texas at Austin.

Gary R. Mormino is a professor of history at the University of South Florida, Tampa. He is the author of *Immigrants on the Hill: Italian Americans in St. Louis, 1882–1982* and coauthor of *The Immigrant World of Ybor City: Italians and Their Latin Neighbors in Tampa, 1885–1985*.

Gregory B. Padgett is an associate professor of history at Eckerd College.

Lawrence N. Powell is an associate professor at Tulane University. Among his publications are *Troubled Memory: Anne Levy, the Holocaust, and David Duke's Louisiana* and *New Masters: Northern Planters During the Civil War and Reconstruction.*

Houston B. Roberson is assistant professor of African American history at the University of the South.

James Patterson Smith is an associate professor of history at the University of Southern Mississippi. He is coauthor of *Beaches, Blood, and Ballots: A Black Doctor's Civil Rights Struggle* and the 1997 recipient of the *Journal of Negro History*'s Carter G. Woodson Award for best article.

Index

Russian and Soviet Music
Essays for Boris Schwarz

Russian Music Studies, No. 11

Malcolm Hamrick Brown, Series Editor

Professor of Music
Indiana University

Other Titles in This Series

Russian and Soviet Music
Essays for Boris Schwarz

Edited by
Malcolm Hamrick Brown
Professor of Music
Indiana University
Bloomington, Indiana

UMI RESEARCH PRESS
Ann Arbor, Michigan

Produced and distributed by
UMI Research Press
an imprint of
University Microfilms International
A Xerox Information Resources Company
Ann Arbor, Michigan 48106

Library of Congress Cataloging in Publication Data

Russian and Soviet music.

(Russian music studies ; no. 11)
Includes bibliographies.
1. Schwarz, Boris, 1906-   2. Music—
Russia—Addresses, essays, lectures. I. Schwarz,
Boris, 1906-   II. Brown, Malcolm Hamrick.
III. Series.
ML55.S398 1984   781.747   84-50049
ISBN 0-8357-1545-0

Boris Schwarz
(1906-1983)

Contents

1

Canon for Boris: A Musical Toast
(On the Notes of His Name)

Howard Shanet (U.S.A.)

* Special obbligato for the synod choir-man in Chekhov's <u>Seagull</u>.

2

Introduction

Dear Colleague,

On 13 March 1981 Boris Schwarz celebrated his seventy-fifth birthday—a fact not a little startling to me when I think of Boris. But his unabated energy, enthusiasm, and good cheer notwithstanding, he has indeed attained that venerable seniority, and the fact deserves notice. I propose a volume of essays to wish him *mnogoletie* ["many happy returns"] and to honor *one* aspect of his multifaceted career as a musician and musicologist. I have in mind Boris's scholarship in the area of Russian and Soviet music, therefore, I propose that a "Russian Connection" provide the unifying theme for all the essays to be included in the *Festschrift.*

The above invitation to make a seventy-fifth-birthday offering to Boris Schwarz achieved its purpose well, despite the thematic restriction placed on prospective contributors. The collection of essays gathered here from among Boris's friends, colleagues, and former students testifies eloquently to an abiding respect and affection for him. Many more contributors would gladly have joined us in testimony had they been given complete freedom in the choice of a subject. Still others were invited and might easily have written on the given "theme," but circumstances prevented their participation. All of us, participants and would-be participants alike, raise our voices in a chorus of "*Da zdravstvuet!* Long live!" and share *con amore* in this belated presentation to Boris Schwarz of a special birthday present with a "Russian Connection."

It's not the first "Russian Connection" in Schwarz's life. He was born in St. Petersburg, Russia, into a family of musicians: his father and four of his father's brothers and sisters were graduates of the St. Petersburg Conservatory; and there were professional musicians on his mother's side as well. During his conservatory years, Boris's father, Joseph, a noted concert pianist, student of Esipova and winner of the Rubinstein Prize, had been close to Leopold Auer (he even concertized with Auer), Efrem Zimbalist, and Mischa Elman, and it seemed only natural that his son should play the violin. Young Boris was never given any choice....

Barely six years old, Boris was transplanted from Petersburg to Berlin—new language, new environment, a difficult adjustment. He received there most of his education, general and musical. Although he studied violin with the eminent Carl Flesch, it was really his father who guided his development as a musician. Joseph was his son's constant piano partner, taught him the chamber music repertoire, and was the boy's tutor and mentor.

At age fourteen, Schwarz made his debut as a concert violinist and played publicly for the next five years. His debut as a soloist with Pasdeloup and Lamoureux was preceded by a study-year in the French capital (1925-26)—perhaps the most important period of learning and growing in the young man's life—which included lessons with the celebrated Jacques Thibaud and Lucien Capet, as well as courses at the Sorbonne. Afterwards, he began to concertize extensively throughout Europe, including a six-week tour of Soviet Russia in 1930 (as far as Baku and the Ukraine) that reawakened his interest in his native language and laid the foundation for his later preoccupation with Soviet music and musical life.

In September 1930, Schwarz returned to Berlin where he entered the University as a student of musicology, considering the field as "complementary" to his career as a concert violinist. This move established decisively the most characteristic feature of Boris Schwarz's life as a musician—the coexistence of performer and historian. He qualified for the seminar of Arnold Schering, who was aware of his student's background as a violin player and guided his research in that direction. It was Schering who recommended Schwarz's dissertation topic: "Die Entwicklung der französischen Violinmusik von der Klassik zur Romantik." During his years at the University of Berlin (1930-36), Schwarz also had classes with Johannes Wolf and Curt Sachs; but he never put aside his activities as a performer. Meeting Prokofiev in 1932, the twenty-six-year-old violin virtuoso and aspiring musicologist impressed the Russian modernist by playing Prokofiev's First Violin Concerto for him.

Then came the year 1933 and Hitler's "new order." Classified as a "non-Aryan," Schwarz's professional activities as performer and teacher were strictly curtailed by new laws. His foreign travels were limited because he was now handed a stateless-person passport. Finally, his hope to complete the doctorate at Berlin was shattered when he was denied admission to the oral examinations, despite the fact that Schering had already accepted his dissertation. It was a bleak time. Then, late in 1935, Schwarz received a letter from Princeton, New Jersey, signed "Elsa Alberti," the pseudonym used by Mrs. Albert Einstein when she corresponded with Germany. Young Schwarz and his father had often played chamber music with the renowned physicist during the 1920s, and now his wife was concerned about their friend's well-being. Would Schwarz like to have an affidavit from the Professor which would allow him to come to America and escape the Nazi terror?

A new life began for Schwarz when he arrived in New York in July 1936. Goodbye musicology—he had to make a living. With his first audition, he landed a job as concertmaster of the Ballet Russe de Monte Carlo, meaning not only a season at the Metropolitan Opera House but also a cross-country tour from the Atlantic to the Pacific and from Canada to Mexico. The job enabled him to salvage his parents from Germany within seven months, and on the strength of his *own* affidavit. His second job was as concertmaster of the Indianapolis Symphony Orchestra, just reorganized in 1937 under Fabien Sevitzky. While in Indianapolis, he also organized a string quartet, and for four summers taught and played at the National Music Camp in Interlochen, Michigan. It was there that he met Patricia, his Michigan-born wife.

Schwarz liked Indianapolis, but he could not get along with Sevitzky and decided to make a change. Engaged as a first violinist with Toscanini's NBC Symphony Orchestra for the 1938-39 season, Schwarz found the experience extraordinary, never to be forgotten, but it also convinced him that he did not wish to devote his life to orchestra playing.

Daniel Gregory Mason, whose Violin Sonata Schwarz had played, encouraged him to seek admission to Columbia University. His academic record at Berlin University was evaluated, and in September 1940 he was admitted to Columbia as a doctoral student with advanced standing. His class was Paul Henry Lang's first group of doctoral students, and Schwarz's colleagues included Dika Newlin, Ruth Rowen, and William Crosten. Still making a living as a violinist and conductor, he now started to rebuild his musicological base under Lang's supervision.

In mid-1941, Douglas Moore, who was department chairman at Columbia, recommended Schwarz for a vacancy at Queens College, the newest of the four city colleges of New York. The position called for a combination of violinist and conductor, plus historian. Schwarz got the job. He was to conduct the student orchestra, teach the history and performance of chamber music, and participate as well in the grandiose experiment of teaching "music appreciation" as a *required* subject for *all* students at the college.

Schwarz worked hard, worried a lot, and often felt frustrated by the novel experience of lecturing in a language not his own and dealing with undergraduate students of a totally different background. Then came Pearl Harbor and the enormous tensions of the Second World War. Schwarz was classified "4F" and assigned part-time to teach conversational German to young uniformed members of the Army Specialized Training Program. Graduate work at Columbia naturally slowed down during this period, and Schwarz was not able until 1949 to defend his dissertation on "French Instrumental Music between the Revolutions, 1789-1830."

By then, Schwarz had received tenure and promotion at Queens College. He was twice elected deparment chairman (1948-51, 1952-55). In 1946 he founded the Queens College Orchestral Society, a college-community

organization independent of the student orchestra, which he conducted for over twenty-five years. Perhaps his proudest achievement as a performing musician-academic was the establishment of the Queens College Faculty String Quartet (1952), which he headed as first violinist. He and his colleagues in the quartet—violinist Albert Mell, violist Carl Eberl, cellist Alexander Kouguell— managed to integrate their ensemble into the music curriculum at Queens with such courses as "The String Quartet in History and Performance" and "The String Quartets of Beethoven," during which the members of the quartet discussed the music with the students, then performed it in class. The Faculty Quartet also performed at various colleges and universities on the East coast.

Outside of the college, Schwarz joined the Piano Quartet of the *New Friends of Music,* which gave some thirty concerts in the East and Middle West in 1950-51, but after a year, he left the ensemble, having realized that he could not combine touring as a professional player with teaching.

In 1952, Schwarz received a Ford Foundation Grant for research in chamber music. He spent part of that year in Italy where he collected a great many microfilms of early chamber music, but the projected book did not materialize. Then in 1959-60, he received a Guggenheim Fellowship for research in Soviet music history and musicology. He planned a collection of abstracts and full translations of significant Soviet contributions in the field of historical musicology, but publishers showed no interest in such a project. The possibility of a book on the broader subject of music and musical life in Soviet Russia was suggested instead. In 1962, Schwarz received an ACLS Exchange Fellowship with the Soviet Academy of Sciences, and he spent the fall of that year in Moscow and Leningrad collecting the material needed for his *Music and Musical Life in Soviet Russia, 1917-1970.* The first edition of the book appeared in 1972 to general critical acclaim; it was awarded the ASCAP prize for 1972-73. A German translation appeared in 1982, and an updated American edition in 1983.

Returning from his research in the Soviet Union in 1963, Schwarz was eager to share his experiences with his students at Queens College. He introduced a course, "Russian and Soviet Music from Glinka to Shostakovich," which attracted a large cross-section of students. Somewhat later, he and a colleague specialist in literature introduced a seminar, "Russian Music and Literature in the 19th and 20th Centuries." Schwarz continued to teach this course even after his retirement in 1976, following thirty-five years on the faculty of the City University of New York. In recognition of his outstanding service to the Music Department at Queens College, a "Boris Schwarz Scholarship" was established in 1981.

Always the musician performer-*cum*-music historian, Schwarz's most recent book, *Great Masters of the Violin* (Simon & Schuster, 1983), seems to synthesize his lifelong dual professional commitments. Like the performer he has always been, he wants to reach his audience, to communicate, to share his

enthusiasm for music and musicians. His writing style in English—his *third* language, it must be remembered!—possesses vividness, directness, and distinctive personality. No wonder *Great Masters of the Violin* has been selected as an offering by two book clubs (the Music Book Society and the Performing Arts Society). But however engaging and enjoyable to read, Schwarz's writing is unfailingly informed by an impeccable scholarship, whatever the subject, be it the history of the violin and violinists, Russian music and musical life, or any other of the various topics encountered in his lengthy bibliography.

We pay tribute, however, not just to the man's distinguished scholarly record, which, after all, speaks eloquently for itself, but also to the man himself—humane, warm, and always generous with his time and professional expertise.

Da zdravstvuet Boris Schwarz ! We wish you *mnogoletie!*

It is my happy duty to recognize those persons who have made our tribute a reality and to thank them publicly for their help:

Ms. Nancy Basmajian completed the preliminary copy editing of Dr. Detlef Gojowy's essay on Roslavets and insured its idiomaticity.

Mr. John Wesley Clower worked closely with Professor Joachim Braun, serving not only as editorial adviser, but also as copy editor and typist in readying Professor Braun's contribution for publication.

Professor Laurel Fay kindly volunteered to translate Professor Grigory Shneerson's essay from the original Russian, in addition to contributing her own essay to our birthday collection.

Professor Lev Ginzburg's essay was also submitted in Russian, and I am most grateful to the colleague whose thoughtful and timely assistance saved me from having to translate it myself.

Mr. K. Robert Schwarz, our honoree's son and a former graduate student in musicology at Indiana University, wanted to share in our tribute to his father and willingly took over the task of assembling a complete bibliography of the writings of Boris Schwarz.

Both Professor Lev Ginzburg and Professor Grigory Shneerson passed away not long after having sent in their contributions. I regret that they cannot share our satisfaction in the project's completion.

Finally, to all of the authors whose private labors have created the real substance of our public birthday offering, I extend sincere thanks and warm appreciation. Your words, gathered now between these covers, symbolize the admiration and affection which we feel so deeply for a true musician-scholar and ageless friend.

Malcolm Hamrick Brown
Indiana University, Bloomington
September 1983

Boris Schwarz died unexpectedly on 31 December 1983, at a time when this volume of birthday essays was already in press. Active and productive to the end, Schwarz had joyously celebrated his *Great Masters of the Violin* at a publisher's party on 14 December 1983, and in the same period he had completed an article, "Khandoshkin's Earliest Printed Work Rediscovered," for a *Festschrift* honoring Gerald Abraham. As saddened and bereaved as his family, friends, and colleagues may feel, we should be consoled that when his time came, Boris and we were spared a lingering goodbye. He knew about our volume of birthday essays and the scholarly affection it expresses warmed his heart. Our tribute has been brusquely transformed into a memorial, which we offer in token of deepest sympathy to our honoree's wife, Patricia, and two sons, Joseph and Robert.

MHB
January 1984

3

The Melodies of the Ninth-Century Kanon
for St. Demetrius

Miloš Velimirović (U.S.A.)

The celebration of the feast of St. Demetrius (26 October, Old Style), the "protector" of the city of Thessaloniki in Northern Greece, dates from at least the fifth century A.D., commemorating a native of Sirmium (presently Sremska Mitrovica in Yugoslavia) who was martyred for Christianity during the rule of Diocletian's co-emperor Maximian.[1] The earliest known sanctuary dedicated to this saint appears to have been built in the second half of the fifth century and was partly destroyed by fire in the seventh century; thereupon it was rebuilt as a five-aisled church of sizable dimensions measuring 43 × 33 meters (ca. 141 × 108 feet). It is the rebuilt form of this church and the form of ritual practiced in it that must have been known to Constantine and Methodius before they departed on their mission to Christianize the Moravian Slavs;[2] the later history of this church is a subject outside the scope of this investigation.

Among the writings attributed to the "Slavic Apostles," as Constantine (who before his death in 869 became a monk, Cyril) and Methodius are often called, there is a *Kanon* for the feast of St. Demetrius, which they presumably prepared for their missionary activity. Ever since the first publication of the *Kanon*'s text, by Gorsky in 1865, it has been singled out as being different from the standard *Kanon* for that feast as found in the *Menaia,* the service books of the Greek Orthodox Church, which were used in the Byzantine religious tradition.[3] Gorsky published only a fragment of the text. Then in 1886, Jagić published the full text, mentioning that he knew of no Greek parallel for it.[4] Subsequently the text was re-edited in the catalog of Slavic manuscripts in the Synodal Library in Moscow.[5] Since then philologists and literary scholars who have studied this *Kanon* have made differing attributions, and opinions still vary about whether the author was Constantine/Cyril or his brother Methodius. The most authoritative discussion of this earliest known example of original Slavonic liturgical poetry (as distinct from texts translated from the Greek and thereafter utilized in religious services in the Old-Church Slavonic

language) is that by Roman Jakobson published in 1965 under the title
"Methodius' Canon to Demetrius of Thessalonica and the Old Church
Slavonic Heirmoi."[6]

The only study so far known which has dealt with the musical notation of
the *Kanon* as recorded in Moscow MS 435(160), the October *Menaion* from
the very end of the eleventh century, is that by Ladislav Mokrý, which was
presented at the 1964 conference on Old Slavonic music in Bratislava and was
subsequently published in 1966 in the proceedings of that symposium.[7]
Although unable to solve the problem of the *Kanon's* melodies, Mokry's study
did point out, as did Jakobson's, (and as was obvious ever since the publication
of the poem's extensive text) that before each of the *Odes* appeared an
indication of the "model" that was to be used by the singer when chanting the
text of the *Kanon* for St. Demetrius.

It may be appropriate to restate briefly a few basic points about the *Kanon*
as a poetic and musical genre in the Byzantine musical tradition. The poetry of
the *Kanon*, and by implication its accompanying melodies, began to be written
in the late seventh century, and in the eighth century, a number of important
poets cultivated the genre, among them Andrew of Crete, John of
Damascus, and Cosma "the Melodos."[8] Their poetry together with the Early
Byzantine neumatic notation of the melodies can be traced in the earliest
musical MSS *from the middle of the tenth century onward;* there are no earlier
known Byzantine musical manuscripts in existence.[9]

Any citation in manuscript sources of a *Kanon* text that dates from earlier
than the tenth century can be taken as indirect proof of the existence of
melodies that accompanied the text, *even though those melodies may not yet
have been notated.* Likewise, any citation of text *incipits* by themselves in Old-
Church Slavonic translation from a Greek-language *Kanon* can be taken as
proof that the *full text* of the Byzantine original also existed in Old-Church
Slavonic translation, along with the melodies taken over by oral transmission
from the Greek original. Therefore, as Jakobson has inferred, a citation of text
incipits translated into Old-Church Slavonic from Greek-language *incipits* of a
specific Byzantine Kanon which can be identified as having served as the model
for the Slavonic *Kanon* to St. Demetrius not only represents proof of the
existence of the full text of that *Kanon* in the Byzantine tradition, but also
proof of its full-text translation into Old-Church Slavonic and, by implication,
the oral transmission of the melodies associated with the Byzantine original.
The model in the case under discussion is the Greek *Kanon* in the Fourth Mode
(echos tetartos) for the feast of the Assumption of the Virgin, celebrated on 15
August in the church calendar.[10] This particular Greek *Kanon* is well known,
and it appears in numerous musical manuscipts from the middle of the tenth
century onward. Therefore, this "model" *Kanon* can easily be studied with its
melodies, which, beginning in the late twelfth century, can be transcribed into
modern musical notation without any serious problems. The fact that this

Kanon served as the model for the Slavonic *Kanon* for St. Demetrius implies that already in the ninth century the Christianized Slavs were acquainted with the melodies of that particular Greek *Kanon* and that in their own new Slavic creation, they chanted the text and its associated melodies in emulation of the Greek model.

The following steps are necessary to reconstruct the process described above and to retrieve the melodies to which the *Kanon* for St. Demetrius was sung:

1. Since the Greek text of the *Kanon* for the Virgin can easily be located, it is necessary to locate the Slavonic text which represents the translation of the Greek *Kanon*.
2. The Slavonic *Kanon* to the Virgin must then be compared to the *Kanon* for St. Demetrius.
3. Finally, the points of contact and the relationship of the neumatic notations must be established, followed by a tentative transcription into modern notation, which will thus make the *earliest example of Slavic poetry* resound again as it did centuries ago.

Through a set of circumstances, both fortunate and unfortunate, it has been possible to mesh available data and pursue this effort to what can be viewed, even if only in part, as a plausible reconstruction of the process whereby a set of Byzantine melodies was transmitted into the new Slavonic musical tradition.

The first step is a relatively easy one. The poetic and musical genre of *Kanon* consists of nine *odes*; each *ode* in turn consists of a "model-stanza," designated as *"heirmos,"* and its melody is then to be used in chanting the subsequent stanzas (known as *"troparia"*) within that single *ode*. The melodies for each *heirmos* of an *ode* are found in a type of Byzantine musical manuscript known as the *Heirmologion,* and the neumes that accompany the text in these MSS may serve as a virtual textbook example of the evolutionary process from tentative to specific designations of melodies in the history of neumatic notation and its use in Byzantium. By following the now accepted procedure in the study of Byzantine music, we can transcribe the melodies of each of the individual *heirmoi* as found in neumatic manuscripts from *ca.* 1200 A.D. onward.

The Slavic *Heirmologia* represent something of a problem, yet fortunately enough, there is one nearly complete manuscript of this type with neumatic notation from the 12-13th century, now in Moscow and known from its previous location as the "Voskresensky *Heirmologion.*"[11] While the structure and disposition of texts differs from most contemporaneous Byzantine manuscripts, it is nevertheless possible to locate within it all of the *heirmoi* for each of the *odes* that constitute the translation of the Greek *Kanon* for the feast of the Virgin. In short, we have access to the necessary Slavic translation

and its accompanying neumatic notation as used in the earliest layer of the notated Slavic musical tradition. While the neumatic notation found in Slavic musical manuscipts remains unreadable and cannot be transcribed directly, inferences are possible about the relationship of its implied melodies to those of contemporaneous neumatic notation in Byzantine sources, and a degree of plausibility in identifying "melodic counterparts" can be achieved. Therefore, the first step in this inquiry is to present the relationship of the Greek *Kanon* for the feast of the Virgin to its translation into the Old-Church Slavonic language and its accompanying musical notation. Table I demonstrates this relationship rather clearly and there can be no doubt whatsoever that the Slavic adaptors, in this case Cyril and Methodius and their assistants (assuming that the magnitude of the undertaking transcended the time available to a single person or even two persons involved in this type of project), skillfully created a poetic structure which, while differing in a number of details from the Greek original, nevertheless represents an impressive linguistic achievement.[12]

While the purely textual comparison of the syllable-count and the disposition of stresses and lengths are beyond the scope of this study, they may nevertheless be observed and followed easily in the example containing the *heirmos* for the First *Ode* of the *Kanon* for the feast of the Virgin. The crucial problem, however, concerns the neumatic notation. As has already been stated, there are no known Byzantine musical manuscripts before the middle of the tenth century, in other words, roughly a century *after* the period of Cyril and Methodius' mission to the Slavs. There can be no doubt that in their time the melodies were transmitted by an oral tradition which continued in force even after the melodies came to be supplied with neumes indicating their upward and downward movement. Although discrepancies do exist between individual manuscripts in the transmission of some *heirmoi*, there was nevertheless a rather stable melodic tradition which preserved the basic outline of the melodic skeletons, regardless of whether the melodies were learned orally or from their written form by means of neumatic notation. The presence of variants may well testify to the need for "adjusting" the melodies as a consequence of deviations in oral transmission which a new copyist then attempted to "fix" in his manuscript so as to reflect in writing what he had *heard* rather than what he had seen in another manuscript.

Basing ourselves on experience gained in the study of neumatic notation in the Byzantine musical tradition that spans at least five centuries (from the mid-tenth to the mid-fifteenth) and observing the *gradual evolution of melodies*, we can assume that a melody notated in the tenth century is probably essentially "the same" as that which was chanted in the ninth century; we accept this as our working hypothesis. If such a hypothesis is indeed acceptable, then we have for our purposes identified the "genealogy" of the Greek melody which was obviously in use (but with an always present possibility of minor modifications!) from a pre-notational stage down the centuries to the period

when we can find it and chant it directly from the readily decipherable manuscripts.

We are assuming that both Cyril and Methodius were familiar with the melodies used in the services of the Greek church. Yet they were unable to write them down, since no form of musical notation was in use in their lifetimes. Questions therefore arise about the appearance of neumatic notation in Slavic musical manuscripts and about the possibility of inferring the outlines of such melodies, let alone about their transcription into modern notation. In order to answer such questions we must remember that in Byzantium the melodies were written down only in the mid-tenth century and that the transmission of neumatic notation to the Slavs took place in Russia in the eleventh century. For at least two centuries we have to infer the presence of an oral tradition which transmitted melodies until the time when they began to be written down. For the tentative transcription of these melodies we shall submit documentation supporting our working hypothesis.

The process of converting the Slavs to Christianity extended over decades if not centuries. While the earliest documented and best known missionary activity was that of Cyril and Methodius, who translated service books and transmitted Byzantine religious practices to the Moravian Slavs, the crucial documentation for our purposes comes from Russian sources. The Russians were "officially" converted to Christianity in 988 A.D. This is the same period in which the use of neumatic notation may already be found in Byzantium. Turning to the Russian domain, good reasons exist to trace the beginnings of an intensive writing and copying of musical manuscripts in Russia to approximately the middle of the eleventh century. Indeed, the paleographic study of neumatic notation in Slavonic manuscripts of Russian origin appears to support the statements encountered in the Russian *Primary Chronicle* that describes a flowering of literary activities, especially of translating and copying manuscripts, during the reign of Yaroslav the Wise, who ruled until 1054 A.D. In short, the earliest use of any kind of neumatic notation among the Slavs seems to date from about the middle of the eleventh century, although most of the sources still extant date from a somewhat later period—from the latter part of the eleventh and, more profusely, from the twelfth and thirteenth centuries.[13]

The examples of neumatic notations in table 1[14] clearly show that the relationship of the neumes in both Byzantine and Slavic musical manuscripts is rather close, and while by no means identical in every detail, it is sufficiently close to presume the use of *similar* melodic outlines in this hymn, at least in the crucial parts of the text, i.e., at the beginnings and endings of verses, while in between, some variation in the neumes is observable. The presence of signs for stresses and lengths, especially at the endings, is sufficient proof of the near identity of the melodic outline which, while Byzantine in origin, was emulated to say the least, in the Slavic version of the *Kanon* to the Virgin.

Table 1 presents the four verses of *Heirmos* for *Ode* 1 of the *Kanon* for the Virgin. In its central and framed part appears the Slavic translation of the Greek text (located above the frame) with its neumatic notation as found in the Voskresensky *Heirmologion*. Above and below the Slavic version are Greek versions of the same *Heirmos* from a variety of manuscripts arranged in chronological order with the earliest one on top. Strictly speaking, the Slavic version *(Vos)* should be placed above *Ga* and below the four oldest Greek *Heirmologia*. It might be added, were one to ignore the Slavic version, that the succession of neumatic notations reveals a progressive decipherability of neumes, and that a slight variant of the melody makes its appearance with the advent of the last two manuscripts from the early fourteenth century.

Even a cursory examination of table 1 reveals substantial similarities in the manuscripts at crucial points. To start from the beginning, an indication of raised pitch on the second syllable of the Greek text has its counterpart on the third syllable of the Slavic text. The stress and raised pitch appear in both the Slavic and the multiple Byzantine versions on the fifth syllable of the first verse. At the ending of the first half-verse, the Slavic version introduces length (the neume called *diple* in Byzantine tradition);[15] then, on the sixth syllable from the end, all versions have a stress followed by two unstressed syllables. The antepenultimate syllable is again stressed, and all versions end with a long sound which in some versions is modified into a melisma (in *Ku-3, Delta* and *G*). In the second verse, note the stress on the second syllable. The rest of the second verse reveals some differences, although there is a stress on the eighth syllable in Greek, shifted in Slavic to the ninth syllable. At the ending, the time-extension is prominent in all versions, curiously enough, the last neume in the Slavic version is identical to that in two of the oldest Greek versions, *P* and *S*.

In the third verse the Slavic text has four syllables against five in Greek, still the phrase ends with lengths and this time *L* and *Vos* share an identical neume to round up the segment. Two syllables later all versions show stressing and raising of pitch. In the concluding five syllables of all versions, the fifth syllable from the end is unaccented, the fourth accented, and the third is unaccented with lowering of pitch. The penultimate syllable in *P* is accompanied by the neume *bareia,* which also appears in *Vos,* as well as in a few later manuscripts. The presence of *diple* is clear in several sources, including the Slavic.

The concluding fourth verse again indicates stress and raising of pitch on the second syllable in all versions. The next five syllables in the Slavic version contain a simple sign repeated, and while it is probably derived from the Byzantine *ison* (indicating repetition on the same pitch), it is used here probably to designate an unaccented syllable without pitch value. In the next two neumes of the Slavic version, a melodic movement indicated in Byzantine sources with the *dyo kentemata* is shifted one syllable later. The concluding

three syllables introduce lengths in all versions, and the last neume in *Vos* is again identical to that in *P*.

The syllable count of these four verses reveals the following relationships:

verse	1	2	3	4
Greek	16	14	12	13
Slavic	17	14	11	13

In short, the full Slavic text matches in length and in the number of syllables its Greek model, a total of 55 syllables. The verse structure is retained, and while the first verse in the Slavic translation is one syllable longer, the third verse is one syllable shorter, thus compensating in the total count. The neumatic notation demonstrates the molding of the Slavic melodic outline in emulation of its Greek model. The important point to keep in mind is that here we have an *adaptation process* and not a slavish copying. When the text requires it, the stresses are shifted, and length is introduced when demanded by the prosody of the new language.

The same procedure could be repeated for the remaining seven *odes* of the *Kanon* (since this *Kanon* lacks the "second *Ode*" the total number in this case is only eight *odes*!) but a single additional example will suffice to further demonstrate (table 2) the relationship of the Slavic version to three of the Greek versions—*L* and *P*, two of the oldest, and *O*. The *Heirmos* for *Ode* 4 of the same *Kanon* for the feast of the Virgin shows this syllable count:

verse	1	2	3	4	5
Greek	11	10	12	8	10
Slavic	13	11	14	8	10

This time the Slavic version is five syllables longer than the Greek original. A visual comparison of neumatic notation again reveals the presence of stressed and long syllables in most instances at the very same places. At the same time, however, there are clear examples of adaptation from one language to the other and an ignoring of some types of neumes. For example, the *bareia* in the first and third verses of the Greek is missing in the Slavic notation, while in the fifth verse that neume is absent from the Greek version yet the Slavic melody introduces it.

The closeness of the Slavic and Greek versions is clearly demonstrable, although it does seem that the melody of the Slavic version may have undergone some variation. While the neumatic notation in all the manuscripts suggests similar melodic outlines, the Slavic version obviously contains a few melodic turns for which there are no counterparts in the Greek model. On the basis of this point, it may be argued that although the religious ritual was

followed in the takeover of the Greek text and manner of singing, the actual Slavic chant, in practice, from the outset *both emulated and at the very same time introduced original interpretations.*

Having demonstrated the dependence of the Old-Church Slavonic version of the *Kanon* for the feast of the Virgin on its Byzantine model and the near-identity of the melodies in both traditions, the next step is to compare the Slavonic version of the *Kanon* for the Virgin—which was to become a model in its turn—with the *Kanon* for St. Demetrius as it was created by the Slavic Apostles. If ever there has been a need for a clear case of dependence on a pre-existing model for the "creation" of a new work, then the ensuing comparison of these two Slavonic *kanons* can serve as a textbook example.

Regardless of the fact that the neumes that accompany the *Kanon* for St. Demetrius are of a much later date than the actual period of Cyril and Methodius' activity, the fact is that their *Kanon* is based on the tunes of the Slavonic *Kanon* for the Virgin. For this reason, the scribes who entered neumatic notation chose to notate both *kanons* in a nearly identical way, reflecting an enduring practice over the centuries. The minor differences which do appear are of no great significance, and where discrepancies occur, they undoubtedly reflect the consequences of a still lively oral tradition (since the number of "literate" singers actually trained to read neumes must have been insufficient to satisfy the needs of a rapidly growing church). Nevertheless, the basic melodic outlines and melodic formulae are preseved without significant deviations, and our inquiry into the relationship of the Slavic "mirror" to its Slavic "image" confirms the dependence of the *Kanon* for St. Demetrius on its model, the Slavic translation of the Greek *Kanon* for the feast of the Virgin. This is demonstrated in tables 3, 4 and 5, which show the relationship of the *Heirmoi* for *Odes* 1, 4 and 7.

In these tables the *siglum Vos* stands for the Voskresensky manuscript containing the Slavic version of the *Kanon* for the Virgin, while *M* stands for the Moscow *Menaion* for the month of October containing the notated version of the *Kanon* for St. Demetrius.[16] A comparison of these two *kanons* reveals the very same procedure which had been utilized earlier by the adaptors from Greek into the Slavonic language. As the new text was being composed, it had to be fitted to a pre-existing model using the model's melodic formulae. Deviations from the model were to be taken for granted if the new text required slight adjustments. It may be instructive to start with a comparison of the syllable count between these two Slavic *kanons* in the case of the *Heirmos* for *Ode* 1:

verse	1	2	3	4
Kanon for the Virgin	17	14	11	13
Kanon for St. Demetrius	16	16	15	13

The process is again clearly demonstrated: the *Heirmos* for Ode 1 in the *Kanon* for the Virgin has a total of 55 syllables, while its "descendant," the *Heirmos* for *Ode* 1 in the *Kanon* for Demetrius, has a total of 60 syllables, yet the relationship betwen the two texts with their accompanying neumatic notation clearly reveals the dependence of the newly created *Kanon* on the flow of the melody of its model. The two subsequent examples for *Odes* 4 and 7 illustrate the same procedure with additional documentation and need not be discussed further, as a study of them will confirm the results already stated. It is sufficient to direct attention to the endings of verses in each of these examples to reinforce the points made.

Once the new *heirmos* for the *first original poetic creation in the Old-Church Slavonic language* was composed, the traditional structure of the *ode* in a *kanon* required the composition of additional stanzas for the *ode's* completion. These stanzas, or *troparia,* were seldom notated, as it was taken for granted that the singers would adapt the melody of the *heirmos* to the chanting of the text of the *troparia.* That is why in the Byzantine tradition only the *heirmoi* were notated and assembled in the type of musical manuscript known as the *Heirmologion.* However, in the musical manuscript containing the notated version of the *Kanon* for St. Demetrius, we are extremely fortunate to find not only the *heirmoi* but the *troparia* also notated, and a glance at one of the *odes* in its entirety may serve as an additional example of the process of adaptation of the new text to the basic melody to which the *heirmos* was sung. Table 6 contains the first two verses of the *Heirmos* for *Ode* 1 and the corresponding first verses of the three *troparia* for *Ode* 1 of that *Kanon.* The equivalence of the melodies is beyond question, since it is the fundamental rule that the *troparia* which follow a *heirmos* are to be sung to the very same melody. Still there are some minor differences as well, which confirms the long accepted finding that the tradition of Byzantine chanting embraced a large and flexible body of melodic formulae which could be used and adapted to a given text, either by contraction or expansion of the basic formulae, thus serving essentially as melodic skeletons for the chanting of the text.

An examination of the text and of the neumatic notation in table 6 further demonstrates that in the case of a single *ode,* the stanzas may differ in syllable count, nevertheless, despite this, the melodic content, i.e., the neumatic notation, of each stanza remains the same. The process of adapting a melody to a new text allowed the possibility of adjustments and even slight departures from the original melody without violating in the least the conventions of the well established singing practice. The singer took it for granted that the melody would by the "same," even if a microscopic analysis disclosed a lack of "identity" to the last dot. It is the outline that counts, and details are insignificant. By the same token, it is to be assumed that in performance by different singers, each singer was allowed latitude for individual interpretation

Ex. 1   Possible underlay of the Slavic text for the *Heirmos* for
         Ode 1 from the *Kanon* for Demetrius beneath Byzantine
         melodies for the *Heirmos* for *Ode* 1 from the *Kanon* for the
         Virgin

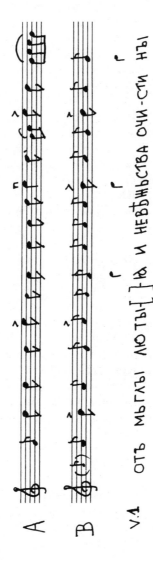

v.1   отъ мьглы люты[ ]ıа и невѣжьства очи-сти ньı

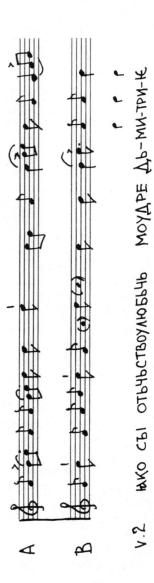

v.2   ıако сьı отъчьствоуıюбьчь моудре дь-ми-три-к

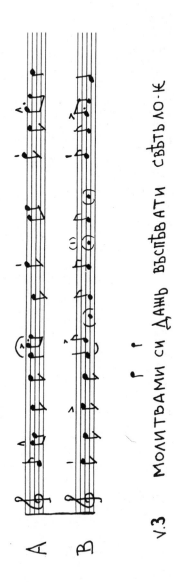

v.3 молитвами си даж въспѣвати свѣтьло-к

v.4 твоѥ тържество [ ] въ дьньшьни-и дьнь.

Table 1. *Kanon* for the Virgin, *Ode 1—Heirmos*, verse 1

Ἄνοιξω τὸ στόμα μου καὶ πληρωθήσεται πνεύματος

ОТВЬРЗЬ ОУСТА МО-Ѩ И НАПЪЛНѦТЬ СѦ ДОУХОМЬ

Although the text for this *heirmos* is missing in *S*, the melody is nevertheless preserved with a different text. The neumatic notation has been adapted to this text in the Table. For data about this case see Jorgen Raasted, *Hirmologium Sabbaiticum*, MMB, Main series, vol. 8, 1. Pars suppletoria (Copenhagen, 1968), p. 49. Manuscript *E*, as is clear from the Table, contains only the incipit of the text.

Table 1. *Kanon* for the Virgin, *Ode 1—Heirmos*, verse 2

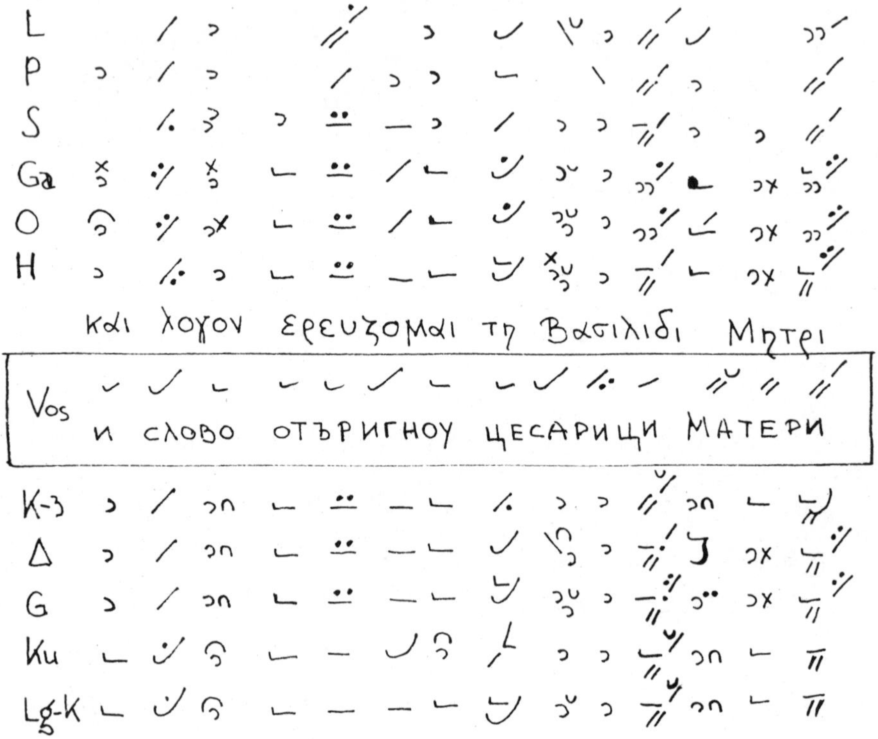

L

P

S

Ga

O

H

καὶ λόγον ἐρεύζομαι τῇ βασιλίδι Μητρι

Vos

и слово отърнгноу цесарнцн Матери

K-з

Δ

G

Ku

Lg-K

Table 1. *Kanon* for the Virgin, *Ode 1—Heirmos,* verse 3

καὶ ὀφθήσομαι φαιδρῶς πανηγυρίζων

и ꙗвлю сѧ свѣтьло тържьствоую

Table 1. *Kanon* for the Virgin, *Ode 1—Heirmos,* verse 4

Καὶ ᾄσω γηθόμενος ταύτης τὰ θαυμάτα :—

И ВЪСПОЮ РАДОУѦ СѦ СИ- Ѧ ЧЮДЕСА :—

Table 3. Slavic *Heirmos* for *Ode* 1 from the *Kanon* for the Virgin *(Vos)*
and the *Heirmos* for *Ode* 1 from the *Kanon* for Demetrius *(M)*

Vos
f.88г ОТЪВЬРЗЪ ОУСТА МОЮ . И НАПЪЛНѦТЬ СѦ ДОУХОМЬ

M
ОТЪ МЬГЛЫ ЛЮТЫЮ И НЕВѢЖЬСТВА ОЧИСТИ НЪI

Vos
И СЛОВО ШТЪРИГНОУ ЦЕСАРИЦИ МАТЕРИ

M
ЮКО СЫ ОТЬЧЬСТВОЛЮБЬЧЬ МОУДРЕ ДЬМИТРИЮ

Vos
И ЮВЛЮ СѦ СВѢТЬЛО ТЪРЖЬСТВОУЮ

M
МОЛИТВАМИ СИ . ДАЖЬ ВЪСПѢВАТИ СВѢТЬЛОЮ

Vos
И ВЪСПОЮ РАДОУЮ СѦ СИѦ ЧЮДЕСА :—

M
ТВОЮ ТЪРЖЬСТВО ВЪ ДЬНЬШЬНИ- И ДЬНЬ .

Table 4. *Heirmos* for *Ode* 4 from the *Kanon* for the Virgin *(Vos)* and the *Heirmos* for *Ode* 4 from the *Kanon* for Demetrius *(M)*

Vos f.98г НЕИСЛѢДЬНОУ ·ОУМОУ БОЖИЮ СЪВѢТОУ

M КЪТО ЖЕ ИКО ОУСЛЫША ТЫ ВЪЗИСКАИ

Vos ИЖЕ ѠТЪ ДѢВЫ ВЪПЛЪЩЕНИИ · ТЕБЕ ВЫШЬНА·А·ГО

M ВЪХОДЪМЬ ГОСПОДА РЕЧЕ · ИЗИДЕ ДОУША МОИ ИГО РАДИ

Vos ПРОРОКЪ АМВАКОУМЪ. ДИВА СА ВЪПИИ АШЕ

M ТѢМЬЖЕ ТЕПЛОЮ ДЬМИТРИИ ТОМОУ

Vos СЛАВА СИЛѢ ТВОИИ ГОСПОДИ ·;·—

M ПОСЛѢ — — — ДОВА ЛЮБЪ—ВИ · Ю

Table 5. *Heirmos* for *Ode* 4 from the *Kanon* for the Virgin *(Vos)* and the *Heirmos* for *Ode* 7 from the *Kanon* for Demetrius *(M)*

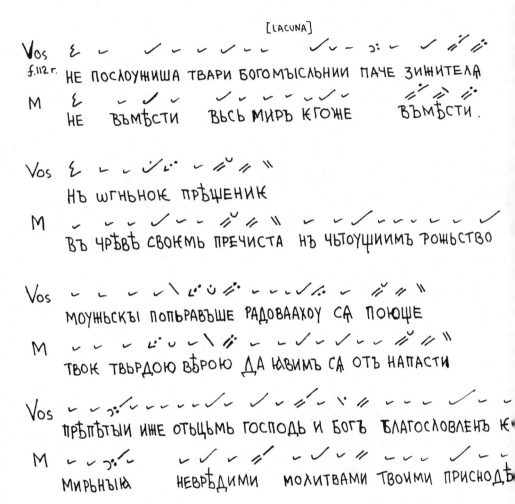

Verse 2 is an interesting example of expansion of the text which in the *Kanon* for Demetrius is twice as long as its model and has no neumatic counterpart in the model. The relationship of the neumatic notation clearly indicates that the division of text has to be made as in the Table.

Table 6. *Heirmos* and *troparia* for *Ode* 1 from the *Kanon* for Demetrius

① ОТЪ МЬГЛЫ ЛЮТЫИХ И НЕ ВѢНЬСТВА ОЧИСТИ НЫ — 16

② РЕЧЕНА БЫША ДИВЬНА И ВЪ БАРѢХЪ ТВОИ ЧЮДЕСА — 18

③ ВЕЛЬМИ ПРОСВѢТИЛА ЄСТЬ И КРАСЬНООБРАЗЬНО ПОКАЗА — 20

④ ЧЬРТОГЪ БОЖЬСТВЬНЫИ ІАКО РОЖЬШИ ЖЕНИХА ХРИСТА — 18

① ІАКО СЫ ОТЬЧЬСТВОУЛЮБЬЧЬ МОУДРЕ ДЬМИТРИЄ — 16

② ВАРВАРЫ БО ПОГОУБИ ВЬСА ПРИШЬДЪША НА ДОСТОІАНИЄ — 18

③ МОУДРОСТЬ ЧЬРПАВЬШИ ПИВА НЕ БЕСЬНААГО — 15

④ ПРИЗЪВАВЪША АГО ВЬСА ВѢРЬНЫІА — 13

The second verse of the first *Troparion* (designated with number 2 in the Table) clearly has 19 syllables of text but only 18 neumes which we have counted.

of the given melody and that uniformity in performance was an exception rather than the rule.

The final point of this inquiry deals with the exploration of the possibility of reconstructing the melodies of the Slavic *Kanon* for St. Demetrius in modern notation. The neumatic notation in the Slavic manuscript containing this *Kanon* remains unreadable by itself; however, on the basis of its dependence on the Greek *Kanon* for the Virgin, which in its late Byzantine version can be read and transcribed relatively easily into modern notation, we can by inference make a plausible attempt to retrieve the tunes to which the ninth-century text may have been chanted.

The plausibility of this exercise rests on the question of the stability of the Byzantine musical performance tradition which had preserved and transmitted the Greek *Kanons* through the centuries while neumatic notation was evolving into a more precise method for recording pitch and length. Byzantine melodies can be transcribed from manuscripts that date from the late twelfth and early thirteenth centuries onward. Paleographic analysis of the neumes from this time and their comparison with earlier manuscripts allows for a tentative, and by no means definitive, transcription which may be "valid" for melodies of earlier periods. By juxtaposing Greek and Slavic texts and adjusting their relationships when the syllable count differs, it should be possible to place the Slavic text beneath the Greek melodies and to obtain at least a partial glimpse into the melodic turns which might have been sung by the contemporaries of Cyril and Methodius in chanting the new poetic creation of the "Slavic Apostles." Example 1 thus suggests a potential melodic outline for the tune of the *Heirmos* for *Ode* 1 of the *Kanon* for Demetrius, based on the Byzantine manuscripts presented in table 1.

In the *Heirmos* for *Ode* 1 of the *Kanon* for St. Demetrius, the syllable count is longer than in its own Slavic model, as we have seen, and therefore also longer than the Greek text of its ancestral Byzantine model, whose melody served as the starting point of this inquiry. Adaptation is thus necessary to "fit" the new Slavic text to the ancestral model tune. An examination of the structure, verse by verse, reveals the following situation: the first verse of the Demetrius *Kanon* possesses the same number of syllables as the first generation Greek prototype, while the disposition of its text corresponds essentially to that of the second-generation Slavic translation from the Greek. The second verse of the Demetrius *Kanon* is two syllables longer and thus requires the insertion of additional syllables in the melodic outline of either the earlier Greek or Slavic versions of the melody. An attempt to sing the new Slavic text either with the melody "A" (which represents a composite of the notation in Byzantine musical manuscripts *K-3, Delta* and *G*) or with the melody "B" (which is a composite transcription of the essentially 14th-century "Kukuzelian" melody in manuscripts *Ku* and *Lg-K*) reveals that both can accommodate the *Heirmos*

for *Ode* 1 in the *Kanon* for St. Demetrius. (As a personal side remark, this writer finds melody "A" much more interesting if not more "beautiful" than melody "B.")

In the case of the first verse, the opening syllables of the Demetrius *Kanon* are closer to the Slavic translation of the Greek, needing only the insertion of a repeated note at the beginning, with one tone of the melody skipped, to compensate for the change. In the second verse, two additional syllables must be accommodated, but they can easily be fitted in without changing the melodic outline, as has been done in melody "B" of example 1. The same type of expansion of three syllables is required in the third verse. As for the fourth verse, the process of adaptation corresponds to that confronted in the first verse—the opening note is repeated and another one omitted in the course of the verse. Thus, as shown here, the method of adaptation is not a complicated one, and the professional singers who chanted these melodies in the Middle Ages could easily handle this type of adjustment, keeping in mind the disposition of stresses in the text which was being sung.

There is, however, one important aspect which has not yet been mentioned with regard to the neumatic notation in the Slavic versions. By going back to table 1 and re-examining the disposition of neumes in the Slavic translation of the original Greek, it may be noted that with two exceptions (stress on the sixth syllable of verse 2 which is eliminated in verse 4; and added length on the sixth syllable from the end in verse 4, which is missing in verse 2 at the corresponding place), the sequence of neumes in verses 2 and 4 in *Vos* is identical. If one is to assume that the identical notation implies the use of an identical melody, an important new element appears, namely that the organization of the Slavic melody does not follow its Byzantine model and that in actuality we are faced with an act of original creation and rhyming of melody (especially at the endings of verses 2 and 4) which is absent in the Byzantine model. An experiment at singing the Slavic translation of the Greek *Kanon* to the Virgin suggests, to this writer at least, that the melody of the fourth verse, as transcribed in version "B," example 1, is more suitable for *both* verses 2 and 4 of the Slavic translation than the respective Greek melodies for the second and fourth verses. As it turns out this "rhyme" disappears in the process of adapting still another text, such as that for the *Kanon* for St. Demetrius, and in this latter case, either melody "A" or melody "B" seems to satisfy the needs of the new text.

Our investigations have demonstrated that there is a way, even if a roundabout one, to obtain insights into the melodies which may have been chanted in the ninth century among the Slavs, as well as among the Greeks. It has once more been demonstrated that the process of adaptation from one language to another is an intricate one and often much more sophisticated than has generally been assumed. Further, in some examples at least, one can discover a reordering of the neumes, and the verses themselves can at times

appear with identical sequences of neumes, which suggests the use of the same melodies, all of which represents a departure from the model to produce a new poetic and also a new musical creation with rhymes. While the ingenious artistic mind would have craved originality then no less than now, it should not be forgotten that in the Byzantine religious tradition, whether one was dealing with icon painting (where the repertory of subjects was limited) or with the chanting of hymns (where the repertory of melodic formulae and poetic structures was predetermined by calendaric and other considerations), it was customary to create new works on the basis of pre-existing models. Such a procedure in no way detracts from the greatness or the importance of the achievement by the author of the *Kanon* for St. Demetrius. The fact itself that the poet created a new text not translated from a Greek source represents a "Slavic response" to Byzantine influence, not even to mention the occasional original melodic rhyme which was entirely absent in the Byzantine model. Cyril and Methodius acted in accord with the accepted practices of their own era, yet at the very same time they laid the foundation for the future growth of a new, Slavonic tradition in religious poetry and music. It is from such beginnings that emerged in later centuries the magnificent body of musical traditions that flourished in Russia, and also among the other Slavic ethnic groups as well.

Notes

1.   R. Aubert, "Démétrius (Saint) de Thessalonique," *Dictionnaire d'histoire et de géographie ecclésiastique,* Vol. 14 (1960), cols. 1493 ff.

2.   There is an enormous amount of literature on this subject. The basic study of the lives of the Thessalonian brothers is that by F. Dvornik, *Les légendes de Constantin et de Méthode vues de Byzance* (Prague, 1933).

3.   A.V. Gorsky, "O drevnikh kanonakh sviatym Kirllu i Mefodiiu," in *Kirillo-Mefodievskii sbornik v pamiat' o sovershivshemsia tysiachiletii slavianskoi pis'mennosti i khristianstva v Rossii,* ["About the old kanons to the Saints Cyril and Methodius," in *Cyril-Methodian volume commemorating the thousand-year anniversary of Slavic literature and Christianity in Russia*] (Moscow, 1865), pp. 271-96.

4.   V. Jagić, *Sluzhebnye minei za sentiabr, oktiabr i noiabr v tserkovno-slavianskom perevode po russkim rukopisiam 1095-1097 g.* [Service Menaia for September, October and November in Old-Church Slavonic translation according to Russian manuscripts of 1095-1097] (St. Petersburg, 1886), pp. 186, 237.

5.   A. Gorsky and K. Nevostruev, *Opisanie slavianskikh rukopisei Moskovskoi Sinodalnoi biblioteki, Otdel III: Knigi bogosluzhebnyia (chast' vtoraia)* [Description of Slavic manuscripts in the Moscow Synodal Library, Section III: service books (Pt. II)] (Moscow, 1917), p. 21 ff. More recently the Bulgarian scholar Bonyu St. Angelov has discussed and published the full Slavonic text of the services for the feast of St. Demetrius on the basis of a large number of manuscripts (which, however, as we understand it, do not contain musical

notation). See his "Kanon na Dimitur Solunski," in *Iz starata bulgarska, ruska i srbska literatura* [From Old Bulgarian, Russian and Serbian literature] (Sofia, 1958), pp. 19-35; the text of the Kanon is to be found on pp. 26-33.

6. In *Sborník Prací Filosofické Fakulty Brněnské University* [Proceedings of the Philosophical Faculty of the University of Brno], R. XIV = řada uměnovědná (F), č.9 pp. 115-21.

7. "Der Kanon zur Ehre des hl. Demetrius als Quelle für die Frühgeschichte des kirchenslavischen Gesanges," in *Anfänge der slavischen Musik*, Slowakische Akademie der Wissenschaften, Institut für Musikwissenschaft, Symposia I (Bratislava, 1966), pp. 35-41. Mokrý also included the facsimile of the beginning of the Kanon from the Moscow MS 160, fols. 197v-198r.

8. For the names of poets and of technical terms relating to the *Kanon, Heirmos,* and *Heirmologion,* see the respective entries in *The New Grove Dictionary of Music and Musicians* (London, 1980). See also my detailed discussion of the origin and structure of the Kanon in "The Byzantine Heirmos and Heirmologion," in *Gattungen der Musik in Einzeldarstellungen—Gedenkschrift Leo Schrade,* Series 1 (Bern & München, 1973), pp. 192-244.

9. Oliver Strunk, *Specimina notationum antiquiorum,* Monumenta Musicae Byzantinae, Serie principale, vol. 7—Pars suppletoria (Copenhagen, 1966), pp. 11-14.

10. Its Greek text begins "Anoixo to stoma mou," and some early MSS carry an attribution to John the Monk, while others refer to Cosma the Monk as its author. In later MSS, the *Kanon* is listed without the name of an author but with the designation for its use on the feast of the Assumption of the Virgin.

11. I have described briefly this otherwise inaccessible manuscript in my "Struktura staroslovenskih muzičkih irmologa" (The structure of Old Slavonic musical heirmologia), in *Hilandarski Zbornik,* v. 1 (Belgrade, 1966), pp. 139-61, see especially pp. 148-49. Professor Roman Jakobson also utilized this manuscript in his above-mentioned study; I am deeply indebted to him for most generously placing at my disposal photostats of the pertinent pages of this manuscript containing the Slavic text of the *Kanon* for the feast of the Virgin. Without his assistance this study could not have been documented with the crucial source which served as an intermediary in the process described in this study.

12. I do not pretend to have competence to decide which of the Slavic Apostles, Cyril or Methodius, might have been the author of the text of the *Kanon* for Demetrius. This is a problem for linguists and literary scholars, and, regardless of the outcome, the main point is that the *Kanon* originated in the second half of the ninth century.

13. I have written several times about this relationship, starting with my *Byzantine Elements in Early Slavic Chant,* in *Monumenta Musicae Byzantinae,* Subsidia, vol. 4 (Copenhagen, 1960), and especially in my paper "The Influence of the Byzantine Chant on the Music of the Slavic Countries," in *Proceedings of the XIIIth International Congress of Byzantine Studies, Oxford, 5-10 September 1966* (London, 1967), pp. 119-47. More recently I read a paper at the annual meeting of the American Musicological Society, Boston, November 1981, under the title "Byzantine Chant and Early Slavic Musical Creativity." A paper entitled "The Slavic Response to Byzantine Musical Influence" was presented at the congress *Musica Antiqua Europae Orientalis,* in September 1982 in Bydgoszcz, Poland.

14. The neumatic notation in table 1 is reproduced from Byzantine MSS and the Voskresensky Heirmologion *(Vos).* These are the *sigla* of the sources:
L: Mt. Athos, Lavra, MS. B. 32, mid-10th century.

P: Patmos, St. John's Monastery, MS. 55, second half of the 10th century.

S: Jerusalem, Greek Patriarchate, St. Sabas collection, MS. 83, from *ca.* 1100; this MS is now available in facsimile in MMB series.

E: Mt. Athos, Esphigmenou, MS. 54, *ca.* 1100.

Ga: Grottaferrata, MS. E. g. III, 12th century.

O: Paris, Bibl. Nat., Coislin 220, 12th century.

H: Mt. Athos, Iviron, MS 470, late 12th century; published in facsimile in MMB series, 1938.

K-3: Mt. Sinai, St. Catherine's Monastery, MS. 1258, dated 1257 A.D.

Delta: Mt. Athos, Lavra, MS D .35, late 13th century.

G: Grottaferrata, MS. E. g. II, dated 1281; published in facsimile in MMB, Rome 1951.

Ku: Mt. Sinai, St. Catherine's Monastery, MS 1256, dated 1309.

Lg-K: Leningrad, State Public Lib., MS. 121, dated 1302.

15. For the shapes and names of the Byzantine neumes see "Byzantine neumatic notations," in *New Grove,* vol. 13, pp. 144-49.

16. I wish to express my deepest appreciation and thanks to Mr. Nicolas Schidlovsky, who during his stay in Moscow in 1979-80 managed with great difficulty to obtain microfilms of pertinent folios containing the Slavic *Kanon* for St. Demetrius with the neumatic notation. Despite his effort to secure a complete film, only the *recto* pages of the folios were photographed, leaving the *verso* pages unrecorded on the film. Without Schidlovsky's generous willingness to obtain this microfilm, my study could not have been undertaken.

4

Glinka's Tour of Folk Modes on the Wheel of Harmony

Ruth Halle Rowen (U. S. A.)

In harmonizing the Caucasian *Lezghinka,* Glinka was a traditionalist, a classicist, and a romanticist. He absorbed authentic melody, organized his musical forces carefully, and gave free vent to his imagination. The result, in the fourth act ballet from his opera *Ruslan and Ludmila,* was a harmonization at once disarmingly simple, logical, and enticing.

Glinka had culled the ideas for his opera at the social gatherings of friendly literary enemies. In the late 1830s members of opposing artisitic factions intermingled at each other's homes to discuss and shape, however informally, the paths of Russian creativity. Both Mikhail Glinka and Alexander Pushkin were guests at one such evening, hosted by Prince Alexander Shakhovskoy.[1] Pushkin had already written his lengthy epic, *Ruslan and Ludmila* (1820), and Glinka was in the act of setting one of Pushkin's more recent short romantic lyrics, *Gde nasha roza?* [Where is our rose?]. Prince Shakhovskoy, an imperial playwright and director, was writing theatrical fairy scenes based on a group of Pushkin's poems to be performed with music, dance, and staging.

Shakhovskoy and Pushkin were associated with opposing literary movements, both aimed toward furthering the cause of Russian letters. Since the beginning of the eighteenth century, the written language had drawn from many sources, including the Church, the bureaucracy, and the multitude of Russian folk dialects. In addition, the language of polite society often borrowed words directly from the French, Italian, the English, the German, and the Dutch. Shakhovskoy was a member of the Conversation Society of Lovers of the Russian Word, a group which favored the archaic Church Slavonic style over the newer foreign influences. They ferreted out native Slavic roots from the old Byzantine chronicles which had survived the Tatar invasion. Pushkin allied himself with the Arzamas, a literary group named for Nikolai Karamzin, who veered toward the Gallic expressions in the speech of genteel society.

Pushkin had fun ridiculing four authors who were in the forefront of retaining what he considered to be an outmoded style of Russian linguistic usage. Since their last names all began with the same letters, Pushkin dubbed them "the Poet-Princes *Sh.*" In addition to Prince *Sh*akhovskoy, there were Vice Admiral Alexander *Sh*ishkov, the Minister of Education who headed the Conversation Society, Peter *Sh*alikov, and Sergei *Sh*irinsky-*Sh*ikhmatov.[2]

In his narrative poem *Eugene Onegin* Pushkin facetiously apologized to Shishkov for using an untranslatable French expression to describe a lady's entrance at a ball. Preceding a haughty general, she comes forward unhurried, unaffected, and unpretentious. In contrast to the other, more devious ladies of society,

> She seems the image quite perfected
> Of *comme il faut*—Shishkov, berate
> Me if you must: I can't translate.[3]

In the same poem he also mocked Shakhovskoy, the poet-prince who was to bring Glinka to Pushkin's brief attention. For the same stage where the grandeur of Corneille's French tragedies was translated into Russian by Pushkin's friend Katenin, Shakhovskoy routinely pumped out caustic comedy as noisy as a swarm of bees.[4]

When the subject of *Ruslan and Ludmila* came up at Shakhovskoy's memorable party, Pushkin's anticipation of imitative flattery without consultation may have caused him to indicate that he expected to make some changes in his narrative. Unfortunately, by the time Glinka sought to gain further elucidation from Pushkin as to what he had in mind, the latter had already been fatally wounded in a romantic duel that he fought in February 1837. Despite this disappointing setback, Glinka continued to make plans for what was to develop into a full-scale opera.

The music that Glinka envisioned for the *Ruslan* tale was by then assuming proportions too overpowering for a comfortable composer-poet relationship with Shakhovskoy. Glinka knew the limits of Shakhovskoy's potential for collaboration from the plays and librettos which the prince wrote for the imperial theatrical companies. Shakhovskoy usually relied on the solidly established talents of Catterino Cavos to supply and compose the incidental music for his plays.

Cavos, Italian by birth and training, was appointed in 1806 to direct the Imperial Russian Opera Company. He held the operatic and orchestral command over a period which spanned from the reign of Tsar Alexander I (1801-25) into that of Tsar Nicholas I (1825-55). Cavos's duties involved composing for the French, Russian, and Italian troupes, and also for the ballet. He immersed himself in Russian subjects from the start. In the year of his appointment Cavos composed a one-act comic opera to Shakhovskoy's

libretto, *Liubovnaia pochta* [Amorous mail], and a four-act opera, *Ilya Bogatyr* [Ilya the Bogatyr] to a libretto based on Russian folklore by Ivan Andreevich Krylov. In 1812 Shakhovskoy provided Cavos with a libretto in the Ukrainian national character, an opera-vaudeville entitled *Kazak-stikhotvorets* [The Cossack poet]. That year Cavos also composed a ballet with national overtones, *Opolcheniie, ili Liubov'k otechestvu* [The National Guard, or Love for the Fatherland]. Cavos continued his interest in the use of Russian folk melody in his opera *Ivan Susanin* (1815) to a libretto by Shakhovskoy. In 1836 Cavos conducted the initial performance of Glinka's opera to the same story. Glinka had been urged to change the name of his *Ivan Susanin* to *Zhizn' za tsaria* [A Life for the Tsar], which he did when he received permission to dedicate his opera to the reigning emperor.

The prospect of transforming Pushkin's epic poem of six cantos into an opera was a much greater challenge than the composition of a song to the stanzas of Pushkin's twelve-line romantic lyric. From his composition of *A Life for the Tsar* Glinka had gained experience in assembling a libretto by enlisting the aid of the then current imperial artistic coterie. That eclectic group now included Alexander Gedeonov, director of the St. Petersburg theaters, Valerian Shirkov, cultural attaché in the suite of the Tsar, Nikolai Markovich, historian of the Ukraine and folklorist, and Nestor Kulkolnik, playwright and poet. Together with Glinka himself, they contributed new verses to be combined with selections from Pushkin's *Ruslan and Ludmila.* An overall plan was proposed by the son of the office director for the Transport Council. This was the bureau at which Glinka worked as undersecretary to fulfill his obligation to the civil service. Glinka was greatly indebted to Alexander Bakhturin, the director, for many of his musical contacts. The younger Bakhturin, Konstantin, a poet, mapped his sketch for *Ruslan* in a drunken flash, while a guest at a party in Kulkolnik's apartment. Glinka adopted the plan and proceeded to put the opera in shape.

The cultural milieu in which Glinka circulated had artistic as well as literary devotees. One of the *Ruslan* librettists, Shirkov, wrote poetry easily and also had a talent for drawing; his cavatina verses and his sketching both sparked Glinka's Russian genius. When Ludmila's Cavatina, to Shirkov's words, was performed at St. Petersburg in 1838, the Polish violinist, Charles Lipinski, proclaimed it as truly Russian music. Although Shirkov's guidance in water colors did not make an artist of Glinka, one of their outdoor painting sessions started Glinka on *Kamarinskaia,* an instrumental fantasy contrasting a Russian wedding song with a Russian dance tune.[5]

Another artist, Ivan Aivazovsky, provided Glinka with three Tatar melodies that he used for *Ruslan and Ludmila.*[6] The seascape painter, remembered by Glinka as Gaivazovsky, was a frequent participant at Kulkolnik's gatherings.[7] Glinka wove two of the Tatar melodies into the Caucasian *Lezghinka* in the fourth act sequence of *Oriental Dances.* He

adapted the other melody, which was vocal rather than instrumental in nature, to the third act scene dominated by Ratmir, the Tatar Prince of the story.

As Glinka addressed himself to every aspect of the opera's eventual production, he felt a strong compulsion to oversee not only the singing and instrumental performance, but the staging and dancing as well. The composer hand-picked the singers and rehearsed the choruses. However, when he tried to supply the French choreographer with a live pattern for the Russian *lezghinka,* Glinka met with stubborn resistance.

Glinka sought to find someone who knew first-hand how to dance the *lezghinka.* Alexander Gedeonov's son, Misha, helped out. Misha, one of the theatrical censors, introduced Glinka to Pavel Kamensky, a translator in his father's office, who could actually perform the dance in the traditional manner. Glinka decided that he had to bring Kamensky together with Titus, the reigning ballet master. Titus, who had been responsible for such dances as the polonaise, the cracovienne, the mazurka, and the pas de quatre in Glinka's *A Life for the Tsar,* was more interested in furthering the style of ballet with which he was familiar than in learning how to imitate the folk of the eastern steppes. However, the *Oriental Dances* of the fourth act, designated as Turkish, Arabian, and Lezghian, were in direct contrast to *Ruslan's* third act dances of Naina's maidens in the French ballet style. Glinka had clearly differentiated the musical settings of the East from the West in *Ruslan and Ludmila,* and was determined for the dances to reflect the distinction likewise. He was satisfied for Titus to choreograph the conventional dances of the west, but not those of the romantic orient.

Glinka overcame the impossible by nationalistic means. He invited the Frenchman to a dinner at a Russian home, surrounded him with Russian guests, and tickled his palate with dishes ordered from a French restaurant. The other guests included the Gedeonovs, father and son, as well as Konstantin Bulgakov, a Guards officer and amateur singer skilled at performing Glinka's romances. After dinner Glinka had the Russian Kamensky dance the lezghinka so that Titus would understand how to stage the dance in the eastern manner. Looking ahead to the production, Glinka had already chosen the dancer, Elena Andreianova, a protégée of the Director of Theaters, to perform the solo of his *Lezghinka.* The ruse worked and Glinka had his way.

Neither Glinka's precaution to preserve the character of the Tatar dance, nor the use of an authentic Caucasian tune, was the most important element in the Russian nature of *Ruslan and Ludmila* as a work of art. Although outward manifestations of nationalism may satisfy the audience at the time when a work of art appears, they may not be enough to warrant continued appreciation into posterity. The tale of Ruslan itself did not stem from Russian roots. Pushkin's original success with the poem arose from its contemporary appeal rather than from its national, ancestral or folkloristic significance.

While composing *Ruslan and Ludmila* Pushkin also wrote some liberal poems which did not meet with the approval of the censors. When he was sent to southern Russia in political exile, Pushkin attributed his plight to the vengeance of jealous people for whom nothing he wrote could "smell of Russia." He mused about this in a letter written from exile on 23 March 1821 to Anton Delvig, a fellow poet in St. Petersburg. Pushkin went on to say, "No matter what I may ask of the censorship, Timkovsky groans."[8] Ironically, Ivan Osipovich Timkovsky was the very censor who passed *Ruslan,* a work which posterity considers as Russian to the core.

In the meanwhile, up north in St. Petersburg, Nikolai Gnedich, a classicist engaged in translating the *Iliad,* was attending to the publication of *Ruslan.*[9] Without Pushkin's knowledge, the artist Alexei Olenin had provided a frontispiece for the first edition.[10] When Pushkin received a copy, he was overjoyed with the appearance. He sent a letter to Gnedich admitting that he took childish delight for four days in admiring the printed verses, the vignette, and the binding. Olenin's montage illustrated the outstanding features of the story. Ludmila, the daughter of Prince Svetozar of Kiev, lies asleep under the spell of her abductor, the wicked dwarf Chernomor. Surrounding the sleeping princess are her three suitors, Ruslan, the brave knight, Farlaf, the cowardly warrior chief, and Ratmir, the Tatar prince from the East. Her father had offered her hand in marriage to the suitor able to free her. In the vignette, musicians playing the horn and drums are perched at the edge of the cloud on which Ludmila rests. Below the cloud, the giant Head, brother of Chernomor, blows up a storm through pursed lips, his cheeks puffed out with the effort. As a stage prop in the opera, the giant Head was to house a male chorus, whose singing would enhance the effect of the storm raging amidst thunder and lightning. In the illustration, the arc of wind spreading from the Head's mouth frames a picture of Ruslan galloping on horseback in the opposite direction, aiming the shaft of an oversized spear along the upper line of the wind's arc, toward the Head's mouth.

The tale of *Ruslan and Ludmila* was not part of the Russian literary heritage when Pushkin wrote his narrative poem. Pushkin had observed in a review of Karamzin's *The History of the Russian State* that this voluminous work had suddenly caused Russian society to discover that the country had a history.[11] When the first volumes appeared in 1818, three thousand copies were purchased in one month, a sale which exceeded even Karamzin's expectations. Karamzin, however, did not get past the year 1612 in his cultural history, and he unearthed but one prominent Russian ancient literary work in the process: In the manuscript *Slovo o polku Igoreve* (The Tale of Igor's Campaign), the anonymous author quotes songs which had been chanted in oral tradition by bards into the eleventh century. Since Russian literature was associated with the Eastern practices of Greek Orthodoxy well into the seventeenth century,

the cultural eras about which Karamzin wrote had not yet come under Latin influence. Therefore, the Russian literary style tinged with Gallicisms which Karamzin advocated may have affected his own nineteenth-century writing, but it had no place in the history covered by his books.

The Russians were not affected either by the eastward traffic of the Crusades or by the wave of allegorical and satirical poems, legends, folk tales, romances, and *mystères* flooding Renaissance Europe. When the Tatars pushed in on Russia from the eastern steppes, the only significant Russian literature that confronted them was the chronicle of the Byzantine Church, which they respected and left undisturbed. In the quest for a Russian national literature, therefore, Pushkin welcomed foreign inspiration. He admitted looking toward Ariosto's *Orlando* while writing *Ruslan*.[12] Nationalism for Pushkin was not a matter of seeking a subject from Russia's history or of using Russian clichés to express oneself in the Russian language.

Ruslan is a romance of adventure whose stock characters had appeared in numerous folk settings in France, Italy, and England to the West, and in Persia to the East. The physical prowess and endurance of the hero, his love for a high-born maiden, and his persistence in achieving his objective, all enveloped in an aura of magic and mystery, had widespread appeal. Pushkin's rendition of the tale and Glinka's creation of the music are national in quality, not because of the locale of the story or the replica of native melodies, but because of the artists' ability to identify in thought and feeling with the people of their country. Both were eager to glean all that they could from near and far.

At the age of ten Glinka would pick out the tonics and dominants on a violin or a small flute when his uncle's serf orchestra came to play dances for family celebrations. He preferred poking at the harmonies to dancing such dances as *écossaises, matradurs, quadrilles,* and *waltzes.*[13]

His uncle's luxury of having a private orchestra was not unique. Numbers of the landed gentry had large instrumental ensembles at their residences.[14] The performers in these orchestras were usually serfs whose musical qualifications had been checked in advance: along with an individual's distinguishing features, such as height and color of hair and eyes, a prospective serf owner was supplied with information as to the vocal part the person sang and whether he played the fiddle. Since innate musical talent knows no barriers, these performers were not prevented from infiltrating their new habitat with their native music or with musical experiences gained in a previous situation. As there was no uniform instrumentation, the musicians had to improvise and to make up their own arrangements, often playing popular operatic airs and dances of the day.

The dances that Glinka recalled in his *Memoirs* were types that came into vogue after the suite and the *contredanse* had taken their course. They were generalized categories, not specific pieces. The *écossaise* in duple time and moderate tempo, the *waltz* in triple meter, and the *quadrille,* which fluctuated

back and forth between six-eight and two-four meter, concluding in a fast *galop,* were all real dances. They made their way from European to Russian parlors before they were played by Glinka's uncle's orchestra. The other dance which Glinka singled out, the *matradur,* seems to combine the Sanskrit word *matra* with the Latin root, *dur.*

Matra is an Indian unit of time that may have been measured as five syllables, each lasting for the twinkling of an eye.[15] According to the ancient principles of dance, a metrical pattern of four feet comprising 12, 18, 12 and 15 *matras,* respectively, is applicable to a woman who defies her husband, speaks harshly, and is inconstant.[16]

Dur, the other part of the dance term, as used by the ancient Romans, also denoted attributes that were rude, uncouth, and harsh to the senses. Since the days of Guido d'Arezzo the name for B natural was *B dur* because of the dissonance of the tritone from F to B. The consonance of the perfect fourth from F to B flat, on the other hand, was *molle,* soft, not hard. Closer in time to Glinka was the Frenchman, Jean Jacques Rousseau, who declared that anything which offended the ear with its harshness was called *dur.* However, Rousseau was not about to dispense with the *dur* intervals. He concluded that if the tritone *(le Triton)* and the augmented fifth *(la Quinte superflue)* are used skillfully, their mystery adds to the expression.[17]

Having *matradurs* in their repertoire was as natural for the Russians as playing waltzes was to the Viennese. With the instinctive equanimity of an unbiased ear, young Glinka found the tonic-dominant foundation for consonance and dissonance in the modal phrases of both the Orient and the Occident. His innate proclivity toward expanding his harmonic horizon was subsequently brought into perspective during nearly five months of study with Siegfried Dehn in Berlin. Dehn summarized the science of harmony, melody, and instrumentation for Glinka in longhand, placing this valuable digest of information in four little notebooks. Glinka wanted to show his appreciation for the enlightenment by having the notebooks printed so that others could benefit likewise. Dehn declined the suggestion, preferring to spell out the triads in his own publication.[18]

Dehn was a consummate musician and scholar. He had made a study of ancient and medieval music and was transcribing the Lassus *Penitential Psalms* into modern notation. He also edited J.S. Bach's instrumental works, including the Brandenburg Concertos, and analyzed fugues from the *Well-Tempered Clavier.* He consolidated the historical and practical knowledge of mode and harmony thus gained into the introduction to his *Theoretisch-praktische Harmonielehre.*

Dehn's concept of what is called *Tonart* in German does not translate readily into English. For him *Tonart* is a circuit *(Inbegriff)* of eight tones, each of which is situated at a relative distance from the main tone or ground tone taken as the norm. The characteristic nature *(Art)* of such a mode springs from

the way that these eight tones determine a scale. He classifies the basic tones either as natural sounds emanating from the human voice or as artificial sounds produced on musical instruments. He shows how both are related to the Greek system and to the Guidonian gamut.

The Greek vowel syllables for a tetrachord, τε,τη, τω, τα, were vocal in nature.[19] The succession of these four vowels within the tetrachord varied, depending on the starting tone and the use of B natural or B flat. The Greek octave scale, A B C D E F G A, with A as the *mese* or central tone, was instrumentally derived on the monochord. Similarly, the Latin syllables of the Guidonian hexachord, *ut, re, mi, fa, sol, la,* were affected by vocal pronunciation, while the harmonic and arithmetic divisions of the octave, the fifth-fourth and the fourth-fifth, were calculated according to instrumental tuning.

According to Dehn, *Tonkunst* (musical composition) evidences two different ways *(Arten)* in which the eight tones of a C scale are harmonically related. The *Durtonart* (German for major mode) derives its name from Guido's "hard hexachord" *(hexachordum durum)*, with the square B, i.e., the B natural. The *Molltonart* (German for the minor mode) harks back to the "soft hexachord" *(hexachordum molle)* with the rounded B, i.e., the B flat. Since the central tone of Guido's system was C, with the *hexachordum durum* on a G a fifth above and the *hexachordum molle* on F a fifth below, Dehn uses the tonic C for both the major and minor modes. The major mode, C, D, E, F, G, A, B, C, is equivalent to a reordering of the tones of the spiral of perfect fifth, B, E, A, D, G, C, F, into a scale with C as the tonic. The harmonic minor mode, C, D, E flat, F, G, A flat, B natural, C, is a transposition of the Greek octave system from A to C, with the subtone of the mode raised to a subsemitone. Hence Dehn concludes that the difference between the major and minor modes is shown in the distances of their third and sixth degrees from the ground tone.

European medieval chant and contrapuntal practice had long recognized the choice of either the natural subtone or the fictitious subsemitone below the octave or the fifth. Despite this option, modal diversity persisted in polyphony through the seventeenth century. However, in eighteenth-century European compostion, the raising of the seventh step of the scale to a leading tone became indispensable, since it was the means for creating a major dominant chord. With the use of the major seventh degree in both modes, and the alignment of the minor third and sixth degrees as chromatic alterations of the parallel major intervals, the multiplicity of modes fairly dwindled away. The textural fracture between East and West was compounded by a rigid, unaccommodating system of chords. If the monophonic modal melodies of the East were to be accompanied at all, they needed harmonies suited to their nature and tunings.

Glinka logically followed a course for harmonization that was based on mode. When he composed in the European major and minor modes, he adhered to the customary rules that had bound the likes of Salieri into

harmonic servitude. Pushkin had already characterized Salieri's plight. At the opening of his play, *Mozart and Salieri,* Salieri, in an immortal soliloquy, attacks the lack of justice on earth and in the heavens, a concept as clear to him as any simple scale.[20] He berates himself for having set up craftsmanship as a pedestal for art. His fingers had obeyed him with cold agility, but had stifled the sounds, dissecting them like a corpse, and had proved the harmony according to algebra. Only then, having tested the sounds scientifically, had he dared to give vent to his creative fancy. When Gluck apeared, he had relinquished his discoveries without malice, to follow in the master's footsteps. Salieri had not been envious when he initially sensed Iphigenia's opening harmonies, or when Piccinni captivated the ears of frivolous Paris. But now, for the first time he is envious. Everything comes so easily to this genius Mozart who can even joke when an ugly itinerant fiddler ruins his *Voi che sapete.*

Glinka took his cue from Mozart rather than Salieri. Glinka listened to the itinerant fiddlers and serf bands playing the popular song and dance tunes in the rough and ready manner of the folk. He would harness the harmonies inspired by the East along with the Western harmonies that frivolous Paris enjoyed so much. With an Oriental harmonic wind band playing on stage and a European orchestra dominated by strings playing in the pit, he proceeded to intersect the parallel lines of major and minor with the circles of the *hedjaz* and *ziraskend* modes.

The scene in the fourth act of *Ruslan and Ludmila* is set in the gardens of the magician, Chernomor. The march procession begins at the back of the stage, with the musicians blowing on their instruments as they come forward. They are followed by the slaves and subjects of the magician. Chernomor's monstrously large beard heralds his entrance visually before he appears carried in on pillows by Moorish attendants. During the course of the procession, Ludmila, having been placed under Chernomor's magic spell, comes gradually to her senses. She gestures her unwillingness when Chernomor wants to seat himself near her on the throne.

The musicians are functioning here as members of Chernomor's military band. Their group, comparable to a regimental band financed by the purse of a local prince, is playing what was known as "harmony music."[21]

At the end of the eighteenth century the military band usually had two horns, two bassoons, one trumpet, and a serpent. Before Glinka composed *Ruslan and Ludmila,* the trumpet was a natural instrument, restricted to tones of the harmonic series sounding above the fundamental at the octave and its fifth, and at the double octave with its major third and perfect fifth. Glinka recalled hearing the sound of the natural trumpet in a regimental band as late as the year 1828, when some friends joined him in a public serenade.[22] The entertainment took place under the auspices of Prince Vasily Petrovich Golitsyn, who lived near the Black River. The Prince provided two barges illuminated by lanterns for the occasion. The barge which accommodated the

singers and the chorus had a small piano on which Glinka played accompaniments. The other barge was for the trumpeters of the Horse Guards Regiment. Glinka later reminisced about the harmonious tones of the resonant trumpets, not yet marred by the false sounds produced by valves. It was for such natural trumpets, capable of playing only tones of the harmonic chord of nature, that Glinka originally wrote the march and finale for *A Life for the Tsar*. Afterwards he sorely regretted that the natural instruments were passing out of use in favor of the valve trumpet.

Glinka may not have been as charmed by the timbre of the old wind bass as he was by the tone color of the natural trumpet. The serpent, made of wood and covered with leather, had long reigned as the bass of the harmony band. This B♭ instrument had raucous tones which unevenly encompassed a three-octave range of the B♭ major scale.[23] The most prominent tones, *d, a,* a fifth above, and *d,* at the octave, had to be subdued when they were not being featured. Nevertheless, the serpent had the advantage of melodic capability over the harmonic leaps of the natural brass instruments, an asset which was of importance to the close harmony of the miliary band. Glinka may have acknowledged the influence of the serpent in the wind band when he chose a key with *d* as the tonic and *a* as the dominant for the Overture and Finale of the entire opera.

The March starts on the tone *b* and winds its way around the jagged musical circumference of alternating fifths and fourths. As Chernomor circles the wheel of harmony, *b-e-a-d-g-c-f,* all of the natural tones appear. The intervals of the fourth and the fifth are indelibly impressed on the listener's mind by favoring harmonic tones at strategic points. Subsidiary harmonic motions are absorbed into the main stream of the cycle.

At first the stage band plays alone, without reinforcement from the orchestra in the pit. True to the tradition of "harmony music," Glinka did not assign the parts to individual instruments. The opening phrase of the March is an unaccompanied melody played in symphonic octaves by the entire ensemble (ex. 1). Its characteristic one-measure motive adorning the descent of the interval of a fifth launches Glinka on an endless cycle of fifths, whose only dissonant link, the tritone, connects the Trio to the March.

Harmonically the first period outlines an octave within which there is a descending fifth from *b* to *e* in the first phrase, and an ascending fourth from *a* to *e* in the second. The high *e* at the close of the period is underscored by its subsemitone *d♯,* while the *e* an octave below is reached by the motion of a descending fourth from *a* terminating in the semitone *f* down to *e.*

The second period of the March parallels the first, with an exact repetition of the opening phrase and a changed ending for the conclusion (ex. 2). The cadential chromatic descent of a fourth from *a* to *e* in the last two measures of the first period is replaced by the downward leap of a fifth from *g* to *c* at the close of the second period.

Ex. 1   Chernomor's March, First Period

After an eight-measure interlude the March is repeated with a transfer of the final phrase from a bass trio of wind instruments to a four-voiced setting for the entire string section of the orchestra. In the process Glinka clarifies the harmonic progression. The original statement had a melodic bass common to the close harmony of the wind band. In the progression *a-d-g-c* the tone *d* of the harmonic cycle was the top voice of a dominant seventh chord in $^6_5$ inversion (ex. 2). In contrast, at the *Fine* of the entire March, *d* is the root of a triad (ex. 3). At the conclusion. Glinka leaves no ambiguity about his intention to establish the harmonic progression, *a* to *d*. The first tone of the string basses is *a*, not the subsemitone *g♯* of the wind bass. The string bass tone *a* leaps directly up the fourth to *d* before descending the decorated fifth to *g*. At the harmonic goal on *c* the *pizzicato* strings are reinforced by the wind band playing its characteristic dotted motive.

The Oriental modes which enunciate the harmonic progressions emphasized in Glinka's March may be found in Laborde's *Essai sur la musique ancienne et moderne.*[24] In the eighteenth century French scholars had been unraveling old Persian, Turkish, and Arabic writings to gather their information about the eastern modes. Glinka absorbed the musical phraseology from the living practice.

Theory and practice coincide in Glinka's use of the *hedjaz* and *ziraskend* modes. The individual harmonic cycle of each of these modes is reproduced in Laborde's *Essai* according to the Arabic manuscript of Schemseddin. The modes are explained in terms of the 7 natural pitches, numbered successively 1 through 7 and identified with Arabic letters corresponding to ABCDEFG. You establish a starting tone, ascend or descend gradually or quickly, by step or leap, move rapidly from one essential tone to another, and close on a final tone.

Ex. 2   Chernomor's March, Second Period

Ex. 3   Chernomor's March, Final Phrase

Only the pitches of the intervals which specifically determine the mode are given.

In the *hedjaz* mode you start on the tone *e*. Descend quickly through all the tones to *b*, whence you ascend quickly to *e*. Descend again quickly to *c*, where you stay for some time. And you finish with a final on *b*.[25] Glinka conforms to this scheme in the March by establishing the *e-b* relationship in the first period, and the *e-c* relationship in the second. Glinka characterizes the clash between *g♯*, a harmonic of *e*, and *g♮*, a harmonic of *c*, as a manifestation of the magic of Chernomor. The augmented fifth from *c* to *g♯* engenders the melodic basis for a whole tone scale. The union of the E-major triad to the C-major triad, whose root is the interval of a major third below, is a stroke of harmonic magic.

The emphatic arrival at C at the close of the March section is Glinka's entry to F at the Trio. There the *ziraskend* mode, with its essential tones, *d, c,* and *f,* takes over. The bass of the first part of the Trio moves chromatically from *f* to *d* and back to *f* (ex.4).

Ex. 4   Trio of Chernomor's March, First Part

The second section of the Trio consists of a four-measure interlude and a repeat of the first part. The capsulated harmonic progression, *f-c-g-d-g-c*, with its scintillating major and minor cross relationship, moves from *f* to *c* (ex. 5).

Having reached *c* in the *ziraskend* mode, Schemseddin says that you should go promptly from there to *f*, whence you descend immediately to *b*. This is the point at which Glinka interlocks the modal circles. At the juncture of the Trio and the March he boldly leaps the cyclic interval of a tritone, from the end of the Trio on *f* to the *b* at the start of the March, a diabolic move worthy of Chernomor.

Ex. 5   Trio of Chernomor's March, Interlude

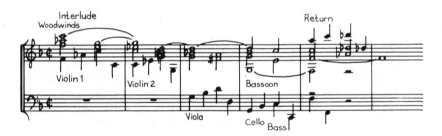

The Trio features the timbre of the *kolokolchikov*, an instrument which derives its name from the Russian word for bell. The sounds of the Russian bell ringers had fascinated Glinka since early childhood, when he tried to imitate them on two copper bowls.[26] Bells sounded the hour, awesome and enchanting in their discordant resonance. In times of alarm "every single story of the cathedral bell tower was studded with people."[27] Soldiers rode to battle to the jingle of bells, and the populace danced to them on festive occasions.

A percussion stick from which little bells dangled signified dignity to the Turks. With the suspension of two horsetails and the Turkish crescent on top, the instrument served to accentuate the beat in their military bands. The

instrument was known as the *Turkist Klockspel* to the Swedish, the *Janitscharspel* to the Danish, and the *Jingling Johnie* to the English. Since the performer had no control over the sounding of pitch on the *Jingling Johnie*, the percussionists of some regimental bands arranged a set of small tuned bells on an iron frame so that the appropriate bells could be struck with a hammer. In Mozart's *Zauberflöte*, Papageno the bird catcher is offered the magic of the tiny bells along with the magic flute. While Papageno attends to his singing on stage, the composed bell part emanates from the orchestra's *Glockenspiel*, a keyboard instrument. When some music from Mozart's *Magic Flute* was introduced at the Paris Opera in a *pasticcio* entitled *Les Mystères d'Isis* (1801), the French used bars of steel instead of bells.

Glinka captures the mysterious magic of the bells in the Trio of Chernomor's March, and again in the Arabian dance. At a signal from Chernomor the dances begin. For the harmonization of the dances, Glinka breaks the circle of fifths at its weakest link, the tritone *f-b*, and spirals off from both tips. *B* heads toward the cyclic tone *f♯* and *c♯* to generate the key signature of two sharps at the start of the Oriental Dances. A seven-measure harmonic tuning of the theater orchestra to fourths and fifths in the *a* octave introduces the Turkish dance. The melody starts on a descent from *a*, delineating the A-major triad which had just been established by the woodwinds and horns in the introduction. In the meanwhile, the initial tone *a* is harmonized by an F♯-major chord whose root has been generated by the final of the mode, *b*. This harmonic revelation is best perceived in the music itself (ex. 6).

Midway in the melody of the Turkish dance, *a*, the subtone of the final, *b*, becomes the dominant of *d*. With the upbeat start of the harmonic leap of a fourth from *a* to *d*, Glinka veers toward a striking resemblance of the *Grossvatertanz*.[28] This sounds like a triadic version of the tune that interrupted Schumann's March of the Davidsbündler against the Philistines at the conclusion of the *Carnaval*. In the March of the German romantic the interloper disappears as the innovative triumphs. Likewise, in the work of the Russian romantic the D-major triad of the natural horns succumbs to the modally propelled minor chord on *b*.

In the subsequent repetition of the Turkish melody, the effect of the harmony is intensified by increased chromaticism and the use of seventh chords, a passionate expression which invades the gentle Grandfather's Dance as well. From *d* at the conclusion of the Turkish dance Glinka progresses harmonically to *a* for the Arabian dance. The key signature now includes the next sharp in the harmonic spiral, *g♯*. The diatonic, scalewise Arabian melody emphasizes the harmonic tones *e-b* and *a* (ex. 7).

Again there is a tuning. This time both the harmony band and the theater orchestra are involved. They traverse the descending harmonic leap from *d* to *a* and its ascending intervening chromatic tones. Glinka is about to explore the varying degrees within the harmonic fourth. The first tune of the *Lezghinka*

Ex. 6   Turkish Dance

Ex. 7   Arabian Dance

radiates fourths in both directions from the tone *d* (ex.8). Each melodic fourth contains an augmented second flanked by semitones above and below. Glinka harmonizes the resulting heptatonic scale with the D-major chord which contains an *f♯*, and the neighboring G-minor chord which has a *b♭*. The two-measure harmonized melody is first stated by the stage orchestra and is then repeated alternately by theater orchestra, stage orchestra, and theater orchestra. The theater orchestra joins the winds on the *sforzato* chord at each repetition, thus welding all four statements of the theme together. The multiple stops of the violins on the upbeat *sforzato* are reduced to a single line as the entire violin section continues with the melody in unison. This insoluble wind-string accentuation of the beat is dynamic orchestral staging at its best.

After the quadruple statement of the heptatonic sixteenth-note galop, there is a chromatic descent from *f♯* to *d*, accompanied by a timpani motive on

Ex. 8   *Lezghinka,* First Melody

the root *b.* On repetition, the identifiable pitch of the kettledrum is reinforced by the indefinite pitch of the *tambourine militaire.*

The other Caucasian melody of the *Lezghinka,* which enters immediately, describes the interval of a fifth with a triadic division at the third (ex. 9). This contrasting tune initially appears accompanied by the intervallic drone of a fifth on the tones *d-a.* Here the neighboring G chord has a major third, *b♮.*

In the course of the *Lezghinka,* the two themes are intertwined, dissected, transposed, reorchestrated, amplified, diminished, ritarded, and accelerated. César Cui called Glinka's *Lezghinka* "the most lively musical incarnation of oriental emotion, as wild as a desert steed."[29]

At a tempo change from *allegro vivo* to *animato,* the wind band announces the second theme *fortissimo,* in the key of *B♭* major. Syncopations in the bass drum and cymbals clash boldly with regular accentuation of fleeting diatonic scales. At the close of the section, the *b♭-d* motive in the stage band vies with the *d-f♯* motive in the orchestra (ex. 10). An augmented second down from *f♯* slips into the orchestral decoration via the *e♭* of the reigning key. The wind

Ex. 9   *Lezghinka,* Second Melody

Ex. 10   *Lezghinka,* Close of the Animato

band again insists on the *b♭* motive. When the orchestra reaches from *d* for the tritone, *g♯,* the leading tone to *a,* it is time for another tuning.

The woodwinds and brasses of the orchestra have just united with the stage band in sounding *a,* the central tone of the harmonic system. The tempo shifts from *animato* to *vivace assai,* the meter changes from $\frac{2}{4}$ to $\frac{3}{4}$, and the key signature, B♭ major, returns to D major. Now the first violins tune the descending fifth from *e* to *a,* and the basses ascend the fifth from *g* to *d.* The flute, oboe, and B♭ clarinet pronounce these cyclic tones in emphatic harmonic leaps, and then proceed to fill in the ascending fourth from *e* to *a* with the intervening chromatic intervals, *e-f♮-f♯-g♮-g♯-a.* Soon the B♭ clarinet shows its preference for *f♮* by breaking away from the others. It blatantly spirals off from *f* in the direction of the flats, and warms up on its tonic arpeggio, the B♭ major triad. Then the violins, taking their cue from the high *b♭* of the clarinet, top it with an *e♭* a perfect fourth higher. In the meanwhile, the cellos and double basses tune to *c,* the fundamental root of the tonal system.

The closing *presto* revels in the ever present conflict between *b♭* and *b♮,* the opening tone of Chernomor's March. After spiraling from *e* up to *b,* the strings reverse their direction on a swift harmonic flight from *b-e* to *e-a* to the *d*

tremolo on which the *Lezghinka* ends. The wheel of harmony has turned full cycle.

The March and Oriental Dances are works of genius and a didactic compositional triumph. The Greeks had accommodated $b\flat$ and $b\natural$ with separate tetrachords. Guido had constructed different hexachords to take care of them, the *durum* for the natural b a tritone away from f, and the *molle* for the flat b, a perfect fourth from f. Dehn's *Tonarten* favored $b\natural$ to the detriment of $b\flat$, to retain the dissonant bite of the f-b tritone. Glinka recognized the need for both, with harmonic motion heading toward $b\natural$ in one direction and $b\flat$ in the other. He satisfied the Russian penchant for the sound of the fifth by harnessing its conflicting tunings, natural and artificial, to the will of the composer.

Glinka's success with the orchestral medium derives from a performance practice that clarifies rather than veils the harmonic structure and modal line. He did not seek bombastic effects through multiple reinforcement of the instruments on each part in the score in the manner of Berlioz. Instead of calling for amplification of the size of the orchestra to proportions where the increase of instruments was self-defeating, Glinka thought in terms of an orchestra close to the essntial nature of the musical texture. Brilliance of sound came from the contrast and mixture of tone color rather than from the number of players involved. The placement of the wind band on the stage and strings in the orchestra pit for the opera was therefore more satisfying for Glinka than his own version of the *Lezghinka* for a single orchestra. Berlioz performed the concert arrangement with an enormous orchestra in the huge amphitheater on the Champs Elysée at Paris in 1845. Although Glinka was most grateful to Berlioz for recognizing the work of a Russian composer, he later complained that the players could not hear each other and that the audience heard only the instruments closest to the individual listener.

Glinka composed the intonation of the folk into art music. He penetrated beneath the surface, tuning the harmony to the tradition rather than to a superficial characterization of it. In the March and Oriental Dances from *Ruslan and Ludmila* Glinka masterfully portrayed the modal propensities of the Russian people as he made his way along the international harmonic cycle common to the people of all countries.

Notes

1. *Mikhail Ivanovich Glinka, Memoirs*, trans. Richard B. Mudge. (Norman, Oklahoma, 1963), p. 121.

2. *The Letters of Alexander Pushkin*, trans. J. Thomas Shaw. (Bloomington and Philadelphia, 1963), pp. 60, 67-68.

3.   Alexander Pushkin, *Eugene Onegin*, chapter 8, stanza 14. English translation in *The Poems, Prose and Plays of Alexander Pushkin*, trans. and intro. by Avrahm Yarmolinsky (New York, 1936), p. 281. Russian text in A.S. Pushkin, *Sochieneniia*, [Works] (New York, 1944), p. 161.

4.   *Eugene Onegin*, chapter 1, stanzas 18-20. English trans. in Yarmolinsky, pp. 119-20; Russian, p. 114.

5.   Glinka, *Memoirs*, trans. Mudge, pp. 137, 151. Shumann dedicated his *Carnaval* to Lipinski.

6.   David Brown, *Mikhail Glinka* (London, New York, Toronto, 1974), p. 186.

7.   Glinka, *Memoirs*, trans. Mudge, p. 122.

8.   *The Letters of Alexander Pushkin*, p. 82.

9.   Ibid., pp. 83-84.

10.   Alexei Nikolaevich Olenin (1763-1843) was President of the Academy of Arts. The frontispiece is reproduced in Jean-Louis Backès, *Pouchkine par lui-même* (Bourges, 1966), p. 23.

11.   The review, which appeared in *Northern Flowers* for 1828, is in *The Critical Prose of Alexander Pushkin*, ed. and trans. Carl R. Proffer (Bloomington and London, 1969), p. 53.

12,   Ibid., pp. 103-4.

13.   Glinka, *Memoirs*, trans. Mudge, pp. 7-8.

14.   Alfred J. Swan, *Russian Music and Its Sources in Chant and Folk Song* (New York, 1973), p. 58.

15.   Bharata-Muni, *The Natyasastra*, trans. Manomehan Gosh (Calcutta, 1961), V.2, chapter 31, "On the Time-Measure," footnote.

16.   Ibid., V. 1, chapter 16, "Metrical Patterns," Nos. 169-70.

17.   J.J. Rousseau, *Dictionnaire de Musique* (Paris, 1768), p. 184.

18.   Siegfried Dehn, *Theoretisch-praktische Harmonielehre* (Berlin, 1840).

19.   Ibid., p. 15. Also see *Handbuch der Notationskunde* (Leipzig, 1913; reprint, Hildesheim, 1963) p. 28.

20.   Pushkin, *The Poems, Prose and Plays*, pp. 428-30; *Sochieneniia*, pp. 236-37.

21.   Heinrich Christoph Koch, *Musikalisches Lexikon* (Rudolstadt, 1802), pp. 737-38.

22.   Glinka, *Memoirs*, trans. Mudge, pp. 45-47.

23.   Hector Berlioz, *Grand traité d'instrumentation et d'orchestration* (Paris, 1844), p. 230.

24.   Jean Benjamin de Laborde, *Essai sur la musique ancienne et moderne* (Paris, 1780), Vol. 1, p. 174.

25.   Ibid., pp. 189-90.

26.   Glinka, *Memoirs*, p. 4.

27.   Pushkin, *Boris Godunov*, in Yarmolinsky, p. 40.

28.   See *Kehraus oder Grossvatertanz* in Ludwig Erk and Franz Böhme, *Deutscher Liederhort* (Leipzig, 1893; reprint, Wiesbaden, 1963), Vol. 2, p. 721.

29.   César Cui, *La Musique en russie* (Paris, 1881), pp. 37-38. Trans. in R.H. Rowen, *Music Through Sources and Documents* (Englewood Cliffs, New Jersey, 1979), pp. 299-301.

5

Robert Schumann's Russian Poems

Edward V. Williams (U.S.A.)

Schumann's sketch of the Kremlin (made during the 1844 concert
tour of Russia) in the Robert-Schumann-Haus, Zwickau

On 9 April, 1844 (New Style) Robert and Clara Schumann entered Moscow.
They reached the old capital of Russia almost thirty-two years after Napoleon
Bonaparte and only eight years after Auguste Montferrand had raised the Tsar
Bell out of its casting pit in the Kremlin and had set it on a granite platform at
the foot of the Ivan Velikii [Ivan the Great] Bell Tower. The Schumanns,
among the most illustrious in a succession of European composers and
musicians who visited Russia during the reign of Nicholas I (1825-55),[1] had
undertaken the journey from Leipzig to St. Petersburg and Moscow in the
winter and early spring of 1844 for financial reasons.[2] During this Russian trip,
which was planned as a concert tour for Clara,[3] Robert's role, as Zhitomirsky
has aptly described it, was solely that of *sputnik* [traveling companion]. He was
introduced to Russian society as the pianist's husband and remained in his
wife's shadow throughout the tour.

As the Russian cleric had admonished the bell founder for his lack of humility, the poet in the fourth poem rebukes Napoleon, whose unbridled ambition has brought misery, not freedom, to countless millions across Europe. Like the bell founder, the emperor turns away from the burning city that he cannot face. In this poem, just as the Russian tsar had felt compassion for the damaged bell and ordered it raised, Schumann claims expiation for Napoleon through his humiliating defeat and exile. Like the bell confined below ground within its pit in the Kremlin, Napoleon's remains are committed to the earth on St. Helena. And, like Nicholas I, who had decreed the raising of the great bell in 1836, Louis Philippe of France decrees the removal of the emperor's remains from St. Helena to Paris and to honorable interment beneath the dome of the Hôtel des Invalides. The silent prayer that the mute bell has dreamed on Easter morning in the Kremlin is paralleled in the soft voice from the tomb of Napoleon that addresses the emperor's former comrades gathered to pay him homage on the anniversary of his death.

Among the vivid details in Schumann's poems is the palpable presence of the city of Moscow as a linking device between the fate of the bell founder and that of Napoleon Bonaparte. The atmosphere in the old capital of Russia fascinated the Schumanns, and Robert felt such a strong attraction to the Kremlin that he was drawn there almost daily from the Hotel Dresden. Of their first evening in Moscow, Clara wrote: "Since I did not feel too well, I was not able to accompany Robert when he set out to look at the Kremlin. Robert returned home ecstatic, and I shared his enthusiasm when I had a look at the wonderful Kremlin myself."[19] Moscow's appeal to the Schumanns was in large measure attributable to its exotic color. On 11 April (N.S.) Clara remarked that the city was distinctive and the commotion in its crowded markets reminiscent of Asia.[20] Earlier she had compared the city to a tale from *A Thousand and One Nights,* and a week later wrote that "each visit to the Kremlin inspired and enriched Robert's creative imagination."[21]

In calling the trip to Russia his "journey to Lapland," Robert betrayed his notion of Russia as a country on the frontier of civilization, perhaps even a semi-barbaric nation.[22] The composer's imagination had already been stirred before the Russian trip during his work on the secular oratorio, *Das Paradies und die Peri,* opus 50, which had received its première in Leipzig in December of 1843, shortly before he and Clara left Germany for the Baltic cities. Based on a German translation of a poem from Thomas Moore's *Lalla Rookh,* the *Peri* was Schumann's first major work for chorus, soloists, and orchestra. It was also one of his rare excursions into that region of the Romantic mind that Russian composers would so richly endow with their Oriental exoticism.[23] The *Peri,* herself an outcast from Heaven, who journeys to India, Egypt, and Syria, won Schumann's complete sympathy.[24] In the Chorus of Houris, for female voices at the beginning of Part III, Schumann drew upon the highly colored

musical idiom and imaginative instrumental scoring of nineteenth-century pseudo-Orientalism.

Three times in his Russian poems, Schumann apostrophizes the magical effect that Moscow exerted on him: "Wunderstadt im Osten," "Russlands Wunderstadt," and, through the exclamations of Napoleon's soldiers, "die Wunderstadt/ Die sich nun auch ergeben hat."[25] In his first poem he juxtaposes the hubbub in the city, whose markets had evoked in Clara thoughts of Asia, to the raucous voices of thousands of bells ringing overhead in their towers.

> And a thousand small bells joyously greet
> The day, to celebrate the day of
> Their sister's birth; in dense crowds
> The throng is drawn to Ivan's Square,
> The metropolitan and priests
> Surround the place, where the founder
> Is to cast the bell....[26]

This mass of Russian humanity, gathered to witness the casting of the bell, finally absorbs the dejected founder.

> And as the crowd disperses,
> He is lost amid the throng.[27]

The poet also contrasts the crowds of Russians in the first poem with the unnatural quiet which greets Napoleon in the deserted city, described in the third and fifth poems.

Schumann's center of interest lies in the Kremlin in all but the fourth poem, which concerns neither Moscow nor Russia. Like many others before and since, he perceived the power of the Kremlin in Russian consciousness during his few weeks in Moscow. The Kremlin he imagines as a fountainhead from which the city flows, and at its source, "on her highest, most beautiful place" stands the great bell, "in the midst of many cathedrals, near the treasury close to the crown jewels of the empire."[28] To Napoleon, Russia's enemy, both the Kremlin and Moscow appear as menacing. The Kremlin stands before him like a dark island in the midst of an ocean of fire, while Moscow is personified as a bride who has rejected him with "a kiss of flame."[29] Schumann further relates Napoleon's isolation within the Kremlin to his exile on St. Helena. As the flawed bell stands at last on its pedestal within the Kremlin walls, Napoleon's ultimate restitution will be found in Paris beneath the dome of the Hôtel des Invalides.

Schumann's consciousness of Napoleon began almost in infancy. In 1812 Zwickau, the small town in Saxony where the two-year-old Robert lived with his parents and four siblings, lay ·directly on the *Grande Armée*'s route to

Moscow. In the spring of 1813, the survivors of the Russian campaign again marched through Zwickau on their way back to Paris. Both times the army must have passed directly beneath the windows of August Schumann's house, which stood on Zwickau's main square. And six months after the humbled French troops had retraced their steps through the town, residents could hear in the distance some forty miles away sounds from the Battle of Leipzig.[30]

Above Schumann's desk during his student days in Leipzig hung three portraits in gold frames: his father, August Schumann; the novelist, Jean Paul; and Napoleon Bonaparte.[31] On 5 May 1832, the eleventh anniversary of Napoleon's death on St. Helena, the twenty-two-year-old Schumann wrote in a letter to his mother, "Heute ist Napoleons Todestag."[32] The fourth of his Russian poems would eventually incorporate images of his French hero found in two passages from one of his early essays, entitled *Monument für Beethoven:*

> ...no companions among men and women came forth to him [i.e., to Beethoven]: he died in the wilderness of a large city more depressed in spirit than Napoleon, without having a child close by him.[33]

> You fortunate Emperor Napoleon, who rest out there [on an island] in the ocean, that we Germans cannot honor you with a monument for the battles you won from us and with us; you too would rise from the grave with an illustrious roster, "Marengo, Paris, the crossing of the Alps, Simplon," and the dwarf-like mausoleum would indeed collapse.[34]

But the composer's youthful admiration for Napoleon had changed by the mid-1840s to a perception of him as a man drunk with ambition and unconcerned with the well being of the peoples he had conquered and ruled. Schumann's revised opinion is suggested even earlier in a remark he made to Clara in the late 1830s about his friend Adolf Henselt: "Sometimes there is really something demoniacal about him like Paganini, Napoleon or Madam Schröder."[35] By 1841, Schumann's vision of Napoleon had changed to that which he presents at the beginning of the third poem—a man with his arms folded in the presence of fire. In the *Neue Zeitschrift für Musik* of 1841, Schumann drew an analogy between Ludwig Spohr's distinctive idiom in his Sixth Symphony (where he imitates the styles of particular eighteenth-century composers) to the unmistakable identity of Napoleon, even in disguise. "Once Napoleon went to a masked ball; and he had been there hardly a moment before he...clasped his arms together. Like a brush fire the cry spread through the hall: 'the emperor!'"[36]

Among the typically Romantic features of these poems is Schumann's endowment of places and objects with supernatural power. Examples appear in his personification of Moscow as the fiery bride who rejects her French conqueror, in the muted ringing emitted by a broken, clapperless bell, and in the voice from the tomb. The most dramatic instance of this device, however, occurs in the poet's endowment of the dead emperor with power over

the sea, with a force that mysteriously propels the vessel bearing his body toward France through windless skies and becalmed waters.

A dramatic manipulation of light also informs Schumann's imagery in these poems. In the first he skillfully contrasts the sunlight of Easter morning, the fiery glow from the melting furnaces, and the subterranean darkness which engulfs the bell in its pit. Tongues of fire, which rise from the burning city, illuminate the third poem. The fifth poem opens as the French catch their first glimpse of Moscow's golden cupolas in brilliant sunlight and ends in the flickering light from the fires that spring up in the city after the *Grande Armée* has entered.

As rich as Schumann's impressions of Moscow are in these poems, the composer's Russian experience had no demonstrable influence or effect on his music during the remaining decade of his productive life. But the five Russian poems, written during one of his least fruitful years, occupy a special place among his creative endeavors. Throughout his career the composer was sensitive to and explored the intimate relationship between literature and music. As early as 1828 he had expressed his thoughts on this subject.[37] Even if Schumann did not achieve equal stature in all of the musical and poetic genres he essayed, the breadth of his vision nevertheless commands attention and spans the range from music without poetry to poetry without music. Many of his character pieces for piano from the 1830s stand among the nineteenth century's finest examples of songs without words, and in 1840, his song year, Schumann fused music and German poetry in an incomparable manner. With his music to Byron's *Manfred* (1848), Schumann's poetic imagination had led him into melodrama, that musico-poetic medium in which poetry is declaimed to a musical background or in dialogue with musical interjections.

During his Russian journey in 1844, Schumann, for some reason, was curiously motivated to create a cycle of pure poetry, the word alone without ostensible amplification or commentary in music. But in these five poems, if a statement in a lettter to his father-in-law, Friedrich Wieck, contains any truth, the composer acknowledges his debt to music: "Meanwhile, here is another poetic greeting from Moscow, which I dare not deliver to you in person. It is hidden music *(versteckte Musik)*, since there was neither quiet nor time for composing."[38] In their cyclic conception, Robert Schumann's five Russian poems of 1844 stand as the composer's only poetic *Liederkreis*.[39]

Robert Schumann's Russian Poems

I. The Bell of Ivan Velikii

Moscow, magical city in the East,
A hundred churches are poised upward,
A hundred bells ringing far and near,
Are suspended in their towers.

"Christ is risen," the words ring
Devoutly from many thousands of lips,
"He is risen indeed,"
The words sound forth in a fraternal kiss.[1]
And the sun of the first
Easter day rises over Moscow.

"I too"—speaks an artist reflecting—
"I too would like to create a monument
In honor of the Most High,
Which, with its mighty tongue,[2] will declare
His eternal name everywhere:
May it be a bell the world
Has never seen before; it will crown
The highest point in the Kremlin
To bless generations with its sound,
Humbly bequeathing my name from year to year."

Ring, bell, whenever one of your tsars
Passes through your gates, Moscow,[3]
Ring an alarm, whenever flames of insurrection
Burn within your walls,
Ring, whenever the enemy approaches—
Ring, ring morning and evening.[4]

How the work rises from within,
And struggles toward its perfection!
The master founder labors night and day,
Often embracing the stubborn mass
With the loving warmth of the artist's faith.[5]

Already around the edge of the mold
Flowers bloom in lovely garlands
Already with the master's hand he rounds

The image of the tsar with crown and scepter,
And the tsarina's too, and that the work
May be blessed, above their portraits
Is also placed the image of Jesus Christ.[6]

So the bell rests in its tomb,[7]
Soon to breathe the air of heaven,
The master awaits the blessed hour
That will call forth its form from the earth,
And throughout the city news of this great event
Is already spreading by word of mouth.

And a thousand small bells joyously greet
The day, to celebrate the day of
Their sister's birth; in dense crowds
The throng is drawn to Ivan's Square,[8]
The metropolitan and priests
Surround the place, where the founder
Is to cast the bell, where
Levers and winches are already in place for raising
The enormous load from its dark pit into the light above.[9]

The flames crackle; tenaciously yet softly
The metal melts in the glowing furnace;
Time is needed to tame the resisting metal;
Sweat runs in drops from the founder's brow;
Everyone becomes quiet,
Those who were singing at their work
The jolly apprentices too; the crowd stands rapt,
And silently, before all present, the founder pours.[10]

The work is now finished, the mold is filled,
The fermenting mass now cools,[11]
In order to reproduce faithfully the portraits
That the artist has created.
And soon hands are busy,
With all their strength,
The pulleys take hold
And the lever from its place, where it is poised,
To raise the giant colossus.[12]
Now it rises, first the crown[13]
With beautifully braided loops—
Yet the founder's apprehension mounts,

The bronze reveals an ashen grey[14]
And half discernible the
Images emerge from the surface,
And now halfway on its passage
The bell continues to rise—
Very close to the image of the Saviour,
Is a gaping hole, a piece is missing,
And motionless in the pit
A remnant remains standing—horror
Grips the crowd and founder.[15]

And grieving as he covers his eyes,
As though to conceal the sight,
To avoid the dreadful misfortune—
Like the mother, who in quiet sorrow,
Looks upon her stillborn child,
Her face may not be more painful—
There rushes up to him a man
In a robe who speaks:[16]
"You have sought what you should not have sought,
A baser motive conceals a holy one:
It is not God whom you wished to serve,
You have been a slave to vanity:
So may your name be henceforth cursed,
You, with thousands of others, equally forgotten!
So that your work might be acceptable to God,
First learn to restrain yourself with humility."

And in silence the artist hears these words,
And as the crowd disperses,
He is lost amid the throng.

II. [*The Raising of Tsar-Kolokol*]

In Moscow, Russia's magical city,
There is the legend of a bell,
So gigantic that as it fell
It carried down into the ground
The cupola in which it was hanging, where
It too is now buried, each year
Boring deeper into the earth.[17]
Still other tales are told of it

Thus: that an artist conceived this bell,
Which would count among the very best
And that in being cast it met with misfortune.[18]
And there are still other legends.

Once upon a time the tsar heard of the giant
That sleeps within his Kremlin[19]—
He says: "I want to see the bell."
And he adds a forgiving note:
"The aspiration of the artist, who conceived
This mightiest of objects, must be sanctified,
Whether this object is perfect or not—
It has slumbered long enough in its confining casket
And must be raised up into the light of day
To give the world an eloquent symbol
Of the artist's endeavor."

And as the tsar in his decision
Is quite used to immediate action
In order that what should be done, must be done,
So he also resists discouragement.[20]
Thus strong arms are soon seen
Committed to the work of freeing the bell
That it, like the lowly slave girl,
May be raised up to its dignity,
To thrive in the light of living breath.

Like a hundred streams running
From the Kremlin's rise into the valley,
Where Moscow flows endlessly to the east,
On her highest, most beautiful place—
In the midst of many cathedrals,
Near the treasury close to the crown jewels of the empire[21]—
There it now stands, not suspended to be sure,
Nor ringing—
Yet early on Easter morning when
The concerted ringing of all its younger companions
Greets this holy day,
Some believers have heard there
A touchingly quiet ringing
As though the bell were dreaming its own mute prayer
To the honor of the risen Christ.[22]

III. [*Napoleon in Moscow*]

Bell founder, how similar to you
And to your lot was another master
Whose figure I picture here,
Yes, here, where at every step
The cry of his defeated spirit stalks me.

Of course his profession was not as bell founder
Though related to metal; he preferred to dictate his empires and his peoples
With the language of cannon:[23] "I must have it."
He knew what he wanted and also how to obtain it,
The corpses at his feet attested to his will.

Kremlin, on your battlements
I see him standing with his arms folded.
An ocean of fire engulfing the horizon,
The flames leaping up with renewed strength,
Were hardly extinguished—the city a grave,
And here and there a howling dog,
Seeking its master and a drunken mob
And (only rarely heard) a cry of victory
As though death were pressing it out of the throat...[24]

But to you on the Kremlin did not
A sinister spirit whisper in your ear:
"Have you on your throne kept your word,
Have you given your peoples freedom,
You, who with a single word could raise up millions
You, with your spirit, with your eagle eye—
Have you on your throne done
What you promised to do, Napoleon?
Was it the people, whom you considered,
When you led them, sure of victory, to battle,
Was it for the people's welfare
That you handed over Enghien to the executioner's lead[25]
Was it for the elevation
Of the people that you raised legions
And sent them off toward distant lands—
Or your own?"

No longer can he bear what
Addresses him from the flames, paler
And paler his cheek becomes as
The ruddy flames flare up even redder.
From all houses fire bursts forth.
But at full gallop he
Leaps through the burning Petrovsky Gate,[26]
As though fire had already seized him by the stirrup.

IV. [The Interment of Napoleon]

On hard stone he has done penance,
As you my bell founder; no,
Perhaps his endeavor was not entirely blameless
Have no concern—he has done penance,
When in his last hour on St. Helena[27]
He kissed the picture of his child,
Who had been taken from his father's heart;[28] cherubim
In heaven beheld his grief and spoke:
"He has borne what no mortal has endured."

So he rests a long time [on an island] in the distant sea;
Only the sentinel's call echoes
Monotonously over his grave;
The quiet place hardly discloses that a king,
An emperor was buried here:
And he rested many years.[29] O bell founder, how like
You and your lot is the fortune of this god of war!
Sated with the praise of friends, weary with the scorn of his enemies
Taking only the man,
Clio, history's muse of prophecy, gives her crown
To the hero, with righteous judgment
The shadow... [30] and the splendor.

And to a king, moderate, wise,
She spoke to his heart;[31] It is time
For you, who dedicated his blood a hundred times
In battles for the glory of France,
To return his remains,
Before they are reduced to dust in foreign soil,

To the native shore, to the country (as he has decreed with touching words
in his will)[32]
To the country that he loved so dearly...
Do this and you will have acted justly!

As if the rigid cargo[33] had special power,
The ocean is appeased,
Obligingly wind and waves unite to speed the course
Of the noble vessel; with its masts terribly still
The ship glides over the watery course,
Well done, well done, my Prince de Joinville,
That was truly the most auspicious journey
That you have made for the glory of France.[34]

In the Hôtel des Invalides
Stands a grave quite new
There fresh flowers rain down
Each year on the fifth of May.[35]

Before all that is immortal
These flowers are brought
By those who once were comrades
Of the brave emperor.

And out of the silent tomb
Echo ghostly sounds:
"I give thanks to you my dear
Comrades for this tribute."

And softly he speaks, ever so softly:
"Come to me soon, how long
You have already left me alone,
You, who, like your emperor,
Must always be ready—
Come soon." The last guardsman
Kneels at the emperor's grave
The last tears dampen
The much beloved grave.

So that he should not waver nor flinch,
One didn't need to tell him:
His motionless body
Was carried away forthwith.[36]

[*V*.] *The French Before Moscow*

There from the hill across the Moscow River
There the *Grande Armée* approached.[37]

When they saw the city,
Unfolding before them in the sunlight,
Cupolas without end on the horizon,
Joyfully resounded from front to front,
"Moscow, Moscow, the magical city,
Has now surrendered too."

They drew closer, they cried loudly:
"To be sure the general has granted us
The most beautiful bride
After the torturous journey.
Here a life of pleasure is possible.
We'd like to be inside—the sooner the better."

Yet they waited a long time as though rooted to the spot
They said: "A city councilman must come forth
With the key to the city in his hand—"
But none appeared.[38]

For two whole hours they waited,
The emperor grew angry; he himself
Sprang through the gate
As though the city were his already.

There was not a single person to be seen
Suddenly he shuddered,
As inside the Kremlin,
He sat on the throne
Of Tsar Alexander,
It was as though it burned.

And as he saw in the distance
A bright speck—
He exclaimed, "That is not a star."
And as he looked again
The small point was a spark.
He spoke, "I don't like what I see."

And when he looked for the third time,
From all sides welled up cries of "Fire"
And the monstrous flames
Rose more and more furiously.
And for him the outcome was clear:
He sat in the house of his enemy,
Sulfur and fire greeted him instead of
...[39] and honor.

The emperor cried out loudly:
And he stamped his foot on the floor.
"Rostopchin, you traitor,[40]
You have laid this for me
If only I had never trusted you
and your treacherous madmen
Now my war is lost."

And on the...[41] hill,
Where it first beheld
The demonic fairy
The army was soon seen
Marching back. —Trust no bride,
Who gives herself so easily
Trust no one no matter how beautiful she may be;
Napoleon wished to embrace her, the splendid prize;
The gloomy specter returns the greeting
With a kiss of flame
And without mercy pursues him,
Hardened in grief,
Through many a city and country.

Moscow, 13/25 April [18]44

Notes to the Text

1.   The Schumanns had been preceded in Russia by Ole Bull (1838 and 1841), Sigismond Thalberg (1839), Franz Liszt (1842), and Pauline Viardot-Garcia (1843). John Field died in Moscow in 1837, and the next year Adolf Henselt arrived in St. Petersburg where he would live for the next forty years. Henselt, a friend of the Schumanns, introduced the Leipzig couple to society in the Russian capital. Berlioz did not pay his first visit to Russia until 1847.

2. The Schumanns left Leipzig on 25 January 1844 (N.S.) On route to Russia, they passed through the Baltic cities of Königsberg (now Kaliningrad), Mitau (now Jelgava, Latvia), Riga, and Dorpat (now Tartu, Estonia). Clara presented concerts in each of these cities. They reached St. Petersburg on 4 March (N.S.) and remained there until 2 April. On their way from St. Petersburg to Moscow, they stopped overnight in Novgorod; and in Tver (now Kalinin) they visited a maternal uncle of Robert, who was serving the Russian army there as a regimental doctor. The Schumanns were in Moscow between 9 April and 8 May (N.S.) and then returned to St. Petersburg. They sailed from Kronstadt on 18 May and reached Leipzig on the 30th. D. Zhitomirsky, *Robert i Klara Schumann v Rossii* [Robert and Clara Schumann in Russia] (Moscow, 1962), pp. 96, 121, 146, 149, 169, 174, and 176; hereafter, *Schumann v Rossii.*

3. Vladimir Vasilevich Stasov, "Liszt, Schumann and Berlioz in Russia," in *Selected Essays on Music,* trans. by Florence Jonas (London, 1968), p. 142; hereafter, Stasov.

4. A table of Schumann's works that were performed in his presence, the names of the performers, and the occasions appear in *Schumann v Rossii,* p. 23-25.

5. Stasov, pp. 144, 145. Schumann was present at a soirée that Glinka also attended and met the fifteen-year-old Anton Rubinstein. *Schumann v Rossii,* pp. 92, 133, 144, 197. The diary does not record any conversation between Schumann and Glinka.

6. Stasov, p. 145.

7. Ibid., pp. 145-46.

8. F. Gustav Jansen, ed., *Robert Schumann's Briefe,* neue Folge (Leipzig: Breitkopf und Härtel, 1886), p. 202. The Empress of Russia, consort of Nicholas I, was the princess Charlotte Louise, daughter of Friedrich Wilhelm III, King of Prussia.

9. *Schumann v Rossii,* p. 167.

10. The Schumanns' diary of their Russian tour is published in its entirety in a Russian translation by P.G. Pechalina, on pp. 94-176 of Zhitomirsky's study cited above. Excerpts from the diary had previously appeared in Russian translation in an article by P. Pechalina and D. Zhitomirsky, "Schumann v Rossii," *Sovetskaia muzyka* no. 7 (1954), pp. 60-73. Highlights of the Schumanns' Russian tour are contained in Georg Eismann, "Robert und Clara Schumanns Reise nach Russland," *Musik und Gesellschaft* no. 4 (1954), pp. 2-5.

11. The original German copy for all five poems, preserved in the Schumanns' diary in the archives of the Robert-Schumann-Haus in Zwickau, was published by Georg Eismann, "Robert Schumanns Moskauer Gedichte," *Beiträge zur Musikwissenschaft* no.1 (1959), pp. 32-40. I am indebted to Dr. Schoppe of the Robert-Schumann-Haus for directing me to this source. Two of the five poems had appeared earlier in Georg Eismann, ed., *Robert Schumann: Ein Quellenwerk über sein Leben und Schaffen,* v. 1 (Leipzig, 1956), pp. 140 ff. Three of the five (nos. 2, 3, and 5 in Eismann) were published in L. Ozerov's Russian translation as "Stikhotvoreniia R. Shumana" [R. Schumann's poems], *Sovetskaia muzyka* no. 9 (1954), pp. 78-79. These same three translations are included in the notes to the Schumanns' diary in *Schumann v Rossii,* pp. 200-4.

12. During 1844 Schumann suffered one of the most severe of his frequent depressions. Melancholia set in on the way to St. Petersburg and continued throughout the Russian trip. Russians who entertained the Schumanns found Robert withdrawn and uncommunicative at social gatherings. Stasov, p. 144. In 1844, aside from the five poems he wrote in Moscow, Robert composed some of his music for Goethe's *Faust.*

13. Letters, essays, and other literary works from Schumann's youth are published in Alfred Schumann, ed., *Der junge Schumann: Dictungen und Briefe* (Leipzig, 1910). Schumann's later work as a music critic for *Neue Zeitschrift für Musik* is thoroughly studied in Leon Plantinga, *Schumann as Critic* (New Haven, 1967).

14. I gratefully acknowledge the interest and many valuable suggestions of my colleagues, Joan Holmes and George Lawner, in the translations of these poems.

15. Eismann, "Robert Schumanns Moskauer Gedichte," p. 32. On p. 40, Eismann has reproduced the final page of the fifth poem in Robert's hand.

16. Schumann presents the events in his five poems without regard to their historical sequence. By placing the poem on the raising of the Tsar Bell (1836) before the third poem on Napoleon in Moscow, Schumann gives the impression that Montferrand had already raised the bell from its pit and had set it on its platform in the Kremlin before Napoleon's arrival in 1812. If the events in the poems were to be ordered according to historical chronology, a number of adjustments would need to be made.

17. In Eismann's opinion, Schumann's poems are "of slight artistic merit," and "the last two [nos. 4 and 5] are frankly weak." "Robert Schumanns Moskauer Gedichte," p. 32.

18. The theme of redemption in German music is most prominent in Richard Wagner's operas and music dramas. In *Das Paradies und die Peri*, which Schumann had just completed in 1843, and in the final scene of his music for Goethe's *Faust*, on which he was working in 1844, redemption through expiation dominates the concluding passages of both works. The repentant Peri gains admission to paradise through her tears; the entire third part of Schumann's *Faust* is devoted to the hero's transfiguration and to choral praise for his redemption.

19. *Schumann v Rossii*, p. 149. Cf. Berlioz's characterization of Moscow in his memoirs of 1847 as a "semi-Asiatic city." David Cairns, trans. and ed., *The Memoirs of Hector Berlioz* (London, 1969), p. 429.

20. *Schumann v Rossii*, pp. 149-50.

21. Ibid., pp. 149, 156.

22. Stasov, p. 143.

23. Schumann's *Paradies und die Peri*, in fact, was "well known to the Balakirev circle, and Balakirev performed excerpts from it at his concerts in 1863 and 1864." Gerald Abraham, ed., *Schumann: A Symposium*, reprint ed. (Westport, Conn., 1977), p. 284, n. 1.

24. Jansen, *Robert Schumann's Briefe*, p. 194.

25. Eismann, "Robert Schumanns Moskauer Gedichte," pp. 32, 35 and 38.

26. Ibid., p. 33.

27. Ibid., p. 34.

28. Ibid., p. 35.

29. Ibid., p. 39.

30. Alan Walker, *Schumann*, The Great Composers (London, 1976), pp. 13-14.

31. *Schumann v Rossii*, p. 204.

32. Schumann, *Der junge Schumann*, p. 232.

33. Ibid., p. 77. Napoleon's own son, the Duke of Reichstadt, who survived him, was not on St. Helena at the time of his father's death, contrary to Schumann's implication in the fourth poem.

34. Ibid., p.76.

35. Joan Chissell, *Schumann* (London, 1956), pp. 45-46. Wilhelmine Schröder-Devrient, a German soprano, experienced her greatest triumph in the role of Leonore in Beethoven's *Fidelio* in 1822.

36. Plantinga, *Schumann as Critic,* p. 153.

37. Ibid., p.179.

38. Jansen, *Robert Schumann's Briefe,* p. 206.

39. In the translations which follow, Schumann's own punctuation in the German has been preserved.

Notes to the Poems

1. *"Khristos voskrese!"* (Christ is risen!) is the traditional greeting on Russian Easter to which the response is "Voistinu voskrese!" (He is risen indeed!). Kisses on the cheeks were exchanged on the streets between strangers. Even the tsar greeted his servants and staff in this manner on Easter.

2. The Russian word for bell clapper is *iazyk* (tongue). Here Schumann also uses "tongue" (Zunge).

3. During the seventeenth century the great Kremlin bell was struck to announce the tsar's ceremonial entries into and departures from Moscow. Petrus Petrejus of Erlesund, "Istoriia o velikom kniazhestve moskovskom . . . " [History of the great Muscovite principality] part 1 in *Chteniia v Imperatorskom obshchestve istorii i drevnosti rossiiskikh pri Moskovskom universitete* [Readings in the Imperial Society of Russian History and Antiquities at Moscow University], 1865, kn. IV, p. 18; Adam Olearius, *Vermehrte neue Beschreibung der muscowitischen und persischen Reyse* (Schleswig, 1656; reprint ed. by Dieter Lohmeier, Tubingen: Max Niemeyer Verlag, 1971), p. 147; and Paul of Aleppo, *Puteshestvie antiokhiiskago patriarkha Makariia v Rossiiu v polovine XVII veka* [Journey of the Antioch Patriarch Makarius to Russia in the mid-seventeenth century], vyp. IV (Moscow: Universitetskaia tipografiia, 1898), pp. 91-92.

4. Another bell, the alarm bell *(nabatnyi kolokol)*, which hung in the Kremlin's Nabatnyi Tower facing Red Square, sounded the tocsin in Moscow. I.M. Snegirev, "Moskovskii Tsar'-kolokol" [Moscow's Tsar Bell], *Russkiia dostopamiatnosti* [Russian memorabilia], no. 3 (1880), p. 27.

5. Schumann in this poem is speaking of the great bell of Ivan and Mikhail Motorin, father and son, which still stands in the Kremlin on its granite platform at the foot of the Ivan Velikii Bell Tower. Ivan Motorin received the commission for founding this bell in August of 1730 from Empress Anna Ivanovna; he designed the bell and supervised the construction of its mold between 1730 and 1734. His first attempt to cast the bell on 29 November 1734 (O.S.) was unsuccessful, and he died the following August. His son, Mikhail Ivanovich, assumed direction of his father's project and, using the same mold, achieved a successful casting of the bell on 25 November 1735 (O.S.), almost a year to the day after his father's attempt. This bell is known today as *Tsar'-kolokol* (The Tsar Bell). G.A. Boguslavskii, *Tsar'-kolokol* [The tsar bell] (Moscow, 1958), pp. 17, 32-35.

6. The decorations on the bell's surface consist of several horizontal bands of floral friezes, two full-length portraits on opposite surfaces of Tsar Aleksei Mikhailovich (1645-76) and Empress Anna Ivanovna (1730-40), who commissioned the bell at the beginning of her reign. Above each of the imperial portraits are icons, including a central oval medallion with the image of Jesus Christ. Between the portraits of the tsar and the empress, are cartouches with inscriptions. The various elements in the bell's decorative system are linked by floral garlands.

7. The bell mold actually rests in the pit. The metal that will create the bell has not yet been poured into the mold.

8. Cathedral Square at the heart of the Kremlin, on which face its cathedrals, palaces, and bell tower.

9. The apparatus and machinery constructed above the pit was only for lifting the cope or outer mold, and once the bell had been cast for raising it slightly from the floor of the pit, so that its lip could be cleaned. The empress intended that Motorin's bell would be raised vertically into a special tower to be built directly above its pit. These plans, however, were never realized. Ernest Morris, *Bells of All Nations* (London, 1951), p. 158.

10. The pouring of molten bronze from the four furnaces into the mold began at 1:13 A.M. on the morning of 25 November 1735 (O.S.); by 1:49 A.M., thirty-six minutes later, the last of the four furnaces had emptied. With an average flow of six tons of metal per minute, Mikhail Motorin's rate of casting his father's bell was one of the most rapid on record up to that time. N.N. Rubtsov, *History of Foundry Practice in USSR,* trans. from the Russian (New Delhi, 1975), p. 478.

11. The newly-cast bell cooled several days in its mold buried in the pit. Before casting, Motorin had filled the pit with packed dirt to support the mold when the metal was poured. The mold, therefore, had to be excavated after the metal had cooled and hardened, before the cope could be removed and the bell revealed.

12. The Motorins' *Tsar'-kolokol* is the largest and heaviest bell ever cast. After loss of metal through burning during the casting process, the bell's weight has been calculated at close to 12,000 *puds,* which is equivalent to 433,356 pounds or 216-2/3 tons. The height of *Tsar'-kolokol* is slightly over 19 feet, and its lower diameter is 19-1/3 feet. The thickness of its wall at the sound-bow (the point where the clapper would have struck the bell) is 2 feet. Schumann, in this portion of his poem, has omitted an entire century of the bell's history from 1735, when it was founded, to 1836, when Montferrand raised the bell to ground level. During these hundred years the bell remained in its subterranean home.

13. The crown, also known as the cannons, of a bell is the loops by which a bell was suspended from a beam or girder in a bell tower.

14. The color of a bronze bell when removed from its mold is a silver-grey. After aging in a tower for some time, the bronze corrodes to a grey-green tone. John Camp, *Bell Ringing: Chimes-Carillons-Hand Bells: The World of the Bell and the Ringer* (Newton Abbot, England: 1974), p. 86.

15. At this point Schumann begins to weave his own legend of *Tsar'-kolokol* to establish the motivation for his moral at the end of the poem. When Motorin's bell was removed from its mold, it was a perfect instrument. The bell was only damaged a year and a half after its founding, during the Trinity Fire on 29 May 1737 (O.S.). When burning timbers from the shed over the pit began to fall down on the bell and to overheat the metal, fire fighters in the Kremlin rightly feared that it would soon be reduced to a shapeless mass, since bronze has a relatively low melting point. To extinguish the fire in the pit around the bell, they began to

pour in water. They put out the fire, but later discovered to their dismay that when the cold water had hit the red-hot metal, the damage to the bell was mortal. A 12-1/2-ton chunk was thrown off from the sound-bow, and the bell sustained a number of cracks and fissures as well. Boguslavskii, *Tsar'-kolokol* [The Tsar Bell], p. 38. Schumann's testimony notwithstanding, the piece broken off from the sound-bow is not even close to the icon of Jesus Christ above the head of Alexei Mikhailovich, but rather, cuts into one of the inscription cartouches.

16. The person in a robe, who addresses the bell founder, is presumably a Russian priest, monk, or cleric of some kind.

17. John Murray transmits the following false information on *Tsar'-kolokol,* a version of which may be reflected in this passage from Schumann's poem: "It is said that the tower in which it originally hung was burnt in 1737, and its fall buried the enormous mass deep in the earth, and broke a huge fragment from it." *Hand-book for Northern Europe; including Denmark, Norway, Sweden, Finland, and Russia,* new ed., part II: Finland and Russia (London, 1849), p. 551.

18. For an explanation of the way in which the bell was damaged, see note 15.

19. Although Schumann begins this section in the manner of the German *Märchen (Es hört der Kaiser von dem Riesen),* the Russian tsar to whom this statement applies was Nicholas I (1825-55). His empress had already received Clara Schumann at the Winter Palace in St. Petersburg where she had played for the imperial court. *Schumann v Rossii,* p. 140. In the translations of these poems, the German *Kaiser* has been rendered "tsar," when referring to the Russian sovereign, and "emperor," when used to designate Napoleon.

20. Nicholas I had commissioned the French architect and engineer, Auguste Montferrand to raise Motorin's bell from its pit so that it could be displayed on ground level at the foot of the Ivan Velikii Bell Tower. The entire operation of 1836 is chronicled in Montferrand's *Description de la grande cloche de Moscou* (Paris, 1840).

21. The treasury of Russia is housed in a wing of the Kremlin Palace, *Oruzheinaia Palata* (Armory), which is located between Cathedral Square and the Borovitsky Gate.

22. Nikolai Olovianishnikov cites a legend among the Old Believers, a schismatic sect, that on the Day of the Last Judgment, *Tsar'-kolokol* will rise from its platform and begin to ring. *Istoriia kolokolov i kolokololiteinoe iskusstvo* [The history of bells and the art of bell founding], 2nd ed. enl. (Moscow, 1912), p. 192.

23. One of Napoleon's first military achievements was his notable victory as commander of a cannon battery at Toulon in the autumn and early winter of 1793. Vincent Cronin, *Napoleon Bonaparte: An Intimate Biography* (New York, 1972), pp. 73-76.

24. Napoleon and his *Grande Armée* reached Moscow on 14 September 1812 (N.S.), only to find the city of almost 300,000 virtually abandoned. Shortly after their arrival, mysterious fires began to break out and soon raged out of control. André Castelot, *Napoleon,* trans. Guy Daniels (New York, 1971), p. 426-27.

25. Louis Antoine Henri de Bourbon-Condé, Duc d'Enghien, was a French counter-revolutionary, who was falsely implicated in the Cadoudal-Pichegru conspiracy. Napoleon ordered Enghien's arrest on 15 March 1804, and, after a mock trial, he was executed on 21 March. Napoleon, through his execution of Enghien, sought to discourage royalist conspirators in their activities to restore the House of Bourbon. Cronin, *Napoleon Bonaparte,* pp. 242-44.

26. Schumann's reference here to Napoleon's ride through "the burning Petrovsky Gate" is not clear. Although a Petrovsky Tower stands in the Kremlin wall, which borders the Moscow River, it does not contain a gate. When Napoleon mounted his horse and entered the Kremlin on 15 September (N.S.) he rode through the Kutafia and Troitsky (Trinity) Gates, the entrance through which most tourists pass into the Kremlin today. Following his flight from the Kremlin, when threatened by the fire, Napoleon took up residence in the Petrovsky Palace on the outskirts of Moscow. Schumann may be referring to Napoleon's gallop through the gates of the (old) Petrovsky Palace.

27. From 1815 until his death in 1821, Napoleon lived in exile on St. Helena, an island in the South Atlantic under English control.

28. Schumann is speaking here of Napoleon's son and heir, the former King of Rome. At the time of Napoleon's death on St. Helena, his son bore the title, Duke of Reichstadt, and was living in Vienna.

29. Napoleon was buried beside a stream on St. Helena from 1821 until 1840.

30. Schumann's manuscript is illegible.

31. Louis Philippe ruled France between the revolutions of 1830 and 1848.

32. In his last will and testament, drafted on 15 April 1821, Napoleon wrote: "It is my wish that my ashes repose on the banks of the Seine, amid the French people whom I have loved so well." Castelot, *Napoleon,* p. 602.

33. *Die steife Last,* meaning Napoleon's remains.

34. In 1840 Louis Philippe sent his son, François, Prince de Joinville, on the frigate, *La belle Poule,* to St. Helena to accompany the return of Napoleon's remains to Paris. A sumptuous funeral procession in mid-December of 1840 was followed by Napoleon's final interment beneath the dome in the Hôtel des Invalides.

35. Napoleon died on St. Helena 5 May 1821.

36. The final verses of Schumann's poem recall the conclusion of Heine's ballad, *Die beiden Grenadiere,* which the composer had set in 1840.

37. The French caught their first glimpse of Moscow from Obeisance Hill near Fili, southwest of the Kremlin on 13 September 1812 (N.S.). The brilliant autumn sunlight on the hundreds of cupolas and towers dazzled the army as it looked out on this panorama. Cronin, *Napoleon Bonaparte,* p. 319.

38. On 15 September when Napoleon entered Moscow, it was practically a deserted city. No Russians came forth either to challenge the presence of the French or to surrender the city. Castelot, *Napoleon,* p. 427.

39. Schumann's manuscript is illegible.

40. Count Fyodor Vasil'evich Rostopchin (1763-1826), Governor-General of Moscow, had ordered the city evacuated before the arrival of the French. Moreover, he had ordered all fire hoses and pumps removed from Moscow and left the French only buckets to fight the conflagrations. Rostopchin is also alleged to have organized the incendiaries, who set the fires throughout the city. Cronin, *Napoleon Bonaparte,* p. 320.

41. Schumann's manuscript is illegible.

6

"The Present in the Past":
Russian Opera and Russian Historiography, ca. 1870

Richard Taruskin (U.S.A.)

"Now *there* is a page of history," Nikolai Kostomarov is supposed to have exclaimed at the conclusion of *Boris Godunov*. For Stasov, who overheard (or perhaps elicited) the famous historian's remark, there could be no higher praise, and he advertised it repeatedly in his writings on Musorgsky.[1] Both the comment and the importance accorded it were symptomatic of the time. The seriousness with which historical drama and even historical opera were considered by educated Russians was one of the hallmarks of the Alexander II period, when the positivist outlook reached the high water mark and art was seen as bearing an obligation, in Chernyshevsky's words, to embody a content "worthy of the attention of a thinking man."[2] The "thinking realist" was as much the literary archetype of the moment as the "superflous man" had been a generation back, and the epithet was applied (not without some irony) to the composer of *Boris* by Herman Laroche in a surprisingly favorable review.[3]

The attitude of high seriousness with which people went to the theater in those days was a very self-conscious, somewhat affected thing. So was historicism. The two met in the pages of the *Vestnik Evropy* [The European Herald], a "thick journal" of historiography and liberal opinion. The very first issue contained a learned exchange between Kostomarov and Stasov on the historical verisimilitude of the production of Serov's opera *Rogneda*.[4] The editor, Mikhail Stasiulevich, saw fit to introduce it with this half-apologetic yet optimistic note:

> Perhaps a few of our readers will be surprised that in our "Historical Chronicle" section we speak of the theater and of scenic productions, even though the journal is devoted specifically to historical scholarship. But such doubts will not visit those who, like us, think of the theater not as an idle amusement, but accord it a high significance among the organs which motivate and develop the intellectual life of man, and, consequently, have an influence on the history of societies.[5]

This positivistic, melioristic esthetic was echoed a year later by Kostomarov himself, in the pages of the same journal, when he affirmed that "the theater has the means to disseminate throughout society information on past life, just as it can acquaint [society] with the trends and notions of the present; just as, in general, it can serve as an important weapon in broadening the intellectual horizon of society."[6] The view of art as a didactic tool, the very attitude a younger generation would brand a "slap in the face of Apollo,"[7] was among the factors contributing most to the efflorescence of historical drama at this particular juncture in Russian literary history. Relaxation of censorship was another, though the censor continued to exert a stronger grip on the theater than on printed literature (and stronger yet on opera, in curious ways we shall examine).

The stunning achievement of Nikolai Karamzin (1766-1826), the littérateur turned "Official Historiographer," had also played a part. His monumental *History of the Russian State,* which appeared in twelve volumes beginning in 1818 (the last one was published posthumously), had an electrifying effect on Russian intellectual life. Intensely monarchist and nationalist, it made as important a contribution to the development of Russian national consciousness as it did to the development of historicist thinking in the land. It provided a prime underpinning to the concept of official nationality, the dominant ideology of the reign of Nikolai I (which received one of its classic artistic expressions in Glinka's *A Life for the Tsar* of 1836). Its impact on imaginative literature was immediate: it began, in fact, before the *History* was even complete. Volumes X and XI, covering the reigns of Tsars Fyodor Ioannovich, Boris Godunov, and the False Dimitri, appeared in 1824; Pushkin wrote his famous tragedy in 1825 (though it was not published until 1831). As can be clearly demonstrated (as in fact we shall demonstrate), whatever Pushkin's artistic insights and embellishments may have been, he found not only his subject but its treatment ready-made in Karamzin.

Boris Godunov was the progenitor of the whole line of Russian romantic historical dramas in verse. Such had been Pushkin's intention: with his "Shakespearean" tragedy he had hoped to break the stranglehold of French neoclassical drama on the Russian court theater. Karamzin's vivid portrayal of Boris in his *History* had provided Pushkin with the pretext he had been looking for to attempt the "reform of our stage."[8] If we discount for the moment the minor contributions made to the historical drama in the 1840s by such romantic novelists as Mikhail Zagoskin and Ivan Lazhechnikov, the reform initiated by Pushkin was next taken up by the lyric poet Lev Alexandrovich Mey (1822-62), whose *Tsar's Bride* (1849) and especially *Pskovitianka* [The Maid of Pskov] (1859) marked something of an epoch in the development of the genre, in terms both of period atmosphere and seriousness of treatment.[9] Unlike Pushkin's play, moreover, Mey's were "well-made" and effective and they inspired imitations. What in the forties and fifties had been a trickle turned,

after *Pskovitianka,* into a flood, which reached its peak in the late sixties and early seventies, that is, just when the operas we shall consider were conceived. Dramatists great and small were caught up willy-nilly in this rising tide. Alexander Ostrovsky was temporarily diverted from his true métier, that of realistic domestic dramas in prose, to compose a series of "chronicles" in verse which culminated in a kind of trilogy: *Dimitri the Pretender and Vasily Shuisky* (1867),[10] *Tushino* (also 1867), and *Vasilisa Melentieva* (1868).[11] An actual historical trilogy was the magnum opus of Count Alexei Tolstoy: *The Death of Ivan the Terrible* (1866), *Tsar Fydor Ioannovich* (1868), and *Tsar Boris* (1870). And then there was the work of numerous stringers and hacks like Nikolai Chaev (*Dimitri the Pretender,* 1866; *The Dread Tsar Ivan Vasilievich,* 1868; etc.) and Serov's *Rogneda* librettist Dmitri Averkiev (*Sloboda Nevolia,* 1866). The whole spate is often dismissed by modern critics for its excessive plot complications and superfluous characters (owing to a naive understanding of Pushkin's technique and its Shakespearean model), for its falsification of the conditions of old Russian life through the inevitable introduction of the theme of romantic love (here Pushkin alone had been blameless), and, finally, for its clumsy and stilted rhetoric—"the conventional language of contemporary poetry larded with idioms from old documents and from folklore."[12]

But, superficial though they may have been, these plays clearly answered a real and definite need. A clue to the nature of that need may be gleaned from the subject matter their authors all favored. Without exception the titles given above deal with the late reign of Ivan the Terrible and the "Time of Troubles" *(smutnoe vremia)* that followed it, that is, the period *ca.* 1565-1613.[13] This may be partly explained by the conditions of the censorship, which forbade the appearance of any member of the Romanov dynasty as a character on the stage. The Time of Troubles, then, was the very latest phase of Russian history that could be used by a dramatist, at least if he adhered to Karamzin's "Caesaristic" mode of historiography, which viewed the history of Russia in terms of the personalities of the tsars. And, in those days, who didn't?[14] As to the specific attractions of Ivan the Terrible and Boris Godunov, we have Karamzin again to thank, for his masterly and controversial character portraits of these two titanically flawed personages had turned them into veritable myths. The historical theater of the 1860s was taking an increasingly "psychological" turn (it was the period, after all, that spawned *Crime and Punishment*), and Ivan and Boris provided an endless source of psychopathological speculation on the part of dramatists whose aims ranged from the loftiest (Tolstoy) to the most trivial (Averkiev: "I wanted to show Ivan the Terrible not as the Tsar Ioann, but . . . [as] Vanya, Vanyusha, sweetheart").[15]

Finally, we may recall the social and civic themes with which we opened this essay. Belinsky had observed in 1846 that "the study of Russian history has never had so serious a character as it has taken on recently," and went on to one

of his most famous dicta: "We question, nay, we interrogate the past for an explanation of our present and a hint of our future."[16] All this was even more true in the 1860s. It was for Russia a new time of troubles, a period of social unrest unprecedented within living memory, brought about by the disastrous Crimean War, by the Emancipation, and by nationalist uprisings on the peripheries of the Empire. Art sought "relevant" themes, and in all media one can observe the swing away from the Kievan period as favored historical epoch to that of the Time of Troubles, matching the general swing from romanticism to realism as the reigning esthetic.

That opera lagged a bit behind the spoken drama until the end of the sixties can be seen from the standpoint of *Rogneda,* which had a Kievan setting though it was produced as late as 1865, and which celebrated an "official nationality" hardly less egregious than that of *A Life for the Tsar.* For many, that was merely in the nature of the operatic beast. Kostomarov, though his admiration was sincere, greeted Serov's work in a way that appears in retrospect to be unwittingly patronizing:

> Such a remote period as the time of Vladimir [the tenth-century Kievan prince who Christianized Russia], virtually impossible for drama [owing to the absence of a sufficient fund of information for realistic treatment], suits opera better, as it generally seems that where the dramatic kernel is shrouded in an epic atmosphere, opera must replace drama, and will thus serve as a musical interpretation of such historical facts as would be, by virtue of the remoteness of their epoch, hardly accessible even to the strongest dramatic talent. And in that case it is necessary that any opera with a historical subject, both in content and in its musical idea, leave us with the impression precisely of a historico-epic image, through which the subject may be conveyed to us out of the depths of the past, and in which it may be grasped and reproduced by artistic creation.[17]

But this, on second thought, is only the standard idealist view of music as an art with the "capacity to reach back into prehistory," as Vischer, for one, put it.[18] Nor is it so far from what Wagner had to say on the matter. In *Opera and Drama* he had declared historical verisimilitude and "realization" of feeling irreconcilable, and had deplored the historical drama (which to a musician, of course, meant the French grand opera) as "romance turned to politics."[19] Serov, his Russian admirer and the author of *Rogneda,* followed Wagner in this view (no doubt consciously), going so far in one critical essay as to rule out Pushkin's *Boris Godunov* as a viable operatic subject, since the title character was one in whom "rational thought predominates," and this was "an element unmusical in essence."[20] Elsewhere Serov rejected Ostrovsky's *Dimitri the Pretender* for a similar reason: "it is a brilliant subject to be sure, but in essence not very musical. Politics plays the chief role in it and music, by virtue of its open, candid nature, is but a poor elucidator of political and diplomatic intrigue. Give us rather something *simpler,* more heartfelt."[21] We seem to be dealing here with what Dahlhaus has characterized as the "neoromantic" plight

of music in the latter nineteenth century: "romantic in an unromantic age dominated by positivism and realism."[22] And yet, as anyone who knows the standard operatic repertoire is aware, there were composers in Russia only too eager to embrace positivism and realism and to try their hands at the new historical drama without compromise. Their unprecedented success can be preliminarily measured in the startling paragraph with which Prince Mirsky concluded his not-too-admiring survey of the Russian costume play:

> The principal interest of all this drama is its connection with the far more vigorous growth of the Russian opera; Rimsky-Korsakov's librettist, Belsky, was one of its best writers, and above all it can claim kinship with the greatest Russian tragic poet of the period, Modest Musorgsky. Musorgsky himself wrote the libretto of *Khovanshchina* and adapted with great skill Pushkin's *Boris Godunov* to make his popular opera. That he had dramatic as well as musical genius cannot be denied, but the literary historian unfortunately has no right to appropriate him or to sever the dramatic from the musical texture of his dramas.[23]

The mention of Belsky is both inappropriate and anachronistic, no doubt motivated by personal regard.[24] But Rimsky's first opera, *Pskovitianka*, after Mey's play, was one of the most remarkable achievements of the early "kuchkist" period (it is dedicated, in fact, to "my dear musical circle"). It stands with *Boris*, its exact contemporary, as the kuchkist opera *par excellence:* seeking as little compromise as possible with operatic convention, it attempts to harness music's power to realize not only transcendent feeling, but that "content worthy of the attention of a thinking man" which sets realist art apart from romantic. Like *Boris* and *Khovanshchina* it is not only "historical drama" but drama about history, in which the past is treated and confronted in the light of advanced historiographical thought, and in which an attempt is made to contribute to historical understanding.

We shall focus on *Pskovitianka* and *Boris* primarily from this standpoint, and, rushing in where Mirsky feared to tread, we shall (particularly in the case of Musorgsky's so much better known work) to a considerable extent sever the "historiographical" from both the dramatic and the musical textures of the operas. Our method will be comparative. But instead of comparing Rimsky's opera with Musorgsky's directly (except briefly, when passing from one to the other), we shall compare *Pskovitianka* with another exactly contemporaneous work, Tchaikovsky's *The Oprichnik*, which, like *Pskovitianka*, was concerned with Ivan the Terrible; and we shall compare *Boris* not with any other opera but with its own first version. Our goal in both cases will be to place the operas in a precise historical as well as historiographical context and to show how the composers, unlike their "neoromantic" comtemporaries, saw themselves as aspiring participants in their country's intellectual life.

II

In the *Vestnik Evropy* article we quoted from above, Kostomarov went on to say:

> One has to allow the dramatist who deals with historical personages to invent whatever he likes, but only on the condition that the historian would say, "although history says nothing about this, the progress of events, the nature of the characters, the spirit of the era and the customs of the time are all presented by the poet just as they must have been." That, in our view, is what one must demand of a historical drama.[25]

It seems a pious Aristotelian platitude (and all the more so since the object in view was *Rogneda*). Yet it contains the seeds of controversy without end, since historians inevitably differ, and never more than they did in the Russia of Alexander II's time. If from the civic point of view the most important of these controversies concerned an area that was off-limits to the drama—the reforms of Peter the Great and the church schism—the one that most closely concerned artists and dramatists was the one that revolved around the character and the place in history of Ivan the Terrible. It began in 1821 with the publication of the ninth volume of Karamzin's *History*. Up until then Karamzin had behaved like a servile aristocratic historian, foreshadowing Nikolaian ideology and (in words attributed to Pushkin) "proving the necessity of autocracy and the delights of the knout."[26] But although Karamzin did indeed view the autocracy as necessary, emphasizing again and again that "whenever the power of the sovereign was emasculated, Russia fell apart and her subjects turned into slaves,"[27] he had his doubts about the knout, especially when wielded by a sovereign with no respect for law. Having himself suffered under the despotic rule of Paul I, Karamzin passed a harsh judgment on the "unenlightened" sixteenth-century despot, summing it all up in a ringing passage that completely captivated the imagination of his contemporaries:

> Amid other sore trials of Fate, beyond the misfortune of the feudal system, beyond the Mongolian yoke, Russia had also to endure the terror of an Autocrat-Torturer. She withstood it with love for the autocracy, for she believed that God sends plagues, earthquakes and tyrants alike; she did not break the iron scepter in Ivan's hands but bore with her tormentor for twenty-four years, armed only with prayer and patience, in order to have, in better times, Peter the Great and Catherine the Second (History does not like to name the living [i.e., Alexander I, Karamzin's patron]). In magnanimous tranquility martyrs died on Red Square like the Greeks at Thermopylae, for their fatherland, for Faith and Loyalty, without even a thought of rebellion. In vain did some foreign historians seek to excuse Ivan's cruelty by writing of the conspiracies he crushed by means of it: these conspiracies existed only in the Tsar's troubled mind, as all our chronicles and state papers attest. The Clergy, the Boyars, the distinguished citizenry would not have summoned the beast from his lair at Alexandrovo had they been planning treason, of which they were accused just as absurdly as they were of sorcery. No, the tiger revelled in the blood of the

lambs—and the victims, perishing in innocence, in their last look at the impoverished land, demanded justice and a loving memory from their contemporaries and posterity!

Despite all hypotheses and speculations, the character of Ivan, beneficent Hero in his youth and ferocious bloodsucker in his manhood and old age, remains an enigma, and we would doubt the veracity of the most trustworthy accounts of him if the chronicles of other nations did not present us with examples just as astonishing: if Caligula, a *model sovereign* and a *monster*, if Nero, disciple of the wise Seneca, the *object of love* and the *object of disgust*, had not reigned in Rome. They were pagans; but Louis XI was a Christian and yielded to Ivan neither in ferocity nor in outward piety, by which both of them sought to expiate their iniquities. Both were pious out of fear, both were bloodthirsty and lecherous, like the Asiatic and Roman torturers. Miscreants beyond the law, beyond rule and all rational probability, these horrible meteors, these will-o'-the-wisps of unrestrained passion illumine for us through the ages the chasm of potential human depravity—to see it is to shudder! The life of a tyrant is a calamity for mankind, but his History is always useful to Sovereigns and peoples: to nurture aversion to evil is to nurture love of virtue—and glory to that time, when a historian armed with truth can, in an autocratic government, expose to shame such a ruler, may his like never again be seen! The grave is insensible: but the living dread the eternal damnation of History, which, while not reforming villains, can sometimes prevent misdeeds, always possible since wild passions rage even in times of civic enlightenment, commanding the mind to keep still or else in a servile voice to justify its crimes.[28]

This totally unexpected diatribe burst like a bombshell on the Russian intellectual community. "What an Ivan! What a Karamzin!" exclaimed Ryleev, the future Decembrist,[29] while at the other end of the political spectrum there were outraged condemnations: "A well-described virtue attracts people to goodness but it serves no purpose to expose and magnify forms of evil."[30] At least one purpose was served, however: a figure of epic proportions was bequeathed to Russian artists in all media, and to dramatists above all.

An excellent example of Karamzin's Ivan on the Russian stage can be found in Ivan Lazhechnikov's tragedy, *The Oprichnik* (1834), on which, some three decades later, Tchaikovsky was to base his opera. Lazhechnikov (1792-1869) was primarily a novelist who favored exotic and patriotic themes after the fashion of his time. His *Basurman* [The infidel] (1838), which Serov briefly considered turning into an opera in his extreme youth,[31] had contained a vivid, if trivially "realistic" portrait of Ivan III ("The Great," grandfather of "The Terrible"), drawn strictly from imagination, which sympathetic critics liked to contrast with the stilted magnificence of Pushkin's *Boris Godunov* on the one hand, and, on the other, the hazy romanticism of Lermontov's *Song of the Tsar Ivan Vasilievich* [i.e., the Terrible], *the Young Oprichnik, and the Brave Merchant Kalashnikov* (turned into an opera by Anton Rubinstein in the late seventies).[32] Meanwhile, the sensibilities of the defenders of official nationality were affronted. A review by the ultraconservative editor Thaddei Bulgarin suggests that the portrait of Ivan III in *Basurman* was a kind of dry run at that of Ivan IV in *The Oprichnik*, and was probably already heavily influenced by the description of the latter in Karamzin's *History:*

Ioann III is depicted in frantic terms, as one who flies into a fury at every word, seizes his nobles by the throat, curses them in the most extreme language, orders them beaten, rounded up, thrown into dungeons, picks fights but is really a coward who fears war, works solely by treachery, through his base courtiers. Shame and disgrace! This is our great Ioann!... It's unnatural and revolting. Ivan wasn't like that!...[*He*] *never bragged and never chattered about nonsense, but did his deeds heroically.*[33]

Undeterred, Lazhechnikov immediately embarked upon *The Oprichnik*, attracted particularly by the figure of Ivan the Terrible: "No one can dispute the fact," he boasted at the time of the belated première of the play, "that I was the first to think of putting the gigantic figure of Ivan on the stage."[34] His portrayal this time was so extreme as to provoke the censor, and the play remained unpublished until 1859, unperformed till eight years later. Though trouble with the censor lends an inevitable glamor, all agree that Lazhechnikov's *Oprichnik* was no masterpiece. It concerns one of the murkiest and least understood phases of Ivan IV's reign, but its virtues are those of the well-made play; it broadened no one's intellectual horizon.

The *oprichnina*, or *oprichina* (from *oprich*, a thing apart) was Ivan's personal domain within Russia, created by decree in 1565 as an administrative entity distinct from the *zemshchina*, or territories belonging, as before, to hereditary landowners. Within the *oprichnina*, land was held by a special class of "serving people" known as the *oprichniki*, (sing., *oprichnik*), sworn to stringent vows of personal loyalty to the Tsar (for which reason they are often erroneously described as the Tsar's bodyguard), who were assigned special tasks of surveillance over the rest of the population and of "tracking down traitors."[35] The quasi-monastic life of the oprichniki, their dread hound's-head-and-broom insignia, their documented excesses of zeal (or of simple plunder) in carrying out the Tsar's program, contain all the makings of lurid melodrama, and Karamzin certainly did not miss his opportunity:

It quickly became apparent that Ivan had sacrificed all of Russia to his oprichniki. They were always right in court, on them there could be neither judgment nor restraint. An oprichnik, or hellhound [*kromeshnik*]—for so they came to be called, as if they were monsters of hellish darkness—could with impunity oppress and plunder his neighbor.... In a word, the people of the *zemshchina*, from courtier to townsman, were disenfranchised, helpless before the oprichnik. The former were prey, the latter predators, and all so that Ivan might count on the zeal of his highwaymen-bodyguards in any new, murderous plan he might think up.[36]

This indignant view of the *oprichnina* as the instrument not of reform, whether administrative, political or social, but of terror inflicted by a paranoiac sovereign on an innocent populace, was taken over not merely uncritically but enthusiastically by Lazhechnikov as the background to his tragedy. He gave the piece a veneer of historical authenticity by drawing the names of his characters from Karamzin (e.g., the leading oprichniki Viazemsky, Basmanov, and Skuratov), by having the oprichniki referred to as "kromeshniki," and by

citing footnote references to the *History of the Russian State* to justify or document such matters as the abduction of Boyar maidens and wives to the Tsar's *sloboda,* or retreat,[37] the ubiquity of spies and informers, the nature of the oprichnik oath, even the sport of bear wrestling. But despite this apparent diligence, Lazhechnikov really took from Karamzin little more than a hackneyed backdrop. The main plot line is adapted from a familiar stock situation.

It runs as follows: the young boyar Andrei Morozov joins the oprichniki with the object of settling accounts with Prince Zhemchuzhny, who has cheated Andrei and his mother out of their inheritance, and with whose daughter Natasha he is in love (she, of course, is plighted to another). But when she finds out that he has joined the hated band, Natasha rejects him. In despair, Andrei petitions the Tsar for release from his vows. Ivan hypocritically assents, with the proviso that Andrei remain an oprichnik until after his wedding feast. In the midst of the celebration, the Tsar sends word that he wishes Natasha brought to his chambers alone. Andrei forgets his oprichnik discipline and insists upon accompanying his bride against the Tsar's orders, which gives Ivan the pretext to have him murdered. Natasha, throwing herself at the fatally wounded Andrei, herself falls accidentally upon a sword and is killed. As for Andrei's mother, she drops dead on the spot upon discovering that her son has joined the oprichniki.

It is obvious that this is no historical drama at all, but a drama of Fate after the German romantic model.[38] Historical personages and conditions are merely the tools of the stars in their conspiracy against the pure love of a Russian Romeo and Juliet. The bloody denouement has the same character and significance as in, say, Heine's *William Ratcliff* (operaticized by César Cui)—the inexorable working out of implacable forces beyond the protagonists' control. The Karamzinian persona of Ivan-aş-evil-genius was a convenient Fury and little more. Shown as he is only in domestic surroundings and concerned with trivial affairs, the Tsar emerges as a petty sadist, while the oprichniki are reduced to a band of rowdies and roisterers, a medieval motorcycle gang.

All of this rendered Lazhechnikov's *Oprichnik* excellently suitable to Tchaikovsky's creative strengths and needs. The composer attended the play's first Moscow production, three weeks after the belated première in St. Petersburg in September 1867. He remembered it as a play sufficiently close in setting to Ostrovsky's *The Voyevoda* to accommodate the transfer of music from his unsuccessful first opera.[39] The fact that the historical data in *The Oprichnik* were merely circumstantial and of little specific relevance to the central, "universal" love-fate intrigue was for Tchaikovsky not a minus but a plus. In the opera, in fact, the purely historical element shrank to even less significance than in the play, both for reasons outside the composer's control and for reasons very much within it, as he wrote his own libretto.

To begin with, the figure of Ivan himself had to be removed for legal reasons. So his functions were taken over by the oprichnik Viazemsky (rechristened Viazminsky in the opera, perhaps also in deference to the censor). The latter, not Ivan, administers the oath to Andrei, and this necessitated a further change in the plot. In Lazhechnikov's play Ivan exercises his arbitrary power and grants Andrei the exceptional favor of exemption from the requirement that he renounce all ties with his mother.[40] Viazminsky could not do this in the opera, and so Andrei must renounce her, which motivates the maternal curse that replaces Natasha's rejection and forms the climax of the third act. Also absent in the opera were the scenes that showed the oprichniki in action, whether plundering the *zemshchina* (Act II, sc. i-iv) or leading their peculiar monkish life at the Tsar's retreat (Act III, sc. iv-v). The latter aspect of the oprichniki was all summed up operatically in the quasi-religious chorus that prefaces the oath-taking scene (Act II, sc. ii), while the former was reduced to a few shouts of "Hoyda, hoyda" in the first and third acts.

Far more interesting were the changes Tchaikovsky made for reasons of artistic principle. As is usual in operatic adaptations, the cast of characters was radically scaled down (from thirty-two to eight) and the action was notably streamlined. Tchaikovsky succeeded in reducing the plot of his opera to a set of pliant stock elements that could be freely and effectively rebuilt and reordered so as to conform to a very specific and in its day highly regarded set of dramaturgical conventions, i.e., those of Scribe's grand opera libretti. From this point of view, and despite the ridicule *The Oprichnik* continues to elicit even from those most kindly disposed toward the composer, Tchaikovsky's adaptation of Lazhechnikov was quite impressively skillful, demonstrating not only his intimate acquaintance with Scribe's structural methods (as embodied at their most mature in *Le Prophète* and *Les Huguenots*), but a decided dramaturgical flair of his own. Everyone quotes Gerald Abraham's bon mot that *The Oprichnik* was "Meyerbeer translated into Russian."[41] But the translation really took place at the precompositional level (there is not, nor did Abraham mean to imply that there was, much musical resemblance between the Russian composer and his cosmopolite forebear). And it is therefore much more interesting than the notorious comment would suggest. Moreover, as the first deliberate and principled attempt to "translate" the most complex and imposing international operatic method of its day into Russian, *The Oprichnik* deserves a far closer and more respectful look than it has yet received.

III

There is not space for a look that is both close and comprehensive, so let us focus entirely on the act which most closely reveals Tchaikovsky's operatic methods, the third. It is a classic Scribian act. As the baroque opera is often referred to as "exit opera," so may the French grand opera be termed "entrance

opera." After an opening decorative chorus, a soliloquy, or both, an act is typically given a steadily mounting tension through a progressive accumulation of characters, each of whose entrances marks an abrupt shift in plot. The final peripeteia is musically fixed by a huge ensemble with chorus, the latter now taking on a more active role, often, moreover, divided into various (and oft-times opposing) groups.

In order to achieve this dramaturgical rhythm in his third act, Tchaikovsky made quite free with Lazhechnikov's plot. Events from numerous scenes in the original play were telescoped. Some of them bore only a slight resemblance to Lazhechnikov's scenario. Others were contrived for the occasion.

After a brief, agitated entr'acte (which contains some striking common-tone progressions of the kind made famous by the Coronation scene in *Boris Godunov*), the curtain goes up on a typically Scribian "scenic tableau":[42] a quite lengthy formal choral lament, in which the people of Moscow bewail Russia's "orphanhood" (i.e., the Tsar's retreat from Moscow to his abode at Alexandrovo). The opening and closing quatrains of Tchaikovsky's text are worth quoting for their ironic contrast with the libretto of *Pskovitianka*, to which we shall presently turn:

Vremena nastali zlye:	Evil times have come:
Nas pokinul tsar' otets.	Our father Tsar has left us
I volkov golodnykh staia	And a pack of famished wolves
razoriaet nas v konets.	Is bringing us to ruin.
Nas pokinul pastyr' dobryi	Our good shepherd has left us,
Stado zhalkoe svoë,	His poor, forsaken flock,
Bed velikikh preispolnil	Horrendous woes have overwhelmed
Nashe gor'koe zhit'ë.	Our bitter existence.

The idea for this chorus came apparently from the speeches of the boyars Fyodorov and Viskovatov in Lazhechnikov's Act III, sc. iii.[43] Morozova (Andrei's mother) now enters and soliloquizes an arioso about her loneliness. This material is drawn from Lazhechnikov's Act II, sc. vi (Morozova alone). She is taunted by a little chorus of street urchins (the Boris-like progressions return here, and the resemblance of this scene to that of the taunting of the Holy Fool [*iurodivyi*] in *Boris* has often been remarked[44]). The text for this chorus (plus one line for "five basses [who] come out on stage and chase the urchins away") is taken from Lazhechnikov's Act III, sc. i.

The next entrance, and the plot situation it introduces, is Tchaikovsky's invention. Natasha, having run away from home, comes rushing onstage and seeks protection from Morozova. This episode may have been tenuously suggested by Andrei's abduction of Natasha in Lazhechnikov, Act IV, sc. i. And if so, then we have so far elements derived from three different acts of the

immobilized state.[46] Again as in *Ruslan,* the chorus is brought into play at the end of the quartet. But whereas in Glinka's opera the choral entrance provided nothing more than a coda, in Tchaikovsky's it forms a bridge to a new level of musical intensity: the monster *morceau d'ensemble avec choeurs,* a gigantic tableau, huge both in volume and in emotional weight, the crowning moment for which the whole preceding action had been a strategic preparation, an enormous dramaturgical upbeat (pp. 250;275). Like all Scribe-engineered musical climaxes, it take place in a complete dramatic stasis. Further development of action waits while the mood of agony is fixed and monumentalized at length by the impressive music.

When the mood had run its course, the action is resumed with a recitative by Basmanov over the oprichnik leitmotive. He suggests the only possible way out for Andrei: to plead with the Tsar for release. The idea is received enthusiastically by all, producing an instant change in affect and sending the *morceau d'ensemble* on to new heights of volume. All are now in agreement and join voices in one monolithic chordal mass: "To the Tsar! To the Tsar! He is God's chosen one! He is our lord and master! . . ." (pp. 262;286). Tchaikovsky works this into a lengthy musical coda, which ends with the exit of all the principals, the chorus meanwhile continuing its celebration in a second coda, *tempo vivace,* as the curtain falls.

The third act of *The Oprichnik* is a kind of monument to convention. In it, Tchaikovsky can be seen as a genuine musical counterpoint to Lazhechnikov: a sure-handed, highly professional if not overly subtle dramatist who knows how to harness to their maximum effect the theatrical methods of his day. The operatic esthetic within which he operated regarded the radical transformation of material appropriated from the spoken drama as a foregone conclusion (Meyerbeer: "One does not redo what has already been done perfectly").[47] The musical stage had its own requirements which differed considerably from those of the spoken stage. And the esthetic within which Lazhechnikov had operated regarded the radical transformation of historical fact for the sake of theatrical effect as equally to be taken for granted. But by the late 1860s all of these assumptions were being fundamentally questioned by radical artists, as was the view of history Lazhechnikov had taken as his starting point.[48]

IV

Karamzin ended his assessment of Ivan the Terrible with a passage that was to prove extremely suggestive to historians of a later generation:

> But let us give even the tyrant his due: even in the very extremes of evil Ivan looms as the specter of a great monarch, zealous, tireless, often shrewd in his political activity. Though (despite the fact that he always loved to compare himself with Alexander the Great) he hadn't even the shadow of courage in his soul, he remained a conqueror. In his foreign policy he

steadfastly followed the grand designs of his grandfather. He loved the truth in courts of law, not infrequently tried cases himself, heard grievances, read documents and made decisions without intermediaries. He punished oppressors of the people, unscrupulous dignitaries and usurers, both corporally and by shaming them.... Ivan showed respect for the Arts and Sciences, showing favor to educated foreigners. He founded no Academy, but promoted the education of the masses through the propagation of church schools, where even laymen learned to read and write, learned Law and even History.... Finally, Ivan is celebrated in history as a lawgiver and as a founder of the state.[49]

This last distinction was for historians of a certain stripe sufficient to redeem all the rest, even (or especially) the *oprichnina*. In the 1850s the influence of German idealism and German historicism began to make itself felt in Russian historiography. The school of historical writing known as "statist" appeared, which took over from Hegel and Schelling the idea that all of history points in the direction of the nation states of the post-Napoleonic period, and that historical judgments should be made not on the basis of contemporary morality but on the "objective" basis of this teleology. The state was a concept that transcended the personalities and the actions of rulers; any atrocity, any excess could be justitifed by the historian if it made a positive contribution to overriding historical processes.

Russian historians like Konstantin Kavelin (1818-85) and especially Sergei Solovyov (1820-79) believed in Hegel's concept of the world-historical individual, whose actions, whatever their ostensive immediate motivation, accorded with the demands of progress, that is, the progressive realization of freedom as vouchsafed in the nation-state. "The great man," in the words of Solovyov, "always and everywhere... satisfies the needs of the nation in a certain time.... The activity of the great man is always the result of all the previous history of the nation."[50] Accordingly, Solovyov "made an attempt to discover some political meaning in the series of events [i.e., those of the years 1565-72], which his fellow-historian [Karamzin] had taken to be nothing but a succession of horrors and acts of insanity."[51]

This was the first serious challenge to Karamzin's hitherto unassailable historiographical preeminence, and it centered around the figure of Ivan the Terrible. The *locus classicus* of the "statist" interpretation of Ivan's reign was the sixth volume (1856) of Solovyov's supremely ambitious twenty-nine-volume (!) *History of Russia from the Earliest Times*. This most comprehensive history of Russia ever attempted by a single author was a deliberate attempt to supersede Karamzin. It began coming out in 1851 and continued at the rate of a volume each year up to the author's death, by which time he had reached the year 1774. "Ivan the Terrible has long been an enigmatic figure in our history," wrote Solovyov." For a long time his character and deeds have been an object of controversy." The reason for the controversy lay in "the immaturity of historical science, the disinclination to give attention to the connection, the causality of phenomena."[52] The founder of the *oprichnina* emerges as a

farseeing reformer: "The age posed important problems, and at the helm of state stood a man whose character equipped him to move resolutely toward their solution."[53] However great and real the cruelties with which Ivan realized his policies, the struggle with the boyar class was historically determined, inevitable, and hence, "progressive."

And what were these policies? The statists located them first and foremost in Ivan's lengthy epistles to the renegade boyar Prince Andrei Mikhailovich Kurbsky, who had defamed and reviled him from his Lithuanian sanctuary, and whose treacherous defection is generally considered by modern historians to have been the efficient cause of the drastic administrative measures that led to the institution of the *oprichnina.* Kurbsky had challenged Ivan's right to rule autocratically. Ivan answered at furious length, defending not only his divine right, but his holy duty to wield his power without division or limit, as had his forebears, who "from the beginning . . . have ruled all their dominions, not the boyars, not the magnates." He bolstered his point with references to Greek and Roman history, showing in a passage that obviously impressed Karamzin, that unless "under one authority," nations and empires inevitably fell from greatness. And, of course, Ivan cited copiously from the Bible: "Bethink yourself: did God, having led Israel out of captivity, appoint a priest to command over men, or numerous governors? No, he made Moses alone lord over them, like a Tsar."[54]

Defense of his autocratic power, his assertion of it against the claims of the once-powerful boyars, and his consolidation of it throughout the length and breadth of his domain (which increased insignificantly in territory during his reign) constituted Ivan's primary domestic policy, and in this he was a profoundly "historical" figure in the eyes of Solovyov. One of his greatest exploits in pursuit of this policy was the ruthless destruction in 1570 of the ancient city of Novgorod, on suspicion of conspiring with Poland. For this, of course, Ivan was reviled by Karamzin, who bewailed the fate of one of Russia's great political entities, with her remarkable republican traditions (smashed by Ivan's grandfather Ivan III, "The Great") and her ties to the West through the Hanseatic League. But there can be no question that Ivan's bloody act strengthened the Muscovite state, and so for Solovyov it counted as one of Ivan's typically resolute solutions to the problems of his age.

The new image of Ivan as forerunner of Peter the Great, as visionary statesman and progressive historical force, quickly found expression in the arts. One thinks, for example, of Antokolsky's famous marble statue (1870), which depicts the Tsar seated deep in thought, a commanding figure of strength and determination, but of great intelligence and obvious wisdom as well. The first play to embody the new Ivan was Mey's *Pskovitianka,* composed only three years after Solovyov's third volume had appeared. With Rimsky-Korsakov's adoption of Mey's play for operatic treatment early in 1868 at the suggestion of Balakirev and Musorgsky[55] (and while the play was still under the

censor's ban), musicians now entered what was an arena of vital and vigorous intellectual debate.

Pskovitianka was the first attempt in the realm of fiction to "explain" the actions of the Grozny [Terrible, or threatening] Tsar along lines suggested by the new teleological historiography. Mey's Ivan seems to have read both Solovyov and Karamzin. He ponders and juxtaposes his various historiographical images. In one speech the Tsar deftly summarizes the "popular" view of his character and reign in terms patently Karamzinian: "A bloodthirsty blackguard, persecutor of the boyars and his zealous servants, a torturer, a killer, a monster!..."

Gotov ia vsiu ikh pesen'ku propet':
"On, mol, kakoi: chem tol'ko kto pravee,
Tem na sude ego i vinovatei;
Kto zhitiem, voistinu molchal'nym
I monastyrskim, gospodu ugoden,
Tot u nego—khanzha i litsemer;
Kto lestiu gnushaetsia—zavistnik,
A kto stoit za pravdu, po prisiage
I tselovan'iu krestnomu—otmiotnik,
Zlokoznennyi izmennik i predatel'!...
I vot, mol, on muzhei, toliko doblikh,
Preslavnykh tsartsva russkogo singklitov,
Vserodno istrebliaet, aki zver',
O nem zhe nam glasit Apokalipsis...
Ni vozrasta, ni pola ne zhaleet:
Grudnykh mladentsev, startsev
   bespomoshchnykh,
Nevinnykh dev terzaet liutoi mukoi
I teshitsia ikh krov'iu, so svoeiu
Kromeshnoi t'moi, chto satana s besami..."[56]

[Word for word I'll sing you their whole song:
"This is how he is: the more you're in the right,
The more guilty in his court you'll be judged;
If in your ways you are truly monklike
And humble, worthy of the Lord,
Then as far as he is concerned—you're a fraud and a hypocrite;
If flattery you shun—you're envious;
If you stand by the truth, swear oaths
And kiss the cross—you're a turncoat,
An insidious recreant and traitor!...
And look how he treats the mighty men,
Glorious defenders of the Russian realm—
He exterminates them one and all, like a very beast;
It is he of whom the Apocalypse forewarns...
He pities neither age nor gender;
Babes in arms, the helpless aged,
Innocent maids he racks with fearsome torture,

Amusing himself with their blood, in his
Hellish abyss, like Satan with his troop of devils..."]

But in a famous address to his son (modelled obviously on Boris's farewell in Pushkin), which Rimsky-Korsakov was to turn into a monologue, Ivan gives his reasons:

To tol'ko tsarstvo krepko i veliko,
Gde vedaet narod, chto u nego
Odin vladyka, kak v edinom stade
Edinnyi pastyr'... Esli zhe podpaskam
Pastukh dast voliu—pogibai vsio stado!...
Ne to chto volki, sami budut rezat'
Da svalivat' vinu svoiu na psov...
Net! tak by mne upravit'sia khotelos',
Rus' skovat' zakonom, chto broneiu.
Da dast li Bog mne razuma i sily?...[57]

[Only that kingdom is strong and great,
Where the people know they have
A single ruler, as in a single flock
There is a single shepherd.... Let the shepherd
Grant the herd boys their will—and the whole flock perishes!
Never mind the wolves; they themselves will do the killing
And lay the blame to the dogs...
No! I would like to rule so that
Rus' will be bound by law, like armor.
But will God grant me the insight and the strength?...]

This direct embodiment of historiographical controversy made *Pskovitianka* a "thinking man's" play, albeit Mey's handling of the Tsar struck more than a few as faintly ridiculous. Apollon Grigoriev, for one, could only laugh: "How comical is this Ivan Vasilievich, discoursing on his theories of government just like Mr. Solovyov,... almost a sweet and tenderhearted Ivan Vasilievich, this."[58] But most found impressive the skill with which the author effected the "organic" integration and interpenetration of historical background and Romantic intrigue. Neither the one nor the other can be viewed as superfluous in *Pskovitianka,* and the play therefore represented a breakthrough to a new level of responsibility and seriousness.

Mey's plot is cleverly contrived so as to provide an answer to some real historical questions. The drama is set in the year 1570, at the time of the Novgorod campaign. The question was: why, having destroyed Novgorod, did the Tsar come with all his retinue of oprichniki to Pskov, the other ancient Russian Hanseatic port, and yet spare it its sister's fate?

In a historical afterword to his drama, which bears the title "Annotations" *(Primechaniia)* in deliberate emulation of the famous documentary appendices

Karamzin had provided for each volume of his *History,* Mey himself indicates that this problem was what had initially attracted his attention to this episode as the basis for a play:[59]

> At first glance this unexpected mercy will seem decidedly enigmatic, and Karamzin was unable to explain it substantively, giving himself up rather to farfetched psychological speculations and even mysticism.
>
> According to him, Ivan Vasilievich visited the hermit monk Nikola Sadlos in the Pechersky Monastery and took fright at the latter's forthright speech.
>
> It was during Lent. Nikola handed the Tsar a piece of bloody meat. "I do not eat meat during the fast," objected Ioann. "You do worse than that, Tsar!" answered the hermit, according to Karamzin, "You drink Christian blood!!!"
>
> And the ruler became not angry and he spared the city of Pskov...
>
> He pitched camp not far from Pskov on the river, and was awakened that first night by the peal of Pskovan churchbells.
>
> "His heart was softened miraculously," once more according to Karamzin, "and..."
>
> ...And Pskov endured longer than Novgorod...
>
> But is this so? Is this the reason?
>
> Hardly.[60]

Mey rejects any ascription of superstition to this Machiavellian Tsar. Nor does he imagine that Ivan could have been taken in by protestations of fealty or hypocritical displays of bread-and-salt. "Tsar Ivan IV was above all else a politician," he avers, following the example of Solovyov. And so Mey prefers to believe that Ivan was motivated by concern lest both Russian Hanseatic cities be destroyed, thus cutting the country off from trade with the West (Ivan as proto-Peter, again). And that Pskov should have been the one spared Mey attributes to the fact that Ivan had personal ties there. Pskov had been conquered and ruled by his father, the Great Prince Vasily Ioannovich, son of Ivan III, and Ivan the Terrible had been there in his youth.[61] Acknowledging that not everyone might find this explanation convincing—sentimentality in a sixteenth-century despot seems a mite harder to swallow even than superstition—the author proceeds to fabricate a plot that will motivate his reading of the events of 1570 even as it provides a central romantic intrigue.

The "Pskovitianka"—maid of Pskov—of the title, the central character of the drama, is an invented, deliberate symbol of the "blood ties" that bind Pskov and Moscow and stay Ivan's hand from carnage. Noting that Ivan had briefly visited Pskov, according to chronicle accounts, in 1555, Mey supposes an affair between the young Tsar and the beautiful Pskovan Boyarinya Vera Sheloga. Mey christens their fictitious love-child Olga—an inevitable, symbolic choice, after the "Cross-receiving Olga" (*Krestopriimnaia Ol'ga),* the half-legendary wife of the tenth-century Kievan Prince Igor, who, born at Pskov, embraced Christianity long before the general conversion of Russia and became her native city's patron saint.[62] Mey's Olga is brought up by her mother's sister Nadezhda and her husband Prince Yuri Tokmakov, who happens to be the

Tsar's viceregent in Pskov. The circumstances of her conception and birth are revealed in Act I of Mey's drama, which takes place in the year 1555.[63]

The rest of the play (and the whole of the opera) concerns the events of 1570. A parallel with Lazhechnikov's *Oprichnik* is immediately suggested by the facile love-triangle that motivates the surface action—a stock coherence-insuring device that few constructors of drama out of history could avoid (not even Musorgsky in *Khovanshchina!*): Olga has been betrothed to the Pskovan boyar Nikita Matuta, who is old enough to be her father (he *is* the father of her best friend, Styosha). But she loves Mikhailo Tucha, the son of a landlord's overseer. When news of the Tsar's imminent arrival with his troops gets out, citizens of Pskov convene a *veche* (republican council),[64] at which an emissary from Novgorod horrifies all with his account of the bloodbath there. In order to escape a similar fate, the council resolves that Ivan shall be met with a show of submission and with petitions for mercy.[65] But Tucha rejects this idea and calls for armed resistance. A band of hotheads joins him and they march off into the woods. Ivan arrives in triumph and is entertained by Tokmakov. He demands refreshment and Tokmakov calls for Olga to give him drink. Upon sight of her, Ivan recognizes Vera's features and knows that he is looking at his own daughter. It is then that he utters the climactic words, "Let the killing cease! There has been too much blood. Make your swords blunt upon a stone: the Lord preserveth Pskov!"[66]

Olga tries to find Tucha to tell him of the Tsar's change of heart, but she is waylaid by Matuta and brought before the Tsar (it is at this point that he "discourses" on his historiographical image). While Olga is with Ivan, Tucha and his band mount an attack. The Tsar orders that Tucha's life be spared for Olga's sake, but his soldiers fire indiscriminately at the rebels and kill them all. When Olga learns that her beloved is dead, she picks up Ivan's own knife and stabs herself. The Tsar sends for his physician (the Dutchman Elisei Bomelius), but he can do nothing for her, and utters the drama's curtain line: "Sovereign! Only the Lord can raise the dead!"[67] Olga dies in her father-Tsar's arms.[68]

The symbolism is pretty thick, but it is effective. Olga's tragic situation—torn between the Tsar, her father, toward whom she feels a strange and inexplicable attraction, and her lover Tucha, the leader of the abortive insurrection—is the predicament of Pskov itself, torn between its independent republican traditions and the historical necessity of submission to Moscow. Olga's death, while melodramatic, epitomizes the historical moment. Not merely a "historical drama," *Pskovitianka* is a drama about history—history conceptualized in the light of Solovyov's Hegelian historiography.

V

It was already a measure of kuchkist idealism (or merely impracticality?) that the youngest member of Balakirev's circle should have chosen to turn into an opera a play that was under the censor's ban. The problem was compounded by an Imperial decree of 1837, which stipulated that while Russian rulers antedating the house of Romanov could appear on the dramatic stage, they could not appear in opera. When Rimsky inquired at the Censorship Bureau as to the reason for this, he was told, "And suppose the Tsar should suddenly sing a ditty? Well, it would be unseemly."[69]

But of course there was no danger of that in a kuchkist opera, as Rimsky and Musorgsky hastened to assure the censor in charge of the case, a certain Fridberg, who in any case was more intent upon toning down the republican trappings of the *veche* scene.[70] Rimsky secured permission for staging his opera by appealing to the Tsar's brother, the Grand Duke Konstantin, for special dispensation.[71] But Fridberg himself had been impressed by the seriousness of Rimsky's opera and in his report (7 January 1872, O.S.) urged that "high-level permission" be secured to circumvent the Nikolaian decree. "This would serve," he wrote in his pompous bureaucratic way, "to encourage young, talented creators (among whom Mr. Rimsky-Korsakov should be counted), to whose lot it falls to vouchsafe the existence of Russian opera, which has just begun to take on an independent character, thanks to the exemplary and typical works of Glinka, Dargomyzhsky, Serov, and others."[72]

Rimsky-Korsakov's *Pskovitianka* is as fully committed to a new conception of operatic dramaturgy as Tchaikovsky's *Oprichnik* is to an old one. Where the Moscow professional viewed opera as an art form with its own peculiar and immutable laws, the St. Petersburg naval cadet was at the time completely under the sway of a realist canon which sought in the name of "truth" to compromise the canons of the spoken theater as little as possible. The outstanding artifact of that tendency was Dargomyzhsky's *Stone Guest*,[73] which was in progress when Rimsky embarked on *Pskovitianka* in 1868, and which he himself was shortly to orchestrate upon Dargomyzhsky's death early the next year.

Accordingly, although Rimsky started out with a conventional libretto after Mey's play by the novelist Vsevolod Krestovsky (1840-95) in hand,[74] he quickly forsook it and worked directly from Mey's text, subjecting it for the most part only to a radical condensation both in length and in the number of characters (from forty-one to eleven), plus interpolating a few "genre" numbers for the chorus.[75] The role of Ivan the Terrible was the most "realistically" conceived one in the opera.[76] The scenes in which he appears are the ones in which the texts are most closely based on the original text of Mey's drama, and

Rimsky's opera comes closest to the ideal of the Dargomyzhskian "play set to music." The role is cast throughout in what Cui liked in his reviews to call "melodic recitative" (no ditties for the Tsar!), usually played off against the leitmotive that follows Ivan wherever he goes, and which in fact had been adumbrating him for two whole acts before his first appearance onstage. This theme, which resembles the opening tune of the familiar "Russian Easter" Overture (and which is thought by some therefore, to be, like it, a derivation from authentic Russian ecclesiastical—i.e., "znamenny"—chant[77]), is actually sung—once only—by Ivan upon his first entrance, but thereafter is predominantly an orchestral theme, against which Ivan usually sings a counterpoint of naturalistic declamation.[78] At climactic moments, Ivan is apt to join his voice to the notes of his leitmotive, but to seemingly random ones which emphasize odd intervals and preclude any hint of lyricism. The classic example is the third act curtain, corresponding to the end of Mey's fourth act, quoted above (ex. 1).[79]

Now the whole purpose of "realistic" declamation was that it enabled the composer to follow faithfully the smallest nuances of feeling. It was a kind of Camerata-like esthetic, its object the exploration and elucidation of character, And that is what made Mey's Solovyovesque Ivan an inviting personage for a kuchkist musicalization. He had many dimensions, and his portrayal by the dramatist had been eminently "psychological." Ivan's Act V disquisitions on statecraft and on historiography were taken very seriously by Rimsky-Korsakov, and however stringently he otherwise condensed and streamlined the action of the play, these passages he preserved and prominently displayed. The opening of the last scene in the opera shows Ivan sitting alone, pondering the events that had befallen him in Pskov. The text, after a short expository preface presumably of the composer's devising, is a condensation of Mey's scene (Act I, sc. i) in which Ivan discusses kingship and statehood with his two closest and dearest, Boris Godunov and the Tsarevich Ioann, Mey further specifying the presence of the scribe Elizar Vylyzgin (who reads to the Tsar from scripture) and a guard of oprichniki crisscrossing the gate at the rear of the set. All of these characters are eliminated in the opera, the Tsar himself taking whatever lines Rimsky chose to retain from their parts (including the passages from scripture). The passage on stagecraft quoted above on p. 94 is set in typical "melodic mold" technique (ex. 2). The mood evoked here is as un-Karamzinian as can be imagined: contemplative, rational, moderate, and full of quiet lyricism suggesting a heart at peace. Though Rimsky's Ivan has often been compared with Musorgsky's Boris, the character that comes first to mind here is Pimen.

Even more Musorgskian is the Tsar's "historiographical" monologue as set by Rimsky later in the same scene, when Ivan is trying to put Olga at her ease. "I can sing you their whole song," the passage begins, and Rimsky sets in as an ironic little "pesenka" or ditty whose passages *all'unisono* and whose non-

Ex. 1   *Pskovitianka,* Act III, sc. iv, conclusion (Nikolai Rimsky-
Korsakov, *Polnoe sobranie sochinenii,* vol. 29a [Moscow:
Muzyka, 1965], pp. 212-13)

    Ivan: Let the killing stop! There has been too much
              bloodshed... Let us make our swords blunt against
              the stones, for the Lord preserveth Pskov!

Ex. 2   *Pskovitianka,* Act IV, sc. v (pp. 248-49)

Ivan: Only that kingdom is solid and strong, where the
         people know they have one ruler, as in a single
         flock there is a single shepherd. I would like to
         have it so that Rus is bound in wise laws as if in a
         coat of armor. But will God give me the
         understanding and the strength?

Ex. 2 (continued)

Ex. 3a.   *Pskovitianka,* Act IV, sc. vii (p. 266)

> Ivan: I can sing their whole song through, word for
>   word! This is what he's like!

Ex. 3b.   Musorgsky, *Kozël* (The Billy-goat, (1867), meas. 14

cadences on tritones over strangely voiced French sixths will bring to mind many of Musorgsky's realistic songs of the sixties, perhaps *Kozël* (The Billy Goat, 1867) above all. When Ivan sings "Vot on, mol, kakoi!" ("That's what he's like!"), one's inner ear resonates with Musorgsky's "Sushchii chort!" ("The very devil!")—and so, one is tempted to think, had Rimsky's. (See ex. 3.)

Rimsky bent so far over backwards to cast Ivan in a new, rounded, humane and unbloodthirsty light that even in the opinion of his kuchkist confrères the role was somewhat vitiated. Borodin, for example, found it "cold."[80] For Cui, the best characterization was that of Matuta (!), the one which so embarrassed Rimsky later that he removed it bodily from the opera. As for Ivan, though Cui praised the role's "sharp, strong, sombre" features, he sternly criticized the handling of the voice in dramatic scenes. Of the confrontation between the Tsar and Olga he wrote:

> If this whole scene were a symphonic picture for orchestra alone, it would make the strongest possible impression. But in point of fact the presence of words, which impart to it a fully defined meaning, makes its effect not deeper but weaker, and the reason is the occasionally incorrect and inept use of the voice. First of all, the voice will often sing some strong melodic phrase which is then completely lost.... Secondly, because sometimes Ivan's speech is too quick and monotonous in rhythm,...and thirdly, because the development of the voice is not knowing enough to give the voice a chance to augment the total sound, and this is necessary if the impression of the scene is to be enhanced.[81]

Sure enough, when Rimsky revised the opera, the role he changed the most was Ivan's: the range was broadened, the tessitura significantly raised, the durations increased, the whole effect inflated. It was not dissimilar to the change Boris's monologue underwent when Musorgsky rewrote his "terem" scene, i.e., the scene in Boris's quarters in the Kremlin, and it had a similar motivation, to cast the character into greater relief. But while the changes certainly do show a far more practiced hand and a far surer gauging of effect, it is only hindsight that judges the original to have been mere "throw-away recitative."[82] What was really thrown away was the Karamzinian stereotype. Rimsky's original Ivan was a more faithful counterpart to Mey's than the more theatrically effective character familiar to this day on the Russian operatic stage. Ivan was not meant to dominate the opera, as (particularly thanks to the example of Chaliapin) he now does.[83]

VI

Who, if not Ivan, did dominate the original version? The chorus. Without exception the reviewers of 1873 singled out the Act II *veche* as the most successful and significant scene in the opera. Critics of the original play had

also singled this scene out, and the censor had obliquely concurred by making it the chief obstacle to the play's production. It was just the kind of scene to capture the imagination of Slavophiles and *pochvenniki*. As Grigoriev put it in 1861,

> The Pskovan *veche* looms heavily over the whole of *Pskovitianka,* and, in the breadth of its conception, its profound attainment of Russian national spirit, its artistic serenity combined with true dramatic content, it crushes before it everything in our contemporary drama except, of course, the plays of Ostrovsky.[84]

The censor, on the other hand, considered that the scene's inflammatory potential outweighed its artistic merits:

> The *veche* constitutes the focal point of the struggle between Pskovan autonomy, in particular the Pskovan *vol'nitsa* [rebels], and Muscovite sovereignty, the lawful power.... The youthful faction at the meeting instigates an actual secession from the lawful power of the Muscovite state, leaving in scorn those who remain submissive, loyal to the Tsar.... All this can hardly make a seemly impression on the mass of spectators.[85]

That the censor's fears were not groundless is indirectly confirmed by Rimsky-Korsakov's recollection of his opera's reception, which strikingly parallels Stasov's report of the reception of Musorgsky's "Kromy" scene. The *vol'nitsa,* according to Rimsky, "struck the fancy of the young students, who could be heard bawling the mutineers' song to their hearts' content up and down the corridors of the [Medical] Academy."[86]

Indeed, thanks in part to the music, the *veche* is even more the focal point of the opera than it was of the play. It was a heaven-sent opportunity for the broad choral dramaturgy so highly valued in kuchkist theory, the one ingredient missing from the Dargomyzhskian operatic recipe. Rimsky's *veche* was the most specifically "kuchkist" music yet written for public consumption, and, after Serov's Shrovetide carnival in *The Power of the Fiend,* it was the most ambitious choral scene in Russian opera (excepting the static epilogue to *A Life for the Tsar*). But where Serov's choral scene had concerned itself chiefly with setting a genre background to the action, Rimsky's *was* the action at the point at which it occurred. The *veche* embodied the crux of the opera's dramatic conflict and projected it on a heroic scale. It attempted a radical and specifically kuchkist solution to the problem of actively integrating the chorus into the unfolding drama, along lines called for in numerous articles by Cui and, perhaps even more to the point, one by Rimsky-Korsakov himself.

Early in 1869, Cui called on Rimsky to pinch-hit for him twice as music reviewer for the *Sanktpeterburgskie vedomosti* [St. Petersburg news]. Once was for the première of his own *William Ratcliff*. The other occasion was the première of the opera *Nizhegorodtsy* [Men of Nizhny Novgorod], a historical opera on a subject dealing with the end of the Time of Troubles, that is, the Muscovite uprising against the Poles under Minin and Pozharsky. The composer was Eduard Napravnik, who had just been engaged as chief conductor at the Maryinsky Theater, and who was slated shortly to direct the première of Cui's opera. The young, idealistic Rimsky's review of *Nizhegorodtsy* had for him the consequence that Cui had sought to avoid: it poisoned relations between Rimsky and the conductor for life.

The review appeared on 3 January 1869 over the initial "N," and treated Napravnik's work as an object lesson in how historical operas were not to be composed. Special attention was accorded the treatment of the chorus. The libretto by Pyotr Kalashnikov, an operatic translator employed by the theater (he would later compose the fourth act of *The Power of the Fiend* for Serov), provided magnificent opportunities in its "scenes of popular agitation" in the third and fourth acts. The effect of these scenes, in which the composer had sought to give the chorus an enormous active role, was vitiated, in the reviewer's opinion, first by the "monolithic" treatment of the choral mass, and secondly by the excessive respect Napravnik had shown "the routine forms of old." "How often," exclaims Rimsky-Korsakov, "do all these procedures work not only against sense, but even against effect!" He gives one rather extreme example:

> Minin, exhorting the people, proposes that they sell their property to raise funds:
> "We must mortgage our wives, our children,
> But we will ransom our beloved country!
> Will you do it?"
> he asks; but the people wait in silence for the orchestral coda. The orchestra sounds the final E-flat, and only then does the chorus shout, "We will!"[87]

In fairness to Napravnik it should be pointed out that the young critic rather tendentiously exaggerated the point, both as to text and as to music. (He even had the key wrong.) Example 4 gives the spot in question as it appears in the vocal score. Similarly exaggerated, but very revealing, is Rimsky-Korsakov's more general critique of the unhealthy influence of conventional libretto construction upon musical dramaturgy. Here the target is not just the poor scapegoat at hand, but the whole dramaturgical procedure and strategy so notably embodied, as we have seen, in the third act of the as yet unwritten *Oprichnik:*

Formal duets, trios, quartets, choruses, all with thoroughly defined endings, often thoroughly contrary to common sense, linked by the insertion of recitatives—that is the format in which most of the operas that exist in the world are written. The text of each number is itself written in such a way as to allow the music to achieve the most uncomplicated "symphonic" form. From this proceed those numberless and senseless repetitions of lines and individual words. From this proceeds the librettist's striving to write such a text that several characters might sing it at the same time, with only the pronouns changed. "How I love you!" sings she. "How you love me!" exclaims he at the same time. "How she loves him!" accompanies the chorus. All operas, unfortunately, are full of such absurdities. Sometimes, because of the dictates of the action, the librettist cannot invent a text with the needed repetitions of lines, but the composer does not despair and forces the text into a routine symphonic frame anyway. From this proceeds the common situation where two completely different texts are sung to the same music. Many similar incongruities were decreed by entrenched routine, but the public listened and enjoyed itself because it had no wish to see in opera anything but a concert in costume. But in the course of time even tastes change. By now it has become impossible to write operas in such forms. We now demand a fully rational text and the total solidarity of text and music. If one gives every number in an opera a discrete, rounded, and uncomplicated symphonic form, with symmetrical layout of sections and repetitions, this goal cannot be achieved.[88]

So here is the crux of the complaint against Napravnik's choral scenes: they are too orderly. In example 4, both Minin's exhortations and the choral responses are cast in eight- and sixteen-bar periods, and they are almost invariably separated by full cadences. Protagonist and chorus practically never overlap or sing simultaneously, except in large, formal, perorative ensembles. Not only that, but choral responses are often parallel-period repetitions of the soloist's phrases. The one exception, which Rimsky-Korsakov calls the "single dramatic moment in all of Mr. Napravnik's music," comes where the composer invokes the old "loi des contrastes" and pits two choruses one against the other. The "people" stand on the town ramparts and listen to the offstage choir that accompanies the wedding ceremony of two of the opera's protagonists. The quick *parlando* commentary of the onstage chorus in juxtaposition with the measured *falsobordone* of the offstage group is effectively handled (see ex. 5). Even this is ultimately an orderly affair, though, and Rimsky finds further cause for complaint in the style of the church choir's anachronistically Bortnianskian music. He praises the orchestration, calling special attention to the "exquisite effect of the woodwinds playing in imitation of the organ, while the gong is struck pianissimo." But he is quick to turn praise to blame even here, noting that such an effect has "little to do with Russian church singing," which is never accompanied.[89]

How ironic, then, that Rimsky began his *veche* scene with a comparable anachronism—the famous *veche* bell, which had been carried off from Pskov by Ivan III some sixty years before the time of *Pskovitianka's* action. But this

Ex. 4   Eduard Napravnik, *Nizhegorodtsy* (1888), Act III, scena
with chorus (no. 19) (Moscow: Jurgenson, 1884), pp. 188-
89.

Ex. 4 (continued)

Ex. 5   *Nizhegorodtsy*, Act III, Prayer (pp. 236-37)

Ex. 5 (continued)

was an anachronism of the right tendency according to the tacit kuchkist double standard, that is, backward rather than forward in time. It imparted a greater aura of antiquity and of national character—of "authenticity," in short—than scrupulous observances of historical data might have achieved.

From the very beginning of the scene, Rimsky's efforts are bent at destroying the orderliness and symmetry that had shackled Napravnik. The chorus enters gradually in response to the tolling bell. A spirit of confusion is created by dividing the singers into five groups who converse among themselves with mounting intensity until all five are singing (shouting) at once to different words:

> Bass I: Who has summoned the *veche?*
> Tenor I: A messenger from Novgorod.
> Bass I: Well, this can bode us no good!
> Soprano and alto: A *veche* has been called, but no word as yet why.
> Tenor I: Well, let the messenger tell us: let him have his word with Pskov.
> Soprano and alto: And here come the boyars with the generals and judges.
> Tenor I: Let him speak! What are we waiting for?
> Bass I: No, my lords! Let's observe the forms and protocols: let the good people all gather first.
> Bass II: By the old peaceful ways!
> Soprano and alto: And the deacons, and the scribes, and the prince-viceregent himself has deigned to come.
> Tenor I: A *veche* has been called, but no word as yet why. Let him speak!
> Tenor II: Really, fellows! Let him speak! What are we waiting for?
> Bass I: The prince-vice regent must come.
> Bass II: No, that's no way! My lords of Pskov, judge: Shall there be a *veche,* or is there no need for one?[90]

In answer to this last question from the second basses, the whole chorus comes together for the first time: "Yes! Yes! Let there be a *veche,* according to the will of all Pskov!" This cry is set to the first of five recurrent, homorhythmic choral "themes" which Rimsky uses for most of the full-chorus utterances. They bind the scene together musically, doing multiple duty with respect to the text. What is unchanging is their affective content. This first motive (A), for example, is used consistently for assertions of popular will (ex. 6). In its other appearances, it take words like "Ring for the *veche!*" and "Let Tucha have a word!"

The other recurrent choral motives are shown in ex. 7. They are handled quite freely, reappearing in many keys and with many modifications in texture, tempo, and harmony. Extended choral passages are often constructed mosaic-like out of these elements. The longest one (vocal score, pp. 118-25), for example, is built on the succession C-B-D-A. Even in these full-chorus passages, the choral mass is often divided against itself, bristling with dissension and dramatic conflict, as far as possible from the conventionally

Ex. 6 *Pskovitianka*, Act II (The Veche), Choral Theme A (pp. 97-99), vocal parts only

"Let there be a veche! It is the will of all Pskov!"

Ex. 6 (continued)

Ex. 7   The Veche, other choral themes

a.   Theme B (p. 105), voice parts only

"What? Have the walls come down? Have the locks become rusty?"

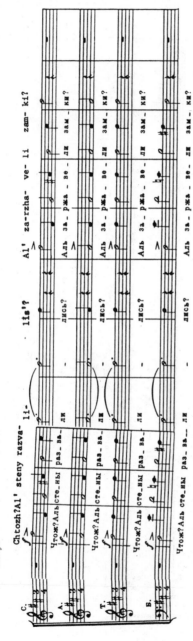

b.   Theme C (p. 106), voice parts only

"For our native Pskov, for our veche, for the sake of old times"

c. Theme D (p. 107), voice parts only

"If it comes to that we will don our shields, lads. Stand by great Pskov."

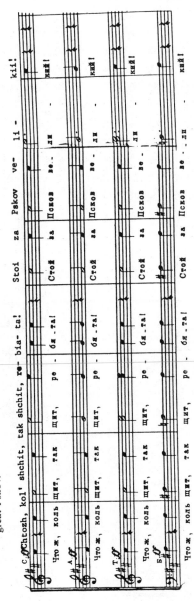

d. Theme E (p. 112), soprani only

"Lord Prince, by thy well-being our Pskov endures"

"monolithic" chorus upon which the kuchka so loved to heap scorn. In the passage just mentioned, for example, the first tenors and first basses, who later will form the core of Tucha's *vol'nitsa*, cut through the texture of the rest of the chorus with cries to give Tucha the floor (see ex. 8). In an even more striking passage, the basses actually attempt to shout the rest of the chorus down (ex. 9).

But extended passages for the full chorus are only a part of the chorus's role in the *veche*. Just as characteristic is the realistic breakup of the chorus into its component sections, who react and interact freely among themselves and with the soloists. One example of this is the muttered exclamations of groups of choristers at the fearful tale of Yushko, the Novgorod messenger (ex. 10). Another is the dialogue between Tucha and the crowd, where the choral repliques are written in a recitative style indistinguishable from Tucha's own (ex. 11).

Cadences rarely separate the utterances of the full chorus and the soloists. The composer dovetails their passages so that they are continually breaking in on one another, maintaining at once a high dramatic tension and a seamless, asymmetrical continuity (ex. 12).

The end of the scene, that is, the secession of Tucha and the *vol'nitsa*, is the most strikingly novel of all. Having announced his intention to resist Ivan the Terrible, and having gathered to his side the first tenors and first basses, Tucha breaks into a mocking "farewell song," for which purpose Rimsky-Korsakov appropriated a folk song from Balakirev's recently published anthology (No. 30: *Kak pod lesom, pod lesochkom*). Tucha sings the part of *zapevalo* (precentor) and the *vol'nitsa* enters on the refrain, maintaining not only the tune, but also the harmony as notated by Balakirev "in the field." Against this the composer pits the anguished protests of Tokmatov in recitative style, along with similar ejaculations from the rest of the chorus, while the orchestra sounds the *veche* bell and reminiscences of the melody to which Tucha had previously sung his call to arms. The resulting combination of almost unretouched folksong, choral recitative and "realistic" orchestral effect makes for a texture that is a very epitome of kuchkist ideals, and the group's tribunes heralded it with encomium upon encomium. The normally tight-lipped Cui, for example, proclaimed:

> You forget that before you is a stage, and on it choristers performing a more-or-less skillfully constructed crowd scene. Before you is reality, the living people, and all of it accompanied by matchless, meaty music from beginning to end. A crowd scene like this has never appeared in any existing opera. Even if everything else in *Pskovitianka* had been completely worthless, this *veche* scene alone would have been enough to give the opera significance in the history of art and a prominent place among the most remarkable of operas, and its author a place among the best of operatic composers.[91]

Once again it should be emphasized that what prompted this remarkable musico-dramatic concatenation was Mey's original text, unmediated by any

Ex. 8   The Veche, pp. 119-20

Chorus (Theme C): Come, milords, let us meet him in peace! We
          have made no seditious alliances! Why should
          Ivan Vasilievich turn in anger against Pskov?
Bass I: But we would have it differently!
Tenor I: Hey there, Mikhailo Andreich, thou overseer's son!

Ex. 9   The Veche, p. 132

Soprano, alto, tenor (Theme C): For our great Pskov, for
our native Pskov, for the sake of old times!

Basses: Not so fast! Quiet! Wait! Quiet! Quiet! Wait, I say!

Ex. 10   The Veche, pp. 103-4

Yushko (The Novgorod Messenger): Soon it will be a
month since the victims were thrown from the bridge into
the seething whirlpool. Babies were tied to their mothers
and both were thrown in the water.

Altos: My God!
Tenors: Could it be true?
Sopranos: Could the Tsar punish so harshly?
Basses: You're lying!
Tenors: As if children were also guilty...

Ex. 10 (continued)

librettist and handled with a literalness that was unprecedented in historical opera. Like Ostrovsky,[92] Mey himself had realized the theatrical potency of folk songs and had thought up the idea of having the mutineers march off to the strains of one. He had even directed that Tucha produce a balalaika to accompany it.

After the mutineers have marched off, Rimsky appended a little epilogue for the portion of the chorus remaining onstage. It has no analogue in the original drama: "Thy end is coming, great Pskov! Heavy is the hand of the Grozny Tsar!" This little passage would hardly merit special notice except that it prefigures the larger choral epilogue that brings the whole opera to an end. This epilogue-conclusion, which has been pointed to with a certain wry admiration as "the most 'ineffective' end of any opera in existence,"[93] sits oddly with the rest of the work. It was suggested, and its text composed, by Vladimir Nikolsky (who suggested something very similar to Musorgsky: the *iurodivyi* or Holy Fool, at the end of the Kromy scene), and though it is modest in length, it has an effect similar to that of the choral epilogue to *A Life for the Tsar.*[94] After all the action of the opera has been completed, and Ivan the Terrible is grieving over Olga's corpse, Rimsky-Korsakov brings the chorus onstage (rather improbably, that is, into Ivan's inner sanctum), to sing a lament that spells out, none too subtly yet touchingly, the equation of Olga's fate and Pskov's, the symbolic underpinning of the whole foregoing drama:

Ex. 11   The Veche, p. 127

Tucha: As if we did not fend off those awful Lithuanians!
        As if we spared the Germans our battle-axes!
        Why should we now hang our heads?

Tenors: We haven't done anything! Lithuania, indeed!

Basses: Like hell we spared them!

Ex. 12a.   The Veche, p. 101 (Chorus interrupts solo)

Yushko:...keep its memory alive.

Chorus: Oh my God! Great Novgorod, dear Novgorod,
can it be thy end has come?

b. The Veche, p. 109-10 (soloist interrupts chorus)
   Chorus: Hey, a veche, a veche!
   Boyar Matuta: Quiet, milords of Pskov! Our viceregent
   has the floor!

Liudi pskovskie pravoslavnye,
Sovershilas' volia bozhiia.
Za svoi rodnyi Pskov, za liubov' svoiu
Otdala ty zhizn', krasu, molodost'.
Liudi russkie, liudi pskovskie!
Pozabudemte raspriu staruiu
A pomolimtes' o dushe eë.
Da prostit ei gospod' grekhi eë,
Bozh'ei milosti net kontsa vo vek.

Orthodox people of Pskov,
God's will is done.
For they cherished Pskov and for thy love
Hast thou laid down thy life, thy beauty, thy youth.
People of Russia, people of Pskov!
Let us forget our ancient strife
And pray for her soul.
May the Lord forgive her her sins,
For God's mercy is everlasting.

Like the *iurodivyi's* lament on the battlefied, this curiously impersonal little choral sermon on the theme of reconciliation is the musico-dramatic equivalent of the historian's *primechanie*. It is a perfect encapsulation of the "statist" view of the events of 1570 in Novgorod and Pskov. The triumph of the Tsar's absolute power, though purchased at a painful price, was inevitable and just. It was the working out of historical necessity. It was, in short, God's will.

VII

Among the most fervent admirers of Rimsky's achievement in the *veche* scene was a close friend and fellow kuchkist, who for a short but significant time was also his roommate and hence knew the scene earlier and better than anyone else. On 18 June 1870, Musorgsky wrote to the Purgold sisters:

Before [Rimsky-Korsakov's] departure from Petrograd I went to see him and experienced something extraordinary. This something is none other than a milestone in Korsinka's talent. He has realized the dramatic essence of musical drama. He, that is, Korsinka, has concocted some magnificent history with the choruses in the *veche*—just as it should be: I actually burst out laughing with delight.[95]

Indeed, it took another composer facing the same problems to realize the full import of the scene. At the time Rimsky wrote his *veche*, Musorgsky was between versions of *Boris*. It had been submitted to the Imperial Theaters Directorate, whose Opera Committee, as everyone knows, rejected it in February 1871, on the grounds that there was no prima donna role. But of course the changes Musorgsky made went so much further than anything required or envisioned by the Committee that one can only conclude that the impetus that caused him to rethink his opera lay elsewhere. According to

Stasov, the scene at Kromy, in which the people are shown in the act of rebellion, and which had nothing to do either with the Committee's wishes or with the Pushkin tragedy on which the first version of the opera had been so closely modelled, was conceived "during the winter of 1870-71." In the fall of 1871 Musorgsky and Rimsky moved in together, sharing a furnished room in an apartment belonging to the Conservatory professor Nikolai Zaremba. According to Rimsky's account, during the time they lived together, *Pskovitianka* was orchestrated and the Polish Act and Kromy scene were added to *Boris*.[96] The Kromy scene in completed full score bears the date 23 June 1872.

All this circumstantial evidence merely confirms an idea which knowledge of the two scores already compels: that the Kromy scene was inspired by, and was written in emulation of Rimsky's *veche*. The parallels are far-reaching and astonishing: the portrayal of the crowd in revolt; the effect of mocking glorification; perhaps above all the use of folk song as an integral part of the action.[97] The song of the *vol'nitsa* at the end of the *veche* found echo in two Kromy numbers, the very ones Stasov claimed he heard the students singing:[98] the choral song about the falcon (the mocking of the boyar Khrushchov) and the "revolutionary" chorus, "Raskhodilas', razgulialas'." Like the *vol'nitsa* chorus, both of them incorporate tunes collected by Balakirev[99] and work them up into large scale numbers which (unlike the *Slava* in the Coronation scene) carry action. This was a new kind of choral dramaturgy for Musorgsky: in the first version of *Boris* the crowd had been treated as if a single Dargomyzhskian character, in recitative declamation.

The fact that the correspondence between Rimsky's *veche* and Musorgsky's "tramps"—and the importance of the former as background, subtext, and perhaps even efficient cause of the latter—has remained as unremarked as it has, reflects a number of bad habits that have affected Musorgsky research. First, he is often treated as a complete *naif* without a historical context. Second, when antecedents are sought they are usually sought in the realm of ideology, not in prior music or opera. Third, when Rimsky-Korsakov is thought of in conjunction with Musorgsky it is all but invariably in connection with their "posthumous" relationship, in which they are often viewed as antagonists. Thus, the Kromy scene is usually treated by Soviet writers (and not only by them) as a kind of direct reflection of "populist" thought: as an unmediated response to the peasant uprisings of Musorgsky's own time, or else as a kind of musicalization of the writings of Shchapov, say, or worse, of Khudiakov.[100] And attempts are often made to show why the Kromy scene is a kind of complement to the scene at St. Basil the Blessed in the first version, rather than—as the sheer physical evidence of the manuscripts already proves—its replacement. The impulse to write Kromy, it should be clear, was not only an ideological one or a historiographical one. It was also a musical one: the wish to replace one form of choral dramaturgy with another.

But even if we acknowledge this much, a historiographical problem remains. Having determined to write a scene of popular rebellion on the order of Rimsky's *veche,* Musorgsky was faced with a task Rimsky had not encountered. The *veche* scene was provided ready-made within the play from which Rimsky adapted his libretto. The scene Musorgsky wanted to write had no counterpart in Pushkin's *Boris Godunov.* To motivate and justify it, Musorgsky was forced to do something unprecedented in Russian opera: he went directly to historical sources (as he and Stasov would do later, of course, for the whole of *Khovanshchina*) and made an original selection and interpretation. In the end, his scene thus attained an authenticity his immediate model (that is, Rimsky's *veche*) had neither possessed nor needed. The obvious question: what in fact were his sources?

Before attempting an answer it will be necessary to identify and characterize the historiographical tradition within which Pushkin had worked, so as to show the distance between the Kromy scene and Pushkin's drama, and hence the distance between Kromy and Musorgsky's own first conception of the opera. Once again we shall be dealing with Karamzin, for he was Pushkin's sole source.

It is well known by now that twentieth-century historians have rejected the premise on which Pushkin based his play: that Boris Godunov had engineered the murder of the Tsarevich Dimitri, Ivan the Terrible's youngest son, so as to pave his own way to the throne. George Vernadsky, summarizing this new view of the events of May 1591 (largely from the work of V.I. Kleyn and Sergei Zavadsky), has called attention to the fact that the documents which implicate Boris all come from the early Romanov years and must be treated as Romanov propaganda, while there is no serious reason to doubt the veracity of the one important document contemporaneous with the events, the *Sledstvennoe Delo,* an investigative report prepared by a commission headed by Prince Vasily Shuisky, which attributed the Tsarevich's death to a self-inflicted stab wound.[101] But Karamzin thought otherwise. He rejected the *Delo* as a Boris-instigated falsification and believed the testimony of the post-1613 chronicles. On the basis of his assumption of Boris's guilt, he created another vivid historiographical figment to rival the bloodthirsty Ivan—this time a wise, just ruler tragically doomed by his one misdeed. Karamzin ends his first chapter on the reign of Boris Godunov with this singing peroration:

> But the time was approaching when this wise sovereign, rightly acclaimed throughout Europe for his high-minded policies, his love of enlightenment, his zeal to be a true father of his country, finally for the fine conduct of his social and familial life, would have to taste the bitter fruit of lawlessness and become one of the most astounding victims of heavenly judgment. Its harbingers were the inner anxiety of Boris's heart and the various calamities against which he as yet still intensely struggled with all the steadfastness of his spirit, only to find himself all at once feeble and as it were helpless against the ultimate manifestation of his awesome fate.[102]

Here we have, as the Russians would say, the whole *zamysel'*, the whole conception of Pushkin's drama and its tragic protagonist. Even Karamzin's rhetoric found its way into some of Pushkin's most famous lines. The very next paragraph in the *History*, the one that begins the second chapter on Boris, starts with a phrase that will bring both Pushkin and Musorgsky forcefully to mind:

> Having attained his ends, having risen from petty servility to the heights of power by dint of tireless effort and inexhaustible resources of guile, perfidy, intrigue and villany, could Boris enjoy to the full the grandeur his soul had so craved—a grandeur purchased at so high a price? And could he enjoy the pure satisfaction of the soul, a soul so beneficent toward his subjects and therefore so deserving of his country's love? At best, not for long.[103]

Dostignuv tseli [Having attained his ends], . . . *Dostig ia vysshei vlasti* [I have attained the highest power], . . . this was the model for the great central monologue (Pushkin's scene 8, combined in Musorgsky's first version with Pushkin's scene 11) in which the "Tsar-Herod" bares to the audience the soul so dramatically described by Karamzin. Pushkin was chided by Belinsky for his "slavish adherence" to the Official Historiographer, but of course his motives in writing *Boris* were hardly those of a historian. Few plays were so purely literary in conception and execution, and even Musorgsky assumed that "Pushkin wrote *Boris* in dramatic form, [but] not for the stage."[104] One may hesitate to hold with the modern formalist that Pushkin's tragedy, "a premeditated and experimental work," was "written not so much for the subject as for the literary form,"[105] and still conclude that for the poet the subject consisted not in the facts of history but in the tragic character of the protagonist and in the theme of nemesis, all wholly set forth by Karamzin in prose that, in the words of Musorgsky's friend and adviser, the Pushkinist V.V. Nikolsky, already "reads like poetry."[106]

Now if this be a drama of nemesis, who, to use Mirsky's word, was the "Eumenid"? Quite obviously, the False Dimitri, and not, as is so often supposed, "the people." The widespread conception, based on knowledge of the second version of Musorgsky's opera, that Pushkin's drama already embodied the theme of kingship and legitimacy, of the relationship between ruler and ruled, is quite erroneous. And the idea that the source of this conception lay in Karamzin is still more so. Karamzin's conception of legitimacy derived from anything but "the consent of the governed" (cf. his treatment of Ivan IV), and "the people" play no active or essential role at any point in his narrative. Neither do they play such a role in Pushkin. And neither did they play any such role in Musorgsky's first conception of his opera. Soviet critiques of Pushkin's play, as may be expected, always fabricate a "social" or "civic" subtext. But even ostensibly un-Soviet, revisionist interpretations often commit the same error. Orlova and Shneerson, for example, assert that "the

dramatic conflict of Musorgsky's opera, as well as of Pushkin's tragedy, is based on the confrontation of the people with the 'criminal Tsar Boris,'"[107] and go on to emphasize the famous stage direction with which the drama ends: *Narod bezmolvstvuet* [The people keep silent]. Following the traditions of Soviet criticism, they call this a "sinister stillness pregnant with menace," and claim that "behind this brief phrase, we feel the invisible presence of the poet-seer who foresees the misfortunes and upheavals to come.[108] But it has long been a matter of common knowledge that the poet-seer inserted the famous closing direction at the behest of the censor. Pushkin's intended ending was to have been the crowd acclaiming the False Dimitri on command, as earlier it had acclaimed Boris. The people, then, for Pushkin as for Karamzin, remained passive to the end.

Nowhere is the passivity and impotence of the people more apparent than in the scene at St. Basil the Blessed, often touted as the scene that shows Tsar and people in sharpest confrontation, and which therefore is often viewed as the heart of the dramatic conception of play and opera alike. Its kernel in Karamzin was an incident wholly unrelated to the matter of the Tsarevich Dimitri: Boris's encounter with a *iurodivyi* following the death of his own firstborn son in 1588, ten years before he became Tsar.

> Godunov, . . . having at the time only one infant son, took him recklessly with him, though the boy was sick, to the church of St. Basil the Blessed, paying his doctors no heed. The infant died. At the time there was in Moscow a fool in God *(iurodivyi),* esteemed for his real or imaginary holiness. Walking naked through the streets in bitter cold, his hair hanging long and wild, he foretold calamities and solemnly calumniated Boris. But Boris held his peace and dared not do him the smallest harm, whether out of fear of the populace or because he believed in the man's holiness. Such *iurodivye,* or blessed simpletons, appeared frequently in the capital wearing chains of penance called *verigi.* They were privileged to reproach anyone, no matter how important, right in the eye, if their conduct was bad. And they could take whatever they wanted from shops without paying. The merchants would thank them for it as if for a great favor.[109]

Pushkin (and following him, Musorgsky) tied this story to the events of 1604 in the following way: seizing upon another choice item from Karamzin, that Boris, in response to the growing threat from the False Dimitri, ordered memorial services for the slain Tsarevich and anathema services for Grishka Otrepiev,[110] the poet had Boris emerge from St. Basil's after such a service to be greeted by a howl from the starving populace: "Bread, give bread to the hungry, batiushka, for Christ's sake!" There follows the searing exchange between the Tsar and the *iurodivyi,* who is usually portrayed as the voice or personification of the people.[111] Boris is confronted with his crime: the *iurodivyi* asks him to have the little boys killed who had stolen his kopeck, just as he had had the little Tsarevich killed. As in the incident cited above, Boris does not react to this unspeakable offense; instead he asks the *iurodivyi* to pray for him. But, the *iurodivyi* says in refusal, "Our Lady forbids us to pray for the Tsar-Herod."

Now even in this scene the crowd is passive. Boris is still their *batiushka,* "little father." The people do not threaten him, rather they go down on their knees to him in supplication. And when the *iurodivyi* refuses to pray for the Tsar, the crowd, according to *Musorgsky's* stage direction, "disperses in horror."[112] The *iurodivyi* is at best an ambiguous figure; to see him here as the people's spokesman is an unwarranted extrapolation. One detail, in fact, positively separates him from the crowd. In the beginning of the scene the chorus indicates its belief in the False Dimitri's legitimacy; that is, they believe that he is the real Dimitri, alive and well. The *iurodivyi,* on the other hand, knows that the Tsarevich is dead by Boris's hand. How, in the face of this, can one go on seeing his words as the voice of the people? Clearly, the *iurodivyi* is no such thing, but rather the voice of Boris's remorse.

Quite the best evidence that this interpretation is correct is the very fact that having written the scene at Kromy, Musorgsky deleted the one at St. Basil's—physically ripped it out of his score, in fact—and, moreover, made conflation impossible by recycling the episode of the *iurodivyi* and the boys, along with the *iurodivyi's* concluding lament.[113] Indeed, the two scenes, meant originally to occupy the same (penultimate) position in the opera's sequence of scenes, are ideologically incompatible, and one has to wonder at the ingenuousness of those who claim that "what caused Musorgsky to delete one of the best scenes remains unknown."[114] For with Kromy, and only with Kromy, did Musorgsky finally introduce the theme of conflict between Tsar and people into his opera as motive force in the drama, and in Kromy (and only in Kromy) can one speak accurately of the people as the real tragic hero of the opera (their tragic flaw being their credulity).

So, clearly, the Kromy scene had little to do with Pushkin. It is true that the penultimate scene in the original drama ends with the crowd, having been incited to riot by the speech of the poet's namesake, the boyar Pushkin, rushing off toward the palace now occupied by Boris's helpless son, shouting, "Bind him, drown him! Hail Dimitri! Crush the race of Godunov!"—an episode that comes straight out of Karamzin, and, *mutatis mutandis,* went straight into Musorgsky. But the relationship of these events to those in the Kromy scene is at best oblique. The violence is being committed not spontaneously but at the behest of Dimitri's minion; the angry mob is one of Muscovites at home, not tramps in the woods; finally, the target is Fyodor Borisovich, not the boyar Khrushchov.[115] Something perhaps a bit closer to Musorgsky's scene is suggested in the scene immediately preceding in Pushkin, when the boyar Pushkin, conferring with the boyar Basmanov (another defector to the Pretender's cause), confidently predicts victory, and on these grounds:

... Basmanov, dost thou know
Wherein our true strength lies? Not in the army,
Nor yet in Polish aid, but in opinion—
Yes, popular opinion. Dost remember

> The triumph of Dimitry, dost remember
> His peaceful conquests, when, without a blow
> The docile towns surrendered, and the mob
> Bound the recalcitrant leaders?[116]

But that is all one finds in Pushkin—a suggestion, not a conception, hardly a *zamysel'*. The first actual spark of the eventual scene at Kromy may have been touched off, interestingly enough, by a couple of lines on the Pretender's progress which Musorgsky himself inserted into the text of the scene at St. Basil the Blessed: "He's already gotten as far as Kromy, they say. — He's coming with his troops to Moscow. —He's blasting Boris's troops to smithereens."[117] Even this, however, is rather far from the eventual "revolution scene." It refers to the siege and pitched battle described in detail by Karamzin, at which Dimitri's Polish troops were joined by several hundred Don Cossacks. It was they who had bound and taken prisoner the boyar Khrushchov, whom Boris had sent to lead them against the Pretender. They presented Khrushchov to Dimitri as a trophy at Kromy. This was, at least according to Karamzin, the turning point in the Pretender's campaign.[118]

Was it in Karamzin, then, that Musorgsky found the makings of his Kromy scenario? Most historians agree it was, taking their cue from Stasov's account of the planning of the scene, in which he claimed to have been a direct participant.

> Karamzin's story of the popular rebellion and of the Jesuits Czernikowski and Lawicki was decided upon by us as the basis for the magnificent scene of the people jeering at the boyar Khrushchov, the commander at Kromy, and for the scene of the people's settling of accounts with the Jesuits at the moment the victorious Pretender approaches with his troops.[119]

But there is no such story in Karamzin. What there is is the vivid description of the siege at Kromy to which we have referred (and which was fairly irrelevant to Musorgsky's concerns), the mere names of the Jesuits (given at the end of note 240 to Volume 11), some documents from which Musorgsky derived the rhetoric of Dimitri's proclamation at the end of the scene,[120] and some scattered references to the famine of 1604 and the widespread unrest it caused among the people. One of these references is interesting for its mention of "tramps" *(brodiagi),* the word Musorgsky used in his correspondence to refer to the Kromy scene:[121]

> Whereas in good times the nobility willingly augmented their retinues, in times of famine they began to disperse them. Their temper turned toward executions and cruel punishments! Even people of good conscience expelled their servants from their homes, or at best forced them to take a leave.... The unfortunate perished, or else turned to robbery together with many exiles of the nobility, Romanovs and others, who were condemned to lead the lives of tramps (for no one dared take in the servants of the disgraced)—together with Ukrainian

fugitives, wandering far from their nests into the heart of Russia in quest of plunder. Gangs appeared on the highways,...people were robbed and murdered at the very outskirts of Moscow.[122]

But as this phenomenon is described by Karamzin, it had little to do with the progress of the False Dimitri. The one concrete borrowing attributable uniquely to Karamzin that may be verified in the scene at Kromy is the reappearance in that scene of the monks Varlaam and Missail, both of whom are named by Karamzin among the Pretender's supporters.[123] And that is all, despite the fact that the earliest printed libretto of the Kromy scene carried a number of footnote references to the Official Historiographer. These have been shown to be "fictitious" (presumably for the benefit of the censor) by Orlova and Shneerson, who, though they attempt to prove the derivation of Kromy from Karamzin, admit that "revolt is not even mentioned in [his] history."[124] Indeed, missing altogether from Karamzin is the crucial factor: any sense that "the people" played any active "revolutionary" role which may have contributed to the fall of Godunov and the triumph of the False Dimitri. The closest Karamzin ever comes to such an idea is the following rather caustic remark:

In the cities, the villages and along the highways, proclamations of Dimitri to the inhabitants of Russia were circulated, containing news that he was alive and would soon be among them. The people were astonished, not knowing whether or not to believe it. But the tramps, the good-for-nothings, the robbers long since inhabiting the northern regions, rejoiced: their time was coming. Some came running to the Pretender in Galicia; others ran to Kiev, where...a banner had been set out to rally a militia [*vol'nitsa*].[125]

But this passage already suggests Karamzin's harsh judgment of the "tramps." They were an anarchic element at best, not a "historical force." Here is a fuller description:

It was not a host that assembled against Boris, but a scum. An entirely insignficant portion of the [Polish] nobility, in deference to their king,...or else flattering themselves with the thought of deeds of derring-do with the exiled Tsarevich, showed up in Sambor and Lvov. Also there hurried thither all manner of tramps, hungry and half-naked, demanding arms not for victorious battle, but for plunder and favors, which Mniszek granted generously in hopes for the future.[126]

This is the riff-raff from which Musorgsky is supposed to have taken inspiration. Not that the point is one of moral attitude, for Musorgsky, too (as Orlova and Shneerson quite rightly point out), judged his "tramps" harshly.[127] The point is that Karamzin altogether minimized the importance of the "people"—tramps or otherwise—as a historical force, and never drew an unambiguous connection between the famine-inspired lawlessness in the

Russian countryside and the progress of the False Dimitri. In order to find an authentic historiographical sanction for a choral scene to match Rimsky's *veche,* or on a more philosophical plane, to find an account which viewed the people, as he did, as a "great individual, inspired by a single idea,"[128] Musorgsky would need a historian who viewed the people as an essential, motivating force for the events of the Time of Troubles, not a mere reactor to those events, as in the accounts both of aristocratic historians like Karamzin and "statists" like Solovyov.

There was such a man, and his name was Kostomarov—the very one whose admiring comments about Musorgsky's opera furnished us with one point of departure. He and Musorgsky were well acquainted. Kostomarov was among those named by Musorgsky, in the autobiographical sketch he wrote for Riemann during the last year of his life, as having contributed the most to "the arousal of the young composer's mental activity and to giving it its serious, strictly scientific inclination."[129] Musorgsky further stated, in the same sketch, that Kostomarov participated directly, along with Stasov and Nikolsky, in planning *Khovanshchina* and *The Fair at Sorochintsy.*[130] That would imply that his period of close relationship to the historian began right before those works were planned, or precisely as he was revising *Boris.* It further implies that Kostomarov's influence on the earlier opera was exercised not in person but through his published works. And so we shall find.

Of all Russian historians, Kostomarov showed the greatest interest in theater and the arts as bearers of historical lessons. Besides the articles in the *Vestnik Evropy* from which we quoted in the beginning, in the late sixties Kostomarov wrote many reviews of historical dramas for the newspaper *Golos* [The Voice]. So widely noticed were these columns that in the 1870s Kostomarov was retained (along with Stasov) as consultant on matters of historical verisimilitude by the Imperial Theaters Directorate under Stepan Gedeonov.[131] Of the radical historians of his day, Kostomarov was by far the most influential, thanks to a vivid writing and speaking style that made his books and lectures very popular among students and the liberal-minded intelligentsia. He was the major proponent of the view that the prime historical mover was not Tsar but populace. His idealization of the peasantry made it inevitable that Kostomarov should specialize in the chronicling of popular uprisings. His first big success was *Stenka Razin's Revolt (Bunt Stenki Razina,* St. Petersburg, 1859), one of the first fruits of the liberalized censorship under Alexander II. Its popularity was phenomenal and made its author a hero. In the early sixties his lectures were so appealing to the St. Petersburg University students who crowded his auditorium that more than once Kostomarov was carried out on their shoulders.[132]

Kostomarov's magnum opus was *The Time of Troubles of the Russian State in the Beginning of the XVII Century (Smutnoe vremia moskovskogo gosudarstva v nachale XVII stoletiia),* first published serially in the *Vestnik Evropy* in 1866. It was the most recent authoritative word on the subject when

Musorgsky composed *Boris*. It began at the year 1604, the year of the False Dimitri's victory over the forces of Boris Godunov. In the scene-setting introduction to the main narrative, Kostomarov wrote an extended paragraph which directly related the unrest caused by famine to the progress of the Pretender, thereby setting out the whole *zamysel'* of Musorgsky's Kromy scene:

> If old-timers couldn't remember such a horrible famine in Russia, neither could they remember such vagrancy *(brodiazhnichestvo)* as then was rife. Lords had turned out their servants when it became excessively dear to feed them, and later, when the price of bread had fallen, wanted to get them back. But their former serfs, if they had managed to survive the famine, were living with other masters or else had developed a taste for wandering—and did not wish to turn themselves in. Lawsuits and prosecutions multiplied. Hunted fugitives gathered in gangs. To these tramps were added a multitude of serfs who had belonged to fallen boyars. Boris had forbidden taking them as serfs, and this had been just as hard on them as the prohibition on transfers had been on the peasants. Having been indentured to one master, it was a rare serf who wanted to leave the status of serf altogether; practically all ran away to find another place. These "fallen" serfs gathered at that time by the thousands. Deprived of the right to roam from court to court, they attached themselves to the robber gangs, which sprang up everywhere in varying numbers. Most serfs had no other way of feeding themselves. The only exceptions were those who knew some trade. There were a multitude of fugitives from noble courts, from monasteries, from outlying settlements. They ran wild during the famine, and later, when they were sought by their former masters, they couldn't buy themselves off, especially since so many died in the famine. On the survivors a huge tax was declared before they could be free of their obligations. And so they ran, cursing the extortion, the injustice of the bailiffs and elders, the violent measures of their henchmen. Some ran off to Siberia, others to the Don, still others to the Dniepr. Many settled on the Urkrainian plains and there evaded their state-imposed obligations. The fact that the northern Ukraine had happily been spared the worst of the famine was the reason for an extreme concentration of people in that region. The government began to take measures for the return of the fugitives, and they for their part were prepared to resist. This whole fugitive population was naturally unhappy with the Moscow authorities. They were prepared to throw themselves with joy at whomever would lead them against Boris, at whomever would promise them an advantage. This was not a matter of aspiring to this or that political or social order; the huge crowd of sufferers easily attached itself to a new face in the hope that under a new regime things would be better than under the old.[133]

Kostomarov presents not a scum, then, but a mass of the insulted-and-injured with whom one can (and he does) sympathize. As for the people as an active force which, when aroused, can threaten Tsars, consider Kostomarov's description of the gang of Khlopka Kosolapy (and substitute the name Khrushchov for Basmanov):

> Khlopka did not limit himself to attacking travelers on the highway: with an enormous gang he went straight to Moscow, threatening to annihilate the throne, the boyars and all that was sanctioned by authority, powerful, rich and oppressive in Russia. In October 1603, Boris sent troops to destroy this gang, under the leadership of the *okol'nichii* Ivan Fyodorovich Basmanov. They had not gotten far from Moscow when suddenly "thieves" fell upon Basmanov. They attacked the Tsar's troops on a path that cut through the underbrush. Basmanov was killed.[134]

And as for Khrushchov himself, the story of his capture by the Don cossacks and his acceptance of the False Dimitri (which last is part of the action of Musorgsky's Kromy scene) is related by Kostomarov in much greater detail than in the work of any previous historian:

> Here [on the left bank of the Dniepr near Kiev], there came again to Dimitri emissaries from the Don cossacks with representations of the willingness of the whole independent population of the Don basin to serve the miraculously spared Tsarevich. As an earnest of their fidelity they lay at their feet the nobleman Pyotr Khrushchov, who had been sent by Boris to incite them against Dmitri. The prisoner, brought before him in shackles, no sooner caught sight of the Pretender than he fell at his feet and said, "Now I see that you are the natural born, true Tsarevich. Your face resembles that of your father, the sovereign Tsar Ivan Vasilievich. Forgive us, Lord, and show us mercy. In our ignorance we served Boris, but when they see you, all will recognize you."[135]

Finally, Kostomarov narrates several incidents that furnished Musorgsky with the model for his chorus of mockery. They relate, actually, to the period immediately following Boris's death, when his son and family were routed from the palace. Here are two:

> Meanwhile, on the other side of the river there were still those who, having sworn loyalty to Boris's widow and son, wished to remain true to their vows and persuaded others in the name of church and duty not to turn traitor. They reviled Dimitri, proclaiming, "Long live the children of Boris Fyodorovich!" Then Korela shouted: "Beat them, beat them, not with swords, not with sticks, but with poles; beat them and say, 'There you are, there you are! Don't you be picking fights with us!'" This appealed to the assembled troops, especially the ones from Ryazan. The Godunovites were turned loose, and the Dmitryites chased them with laughter and beat them, some with whips, some with sticks and some with fists.[136]

> [The supporters of Boris] were robbed and plundered without any mercy, from those marked by the people's hatred even the clothing was ripped, and many were seen that day—so eyewitnesses report—covering their nakedness as Adam did, with leaves. The mob, who had suffered long and much, who had been so long humiliated, rejoiced in this day, amused themselves at the expense of the noble and wealthy, paid them back for their former humiliation. Even those who had not sided with the Godunovs suffered on that day; it was enough to have been rich. And the general plunder and drunkenness continued until nightfall, when all slept like the dead.[137]

So when Kostomarov said of *Boris* that it was a "page of history," one understands what he meant—it was a page of *his* history. That he was referring to Kromy, the scene that concludes the opera, goes without saying. The difference between Kromy and the rest of *Boris* was precisely the difference between Karamzin and Kostomarov. As one of Musorgsky's intimates, Alexandra Molas (née Purgold), put it much later to the young Boris Asafiev, "the Kromy Forest scene arose in connection with the fact that Musorgsky [wished to] recast the denouement of his tragedy in keeping with the burgeoning populist *(narodnichestvennye)* tendencies" of the time.[138] This

much is true; but it will not do to assert with Asafiev that "precisely that which Nikolai I's regime did not permit Pushkin to do, was done here by Musorgsky."[139] For Musorgsky's conception derived from a historiographical viewpoint that did not so much as exist in Pushkin's time, nor indeed until the 1860s. It was as much a denial of Solovyov's "statism" as the latter had been of Karamzin's absolutism, the source of Pushkin's view of the Time of Troubles and, at first, of Musorgsky's, too.

All of the foregoing notwithstanding, to claim that the Kromy scene is an example of ideologically committed *art engagé* would be facile. The evidence, as we have seen, suggests a rather more tortuous conception, in which Musorgsky's initial stimulus may have been musical, not political, not an a priori commitment to populism but admiration for Rimsky-Korsakov's choral dramaturgy in that quintessentially "statist" opera *Pskovitianka,* where the theme of popular rebellion had, from the purely historiographical standpoint, sounded a curiously discordant note. If we call Musorgsky a committed populist in *Boris,* we shall have to explain his apparent retreat from that ideology in *Khovanshchina.*[140] This self-created problem has led researchers into endless difficulties: some have seen fit to censure, others to devise elaborate rationalizations. Neither the one nor the other is justified by the evidence. It is enough to view Musorgsky's "populism" on the one hand as an exterior manifestation of his overriding commitment to realism, and on the other, to his alertness to the intellectual currents of his time. It is already sufficient praise to note that for him it was not enough merely to contrive an emulation of Rimsky's *veche* by hook or crook, which he might easily have done by adapting his own scene at St. Basil's. No, he was impelled to seek an authentic historical basis for his crowd music, and he found it in the "tramps" so vividly described by his friend and mentor, Kostomarov.

VIII

"History in a certain sense is the Holy Book of nations," wrote Karamzin at the very outset of his gigantic labors. "It is the chief thing, the indispensable thing. It is the mirror of their existence and their deeds, a tablet of revelations and laws, the testament of the forebears to posterity, the amplification and explication of the present and an example of the future."[141] The new birth of historical studies in the nineteenth century, its significance and its fundamentals of aim and method are among the brightest testimonies and finest fruits of the heightened national consciousness the new century was witnessing everywhere in Europe. In Russia, where that consciousness was newer and stronger, perhaps, than anywhere else, interest in the past became obsessive. Our study of its effect on opera is but a small facet of that general obsession. But the fact that the three most important Russian operatic composers of the latter nineteenth century should have been so directly

involved with the works and issues raised by the three most eminent Russian historians of their time lends a new credence to the oft-heard claim that in Russia the arts mattered more than anywhere else. Musorgsky, it goes without saying, but also Rimsky-Korsakov and even Tchaikovsky viewed themselves in the period around 1870, the most quintessentially "civic" moment in Russian intellectual history, not as "mere" musicians but as participants and contributors to their country's seething intellectual life. If history was the mirror of the nation, what better role for opera than to mirror history if, as Tchaikovsky put it, the composer wished to become "the property not merely of separate little circles but—with luck—of the whole nation"?[142] Though their angles of reflection differed considerably, the three operas we have examined were all honorable constituents of the great mirror that was nineteenth-century Russian art.

Notes

1.   It appears in Stasov's necrological essay of 1881, *Modest Petrovich Musorgskii: biograficheskii ocherk* [Biographical essay] (see Vladimir Vasilievich Stasov, *Izbrannye sochineiia* [Selected works], v. 2 [Moscow, 1952], p. 199), and, a bit differently worded, in *Pamiati Musorgskogo* [In Memory of Musorgsky], an essay marking the fifth anniversary of the composer's death (*Izbrannye sochineniia*, v. 3, p. 34). Though Stasov implies in these articles that the remark was made after a performance in the theater, it seems rather likelier that the occasion for it was an evening at Stasov's own home (30 October 1874), at which Musorgsky played excerpts from his opera to a gathering which included, besides Kostomarov, the writer Daniil Mordovtsev (who had contributed to the text of the "Kromy" scene), Musorgsky's poet friend Arseny Golenishchev-Kutuzov, and the painter Nikolai Ge, who specialized in historical subjects. See Alexandra Orlova, *Trudy i dni M.P. Musorgskogo* [M.P. Musorgsky's works and days] (Moscow, 1963), p. 404, where the date of the gathering is established on the basis of letters.

2.   Nikolai Chernyshevsky, *Selected Philosophical Essays* (Moscow, 1953), p. 379.

3.   "Mysliashchii realist v russkoi opere" [A thinking realist in Russian opera], *Golos*, 13 February 1874.

4.   Part of Stasov's side of it is given in my *Opera and Drama in Russia* (Ann Arbor, 1981), p. 126.

5.   *Vestnik Evropy*, v. 1, no. 1, (1866), p. 84.

6.   "Po povodu noveishei russkoi istoricheskoi stseny [Concerning the newest Russian historical theater], *Vestnik Evropy*, v. 2, no. 2, (1867), p. 94.

7.   Alexandre Benois, "Vrubel'," *Mir iskusstva*, no. 3, (1910), quoted in John Bowlt, *The Silver Age: Russian Art of the Early Twentieth Century and the "World of Art" Group* (Newtonville, Mass., 1979), p. 74.

8.   Cf. the manuscript draft of a preface to the first edition (1831) in D.S. Mirsky, *Pushkin* (New York, 1963), p. 154. Pushkin, of course, was only one of many "Shakespearean" reformers of nineteenth-century drama. Hugo was another, as was Verdi. See Piero Weiss, "Verdi and the Fusion of Genres," *JAMS* 35 (1982), 138-56.

9. Both of these plays were turned into operas by Rimsky-Korsakov, as was Mey's remaining play, *Servilia* (1853), on an ancient Roman subject. Another Russian historical play, on Vasilisa Melentieva, remained unfinished at Mey's death and the manuscript has perished.

10. It was first performed at the Maly Theater in Moscow with an overture and mazurka specially composed by Tchaikovsky, who then began work on another Ostrovsky project, *The Voyevoda*. Though set in seventheenth-century Russia, the latter is not truly a historical drama, since it contains no historical personages.

11. It was precisely when Ostrovsky was hardest at work on these plays that Serov proposed collaboration on what became *The Power of the Fiend*. No wonder Ostrovsky was initially reluctant to go back to one of his "paltry" domestic comedies (*Live Not the Way You'd Like*, 1855) and tried to persuade Serov to undertake something more grandiose—say, a historical drama (see *Opera and Drama in Russia*, p. 153). I should like to take this opportunity to add one choice bit of documentation to the account given in *Opera and Drama in Russia* of the unhappy end of the Serov-Ostrovsky collaboration. There I wrote (p. 167) that "Ostrovsky did not dignify with a response" Serov's "ultimatum," an incredibly rude communication in which the composer set a two-week deadline on the completion of a revised libretto. There was a response, however, and it has just been published:

    After your letter there is no way I can imagine that you have any idea of manners. You write that I am impeding your composing career. The libretto for you I finished long ago; but you have demanded revisions from me, and precisely at a time when I was up to my ears in work that was necessary for my livelihood. But still I did not refuse and did what I could. The rest I proposed to finish up when I was through with my work, and spoke with you about this in Moscow just recently at which time you not only agreed, but asked me not to rush and to set about the completion of the libretto when I was finished with my other affairs. Those were your very own words. And so I have done. Having finished my latest comedy *(A Burning Heart)*, I wrote even before leaving St. Petersburg the second scene of Act III and began Act IV of *The Power of the Fiend*. Judge for yourself whether after all of this your letter, both by its form and by its content, could strike me as anything but altogether bizarre. After all I have just said, it should be obvious that you have rushed into the matter of ultimatums and two-week deadlines. I only ask now that you leave me alone, since it is more than clear to me by now that I cannot possibly have any further dealings with you. You ask me not to blame you for your brusqueness. What's to blame? I am not your subordinate. To a brusque letter anyone has the right to answer even more brusquely, if his upbringing permits it (letter of late December 1868, printed in A.N. Ostrovsky, *Polnoe sobranie sochinenii* [Complete collected works], v. 11 [Moscow, 1979], pp. 295-96).

12. D.S. Mirsky, *A History of Russian Literature* (New York, 1958), p. 254.

13. It may be helpful to explain some of the titles given above: Tushino was the encampment of the second False Dimitri, who led to campaign on Moscow in 1607; Vasilisa Melentieva was Ivan the Terrible's sixth wife, whom he wedded without benefit of clergy; Sloboda Nevolia was the popular name of Ivan's domestic retreat at Alexandrovo.

14. Even later it remained a feature of popular historiography: witness Kostomarov's best seller, *Russian History Through the Lives of its Main Figures (Russkaia istoriia v zhizneopisaniiakh ee glavneishikh deiatelei*, 7 vols. [St. Petersburg, 1873-88], and reprinted continually thereafter up to the Revolution), which clashes curiously with the main thrust of Kostomarov's work, directed as we shall see, very much against the Caesaristic approach.

15. S.S. Danilov, *Ocherki po istorii russkogo dramaticheskogo teatra* [Essays on the history of the Russian dramatic theater] (Moscow, 1948), p. 386.

16.   Vissarion Belinsky, "Vzgliad na russkuiu literaturu 1846 goda" [A Glance at Russian literature of the year 1846], *Polnoe sobranie sochinenii*, v. 10 (Moscow, 1956), p. 18.

17.   *Vestnik Evropy*, v. 1, no. 1, p. 92.

18.   See Carl Dahlhaus, *Richard Wagner's Music Dramas*, trans. Mary Whittall (Cambridge, 1979), p. 80.

19.   Cf. *Richard Wagner's Prose Works* (trans. William Ashton Ellis), v. 2 (London, 1895), pp. 168-79, 197-201.

20.   A.N. Serov, *Izbrannye stat'i* [selected articles], I (Moscow, 1950), 259.

21.   Letter to O. Novikova (August 1866), quoted in A.A. Gozenpud, *Russkii opernyi teatr XIX veka* [Russian operatic theater of the XIX century], v. 2 (Leningrad, 1971), p. 248.

22.   Carl Dahlhaus, *Between Romanticism and Modernism: Four Studies in the Music of the Later Nineteenth Century*, trans. Mary Whittall (Berkeley, 1980), p. 5.

23.   *History of Russian Literature*, p. 255.

24.   Belsky's collaboration with Rimsky-Korsakov only began in 1899, and in all cases involved not historical but fantastic subjects (*Tsar Saltan*, 1900; *Kitezh*, 1905; *The Golden Cockerel*, 1907).

25.   *Vestnik Evropy*, v. 2, no. 2, p. 98.

26.   Cf. A.S. Pushkin, *Sochineniia* [Works] (Moscow, 1964), v. 1, p. 100. The anonymous little quatrain circulated widely in "samizdat," and has been assigned by Pushkinists conjecturally to the year 1818, when volumes 1-8 of Karamzin were issued.

27.   Richard Pipes, "Karamzin's Conception of the Monarchy," in J.L. Black, ed., *Essays on Karamzin* (The Hague, 1975), p. 118.

28.   Nikolai Karamzin, *Istoriia gosudarstva rossiiskogo* [*History of the Russian State* (henceforth HRS)] (St. Petersburg, 1892; rpt. The Hague, 1969), v. 9, pp. 273-74.

29.   Quoted in Alexandra Orlova and Maria Shneerson, "After Pushkin and Karamzin: Researching the Sources for the Libretto of *Boris Godunov*," in Malcolm H. Brown, ed., *Musorgsky: In Memoriam 1881-1981* (Ann Arbor, 1982), p. 251.

30.   Metropolitan Filaret, quoted in J.L. Black, *Nicholas Karamzin and Russian Society in the Nineteenth Century* (Toronto, 1975), p. 148.

31.   A lengthy letter on this early project is excerpted in *Opera and Drama in Russia*, p. 70, n. 37.

32.   S.A. Vengerov, "Ivan Ivanovich Lazhechnikov: Kritiko-biograficheskii ocherk" [A critical biographical essay], in Lazhechnikov, *Polnoe sobranie sochinenii*, v. 1 (St. Petersburg, 1899), p. ciii.

33.   *Severnaia pchela*, no. 47 (1839), quoted in Vengerov, pp. cv-cvi.

34.   Preface to *The Oprichnik* (St. Petersburg, 1867), quoted in Vengerov, p. cxvi.

35.   Leo Yaresh, "Ivan the Terrible and the *Oprichnina*," in C.E. Black, ed., *Rewriting Russian History* (New York, 1956), p. 226.

36.   HRS, v. 9, pp. 54-55.

37.   This in fact had provided the main plot line for Lermontov's *Merchant Kalashnikov* and Averkiev's *Slobodo Nevolia*.

38. Tchaikovsky well understood this. In his last act Natasha sings of nameless forebodings as prelude to her final duet with Andrei and immediately before the Tsar's grisly "test," and the composer built the climax of the duet on a theme from his early tone poem *Fatum* [Fate] (1868).

39. This is the aspect of *The Oprichnik* stressed to the virtual exclusion of all else in most published descriptions beginning with that of Modest Tchaikovsky *(Zhizn' Petra Il'icha Chaikovskogo* [Tchaikovsky's life], v. 1 [Moscow, 1903], pp. 384-92) and continuing with those of Vsevolod Cheshikhin *(Istoriia russkoi opery* [A History of Russian opera] [Moscow, 1905], pp. 289-98), Gerald Abraham, ed., (*The Music of Tchaikovsky* [New York, 1946], pp. 134-38) and David Brown *(Tchaikovsky: The Early Years* [New York, 1978], pp. 222-45). The latter three are all in varying degrees dependent on the first. For information on borrowings from *The Voyevoda* in *The Oprichnik* the reader is referred to any of the above.

40. Act III, sc. viii. Lazhechnikov, *Polnoe sobranie sochinenii,* v. 11, p. 352.

41. *The Music of Tchaikovsky,* p. 136.

42. For the terminology employed in this description I have depended in part on Karin Pendle, *Eugène Scribe and French Opera of the Nineteenth Century* (Ann Arbor, 1979), especially the chapter on "The Technique of Grand Opera and The Transformation of Literary Models" (pp. 465-94).

43. E.g., Viskovatov: "How bitter, how bitter it is for Holy Russia, how like a deserted widow she appears; it seems our Sovereign has forsaken us altogether!" (Lazhechnikov, v. 11, p. 333).

44. E.g., David Brown, *Tchaikovsky: The Early Years,* p. 244. Not that there is any question of influence, for the two operas were composed simultaneously and premièred three months apart in 1874.

45. The first page reference is to the vocal score published by Bessel in 1874; the second is to the standard Soviet edition (P.I. Tchaikovsky, *Polnoe sobranie sochineii* [Moscow, 1940-71], vol. 34).

46. Compare *The Oprichnik,* pp. 258;243 with *Ruslan and Ludmila* (vocal score: Moscow, 1968), p. 81. Glinka's model, it seems pretty clear, was Rossini's Act I sextet, "Fredda ed immobile," from *The Barber of Seville.*

47. Letter to Dr. Schucht (1852), quoted in William L. Crosten, *French Grand Opera, An Art and a Business* (New York, 1948), p. 90.

48. In dealing with Tchaikovsky's *Oprichnik,* Soviet critics and historians are in a double bind for official Soviet historiography regards the *oprichnina* in a favorable light, and Tchaikovsky, as the officially proclaimed greatest Russian composer, can never be wrong. Lazhechnikov's original drama, if viewed through the distorting lens of Marxist-Leninist historiography, can be made to seem a depiction of Ivan's just triumph over the feudal boyars. But when such attempts are made on Tchaikovsky's opera, the result is absurdity. Tumanina tries to make *The Oprichnik* a "popular drama" *(narodnaia drama)* like *Pskovitianka* or *Boris,* praising both Lazhechnikov's and Tchaikovsky's "great sympathy for [their] heroes, drawn from the people" (*Chaikovskii: Put' k masterstvu* [The path to mastery; Moscow, 1962], p. 240), but this distorts Andrei's status beyond recognition. He comes not from "the people" in the sense obviously meant by a Soviet writer, but from the boyars, i.e., the feudal nobility. Lately, responsible Soviet scholars have been calling a halt to the nonsense. Gozenpud writes with grim amusement of interpretations that have at times been made of some standard transformations of the oprichnik leitmotive (which Gozenpud calls the "Tsar's Slava" in the extract that follows):

At culminating points the "Slava" to the Tsar is transformed from its original minor to the major and takes on a triumphant character. From this, certain researchers have come to the conclusion that Tchaikovsky wished to underscore the positive role played by the *oprichnina* in its struggle with the old boyar class. If one agrees with this peculiar point of view, then Andrei's downfall must also be considered a just retribution. After all, he is the son of the boyarynya Morozova who hates the Tsar and he has broken his vows to the same Tsar. Consequently, in condemning him to death, Ivan the Terrible is punishing a traitor *(Russkii opernyi teatr XIX veka* [Russian operatic theater of the XIX century], v. 3 [Leningrad, 1973], p. 120).

49.   HRS, v. 9, pp. 275-76.

50.   Cited in Black, *Karamzin and Russian Society,* p. 179.

51.   K. Waliszewski, "The *Opritchnina* at the Bar of History," in *Ivan the Terrible* (Hamden, Conn., 1966), p. 263.

52.   Sergei Solovyov, *Istoriia Rossii c drevneishikh vremën* [A history of Russia from the earliest times], v. 3, (containing the original vv. 5 and 6) (Moscow, 1963), p. 704.

53.   Solovyov, p. 707.

54.   Citations in this paragraph from J.L.I. Fennell, ed. and trans., *The Correspondence Between Prince A.M. Kurbsky and Tsar Ivan IV of Russia, 1564-79* (Cambridge, 1955), pp. 26-27, 61, 46-47.

55.   See N.A. Rimsky-Korsakov, *My Musical Life,* trans. Judah L. Joffe (New York, 1924), p. 80.

56.   *Pskovitianka,* Act V, sc. x in: L.A. Mey, *Dramy* [Dramas] (Moscow, 1961), pp. 194-95.

57.   Act V, sc. i; Mey, *Dramy,* p. 181.

58.   *Sochineniia Ap. Grigor'eva* [Apollon Grigoriev's works], v. 1 (St. Petersburg, 1876), p. 515.

59.   Here, too, Mey gives a liberal sampling of extracts from the Kurbsky correspondence to "document" the speeches quoted above.

60.   Mey, *Dramy,* p. 201. Cf. Karamzin, HRS, IX:97-98. Solovyov passes over the episode rather cursorily (*Istoriia,* III, 561).

61.   There is substantial documentation to this effect from Pskovan chronicles in Mey's *"Primechaniia,"* though Karamzin and Solovyov are both silent on the matter.

62.   For more on Olga, see George Vernadsky, *Kievan Russia* (New Haven, 1948), pp. 32, 38-42. Karamzin ends his account of the sparing of Pskov with these words: "[Nikola Sadlos] so frightened Ivan, that he immediately left the city; he spent a few days in his camp nearby; he allowed his soldiers to pillage the estates of the wealthy, but commanded them not to touch the hermits or priests; he took only the monastery treasuries and a few icons, vessels, books, and having as it were involuntarily spared Olga's homeland, he hurried to Moscow, where he might slake his unquenchable thirst for torture with new blood" (HRS, v. 9, p. 98). It seems possible that his passing reference to the sainted Olga gave Mey the first glimmer of the idea whence *Pskovitianka* grew.

63.   In adapting Mey's play, Rimsky-Korsakov opted for the "unities" and dispensed with this act, preferring to reveal its contents as needed in strategically placed narratives. In the first of the two revisions of the opera (1877-78, never performed or published), the act was restored, only to be dropped again from the second revision (1891-92) and refashioned into an independent one-act "musico-dramatic prologue to L. Mey's *Pskovitianka*" in 1898. Another change

made in the first revision stands out for its absurdity. Rimsky let Stasov (who was obviously thinking of the St. Basil scene in *Boris*) talk him into including the confrontation between Ivan the Terrible and Nikola Sadlos—the very episode against which the whole of Mey's drama polemicizes! For detailed information on the various versions of Rimsky-Korsakov's opera (only the first of which will concern us henceforth), see Gerald Abraham, *"Pskovityanka:* The Original Version of Rimsky-Korsakov's First Opera," *Musical Quarterly,* v. 54, no. 1 (1968), pp. 58-73.

64. This was an anachronistic touch. Vasily Ioannovich, Ivan the Terrible's Father, had put an end to Pskovan republicanism, and the last *veche* had taken placed in 1507. It was also a forbidden touch, and was one of the factors that caused the censor's ban on Mey's play. In Rimsky's opera, although he makes striking musical use of the famous Pskovan *veche* bell (another anachronism: it had been carried off by Vasily's father, Ivan the Terrible's grandfather, Ivan III), he never uses the word *veche,* replacing it at the censor's behest by the neutral *skhodka,* meeting.

65. This much is faithful to Karamzin: "Coming into the city [Ivan] with astonishment saw that on all the streets, before each house, tables had been set out with viands (following the advice of Prince Yuri Tokmakov). The citizens, their wives and children, all holding bread and salt, bent their knees to the Tsar, blessed him, greeted him, and said, "Great Sovereign Prince! We, your faithful subjects, with zeal and with love do offer you our bread and salt; do with us and with our lives as you will, for all that we have, and we ourselves, are yours, great monarch!" (HRS, v. 9, p. 97).

66. Mey, *Dramy,* p. 179.

67. Ibid., p. 198.

68. In the opera the ending is somewhat modified. Instead of killing herself onstage, Olga rushes out to Tucha and is caught in the gunfire. She is then carried onstage dead.

69. *My Musical Life,* p. 125.

70. Ironically enough, a "ditty" for the Tsar was added much later at Chaliapin's request, for performances of the third (i.e., standard) version of *Pskovityanka* by Mamontov's Private Opera. See the singer's autobiography, *Maska i dusha* [Mask and soul] (Fyodor Ivanovich Chaliapin, *Literaturnoe nasledstvo,* [Literary legacy], v. 1 [Moscow, 1957], p. 300). It was never performed, even by Chaliapin, but it can be found in an appendix to the Muzgiz (the Soviet state music publishers), vocal score of the third version (Moscow, 1967).

71. *My Musical Life,* p. 126.

72. A.A. Orlova and V.N. Rimsky-Korsakov, *Stranitsy zhizni N.A. Rimskogo-Korsakova,* [Pages from the life of N.A. Rimsky-Korsakov], v. 2 (Leningrad, 1971), 68-69. The censor cites three specific precedents for the lifting of the ban, and a curious assortment they are: Serov's *Rogneda,* which includes the Kievan prince Vladimir the Great among its *dramatis personae;* Rubinstein's *The Battle at Kulikovo (Dimitri Donskoi);* and (of all things) Glinka's *Ruslan,* with its purely fictitious Kievan prince Svetozar.

73. For a detailed description and evaluation of its significance, see *Opera and Drama in Russia,* chapter 5.

74. It had originally been prepared for Anton Rubinstein, and Tchaikovsky seems to have had something to do with procuring it for Rimsky. See Gozenpud, *Russkii opernyi teatr,* v. 3, p. 48n, and Abraham, *"Pskovityanka,"* p. 58. Rimsky probably got the idea of transferring the action of Act I to a later narrative from Krestovsky, who had had Vera Sheloga appear in Act IV as a nun who tells her whole story in a lengthy monologue.

75.   These were the songs sung by the maidens to entertain the Tsar in the third act, for which the texts were composed (after models in Krestovsky) by none other than Musorgsky (see Alexandra Orlova and Mikhail Pekelis, eds., *M.P. Musorgsky: Literaturnoe nasledie* [Literary legacy], v. 2 [Moscow, 1972], pp. 211-21, where documentation, texts and settings are all given), and the tableau-like concluding chorus, for which both idea and text came from Vladimir Nikolsky, the Lyceum professor and adviser to the kuchka on the matter of historical opera. Nikolsky also wrote the text of the first scene of Rimsky's Act IV, which portrays Olga's abduction by Matura and the attempted capture of Tucha, events only narrated (by Matuta) in Mey's Act V.

76.   Except, that is, for the minor role of Matuta, who in the scene mentioned in note 75 (one of the earliest to be composed) has music which for studied ugliness can be compared only with Musorgsky's *Marriage,* composed at exactly the same time. See my "Handel, Shakespeare and Musorgsky: The Sources and Limits of Russian Operatic Realism," in *Studies in the History of Music,* v. 1 (New York, 1983), pp. 247-68. An evident embarrassment to the mature Rimsky-Korsakov, the whole scene was eliminated from later versions of the opera.

77.   See, for example, Aleksei Kandinsky, *Problema narodnosti v opernom tvorchestve N.A. Rimskogo-Korsakova 60-70-kh godov* [The issue of national character in N.A. Rimsky-Korsakov's operatic output of the 1860s-'70s] (Moscow, 1956), p. 4.

78.   Even the one time it *is* sung, the peculiarities of the prosody show that the theme was not conceived in connection with the words, but is functioning as what in another context I have called a "melodic mold" ("Tone, Style and Form in Prokofiev's Soviet Operas: Some Preliminary Observations," to appear in *Studies in the History of Music,* v. 2). By this technique an abstractly conceived melodic idea is made to accommodate an infinite variety of naturalistically declaimed texts, and could therefore lend a higher level of musical organization and coherence to a "play set to music." The device is very thoroughly exploited in *Pskovitianka,* in which many scenes set in naturalistic declamation are tied together with a melodic thread—often of folk-like character and in at least one instance a genuine folk song—that runs throughout in the orchestra. The scene that cites the actual folksong is the very first one in the opera, where the exchange between the two nannies is accompanied by the folk song *Ne son moiu golovushko klonit* ("It is not sleepiness that makes me hang my head"), which Rimsky-Korsakov had collected himself, and would publish in his anthology of 1876.

79.   Feality to Dargomyzhsky is proclaimed especially loudly at this moment in the opera: the curtain line is followed by an orchestral postlude based on a whole-tone tranformation of Ivan's leitmotive which practically plagiarizes the music of the statue's entrance in the last scene of *The Stone Guest.*

80.   S.A. Dianin, ed., *Pis'ma A.P. Borodina* [A.P. Borodin's letters], v. 1 (Moscow, 1928), p. 310. Borodin says he is concurring in this opinion with Stasov.

81.   César Cui, *Isbrannye stat'i* [Selected articles] (Leningrad, 1952), pp. 215, 218, 223.

82.   Abraham, "Pskovityanka," p. 69.

83.   When *Pskovitianka* was presented to Paris by Diaghilev in 1909 as a Chaliapin vehicle, the title was actually changed to *Ivan le Terrible* so as to strengthen the parallel with the wildly successful production of *Boris Godunov* the previous year.

84.   Quoted in Gozenpud, *Russkii opernyi teatr,* v. 3, p. 46.

85.   Ibid., p. 47.

86.   *My Musical Life*, p. 113. Compare Stasov: "More than once a crowd of young people would break into song at night on the street, approaching the Liteiny Bridge on the way to the Vyborg side, taking up the chorus of 'glorification of the boyar by the people' and other choruses" (*Izbrannye stat'i*, v. 2, p. 202). James Billington rather exaggerated this phenomenon in his discussion of "populist art": "Enthusiastic students left the theater singing this anarchistic chorus through the streets of St. Petersburg as *Boris* made its spectacular entry into the repertoire early in 1874 on the eve of the mad summer that took them off into Kromy forests of their own" (*The Icon and the Axe* [New York, 1970], p. 410). On *Boris*'s status as putative embodiment of populism see below, and also two essays in *Musorgsky: In Memoriam:* Orlova, "After Pushkin and Karamzin," and Richard Hoops, "Musorgsky and the Populist Age," esp. pp. 289-91.

87.   This and all preceding quotations from Rimsky's review in Nikolai Rimsky-Korsakov, *Polnoe sobranie sochinenii* [Compete collected works], v. 2 (Moscow, 1963), p. 15.

88.   Ibid., pp. 14-15.

89.   Ibid., p. 16.

90.   In this extract the words changed by the censor are reinstated, following the latest vocal score (Moscow, 1965).

91.   Cui, *Izbrannye stat'i*, p. 221.

92.   See *Opera and Drama in Russia*, pp. 144-47.

93.   Abraham, "Pskovityanka," p. 70.

94.   It was, inevitably and rather vulgarly, inflated in the third (standard) version of the opera.

95.   Orlova and Pekelis, eds., *M.P. Musorgsky: Literaturnoe nasledie* [Literary legacy], v. 1 (Moscow, 1971), p. 110.

96.   *My Musical Life*, p. 123.

97.   It was *Pskovitianka* that really put the use of folk song on the operatic map, as embodiment of "the people" in action. But at the same time the opera contained another use of folk song that was universally condemned as naive, even by Rimsky's fellow kuchkists. The Olga-Tucha love duet in Act I was based on a folksong from Balakirev's collection (see Vera Bachinskaia, *Narodnye pesni v tvorchestve russkikh kompozitorov* [Folk songs in the works of Russian composers; Moscow, 1962], pp. 162-63). This was a serious lapse from the point of view of psychological realism. For folk song, in the mouths of operatic characters, can only properly "represent itself," never convey a spontaneous, subjective emotional state. As Laroche put it in his review, "One can hardly justify the introduction of a folk song into an operatic monologue or duet.... In a song a collective entity expresses itself; the whole people is expressed, and this gives the song a certain impersonality. Nothing could be more inimical to those highest dramatic moments wherein individuality is to be limned with all the force of specificity" (quoted in Gozenpud, *Russkii opernyi teatr*, v. 3, p. 50). And as Cui himself wrote, "Why not employ folk song as a source of rich material? Why not develop it, since it imparts such a marvelous local color? True enough, but one must note in this connection that a folk song can be given to a chorus of the people, it can be given even to a single character if that character actually sings a song, but individual feelings cannot be expressed in the sounds of a folk song. Here Olga and Tucha speak of their love, their own feelings, and in this situation the sound of folk song on their lips is wholly out of place" (*Izbrannye stat'i*, p. 219). I.L. Gusin, the editor of Cui's essays, attempts to defend Rimsky-Korsakov on grounds obviously

borrowed from Chernyshevsky: "[Folk song], in its origins, is also an expression of individual feelings." But of course Cui was speaking not of origins, but of songs that have already achieved currency in transmission.

98. See note 86.

99. For identifications, see Bachinskaia, pp. 154-55.

100. Such interpretations are rife even in the most recent Soviet literature. Gozenpud, for example, flatly asserts without documentation that "the conception of the scene at Kromy was influenced not so much by Karamzin's account as by the peasant uprisings of the sixties, which gripped a significant part of Russia," and, "the chorus demanding bread in the scene at St. Basil the Blessed was conditioned not only by the events of the late sixteenth century but also by the famine that had seized many provinces of Russia at the beginning of 1868" (*Russkii opernyi teatr*, v. 3, pp. 72-73). Mikhail Pekelis, in his introductory essay to the second volume of *Musorgsky: Literturnoe nasledie*, in which the libretto of Boris is published with annotations, builds a blatantly factitious case for the influence of the fugitive revolutionary populist Ivan Khudiakov's inflammatory (and anonymously published) historical tract, *Ancient Russia* (*Drevniaia Rus'*, 1867) on the second version of *Boris*, basing his argument on the fact that a different publication of Khudiakov's, his *Anthology of Great Russian Historical Folk Songs (Sbornik velikorusskikh narodnykh istoricheskikh pesen)*, has furnished Musorgsky (through Stasov) with the model for Varlaam's song about the taking of Kazan in the *first* version of the opera ("Musorgsky—pisatel'-dramaturg [writer-dramatist], *Literaturnoe nasledie*, v. 2, pp. 18-20, 26-30). Unfortunately this hypothesis has been accepted uncritically by Hoops in "Musorgsky and the Populist Age" (in *Musorgsky: In Memoriam;* see especially pp. 288-89). For a similarly factitious case regarding the supposed influence of the *narodnik* historian and political exile Afanasy Prokof'evich Shchapov on Musorgsky, see M. Rakhmanova, "Musorgsky i ego vremia [Musorgsky and his time], *Sovetskaia muzyka,* no. 9 (1980), pp. 101-10. Hardly better, of course, is the doggedly revisionist position that would completely deny the influence even of liberal, let alone populist thought on Musorgsky. Orlova and Shneerson's discussion of the *Boris* libretto ("After Pushkin and Karamzin") is a case in point (In *Musorgsky: In Memoriam,* pp. 249-70).

101. See Vernadsky, "The Death of the Tsarevich Dimitry: A Reconsideration of the Case," *Oxford Slavonic Papers,* v. 5 (Oxford, 1954), pp. 1-19.

102. HRS, v. 11, p. 55.

103. Ibid., p. 56.

104. Musorgsky to Golenishchev-Kutuzov, 15 August 1877. *Literaturnoe nasledie,* v. 1, p. 232.

105. Mirsky, *Pushkin,* p. 153.

106. Lecture notes, quoted in Orlova and Shneerson, "After Pushkin and Karamzin," p. 252.

107. "After Pushkin and Karamzin," p. 255. This seems a paraphrase of a passage on the first version of the opera from Gozenpud: "Everything is concentrated on the collision of *two* forces—the people and the Tsar. The theme of enemy intervention is not visually present. Grishka Otrepiev, having jumped from the window of the inn, disappears forever from the stage. The appearance of the Pretender is only alluded to in Shuisky's report, the scene at St. Basil the Blessed, and at the Tsar's Council. The first version of the opera excluded everything that was not directly connected with the central conflict. Boris Godunov perishes because the Tsar-criminal is rejected by the people" (*Russkii opernyi teatr,* v. 3, p. 71). Ultimately, of course, the source of this interpretation is Asafiev. His three articles on the dramaturgy of *Boris* are reprinted in B.V. Asafiev, *Izbrannye trudy* [Selected works], v. 3 (Moscow, 1954).

108. "After Pushkin and Karamzin," p. 266.

109. HRS, v. 10, p. 169.

110. Cf. HRS, v. 11, p. 95.

111. E.g., Gozenpud: "The *iurodivyi* pronounces judgment on the Tsar in the name of the people" (*Russkii opernyi teatr,* v. 3, p. 78).

112. *M.P. Musorgsky: Literaturnoe nasledie,* v. 2, p. 122.

113. That Musorgsky's wishes are regularly flouted in this matter, particularly in performances that pretend to authenticity, in no way changes the fact. Attempts to justify the inclusion of both scenes on grounds that the Kromy scene realizes what is already implicit in Pushkin/Karamzin, or else on the assumption that the versions "do not replace but complement one another" (Pekelis, in *Literaturnoe nasledie,* v. 2, p. 9) are untenable. Altogether preposterous is the claim first made by Asafiev and repeated as recently as Orlova's "After Pushkin and Karamzin," that the scene at St. Basil's was deleted for reasons having to do with the censorship. In that case, why was the far more radical Kromy scene permitted? Such arguments, moreover, fail to consider that when Pushkin's play was finally produced in 1870, the scene at St. Basil's was passed. (For more on the censorship question, see Robert William Oldani, "*Boris Godunov* and the Censor," *19th Century Music,* v. 2, no. 3 [March 1979], pp. 245-53.) One senses that what lies behind the rage to conflate is simply the desire not to lose any of Musorgsky's music. And who can fail to sympathize? But let the rationalizations cease.

114. "After Pushkin and Karamzin," p. 263.

115. Krushchov makes only the briefest of appearances in Pushkin, in a passage from scene 12 that was cut by the censors when the play was first published in 1831. In it, Khrushchov, an early defector to the False Dimitri, appears before the Pretender with news of Boris's condition.

116. Trans. Alfred Hayes, in Avrahm Yarmolinsky, ed., *The Poems, Prose and Plays of Pushkin* (New York, 1936), pp. 406-7.

117. *Literaturnoe nasledie,* v. 2, p. 120.

118. The whole story may be read in HRS, v. 11, pp. 86-87, 104-6.

119. *Izbrannye sochineniia,* v. 2, p. 197.

120. HRS, v. 11, p. 83, n. 217, etc.

121. As he wrote to Stasov, "I acquainted myself in *Boris* with the origins of the Time of Troubles through the tramps" (6 September 1873, *Literaturnoe nasledie,* v. 1, p. 169), meaning through the study of the phenomenon of vagrancy mentioned by Karamzin. The translator of Orlova and Shneerson's article on the sources of *Boris*'s libretto committed a serious error here, rendering the words *v brodiagakh* as "while tramping [through the woods]" ("After Pushkin and Karamzin," p. 267).

122. HRS, v. 22, p. 71.

123. Ibid., v. 11, p. 84 (Varlaam), p. 85 (Missail); also note 224, in which the presence of two orthodox monks among the Pretender's retinue is documented.

124. "After Pushkin and Karamzin," p. 253.

125. HRS, v. 11, p. 85.

126. Ibid., p. 84.

127. "After Pushkin and Karamzin," p. 265: "The scene at Kromy, despite the accepted opinion among Soviet musicologists, does not represent the apotheosis of popular uprising but demonstrates that revolt is a profoundly tragic phenomenon." According to the Golenishchev-Kutuzov's memoirs of the composer, Musorgsky, in his late, "idealistic," period, is supposed to have had second thoughts about his brutal, un-idealized portrayal of his "tramps": "In this act, I, for the only time in my life, slandered the Russian people. The jeering of the people at the boyar—that's a falsehood, that's not a Russian trait. The infuriated people might kill and punish, but they do not mock their victims" (Arseny Golenishchev-Kutuzov, "Vospominaniia o M.P. Musorgskom" [Reminiscences about Musorgsky], in *Muzykal'noe nasledstvo*, v. 1 [Moscow, 1935], pp. 19-20). Quite contrary to Orlova and Shneerson's assertion, at least one eminent Soviet musicologist, deeply committed to the idealization of the people, has called for the suppression of the Kromy scene on this basis. See Yury Tiulin, "Stsena 'pod Kromami' v dramaturgii 'Borisa Godunova'[The Kromy scene in the dramaturgy of Boris Godunov], and answers by E. Frid, B. Yarustovsky, A. Kandinsky, and P. Aravin, all in *Sovetskaia muzyka,* no. 3 (1970), pp. 90-114.

128. Manuscript dedication on title page of the published vocal score, 21 January 1874. *Literaturnoe nasledie*, v. 1, p. 326.

129. *Literaturnoe nasledie*, v. 1, p. 268.

130. Ibid., p. 269.

131. Gozenpud, *Russkii opernyi teatr*, v. 3, p. 20.

132. For interesting oblique references to this, see Stasov's hysterical letter to Balakirev on Stasov's *Judith*: "Immediately, from the very first note Serov became the idol of St. Petersburg, just such an idol as Kostomarov was recently" (17 May 1863). See A.S. Liapunova, ed., *M.A. Balakirev i V.V. Stasov: Perepiska* [Correspondence], v. 1 (Moscow, 1970), p. 199.

133. *Sochineniia N.I. Kostomarova* [N.I. Kostomarov's works], v. 2 (St. Petersburg, 1903), pp. 42-43.

134. Ibid., p. 43.

135. Ibid., p. 83.

136. Ibid., p. 117.

137. Ibid., pp. 127-28.

138. Boris Asafiev, "'Boris Godunov' Musorgskogo, kak muzykal'nyi spektakl' iz Pushkina, [Musorgsky's *Boris Godunov* as a musical spectacle from Pushkin], *Izbrannye trudy,* v. 3 (Moscow, 1954), p. 132.

139. Ibid., p. 137.

140. The curious mixture of romanticism and historicist pedantry that characterizes the libretto of *Khovanshchina* is well reflected in Musorgsky's comments to Golenishchev-Kutuzov on historical drama and on the work of Vladislav Kenevich. See especially the letter of 2 March 1874 (*Literaturnoe nasledie*, v. 1, pp. 177-78).

141. "Predislovie," HRS, v. 1, p. xvii.

142. Tchaikovsky to Nadezhda von Meck, 27 September 1885. Quoted in *The Music of Tchaikovsky*, p. 126.

7

Balakirev: The Years of Crisis (1867-1876)

Edward Garden (Great Britain)

In 1867, at the age of thirty, Balakirev appeared to be at the peak of his career. He headed the most advanced group of composers in Russia, acknowledged as their leader by Musorgsky, Rimsky-Korsakov, Borodin, Cui, and their staunch supporter, the critic Vladimir Stasov, who in that very year referred to them as the "mighty handful" in an article praising Balakirev's conducting of a performance which included some of their compositions given at a Free Music School concert in St. Petersburg in honor of the Slav visitors who had come to Russia for the Russian Ethnographical Exhibition in Moscow.[1] Although Gavriil Lomakin was still technically Director of the Free School, his influence had steadily waned since he had founded the school, jointly with Balakirev, in 1862, and he resigned "for health reasons" early in 1868, when Balakirev succeeded him as Director.[2] The concerts of the School provided a platform for his own compositions and those of his protégés, as well as for radical Western music, in particular that of Berlioz, Schumann, and Liszt. He had written a number of fine works himself, including two overtures in Russian folksongs, an overture and incidental music to Shakespeare's *King Lear,* a group of twenty songs, a book of folksong arrangements of exceptional originality and, for the Slav concert, an overture on Czech folksongs. He was intimately associated with the music of the other members of his circle, which included Borodin's and Rimsky-Korsakov's first symphonies, the latter's "Musical Picture," *Sadko,* and other works. They were inspired by his magnetic personality, and were coaxed and cajoled into writing music of which he would approve, and of which they would otherwise not have considered themselves capable. Without Balakirev, it is very doubtful if the young Musorgsky, then an army officer, the naval officer Rimsky-Korsakov, or the medical chemist Borodin, would have received the encouragement necessary to give them self-confidence to write music which, as it happened, turned out to be startlingly imaginative. His teaching was unorthodox, since he had had no conventional training himself—the St. Petersburg Conservatory had not been founded until 1862, by which time his

own circle was complete. The only series of subscription concerts in St. Petersburg was given by the Russian Musical Society; its conductor was Anton Rubinstein, who was also Director of the Conservatory. Balakirev and his circle disliked the Conservatory and the "routine" teaching procedures employed there. They were scornful of Anton Rubinstein's ability and criticised particulary what they considered to be the reactionary nature of his RMS concert programs.

Unknown to Balakirev, Rubinstein found it very difficult to get on with his colleagues and with the patroness of the Conservatory, the Grand Duchess Elena Pavlovna, née Princess of Saxe-Altenburg, the Tsar's aunt. Rubinstein disliked criticism and on more than one occasion had tendered his resignation, only to withdraw it subsequently. He again informed the committee of his intention to resign in January 1867 but, since this had happened before, nobody took him seriously. His official letter of resignation (from abroad) was not written until the middle of July.[3] The Grand Duchess was by this time in Germany for her customary summer holiday. The music theorist Zaremba, already a professor at the Conservatory, was chosen to become its Director, but he was no conductor. Who should they appoint in this capacity? Who could they find at such short notice?

Balakirev was immediately thought of, especially as both Dargomyzhsky and Balakirev's great friend and admirer, Kologrivov, were on the board of directors. His conducting, not only at the Free School of Music but at other concerts, including the Slav concert, had received very favorable criticism from Cui and Stasov, even if other critics, such as Famintsyn, took a different view. More particularly, he had with great success conducted performances of Glinka's operas in Prague earlier in 1867, and this success abroad considerably increased his reputation. Nor did the amusing stories, circulating in St. Petersburg, of the difficulties he had had to overcome to achieve this success in Prague do his reputation any harm. The vocal score of Glinka's *Ruslan and Ludmila* disappeared mysteriously, so Balakirev accompanied the rehearsal from memory. Some Poles had come to stage a demonstration at a performance of Glinka's *A Life For the Tsar* [*Zhizn' za tsaria*], but their hisses had been drowned by Czech cheers, and Balakirev had made the whole cast "kneel at the prayer 'God save the Tsar,'" as he wrote to Glinka's sister, Ludmila Shestakova.[4] Though opposed to all his ideals, the German-born Grand Duchess was willing to agree with the recommendation of the board that Balakirev should be invited to conduct not more than four of the ten subscription concerts, provided that a well-known foreign conductor took charge of other concerts. At a subsequent meeting of the board,[5] which was attended by Balakirev, it was agreed with his wholehearted approval (according to Rimsky-Korsakov,[6] at his insistence) that Berlioz should be invited to conduct six concerts, and he himself agreed to conduct on the understanding that he would be allowed to choose his own programs.

Thus, in the autumn of 1867, Balakirev had achieved a major breakthrough and seemed to be established as the principal indigenous conductor in St. Petersburg, as well as being a renowned if controversial figure as a creative artist and leader of a radical circle of composers. Yet Balakirev's position was in fact far from secure, and even in his own circle stresses were beginning to show. The daring harmonies in Musorgsky's original version of *Night on Bare Mountain,* with its bold orchestration, shocked Balakirev, who peppered the margin of the score with remarks such as "rubbish" and insisted on substantial revisions if he were to perform it. Musorgsky would not obey Balakirev's directions, writing to him that neither the plan nor the working-out would be altered, for both were carried out in the spirit of sincerity.[7] Rimsky-Korsakov was also becoming more independent and refusing to adhere strictly to the often dogmatically expressed requirements of Balakirev, although he did at the time give up the idea of composing a second symphony, for which he had already written a fine scherzo in $\frac{5}{4}$ time (later to be used in his Third Symphony in C major), because Balakirev found what had been composed of the first movement—only the exposition—unsatisfactory. "Balakirev was totally unable to explain to me at all clearly the defects in form, using, as he often did, not terms borrowed from syntax or logic, but culinary terms, saying that I had sauce and cayenne pepper, but no roast beef, etc."[8] When in the following year Rimsky was composing, instead, his program symphony *Antar,* he wrote to Musorgsky that the hyper-critical Balakirev would hate one of the movements and be dissatisfied with another, and would be unhappy with the lack of a proper allegro with extensive symphonic development. "But I shan't alter anything, for I have expressed an idea, and well at that, and symphonic development is not always apt."[9] Balakirev's relationship with Stasov, though outwardly as cordial as ever, was also showing certain signs of strain, since Stasov found Balakirev's pan-slavophilism distasteful, and Balakirev could not understand his friend's "cosmopolitanism" in this respect;[10] the correspondence between the two began to fall off, and the former intimate relationship was never wholly reestablished. As far as Balakirev's position with the RMS was concerned, he was only a stop-gap conductor. There was no guarantee that he would necessarily be invited to conduct these important concerts the following year. And finally, although he continued to jot down ideas and to extemporize extensively for his friends, effective composition virtually ceased after the overture on Czech folksongs (with the exception of *Islamey* in 1869). In 1866, about one third of the first movement of his splendid Symphony in C major had been written down, and the rest extemporized for his circle. It was not to be completed until the 1890s. The first movement only of a piano concerto in E flat had been written. The second movement was not composed until the end of his life, and Liapunov completed the finale after his death. There were jottings for a *lezghinka* (which became the Symphonic Poem *Tamara*), but these came to nothing for the time being. In 1867, Balakirev

concentrated on his public musical activities, and other activities were pushed into the background and became secondary.

This was unfortunate, not because Balakirev was not an excellent conductor in the right circumstances, but because he did not have the right temperament to conduct the only subscription series in a major city. He saw the chance he had been given as an opportunity to give the public the music which *he* liked, which inspired him to conduct superbly; it was not worthwhile that they should be given the opportunity to hear other music, which was necessarily inferior, since he himself was antipathetic towards it. Nothing composed before the nineteenth century was performed by him, unless a soloist had requested it. He refused point-blank to conduct Haydn, whose music under Rubinstein had become very popular. In a letter written later on to Tchaikovsky,[11] he expressed his sarcastic views on Haydn, and he declared that all his music could do was to induce an inordinate thirst for beer. Similarly, Bach's music was for him cold and dry, and he would have nothing to do with Handel. This attitude infuriated the Grand Duchess, who was herself unable to see any talent in the new Russian music of Balakirev and his circle. If Balakirev had been another Liszt, he would have perhaps been able, slowly, carefully, and tactfully to bring her round. But it would have been necessary for him to try to understand the music which she liked, and he would never have considered this, since the "truth" was with him, and to disagree with him was to be wrong. So deeply had this feeling become part of his personality that he was unable to conduct music which did not profoundly move him. While he conducted excellently Beethoven's Ninth Symphony, which he considered to be a masterpiece, the Eighth Symphony was another matter, as Famintsyn wrote in a review of the first RMS concert of the season conducted by Balakirev: "One cannot help being surprised at the carelessness with which the Beethoven symphony [No. 8] was performed."[12] Famintsyn, an influential professor at the Conservatory, was not favorably disposed towards Balakirev's circle; but it is likely that this review is fair.

The lopsided nature of Balakirev's own programs was not evident in the 1867-68 season, since Berlioz's programs included not only his own compositions, but also a wide variety of other music, including excerpts from Gluck operas. Yet Balakirev's tactlessness had already alienated the Grand Duchess, who tried unsuccessfully to replace him, but was persuaded, by his friends on the board of directors, to agree that he should be appointed as conductor for the following season "for an experimental period of one year."[13] This appointment, such an apparent success, was the real disaster of Balakirev's life. His remuneration was comparatively small, yet he gave up almost his entire time, with the exception of the inevitable piano lessons, to making a success of the concerts. During this period, his circle frequently gathered at the house of Dargomyzhsky, now writing his opera *The Stone Guest* [*Kamenyi gost*] of which they all approved, and Musorgsky, Rimsky-

Korsakov and Cui were also writing operas. Balakirev was occasionally present at these musical evenings, but was often too busy to attend, and in any case he was not able to give assistance in operatic matters, in which Cui was always deferred to.

Balakirev conducted all but one[14] of the RMS concerts in the 1868-69 season. The audiences began to fall off, though the erratic nature of the dates of the concerts (not Balakirev's fault) may have been a contributory factor. Even so, the last concert in the season, at which Beethoven's Ninth Symphony was given, was an outstanding success. Yet the many novelties which he introduced, including Tchaikovsky's feeble Symphonic Fantasia *Fate* [*Fatum*], and Borodin's First Symphony (which was rehearsed to the exclusion of almost everything else in the program), were not to the liking of the majority of the subscription ticket holders, and he made no attempt to sugar the pill. If Balakirev had been wiser he would have introduced such novelties at Free School Concerts, over which he had total control after Lomakin's resignation. But he was convinced that if he were only persistent enough, others would come round to his point of view.

That he did have a good deal of public good will is certainly true. When, in the spring of 1869, he was told that he would not be reappointed as conductor in the following season, there was a public outcry. His cause was taken up both by Tchaikovsky and by the Director of the Moscow Conservatory, Anton Rubinstein's brother Nikolai, for whom Balakirev specially composed the piano fantasy *Islamey,* which Nikolai agreed to perform at a series of Free School subscription concerts organized by Balakirev in direct opposition to the RMS; these concerts were well attended by extremely sympathetic audiences, while the RMS concerts languished. Yet the outcome was unfortunate financially for them both, since the Free School did not really have enough funds to put on more than two concerts in a season, and the RMS, in order to undercut Balakirev, had to reduce the price of its tickets to an uneconomic level at the very moment when the number of its subscribing members fell substantially.[15]

In the period 1867-69 Balakirev had made no attempt to conciliate those who disagreed with him. He alienated Famintsyn irrevocably when that learned professor told him that he had composed incidental music for Schiller's *William Tell.* Balakirev immediately sang the famous theme from Rossini's overture and asked him whether he had included it. According to Rimsky-Korsakov,[16] Famintsyn never forgave Balakirev this sally. Furthermore, in the autumn of 1868, Balakirev would have nothing to do with the attempts of Kologrivov to mediate between himself and Zaremba, averring that his friend displayed a limited understanding of people if he imagined that it was possible to mix "oil and water."[17] Similarly, when it became known that the Free School's concerts could not continue for financial reasons, an invitation to Balakirev to be concerned again (though not as principal conductor) with the

affairs of the RMS in 1870 was scornfully turned down by him. He busied himself with trying to find funds for another Free School series in the season 1871-72; but these concerts turned out to be less successful, since the RMS had modified its programs and included much more new music (including the first Petersburg performance of Tchaikovsky's overture *Romeo and Juliet* with which Balakirev had been closely associated[18]), so that the Free School concerts had much less of a *raison d'être* than previously, especially as Balakirev's successor at the RMS, Napravnik, was an excellent conductor. The Free School subscription series had to be abandoned. Balakirev saw this as his final failure.

Despite the rather perverted pleasure which Balakirev initially took in these battles, he had gradually been becoming more and more depressed as a result of an increasing sense of failure and appalling financial distress. On 6/18 July 1872, he took a job as a clerk with the Central Railway Company, Warsaw line.[19] Two months later, however, he was still in dire financial straits, writing to his friend Zhemchuzhnikov : "My circumstances have not improved, in fact quite the reverse. They are *demanding* my rent, and it must be paid by 1st October at the latest. Besides my rent I must have 40 or 50 rubles to get myself clothes in which I can go out to give lessons, which I have had to postpone until 1st October because I am without respectable clothes."[20] In addition to his clerical work, Balakirev taught the piano on weekday evenings. He abandoned the Free School and its concerts, explaining to Stasov that Rimsky-Korsakov would be quite capable of drawing up good programs and also conducting.

After the failure of his concerts, Balakirev reached the lowest point of his depression, contemplating suicide. Kashkin visited him and found a horrible change. He seemed to "exhale an atmosphere of deep depression,"according to the Moscow musician.[21] He overcame his suicidal tendencies, however, and took refuge instead in an exaggerated form of Orthodox Christianity, which he adhered to for the rest of his life. For the next four years he would see none of his friends. He had hoped to gain promotion in his job so as to be able to stop teaching and concentrate on composition. Unfortunately, it would have been difficult for a man who had been the central figure in the most progressive group of Russian composers of the day, and who had been conductor of the Russian Musical Society and the Free School, to be as it were translated into that well-loved Romantic figure, the poor neglected musician composing in a garret, and in any case he lost his railway job soon afterwards. Not only did he not compose anything at all until he gradually made a reappearance in 1876, but Ludmila Shestakova, worried about the safety of his compositions and sketches, asked him to give them all to her for safe custody.[22] This he did.

It was Glinka's redoubtable sister herself who managed to entice Balakirev from his retirement in 1876, pleading with him to prepare an edition of her brother's operas for publication and urging him to take up again the

composition of *Tamara*. This masterly symphonic poem was not completed until 1882 and is Balakirev's sole composition between 1870 and 1882.

It would be tempting to put forward the view that if Balakirev had not been offered the conductorship of the RMS in 1867 and 1868, then subsequently dismissed, his career might very well have taken a different turn. Certainly this shaped his future and proved in the end to have a very deleterious effect, by cutting off his creative work and eventually alienating him from society for a considerable period of time. Although things might have turned out differently, it is much too simplistic to draw the conclusion that his career would necessarily have been any more successful. Soon after the composition of *Tamara*, he was appointed Director of Music for the Imperial Chapel, a post he held for eleven years until 1894. He devoted himself to it assiduously, but the result was that he composed nothing of any consequence during this period either. It was not until the early 1890s, when he was in his mid-fifties, that he began composing again in earnest, resuming work on his unfinished symphony in C major. The mental creative block, dating from the mid-sixties (with the exception of *Islamey* and *Tamara*) was, as it were, cleared, and as an older man, Balakirev once again composed with the same dedication as he had before the "crisis years." In his middle years, Balakirev was never happy unless he was fighting a battle. As a result of this, as I have shown, he was already provoking unfavorable reactions from his circle before his appointment to the RMS in 1867, and he refused to countenance compromise solutions in his fight with the authorities. After his inevitable failure and isolation and his gradual reappearance, his appointment to the Imperial Chapel heralded the beginning of new battles—to improve the lot of the choirboys, to improve the standard of the music and so on; these skirmishes were never taken to extremes, although he did quarrel with his superior, Count Sheremetev, and his assistant, Rimsky-Korsakov, from whom he finally became totally estranged in the 1890s. In the later part of his life, Balakirev used to assert that because of the trouble he had caused at the Chapel he had received only half the pension he had expected.

In the marvellous creative period at the end of his life, Balakirev took up his pen where he had laid it down in the 1860s. The embattled strife-torn middle years which produced only *Islamey* and *Tamara* were passed over, and the interrupted development of the early years was continued. The C major symphony was completed in exactly the same style; the creative experience gained in *Tamara* was ignored, since in such a different type of piece it was irrelevant for Balakirev. Many fine new pieces were written, such as the magnificent Piano Sonata in B flat minor, of which the first movement is a finely etched delicate mixture of sonata form and fugue, rather different from anything he had composed previously and, in some ways, like Rimsky-Korsakov's later music, more detached than his earlier music. As well as the first movement, the sonata's *intermezzo* is also a particularly good example of this.

Thus we have a picture of a young man, up to his late twenties, and of an older man, from the time of his retirement from the Imperial Chapel in his middle fifties, as a creative artist whose primary activity was composition. The creative "child"[23] developed naturally in the early years, but was nipped in the bud by life itself, which was experienced to the full in all its turbulence, ousting almost completely the urge to compose. This was followed by what might almost be called a second creative childhood, in which the development of the early period gently continued. We should not, perhaps, regret that Balakirev could never have been a single-minded enough composer to develop steadily throughout his whole life, but on the contrary we should be grateful that the young and the old Balakirev left us so much beautiful music, and that the dogmatic, magnetic, argumentative, inspiring, domineering Balakirev helped others to achieve creative excellence, even if this aspect of his personality also produced many enemies and caused him, in the end, to quarrel with all his old friends and former disciples.

It is arguable, then, that Balakirev's personality made the crisis of the middle years inevitable. It is probable that, if this crisis had not taken the form outlined above, it would have taken some other form. That he emerged from the crisis as he grew older might almost be described as a natural part of the aging process. His creative fire had not been permanently extinguished, and in the tranquillity of old age he was able to look back dispassionately at the crisis years and to compose in calm detachment.

Notes

1. V.V. Stasov, *Izbrannye sochineniia* [Selected works], v. 1 (Moscow, 1952), pp. 171-73.

2. M.A. Balakirev, *Letopis' zhizni i tvorchestva* [Chronicle of life and works], compiled by A.S. Liapunova and A.A. Yazovitskaya, (Leningrad, 1967), p. 137.

3. A.G. Rubinstein, *Izbrannye pis'ma* [Selected letters], ed. L.A. Barenboim, (Moscow, 1954), pp. 70-71.

4. Edward Garden, *Balakirev: A Critical Study of his Life and Music* (New York and London, 1967), p. 75.

5. Balakirev, *Letopis'*, p. 130.

6. N. Rimsky-Korsakov, *Letopis' moei muzykal'noi zhizni* [Chronicle of my musical life], 8th ed. (Moscow, 1980), p. 70.

7. M.P. Musorgsky, *Pis'ma* [Letters] (Moscow, 1981), p. 63.

8. Rimsky-Korsakov, *Letopis'*, p. 73.

9. N. Rimsky-Korsakov, *Polnoe sobranie sochinenii* [Collected works], v. 5: *Literaturnye proizvedeniia i perepiska* [Literary works and correspondence] (Moscow, 1963), p. 308.

10. Balakirev to Stasov, 10/22 February 1867, in Mili Alexeevich Balakirev and Vladimir Vasilievich Stasov: *Perepiska* [Correspondence], ed. A.S. Liapunova (Moscow, 1970-71), Vol 1, pp. 247-50.

11. M.A. Balakirev, *Vospominaniia i pis'ma* [Memoirs and letters] (Leningrad, 1962) p. 137.

12. Balakirev, *Letopis'*, p. 131.

13. Ibid., p. 144.

14. At this concert, Anton Rubinstein's brother Nikolai, Director of the Moscow Conservatory, conducted his brother's *Ocean* Symphony and was the solo pianist in Litolff's Fourth Piano Concerto and Liszt's Second Piano Concero, with Balakirev conducting.

15. Robert C. Ridenour, *Nationalism, Modernism, and Personal Rivalry in Nineteenth-Century Russian Music* (UMI Research Press, Ann Arbor, 1981), p. 177 ff. In this study, Ridenour considers the rivalries in commendable detail and deals with the subject accurately and in a wide context.

16. Rimsky-Korsakov, *Letopis'*, p. 72.

17. Balakirev and Stasov, *Perepiska*, Vol 1, p. 258.

18. For a full discussion of Balakirev's relationship with Tchaikovsky, see my article, "The Influence of Balakirev on Tchaikovsky," in *Proceedings of the Royal Musical Association*, Vol. 107 (London, 1981), pp. 86-100.

19. Balakirev, *Issledovaniia i stat'i* [Research and articles] (Leningrad, 1961), p. 47.

20. Balakirev, *Vospominaniia i pis'ma*, pp. 106-7.

21. V. Muzalevsky, *M.A. Balakirev: Kritiko-biograficheskii ocherk* [A Critical biographical essay] (Leningrad, 1938), pp. 58-59. Balakirev refused the offer of a post at the Moscow Conservatory (see N.D. Kashkin, "M.A. Balakirev i evo otnosheniia k Moskve," in *Muzyka*, No. 152 (1913), p. 677ff).

22. Balakirev, *Issledovaniia i stat'i*, pp. 48-49.

23. I have dealt with the psychological aspects of Balakirev's character in detail in my article, "Balakirev's Personality," in *Proceedings of the Royal Musical Association*, Vol. 96 (London, 1970), pp. 43-55.

8

The Russians in Paris (1889-1914)

Elaine Brody (U.S.A.)

When Sergei Diaghilev and his ballet troupe streaked across the artistic firmament of Paris in 1909, his dazzling achievement astonished even the sophisticated citizens of the French capital. No actor, no painter, no artist, no poet, no musician, no dramatist, and not even an impresario when he started, Diaghilev was nevertheless able to surround himself with what was undoubtedly the foremost galaxy of artists ever assembled in any single enterprise. His accomplishments place him in the forefront of the artistic avant-garde of the twentieth century. For Diaghilev as for Wagner in the nineteenth century, his fantasies demanded a synthesis of the arts. "Perfect ballet," he is reported to have said, "can only be created by the fusion of dancing, painting and music." Much more than dance and dancers, however, succumbed to the wizardry of Diaghilev. Fashion, interior design, stage settings, musical compositions, and, in a way, the cultural taste and artistic direction of two nations, France and later America, reveal the impact of his feverish activities. A bare half dozen years after Diaghilev's arrival on the Parisian scene in 1906, Proust would write of the coming of the Russian dancers: "This charming invasion, against whose seductions only the stupidest of critics protested, infected Paris, as we know, with a fever of curiosity less burning, more purely aesthetic, but quite as intense, perhaps, as that aroused by the Dreyfus case."[1]

Diaghilev orchestrated his plans down to the last detail. His first French season found him represented at the Salon d'Automne in 1906 with an assemblage of works of art such as neither Paris nor any other European capital had yet seen. For 1907 he arranged a series of historical concerts aimed at demonstrating the wealth of talent kept under wraps in his native Russia.[2] The following year he prepared to introduce Musorgsky's *Boris Godunov* to the unsuspecting French, another first that was calculated to take them by surprise. And finally, with every artifice he could muster, fortified with funds from friends and patrons[3]—throughout his career he was lavish with other people's money—he landed in the French capital with a troupe of dancers,

scenic designers, choreographers, musicians, and artists who would change the course of dance in Western Europe.

In the twenty years of his reign in Paris, from 1909 to his untimely death in Venice in 1929 at the age of fifty-seven, this single individual controlled the destinies of his group much as a puppeteer manages his marionettes. An elitist, a cultural snob, he gave no thought to the masses, preferring to socialize with and perform for the upper classes. (As if to reaffirm his mental image of himself, Diaghilev's head was so large that he was obliged always to have his hats made to order. While he gave the appearance of a dandy, his close friends insist that he had but one suit and one cape, both of which he wore until they were practically threadbare.[4]) Diaghilev was very superstitious. A fortune teller once told him he would die on the water. Therefore, when his company left for South America in 1913, he remained behind; but his absence cost him dearly. Out of sight of Diaghilev, while in Buenos Aires, Nijinsky, Diaghilev's first protégé, married the Hungarian dancer Romola de Pulszky from the troupe's corps de ballet. Diaghilev, when he heard, immediately cabled the dancer he was fired. The tenuous thread that kept the great Nijinsky afloat in the real world snapped; within a few months, this remarkable genius was retired to a mental institution, and except for a very few appearances, he never danced again. Diaghilev, with his hypnotic power over artists and patrons and even sovereigns, was unique, and it is doubtful that we shall ever again see his equal. His was a flame that burned very brightly and in so doing extinguished itself.

Most historians pinpoint the appearance of Diaghilev and the *Ballets russes* as the start of a new direction in the history of dance. I see the phenomenon more as the culmination of a movement begun several decades earlier. Further proof that the Franco-Russian musical alliance developed gradually—in the late nineteenth and early twentieth centuries—will be found in the essay that follows.

One of the most enlightening articles concerned with the Franco-Russian interface was written in 1953 by André Schaeffner for Pierre Souvtchinsky's *La Musique Russe*.[5] In "Debussy et ses rapports avec la musique russe," Schaeffner goes over the terrain of Russian music in Paris so carefully that any investigations of this phenomenon must begin with his analysis of the situation. He cites 1873 as the year that saw the beginning of new relations between France and Russia. Liszt was then at Weimar, where his ducal orchestra read over considerable numbers of Russian works and made them known to many foreign visitors, among them Vincent d'Indy.[6] Earlier in the century, Adolphe Adam, after a visit to St. Petersburg, wrote of the extraordinary effect on him of the Russian sacred music that he had heard in the Imperial Chapel.[7] Berlioz, too, on the occasion of his first visit to Russia in 1847, marvelled at the sonority of the basses who sang with the choir.[8] D'Indy, however, appears to have been

among the first of the young Frenchmen in the latter part of the century to have heard live performances of this music, not merely to have read about them.[9]

In 1874, the Conservatoire in Paris received a package of twenty-seven scores including almost all the orchestral works of Glinka, Rimsky-Korsakov's *Sadko* and *The Maid of Pskov,* Tchaikovsky's *Oprichnik,* and various works by Dargomyzhsky, Cui, Serov, Verstovsky, and Liadov—and also Musorgsky's *Boris Godunov.*[10] The presence of *Boris* among these scores makes the copy that Jules de Brayer left at Debussy's of far less importance than had previously been believed.[11] To the first packet of scores mentioned above, the Russians added another hundred scores after the Universal Exposition of 1889, and still another fifty towards the end of 1893. The expositions held in Paris every eleven years from 1867 to 1900—the very first one had been held in 1855—eventually became the arenas for the presentation of new music of other nations. Exotic musical instruments, refreshingly new melodies, and novel approaches to rhythm, soon provided French composers with much-needed inspiration. At the Trocadéro, during the 1878 Exhibition, Nikolai Rubinstein conducted a series of four concerts that included pieces by Glinka, Tchaikovsky, Dargomyzhsky, Serov, and Musorgsky.[12] César Cui contributed a series of explanatory articles on this music in the *Revue et Gazette musicale* from 12 May 1878 to 5 October 1880.[13]

Beginning in 1878, Louis Bourgault-Ducoudray, a French scholar and composer who had travelled to Greece to study ancient and popular Greek music and who had done similar research on the music of Brittany, started teaching music history at the Paris Conservatoire. As early as 1880, he introduced his students to the music of Rimsky-Korsakov and Musorgsky; in 1903 he offered an entire course on Russian music.[14] Like Berlioz before him, Bourgault-Ducoudray was much impressed with Balakirev, with whom he began a lengthy correspondence.[15] Saint-Saëns, too, on his Russian visit, enjoyed the music of Balakirev, formed a good relationship with Tchaikovsky, and although he heard much about Musorgsky and his music, ended by disliking both with equal relish. (The Russian composer, for his part, felt the same about Saint-Saëns.[16]) Saint-Saëns also met with Taneev, when the latter came to Paris on tour in November 1876.[17]

Debussy visited Russia twice while in the employ of Madame von Meck, Tchaikovsky's celebrated patron—first in the period mid-July through September of 1881, and again in August through September 1882.[18] There were few opportunities during the summer months, however, to hear performances of music by the *jeune école russe,* as they were called by the French, although Debussy may possibly have attended concerts at the All-Russian Exposition in Moscow during the latter part of the summer of 1882, which included programs of Russian music conducted by Rimsky-Korsakov. Rimsky mentions in his memoirs that pieces by himself, Borodin, Glazunov,

Tchaikovsky, and Napravnik were performed, but no evidence exists to suggest that Debussy attended any of the concerts.[19]

In the 1880s, Tchaikovsky's name was already widely known in Germany and in France, at least in the urban musical centers. The Russians, particularly the avant-garde, considered his structures too traditional and his style too Germanic, while the composer, himself, felt drawn to Paris and things French. In two letters (10 July 1880 and 5 July 1884) to Tchaikovsky, Madame von Meck, his patron, mentions Debussy's name. In his reply, the Russian composer writes that he's very happy with de Bussy's [*sic*] success in achieving the Prix de Rome. And at the beginning of his relationship with von Meck, when she sent him a photo of Debussy, the older man even commented that Debussy had "something in his features and his hands that vaguely recalls Anton Rubinstein in his youth. May God grant that his destiny be as glorious as that of the King of pianists."[20]

Except in Russia where his works were often performed, the pianist Anton Rubinstein was far better known than the composer. Today, even his remarkable pianistic facility is long forgotten in Western Europe and America. (Most concertgoers think of Arthur, not Anton, when the name Rubinstein is mentioned. They are not related.) Nevertheless, his accomplishments remain a model of the nineteenth-century virtuoso's life style. From Russia, where he was born, he toured Poland, Germany, Holland, Belgium, France, Switzerland, Italy, Austria, Hungary, Denmark, Sweden, England, and crossed the ocean to perform as well in the United States and Canada. An indefatigable traveller and an incomparable virtuoso, he also wrote about a dozen operas, five oratorios on biblical subjects, a ballet, several piano concertos and piano sonatas, half a dozen symphonies, along with numerous smaller works. His multiple talents as pianist, composer, and sometimes impresario made him the envy of his peers. He was not popular with the young Russian school, and he knew it. To a friend he wrote:

> The Jews regard me as a Christian; the Christians as a Jew; the classicists as a Wagnerian; the Wagnerians as a classicist; the Russians as a German, and the Germans as a Russian.[21]

We have no evidence that Debussy heard any of Rubinstein's music, and although Louis Laloy reports that Debussy met Rimsky-Korsakov, Balakirev, and Borodin, we cannot be certain that he did.[22] Nor do we know, as already mentioned, whether or not Debussy attended two concerts in Russian music that Rimsky conducted while Debussy was in Moscow.[23] Conceivably he attended one of the presentations of the "Rossignols de Koursk," a troupe of forty gypsies from Moscow who performed at the Trocadéro and the Orangerie during the Exposition of 1878.[24] Another friend of Debussy, Paul Vidal, describes his enthusiasm for Tchaikovsky and Borodin[25] but says he was not familiar with Musorgsky's work.[26] Surely, the young composer—he was

only eighteen in 1878—would have heard at least one of the six performances of Rimsky's *Sadko,* either at the Exposition, which he visited often or at one of Pasdeloup's numerous performances of the piece.[27] Schaeffner reports that from the fall of 1878 to the spring of 1902—excluding the years 1885-86, when Debussy was away in Rome, and, oddly enough, no Russian music of consequence was performed in Paris—the following works were presented:

Dances from *Prince Igor* (Borodin)	13 performances
Sadko (Rimsky)	12 performances
In the Steppes of Central Asia (Borodin)	10 performances
Capriccio Espagnol (Rimsky)	9 performances
Antar (Rimsky)	7 performances
Tamara (Balakirev)	6 performances
Sheherazade (Rimsky)	5 performances
Night on Bald Mountain (Musorgsky)	2 performances
Second Symphony (Borodin)	2 performances[28]

Pasdeloup, Colonne, Lamoureux and especially Chevillard, after 1897 when he took over from Lamoureux, offered Russian music on their programs. Lamoureux also included historian Bourgault-Ducoudray's Cambodian Rhapsody, perhaps inspired by interest in the Orient, in a concert of January 1889; and in June of that year, Rimsky-Korsakov presented a series of concerts of Russian music.

Schaeffner's investigations virtually come to a halt with the production of *Pelléas et Mélisande* in 1902. Although we would overlap slightly, I decided to begin my investigation with 1889, the year of the fourth Universal Exposition and also the year that French musicians *en masse* made the pilgrimage to Bayreuth. (Perhaps I wanted to prove that Wagner did indeed have some foreign competition among French musicians of this era!) The periodical *Le Guide musical* became my point of departure. Reading, with my assistants, Alex Varias and Colin Denis, through every issue from 1889 through 1914, we were able to obtain a picture of the gradual emergence of Russian music and musicians in Paris.

   Le Guide musical, begun in 1855 and continued through 1917, was first edited by Felix Delhasse in Brussels. Schott of Mainz published this weekly, which appeared every Thursday (and after 1890 on Sundays instead) and distributed it in Brussels and in Paris. By 1865, it could boast of correspondents in numerous European musical centers, and between its pages one could find the thoughtful comments of some of the finest musicians and critics of the day. Advertisements for concerts, for instruments, for books about music, and for musical editions provided readers with considerable information about musical activities in Europe and often in America as well. Guest writers

contributed special essays; centenaries of composers' births or deaths received particular attention; a necrology column kept readers informed of the passing of significant performers and composers; and *nouvelles diverses* carried the kind of gossip about marriages and divorces always of more interest to women than to men. Many an odd item helped to convince me that I was on the right track. For example, in 1878, Jurgenson announced a four-hand arrangement of Berlioz's *Harold en Italie,* nine years after the composer's death, by none other than Balakirev. By 1886, the first item in the journal is a piece on Borodin's Second Symphony, followed by a biographical essay on César Cui. In the issue of 22 April 1886, a portrait of Anton Rubinstein accompanies an article on him that begins, "On dit de Rubinstein qu'il était le Michel-Anges de piano." Maurice Kufferath, the Belgian Wagnerite, who became editor-in-chief in 1887, was an early contributor. By 1887, the journal could list on its masthead Adolphe Jullien, Arthur Pougin, George Servières, Camille Bellaigue and Michel Brenet of France; Ed. Evenepoël, Ed. de Hartog, Felix Delhasse and Kufferath of Belgium; G.P. Harry from England, Egidio Cura from Italy, and the peripatetic César Cui from Russia.[29]

To do justice to all the material I have uncovered would require an article at least three times as long as M. Schaeffner's richly informative piece. Because limitations of time and space do not permit this kind of indulgence, I have simply gathered together the highlights of my survey.

Of several hundred citations culled from twenty-five years (1889-1914) of comment and criticism in the pages of the *Guide musical,* the following selection of items reveals a Franco-Russian musical alliance of relatively long duration. I have translated and summarized most of the material. Occasionally, I have chosen to leave quotations in French, in order to capture the flavor of the original.

"GM, 21 February 1889, p. 63", for example, refers to the *Guide musical,* the issue of 21 February 1889, page 63.

1889

Le *Prince Igor* est donc, selon l'esthétique moderne, une oeuvre décorative. A ce point de vue, elle est remarquable et se distingue des autres oeuvres de ce genre par un coloris pittoresque ou particulier à l'école russe et surtout à Borodine. (GM, 21 February 1889, p. 63.)

[*Prince Igor* is then, according to today's aesthetic, a decorative work. From this point of view, it is noteworthy and differs from other works of this genre through the picturesque or special color of the Russian school and, particularly, of Borodin.]

Thus Marcel Remy describes the newly published edition of Borodin's posthumous opera, completed by Rimsky-Korsakov and Glazunov from Borodin's own sketches. The two sentences, even taken out of context—a

review of the edition and a summary of the opera's plot—encapsulate the French view of what they would soon be describing as "la jeune école russe," a group dedicated to the reform of Russian music through the use of authentic Russian folk and colorful popular tunes, along with occasional references to the melodies of the Russian Orthodox church: a revitalization along the lines that Wagner had advocated for German music and the French Wagnerites, like Catulle Mendès and others, had also prescribed for French composers eager to make their mark. To lessen the impact of Wagner, French composers begin to seek inspiration from their own ethnic and cultural roots. As the century draws to a close, German influence fades. After experiencing the delights of Russian music (as a result of the visits of Russian musicians and pianists at the Exposition of 1889), the French become more amenable to cultural contacts with their neighbor further to the East.[30]

In July 1889, at the Trocadéro, two concerts of Russian music conducted by Rimsky-Korsakov and his young pupil Glazunov are well received by French critics, who deplore the absence of the public from the French capital at the time. They express the hope that Colonne, Lamoureux, and Garcin will see fit to include works of these Russian masters on some of their winter programs. Balthazar Claes, the critic, reminds his readers that Musorgsky's *Night on Bald Mountain* might conceivably be compared with Berlioz's "Witches' Sabbath" from his *Symphonie fantastique* and also with Saint-Saëns's *Danse Macabre*. He points out that the Saint-Saëns piece comes after the Russian master's work—but both of them are indebted to Berlioz's orchestration and his descriptive style.

In the autumn of 1889, Gounod's forthcoming appearance for several concerts in St. Petersburg and Moscow is announced; the French pedagogue and pianist Louis Diémer is also expected there. On the occasion of Anton Rubinstein's fiftieth anniversary of his professional career, Countess Rostopchina, on behalf of the Russian colony and musicians of Paris, sends a congratulatory telegram expressing admiration and good wishes; signatories include A. Thomas, Gounod, Massenet, Saint-Saëns, Delibes and all members of the musical section of the French Institute. The following week, an extensive review of the celebrations accompanying Rubinstein's jubilee calls attention to "the contingents from New York, Chicago, Brussels, Antwerp, Berlin, Vienna, and Paris who have gathered to pay him homage." Countess Louise de Mercy-Argenteau,[31] the celebrated Belgian Russophile and friend of Liszt, proffers her remarks in person.

1890

Maurice Kufferath, famous Belgian Wagnerite who will become editor of the *Guide musical,* heralds Rimsky's imminent arrival in Brussels, where he will conduct a concert devoted exclusively to Russian music. Roger Martin writes:

Les Russes saisissent toutes les occasions de manifester avec éclat leurs sympathies pour les artistes français. On nous écrit de Moscou que Edouard Colonne vient de remporter dans cette ville un succès sans précédent. Le concert qu'il dirige au Conservatoire n'a été qu'une longue ovation pour notre chef d'orchestre et pour les compositeurs français dont les oeuvres défrayaient la moitié du programme. M. Colonne, que la société moscovite voulait à toute force retenir, n'a pu quitter Moscou qu'en promettant de revenir, l'an prochain, donner une série de concerts en Russie. (GM, 13 April 1890, p. 119.)

[The Russians sieze every opportunity to express in a resounding manner, their sympathy for French artists. They write us from Moscow that Edouard Colonne has just won an unprecedented success in that city. The concert he conducted at the Conservatoire was but one long ovation for our conductor and for French composers whose works preempted half the program. M. Colonne, whom the Muscovite society wanted to retain at all costs, was only able to leave Moscow by promising to return, next year, to give a series of concerts in Russia.]

After the concert at Brussels, Kufferath remarks:

Je ne crois qu'il y ait actuellement dans aucun pays d'Europe une réunion aussi intéressante d'artistes connaissant mieux leur métier et plus complètement armés pour apporter au public des sensations plus originales et plus nouvelles. Elle n'est pas plus jeune, la nouvelle école russe. Deux de ses plus éminents disciples, Borodine et Mussorgski, sont morts; les vivants sont César Cui, Rimsky Korsakov; Balakirev a atteint la maturité de l'âge et du talent. [*Glazunov is still young at this period, not yet thirty.*] (GM, 20 April 1890, p. 125.)

[I do not believe that there is currently in any country of Europe as interesting a group of artists, more knowledgeable about their craft and more completely equipped to bring before the public any newer or more original sensations. It is no longer young, this new Russian school. Two of its most eminent disciples, Borodin and Musorgsky, are dead; still living are César Cui and Rimsky-Korsakov; Balakirev has attained the maturity of age and of talent.]

1891

Richepin's *Le Flibustier* with music by César Cui will be produced at the Opéra-Comique.

Rumor has it that the Tsar will establish in Paris an Academy for Russian artists and composers, the counterpart of the French Academy in Rome. It is well known how much the Russian government does for music: Tiflis, Warsaw, Karkov, Kiev, Moscow, St. Petersburg, and other cities all get substantial help. Would that the French goverment did likewise! (GM, 5 April 1891, p. 111.)

In October, Colonne presents works of the Russian school. On 19 November, he prepares once again to leave for St. Petersburg where the

Russian papers list the following program: Beethoven's Fifth Symphony, Grieg's *Peer Gynt* Suite, three excerpts from Massenet's *Hérodiade,* Boccherini's Minuet and Sicilienne, and the Wedding March from *Lohengrin.* Vocalist Berthe Montalant will sing selections from Gluck, Saint-Saëns, Gounod, and Augusta Holmès. (GM, 25 October 1891, p. 270.)

1892

Publisher-impresario Beliaev [Belaïeff][32] organizes two concerts of works by the new Russian school at St. Petersburg. Works featured include some by Rimsky-Korsakov, Musorgsky, Sokolov, Liadov, and Glazunov, whose *Le Printemps* resembles Wagner's "Forestmurmurs" from *Siegfried.* (GM, 14 February 1892, p. 56.)

I. Philipp plays Glazunov's *Novelettes* on a piano program in Paris. (GM, 10 April 1892, p. 131.)

At the Trocadéro, La Société des grandes auditions musicales gives a concert of Russian music, but includes not one piece of Musorgsky, Sokolov, Liadov, Cui, Balakirev, or Dargomyzhsky. They present four works by Tchaikovsky, the "least Russian" of these composers [in the view of Marcel Remy], and a "chorus of the German variety by the Czech Napravnik!" The most important work, Borodin's Second Symphony, is cut. Are they afraid of tiring their audience? The Tchaikovsky concerto is played by Siloty [sic], a newcomer of talent. (GM, 12-19 June 1892, p. 185.)

Lamoureux is invited to St. Petersburg to conduct some music of Richard Wagner and works by composers of the young French school. (GM, 9 October 1892, p. 275.)

The French Académie des Beaux-Arts appoints Tchaikovsky a corresponding member for music. (GM, 4 December 1892, p. 352.)

1893

The journal reports that Colonne has been far more successful in his Russian concerts than Lamoureux. (GM, 1 January 1893, p. 9.)

Tchaikovsky, the most universally admired Russian composer, and Glazunov, the youngest musician of the new Russian school, both have articles devoted to them and their works. Tchaikovsky's newest pieces are advertised for sale. (GM, 8 January 1893, pp. 18-19.)

The visit of the Russian fleet to France has, as its musical counterpart, a *Festival russe* organized by *L'Echo de Paris* at the Châtelet. A critic writes that they couldn't have selected a better person than Colonne as conductor. Russian works already have an undeniable importance in Paris, although they are not so well-known as yet throughout France. Composers whose works are included are Glinka, Serov, Borodin, Cui, A. Rubinstein, Rimsky-Korsakov, Tchaikovsky, Musorgsky, Dargomyzhsky, Liadov, Glazunov, Napravnik, and Balakirev. Their [the Russians] proximity to the Orient has enabled them to study its rich melodies and modalities. They are slowly leaving behind the Italian music brought to Russia in the eighteenth century. *L'Echo* has made careful plans for this festival. The Russian ambassador, the significant members of the resident Parisian Russian colony, Sarah Bernhardt, and several eminent singers—Bréval, Delma (of the Opéra-Comique), Duvivier and Saléza will also attend and/or perform. (GM, 22 October 1893, p. 409.)

Excitement associated with the visit of the Russian sailors permeates every musical event these past few weeks. New works that reek of the Russian Hymn or the Marseillaise flow from composers' pens. Excerpts from Glinka's *A Life for the Tsar* are offered in a soirée at the Opéra.

Unfortunately, Gounod's death on 18 October interferes with some of the festivities and some concerts and recitals turn into memorials for him. (GM, 29 October 1893, p. 422.)

1894

Remy reviews Cui's *Le Flibustier* at the Opéra-Comique and calls it boring—despite the composer's precise theories expressed in his *Musique en Russie* (Paris, 1880), where he calls for the exclusion of Italianisms and extensive patches of instrumental music in opera, the elimination of closed musical forms, and the omission, as well, of duets, trios,[33] and the like. *Le Flibustier* is simply monotonous. (GM, 28 January 1894, p. 105.)

Colonne is recalled three times in St. Petersburg after his performance of Meyerbeer's *Les Huguénots*. (GM, 1 April 1894, p. 329.)

Tsar Alexander III dies of kidney failure on 1 November. A long obituary praises this remarkable sovereign who had been supportive of music. He had an excellent ear, played the cornet and bourdon himself, organized an orchestra of amateurs and had them give benefit concerts as well as play at dinners and balls. He maintained a fine choir in his chapel under Balakirev and Rimsky-Korsakov (see endnotes 7 and 8). The late Emperor did not care for classical eighteenth-century music or Italian opera; he preferred home-grown Russian opera. And although he did not like Anton Rubinstein's music, he supported

the composer because he believed his work was good for Russia's cultural reputation. (GM, 18 November 1894, p. 906.)

The lead article in the journal offers H. Imbert's obituary of Rubinstein, whom he compares very favorably with Liszt.

The Société des concerts will give Rubinstein's works during the 1894-95 season. (GM, 25 November 1894, p. 923.)

1895

Speaking of Napravnik's *Dubrovsky,* the critic writes: "Un nouvel opéra russe est toujours un gros événement." (GM, 27 January 1895, p. 88.)

A season of French opera is announced for the Théâtre Korsch in Russia. The artistic efforts are due to M. Devoyod; the conductor will be Vianesi. The works are *Les Huguénots, L'Africaine, Guillaume Tell, Charles VI, Hamlet, Faust, Rigoletto* [sic], *Mireïlle, Roméo, Lakmé, Werther, L'Attaque du moulin,* and *Carmen.* The occasion represents the first time that the French language will be sung at the Moscow opera house. (GM, 24 February 1895, p. 186.)

Siloti, who has lived for a long while in Paris, is leaving for a German tour on which he will perform piano pieces of the young Russian school. (GM, 27 October 1895, p. 811.)

A supplement dated 1 December is sent to all subscribers; it lists the available publications of Borodin, Rimsky-Korsakov, and Cui.

1896

Scriabin, a young Russian pianist, will give a concert at the Salle Erard on 19 January. (GM, 12 January 1896, p. 29.)

An announcement notifies readers that at the Châtelet, at 2:00 PM, Vinogradsky, director of the Kiev Imperial Musical Society, will conduct a *grand festival de musique russe* at the Concerts Colonne. Works will include the following: the Overture to *Prince Kholmsky* by Glinka; Tchaikovsky's *Pathétique* Symphony; excerpts from Serov's *Rogneda;* Dargomyzhsky's *Little Russian Kazachok; In the Steppes of Central Asia* by Borodin; Rubinstein's *Danses des Bayadères;* excerpts from Rimsky-Korsakov's *The Snow Maiden,* Cui's *Berceuse,* and fragments from Musorgsky's *Boris Godunov.* Berthe Montalant will be the vocalist. (GM, 8 November 1896, p. 739.)

Théodore Radoux, writing on *La Musique et les écoles nationales* declares that the young Russian school derives from Berlioz and Liszt. After all, Berlioz was first recognized in Russia and certainly influenced Borodin. (GM, 15 November 1896, p. 743.)

1897

Albert Soubies writes a lead article on *La Jeune Ecole russe:* "Ces artistes sont à l'égard de la forme, des délicats, mais ils ont en eux une puissance qui, d'habitude, n'appartient pas aux raffinés." (GM, 26 December 1897, p. 867.)

1898

M. and Mme Scriabin will perform his works on 31 January. "We cannot forget the success he had here two years ago." (GM, 30 January 1898, p. 103.)

A surprising series on Tolstoy and Nietzsche appears in the *Guide musical* in issues running from 28 August to 11 December.

Raoul Pugno is recalled nine times after his concert in St. Petersburg. (GM, 4 December 1898, p. 935.)

1899

Glinka's *A Life for the Tsar* is performed in St. Petersburg with Madame Gorlenko-Dolina, a singer and impresario already known in Paris for her customary mastery in the role of Vania. [She had sung excerpts from the opera in a soirée at the Opéra in 1893. See entry for 29 October 1893.] Lamoureux and his son-in-law Chevillard, who took over his orchestra in 1897, will each conduct a concert in St. Petersburg. Several French celebrities are invited. (GM, 29 October 1899, p. 805.)

1900

For the first time, Cui's work receives some negative criticism in the French press. (GM, 7 January 1900, p. 15.)

An advertisement cites the availability of works by Chabrier, Fauré, and Rubinstein. (GM, 7 January 1900, p. 20.)

Ricardo Viñes, a young Catalan pianist, friendly with Ravel since 1888, begins to include a number of works by the young Russians on his programs. (GM, 21 January 1900, p. 57.)

Chevillard acquaints the French with the young Russians at the Concerts Lamoureux. (GM, 18 February 1900, p. 147.)

The Russians complain that they're getting too much Russian music. In Brussels, on the other hand, at the Théâtre de la Monnaie, audiences hear works of Glinka, Rimsky-Korsakov, Glazunov, Taneev, and Borodin and respond with enthusiasm. (GM, 25 February 1900, p. 184.)

Colonne, received favorably in Russia in 1891 and 1894, returns and, with Gorlenko-Dolina acting as impresario, performs music of Bizet, Saint-Saëns, and Berlioz with much success. (GM, 1 April 1900, p. 302.)

Imbert raves about the Russian balalaika orchestras conducted by Andreev at the Universal Exposition of 1900. (GM, 24 June 1900, p. 509.)

In an article on *L'Exoticisme musical à l'exposition universelle,* the writer informs readers that the publisher Hartmann has already issued *Les Musiques bizarres de l'Exposition 1889,* a volume written by Louis Benedictus. [Benedictus is an intimate friend of Judith Gautier.] (GM, 21 October 1900, p. 743.)

1901

Leopold Auer will divorce his wife in order to marry an eighteen-year-old pupil. (GM, 3 March 1901, p. 212.)

Steinway announces that they make pianos for the Tsar of Russia and their advertisement cites endorsements from Rubinstein and other Russians. (GM, 5 May 1901, p. 430.)

Marie Olénine [Maria Alexeevna Olenina] sings Russian songs in Paris. Without Pierre d'Alheim and his wife-to-be Marie Olénine, Musorgsky would have to wait a long time for recognition in France. (GM, 19 May 1901, p. 469.)

Gustave Samazeuilh writes that Musorgsky's *Nursery*[34] has been published in French translation by Froment, 40 rue d'Anjou; and Marcel Boulestine, in the *Courrier musical,* has a penetrating study on them in an issue dedicated to Musorgsky. (GM, 23-30 June 1901, p. 536.)

Lamoureux will give the first performance in Paris of Borodin's *Polovtsian Dances.* (GM, 20 October 1901, p. 751.)

1902

Gorlenko-Dolina, soloist for the Russian Emperor, organizes the twelfth annual concert of French music conducted by Alfred Bruneau. All are warmly received by the Russian audience in St. Petersburg. Pianist Lucien Wurmser and violinist Jacques Thibaud are in the audience along with the Emperor's sister, Russian grand dukes, and the French ambassador. (GM, 19 January 1902, p. 68.)

Colonne and Gorlenko-Dolina organize a *Festival russe* on 23 March at the Théâtre du Châtelet in Paris. She sings excerpts from works by Arensky, Rimsky-Korsakov, Glazunov, and Rubinstein in a concert lasting four and a half hours! (GM, 30 March 1902, p. 295.)

The distinguished lecturer Mademoiselle Biermé gives two lectures on "Russian music since Peter the Great" at the Ecole de musiqe d'Ixelles. (GM, 25 May 1902, p. 472.)

Alfred Bruneau has been sent to Russia by the French Minister of Public Instruction and Fine Arts. Bruneau has just offered the *Revue de Paris* the first of his studies on theaters, concerts, schools, churches, and music in general in Russia.[35] Bruneau analyzes the principal works of several great Russian composers beginning with Glinka. He describes the generosity of Beliaev in his promotion of Russian music and Russian musicians. In this first article, where he describes musical activities in St. Petersburg, Bruneau reports that three lyric theaters present Russian works; concerts are offered on early Russian instruments. Gorlenko-Dolina has organized public performances at which Colonne, Chevillard and Bruneau, himself, are given opportunities to conduct. (Alexander III had two orchestras, and he sometimes played cornet or bass tuba with the players.) The orchestra has a large building with an extensive library as well as an instrument museum. In addition, Bruneau is full of enthusiasm for the St. Petersburg Conservatory founded by Anton Rubinstein. (GM, 28 September 1902, p. 691.)

1903

A report from Kiev indicates that everyday French music acquires a larger audience in Russia. Conductor Vinogradsky, by now well-known in Paris, is, without doubt, one of its principal promoters. In his concerts at Kiev and St. Petersburg, he has performed with customary success the works of several composers unknown until now in Russia, including Lalo's Symphony in G-minor; Bruneau's Overture to *L'Ouragon;* the Prelude from *Armor* by Sylvio Lazzari; the *Enterrement d'Ophélie* by Bourgault-Ducoudray, and the *Danse*

de Platée by Rameau. Not content with offering only French compositions, Vinogradsky has also engaged the French artists Henri Marteau and Mademoiselle Emma Holmstrand, who have sung selections from Berlioz, Messager, and Pierné. (GM, 8 February 1903, p. 133.)

During the entire concert season, Ricardo Viñes plays many selections of Russian piano music.

Alfred Bruneau's *Musiques de Russie et Musiciens de France*, published by Fasquelle, gets good reviews, although the reviewer reminds us that the volume is really a compilation of several of his articles, many of which have already appeared in print. (GM, 12-19 July 1903, p. 544.)

Since the dawn of the twentieth century, many Russians have come to Paris. Today, numbers of them are stranded, without funds, and without the necessary guidance with which to promote their careers and to help propagate their national gifts. Their needs will be met by the newly organized Union des artistes russes à Paris, which will promote events, concerts and expositions. A large but select group, including the Russian ambassador Urusov, will sponsor a concert on 30 May at the Salle d'Athénée in Saint Germain, where the Schor, Krein, and Ehrlich trio, celebrated in Russia, will perform in Paris for the first time. They will play Tchaikovsky's trio composed in memory of Nikolai Rubinstein, his close friend and colleague, and late director of the Moscow Conservatory.

Singer Georges Féderov of the Opéra has sung selections from *L'Africaine* and A. Rubinstein's [song] *La Nuit*. The contralto Mademoiselle Melgunov appeared in selections from Borodin's *Sleeping Beauty*, in the Bohemian song from Koreshchenko's *The House of Ice*, and in A. Rubinstein's *Russalka*; she also sang a song by Taneev. "Colonne should look to his laurels!" (GM, 14-21 June 1903, p. 491.)

Pugno and Auer together tour Russia most successfully. (GM, 15 November 1903, p. 797.)

Imbert complains about a performance of *La Juive*. "Why not mount some modern Russian operas, currently unknown in France?" he asks. (GM, 29 November 1903, p. 828.)

1904

At a meeting of Russian artists on 30 January, Bourgault-Ducoudray, with his customary artistry, traces the history of Russian music and comments on current tendencies. He shows similarities between the folk songs of Brittany

and Russian folk songs. Madame de Mouromzeff, [Nadezhda Alexandrovna Muromtseva] organized this conference. (GM, 7 February 1904, p. 121.)

Arthur Pougin's monograph *Essai historique sur la musique en Russie* is published by Fischbacher in Paris. Imbert in his review calls it a compilation of the work of others, and "Pougin didn't have the decency to cite these references." Octave Fouque, G. Bertrand, Albert Soubies, César Cui, Anton Rubinstein, Alfred Bruneau, and the Countess de Mercy-Argenteau are among those from whom Pougin has lifted material. [Nor did he cite Imbert's own essay on Tchaikovsky!] (GM, 17 April 1904, p. 369.)

On 11 May, Gabrilovitsch will give a concert at the Salle Erard for the benefit of widows and orphans of Russian sailors, victims of the loss of Petropavlovsk. (Gm, 8-15 May 1904, p. 444.)

1905

Announcement of a benefit concert of the Union des artistes russes at the Salle Erard on Sunday, 15 January. (GM, 15 January 1905, p. 40.)

Calvocoressi[36] gives the first of a series of lectures on Russian music at the Ecole des Hautes Etudes Sociales. He discusses works of Glinka, Serov, and Dargomyzhsky. Mademoiselle Rabaïan [*sic*] from the Tiflis Conservatory illustrates some of the songs. (GM, 26 March, 1905, p. 260.)

Viñes includes works by Balakirev in his series of historical piano recitals at Salle Erard. He plays Balakirev's *Islamey* and also Musorgsky's *Pictures from an Exhibition* and repeats his program at the Université Populaire on the Rue du Faubourg Saint Antoine.
Calvocoressi lectures on Russian, and Mlle Babaïan illustrates the vocal works also at the Université Populaire. (GM, 10 December 1905, p. 813.)

Lead article on Félia Litvinne, [real name, Françoise Jeanne Schütz; by marriage, Litvinova] Russian soprano. (GM, 17 December 1905, p. 823.)

Safonov, a pianist and conductor and student of maestro Leschetizky [Polish, Leszetycki], conducts the Lamoureux orchestra in Paris. (GM, 24 December 1905, p. 851.)

1906

February is a big month for Russian music. Calvocoressi writes a leading article on the genius of the Five; their gifts are incorporated in Liapunov, whose

Etudes d'Exécution he compares with those by Liszt. Debussy is indebted to Liapunov; Ravel and de Séverac owe much to Balakirev.[37] (GM, 11 February 1906, p. 105.)

The Conservatoire and the Lamoureux orchestras feature music by Russian composers Borodin, Rimsky-Korsakov, Tchaikovsky, and Balakirev. Gabrilovitch performs.

Julien Torchet says that "Debussy [est] un impressioniste à la façon des peintres Monet et Sisley comme l'a dit si justement H. Imbert, d'un coloris séduisant sans ligne ni dessin, poète de l'irréel et du rêve." (GM, 18 February 1906, p. 128.)

On the fiftieth anniversary of the death of Heinrich Heine, ninety of his poems have already been set by Slavic composers including Cui, Rubinstein, Dargomyzhsky, Borodin, Tchaikovsky, Napravnik, Rimsky-Korsakov, Balakirev, and Glazunov. At the dedication of the Glinka monument in St. Petersburg, a cantata by Balakirev has been performed. (GM, 25 February 1906, p. 159.)

An announcement tells of the availability of Balakirev's works at Jurgenson's,[38] publishers with locations in Leipzig and Moscow. (GM, 27 May, 3 June 1906, p. 406.)

Pierre d'Alheim offers his fifty-fourth recital devoted to works by Musorgsky. D'Indy's *Tableaux de voyage* and Dupont's *Heures dolentes* show the impact of Musorgsky's illustrative music. (GM, 10-17 June 1906, p. 438.)

A concert of Russian music has been given at the Grand Palais des Beaux Arts at the exhibit of contemporary and retrospective Russian art. Félia Litvinne has sung; Selva and Pitsch performed Rakhmaninov's Sonata for cello and piano. Other works included Balakirev's *Islamey*, and excerpts from Glinka's *A Life for the Tsar*, Serov's *Judith*, and Tchaikovsky's *Onegin*, as well as songs by Tchaikovsky and Borodin, and Rubinstein's *The Night Voyager*. (GM, 11 November 1906, p. 706.)

Stasov, Russian critic and writer, died at the age of eighty-two in Russia.[39] He wrote biographies of Glinka, Musorgsky, and Borodin. (GM, 18 November 1906, p. 732)

1907

The Lamoureux concerts conducted by Chevillard will present five concerts of Russian music in May 1907.

16 May: Excerpts from Glinka's *Ruslan and Ludmila* and Borodin's *Prince Igor;* Rimsky-Korsakov's Symphonic Poem "Christmas Eve"; and Tchaikovsky's Second Symphony.

19 May: Excerpts from Rimsky's *The Snow Maiden* and his *Night on Mount Triglav,* an arrangement for orchestra of the third act of the opera-ballet *Mlada;* excerpts from Musorgsky's *Boris* and Borodin's *Igor;* songs of Liadov and his Symphonic Sketch *Baba Yaga,* and Taneev's Second Symphony.

23 May: Tchaikovsky's Fourth and Borodin's First Symphonies; a concerto by Scriabin; excerpts from Musorgsky's *Boris;* and Rimsky's Suite from *Tsar Saltan.*

26 May: Glazunov's Second Symphony; a Rakhmaninov concerto and his cantata, *Spring;* Balakirev's Symphonic Poem *Tamara,* and excerpts from Musorgsky's *Khovanshchina.*

30 May: Scriabin's Second Symphony; excerpts from Cui's *William Ratcliff,* Tchaikovsky's *The Sorceress,* and Rimsky's *Sadko;* Glazunov's Suite *From the Middle Ages,* and a concerto by Liapunov.

Except for the fourth concert of 26 May when Chevillard will conduct, all the others will be led by Artur Nikisch. Singers include Litvinne, Chaliapin, Smirnov and Zbrueva. (GM, 21 April 1907, p. 319.)

Article devoted to *Les Concerts historiques russes à Paris* reveals the extent of Diaghilev's labors for Russian music in Paris. (GM, 2-9 June 1907, p. 419.)

1908

Under the Tsar's patronage, the Imperial Opera of St. Petersburg will give a series of ten Russian operas in Berlin from 20 May to 20 June. At the same time, in Paris from 15 May to 15 June, there will also be a season of Russian operas, beginning with a performance of Musorgsky's *Boris Godunov* conducted by Blumenfeld and with Chaliapin in the title role. (GM, 1 March 1908, p. 196.)

Henri de Curzon devotes an article to *Boris Godunov* at the Opéra and *The Snow Maiden* at the Opéra-Comique. (GM, 24-31 May 1908, p. 423.)

Marie Olénine d'Alheim [Maria Olenina-d'Alheim], who has just written *Le Legs de Moussorgski,* will give her sixtieth recital devoted to Musorgsky's works. (GM, 21-28 June 1908, p. 479.)

Diaghilev has found an heir of Musorgsky and wants to give him royalties. France won't allow it because Russia was not a signatory of the Bern

Convention for international copyright protection. (GM, 21-28 June 1908, p. 484.)

Excerpts are printed from the Tolstoy and Tchaikovsky correspondence. (GM, 29 November 1908, p. 779.)

Louis Schneider, Massenet's biographer, gives a lecture on Russian folk songs, after acknowledging the work of Soubies. "Particularly impressive is the *Chant hébraïque* of Rimsky-Korsakov," he says. (GM, 20 December 1908, p. 833.)

1909

The *Cercle artistique* has an evening devoted to Russian music. Viñes plays works of Liapunov, Musorgsky, Akimenko, and Balakirev. (GM, 7 February 1909, p. 118.)

Announcement that the Châtelet theater will have a series of operas and ballets *russes* with Chaliapin, Litvinne, et al. (GM, 14 March 1909, p. 237.)

Paris, Brussels, Monte Carlo and Lyons all are presenting works of Russian composers. The reviewer particularly likes the *Chant juif* of Musorgsky. (GM, 4 April 1909, p. 354.)

Announcement of the availability of the score of Rimsky-Korsakov's opera *The Maid of Pskov* from Eschig. (GM, 23-30 May 1909, p. 426.)

Henri de Curzon writes a piece on "La Saison russe à Paris." He speaks of the contribution of Diaghilev, Astruc,[40] and Nijinsky who, at eighteen, is so remarkable. They haven't seen his equal in fifty years! He enjoys particularly the *Pavillon d'Armide* (after Théophile Gautier), Benois's sets, and music by the conductor/composer Nikolai Cherepnin. The choreography of Fokine and Petipa "de la famille française," the music of Glinka, Rimsky-Korsakov, Tchaikovsky, Glazunov, Musorgsky, all prove most successful. (GM, 23-30 May 1909, p. 434.)

1910

In a series on the history of the string quartet, the Quatuor Lejeune is to devote five concerts to works by Russian composers at the Salle Pleyel. The first was given on 22 December [1909] the others will be presented on 26 January, 23 February, 16 March, 13 April [1910].

Nancy, Lyons, and Rouen are among other French cities now being exposed to Russian music. (GM, 2 January 1910, p. 10.)

Rimsky-Korsakov's opera *The Golden Cockerel* is given its first posthumous performance in Moscow. Leopold Auer is honored by the Emperor at one of the events commemorating the fiftieth anniversary of the Russian Musical Society, founded by A. Rubinstein in 1860 [in fact, 27 January 1859, O.S.]. (GM, 6 February 1910, p. 116.)

The Concerts Lamoureux presents Rimsky-Korsakov's *Russian Easter Overture* conducted by Chevillard. "Quelle coloration resplendissante. Nuées d'encens!... Cierges innombrables!... Carillons de gloire divine sur des petits thèmes de cinq notes, ayant quelques affinités ce me semble, avec nos vieilles chansons populaires. Avec cela, une virtuosité furieuse qui surprend un peu... Mais quelle belle chose! (GM, 3 April 1910, p. 267.)
[What gorgeous hues! Bathed in incense. Countless number of candles. Divinely glorious chimes playing short themes of five notes, having certain affinities, it seems to me, with our old folk songs. And with it all, a furious virtuosity that surprises slightly. But what beauty!]

Pierné conducts the opera orchestra for several Russian ballets at the Opéra. The French are delighted to see their friends the Russians once again. (GM, 12 June 1910, p. 469.)

Félia Litvinne, at the Société musicale indépendante "n'a jamais chanté avec plus de science et en même temps avec plus de fantaisie *La Berceuse de la Mort* de Moussorgsky." (GM, 19-26 June 1910, p. 492.)

In July [the première had been given on 25 June 1910], the Russian season at the Opéra features Stravinsky's *Firebird,* which borrows its plot from Russian legends. Karsavina triumphs in this most significant work of the season. Fokine is responsible for the choreography; Pierné conducts. Stravinsky is a pupil of Rimsky-Korsakov. (GM, 3-10 July 1910, p. 507.)

The Concerts Colonne for 1910-11 will include works for solo, chorus, and orchestra by several foreigners including Borodin, Glazunov, Balakirev, Rimsky-Korsakov, Musorgsky, Liadov, and Stravinsky. Modern French composers whose works will also be performed include Th. Dubois, G. Fauré, Gabriel Dupont, Paul Dukas, A. Gédalge, V. d'Indy, Ed. Lalo, Albéric Magnard, M. Ravel, and Ch-M. Widor. First performances of works by Saint-Saëns and Cl. Debussy will also be featured. (GM, 25 September-3 October 1910, p. 637.)

Lamoureux gives the première of Balakirev's D-minor Symphony, one of his last works. It received its first performance in Russia on 23 April 1909 [10 April, O.S.] under Liapunov. Analytical article on the symphony appears in this issue. (GM, 20 November 1910, p. 756.)

Lamoureux plays Liadov's *Baba Yaga* and the critic calls it "le tableau musical le plus amusant, le plus spirituel qu'on puisse imaginer." As Gounod used to say, "Ce n'est pas la musique à traverser le soir." (GM, 4 December 1910, p. 798.)

Borodin, Musorgsky, Rimsky-Korsakov, Liadov, Glazunov, and Tchaikovsky are played by both the Colonne and Lamoureux orchestras. Rimsky's *Antar* and *Sheherazade* are favorites.

A lecture on *Félicien David et l'Orientalisme en musique* is given by M. Brancour at the General Psychological Institute. M. Paulet, a tenor, illustrates vocal selections.

Announcement indicates the forthcoming season of the *Ballets russes* organized by Diaghilev and Astruc, and featuring the incomparable dancer Nijinsky. Stravinsky's *Petrushka* and *Firebird,* Cherepnin's *Narcissus and Echo,* Rimsky-Korsakov's *Sadko,* balletic adaptations of Liszt's *Orphée* and his *Fourth Hungarian Rhapsody,* and Weber's *Spectre de la rose* are to be performed. (GM, 5 March 1911, p. 189.)

In Moscow, the Imperial Russian Musical Society has celebrated its fiftieth anniversary during 1910 with more than sixty delegations from all over the world to honor Nikolai Rubinstein's artistic enterprise. Works played include those by Rimsky-Korsakov, Taneev, Scriabin, and Rakhmaninov. In its fifty years the Society in Moscow has offered 670 symphonic concerts and 400 concerts of chamber music. More than 900 students have attended classes at the conservatory in that city, among them some who have become eminent in their field. (GM, 12 March 1911, p. 215.)

The Théâtre Sarah Bernhardt will open a Russian lyric season with Dargomyzhsky's *Russalka,* Rimsky-Korsakov's *The Tsar's Bride* and *May Night,* A. Rubinstein's *The Demon,* and Tchaikovsky's *Queen of Spades* and *Eugene Onegin,* all with two casts, Russian and French. They will alternate languages in their performances. (GM, 30 April 1911, p. 352.)

The Opéra-Comique gives a historic concert devoted to Russian and Scandinavian works, and the critic feels that the Russian pieces have not been well selected. (GM, 14-21 May 1911, p. 390.)

Extensive review of the plot and the performance of Rimsky's *The Tsar's Bride.* (GM, 28 May-4 June 1911, p. 407.)

Russian singer Sonia Garenina gives a recital of songs that are not as well known as those performed by Olenina. Her selections come from works of

Glinka, Grechaninov, Borodin, Arensky, Dargomyzhsky and Rakhmaninov. (GM, 18 May-4 June 1911, p. 413.)

1912

Before the close of the legislature, the Russian ambassador Izvolsky and the French minister of foreign affairs, M. de Selve, sponsor a law to protect literary and artistic works of France and Russia. (GM, 7 January 1912, p. 16.)

Jurgenson in Moscow publishes two volumes entitled *Chants populaires.* A critic calls them marvels of international musical art. (GM, 25 February 1912, p. 159.)

The Toulouse Conservatoire gives a concert of Russian music. (GM, 31 March 1912, p. 260.)

The Theater of the St. Petersburg Conservatory presents Saint-Saëns's *Samson et Dalila* translated into Hebrew by a young student named Ravreb. The work is performed with much success before the top Jewish society of that city. (GM, 21 April 1912, p. 321.)

Diaghilev and Astruc have taken the Châtelet theater for four weeks. Four works, each performed four times, will include the principal ballets of the repertoire. In this, their seventh season, they will feature, besides the usual *Firebird, Spectre de la rose* and *Prince Igor,* Cocteau's *Le Dieu bleu* with music by Reynaldo Hahn. Principal dancers will be Karsavina and Nijinsky. Bakst has done the sets. Ingelbrecht and Monteux will alternate as conductors. (GM, 26 May-2 June 1912, p. 393.)

Balakirev's *Tamara* [a choreographed version] is added to the *Ballets russes* season. Three concerts are offered by Maria Olenina. The critic asks why there are only three, considering her incomparable voice. Last year, seven folk songs published by her publishing house, Maison du Lied in Moscow, were not that interesting.
Professor Natalia Aktzéri of the St. Petersburg Conservatory gives a recital covering the history of the *romance* and naturally includes works by Russian composers. (GM, 9-16 June 1912, p. 421.)

Madame Niktina of the St. Petersburg opera has given a recital; Viñes, who was supposed to perform, was ill. At this recital, Calvocoressi spoke about the current trends in Russian music and explained what the current crop of French musicians owed to the Russian Five. Today's music proves what present day Russians now owe the French. "Avec les pénétrations des écoles

russes, allemandes, et françaises, il est difficile de répondre à la question de M. Calvocoressi," says the journal's critic, "Où va l'école russe aujourd'hui?" (GM, 23-30 June 1912, p. 438.)

1913

In their eighth season in Paris, Nijinsky and the *Ballets russes* have produced some works that are anti-artistic, according to Henri de Curzon. (GM, 25 May-1 June 1913, p. 420.)

Ravel's *Daphnis et Chloë* has concluded the Russian season at the Châtelet. Nijinsky and Karsavina were the principal dancers. (GM, 23-30 June 1913, p. 435.)

Next February, *Orphée*, with text and music by Roger-Ducasse will be choreographed at the Imperial Theater in St. Petersburg. (GM, 30 Sept.-5 October 1913, p. 608.)

Le Guide musical in 1914—until it temporarily ceased publication with the issue dated August 2-9—carried innumerable references to performances of Russian music in Paris, Brussels, and other capitals of Europe. The activities of Russian composers both within and outside of their native land, the visits of French musicians to Russia and performances of French music in Moscow and St. Petersburg continued to make the news.

In the States, that venerable American music critic James Huneker had described the impact of the Russians before the turn of the century. He first heard the music of Musorgsky and Rimsky-Korsakov at a Pasdeloup concert early in December in 1878.[41] Huneker often spoke of these concerts in the Philadelphia *Bulletin* to which he contributed articles. On 29 January 1879,[42] commenting on the differences between the French and German approaches to music, he said: "To be successful in Paris, music has to be embellished with scenery, ballet and costumes, while the Germans, on the other hand, like music for its own sake." Later in 1915, his discerning essay, "A Musical Primitive: Modeste Moussorgsky," appeared in the *Forum* magazine.[43]

Before the outbreak of the War, Stravinsky, the young Russian composer who would emerge as the most significant representative of his country in the twentieth century—albeit mostly in exile—had established himself with Diaghilev and other nostalgic Russian emigrés in Paris. And after the conclusion of the War, came the Americans, engulfing the French capital with still another group of emigrés. Alfredo Casella in his quasi autobiography, *Music in My Time*, commented most succinctly on the changed direction of French music: "However important German teaching may have been in [the]

revival of French instrumental consciousness, it was evident by now that Germany had entered the descending parabola of her formidable musical cycle and that the light of the future must be sought elsewhere."[44]

Notes

1. Marcel Proust, *Remembrance of Things Past* (New York, 1932) v. 2, p. 544.

2. The following excerpt appeared in *The Musical Courier, A Weekly Journal,* 12 June 1907, p. 9. Americans, too, were interested in the events in Paris. This report helps us to understand why.

> It is possibly no exaggeration to state that no place except this city is capable at any one time to bring in personal contact so many universal celebrities as one could see within a few days within the circumference of a small circle—say, the distance comprised in New York in the block from Broadway and 34th Street to the Waldorf—for they were all seen in that sized territory and among them were Nikisch, Chaliapin, Godowsky and Mrs. Godowsky, Kubelik, Ysaÿe, Pugno, Caruso, Smirnov, Sarasate, Farrar, Raoul Gunsburg, Rimsky-Korsakov, Harold Bauer, Kreisler and Mrs. Kreisler, Blumenfeld (conductor at St. Petersburg), Kussevitzsky, Vance Thompson, Dazian, the friend of the late Maurice Grau, Sickesz and about a thousand more...

> See also Alfredo Casella, *Music in My Time,* trans. and ed. by Spencer Norton (Norman, Oklahoma 1955), pp. 75-81.

3. Arnold L. Haskell, *Diaghilev: His Artistic and Private Life* (New York, 1935), p. 142.

4. John J. O'Connor, "TV: Diaghilev on Cable Arts Channel," *New York Times,* 12 July 1982, p. C15. Balanchine, Tamara Geva, Alexandra Danilova and others describe their experiences with Diaghilev in a documentary shown on television's CBS Cable during the summer of 1982.

5. André Schaeffner, "Debussy et ses rapports avec la musique russe" in Pierre Souvtchinsky, ed., *La Musique Russe* (Paris, 1953), pp. 95-138.
   See also Andreas Liess, "Claude Debussy und die 'Fünf'" in *Neue Zeitschrift für Musik,* v. 128, no. 2 (February 1967), pp. 69-77; Roman Pelinski, "Musikexotismus um 1900: Claude Debussy" in *Weltkulturen und moderne Kunst,* ed. Siegfried Wichmann (München, 1972), pp. 412-25.

6. Léon Vallas, *Vincent d'Indy: la jeunesse* (Paris, 1946) pp. 150-59.
   Also, Liszt to Countess de Mercy-Argenteau, 24 October 1884 and 20 January 1885, *Franz Liszts Briefe,* v. 2, ed. La Mara (Leipzig, 1893), pp. 371-72, 375.

7. *France musicale,* July 1840, cited in Arthur Pougin *La Musique en Russie* (Paris, 1904), p. 14.

8. Hector Berlioz, "Vingt-et-unième soirée," *Les Soirées de l'orchestre,* 2nd ed. (Paris, 1854), pp. 268-72. Berlioz, like Schumann, also wrote glowingly of Lvov (1798-1870), a Russian violinist and composer, and composer of the Russian national hymn under the Tsars. His comments may be found in *Les Soirées de l'orchestre,* in the same "twenty-first evening." Another article on Lvov had appeared in the *Revue et Gazette musicale* of 11 October 1840 by none other than Richard Wagner. Wagner did not visit Russia until 1863, but he may have heard Lvov in Leipzig.

9. Schaeffner, pp. 104-6.
    See also the report of an interview conducted by Henri Malherbe on Russian music and French composers in *Excelsior*, 9 March 1911.

10. Bibliothèque du Conservatoire de Paris: nos. 17844 to 17870; *Boris* is registered as no. 17866. This information appears in Schaeffner, *op. cit.* p. 108, f.n. 1.

11. Robert Godet in *En marge de Boris Godounof* (Paris, 1926), pp. 502-4, along with several other writers, has cited Saint-Saëns's copy of the score of *Boris Godunov*—which he loaned to the organist Jules de Brayer and which that gentleman left with Debussy—as the link between Debussy and Musorgsky. It now seems that de Brayer could not have obtained the score before 1876, because Saint-Saëns, in Russia from December 1875, did not return until January 1876. De Brayer's letter about *Boris* to Pierre d'Alheim, another Russophile whom we will meet later, claims incorrectly that he had the score in 1874 (Schaeffner, p. 109).
    Debussy entered the Paris Conservatoire in 1872, at the age of ten. By 1877, he was already using the library. He could well have stumbled upon the score of *Boris Godunov* shortly thereafter. If so, it would mean that the copy of the score he received from de Brayer was the second one available to him.

12. These concerts were presented on 9, 14, 21, and 27 September 1878.

13. Cui, whose father had been a soldier with Napoleon's army in Russia, was himself one of the Russian "Five"; he became one of the more forceful promoters of the Franco-Russian musical alliance. His essays written for the *Revue et Gazette musicale* appeared in book form as *La Musique en Russie* (Paris, 1880); the volume was dedicated to Franz Liszt.

14. A summary of this course, written by one Mlle Daubresse, appears in the *Courrier Musical* of 1902 in the issues of 15 April, 15 May, 1 and 15 June, 1 August, and 1 October. Curiously, Maurice Emmanuel and Louis Laloy, both friends of Debussy, succeeded Bourgault-Ducoudray in his post as teacher of music history at the Conservatoire; both were entranced with the melodies of the East.

15. Edward Garden, *Balakirev, A Critical Study of His Life and Music* (London, 1967), p. 116.

16. James Harding, *Saint-Saëns and His Circle* (London, 1965), p. 142.

17. M.D. Calvocoressi and Gerald Abraham, *Masters of Russian Music* (New York, 1936), p. 440.

18. Edward Lockspeiser, "Debussy, Tchaikovsky et Mme von Meck," *La Revue Musicale* (November 1935); also Lockspeiser's "Claude Debussy dans la Correspondance de Tchaikovsky et de Mme von Meck" in *La Revue Musicale* (October 1937).

19. N.A. Rimsky-Korsakov, *My Musical Life*, trans. from the 5th rev. Russian ed. by Judah A. Joffe and ed. with an intro. by Carl Van Vechten (New York, 1942), p. 260.

20. This letter dates from 14 October 1880, when Debussy was eighteen.
    See also Catherine Drinker-Bowen and Barbara von Meck, *Beloved Friend* (London, 1937).
    In another letter to Mme von Meck (17 February 1883) Tchaikovsky writes: "In the modern French composers, you do not find that ugliness in which some of our composers indulge in the mistaken idea that originality consists in treading underfoot all previous traditions of beauty." Cited in Edward Lockspeiser, "Tchaikovsky the Man" in G. Abraham, ed. *Tchaikovsky: A Symposium* (London, 1945) p. 20.
    See also V. Féderov, "Cajkovskij et la France" in *Revue de musicologie*, v. 54, n. 1 (1968), pp. 19-65.

21. Quoted in Pougin, *op. cit.*, 127.
    One sign of the times, in the 1880s, was a trend towards historical recitals. In 1885, Anton Rubinstein presented a series of seven concerts of historical piano music comprising 193 works by 31 different composers. He played these works both in St. Petersburg and in Moscow in the space of seven weeks. On the morrow of each public concert, he repeated the concert gratis for students at the respective conservatories. All works were played from memory.

22. Louis Laloy, *Claude Debussy* (Paris, 1909), p. 15.

23. Rimsky-Korsakov, *My Musical Life*, p. 260.

24. *Revue et Gazette musicale*, 23 June 1878, p. 198; also Vallas, *op. cit.*, p. 19.

25. Paul Poujaud, yet another friend, had in his possession a copy of Borodin's songs on which Debussy had copied in a French translation of the Russian text. Léon Vallas, *Claude Debussy et son temps* (Paris, 1932), p. 17.

26. Schaeffner, *op. cit.*, p. 117. See François Lesure, ed., "Correspondance de Claude Debussy et de Louis Laloy" in the special Debussy issue of the *Revue de musicologie* (July-December 1962).

27. Rimsky's *Sadko* was performed at the 1878 Exposition. It was also presented by Pasdeloup on 1 and 29 December 1878; on 1 February 1880, 19 February 1882, and 12 May 1883. At the performance of 19 February 1882, a concert devoted to Franco-Russian music, Ernest Guiraud's *Danse persane* was included among the French pieces. Inasmuch as Guiraud was Debussy's teacher at the Conservatoire, the young composer may have attended this concert. Schaeffner, *op. cit.*, p. 118, f.n. 1.

28. Schaeffner, *op. cit.*, p. 118, f.n. 2.

29. Cui's review of Verdi's *Othello* today sounds rather amusing. "Il n'y a presque pas d'inspiration; on pouvait même dire presque pas de musique." He claims that Verdi has copied his Iago from Gounod and Boïto's Mefistopheles!

30. We might do well to note here two significant historical events: first the enthusiastic French response to the visit of the Russian Admiral Avellan who, with his bearded soldiers, had anchored at Toulon in 1893; and second, the Parisian visit of Tsar Nicholas II and his Tsaritsa Alexandra in October 1896, an event that reassured the French that they were no longer alone vis-à-vis the Germans.

31. Countess Louise de Mercy-Argenteau, who promoted Russian music and musicians particularly in Belgium, wrote a biography of César Cui in 1888.

32. Mitrofan Belyayev [Belaïeff] (1836-1904) came from a wealthy family in the timber business. After his father's death in 1888, Beliaev decided to enter the field of music publishing. He had his printing done in Leipzig. Actively promoting concerts of Russian music in St. Petersburg, he arranged for ten symphonic concerts and four chamber music recitals each season. Belyayev's editions proved vital in the development of Russia's national music. See M. Montagu Nathan, "Belaïev, Maecenas of Russian Music," *Musical Quarterly* (July 1918), pp. 450-65.

33. Cui condemned Rubinstein and Tchaikovsky for imitating the Germans and not being sufficiently original. Ironically, Cui's own operatic subjects derived from Heine *(William Ratcliff)*, Victor Hugo *(Angelo)* and Dumas *(Sarrasin)*. He was against the customary repetition of text, closed musical forms, and any kind of ensembles—very much *à la* Wagner. See Pougin, *op. cit.*, pp. 168-69.

34. See Debussy's article on the *Nursery* songs in *Revue Blanche*, 1901.

35. See Alfred Bruneau's *Musiques de Russie et Musiciens de France* (Paris, 1903).

36. M.D. Calvocoressi (1877-1944) was born of Greek parents in Marseilles. He studied music in Paris and in 1916 settled in London. Having learned Russian, he began to promote Russian music and musicians and wrote *La Musique russe* in 1907; he also published monographs on Liszt, Glinka, Schumann, and Musorgsky. See also his *Music and Ballet* (London, 1933) and *Musical Criticism* (London, 1923).

37. Ravel and some friends, who called themselves the Apaches, adopted as their identifying motto, a tune from Borodin's Symphony in B minor. See Hans Stuckenschmidt's *Maurice Ravel* (New York, 1968) p. 55. Stuckenschmidt says that Ravel's compositions were affected by the nationalist Russian school, particularly Borodin (Stuckenschmidt, *op. cit.* p. 185). See also Ravel's piano piece *A la manière de Borodine* (1913) and his orchestration of Musorgsky's *Pictures from an Exhibition* (1922).

38. Pytor Jurgenson (1836-1904) came from an impoverished family and worked first for others selling music. Eventually, he opened his own business, a music publishing concern that became one of the largest in Russia. Through N. Rubinstein he met many leading musicians. He was Tchaikovsky's publisher.

39. Vladimir Stasov (1824-1906) was appointed director of the Department of Fine Arts in 1872 in Russia. He constantly promoted Russian music. On 24 May 1867, in an article in a St. Petersburg paper, he coined the nickname *"moguchaia kuchka"* or "mighty little handful" in reference to Balakirev and his circle; this has been variously rendered in English, but most commonly as "The Mighty Handful" or "The Mighty Five." See V.V. Stasov, *Selected Essays on Music*, translated by F. Jonas (London, 1968).

40. Gabriel Astruc was a French-Jewish music publisher who founded La Société Musicale to promote new music. He convinced the Countess Greffulhe to become its president. The Countess, daughter of Prince Caraman-Chimay, the Belgian Foreign Minister, was the original of Proust's Princesse de Guermantes. Astruc handled—or at least tried to manage— Diaghilev's financial affairs.

41. Arnold T. Schwab, *James Gibbons Huneker: Critic of the Seven Arts* (Stanford, 1963), p. 24.

42. The *Philadelphia Evening Bulletin*, 29 January 1878, p. 2.

43. James Gibbons Huneker, "A Musical Primitive: Modeste Moussorgsky," in *Forum*, v. 53 (February 1915) p. 275.

44. Alfredo Casella, *Music in My Time* (Norman, Oklahoma, 1955). Casella was here referring to the year 1900. However, the stimulation of *la jeune école russe* had, for some time, been nourishing *une nouvelle jeune école française*.

For still another contemporary account of the Russians in Paris, see *Les Ecrits de Paul Dukas* (Paris, 1948) p. 129ff. His piece of October 1893 proves most enlightening.

French Music in Russia (1894-1913):
A Listing of References from the Index of the *Russkaia muzykal'naia gazeta*[1]

prepared by Claudia Jensen (U.S.A.)
under the supervision of Elaine Brody (U.S.A.)

Part I, 1894-1903 (from the *RMG* n. 52 [1903])

Section I

I. Articles and Studies

16. Muzykal'nyia vpechatleniia zagranitsei (aprel'-mai 1897 g.) [Musical impressions from abroad, April-May 1897]. Nikolai Findeizen. Item II on Paris, 1897, cols. 903, 1159, 1263.
19. Muzykal'nyi otdel vsemirnoi parizhskoi vystavki [The musical section of the World Paris Exhibition]. Ivan Lipaev. 1900, col. 745.
38. Zametki. Franko-russkiia simpatii v muzyke [Notes. Franco-Russian sympathetic trends in music]. 1901, col. 1120.

II. History of Music

101. Russkiia i inostrannyia opery, ispolniavshiiasia na Imperatorskikh teatrakh v Rossii, v XVIII-m i XIX-m stoletiiakh [Russian and foreign operas performed at Imperial theaters in Russia in the eighteenth and nineteenth centuries]. V. Stasov. 1898, cols. 4, 121, 276.

III. Articles on musicians and musical compositions

139. Biograficheskaia zapiska o Berlioze [Biographical note on Berlioz]. Dan. Bernar (translated by N.N.V.). 1898, cols. 242, 359, 440.
140. Neizdannaia perepiska G. Berlioza, 1819-1868 gg. [Unpublished correspondence of H. Berlioz, 1819-1868]. Translated by N.N. Voroshilov. [He is probably the translator of item 139.] 1898, cols. 639, 740, 809, 881, 965, 1081.

141a-b. a) Kn. V. Odoevskii o pervom kontserte Berlioza v 1847 g. [Prince V. Odoevskii on the first Berlioz concert in 1847]; b) Kontsert Berlioza v Peterburge. Pis'mo k M.I. Glinke [A Berlioz concert in Petersburg. A letter to M.I. Glinka]. K.V.O. [same as 141a]. 1903, col. 1213.

142. Berlioz v pis'makh k kniagine K. Sain-Vitgenshtein. [Berlioz in letters to Princess Carolyne Sayn-Wittgenstein]. 1903, col. 1217.

144. Berlioz o Glinke. Fel'eton G. Berlioza (1845 g.) [Berlioz on Glinka. A feuilleton by H. Berlioz, 1845]. Translated by A.S.G. 1903, col. 1250.

145. Neizdannoe pis'mo Berlioza [An unpublished Berlioz letter]. V. Stasov. 1896, col. 81.

146. "Freishiutts" Vebera. Stat'ia G. Berlioza [Weber's *Freischütz*. An article by H. Berlioz]. Tr. by M. 1901, col. 1206.

147. "Troiantsy v Karfagene" Gekt. Berlioza [*Les Troyens à Carthage* of Hect(or) Berlioz]. Iu. Kurdiumov. 1900, col. 73.

148. "Rekviem" Gektora Berlioza [Hector Berlioz's *Requiem*]. V. Shol'ts. 1900, col. 265.

149. Fantasticheskaia simfoniia Gekt. Berlioza. Soch. 14 [The *Symphonie fantastique* of Hect(or) Berlioz, Op. 14]. Rob. Schumann. Annotated translation by A.V. Ossovskii. 1894, cols. 236, 265.

272. Sharl' Guno. Zapiski artista [Charles Gounod, Artist's notes]. Tr. by A.V. Ossovskii. 1895, cols. 445, 524, 586, 704. 1896, cols. 85, 191, 437, 545.

345. Frantsuzskie chudaki (po povodu chestvovaniia Musorgskago v Parizhe) [French oddities (on the occasion of the Musorgskii celebration in Paris)]. Nikolai Findeizen. 1896, col. 453.

346. Mneniia Parizha o Musorgskom [Paris's opinion of Musorgskii]. 1896, col. 1355.

347. Parizhane i Musorgskii [The Parisians and Musorgskii]. P. Veimarn. 1898, col. 183.

378. Sovremennaia frantsuzskaia opera "Sigurd" E. Reie (E. Reyer) [The modern French opera *Sigurd* by E. Reyer]. 1894, col. 63.

451. Tsezar' Frank [César Franck]. O.V. 1898, col. 630.

478. Emmanuel' Shabrie [Emmanuel Chabrier]. 1894, col. 215.

Section II. Music in the Periodical Literature

51. O frantsuzskikh voennykh kapel'meisterakh [On French military conductors]. 1902, col. 593.

91. K novomy izdaniiu sochinenii Berlioza [Toward a new edition of the works of Berlioz]. 1903, col. 1315.

Section III. Chronicle

A. St. Petersburg

4. Gounod, Oratorio; French opera in the Malyi Theater; *Samson, Les Huguenots*. 1894, col. 91.

5. Productions staged by a French troupe: *Sigurd* (Reyer), *Werther* (Massenet), *Damnation of Faust* (Berlioz). 1894, col. 115.

11. *Samson et Dalila*. 1895, col. 145.

13. Lecture on Saint-Saëns by A. Koptiaev at the Conservatory. 1895, col. 278.

19. French quartets. 1895, col. 813.

21. *Werther*. 1896, col. 213.

23. Gounod, *Requiem*. 1896, col. 457.

32.   *Samson et Dalila.* 1897, col. 125.
46.   *Orfeo,* Gluck. 1898, col. 380.

B. The Mariinsky Theater

63-4.   *Les Huguenots.* 1899, cols. 408-438.
120.   *Lakmé.* 1903, col. 897.
125.   Saint-Saëns, Oratorio. 1899, col. 22.
316.   A symphonic gathering in memory of Berlioz. 1903, col. 1262.

C. Moscow

459.   Compositions by Widor. 1903, col. 212.
468.   *Werther* (private troupe). 1903, col. 1033.
471a.   A celebration in honor of Berlioz. 1903, col. 1237.
471c.   Berlioz's *Damnation of Faust.* 1903, col. 1321.

Section V

Printed Music

65.   Delibes, Grande Valse. 1901, col. 689.
206.   Fauré, Sonate op. 13 pour violon et piano. 1889, col. 70.

Books on music in foreign languages

360.   Alheim, P. d'. *Moussorgski.* 1896, col. 399, 1118.
366.   Berlioz, H. *Literarische Werke,* Vols. I, V, XI. 1903, col. 1297.
388.   *Fanfare.* Journal musical, paraissant tous les mois sous la rédaction de Ch. Blosfeld. 1894, col. 274.
415.   Jadassohn, S. *Traité de Contrepoint.* 1897, col. 197.
416.   Jaëll, Marie. *Le mécanisme de toucher.* 1897, col. 1877.
432.   Lavignac, A. *La musique et les musiciens* 1896, col. 510.
434.   Miggé, Otto. *Le secret des célèbres luthiers italiens.* 1896, col. 394.
449.   Pierre, Constant. *Le magazin de musique à l'usage de fêtes nationales et du Conservatoire.* 1896, col. 392.
       _____. *B. Sarette et les origines du conservatoire national.* 1896, col. 392.
451.   Pohl, Louise. *Hector Berlioz's Leben und Werke.* 1903, col. 1296.
462.   Riemann, H. *Dictionnaire de musique.* 1896, col. 142.
466.   Rober, Gustave. *La musique à Paris 1894-1895.* 1896, col. 396.
468.   Romain, Louis de. *Médecin-philosophe et musicien-poète.* 1895, col. 503.
481.   Soubies, Albert. *Précis de l'Histoire de la musique russe.* 1894, col. 22.
       _____. *L'Histoire de la musique russe.* 1896, col. 208.
484.   Tchaikovsky, P. *Catalogue thématique des oeuvres.* 1897, col. 1241.
486.   Valorí, de. *Verdi et son oeuvre.* 1895, col. 503.

Section VI. Photographs and Illustrations

12.   Berlioz. Photograph from 1867. 1903, col. 1212.
13.   Berlioz. Place of birth. 1898, col. 256.
76.   Gounod. 1895, August issue.
191.   César Franck. 1898, col. 631.
240.   The Opera in Paris. 1897, col. 960. (See Section I, No. 16.)
282-83. Facsimiles of pages from the *Journal de Musique* (18th century) and the *Journal pour la Guitare* (1802). 1903, cols. 11, 81.

Part II, 1904-1913 (from the *RMG* [n. 52 (1913)])

96.   "Vakkh, " op[era] Massne [*Bacchus,* an opera by Massenet]. I. Landovskii. 1909, No. 22-23, col. 572.
98.   Opernyi sezon vo Frantsii [The opera season in France]. 1910, No. 12, col. 343.
204.   "Ispanskaia rapsodiia" M. Ravelia [The *Rhapsodie espagnol* by M. Ravel]. 1908, No. 48, col. 1076.
221.   Zh. F. Ramo, kak fortep['ianny]i pedagog [J.-P. Rameau as fortepiano teacher]. H. Riemann. 1904, Nos. 38, 39, cols. 812, 838.
293.   Shkola Franka [The Franck School]. V. d'Indy, 1906, Nos. 40-41, cols. 875, 904.
334.   Reformy Parizhskoi Konservatorii [Reforms of the Paris Conservatory]. 1915, Nos. 42, 47, cols. 1020, 1164. [The RMG contains a number of articles on reforms in the Russian conservatories.]
352.   Kollegi Berlioza [Berlioz's colleagues] E. P-skii. 1906, Nos. 21-26, 29-32, 35-36, cols. 521, 561, 590, 667, 690, 737.
358.   Napoleon i muzyka [Napoleon and music]. By L. 1912, No. 35, col. 676.
365.   Shkola Ts. Franka [The school of C. Franck]. I. Kaplan. 1911, No. 5, col. 116.
375.   Iz Parizha i Londona [From Paris and London]. I. Lipaev. 1909, Nos. 26-29, cols. 609, 631.
376.   Russkaia muzyka za granitsei [Russian music abroad]. 1904-13. [No specific articles listed in index.]
416.   Khronika muzykal'noi zhizni [Chronicle of Musical Life]. Section on France: 1904, cols. 55, 123, 188, 222, 255, 416, 477, 599, 690, 891, 923, 995, 1066, 1139, 1176, 1295; 1905 cols. 37, 111, 180, 245, 366, 398, 596, 691, 790, 828, 931, 965, 1064, 1104, 1134, 1240, 1284; 1906 cols. 28, 133, 165, 229, 293, 390, 418, 512, 551, 614, 643, 707, 763, 827, 894, 923, 956, 1022, 1051, 1113, 1151, 1181, 1215, 1257; 1907 cols. 50, 149, 231, 331, 358, 422, 571, 598, 617, 680, 823, 1033, 1124; 1908 cols. 30, 56, 204, 254, 282, 315, 488, 521, 553, 637, 730, 764, 990, 1196; 1909 cols. 153, 254, 349, 415, 696, 744, 778, 843, 1120, 1152; 1910 cols. 270, 550; 1911 cols. 91, 139, 278, 790, 881, 899, 948, 1029; 1912 cols. 179, 428, 748; 1913 cols. 284, 876.
417.   Chronicle. Section on Paris: 1907, col. 565, 595.
418.   Chronicle. Section on Paris. Correspondent, I. Landovskii. 1909 cols. 572, 643, 869, 1149; 1910 col. 463.
849a.   Kollegi Berlioza. See no. 352.
849b.   Pamiatnik Berliozu [A Monument to Berlioz]. 1912, Nos. 6-7, col. 180.
849c.   Berlioz. 2-aia ch[ast'] orat[orii] "Detstvo Khrista" [Berlioz. The second part of the oratorio *L'Enfance du Christ*]. 1905, col. 283.
849d.   [Berlioz.] "Lelio" *(Lélio).* 1906, col. 1146.
849e.   [Berlioz.] Drei Orchesterstücke aus "Faust's Verdammung." 1905, col. 627.
849f.   [Berlioz.] "Romeo." 1907, col. 413.

855. Bize. "Karmen" [Bizet. *Carmen*]. 1908, col. 45, 1004.

1017. Pamiatnik Gretri [A monument to Grétry]. 1912, Nos. 6-7, col. 180.

1029a. Guno. "Filemon i Bavkida. op[era] [Gounod. *Philémon et Baucis,* an opera]. 1919 [sic.; index only to year 1913, so this is a typographical error. The correct year is not known.], col. 963.

1029b. [Gounod.] Orat[orio] "Redemption" [sic.]. 1907, col. 447.

1043a. K. Debiussi [C. Debussy]. By E. Pengu [French?] 1911, No. 5, col. 124.

1043b. Klod Debiusi. (port[ret]) [Claude Debussy. A portrait]. 1911, col. 127.

1043c. Debiussi [Debussy]. "L'Après midi d'un Faune." 1905, col. 92.

1043d. [Debussy.] "Simf[onicheskaia] poema "Iberiia" [The Symphonic Poem *Iberia*]. 1910, col. 1054.

1043e. [Debussy.] Sochineniia [Works]. 1913, col. 1142, 1166.

1043f. [Debussy.] "More" [*La Mer*]. 1911, col. 398; 1912 col. 1162.

1065. Diuka. "L'Apprenti Sorcier (ork.) [Dukas. *L'Apprenti Sorcier,* for orchestra]. 1905, col. 534.

1082. A. Zhorzh, A. Olenin, M. Ravel. 7 narodnykh pesen. Garmonizatsiia [Seven folk songs. A harmonization]. 1912, col. 542.

1217. Lalo. "Korol' goroda Is." op[era] [Lalo. *Le roi d'Ys,* an opera]. 1906 col. 126.

1281a. Zh. Massne [J. Massenet]. By O.V. 1912, col. 684.

1281b. Zh. Massne i ego ucheniki [J. Massenet and his students]. I. Kaplan. 1911, No. 5, col. 128.

1281c. Zh. Massne. (port[ret]) [J. Massenet. A portrait]. 1911, col. 130; 1912 col. 685.

1281d. [Massenet.] "Ariane." Opéra, 1908 col. 1134.

1281e. [Massenet.] Op[era] "Don Kikhot" [*Don Quichotte*]. 1910, col. 1060.

1281f. [Massenet.] "Manon," op[era]. 1904, col. 185; 1909, col. 955.

1281g. [Massenet.] "Navarrianka," op[era] [*La Navarraise,* an opera]. 1904, col. 91.

1281h. [Massenet.] "Safo," (op[era]) [*Sappho,* an opera]. 1909, col. 1105.

1364. Offenbakh. "Skazki Gofmana," op[era] [Offenbach. *Les Contes d'Hoffmann,* an opera]. 1905, col. 457.

1416a. M. Ravel. By I. Kaplan. 1911, no. 5 col. 132.

1416b. Mor. Ravel (port[ret]) [Maurice Ravel. A portrait]. 1911, col. 132.

1416c. "Ispanskaia rapsodiia" Ravelia [*Rhapsodie espagnol* by Ravel]. 1908, No. 48, col. 1076.

1416d. "Ispanskaia rapsodiia" [*Rhapsodie espagnol*]. 1909, col. 53, 1240.

1416e. [Ravel.] Str[unnyi] kvartet [String quartet]. 1909, col. 178.

1416f. See no. 1082.

1420a. K 140-l. smerti Ramo [On the 140th year of Rameau's death]. Editors. 1904, No. 38, col. 810.

1420b. Debiussi o Ramo [Debussy on Rameau]. 1908, No. 30-31, col. 627.

1420c. Zh. F. Ramo, kak fortep ['iannist] i pedagog [J.-P. Rameau as pianist and pedagogue]. H. Riemann. 1904, Nos. 38-39 (no col. given.)

1420d. Zh. F. Ramo (port[ret]) [J.-P. Rameau. A portrait]. 1904, col. 809.

1420e. Ramo. Konts[ert] A-dur [Rameau. Concerto in A major]. 1908, col. 918.

1436. Frantsuzskii sonet N.A. Rimskomy-Korsakovy [A French sonnet to N.A. Rimskii-Korsakov]. By H. Allorge. 1907, No. 7, col. 215. [This is item 26 under number 1436.]

1436. Snégourotschka. Traduction française. 1908, col. 856. [This is item 45 under number 1436.]

1454. Pamiati Zh. Zh. Russo [In memory of J.J. Rousseau]. 1912, No. 27, col. 590.

1484a. K.S.-Sans [C. Saint-Saëns]. By I. Kaplan. 1911, No. 5, col. 113.

1484b. K.S.-Sans (port[ret]) [C. Saint-Saëns. A portrait]. 1911, col. 113

1484c. Karrikatura: S.-Sans v Samsone [Caricature: Saint-Saëns in *Samson*]. 1911, col. 115.

1484d. Statuia S.-Sansa v Dieppe [A statue of Saint-Saëns in Dieppe]. 1911, col. 116.

1484e.   Sen-Sans. "Frina," op[era] [Saint-Saëns. *Phryné,* an opera]. 1906, col. 919.
1484f.   [Saint-Saëns.] 3-ia simf[oniia] (s org[anom]) [Third Symphony (with organ)]. 1908, col. 1129.
1484g.   [Saint-Saëns.] Bibleiskaia poema "Potop." (The Biblical poem *The Flood.*) 1909, col. 338.
1484h.   [Saint-Saëns]. Frp. [Fortep'iannoe] trio e-moll [Piano trio in e minor]. 1909, col. 1203.
1484i.   [Saint-Saëns]. Septet, E♭ Major, op. 65. 1909, col. 1204.
1569.   E. Fetis. 1909, no. 8, col. 205.
1580.   G. Fore. Siuita "Pelleas i Melissanda" (ork.) [G. Fauré. *Pelléas et Mélisande,* suite for orchestra]. 1906, col. 17.
1584a.   See item 365.
1584b.   See item 293.
1584c.   Ts. Frank. Orat[orio] "Blazhenstva" [C. Franck. The Oratorio *Beatitudes*]. 1907, col. 1140.
1584d.   [Franck.] Simf[oniia] d-moll. 1905, col. 283.
1584e.   [Franck.] Eros i Psikheia (ork.) [*Eros et Psyché,* for orchestra]. 1904, col. 985.
1626.   E. Shabrie (port[ret]) [E. Chabrier. A portrait]. 1911, col. 117.
1629a.   A.L. Sharpant'e [A.L. (sic) Charpentier]. 1911, No. 46, col. 963.
1629b.   Sharpant'e. Op[era] "Luiza" [G. Charpentier. *Louise*]. 1911, col. 848.
1630.   M.K. Sharpant'e [M.K. (sic) Charpentier]. 1912, Nos. 29-30, col. 614.
1648a.   E. Shosson (port[ret]) [E. Chausson. A portrait]. 1911, col. 118.
1648b.   Th. Shosson. Konts[ert] dlia skripki [Th. (sic) Chausson. Violin Concerto]. 1907, col. 1165.
1675a.   V. d'Endi [V. d'Indy]. By I. Kaplan. 1911, No. 5, col. 119.
1675b.   V. d'Endi (port[ret]) [V. d'Indy. A portrait]. 1911, col. 121.
1675c.   d'Endi. Poema "Vallenshtein" [d'Indy. The poem *Wallenstein*]. 1905, col. 92.

Reviews of Books: Russian

1806.   R. Rolan. Zhizn' Betkhovena [R. Rolland. *The Life of Beethoven*]. 1913, col. 25b.

Reviews of Books: French

1849.   l'Année Musicale, 1911. 1913, col. 43b.
1850.   P. Aubry. Trouvères et troubadours. 1911, col. 139.
[1854.   H. Berlioz. Memoiren. 1906, col. 989.]
1855.   M. Brenet. Haydn. 1909, col. 510.
1856.   M. Brenet. Palestrina. 1906, col. 29.
1864.   H. de Curzon. L'évolution lyrique du théâtre les differents pays. 1909, col. 684.
1865.   M. Delinès. La Pskovitaine. 1909, col. 575.
1866.   M. Delinès. Boris Godounoff. 1909, col. 749.
1872.   E. Ergo. Dans les Propyles de l'instrumentation. 1909, col. 620.
1877.   V. d'Indy. Beethoven. 1913, col. 37b.
1878.   V. d'Indy. C. Franck. 1906, col. 958.
1887.   L. Laloy. La musique chinoise. 1911, col. 142.
1888.   L. Laloy. C. Debussy. 1911, col. 855.
1889.   Landowska. Musi. [*sic*] anciennes. 1909, col. 844.
1897.   M. Olénine d'Alheim. Le Legs de Moussorgsky. 1908, col. 1063.
1898.   I. Paderewsky. A la memoire de F. Chopin. 1911, col. 882.

1902. I. Prod'homme. Escrits de Musiciens. 1913, col. 38b.
1903. I. Prod'homme et Dandelot. Gounod. 1912, col. 828.
1905. E. Richter. Traité de Fugue. 1906, col. 30.
1913. O. Séré. Musiciens français d'Aujourd'hui. 1912, col. 827.
1916. I. Stainer. La Musique. 1913, col. 57b.
1919. M. Unschuld v. Melasfeld. La main du pianiste. 1904, col. 56.
1920. G. Villare. Bizet. 1913, col. 37b.
1923. R. Wagner. Oeuvres en prose. 1908, cols. 110, 795.
1995. Literaturno-muzykal'naia konventsiia Rossii s Frantsiei [A literary-musical convention between Russia and France]. 1912, No. 10, col. 244.
2071. Vyezd frantsuzskikh artistov iz Moskvy, karrik[atura] Venetsianova (1812 g.) [The flight of the French artists from Moscow, a caricature by Venetsianov (1812)]. 1912, col. 644.
2082. Frantsuzsk[ii] tanets nach[ala] XIX v. [French dance at the beginning of the nineteenth century]. 1912, col. 668.

Note

1. The listing here follows exactly the organization of the *RMG's* printed indexes, reflecting the differences found there between the index for 1894-1903 and the one for 1904-13 (bound into the middle of the volumes of issues for 1914 in the collection of the New York Public Library). Each page of the *RMG* contains two columns; the column number of the beginning of each article is cited in the entries. Typographical errors occur frequently in the printed index; our listing gives the items as printed. The letter "b" after a few of the entries from the year 1913 indicates that the article in question appeared in a supplement at the end of that year, which contained a whole series of book reviews. The supplement had its own series of column numbers, therefore the distinction is important. For detailed information on the publication history of the *RMG,* see G. Abraham, "Musical Periodicals in 'Bourgeois Russia'," in *Music and Bibliography: Essays in Honor of Alec Hyatt King* (London and Ridgewood, NJ, 1980), pp. 193-205.

10

Dostoevsky in Music

Gerald Abraham (Great Britain)

One doesn't readily associate Dostoevsky with music as one does Tolstoy or Turgenev. Hermann Laroche tells of an evening with Tchaikovsky and Serov when "Dostoevsky talked a lot of nonsense about music, as literary men, who know nothing about it, will."[1] And for his part, Tchaikovsky told his brother in May 1879 that he had been reading the latest instalment of *Karamazov* in the *Ruskii vestnik* and found it "beginning to be intolerable. All the characters are crazy," while in August 1881 he was "longing for it to end as soon as possible. Dostoevsky is highly gifted but an antipathetic writer. The more I read, the more he weighs on me."[2]

Dostoevsky's writings certainly do not cry out for musical treatment; nevertheless, they have been given it. The earliest was probably Henri Charles Maréchal's incidental music for a Parisian adaptation of *Crime and Punishment,* a book that has inspired at least two operas, Heinrich Sutermeister's *Raskolnikoff* (1948) and *Delitto e castigo* (1926) by a rather obscure Italian, Arrigo Pedrollo. *The Brothers Karamazov* had been put on the opera stage by Otakar Jeremiáš (*Bratři Karamazovi,* 1928) and Boris Blacher has extracted from it a "scenic oratorio," *Der Grossinquisitor* (1948). Perhaps the most recent was *Myshkin* (1970), taken from *The Idiot* and composed expressly for television realization by the young American, John Eaton (telecast nationally on the American Public Broadcasting Service in 1973). But all these have been eclipsed by two operas that appeared in 1929 and 1930: Prokofiev's *Igrok* (*The Gambler,* composed in 1915-16, but only produced, in a much revised form and with French text, in Brussels in 1929; in Moscow in 1968) and Janáček's *Z mrtvého domu* (*From the House of the Dead,* composed in 1928), neither work an ideal subject for musical treatment.

Both Prokofiev and Janáček were their own librettists, and while *The Gambler* strikes one as a very difficult opera subject, *The House of the Dead* would seem an impossible one had not Janáček proved otherwise. Both books are autobiographical. *The House of the Dead* is not even a novel, but a lightly disguised account of Dostoevsky's experiences and fellow prisoners—with

Gorianchikov as the "Dostoevsky" figure—in Siberia during 1850-54; in *The Gambler* the narrator, Alexei, is clearly Dostoevsky himself and Polina the sado-masochistic Polina Suslova of real life, while Babulenka is based on a rich aunt, Dostoevsky's mother's sister. "Roulettenburg" is Wiesbaden and the "Schlangenberg" the Neroberg. The figures who surround Alexei and Polina— the pair of French sharpers, the foolish General whom they have marked out as their prey, the wooden Englishman—are hardly more than caricatures. In *The House of the Dead,* it is the "other" figures who are important; in the book, Gorianchikov is observer rather than character. The characters are the young Tatar Aley, Skuratov the Old Believer, the unhappy Shiskov, and the rest. But Janáček hardly allows them to interact or even to preserve their Dostoevskian identities; their histories and characteristics are transferred from one to another;[3] each occupies the front of the stage for a while and then retires, or dies. There is no drama, not even a story (except those told by individuals). But if they do not react on each other, Janáček's powerfully searching music, "truthful" in the Musorgskian sense, acts on them and brings them to tragic life, creating a masterpiece.

Prokofiev's *Gambler* is no masterpiece. But it is a fascinating experiment that has so far received little critical examination in the West. Just before the First World War, Dostoevsky was enjoying a revival of popularity signaled by the performance in the Moscow theaters of dramatized versions of *Karamazov, Demons,* and *The Idiot.* The last of these temporarily attracted Miaskovsky as a possible opera subject, and his younger friend Prokofiev began to contemplate a *Gambler.* Other projects intervened, but in September 1915, encouraged by Albert Coates who was then very influential at the Maryinsky Theater, Prokofiev reread the book, prepared a libretto, and began the composition. "I started in the middle of Act I, from the words 'dobrodetel'nyi fater' [virtuous father],"[4] that is, with Alexei's sarcastic onslaught on German "virtues"; everything German was of course anathema at the time. He intended to keep as closely as possible to Dostoevsky's own text, which he considered "clearer, more vivid and more convincing than any verses,"[5] setting it as faithfully as Musorgsky has set Gogol's *Marriage.* But he naturally found at once that he had to cut drastically. Even the two opening words of Alexei's monologue are hacked out of fifteen by Dostoevsky, and after the account of how the "virtuous father" blesses the son and dies, Prokofiev breaks off with "and so on, and so on." Not only the words but the narrative and action had to be altered and compressed; Act I opens in the middle of chapter 4 of the book. Scene changes had to be avoided: in chapter 6 of the book, the General summons Alexei to his room for a dressing-down, in De Grieux's presence, for insulting the German Baroness; in chapter 8, Alexei has a long conversation with Mr. Astley in the park; in chapter 7, he has a confrontation with De Grieux in his own room; in Chapter 9, Babulenka appears outside the hotel, is greeted by Alexei, and then carried up to the General's room on the third floor. In the opera all this is transacted, in that order, in the vestibule of the hotel.

Above all, the Alexei/Polina relationship had to be emphasized as the center of gravity.

Prokofiev soon completed this operation and set about the music, banging it out on his mother's piano.[6] The vocal score was finished early in April 1916; it had taken only five and a half months. Teliakovsky, the Director of the Imperial theaters since 1901, had misgivings about the work but allowed himself to be persuaded by Coates; Prokofiev was given a contract and an advance fee, a hundred lithographed copies of the vocal score were prepared for the singers, and Prokofiev set about the orchestration, "doing about 10 pages a day, in more transparent passages as many as 18."[7]

The war situation was bad, but Meyerhold was prepared early in 1917 to put on a production at the Maryinsky without costume. But some of the singers objected to the difficult tessitura of their parts and, of course, greater events supervened, so that in the end, the first version of *The Gambler* was never produced at all.

Prokofiev put the score aside, and it was only in the spring of 1927 that contact with Meyerhold in Leningrad turned his thoughts back to it. He retrieved the Maryinsky score from its library and embarked on what he described as "essentially a complete recomposition,"[8] which he completed in Paris on 6 March 1928. This was first performed with French text in Brussels at the Théâtre de la Monnaie on 29 April 1929, and the vocal score was published by the Editions Russes de Musique the following year. In 1931, the composer constructed a symphonic suite of *Portraits* from materials drawn from the opera[9]—"Alexei," "Babulenka," "The General," "Polina," with a final "Dénouement" *(Razviazka)* on the two entr'actes of Act IV.

Lacking access to the 1916 version but relying on the detailed study by Boris Yarustovsky,[10] we can gather that the first version—even more than the second—was based on dialogue adapted from Dostoevsky's text. In the final version the recitative is sometimes softened into arioso, particularly in the more emotional Polina-Alexei scenes and in the music of Babulenka, not only in the actual theme of "Russia" closely associated with Babulenka, but also in other of her music, for example:

Ex. 1

[My home in Moscow, you yourself know, is a palace.]

(The derivation of her voice-part from the orchestral "background" is typical of the whole score.)

The most striking difference between the two versions is in the penultimate scene. In an interview printed in the *Birzhevye vedomosti* for 12 May 1916, Prokofiev had expressed his pride in the original version:

> The *"clou"* of the opera, undoubtedly, is the scene in the casino. It has no chorus—for a chorus is neither flexible nor good theater—but it demands numerous participants— gamblers, croupiers, onlookers, each of whom has a clearly delineated character. All this, with the extreme rapidity and complexity of the action, will demand very considerable care in the production.
>
> I allow myself to consider that the casino scene represents something perfectly new in the literature of opera as regards both the idea and the carrying out. And it seems to me that in this scene I have successfully realized what I intended.[11]

In 1927 Prokofiev felt differently. Some characters—thieves, police— were taken out, the director of the casino was brought in—his entrance replacing the "arrest" episode—and instead of being given numbers ("First gambler," "Second gambler," and so on) the players were differentiated in character ("Hunchbacked gambler," "Ailing gambler," "The so-so lady," "The venerable lady," "The fat Englishman"). Prokofiev now introduced the delightful touch of the sixteenth-note figure on flute and piano, with *pizzicato* and oboe accompaniment, suggesting the rolling of the roulette ball and its drop into the hole: three bars the first time, five the second, and seven the third, a nice heightening of the tension. But the most important change in Act IV was the introduction of a chorus "behind the scenes or in the orchestra," not in the casino scene itself but in the second of the two entr'actes which frame it. The chorus begins and ends with the unison cry, "Won two hundred thousand!" an echo of the gambling scene, which the orchestra alone had sounded in the first version. And it is with this phrase, though with different words ("The red came up twenty times in a row!") that Alexei ends the opera.[12]

Ex. 2

[Won two-hundred thousand!]

Some of the other cross-references in the score, mostly in the 1928 version, are less obvious. Near the beginning of Act III (No. 321), Blanche sings a brief phrase which is referred to at greater length in another scene between her and the General at the very end of the Act, but not many listeners are likely to catch the connection. A passage in Alexei's soliloquy at the beginning of Act IV,

scene 3 (No. 580), "Ha! the roulette looks mournful after the incursion of the 'Tartar horde!'" repeats in voice-part, harmony, and orchestration, but a semitone higher—the same passage in which, near the beginning of Act I (No. 69), he had expressed his wish to take the Marquis by the nose. Even less clear is the employment in the love-duet of the last Act (No. 614) of the orchestral figure that had accompanied Alexei's outburst against the Marquis in Act II (No. 234). Or the reference to Alexei's insult to the German baroness from Act I (No. 131) when Polina throws the money in his face at the end (No. 624). There is perhaps more point in the musical connection of Polina's hysteria in the last scene of the opera (No. 604) with her anger against the Marquis in Act IV, scene 1 (No. 446). Yet another melodic-harmonic progression, always in strings, heard in Act I when Alexei tells Polina, "You overwhelm me!" (No, 83), "You make me feverish" (No. 93), returns in Act II at the moment he tells Astley that when she has wheedled the money out of the Marquis she will throw herself on his neck, "On his neck! Understand, on his neck—that money-lender!" (No. 204), and again later in the same scene, just before the Marquis enters, "She's capable of every horror in life and passion, she...she..." (No. 209). The progression is hardly striking enough to recall its earlier appearance to the listener; it is essentially a compositional rather than a dramatic device. The same may be said of the theme occasionally associated with the General, heard on cellos and basses when he first notices Alexei in Act I (No. 106); it opens Act II, recurs when he denounces Alexei for his behavior "to me and my family" in Act III (No. 332), and again at his similar outburst against Babulenka after her final exit (No. 397). But this is hardly a leitmotive.

Prokofiev achieves characterization mainly by word-setting rather than by such orchestral devices. It is true that his vocal lines rest very largely on the orchestral fabric, but in the first place, as we have seen, his primary concern was to transmit Dostoevsky's text: "clearer, more vivid, and more convincing than any verses." "And for that reason," he added, "the orchestration will be transparent so that every word will be audible, something particularly desirable in view of Dostoevsky's text." One might put it that the orchestra provides the bone structure of *The Gambler,* the voice-parts the flesh and blood. And it is here that Prokofiev places himself in the line of Dargomyzhsky and Musorgsky, and side by side with Janáček. The changing moods of Polina, the varying shades of Alexei's passion, the falseness of Blanche and De Grieux, the sincerity—and anger—of the old grandmother, the dry Englishness of Mr. Astley, are masterpieces of musical characterization within the limited framework provided by the semi-comic action and shallow characters. There is no scope for the power and breadth and emotional depth Prokofiev was to show in, for instance, *War and Peace.* But the liveliness of his comic invention may be demonstrated by his treatment of the ridiculous General, whose voice-part almost deserves a study on its own. Here it may suffice to quote some of the treatments of his ejaculatory syllables: (a) the amorous "Oh, yes!" to Blanche in

Act I; (b) his bewildered, "Eh?" [*A!*] when startled by Alexei over the matter of
the duel in Act II; (c) his stutter when confronted by Babulenka; (d) his horror
when he hears of her intention to visit the casino; (e) his anguish over Blanche's
"ingratitude."

Ex. 3

It was such things as this that prompted Meyerhold to say that Prokofiev's
"free recitative demands a dramatic actor. There are notes, it is necessary to be
able to read them and to have a good vocal delivery [*postavlenie golosa*], one
must know how to sing: nevertheless it is impossible to say that this is an opera,
impossible to say that it needs opera singers since every customary opera singer
with his *bel canto* would be a failure here."[13]

Notes

1.   Hermann Laroche, *Izbrannye stat'i v piati vypuskakh* [Selected articles in five parts], Part 2:
      P.I. Tchaikovsky (Leningrad, 1975), p. 294.

2.   Pyotr Illich Tchaikovsky to Modest Illich Tchaikovsky, 20 May/1 June 1879, Tchaikovsky,
      Polnoe sobranie sochinenii: Literaturnye proizvedeniia i perepiska [Collected works:
      Literary works and correspondence], v. 8: *Pis'ma (1879)* [Letters (1879)] (Moscow, 1963), p.
      226; Pyotr to Modest, 23 August 1881, ibid., v. 10: *Pis'ma (1881)* (Moscow, 1966), p. 202.

3.   See my *Slavonic and Romantic Music* (London, 1968), pp. 96-97.

4.   *S.S. Prokofiev: Materialy, dokumenty, vospominaniia,* comp. & ed. S.I. Shlifshtein, 2nd ed.,
      rev. & enl. (Moscow, 1961), p. 153.

5.   *Sergei Prokofiev, 1953-1963,* comp. & ed. I.V. Nestyev & G. Ya. Edelman (Moscow, 1962), p.
      297.

6.   Ibid., p. 36.

7.   Ibid., p. 37.

8. Israel Nestyev, *Zhizn' Sergeia Prokofieva* [Sergei Prokofiev's life], 2nd ed., rev. & enl. (Moscow, 1973), p. 281.

9. On his curious method of working, see Nestyev, *Zhizn',* p. 324.

10. Boris Yarustovsky, "'Igrok': Tragediia-satira" [*Igrok:* A satirical tragedy], *Sovetskaia muzyka,* no. 4 (1970), pp. 103-14, and no. 6 (1970), pp. 64-76; Yarustovsky, *Ocherki po dramaturgii opery XX veka* [Essays on operatic dramaturgy in the XX century] (Moscow, 1971), pp. 99-114.

11. *Prokofiev, 1953-1963,* p. 298.

12. The distant objectivization of Alexei's memory of the croupiers' cries near the beginning of the final scene is yet another addition to the second version.

13. *Prokofiev, 1953-1963,* p. 94.

11

The "Czech Quartet" in Russia*

Lev Ginzburg (U.S.S.R.)

The concert activities of the renowned ensemble of Czech musicians, known in the history of world musical culture as the "Czech Quartet" [perhaps better known as the Bohemian String Quartet], spanned a period of over forty years. Its original members were Karel Hoffmann, Josef Suk, Oscar Nedbel, and Hanuš Wihan; over the years there were some changes while preserving its best traditions. The "Czech Quartet" appeared in a country of old and rich traditions in the field of quartet culture. These traditions are deeply democratic and their roots reach into the practice of folk music making. The well-known Russian musical activist, author of the first monograph on Mozart, Alexander Ulybyshev (1794-1858), remembering his visit to Czechia in the first half of the past century, wrote:

> Travelling through Czechia, I met at various inns peasants playing Haydn quartets, and one could listen to those shirt-sleeved amateurs with pleasure.[1]

Professional quartet playing in Czechia developed side by side with the development of quartet music and particularly the creativeness of Smetana and Dvořák. The peak was reached at the end of the past century with the "Czech Quartet."

The Czech Quartet had its origin within the walls of the Prague Conservatory, in the quartet class of the noted Czech cellist Prof. Hanuš Wihan (1855-1920). The ensemble consisted of students of Prof. Anton Bennewitz: Karel Hoffmann (1872-1936), Josef Suk (1874-1935), and Oscar Nedbal (1874-

---

*This essay was printed in a Czech translation in a collection by Soviet and Czechoslovak musicologists, entitled *Česká hudba světu, svět české hudbě* (Praha, 1974). More about the Czech Quartet and its members in the book; Lev Ginzburg, *Ganush Vigan i cheshskii Kvartet* [Hanuš Wihan and the Czech Quartet] (Moscow, 1955).

1920), and a student of Wihan, Otakar Berger (1873-1897). Within a brief period, Wihan succeeded in shaping the quartet style of his talented young musicians and to fire their enthusiasm for this exalted art, he developed their taste and their love for the quartet repertoire, especially for the classical literature. Soon, in 1893-94, Wihan replaced the cellist Berger who fell ill and died a few years later, but he remained the artistic leader of the quartet and the mentor of his young partners.

Already in 1891 the quartet was heard successfully in a public concert, but made its debut under the name *Czech Quartet* the following year (13 November 1892). "The first concert of the *Czech Quartet* went brilliantly," wrote the noted Czech composer Joseph Boguslaw Foerster after the debut:

> The splendid works of Dvořák and Schumann were heard in such a coordinated interpretation, in such an exemplary manner with regard to understanding and plasticity of treatment that we do not remember having heard since the last concert of the *Florentine Quartet*. Crystal-pure intonation, warmth of phrasing, precision and fire of rhythm, and the expressive emphasis of the thematic lines insure the success of the young artists. Here, everything flows out of one soul because each member of the quartet knows every detail not only of his voice, but of the other three voices, and by this study of the score absorbed the essence of the composition. It is remarkable how unobtrusively, yet expressively every voice knows how to present the themes, how the others yield, how every imitation and every thematic embellishment acquire significance, yet these details do not obscure the main trend of thought. Director Bennewitz, Professor Wihan and all the other teachers of these exquisite musicians can take pride in the result of their work.[2]

In this manner, the dominant musical principles and the basis of quartet style were established right at the outset, and they guided the artistic depth and realistic direction of the Czech Quartet and of its creative interpretation which insured its world-wide recognition.

The signifiance of the *Czech Quartet* reaches far beyond the borders of the homeland of its remarkable members. Having acquired a reputation as an outstanding ensemble by its artistic interpretations, the Quartet concertized with immense success in almost all the European countries. Having mastered an enormous repertoire, the Czech Quartet acquired its fame for the performances of the classics, especially Czech and Russian, and of course the quartet *oeuvre* of Beethoven. The Czech Quartet gave exemplary renditions not only of the quartets by Smetana and Dvořák, Suk and Novák, Foerster and Fibich, but also Beethoven and Schubert, Tchaikovsky and Borodin, Taneev and Glazunov.

The history of the Czech Quartet contains vivid incidents connected with its concert tours in Russia, meetings with Russian musicians and listeners. The Quartet enjoyed visiting Russia where the reception was always friendly and warm. They introduced the works of Czech composers to the Russian public and, in turn, became acquainted with Russian music and musicians.

During the years 1895-1912, the Czech Quartet visited Russia no fewer than twelve times; they played not only in St. Petersburg and Moscow but also in Kiev, Kharkov, Saratov, Tula, Kursk, Yekaterinoslav, and many other cities in Russia (including the Caucasus, the Baltic States, and other regions of the country).

The Czech Quartet was first heard in Moscow and St. Petersburg in 1895. The debut concerts in Moscow, on 31 January and 2 February, aroused immense interest among Russian musicians and music lovers. They played Beethoven's Opus 59 No. 1 and Schubert's A minor, Smetana's "From My Life" and Dvořák's E-flat Major and C major quartets; in addition, the Czech musicians presented the First Quartet in B-flat minor by Taneev, dedicated to his teacher Tchaikovsky. From then on dated the fruitful, creative friendship of the Czech Quartet players with the distinguished Russian composer, Sergei Taneev (1856-1915).

The violist of the Quartet, Oscar Nedbal, reported in a letter to his sister, that the Quartet members met Taneev at a farewell banquet in Moscow. Asked what he would wish the quartet to do for him, the composer replied, "Always to hear my quartet played in such a beautiful performance."[3]

After the Quartet's first concert in Moscow (among their encore pieces was Tchaikovsky's *Andante cantabile* from Opus 11), the Moscow critic and composer A.N. Koroshchenko wrote:

> Rarely one carries away such strong impressions born out of an unusual artistic unity.... All members, and each individually, are undoubtedly outstanding talents possessing rare musical powers. Because of their constant musical collaboration, they are welded together to such an extent that their single individuality and subjectivity are somehow effaced and, joining one with another, form a new unit which is so solidly harmonious that the four instruments are, as it were, transformed into one gigantic instrument played, not by four individuals, but by one person.... This interpretation was not only fiery, absorbing, and full of life, but it was truly *inspired;* the listener, even the simple music lover, could not remain indifferent toward such playing because unwillingly it took possession of his soul by its poetic fervor; one wished to listen and listen without end....[4]

In St. Petersburg, the Quartet first appeared on 6 and 18 February 1895. Smetana's "From My Life" was heard, as well as the previously named quartets by Dvořák, Beethoven, and Schubert, in addition to the Second Quartet by Tchaikovsky. (Among the encores was Glazunov's Novelette "Orientale.")

Reviewing the St. Petersburg concerts of the Czech Quartet, the noted Russian critic Alexander Ussovsky—a perceptive and sensitive musician—immediately singled out the most characteristic traits of its style, which of course acquired more depth and breadth in future years:

> The recently founded Bohemian [Czech] Quartet represents an outstanding phenomenon, despite the youth of its members. One cannot imagine anything more closely suited to the

chamber ideal, in fact even bringing it to realization. The four instruments of the Czech artists fuse into one organism, firmly intertwined and finished; the individual disappears to serve the group in order to reproduce minutely the thought and print of the work. And if occasionally one instrument dominated above the others, it is because the work requires it, because the composer planned it that way. This Quartet proves what can be achieved by dedication to a task and an idea, while renouncing individualism, artistic vanity, and egotism. Perhaps each member of the Quartet could not compete individually with world-famous "soloists" in terms of virtuosity, brilliance of technique, etc. But honestly, how much higher stands each of the Czech artists, musically speaking, than those people displaying their *tour de force* pieces. . . .

Side by side with the striking harmoniousness of the Bohemian Quartet, one admires its rare sonority, reaching at times an organ-like richness. . . . The youth of the artists lends their interpretation a lot of fire and enthusiasm, immediately winning over the listeners, yet there is never any lack of self-control. With regard to warmth of musical temperament, the first place belongs to the violist, O. Nedbal, a fine musician with a beautiful rich tone.[5] One must also draw attention to the original concept of certain works and to novel nuances and details displayed by our guests. For example, the entire Scherzo of Tchaikovsky's Second Quartet was played in a manner entirely different from what I previously heard in performances of Petersburg or Moscow quartets, even different from the famous old Brodsky Quartet. The Scherzo acquired a kind of mellow and matte color, instead of sharp and shiny as is customary; at times, one could hear gentleness and even sorrow instead of unconcern and boldness. Or, for example, in the Andante of the same quartet at the beginning of the middle part, the markings in the syncopated theme of the violin on each note were rendered particularly well and originally, like deep and sorrowful—yet somehow suppressed—sighs. Let me say that from the point of view of unity, firmness, and finesse the performance of the Tchaikovsky Quartet was truly ideal. . . .[6]

Furthermore, the critic pointed out that the guests set an example for the Petersburg Quartet in paying attention to Russian music, namely Tchaikovsky and Glazunov.

In fact, the Czech Quartet had all three Tchaikovsky Quartets in its repertoire, including No. 3 in F Major dedicated to the memory of Laub. In further performances, the Czechs included the quartets of Borodin, Rubinstein, Davydov, Arensky, Afanasiev, Cui, Taneev, Glière, Ippolitov-Ivanov, as well as Tchaikovsky's Sextet, Glière's Octet, the quintets of Taneev and Arensky, the trios of Tchaikovsky, Taneev, and Akimenko. The Czech ensemble also occasionally included sonatas: thus, Oscar Nedbal played Anton Rubinstein's Viola Sonata Opus 49 in F minor.

Such broad inclusion of Russian chamber music was due to a considerable degree to the influence of Hanuš Wihan. "He had a particularly close and warm relationship to Russia,"[7] we hear from one of his last students, Boguš Heran. "His expansive character felt very close to the Russian temperament. He loved everything related to Russia, including Russian music. Thanks to him, the basic repertoire of the Czechs included the quartets of Russian composers which, next to the Czech composers, represented their playing most advantageously."[8]

After the already mentioned Moscow performance of the Taneev Quartet No. 1, the composer entered into his diary, "They played incomparably; it was a tremendous joy to hear my work in such a superb performance."

When, in October 1897, the Czech Quartet played Taneev's Second Quartet (C Major), he wrote to the publisher M.P. Balaïeff (Beliaev) on 12 October 1897, "The performance was the height of perfection." And in a letter to V.I. Maslova (October 20) he said, "On the second the Czechs played my quartet with great excellence."

The Czech Quartet was the first performer of Taneev's Quartet No. 4 (A minor), which the grateful composer dedicated to this ensemble. The premières of this work took place in Riga and Berlin in the autumn of 1900, and in St. Petersburg on 27 December of that year. Together with the composer, the Czech Quartet brilliantly premièred the Piano Quartet (G minor) by Taneev in Moscow in January 1912. This particular performance signaled the beginning of the general appreciation of this beautiful work which received the Glinka Prize the same year. Even before that, in November-December 1911, the Quintet by Taneev was played in Berlin, Düsseldorf, and Frankfurt/Main by the Czech Quartet and the composer at the piano.

In 1908 and 1911, Sergei Taneev concertized repeatedly with the Czech Quartet in Russia and abroad, playing in Prague, Vienna, Berlin, and other cities. Particularly satisfying were the great appearances in Prague which were exceptionally successful. For several decades, the Czech Quartet was the chief pioneer on behalf of Taneev's chamber music, both in Russia and abroad.

Appearing with the Czech Quartet was also occasionally a student of Taneev, Sergei Rachmaninov, as well as Rachmaninov's piano teacher (and, incidentally, cousin) Alexander Siloti.

In our days, another student of Taneev, Reinhold Glière (a revered Soviet master) remembered with gratitude "that outstanding ensemble which pioneered the classical works of Russian composers," and reminisced about the artistic pleasures provided by the Moscow concerts of the Czech Quartet. "We students of the Moscow Conservatory (he added) particularly cherished the performances of the piano-chamber music of Sergei Ivanovich Taneev played with participation of the composer as pianist."

In the diary of Sophia Andreevna Tolstoy, wife of Lev Tolstoy [and Taneev's confidante], we find the following entry about the Second Quartet by Taneev as played by the Czech artists:

> The Quartet concert was particularly fine. The Beethoven quartet was played superbly; the quartet of S. Taneev was a real triumph of music. . . . The composer was called out twice, the applause was meant for him and for the Czechs who played the quartet to perfection.[9]

Lev Tolstoy himself was enchanted with the playing of the Czech Quartet; in fact, the Czech musicians became acquainted with Taneev at the Tolstoy home.

One of the Quartet members left the following description of a meeting with the great writer which took place late in 1896:

> Professor Jan Hřimalý[10] drew Tolstoy's attention to the Czech Quartet playing in Moscow in December of last year.... Tolstoy listened very attentively to the performance of Beethoven's C♯ minor Quartet [Opus 131], sitting not in the hall but in the artist's Green Room. At the end of the concert he warmly praised the performance.... The next day we were invited to the Tolstoy home where we were received with great warmth by the family of the writer. We played quartets by Schubert, Beethoven, and Haydn. During the supper we met the composer Taneev.... Tolstoy expressed the following thoughts on music, "I passionately love music. People judge me wrongly, I guess, because I wrote the *Kreutzer Sonata*, saying that I do not like it. In the classical era music reached its highest development and I am the greatest admirer of this music. Beethoven, the Old Haydn, the poetic Schubert and Mozart are my favorite composers...." As farewell Tolstoy gave us a photo of his—an amateur picture—with his signature.[11]

A few years ago I saw this photograph with a warm dedication on the wall of the studio of the first violinist Karel Hoffmann in Prague where the Quartet used to rehearse. (The studio, containing memorabilia of the Quartet, was kindly shown to me by Hoffmann's daughter, Dagmar Shetlikova.)

One of Tolstoy's friends, the publicist V. F. Lazursky, wrote in his memoirs, "When the Czech Quartet (whose concert Lev Tolstoy attended) offered to play in the Tolstoy home, it was accepted with joy and by the whole family. The Czechs played Beethoven, Schubert, and Haydn. Lev Nikolaevich (Tolstoy) was enchanted: 'So clear, so transparent,' he said."[12]

The attendance of Tolstoy at the concert of the Czech musicians was the only time that the author was present at a public concert (though he did not sit in the hall). We know this from the pianist Professor Alexander Goldenweiser, who was close to Tolstoy and who also testified to Tolstoy's enjoyment of the Quartet performances.

As for his personal reminiscences about the concerts of the Czech Quartet, Professor Goldenweiser told the following to the author of this essay (1955):

> From the very first visit, the "Czechs" had an outstanding success and became the darlings of the Moscow public. The interpretations of the Czech Quartet were distinguished by vivid artistic temperament, genuine enthusiasm, lively and elastic rhythm, faultless ensemble, and beautiful sound. The Czechs became perennial guests of the Moscow concert stage.... Each of their visits was for Moscow's quartet public, very numerous at the time, a true music festival. Despite the fact that half a century has passed since then, I still cannot forget the marvelous performances of this outstanding ensemble.

The Czech Quartet performed repeatedly for the Belaïeff circle, at the famous quartet "Fridays" of Mitrofan Belaïeff,[13] where the Czech musicians could meet Nikolai Rimsky-Korsakov, Alexander Glazunov, Anatoly Liadov, and other composers. The quartet maintained friendly relations with Belaïeff

as can be seen through Oscar Nedbal's letters to him, preserved in the Glinka Museum in Moscow.

One of the letters (17 June 1899), written on behalf of the Quartet, says: "We are in such sympathy with your noble enterprise that we are always ready to play at your soirées."

The quartet works of Glazunov, side by side with those of Tchaikovsky, Borodin, and Taneev, occupied an important place in their repertoire which they also popularized abroad. When, in 1899, the Czech Quartet was heard at a Belaïeff soirée, the program consisted of Glazunov's Quartet No. 2, Taneev's Quartet No. 2, and Borodin's First. One could read in the *Russkaia muzykal'naia gazeta* about the "staggering force of the incomparable artistic ensemble," which brought out "with brilliance all the beauties and all the positive qualities" of the compositions named. "The interpretation [according to the reviewer] was no longer the transmission in the usual sense of the work, but the realization of that ideal shape about which, perhaps, the brain of the composer dreamed at the moment of creation...."[14]

The same year, 1899, (19 September), the well-known Czech musician Boleslav Kalensky wrote to Glazunov from Prague, "We heard your Second Quartet played in an uncomparable performance of our Czech Quartet."[15]

Side by side with the works of Beethoven and of Czech composers, notably Smetana and Dvořák, it was the classical Russian quartet repertoire that played an important part in shaping the interpretive style of the Czech Quartet, influencing its realistic artistic approach. Russian critics often praised the art of the Czech Quartet in interpreting works from this repertoire. Not only A.V. Ussovsky (mentioned earlier), but also César Cui and many other musicians spoke about the ideal performances of Tchaikovsky's Quartets by the Czechs:

> The rendition of the Czech Quartet represents pure perfection [wrote Cui], all four artists play like one person, no one pushes forward or dominates the others...the resulting ensemble is ideal and the impression is enchanting.... Here we have four lives, dedicated to one aim: to perform music as perfectly as possible. The Quartet is not only a triumph of discipline but at the same time a triumph of specialization.[16]

Equally high was the recognition accorded to the Czech Quartet for their interpretations of the Czech quartet repertoire (some of which was heard for the first time in Russia), as well as Beethoven. In 1910, the Czech Quartet presented complete Beethoven cycles in Moscow and St. Petersburg. Remarking on the finish and subtlety of their performance, a Moscow critic wrote:

> In the rendition of the famous [Beethoven] quartets one is amazed, aside from the marvelous ensemble which is the result of years of collaboration, by the stylish interpretation combined with the freedom of approach.[17]

The concerts of the Czech Quartet in Russia ceased because of the tense international situation which soon led to World War I. But through the year 1912 the Czech musicians visited Russia where they always found a warm, friendly welcome.

In a letter dated 18 March 1910 and addressed to the Russian Musical Society (RMO), the Quartet's leader, Karel Hoffmann, expressed the thanks of the ensemble for the Society's assistance in arranging concerts in Odessa, Kharkov, Voronezh, and other cities, and spoke with special warmth about the Moscow visit. He wrote, "The stay in Moscow was particularly agreeable, and we remember with pleasure the big success and the good people."[18]

Up to the last appearances of the Czech Quartet in Russia, the Russian critics noted the preservation of a freshness and an animated emotionalism characteristic of the Czech's approach to music. In 1912, a Moscow critic called the Quartet's concert series "a true festival for all lovers of real chamber music." At that time, the concert announcements of the RMO bore the designation "The Old Czech Quartet" to distinguish it from newer quartet ensembles of Czech musicians. A Moscow critic objected to this epithet. Noting the unchanged ability of the Quartet to penetrate into the artistic thoughts of the composer, he wrote, "One can only wish that every chamber ensemble, even the youngest, be as young in spirit as this 'old' Czech Quartet which shows not the slightest sign of elderly decrepitude."[19]

At the time of the Moscow visit in 1912, the Russian artist M.F. Shemyakin (1875-1944) made a drawing of the Czech Quartet while rehearsing at the apartment of Professor Jan Hřimalý.[20]

In concluding this essay on the Russian ties of the Czech Quartet, one fact deserves to be remembered. When the revolutionary situation created in Czechia and Slovakia under the impact of the Socialist Revolution of October 1917 led to the proclamation of national independence for Czechoslovakia in 1918, a festive concert was arranged in Prague dedicated to this historic event. At this concert, the Czech Quartet performed the Second Quartet by Alexander Borodin.

The historic significance of the Czech ensemble can be measured by its artistic achievements, the creation of its own performance style, distinguished by depth and truthfulness, sincerity and inspiration, and a spirit of enlightenment displayed in creative advocacy of the classical quartet repertoire. At the same time one must underline the valuable contribution of the Czech Quartet toward the development of traditional and fruitful Russo-Czech musical ties.[21]

Notes

Because of Professor Ginzburg's death, it has been impossible to verify with him questions that have arisen with respect to bibliographic information in the citations accompanying his essay. The information given here is reproduced exactly as it appears in the typescript submitted by Professor Ginzburg.

1. A. Ulybshev, *Novaia biografiia Mozarta* [A new Mozart biography], trans. M. Tchaikovsky (Moscow, 1890), p. 145.

2. *Narodni listy,* 26 October 1892.

3. Miroslav Šulc, *Oscar Nedbal* (Prague, 1959), p. 48.

4. *Moskovskie vedomosti,* 12 February 1895.

5. The tone quality of O. Nedbal is also stressed in the review published in *Novoe vremia,* n. 6806 (1895).

6. *Russkaia muzykal'naia gazeta* (1895), pp. 203-4.

7. Wihan once studied with the famous Russian cellist K. Davydov and called himself his successor (see L. Ginzburg, *Ganush Vigan i cheshskii kvartet* [Hanuš Wihan and the Czech Quartet], Moscow, 1955).

8. Bohuš Heran, *Hanuš Wihan* (Prague, 1947), p. 24.

9. *Dnevnik S.A. Tolstoi* [S.A. Tolstoy's diary], Part 2 (Moscow, 1929), p. 183.

10. Jan Hřimalý (1844-1915), noted violinist, studied at the Prague Conservatory. From 1869 he lived in Moscow where he was for over forty years professor at the Conservatory. He succeeded Laub in heading the Moscow Quartet.

11. *Utro,* n. 22 (1897), reprinted from a contemporary Vienna newspaper.

12. V. Lazursky, *Vospominaniia o Tolstom* [Reminiscences of Tolstoy] (Moscow, 1911), pp. 65-66.

13. M.P. Belaïeff [Beliaev] (1836-1904), an important musical figure and publisher, pioneer of Russian music, in whose St. Petersburg home took place musical soirées and where noted Russian composers assembled.

14. *Russkaia muzykal'naia gazeta* (1899), p. 250.

15. Original in the Saltykov-Shchedrin Library, Manuscript Division, Leningrad.

16. *Novosti i Birzhevaia gazeta,* n. 280 (1897).

17. *Muzykal'nyi truzhenik,* n. 6 (1910), p. 18.

18. Original in the Glinka Museum, Moscow.

19. *Studia,* no. 16 (1912), p. 12.

20. Original in the Tchaikovsky Museum, Klin.

21. We may mention that the former member of the Czech Quartet, Oscar Nedbal, was one of the first Czechoslovakian musicians to have concertized in the Soviet Union; in 1924 he appeared as conductor of nine symphony concerts in Baku.

Half Time for Nikolai Roslavets (1881-1944): A Non-Love Story with a Post-Romantic Composer

Detlef Gojowy (F.R.G.)

It was in the years 1961-65, after having started my research in Soviet music with a study of the young Shostakovich, that I wrote a dissertation about contemporary music in the early years of the Soviet Union, 1917 to 1930.[1] Locating the scores and other materials from this period turned out to be relatively easy, because the entire output of the Soviet State Music Publishers (Muzgiz) in the area of contemporary music was issued jointly, beginning in 1927, with Universal Editions in Vienna. This largely accounts for the fact that scores by the modern Soviet composers found their way into Western libraries, and in particular into the former Preussische Staatsbibliothek in Berlin (after the Second World War, divided into the Deutsche Staatsbibliothek in East Berlin and the Staatsbibliothek Preussischer Kulturbesitz/Marburg, now West Berlin). Among the composers represented in this joint publication project were Anatoly and Boris Alexandrov, Boris Asafiev, Nikolai Chemberdzhi (or Tchemberdzhi), Vladimir Deshevov, Alexander Dzegelyonok, Anatoly Drozdov, Sergei Yevseyev (or Evseev), Samuel Feinberg, Mikhail Gnessin, Dmitri Kabalevsky, Yuri Karnovich, Klimenty Korchmaryóv, Alexander Krein, Boris Liatoshinsky, Genrikh Litinsky, Arthur Lourié, Yuli Meitus, Dmitri Melkikh, Nikolai Miaskovsky, Alexander Mosolov, Leonid Polovinkin, Gavriil Popov, Sergei Protopopov, Joseph Schillinger, Vissarion Shebalin, Vasily Shirinsky, Sergei Vasilenko, Alexander Veprik, Boleslav Yavorsky, and Alexander Zhitomirsky.

Of particular interest were the scores of Nikolai Roslavets, a Ukrainian composer born in 1881 who started as a music autodidact, studied with Vasilenko, Ilyinsky, and Hřimalý at the Moscow Conservatory, and eventually became one of the leading figures of Soviet modern music in the 1920s. The strength and logic of style in such works as *Trois compositions* (1914) and *Deux compositions* (1915) revealed Roslavets as one of the outstanding and

most interesting Russian composers of the period. In an autobiographical article published in *Sovremennaia muzyka* (March 1924), the journal of the Association for Contemporary Music [Assosiatsiia sovremennoi muzyki—the ASM], Roslavets spoke about his "new, efficacious system for organizing sounds,"[2] which appeared to be similar to Scriabin's reliance on a central chordal complex; but Roslavets declared his method to be independent of either Scriabin or Schönberg. It was based on chords of six to eight or more tones, used by Roslavets as substitutes for the functional relationships of classical tonality, which he did not reject but rather tried to expand. These "synthetic chords" of specific and invariable intervallic structure could be transposed not only to the seven pitches of the classical diatonic scale, but also to all twelve degrees of the chromatic scale. Through systematic application of such transpositions, Roslavets's compositions revealed elements similar to dodecaphonic serial thinking as early as 1914-15 in the works mentioned above. For this reason, George Perle has classified Roslavets's system, together with that of Scriabin, as "nondodecaphonic serial composition."[3] I cannot entirely agree with this designation, since it seems to imply that the Russian system amounted merely to a kind of pre-figuring of the fully developed twelve-tone system. In reality, the Russian system, which had already been identified as such in Scriabin's work by the Polish musicologist Zofia Lissa in the 1930s,[4] stands as an independent method with its own principles. A series or row, whether dodecaphonic or not, is defined by the invariable order of its members. But in the tone complex, as used by Scriabin and Roslavets, the order of its elements remains free; the complex is defined only by its intervallic structure. Composition based on the manipulation of tone complexes may at times approach the technique of twelve-tone writing, as happens occasionally in Roslavets as a consequence of his particular choices of scale degree for transposition of a tone complex. This, however, occurs fortuitously, not out of necessity. The method may also generate other structures unrelated to twelve-tone procedures.

The immediate publication of my completed dissertation was out of the question in 1965, so I decided to seek publication of the results in the periodical literature; and since the clarification of Roslavets's compositional system seemed to me the most important result, I wrote an article on it which was accepted by the editor of *Die Musikforschung* in 1966. The next year I was granted a fellowship from the Deutscher Akademischer Austauschdienst to continue my research in Moscow and Leningrad, where it was possible with the cooperation of Soviet colleagues to fill out Roslavets's work list with many titles found in the Lenin Library and in the conservatory libraries in both Moscow and Leningrad. Meanwhile, the article accepted for publication in *Die Musikforschung* still had not appeared. I was told that the editors feared creating problems for their East German colleagues if they published an article about such an unacceptable Soviet composer. It should be remembered that

during this particular period, the Gesellschaft für Musikforschung existed in *both* Germanies, and the West German members of the editorial board felt obliged to behave diplomatically.

The "limpid stream" of Soviet experimental music flowing into German libraries had dried up in the early 1930s, not only because of Hitler's cultural policy, which halted cataloguing of Soviet music, but also because the stream had started to dry up at its source; the flood of scores co-produced with Universal Editions was also being stemmed at home. Roslavets had been affected along with the other "modernist" composers of the 1920s; only one short song by him, entitled *Tabachok* (1942), was published after 1930. All of his other works have remained unpublished to the present (this statement is written in June 1984). As early as the 1920s Roslavets had been under heavy attack by the Association of Proletarian Musicians,[5] but after 1930, his name either vanished completely from Soviet *lexica* and literature about music or was mentioned only in critical terms. The very idea of avant-garde music, which was still being praised for its Marxist aspects in Soviet periodicals of the 1920s, now fell from favor and became suspect in Soviet society. All attempts by Western musicologists to investigate experimental music in Soviet Russia became subject to the charge of being "one-sided" and anti-Soviet.

Following the invasion of Czechoslovakia in 1968, the East German sector of the Gesellschaft für Musikforschung was obliged to leave the society and to form its own association, the Verband deutscher Komponisten und Musikwissenschaftler. This event gave the editors of *Die Musikforschung* the freedom to publish my article "Nikolaj Andreevič Roslavec, ein früher Zwölftonkomponist."[6] The compositional system of this early dodecaphonist aroused so much interest that other periodicals printed articles about him, among them the Czechoslovakian *Hudební Rozhledý*, no. 20 (1969) and the West German *Musik und Bildung*, no. 12 (1969).

In the autumn of 1970, while I was working for the German Music Council, I accompanied an official delegation of the Soviet Composers' Union from Hamburg to Bremen. The delegation, headed by the Union's chief administrative officer Tikhon Khrennikov (the First Secretary) also included the composers Rodion Shchedrin, Arno Babajanian (or Babadzhanian), and Karen Khachaturian. Relations were cordial, and on parting, I gave each member of the group an offprint of my article on Roslavets. I learned later, however, that Khrennikov had gathered up the copies and never returned them to the other composers.

An official attack against unwelcome investigations, my own included, was subsequently published in *Sovetskaia muzyka* (no. 11, 1970), the organ of the Soviet Composers' Union, under the heading "They run to the rescue and, in the process, become thieves."[7] Signed by the anonymous "Journalist," who often carps at unwanted Western preoccupation with Soviet music, the article launched an assault against bourgeois "Kremlinologists," such as Fred K.

Prieberg, Harold Schonberg, Ronald Hinley, Irvin Hoy, Abraham Bramberg, and myself. The "Journalist" evidently regarded the program in the 1920s of modern-music publication by the Soviet State Music Publishers, perhaps indeed forgotten in the USSR, as a figment of my imagination:

> Who are these musicians who outstripped the acknowledged "maîtres" of the New Viennese school by years and decades and anticipated other systems of even the present-day avant-gardists? Gojowy names them: Arthur Lourié, Yefim Golyshev, Nikolai Roslavets, Sergei Protopopov, Joseph Schillinger, Arseny Avraamov—he names them, or rather he lumps them together without any concern for the question of "who is who" among those he has "discovered," composer or theorist, undistinguished emigré hack or committed, though misguided, Soviet musician. For Gojowy, sensation alone is important: Russia—the homeland . . . of avant-gardism.

"Avant-gardism," as defined by Grigory Shneerson in the new Soviet *Musical Encyclopedia,*[8] is not a positive term in the current Soviet musical lexicon, but rather a perjorative, like "left-wing art" in the '20s, or "modernism" and "formalism" in the '30s and '40s.

The "Journalist" renewed his attack in *Sovetskaia muzyka,* no. 3 (1982), under the heading "On the Path of Political Business."[9] Citing the earlier article in the same journal, the "Journalist" again takes aim at all work on Soviet and East European topics by Western musicologists. His targets this time include the Yugoslav musicologists Jelena Djurić-Milojković and Nadezhda Mosusova and the Estonian musicologist Harry Olt, whose book on Estonian music was published as a Swedish-Estonian copublication in Tallinn. The "Journalist" judges all investigations of early Russian dodecaphonic music to be "non-serious," because

> the criteria used for the selection and evaluation of the works examined always turn out to be the very same things, "novelty" and "progress." For lo these many years, "novelty" and "progress" have been pointlessly and exclusively associated with the New Viennese School and the West European avant-garde, the "homeland" of which is now declared to be Russia. The whole affair is so utterly futile and unscientific, as even many Western scholars acknowledge today. Such a perverted "historical conception" naturally leads to blatant ideological trickery.

Attitudes such as these may well explain why Roslavets's work has remained forgotten and defamed in his own country for nearly half a century. Until recently, all attempts by Western publishers and concert promoters to obtain, for example, the score of his Violin Concerto (1925) have failed. Roslavets's legacy, his unpublished manuscripts in Moscow's Central State Archive for Literature and Art (TsGALI), remain unpublished and, so far, inaccessible to international musicological research.

Nonetheless, Soviet musicologists are evidently beginning to rediscover the music of Roslavets and his period. Perhaps the first neutral mention of him

is found in the two-volume collection of material devoted to Nikolai Miaskovsky (*Autobiography. Articles, Notes, and Reviews*, v. 2 [Moscow, 1960]), where Miaskovsky's journal reviews of Roslavets's early works are reprinted (pp. 179-81, 208), together with some information about the composer (pp. 501-2).[10] The date of his death, then unknown, is given as "194?"[11] (Grigory Mikhailovich Shneerson informed me in a letter dated 31 July 1964 that Roslavets died on 23 August 1944 in Moscow.)

The "Journalist's" attacks made it a matter of speculation whether Roslavets would be included in the new Soviet *Musical Encyclopedia*, but M.M. Yakovlev did indeed contribute an article devoted to Roslavets. In it he states that Roslavets

> created the first atonal compositions in Russia: a sonata for violin and piano (1913), cycles of art songs on texts by Russian poets (1913-14), and a *Poem* for violin and piano (1913). In the years 1913-15 he formulated his "new system of organizing sounds" similar to the principles of Schönberg, based on a theory of tone complexes ("synthetic chords"). Using this system, Roslavets composed a series of important orchestral and chamber works between the years 1919 and 1924. In the works from the late 1920s, one can find an attempt to simplify his expressive means.... From 1931 to 1933 he lived in Tashkent, and at the end of the '30s he returned to Moscow where he taught at the Musical Polytechnical School and for the Military Band Directors' Course...."[12]

Here for the first time we learn something of his life after 1930, a period previously obscured by misinformation. Roslavets, the leading figure of contemporary Soviet music in the 1920s, editor of the Marxist and progressive journal *Musical Culture* in 1924, and board member of the Association for Contemporary Music (the Soviet section of the ISCM), had become a "non-person" under the cultural policy of the era of Stalin and Zhdanov. Lacking information, rumors develop. He was said to have been exiled to Siberia and to have died there; this version, in fact, is offered (as an "unconfirmed report") in *Die Musik in Geschichte und Gegenwart*. The truth appears to be that he was pressured, like many fellow composers in the 1920s, to leave the main centers of Moscow and Leningrad for the provinces, where he collected folk music and helped to develop local music institutions. We learn more details about his fate after 1930 in the book, *In the World of Music* [V mire muzyki] (Moscow, 1981; p. 5.):

> Roslavets went to Uzbekistan in 1931, where he became one of the first Russian musicians to contribute to the development of musical culture in Middle Asia. He was director of the Radio Center of the Uzbek Soviet Republic and conductor of the Uzbek Music Theater. He composed music based on [Uzbek] national melodies and rhythms. His ballet *Pakhta* ["Cotton peasant"], dedicated to the struggle for independence of the cotton industry in the USSR and his symphony, "Soviet Uzbekistan," composed for the 15th anniversary of the October Revolution, were performed with great success under his baton. He was awarded an honorary diploma by the government of the Uzbek Republic.

In November 1933, he returned to Moscow as a producer for the All-Union Radio Committee (1933-35) and as director of the All-Russian Concert Association (until 1939); from 1936, he served as head of the section of scientific collaborators in the trade union RABIS. He taught composition in the Musical Polytechnical School, lectured to military band directors, and continued to compose. During these years he wrote important theoretical works, such as "Counterpoint" and "Fugue," which remain unpublished. Although he was seriously ill during the Second World War, he became intensely involved in the general struggle and composed patriotic songs dedicated to the defenders of his country....

It would seem that Roslavets's name and work deserve to be remembered by future generations; moreover, the question of his music must be considered. Do his best works merit a new critical evaluation, or do they, perhaps, deserve even more: a revival in the concert repertory? The answer to this question lies in the future....

Recently some of Roslavets's works have been performed in "closed" concerts, together with works by other twentieth-century composers. On 15 March 1980, his *Nocturne* for oboe, harp, two violas, and violoncello (1913) was performed in Moscow at the Composers' Union by the ensemble, Soloists of the Bolshoi Theater, on a program that also included the *Zodiac* cycle by Karlheinz Stockhausen, Stravinsky's Septet, Hindemith's Chamber Music No. 6, and Seven Pieces by Charles Ives; Alexander Ivashkin provided the introductory commentary for the works. Another concert, this one devoted to the compositions of Roslavets and Leonid Polovinkin, took place in the same hall on 27 December 1980; it featured prize-winners of international competitions in performances of Roslavets's *Three Compositions* for piano, *Meditation* for violoncello and piano, some of the art songs, *Three Dances* for violin and piano, and, again, the *Nocturne*. This program was introduced with a lecture by the young musicologist Marina Lobanova.

The most extensive Soviet research on Roslavets to date is found in a graduation thesis written in 1981 by A. Puchina, a student at the Moscow Conservatory working under the supervision of composer and theorist Edison Denisov: "The Concerto for Violin and Orchestra by Nikolai Roslavets and Its Place in the Composer's Compositional Legacy."[13] Puchina quotes extensively from Western writings about Roslavets; but unlike her Western colleagues, she also had access to the manuscripts in the Roslavets Fond (No. 2659) at the Central State Archives of Literature and Art (TsGALI; this fund contains the composer's music manuscripts, along with other papers, including his theoretical sketches for the "synthetic-chord" system). In addition to her investigation of the Violin Concerto, Puchina also surveys Roslavets's articles on music, his musical philosophy and materialist aesthetics, and his critical ideas about contemporary Soviet music criticism. Her study can be regarded as the first important step in the Soviet rehabilitation of this great Russian and Soviet musician.

A further step in the same direction has been the first reprint of some of his early piano compositions, along with pieces from the 1920s by Deshevov,

Polovinkin, and Mosolov, in *Works of Soviet Composers.*[14] Edited by V.
Alekseeva and with a preface by N. Kopchevsky (known in the Soviet Union as
the editor of J.S. Bach's *Art of the Fugue*), the booklet contains three of
Roslavets's *Five Preludes* (1919-22) and his *Poem No. 2* (1915), all for piano.

Yuri Kholopov, author of books on twentieth-century harmony as found
in the works of such composers as Prokofiev, Hindemith, and Messiaen, has
contributed an important appreciation of Roslavets's atonal system in his
article, "The Problem of New Tonality in Russian and Soviet Theoretical
Musicology."[15] He provides an analysis of the song "Thou Didst Not Leave"
[Ty ne ushla] (1913) from the set *Three Compositions* on texts by Alexander
Blok, discovering in this song "preformations of the series."

Thanks to research by Soviet musicologists, we now know the titles of the
unpublished works by Roslavets in TsGALI, Fond No. 2659. The following list
of these manuscripts completes the list of published works in *Die
Musikforschung,* v. 22 (1969), pp. 36-38.

Table 1.   Central State Archive for Literature and Art (TsGALI), Fond
No. 2659

No. Title	Year of Composition	No. of Sheets
Orchestral Works		
1. *Rêverie* for Violin and Orchestra. Score.	1907	23
2. Symphony in C Minor. Score.	1910	74
3. *V chasy novoluniia* [In the Hours of the New Moon]. Symphonic Poem for Large Orchestra. Score.	1910s	75
4. The same. Orchestra parts.		87
5. Symphony in four movements. Without beginning and ending. Score.	1922	88
6. Symphony No. 2 for Orchestra and Chorus. Unfinished. Score and sketches.	1923	39
7. Concerto No. 1 for Violin and Orchestra. Sketches for the violin-piano score.	1928	8
8. Chamber Symphony. Unfinished. Piano score with notes for the orchestration.	1926	25
9. Concerto for Violin and Orchestra, in four movements. Without beginning. Piano score.	1927	53
10. *Komsomol'skaia.* Symphonic Poem for Orchestra, Chorus, and Piano solo. Sketches for the score.	1928	16
11. Orchestral work, without title. *Lento.* Unfinished. Score.	1920-30?	54
12. Orchestral work, without title. Unfinished. Score.	1920-30?	36

Table 1 (continued)

13.	*Geroia* [Song of the Hero]. Song arranged for orchestra.	1932-33	5
14.	Concerto for Violin and Orchestra, in three movements. Score	1936	52
15.	*Uzbekistan*. Symphonic Poem. Piano score with notes for the orchestration.	1930s	1
16.	Orchestral work. Unfinished. Score.	1930s	30

Chamber Works

17.	*Menuet* for String Quartet.	1907	2
18.	*Romance, Rêverie, Morgenstimmung,* Sonata (beginning), *Gavotte, Elégie, Sérénade*, etc. Pieces for violin and piano.	1908	34
19.	*Serenada* for Two Violins.	1909	2
20.	*3 Poèmes* and *Romance-arabesque* for Violin and Piano.	1909-10	19
21.	*Tantsy belykh dev*/*Danses des vièrges blanches* for Violin and Piano.	1912	21
22.	Quartet/Quatuor No. 1. First violin part.	1913	9 pages
23.	Quartet, second and third movements. Score and piano score.	1916	37
24.	Sonata No. 2 for Violin and Piano.	1917	33
25.	Quartet No. 2. Incomplete. Score.	1919	60
26.	*Liricheskaia poema*/*Poème lyrique* for Violin and Piano.	1910s	11
27.	Trio No. 2	1920	31
28.	Sonata No. 2 for Violoncello and Piano.	1922	20
29.	Piano Quintet for Two Violins, Viola, Violoncello, and Piano. Score.	1924	10
30.	Sonata No. 1 for Viola and Piano. Incomplete.	1928	9
31.	Sonata for Viola and Piano.	1926	21
32.	Trio. Violin and violoncello parts.	1927	24
33.	Quartet. Fragments of the score.	1929-31	17
34.	*7 Pièces* for Violin and Piano: *Etude mortele*, Etude in E-flat Major, Canon, *Fuga, Adagio, Preliudiia, Romanticheskaia poema* [Romantic poem]	1920s	7+29
35.	Quartet for Four Domras, on themes of Chechen folk songs. Score.	1934-35	8
36.	*Invention* and *Nocturne* for Violin and Piano.	1935	2+8
37.	Quartet No. 4. Unfinished. Score.	1939	37
38.	*Potpourri-Fantasie*, on themes of Soviet popular songs, for Xylophone and Piano.	1939	8
39.	Sonata No. 2 for Viola and Piano.	1930s	28
40.	*Legenda* for Violin and Piano.	1940	29

In addition to these manuscripts in TsGALI, the Glinka Museum of Musical Culture (GMMK) in Moscow possesses the following works by Roslavets in its Fond No. 373:

Table 2. Glinka Museum of Musical Culture (GMMK)

Title	Year of Composition
String Quartet	1910
Sonata for Violoncello and Piano.	1921
Dance for Violin and Piano.	1935
Kolybelnaia [Lullaby] for Violin and Piano.	1935
Scherzo for Violin and Piano.	1935
Valse for Violin and Piano.	1935
Quartet No. 5 in E-flat Major.	1941
24 Preludes for Violin and Piano.	1941-42
Legenda for Violin and Piano in D Minor.	n.d.
Rondo and *Polonaise* for Violin and Piano.	n.d.

The title of my essay suggests that, in my opinion, we have at long last reached "half time" with respect to serious musicological investigation of the musical legacy of Nikolai Roslavets. The gradual rehabilitation of his name and his work in the Soviet Union seems to open now the possibility that access to his manuscripts and papers will finally be granted to both Soviet and Western musicologists. In this eventuality, we can also hope that the extensive research remaining to be done will no longer be limited by political arbitrariness and that, perhaps, Roslavets can belatedly assume his rightful place in the international history of musical experimentation in the early twentieth century.

Notes

1. "Moderne Musik in der Sowjetunion bis 1930," Phil. Diss. Göttingen 1966; now published as *Neue Sowjetische Musik der 20-er Jahre* (Laaber, 1980).

2. "Nik. A. Roslavets o sebe i o svoem tvorchestve" [...about himself and his work], *Sovremennaia muzyka*, no. 5 (1924), pp. 132-38.

3. George Perle, *Serial Composition and Atonality: An Introduction to the Music of Schoenberg, Berg, and Webern* (Berkley and Los Angeles, 1962), p. 41.

4. "Geschichtliche Vorformer der Zwölftontechnik," *Acta Musicologica*, v. 7 (1935), pp. 15-21, quoting "Harmonyka A. Skriabina," *Kwartalnik Muzyczny*, no. 8, pp. 320-53.

5.   Lev Kaltat, "O podlinno-burzhuaznoi ideologii gr. Roslavtsa" [About citizen Roslavets's genuine bourgeois ideology], *Muzykal'noe obrazovanie*, no. 3-4 (1927), pp. 32-43; Victor Belyi, " 'Levaia' fraza o 'muzykal'noi reaktsii' " ["Left-wing" phrases about "musical reaction"], *Muzykal'noe obrazovanie*, no. 1 (1928), pp. 43-47; Viktor Belyi, "Printsipial'nye voprosy razvitiia natsional'nykh muzykal'nykh kul'tur" [Fundamental questions about the development of national music cultures], *Proletarskii muzykant*, no. 6 (1931), pp. 1-12.

6.   *Die Musikforschung*, v. 22 no. 1 (1969), pp. 22-38.

7.   "Begut spasat', a spasaia—voruiut" [They run to the rescue and, in the process, become thieves], *Sovetskaia muzyka*, no. 11 (1970), pp. 141-44.

8.   "Avangardizm," *Muzykal'naia entsiklopediia*, v. 1 (Moscow, 1973), columns 26-27.

9.   "Po puti politicheskogo biznes" [On the path of political business], *Sovetskaia muzyka*, no. 3 (1982), pp. 102-4.

10.   S. Shlifshtein, comp., ed., & commentary, *N. Ya. Miaskovsky: Stat'i, pis'ma, vospominaniia* [Articles, letters, and reminiscences], v. 2: *Avtobiografiia. Stat'i, zametki, otzyvy* [Autobiography. Articles, letters, and reminiscences] (Moscow, 1960), pp. 179-81, 208.

11.   Ibid., pp. 501-2.

12.   "Roslavets," *Muzykal'naia entsiklopediia*, v. 4 (Moscow, 1978), columns 711-12.

13.   A. Puchina, "Kontsert dlia skripki s orkestrom N. Roslavtsa i ego mesto v tvorcheskom nasledii kompozitora" [The concerto for violin and orchestra by N. Roslavets and its place in the composer's compositional legacy], a graduation thesis submitted at the Moscow State Conservatory, 1981.

14.   *Proizvedeniia sovetskikh kompozitorov* [Works of Soviet composers] (Moscow, 1981).

15.   Yuri Kholopov, "Problema novoi tonal'nosti v russkom i sovetskom teoreticheskom muzykoznanii" [The problem of new tonality in Russian and Soviet theoretical musicology], *Voprosy metodologii sovetskogo muzykoznanii* [Questions of methodology in Soviet musicology] (Moscow, 1981), pp. 100-126.

13

On Translating a Russian Opera

Joseph Máchlis (U.S.A.)

My work as an opera translator began with the NBC Opera Company, which in the late fifties presented a series of coast-to-coast telecasts of both standard and new works. These were given on Sunday afternoon and aimed to acclimate opera, an essentially European form, to the needs of the American public. Samuel Chotzinoff was the animating spirit behind the project, along with the conductor Peter Herman Adler. Their aim was not so much to present opera on television as to create a new genre—television opera; in effect, to transform a succession of more or less static "numbers" into a fluid form that would take advantage of the possibilities offered by television. They learned much from the techniques of Broadway and Hollywood. Since our performers sang into microphones, they did not have to have the greatest voices in the world. They did have to know how to act and had to look the part. Our Mimi was blond and properly fragile, Rodolfo dark and handsome, Musetta vivacious, Marcello smolderingly jealous. Our director, Kirk Browning, showed endless ingenuity in keeping the camera moving while the action stopped because of an aria or duet. And the language, of course, had to be English.

All this set off a furious debate as to whether opera should be presented in the original tongue or in the language of the audience. The problem existed only in the English-speaking world. In Prague all operas were in Czech; at the Bolshoi and Kirov theatres, I heard *Carmen, Il Trovatore,* and *Lohengrin* in Russian. And several generations of Austro-Germans grew up singing *Wie eiskalt ist dein händechen* without realizing that the line was really *Che gelida la manina.* Behind the debate lay the deeper problem of attitude. For Europeans, opera was a dramatic form that was part of a living theater; hence the audience had to experience each line as it floated across the proscenium. In England and the United States, on the other hand, opera remained a musical rather than dramatic experience. As long as the listener had a vague idea what the plot was about, it didn't much matter what the characters said. No wonder Dr. Johnson called opera "an expensive and irrational form of entertainment" that inspired

Addison's famous dictum: "There is no Question but our great Grandchildren will be very curious to know the Reason why their Forefathers used to sit together like an audience of foreigners in their own Country and to hear whole Plays acted before them in a Tongue which they did not understand." Men of letters failed to understand that in opera the ultimate truth resides in the music rather than the words.

However, when the NBC Opera Theater decided to give the American première of Prokofiev's *War and Peace,* there was no question in anybody's mind as to which language should be used. It obviously made no sense for young American singers to learn the work in a language of which neither they nor their public had the remotest idea. As I neither spoke nor read Russian, I was given a literal translation so that I knew what each word of Prokofiev's text meant. (When I translated two other Russia operas for the New York City Opera, *Boris Godunov* and Prokofiev's *The Flaming Angel,* I had the French and German translations to fall back on.) Actually, in all the singing versions I prepared for NBC, the translating was the least important part of the job. My task was to find words that would sing easily and convey the thought behind the music. The time had come to get away from the stilted, pseudo-poetic verbiage that had given rise to a special language best characterized as "librettese." We had to end forever the "pleasure-measure treasure-leisure" syndrome. The English had to be modern and simple, to avoid on the one hand the pretentiously archaic, on the other the carelessly vernacular. High notes needed open vowels like *ah* rather than constricting ones like *ee* (although Puccini himself, interestingly, did not always observe this rule, possibly because Italian is so singable a language). The prosody had to be faultless, with the accented syllable of the words falling easily and naturally on the principal beat of the measure. I soon realized that not all the words had to be heard: prepositions and conjunctions could fall by the wayside as long as the nouns and verbs came through. The best result was attained when the key word floated in on the crest of the melodic curve. Hence the translation had to be done not only metrically, according to the pulse within the measure, but more broadly according to the shape of the musical phrase. At the NBC Opera Theater, I worked closely with the singers at rehearsal, and many changes were made on the spot in response to an objection from them that a certain vowel did not lie well for their voice, or was too high, or too low. In short, the final version was arrived at—once the basic script was handed in—through a series of imperceptible changes made in response to concrete requests. In this sense, I regarded my texts as singing versions rather than translations, so it was that when the libretto of *War and Peace* was issued together with the recording, I included the following footnote: "While every effort was made to remain faithful to the spirit of the original, the immediate goal was to produce a singable version of the opera rather than a word-for-word translation."

By the time I tackled Prokofiev's opera I had undergone a fairly arduous apprenticeship by translating *La Bohème, La Traviata, Rigoletto, Fidelio,* and Poulenc's *Dialogues of the Carmelites.* I prepared myself for the new assignment by rereading the novel, in Edwin Muir's fine translation. Armed with the vocal score, I set to work.

Prokofiev had composed the music of his opera as the Nazi armies were speeding toward Smolensk—the same route that Napoleon's army had followed a century and a quarter earlier. "This opera," he stated, "was conceived before the war, but the war made it compelling for me to complete it. Tolstoy's great novel depicts Russia's war against Napoleon. Then, as now, it was not a war of two armies but of peoples."

The opera occupied him intermittently during the last twelve years of his life. That he faced formidable difficulties in writing it is attested to by the fact that he produced four variants of *War and Peace.* Malcolm Hamrick Brown has chronicled the opera's artistic and political vicissitudes in its evolution from Prokofiev's original conception (completed in piano score on 13 April 1942) to the "final variant, sanctioned by the composer not long before his death...."[1] This latter was the version I worked on for the NBC Opera Theater.

The opera includes in its frame both the lyricism of the "peace" scenes (Part I) and the epic-heroic tone of the "war" part (Part II). The music veers from romantic expressivity to great choral frescoes that have a remarkable brightness of color and outdoor feeling. The opening scene is set in the garden of Count Rostov's estate on a night in May when Prince Andrei Bolkonsky, who is visiting the estate on business, catches a glimpse of Natasha on the moonlight balcony. He is in mourning after the death in childbirth of his young wife. The mood of sorrowful resignation is set in his opening aria:

> Gentle night, so fragrant and tender,
> Yet a sadness fills my heart.
> I seek in vain for a glimpse of happiness.
> This morning, riding through the forest,
> Spring arrayed in all her beauty,
> I could see the tender blossoms
> Swaying in the fragrant air.
> Standing before me a giant oak tree
> With its body deformed by age,
> Its branches heavy with an ancient grief.
> Suddenly it came to me that
> Life was pain and sorrow...

Natasha, unable to sleep, appears on the balcony as we hear a melody in Prokofiev's most lyric vein—the "love theme" that is associated with her throughout the score. The scene is steeped in nature poetry and the music mirrors Andrei's delight as he gazes up at her.

Next is a scene of external brilliance: a ball at a nobleman's mansion. Against a choral background the main characters are introduced: the kind-hearted Pierre Bezukhov; his beautiful wife, the evil Countess Helene; Natasha's father, Count Rostov, and her cousin Sonya. Here Natasha utters the famous lines in which Tolstoy so aptly captured the feelings of a shy young girl at her first ball: "Can it really be that no one will ask me to dance? Will they pass me by and let me sit by the wall all alone?" Pierre asks Prince Andrei to dance with her. As he approaches Natasha, the music recalls the romantic ardor of the opening scene.

When the third scene opens Andrei has already proposed to Natasha and been accepted. Count Rostov and Natasha arrive to pay their respects to Andrei's father. Prokofiev vividly delineates the protagonists: the tyrannical old Prince, who had hoped for a more brilliant match for his son; Andrei's sister Marya, who is unmercifully bullied by her father; Count Rostov, no match for the Prince in either social position, wealth, or strength of character, who takes the easy way out and disappears; and Natasha, who is left alone to face the ogre. Andrei is abroad, having promised his father to wait a year before he marries Natasha. Her soliloquy eloquently expresses her bewilderment, and foreshadows the anguish that awaits her:

> What right have they to examine me?
> To see if I am good enough to marry Prince Andrei?
> God, if only he were here!...
> Perhaps this very day he'll return.
> I will glance up in my room and suddenly see him—
> His eyes, his face, his handsome features wreathed in a smile.
> Ah, I would be utterly lost without his love!
> My heart is filled with fear and sadness,
> I am so afraid for him, for myself,... so afraid.

In Scene Four we meet the villain of the piece, the brother of Countess Helene, the unscrupulous Anatole Kuragin. Helene is giving a party. Anatole has become infatuated with Natasha; his worldly sister encourages the affair. Natasha, feeling deserted by Andrei, accepts the letter in which Anatole expresses his feelings. He is handsome and charming. Alas, she finds him irresistible.

In the first four scenes Prokofiev has been a painter of moods. Now action takes over. The music of Scene Five assumes a dark "masculine" color as Anatole, planning his elopement with Natasha, takes leave of his boon companion Dolokhov. In Scene Six the ill-starred elopement is foiled by Akhrosimova, in whose care Count Rostov had left Natasha during his absence from Moscow. She discovers that Anatole is married and that she has been compromised by a cad; her future with Andrei is irretrievably ruined. Distraught, she pours her heart out to Andrei's best friend, Pierre, and wishes

to die. Part I ends with the poor girl's despairing cry to Sonya, "Help me, I've taken poison."

In the second part, as Prokofiev pointed out, "The people themselves are the hero of the opera." Here the central figure is Field Marshal Kutuzov, who incarnates the spirit that defeated Napoleon. The music, martial in tone, features stirring choruses of the kind familiar to the world through the cantata *Alexander Nevsky*. Prokofiev takes full advantage of the rich bass sonorities for which Russian choruses are famous. Scene Seven, before the Battle of Borodino, opens with a rousing chorus of the peasant guerrillas. Andrei, in a moving aria, broods on Natasha's betrayal and has a premonition of death. The Field Marshal arrives and is greeted with rapturous enthusiasm by his soldiers. This is followed by Pierre's soliloquy, which reveals an idealistic dreamer who still cannot comprehend the nature of evil. He has always stood apart from life, the eternal observer. Now for the first time he is impelled to become a participant. In his admiration for the selfless soldiers about him we meet Tolstoy's idealized vision of the peasant:

> They are noble and unselfish;
> They go through life without complaining.
> I must learn to be like them
> And become a simple soldier.
> I must enter their brotherly life,
> A life filled with faith and simplicity,
> And partake of the spirit that makes them strong and courageous...

The scene ends with a mighty chorus that must have had a shattering impact upon Russian audiences in 1942:

> Our people brave and true—
> We wage the bitter fight for our beloved land,
> For freedom and honor! We will never yield!
> Kutuzov leads us in this holy war against the foe.
> For our dear homeland we will die!

Scene Eight, which takes place during the Battle of Borodino, views the action from the French side. Napoleon himself is the central figure. True, neither he nor his marshals lend themselves readily to operatic treatment, nor is the hectic activity of a battlefield conveyed easily in terms of music drama. One cannot but admire the adroitness with which Prokofiev carries off the scene. The same problem is encountered in Scene Nine, when Kutuzov and his generals hold a council of war to decide whether to defend Moscow against the French or to abandon it. This episode, however, serves to introduce one of the lyric high points of the score, the Field Marshall's eloquent apostrophe to Moscow. Here Prokofiev becomes the national artist addressing his beleaguered people and lifting their spirits with his promise of victory:

Fairest Moscow, your thousand towers shine
Bright and golden in the sun,
As you lie gleaming before us, lovely Moscow...
Glorious Mother Moscow enthroned in gold and white,
You shall never know defeat!
You may know suffering now,
But your sons will never be vanquished!
Our Russian land shall be strewn with the bodies of our enemies
When our mighty people rise to crush the foe!

Andrei is mortally wounded in the battle. His deathbed scene brings the emotional climax of the opera. The music suggests his delirium through the repetition of an ostinato figure on two meaningless syllables: "piti piti piti piti...." An invisible chorus underlines the irrational sounds he is hearing. Natasha comes to his sickbed, overwhelmed with remorse. This is the heart of the Tolstoyan novel, whether in *War and Peace, Anna Karenina,* or *Resurrection,* when one character who has wronged another begs forgiveness. In the duet of the lovers Prokofiev has met the challenge of one of the great scenes in European literature; the music matches Andrei's compassionate understanding. Characteristic is his last line: "To sleep.... Yet love will conquer death, for love is life."

The opera ends on the road to Smolensk with a hymm to victory and to the Field Marshal:

Hail to all who defended our land!
Hail to those who fought and bled!
In that fateful hour they were steadfast and brave...
Glory to our sacred motherland,
Hail Field Marshal Kutuzov and those who fought beside him!

In *War and Peace* one of the truly creative musicians of the twentieth century undertook to capture the grand gesture, the sweep and élan that are of the essence in a national opera. The work soon established itself as a staple of the repertory in the Soviet Union and aroused considerable interest abroad. The Metropolitan Opera wanted to produce it in the early 1950s, but Winston Churchill's speech about the iron curtain aborted that plan. Thus *War and Peace* became one of the first casualties of the cold war. The NBC production marked its introduction to the American public, and was followed two decades later by Sarah Caldwell's in Boston. The work scored a resounding success in New York when the Bolshoi Opera brought over its magnificent production.

At the moment we are witnessing an upsurge of interest in the music of Shostakovich and Prokofiev. Signs are not wanting that the time is ripe for this major work to take its rightful place in our lyric theater.

Notes

1.   From the editorial notes to S. Prokofiev, *Sobranie sochinenii* [Collected works], ed. N.P. Anosov, et al., vols. 6a, 6b, 6v: *Voina i mir* [War and peace], ed. D. Shostakovich (Moscow, 1958), p. 8; quoted in Malcolm Hamrick Brown, "Prokofiev's *War and Peace:* A Chronicle," *The Musical Quarterly,* v. 63, no. 3 (July 1977), p. 321. Professor Brown informs me that a Soviet study of the different versions of the opera came into his hands after his own article was already in press and that the Russian-language piece provides far more detail about the changes than he was able to present: A. Volkov, "Voina i mir" Prokofieva: Opyt analiza variantov opery [Prokofiev's "War and peace": An attempt at analyzing the opera's variants] (Moscow, 1976).

14

The Punch in Shostakovich's *Nose*

Laurel E. Fay (U.S.A.)

In studies of Dmitri Shostakovich's creative output, far more attention has been paid to the events surrounding the condemnation, in January 1936, of Shostakovich's second opera, *Lady Macbeth of the Mtsensk District* and the ominous ramifications for his career and for the future of Soviet music, than to his earlier effort in the genre, an adaptation of Nikolai Gogol's short story, "The Nose." A self-consciously experimental work, *The Nose* was a product of the exciting creative atmosphere of the Soviet artistic world in the 1920s. Musically, it was one of Shostakovich's most radical scores. As theater, it attempted to explore new directions in musical drama, absorbing the influences of the most innovative artists of the day in a distinctively original manner. The controversy which greeted the work's production in 1930 was predictable, given the extreme aesthetic positions reflected in Soviet criticism of the period; while the opera had its enthusiastic supporters, it was also attacked as a travesty on the operatic genre, the "hand bomb of an anarchist."[1] To a certain extent, this reaction was anticipated by Shostakovich and his supporters, and the path from composition to performance was carefully prepared. In 1930, opposing critical reactions—however virulent—could still be aired in public: they provide an illuminating reflection of the cultural and political milieu, as well as of Shostakovich's youthful creative boldness.

Shostakovich began work on *The Nose* in the summer of 1927 at the age of 20. He had already been acclaimed as a bright new talent in Soviet music after the premiere of his First Symphony in 1926. But the news of his work on an opera was greeted with great interest not only because of the composer's talent. The venerable Russian tradition of opera—that genre of paramount importance to the nation's composers from the time of Glinka—had yet to find a promising continuation in the Soviet period. While critics hotly debated the aesthetic and technical issues appropriate to the ideal Soviet opera, focusing on the topics and treatment suitable to the embodiment of the new socialist reality, the repertory of the opera theaters remained dominated by the "classics" of

nineteenth-century Russian and Western composers.[2] The situation was further complicated by a feeling of stagnation which had crept into the productions of the academic theaters even before the revolutions of 1917. The extent of this feeling can perhaps be judged by the tremendous success of the operatic parody, *Vampuka, The African Bride; A Model Opera in All Respects,* with music by the little-known composer Vladimir Georgievich Erenberg (1875-1923), which had been produced at the Crooked Mirror Theater in St. Petersburg in 1909.[3] Between 1909 and 1927 this spoof ran for over a thousand performances[4] in Moscow, Tiflis, and Riga, as well as in St. Petersburg/Petrograd/Leningrad. The comical term "vampuka," and its various derivatives, entered the critical vocabulary and became synonymous with ridiculous operatic stereotypes and excesses. It was not without justification that the critic Bogdanov-Berezovsky prepared his readers for the premiere of *The Nose* with the words "Shostakovich has taken into account the crisis of contemporary opera, consisting in its isolation from the contemporary accomplishments of the dramatic theater. In his opera there is not a whit of 'vampukism.' So much so that certainly many will not recognize his work as an opera."[5]

The "crisis" of contemporary opera in the Soviet Union stood in sharp contrast to the vitality of the dramatic theater with its innovative post-revolutionary productions—many of which made significant use of music—by such vanguard directors as Stanislavsky, Nemirovich-Danchenko, Tairov, Vakhtangov, and, above all, Vsevolod Meyerhold. At the same time, bold steps were being taken in the development of Soviet film by Sergei Eisenstein and others. The desire to find equivalently fresh and original perspectives in the realm of opera was further stimulated by productions of a number of modern Western works in Leningrad: Schreker's *Der ferne Klang* (1925), Prokofiev's *Love for Three Oranges* (1926), Berg's *Wozzeck* (1927) at the former Maryinsky Theater, and Krenek's *Der Sprung über den Schatten* (1927) and *Jonny spielt auf* (1928) at the Maly. In writing his "experimental" opera, Shostakovich, who avidly followed all the latest cultural developments, was influenced by many of them, most notably by the theatrical principles of Meyerhold.

In light of the pressures and high expectations placed on the would-be composer of a Soviet opera, it is understandable that Shostakovich felt obliged to justify his choice of a libretto that was neither revolutionary nor Soviet:

> There were several reasons why I turned to Gogol for an operatic plot. Soviet authors had created a number of major and highly significant works but since I am no writer, it was difficult for me to make a libretto out of any of these works. None of the authors would help me: some had no time, others were too busy, still others (and if I am mistaken, let the writers who I have approached tell me so) were not sufficiently interested in the development of Soviet opera. It would have been much easier for me to use for the libretto some shorter

work, but I did not find in our contemporary literature anything suitable for an opera. There was nothing but to go to the classics.

I thought that an opera on a classical subject would be more acceptable in our time if it was satirical, so I started looking for a plot in the work of the "Three Whales" of Russian satirical literature—Gogol, Saltykov-Shchedrin, and Chekhov.

Finally I chose "The Nose" by Gogol.[6]

Gogol's grotesque short story was an improbable choice for scenic representation.[7] The story, anecdotal in nature, tells of a petty bureaucrat, Major Kovalev, who wakes one morning to discover that his nose is missing from its accustomed place, leaving a spot that is perfectly flat. There follows his ludicrous attempts to locate the missing appendage which has meanwhile undergone metamorphosis into a person of higher rank than its ostensible "owner." This discrepancy in rank adds to Kovalev's nightmarish frustration and agony, while the personified nose exploits the situation to scandalize the residents of St. Petersburg. Once the nose is captured—and mysteriously restored to its original form—the problem remains as to how to re-attach it to Kovalev's face. The uncomfortable situation is miraculously resolved when the hero wakes to find his nose back in its proper place.

"The subject of 'The Nose' attracted me by its fantastic and absurd content, expounded by Gogol in strictly realistic tones....,"[8] Shostakovich declared, and he also enumerated other reasons for his attraction to the story, including its powerful satire of the period of Nicholas I, its clear and expressive language, and the variety of interesting possibilities for theatrical spectacle.[9] With the help of Georgy Ionin, Alexander Preis and, to a lesser extent, Evgeny Zamiatin,[10] he fashioned a libretto consisting of ten scenes arranged into three acts, using a principle of "literary montage." Much of Gogol's dialogue was retained intact and narrative portions of the story were transformed into monologue or dialogue. Where the situations or text in the original proved insufficient, the librettists fleshed them out with interpolations from a number of other Gogol works, including *The Marriage,* "The Fair at Sorochinsk," "May Night," and *Taras Bulba.* They made a conspicuous departure from Gogol in only one instance; for the song of Kovalev's servant Ivan (scene 6), they turned to Dostoevsky, taking the text "An invisible force ties me to my beloved" from the character Smerdiakov in *The Brothers Karamazov.*

The careful focus on language was not incidental, but related directly to Shostakovich's dramatic intent. In numerous interviews and articles concerning his opera, he emphasized that "music in this spectacle does not play a self-sufficient role. The stress is on the presentation of the text."[11] Elsewhere he spoke of the equal balance between the elements of music and theatrical action in the opera, his attempt to forge their synthesis, and described the process of composition as the "musicalization" of the pronunciation of Gogol's words.[12] He even spoke of his composition not as an opera, but as a symphony:

"I symphonized Gogol's text producing not an 'absolute' or 'pure' symphony but a 'theatre symphony' as represented by Vsevolod Meyerhold's production of *Inspector General.*"[13] He elaborated on this idea: "The music is not divided into individual numbers but flows in a single symphonic current and there is no system of leading motives. Interruptions occur only in between acts. Each act is a movement of a single musico-theatrical symphony."[14]

What is left to the imagination in Gogol's story must, of necessity, be made concrete in the operatic context, and attention is thus focused on the noseless Kovalev, on the one hand, and on his larger-than-life, personified "Nose," on the other. The calculated effect of the opera is dependent, to a great extent, on the complex interaction of the visual, textual, and musical components. Shostakovich's intent was to preserve the tone and realistic quality of the Gogol original:

> I did not feel it necessary to strengthen Gogol's satirical text with "ironic" or "parodistic" coloring in the music. On the contrary, I gave it a completely serious musical accompaniment. The contrast between the comic action and serious music of a symphonic character is meant to create a special theatrical effect; this device seems all the more justified since Gogol himself describes the comic incidents of the plot in an intentionally serious, elevated tone.[15]

This claim has proved baffling to most interpreters of the opera; Shostakovich's score is permeated, in fact, with ingeniously graphic musical evocations of snoring, shaving, and other "sound" effects, as well as unmistakably parodistic and comic treatment of familiar genres, such as march, waltz, galop, and sentimental romance.

While a detailed analysis of the musical style of the opera is beyond the scope of this study, some aspects should be mentioned.[16] The musical idiom of Shostakovich's opera is essentially non-tonal and non-lyrical. The vocal writing is declamatory, angular, and requires a wide range of unusual vocal techniques, including the "pinched" nasal quality with which, appropriately, the "Nose" is expected to sing. The scoring calls for individual winds and brass plus a large assortment of percussion. Among the unprecedented features of the opera is an interlude scored for nine unpitched percussion instruments, and coloristic writing and percussive techniques are pervasive.

The dimensions of the opera are almost grotesquely impractical. The work is scored for a minimum of seventy-eight solo singing roles, nine spoken roles, chorus and orchestra. As Shostakovich indicated, many of the parts are brief enough to allow for the doubling, tripling, quadrupling, etc., of roles, but even so, approximately thirty soloists are needed, and, of course, they must be costumed for the total number of roles. All this poses intriguing creative and economic problems for the producer and designer, and may explain, in part, why the opera proved so time-consuming to produce.

The analogy, mentioned earlier, with Meyerhold's legendary production of Gogol's *Inspector General,* as well as with the musical principles inherent in the director's theatrical approach, is by no means superficial. Meyerhold's innovative and controversial staging had excited the imaginations of the country's most original artists. One of these was the eminent musicologist and composer Boris Asafiev, under whose influence Shostakovich composed *The Nose.*[17] Asafiev was an enthusiastic propagandist of Meyerhold and, in particular, of the latter's production of *Inspector General.*[18] Asafiev had also arranged the music for Meyerhold's production of Griboedov's *Woe from Wit* in 1928. He expressed his frustration at the negative reviews of the latter production, in a letter to Meyerhold at the time, addressing as well an essential problem of integrating music and theater:

> But here's where the trouble starts. Musicians understand music only as music, a piece of craftsmanship, and the public understands music as pleasant entertainment, something that soothes or shakes up the nerves. In the theater, music, as far as the public is concerned, is only a lulling background or an annoying accompaniment that gets in the way of "what the words mean." And that's the whole problem. Music as a living impulse, music included in a dramatic production as an integral element in the dialogue—that, alas, no one understands.... So. Our society rejects the notion of music as an organic part of the performance, as an element of the dialogue, as a symphonic moment. As usual, you have gone far beyond the era and the age. But what's to be done now? How can we proceed in order to make the notion understandable? Of course it could be made totally understandable only in a situation where the actor was also a real musician/improvisor and actually found the stimulus for his lines in the music. It's possible.[19]

Shostakovich's "musico-theatrical symphony" explored this very possibility. Starting with a fundamentally musical genre, he wrote a work which makes sophisticated theatrical demands on the performers. His singers must become actors. The words and action are "integral elements" in the opera, not an "annoying accompaniment" that gets in the way of the music.

At the time Shostakovich began work on *The Nose,* he had not yet met Meyerhold, and when he first saw the latter's production of *Inspector General* is not known.[20] There can be little doubt, however, that he was well aware—through his contacts with Asafiev, as well as through the extensive journalistic coverage given the production—of Meyerhold's creative principles. Meanwhile, the conductor Nikolai Malko, hoping to drag Shostakovich away from his employment in movie houses and place him in Meyerhold's theater, had introduced the director to Shostakovich's First Symphony.[21] The effort did not pay off immediately, but in the winter of 1927-28, Shostakovich was engaged as pianist in the Meyerhold Theater in Moscow. While there, Shostakovich lived in the Meyerholds' apartment and continued work on *The Nose,* completing Act I and sketches of Act II, under the encouraging eye of his host.[22] Shostakovich immersed himself in theatrical life

above and beyond his official duties: "I go to the theater whenever I can. . . . The play which impresses me the most is still *The Government Inspector* [i.e., *Inspector General*] at Meyerhold's theater. I have now seen it through about three times. Seven times in all. And the more I see it, the more I like it."[23] Shostakovich's return to Leningrad in the spring of 1928 did not mark the end of his work with Meyerhold; in 1929 he wrote the music for Meyerhold's production of Mayakovsky's *The Bedbug*.[24] But an advertised production by Meyerhold of *The Nose*, planned for the Bolshoi Theater,[25] went unrealized.

Extensive parallels have been drawn between Meyerhold's concerns with the rhythm, pacing and "musical" structure of his dramatic productions and the composition, as well as the eventual production of Shostakovich's opera.[26] The analogies are indeed striking and did not escape the opera's early critics. A large number of other influences, however, were also detected in the opera. Foremost among these was the continuity in the tradition stemming from Musorgsky's unfinished setting of Gogol's *The Marriage*. Above and beyond the common choice of a Gogolian libretto, the approach to the setting of the text—stressing a musical reproduction of the intonations of the language—and the avoidance of conventional operatic approaches—arias and "number" structure—were perceived as analogous. The musical style of *The Nose*, however, borrowed little from Musorgsky. It owed much more to the advanced techniques of modern Western composers. The list of influential composers cited by the contemporary writers was long and included Stravinsky, Prokofiev, Hindemith, Krenek, and Berg, although no single composer was recognized as a pre-eminent model.

One additional source of inspiration should be mentioned. Even before *The Nose* was staged, critics noticed a "cinematic" quality evident in the pacing and alternation of the scenes and entr'actes which created the effect of a succession of "frames."[27] While it is difficult to trace parallels with specific films or their directors, and Shostakovich's work on his first film score, *The New Babylon*, did not begin until after the completion of *The Nose*, his work as an accompanist for silent movies had exposed him to the latest techniques and accomplishments in the film world. It is not surprising that the impressionable and eclectic composer should find in them a source of inspiration.

Completed in the summer of 1928,[28] *The Nose* was scheduled for production the following season in Leningrad's Maly Theater. Rehearsals, however, stretched out over the next year and a half and the opera did not receive its first public performance until 18 January 1930. In his memoirs Nikolai Malko notes:

> The conductor, Samuel Samosud, held approximately 150 piano rehearsals. He then had some fifty orchestral rehearsals, plus several more for lighting, scenery, and the curtain changes which were sometimes sudden and sometimes gradual. Then there were rehearsals in

costume with scenery and using only the piano for accompaniment. Finally there were eight full dress rehearsals. Then the opera was ready. It was performed many, many times, with tremendous success.[29]

While his figures are almost certainly exaggerated—for instance, the opera received a total of sixteen performances, and its success fell somewhat short of "tremendous"—it is clear that an enormous amount of time and effort went into the preparation of the production.

There are some indications that the performers may have been sceptical initially, both of the work and of the youthful composer:

> The opera has as its basis...an anecdote about Major Kovalev's nose! It was hard to imagine that something sensible and interesting could be made of such an endeavor....[30]

> Shostakovich was known to a comparatively small circle of musicians....[He] had something to be afraid of. In the lobbies the actors recounted that Shostakovich had worked up to then in movie theaters, where he improvised at the piano for silent movies. Of this improvisation they spoke diversely, but all were agreed that the music of the young improvisor was unusually fresh, spiky, dynamic and that it characterized the author as an original musician.... The artists of the theater became unusually interested in the personality of the young composer.[31]

The demands placed on the singers were formidable, a fact duly noted by the work's early critics, and there was some initial resistance to the difficult and unfamiliar musical language. After several months of preparation, however, the performers began to find their parts more grateful, the characterizations convincing, the musical fabric organic and logical. "The ease with which we mastered the musical material in the opera *The Nose* elicited the amazement of the professional musicians."[32]

The theater management, meanwhile, stood solidly behind the production and the composer from the beginning. Samosud, artistic director as well as conductor of the Maly Theater, was committed to the renovation and modernization of operatic theater in Russia, and saw in Shostakovich a promising future. Samosud, along with the producer N. Smolich and the designer V. Dmitriev, would later collaborate again on the first staging of Shostakovich's second opera, *Lady Macbeth of the Mtsensk District.*

In conjunction with the premiere of *The Nose*, a pamphlet of essays was published in which the philosophy and polemical stance of the Maly Theater was clearly articulated:

> With the staging of Shostakovich's opera *The Nose*, the Maly Opera Theater and its Artistic-Political Council are embarking on the path of the decisive Sovietization of the operatic repertory.... And if for some segment of the working-class audience the opera *The Nose* seems unusual in form and difficult in musical style, then that circumstance need trouble neither the working-class viewer, nor us. Soviet opera should not arise by means of

the lowering of artistic quality in comparison with operatic works of the past. The form of Soviet opera should be different from the forms incorporating bourgeois ideology. Our goal, therefore, is to lend every possible assistance to the task of raising the cultural level of the proletarian masses.[33]

The management further expressed its confidence that Shostakovich's opera would come to occupy an esteemed place in the theater's repertory.[34]

The optimistic prognosis had not been issued without careful consideration and testing. In the period between the completion of *The Nose* and its premiere, a number of significant events had taken place. As early as July 1928, articles began to appear assessing the innovative importance of the new opera.[35] Shostakovich himself, with rare volubility, explained the principles and objectives of his opera in a number of interviews and essays.[36] A suite of seven sections from the opera was successfully premiered by Nikolai Malko in Moscow on 25 November 1928. During the winter of 1929, fragments from the opera with accompanying commentary were presented on several occasions to composers' organizations.[37]

On 16 June 1929, a "public hearing" of fragments of the opera, in concert performance, was held during the All-Russian Musical Conference in Leningrad. The hearing was followed by a heated debate, which contained hints of the impending controversy. The talent and mastery of the composer was praised, but Shostakovich was criticized for the complexity of his musical techniques, which made the work inaccessible to the masses, and for the avoidance of a Soviet theme.[38] The composer Daniel Zhitomirsky criticized the opera for its lack of social and ideological relevance to the "students, metal- and textile-workers," who would presumably attend the spectacle, and warned that "with his opera Shostakovich, without a doubt, has strayed from the main road of Soviet art. If he does not accept the falsity of his path, then his work will inevitably find itself at a dead end."[39] Supporters of the work persisted in their defense of the significance of the undertaking and the need to pursue technical progress in the realm of art. The rehearsals continued.

On 14 January 1930—just four days before the premiere—a final "trial balloon" was launched. Before an audience of Leningrad factory workers, three scenes from the opera were presented in the Moscow-Narva House of Culture, with introductions and explanations provided by the composer, the critic Ivan Sollertinsky, the designer Vladimir Dmitriev, and others. In response to questions, Shostakovich explicated his choice of subject, musical and dramatic means, and underscored his commitment to the working-class audience: "I live in the U.S.S.R. Naturally, I actively work for and count on the working-class and peasant spectator. . . . We work for you and seek your help."[40] The acid test—the presentation of the opera to a culturally unsophisticated audience—was an apparent success, and the premiere went ahead as scheduled.

All the elaborate preparations, testing, and educational propaganda on behalf of the opera could not prevent the critical turmoil which its premiere sparked. Shostakovich's opera had been begun just before the instigation of the first Five-Year Plan and at the end of Anatoly Lunacharsky's enlightened tenure as Commissar of Education, in other words, at the end of the "liberal" period in Soviet politics and culture. The opera's production, unfortunately, coincided with the consolidation and rise to power of the "proletarian"cultural organizations, hostile to avant-garde and Western artistic tendencies.[41] It was in this atmosphere that *The Nose* was critically received. The quality of the production or performance was not a paramount issue, nor was the compositional mastery and originality of the composer. The primary issue was political. *The Nose* symbolized one extreme—an extreme which was soon to vanish—in the continuing struggle for the ideological direction of Soviet art.[42] To the critics of the opera,[43] its failure to communicate as a social satire with roots in Soviet reality, its musically esoteric and iconoclastic style, and its total repudiation of classical operatic values stood out as damning features. A common denominator in many reviews was the unworthiness of *The Nose* to be considered a "Soviet" opera at all.

The most prominent champion of the opera was Ivan Sollertinsky. Sollertinsky was a learned and brilliant critic who had become fast friends with Shostakovich in 1927, just as the latter began work on his opera. Like Asafiev, he was an eloquent advocate of the most progressive tendencies in contemporary art, including the theatrical innovations of Meyerhold, and was committed to the renovation of the operatic genre in the Soviet Union. He participated actively in the lengthy preparations for the production of *The Nose*, publishing articles and delivering lectures which helped to interpret and defend the goals of the experiment. In the wake of the storm which greeted the production, he published an impassioned defense of *The Nose,* classifying it as "the first original opera written in the territory of the U.S.S.R. by a Soviet composer."[44] While he did not claim that it would be an enduring masterpiece, he nevertheless saw in it the seeds for the future development of Soviet opera, a compendium of novel techniques, musical and dramatic, which would inspire Soviet composers in their quest for the dynamic and distinctive embodiment of Soviet themes. He concluded his article:

> Does Soviet opera need this? Unquestionably. We will feel the beneficial consequences of the renovation of resources in *The Nose* in the future. *The Nose* is a long-range gun. In other words, it is the investment of capital which isn't immediately compensated, but which later achieves excellent results.[45]

When, in response to Sollertinsky's militaristic metaphor, S. Gres pronounced Shostakovich's opera to be the product of "the childish sickness of leftism," and scathingly labelled it "the hand bomb of an anarchist,"[46] a bomb which would effectively blow up in the face of its proponents, he was only voicing a widely-

held opinion. More charitable reviewers noted that in works composed since *The Nose,* most notably in the Third Symphony "The First of May" (1929) and the incidental music to Alexander Bezymensky's play *The Shot* (1929), Shostakovich had already turned away from the radical musical and theatrical principles of *The Nose.*[47] In a survey of the musical accomplishments of the 1929-30 season, Bogdanov-Berezovsky—an early supporter of the opera—noted with evident relief: "... but it is with great satisfaction that we ascertain Shostakovich's decisive break, after the period of the composition of *The Nose,* with the exclusive sphere of dry formalism, with rational-aphoristic exposition. ..."[48] The consensus of critical opinion was not on Sollertinsky's side.[49] In the Soviet cultural atmosphere of 1930, *The Nose* was not deemed to be an appropriate model for the development of Soviet opera.

The strong language of the debate was worthy of the notorious *Pravda* attack of January 1936 directed at *Lady Macbeth.* From a distance, it is difficult to penetrate the rhetoric and gauge the audience reaction to Shostakovich's opera. Some indication that its success with the general public was not as "tremendous" as Malko claimed, however, can be found in one of Shostakovich's letters, dating from February 1930:

> I had a telegram from mother saying that *The Nose* was sold out on the 8th. I'm pleased, but I fear it isn't true and Mother just wants to cheer me up. I don't know when I'll be back. Most of all I regret missing performances of *The Nose,* but maybe it will still run for a performance or so after I get back.[50]

Shostakovich would have the opportunity to see his opera again. From January through June 1930, it received a respectable fourteen performances. In the following season it was performed twice more before being removed from the repertory. More than forty years would pass before it would receive another performance in the Soviet Union.[51]

Shostakovich's attempt to revolutionize the Soviet operatic stage was a calculated risk which ultimately fell short of its mark. Its uncompromising avant-garde aesthetic failed, at the time, to win it a permanent place in the repertory or to establish a basis for the development of a uniquely Soviet operatic tradition. While the failure must have been a grave disappointment to the composer, the ramifications for Shostakovich's career and reputation were not catastrophic. If anything, he had gained the attention and respect of a circle of scholars and artists committed to progressive developments in Soviet culture. Sergei Kirov, the Communist Party boss of Leningrad, attended a performance of *The Nose.* Samosud recalled a conversation which took place during the intermission:

> He didn't like the opera and somehow justified his opinion. But he spoke with such genuine concern for the future of the theater, the composer, Soviet opera, with such a serious

feeling for all the complexities of the process of compositional discoveries. He spoke about the diversity of art forms, about the need not to fear compositional risk if you set before yourself a great goal. He also spoke about how it is important to remember the whole breadth of interests and demands of our spectators. And when someone remarked that perhaps it doesn't make any sense to show experimental works to the mass listener, the party leader expressed his answer with genuine wisdom; "The proletariat is a broad concept, ranging from the simple worker to Marx...."[52]

In 1930, the personal tastes of political functionaries did not yet exercise a stranglehold on artistic experimentation.

Judged from any standpoint, Shostakovich's second opera was far more accessible and politically palatable than *The Nose*. It also achieved, from 1934 to 1936, an extraordinary degree of critical and popular success. Ironically, at the beginning of 1936, it was *Lady Macbeth,* and not *The Nose,* which was well on its way to becoming the first Soviet operatic "classic." Implicit in the condemnation of *Lady Macbeth* was the excommunication of *The Nose.*[53] During the Stalinist period, *The Nose*—when referred to at all—was characterized at best as a youthful aberration, Shostakovich's misguided seduction by the forces of "decadent Western formalism."

In the 1960s, *The Nose* was produced in Florence, Rome, and Santa Fe, and in a number of German cities. As late as 1966, however, Shostakovich was still doubtful about the value of his early opera:

> I wrote my opera *The Nose* a long time ago, and have forgotten a good deal. I shall have to go back in time and think about it before I can offer my opinion about whether it should be staged again here. To be frank, I have no particular desire to return to it. When the question arose about staging *Katerina Izmailova,* I was glad to do some more work on it, and make a second edition, as it were. But I do not know whether I should return to my first opera, written when I was very young. I shall have to think about it, and take a look at the score....[54]

Just two years later, after hearing a tape of the Berlin production of his opera, he was able to state confidently:

> Forty years have already passed, but I appreciate every measure, I answer for every note, for absolutely everything. Having heard the tape of *The Nose,* I perceive it as new. Maybe everything didn't succeed, but even after forty years I accept this work in its entirety.[55]

Finally in 1974, *The Nose* was the last of Shostakovich's major works to be rehabilitated in his own country, in a production at the Moscow Chamber Opera Theater directed by Boris Pokrovsky.[56] Shostakovich participated enthusiastically in the rehearsal process and made virtually no changes in his original score. The stunning impact and success of this production has stimulated renewed interest in Shostakovich's long-forgotten, but utterly remarkable first opera.

Notes

1.   S. Gres, "Ruchnaia bomba anarkhista" [The hand bomb of an anarchist] *Rabochii i teatr*, no. 10 (21 February 1930), p. 6. The reference here is to the round black bombs, with lighted fuse, characteristically associated with the anarchist movement.

2.   For an overview of the situation, see Boris Schwarz, *Music and Musical Life in Soviet Russia, Enlarged Edition, 1917-1981* (Bloomington, 1983), pp. 63-73.

3.   Yu. Keldysh, ed., *Muzykal'naia entsiklopediia* [Musical encyclopedia], v. 1 (Moscow, 1973), p. 662.

4.   Christopher Collins, "Nikolai Evreinov as a Playwright," in *Life as Theater: Five Modern Plays by Nikolai Evreinov* (Ann Arbor, 1973), p. xv.

5.   V. Bogdanov-Berezovsky, "Sovetskaia opera v predstoiashchem sezone" [Soviet opera in the coming season] *Rabochii i teatr*, no. 36 (8 September 1929), p. 8.

6.   D. Shostakovich, "Pochemu 'Nos'?" [Why *The Nose?*] *Rabochii i teatr*, no. 3 (15 January 1930), p. 11; quoted in "Editor's Note," *D. Shostakovich Collected Works; The Nose*, v. 19, (Moscow, 1981).

7.   Actually, Gogol's short story had been the subject of an earlier dramatization, "Major Kovalev's Dream" by A. Deich, which was staged at the Crooked Mirror Theater in 1915. The production does not appear to have made an overwhelming impression, either on critics or on the public. See *Homo novus* [A. Kugel'], "Zametki" [Remarks] *Teatr i iskusstvo*, no. 41 (11 October 1915), pp. 754-56. In his posthumously published "memoirs" (*Testimony: The Memoirs of Dmitri Shostakovich*, edited by Solomon Volkov (New York, 1979), p. 207) Shostakovich states: "I don't know, maybe Meyerhold did influence the production of my opera *The Nose* that Smolich directed at the Maly Theater. That's another matter, the composer has nothing to do with that. But as far as *The Nose* and myself are concerned, a greater influence was the production of *The Nose* at the famous Crooked Mirror." It is not unreasonable to suppose that the precocious nine-year-old could have seen and remembered this production. But neither he nor his contemporaries noted any connection between the works at the time of the opera's composition and staging, whereas Meyerhold's influence was immediately acknowledged. In light of these facts and the dubious authenticity of *Testimony*, Shostakovich's belated claim must be treated with scepticism.

8.   "'Nos', Beseda s kompozitorom D. Shostakovichem" [*The Nose*, a conversation with D. Shostakovich] *Novyi zritel'*, no. 35 (2 September 1928), p. 14.

9.   Shostakovich, "Pochemu 'Nos'?", p. 11.

10.   Shostakovich indicated that with the exception of the scene of Kovalev's awakening (scene 3), written by Zamiatin, he was exclusively responsible for the libretto of Acts I and II. Shostakovich shared the responsibility for Act III with Ionin and Preis. See D. Shostakovich, "K prem'ere 'Nosa'" [Towards the premiere of *The Nose*] *Rabochii i teatr*, no. 24 (16 June 1929), p. 12.

11.   Shostakovich, "Pochemu 'Nos'?", p. 11.

12.   Shostakovich, "K prem'ere," p. 12.

13.   "Report of Dmitry Shostakovich, post-graduate student of the Leningrad Conservatoire, May 1928" quoted in "Editor's Note," *Shostakovich Collected Works*, v. 19. Gogol's comic masterpiece *Revizor* (translated variously as *Inspector General* or *The Government*

Inspector), was radically adapted and staged with almost tragic overtones, at the Meyerhold Theater in Moscow on 9 December 1926.

14.   Shostakovich, "K prem'ere," p. 12; quoted in "Editor's Note," *Shostakovich Collected Works,* v. 19.

15.   "'Nos', Beseda s kompozitorom," p. 14.

16.   For more detailed information, see G. Grigor'eva, "Pervaia opera Shostakovicha—'Nos'" [Shostakovich's first opera—*The Nose*] *Muzyka i sovremennost',* v. 3 (Moscow, 1965), pp. 68-103; A. Bretanitskaia, "O muzykal'noi dramaturgii opery 'Nos'" [About the musical dramaturgy of the opera *The Nose*] *Sovetskaia muzyka,*no. 9 (September 1974), pp. 47-53; A. Bogdanova, *Opery i balety Shostakovicha* [The operas and ballets of Shostakovich] (Moscow, 1979), pp. 53-108.

17.   D. Shostakovich, "Dumy o proidennom puti" [Thoughts about the path traversed] *Sovetskaia muzyka,* no. 9 (September 1956), p. 11.

18.   Konstantin Rudnitsky, *Meyerhold the Director,* translated by George Petrov (Ann Arbor, 1981), p. 419.

19.   Paul Schmidt, ed., *Meyerhold at Work* (Austin, 1980), p. 149. The letter is dated 27 March 1928.

20.   G. Fedorov speculates that Shostakovich may have been more immediately influenced by another production of *Inspector General,* that of I. Terentiev which premiered in Leningrad on 24 March 1927. He reasons that since Shostakovich would not have been able to see Meyerhold's production performed in Leningrad until September 1927—*after* he had begun his opera—that Terentiev's production may have provided the initial spark for the opera. While his argument is fascinating, he overlooks Shostakovich's comments on the subject and erroneously assumes that Shostakovich could not have had the opportunity to see Meyerhold's production in Moscow. In addition, contemporary critics failed to notice any connection between Shostakovich's opera and the Terentiev production. See G. Fedorov, "Vokrug i posle 'Nosa'" [Around and after *The Nose*] *Sovetskaia muzyka,* no. 9 (September 1976), p. 45.

21.   Nikolai Malko, *A Certain Art* (New York, 1966), pp. 205-6.

22.   Shostakovich recalled an incident which occurred at this time: "A serious fire once broke out at his [Meyerhold's] flat. I was out at the time, but he gathered up all my manuscripts and returned them to me in perfect condition. I was amazed, after all, there were far more valuable things that could have burned." See D. Shostakovich, "Iz vospominanii" [From my recollections] *Sovetskaia muzyka,* no. 3 (March 1974), p. 54; quoted in *D. Shostakovich About Himself and His Times* (Moscow, 1981), p. 321.

23.   Letter to Ivan Sollertinsky, quoted in Dmitri and Ludmilla Sollertinsky, *Pages from the Life of Dmitri Shostakovich* (New York, 1980), p. 50. The exact date of the letter is not given.

24.   A variety of other collaborative ventures was contemplated over the next several years, but none was brought to fruition. See A. Bogdanova, "Rannie proizvedeniia Shostakovicha dlia dramaticheskogo teatra" [Shostakovich's early works for the dramatic theater] in T.N. Livanova, ed., *Iz proshlogo sovetskoi muzykal'noi kul'tury* (Moscow, 1975), pp. 12-13.

25.   See *Rabochii i teatr,* no. 35 (26 August 1928), p. 16 and *Novyi zritel',* no. 40 (6 October 1929), p. 15.

26.   Among other similarities are the extensive use of pantomime and the "polyphonic" layering of stage action. See L. Bubennikovaia, "Meierhold i Shostakovich; iz istorii sozdaniia opery

'Nos'" [Meyerhold and Shostakovich; from the history of the creation of the opera *The Nose*], *Sovetskaia muzyka*, no. 3 (March 1973), pp. 43-48; idem, "K probleme khudozhestvennogo vzaimodeistviia muzykal'nogo i dramaticheskogo teatrov" [Towards the problem of the artistic interaction of the musical and dramatic theaters], *Problemy muzykal'noi nauki*, v. 3 (Moscow, 1975), pp. 38-63.

27.   V. Bogdanov-Berezovsky, "'Nos'—opera D. Shostakovicha" [*The Nose*—D. Shostakovich's opera] *Muzyka i revoliutsiia* no. 7-8 (July-August 1928), p. 55.

28.   Shostakovich indicated that while the work took a year to complete, the time of *actual* composition was slightly more than two months. See "Editor's Note," *Shostakovich Collected Works*, v. 19.

29.   Malko, *A Certain Art*, p. 218.

30.   B.O. Geft, "Kak ia pel v opere 'Nos'" [How I sang in the opera *The Nose*] *Smena*, 25 September 1966; quoted in S. Khentova, *Molodye gody Shostakovicha; kniga pervaia* (Leningrad, 1975), p. 219.

31.   Ibid., p. 220.

32.   Ibid., p. 221.

33.   *Nos, Gosudarstvennyi Malyi Opernyi Teatr* [*The Nose*, State Maly Opera Theater] (Leningrad, 1930), pp. 2-3.

34.   Ibid., p. 3.

35.   See, for instance, Bogdanov-Berezovsky, "'Nos'—opera D. Shostakovicha," pp. 54-56; V. Belaiev, "'Nos'. Opera Shostakovicha" [*The Nose*. Shostakovich's opera] *Zhizn' iskusstva*, no. 48 (25 November 1928), pp. 6-7.

36.   See "'Nos', Beseda s kompozitorom," p. 14; Shostakovich, "K prem'ere," p. 12; idem, "Pochemu 'Nos'?", p. 11.

37.   Khentova, *Molodye gody*, p. 222.

38.   Ibid., p. 223

39.   D. Zhitomirsky, "'Nos'—opera D. Shostakovicha" [*The Nose*—D. Shostakovich's opera] *Proletarskii muzykant*, no. 7-8 (1929), p. 39.

40.   From a transcript of the discussion of the opera *The Nose* at the Moscow-Narva House of Culture on 14 January 1930; quoted in Khentova, *Molodye gody*, p. 223.

41.   For a concise history of the phenomenon, see Schwarz, *Music and Musical Life*, pp. 54-60.

42.   Shostakovich was not alone in feeling the effects of the militant "proletarian" wing. For instance, Mayakovsky and Meyerhold were subjected to furious criticism for the staging of the satire *The Bathhouse*, premiered in Moscow on 16 March 1930. The analogies between the criticisms of Mayakovsky's play and Shostakovich's opera are striking. See Rudnitsky, *Meyerhold*, pp. 462-67.

43.   See, for instance, M. Iankovsky, "'Nos' v Malom opernom teatre" [*The Nose* in the Maly Opera Theater] *Rabochii i teatr*, no. 5 (26 January 1930), pp. 6-7; N. Malkov, "Tak li eto?" [Is it so?] *Rabochii i teatr*, no. 7 (5 February 1930); p. 7; S. Gres, "Sovetskaia opera" [Soviet opera] *Leningrad*, no. 7-8 (November-December 1930), pp. 155-58.

44.   I. Sollertinsky, "'Nos'—orudie dal'noboinoe" [*The Nose*—a long-range gun], *Rabochii i teatr*, no. 7 (5 February 1930), p. 6.

45.   Ibid., p. 7.

46.   S. Gres, "Ruchnaia bomba," pp. 6-7.

47.   See, for instance, N. Malkov, "Tak li eto?", p. 7.

48.   V. Bogdanov-Berezovsky, "Muzyka za god" [Music during the year], *Rabochii i teatr,* no. 37 (5 July 1930), p. 8.

49.   Perhaps sensing the hopelessness of the situation, Boris Asafiev did not participate in the public debate. In 1934, he lamented the fate of the opera: "The fate of the extremely talented opera *The Nose* is profoundly sad. When the youthful composer dared to expose authentic Gogolian existence in music and through it to 'settle accounts' with the 'images of the past' troubling his imagination, then instead of painstaking evaluation, they 'shafted' him, simply accused him of formalism. . . . It's clear that if Shostakovich had told this novella of Gogol in the idyllically naive musical language of Rimsky-Korsakov's *May Night,* he wouldn't have been a formalist . . . " B. Asafiev, "O tvorchestve D. Shostakovicha i ego opere 'Ledi Makbet Mtsenskogo Uezda'" [About Shostakovich's work and his opera *Lady Macbeth of the Mtsensk District*], in *Kriticheskie stat'i, ocherki i retsenzii* (Moscow, 1967), pp. 242-43.

50.   Letter to Ivan Sollertinsky in D. and L. Sollertinsky, *Pages from the Life,* p. 60. Shostakovich was on tour during the early part of the month. The performance referred to, on 8 February 1930, was the fifth performance of the opera.

51.   A piano-vocal score of the opera was issued in a limited edition of 100 copies in Leningrad in 1929.

52.   S. Samosud, "Minuvshee vstaet peredo mnoiu . . ." [The past stands before me . . .], *Sovetskaia muzyka,* no. 9 (September 1965), p. 82.

53.   Vsevolod Meyerhold, parenthetically, was one of very few people who dared to defend Shostakovich publically after the condemnation of *Lady Macbeth.* See Edward Braun, trans. & ed., *Meyerhold on Theatre* (New York, 1969), p. 249. Meyerhold paid dearly for his personal and professional audacity: in 1938 his theater was closed by decree, he was arrested in 1939, and on 2 February 1940, he was executed in prison. See Schmidt, *Meyerhold at Work,* p. xxii.

54.   "Chudesnyi u nas slushatel': Dmitrii Shostakovich otvechaet na voprosy" [We have a marvelous audience: Dmitri Shostakovich answers questions] *Muzykal'naia zhizn',* no. 17 (September 1966), p. 7; quoted in *Dmitry Shostakovich about Himself,* p. 271.

55.   Quoted in Bubennikova, "K probleme," p. 38.

56.   A recording of this production has been released on Melodiya/Columbia M2 34582.

15

The Three Faces of Lady Macbeth

Royal S. Brown (U.S.A.)

The popularity of Dmitri Shostakovich's music with the general listening public has for some time been firmly established. To both the critical and academic communities, on the other hand, the late Soviet composer's output continues to represent problems, most of which, unfortunately, have little to do with the music itself. For throughout much of his career, Shostakovich stood and, even after his death, continues to stand as political symbol. Within the Soviet Union, Shostakovich's music, either because of its audaciousness or because of its intense, and often tragic, expressiveness, was often considered a threat by various powers, although, towards the end of this life, the composer came to enjoy the status of a culture hero who could do no wrong. In the West, Shostakovich has been seen as an example of the pernicious influence a repressive political regime can have on an artist. And so thoroughly do political issues continue to plug the ears of some critics and scholars that the advent of *Testimony,* those highly suspicious memoirs edited by Solomon Volkov, has actually caused some writers to do an about face from negative to positive in their views of Shostakovich's music, as if the protest and anguish expressed in *Testimony's* bitter words (whether Shostakovich's or Volkov's) had not always been expressed with infinitely greater eloquence in much of the musician's *oeuvre.*

The focal work in all this is, of course, Shostakovich's second opera, *Lady Macbeth of Mtsensk,* based on Nikolai Leskov's nineteenth-century short story of the same title. Composed between 1930 and 1932[1] and premièred in Leningrad on 22 January 1934, the opera enjoyed an immediate success and was exported so quickly that it received its first American performance just a little over a year later. But the work also provoked violently negative reactions on both sides of the ocean, culminating in the famous, unsigned *Pravda* attack entitled "Sumbur vmesto muzyki" ("Chaos Instead of Music"), published on 28 January 1936. It has long been assumed in the West that this article, and the one that followed it on 6 February, marked the turning point in Shostakovich's

career, a turning point that allegedly saw the composer metamorphose overnight into a line-toeing court musician for Stalin and his successors.

It is beyond the scope of this essay to show just how erroneous this
judgment is on a purely musical level. Suffice it to say that even a quick perusal
of the Shostakovich output from the *Lady Macbeth* period reveals a definite
turn towards musical conservatism, after the experimentation of such works as
the Second Symphony (1927) and a first opera, *The Nose* (1927-28). The 1934-
35 ballet *The Limpid Stream,* which was the principal object of the second
Pravda blast, shows a thoroughly tonal and utterly characterless harmonic
language and was attacked not for its non-existent musical boldness but for
the flippancy of its tone in treating a serious Soviet subject. It can be argued
that the eye-twinkling satire of such early works as *The Nose,* the *New Babylon*
film score (1928), the *Columbus* Overture (1929), the *Age of Gold* ballet (1927-
30), the innocuous incidental music for a *Hamlet* production, but also the
delightfully naughty chamber-score for Mikhail Tsekhanovsky's unfinished
cartoon opera *The Tale of the Priest and his Servant Balda* (1936), was one very
positive element in Shostakovich's early style to be stifled by the *Pravda* sabre-
rattling. But the shift from the satirical to the tragic vein can already be seen in
the movement from *The Nose* to the more Musorgskian *Lady Macbeth.* And as
successful as the latter work is, it can hardly be said that it ventures, muscially,
into any new territory. Similarly, the Fourth Symphony, begun in 1935 but
withdrawn by the composer in 1936 following the *Pravda* difficulties, marks,
for all its audacities, a return to more conventional symphonic forms that had
appeared in the Second and Third Symphonies. Within the context of
Shostakovich's creative evolution, then, it is difficult not to see the composer's
ultimate musical conservatism, which produced some of the twentieth-
century's great masterpieces, particularly in the symphonic and string quartet
genres, as resulting from anything other than wholly natural processes.

Why, then, did the less musically daring *Lady Macbeth* provoke greater
scandal than more technically *outré* works such as the Second Symphony or
The Nose? The bulk of the answer lies, it seems to me, in the sexual content of
Lady Macbeth and in the musico-dramatic expression of that sexuality. To
begin with, *Lady Macbeth,* which is dedicated to Shostakovich's first wife,
Nina Varzar, is definitely slanted in favor of its heroine and was, in fact,
intitially intended as the first part of a tetralogy devoted to the Russian woman.
Shostakovich took Leskov's naturalistically depicted heroine, Katerina
Izmailova, who, with her lover Sergei, murders her father-in-law, husband, and
a young nephew, and shows her as the victim of a male-dominated, bourgeois
value system. Writing about his opera, Shostakovich even stated that he and
librettist Alexander Preis eliminated the child murder from the story in order to
make Katerina a more sympathetic character.[2] Furthermore, foreshadowing
by some thirty years a principal concern of the woman's liberation movement,
Shostakovich, in his music, and Shostakovich/Preis, in their libretto, stress the

drive towards sexual freedom as a key factor in Katerina Izmailova's attempts to escape from her prison.

It is in Scene 3 of the first act that the opera expresses its sexual theme in the most explicit way, first verbally and then musically in a passage that is surely the most graphic depiction of sexual intercourse ever attempted by a "serious" composer. At the beginning of the scene, Katerina is resigning herself to going to bed alone (her husband is away), even though it is early, since she has nothing else to do. She is encouraged to do so by her crusty father-in-law, Boris Timofeevich, who points out that there is no need to waste candles. After Boris Timofeevich has left, Katerina sings an aria, the most famous of the opera, in which she expresses her longing directly in terms of sexual frustration:

Zherebenok k kobylke *tianetsia* [toropitsia]
Kotik prositsia k koshechke,
A golub' k golubke stremitsia,
I tol'ko ko mne [odnoi (added in 1)] nikto ne speshit.
Berezku veter laskaet,
I teplom svoim *igraet* [greet] solnyshko.
Vsem chto-nibud' ulybnaetsia,
Tol'ko ko mne nikto ne pridet,
Nikto stan moi rukoi ne obnimet,
Nikto guby k moim ne pril'net,
Nikto moiu beluiu grud' ne pogladit,
Nikto strastnoi laskoi menia ne istomit . . .
Unylo, skuchno, i proidet
1 Moia zhizn' bezotradno . . .
Prokhodiat moi dni bezradostnye,
2 Promel'knet moia zhizn' bez ulybki.
1 Nikto, nikto ne pridet . . .
    Nikto, nikto ko mne ne pridet,
2 Nikto ko mne ne pridet.

The foal runs after the filly,
The tom-cat seeks the female,
The dove hastens to his mate,
But no one hurries to me.
The wind caresses the birch-tree,
And the sun warms it with his heat,
For everyone there's a smile from somewhere
But no will come to me.
No one will put his hand round my waist
No will press his lips to mine.
No one will stroke my white breast,
No one will tire me out with his passionate embraces.
The days go by in a joyless procession,
My life will flash past without a smile,
No one, no one will ever come to me,
No one will come to me.[3]

I've no darling, no sweet beloved darling have I.
Day follows day sad and mournful,
My life will pass without a single smile.
No love, no love will be my fate here,
No love will be my fate here.[5]

As for the seduction music (pp. 92-94), although certain changes were effected, such as the replacement of triplet figures by sixteenth-notes, probably in order to make the piano solo sound as full as possible, the first 102 measures basically duplicate the orchestral music discussed above. There is even a piano equivalent of such devices as the downward trombone *glissandi* (F to D above middle C) repeated some eight times as of the sixth measure after rehearsal number 186 in both the original 1932 version and the 1935 piano-vocal reduction. But following the climactic moment in the 1935 version, no attempt is made to reproduce the famous post-coital *glissandi* (contained between numbers 190 and 192 in the 1932 score); significantly, in fact, the score markings in the piano-vocal reduction skip from 189 to 192, at which point Katerina and Sergei begin to sing again. Although, up to here, there are some slight changes in the music and words, the only significant one is the excision of the final measure before the frantic thirteen-bar instrumental conclusion to the scene (beginning at 198 in both scores). In that single excised measure, Katerina's sung "Mily" (Darling) throws a different light on the scene's ending from the one we are left with minus this final expression of passion.

Although there are a certain number of other modifications between the 1932 orchestral partitura (as published by Sikorski in 1979) and the 1935 piano-vocal reduction, none of them are of any substance. There appears, however, to exist yet a further edited version also dating from 1935. In the unsigned, unpaginated preface (in German and English) to the 1979 Sikorski partitura, the writer notes the differences between the 1932 score and a 1935 score published by Muzgiz and by Universal Edition in Vienna (no. 10740). Mentioned in this discussion are the replacement of the orchestral version of the passacaglia Entr'acte, separating Scenes 4 and 5, with a "moderated version played by the organ," and the excision of a "recitativo" sung by Sergei in Scene 3. This unsigned preface also points out that the seduction music "underwent a change in its aggressive orchestration and was considerably shortened." Although nothing can be said about the intended orchestration on the basis of the 1935 piano-vocal score consulted for this essay, we have seen that the latter only reduced the sex scene from 123 to 102 bars. This 1935 piano-vocal score also contains Sergei's "risqué" recitative and at several points in the piano score for the passacaglia Entr'acte between Scenes 4 and 5 indicates some of the orchestral instruments that would be playing. The preface to the Sikorski edition of the 1932 version mentions only the "piano score/libretto" published by Universal in 1935; but it would appear that the writer was also able to consult a full partitura from that period. Whether the additional revisions exist

in both the Universal piano-vocal score and the partitura (should one exist), and whether Muzgiz published a still more bowdlerized piano-vocal reduction in 1935 cannot be verified without further research.

It is not certain at this point just how much of a hand Shostakovich had in the revisions that had already taken place by the time the *Pravda* articles were written. It should be noted, however, that the words for Katerina's aria from Scene 3, while somewhat modified, remain essentially the same in the 1935 and the 1956 versions. On the other hand, in the 1956 revision, not only has the orchestral seduction music been totally replaced by a 16-bar instrumental interlude using a motive that will later reappear in the entr'acte between Scenes 6 and 7, the sexual act itself never takes place, since Katerina and Sergei see Boris Timofeevich walking with a lantern outside the window and "run away from each other in terror."[6] And while Sergei's "risqué" recitativo from the same scene has not been excised, it has been considerably cleaned up so that, for instance, suggestive allusions to babies are replaced with suggestive allusions to books. Numerous other changes appear in the 1956 revision, the most substantial of which are the complete rewrite of the entr'acte between Scenes 1 and 2 and a nearly complete replacement of the one between Scenes 7 and 8.

Lady Macbeth of Mtsensk, then, did not fall victim to a single swing of the ax early in 1936. As a work containing one of the most sexually bold scenes ever to be heard and seen in an opera, *Lady Macbeth* was bound to provoke violent reactions when it appeared in the midst of the sexually conservative 1930s. And if the Soviet Union was able to use political clout to finally get the work suppressed two years after its première, we have likewise seen how in the United States the Philadelphia censors initiated at least one of the cuts that also turned up in the 1935 piano-vocal score (the trombone glissandi). Again, one wonders just how long *Lady Macbeth/Katerina Izmailova* would have remained either intact or even in the repertoire in a country whose movie industry was already governed by the Hays code, had not the Soviet Union conveniently taken care of the problem. That Shostakovich obviously yielded to pressure in his various rewrites of both music and text cannot be questioned. That this pressure came solely from a repressive government out to stifle originality in one of its greatest musical artists is a gross simplification of the issue. As happened with many composers of the twenties and thirties, Shostakovich's genius managed to shock large numbers of people, and it is quite probable that a wholly predictable public outcry, rather than official prodding, prompted the composer to make a few compromises as early as 1934. As a result, Lady Macbeth has at least three faces to show: one from 1932, one from 1935, and one from 1956. It is thanks to Mstislav Rostropovich, who in 1979 somehow unearthed the 1932 version, that we can again see the best of those faces.

Notes

My deep thanks to G. Schirmer in New York for the loan of the Sikorski partitura.

1. Sophia Khentova offers the following precisions on the dates of composition: the first act was begun on 14 October 1930 and completed on 5 December 1931; Act II: 19 November 1931 - 8 March 1932; the third act was begun on 5 April 1932 (no completion date is given), with the fourth act—and the entire opera—reaching completion in the composer's native Leningrad on 17 December 1932. See *Molidie godi Shostakovicha* [Shostakovich's early years], Bk. 1 (Leningrad and Moscow, 1975), pp. 311-12.

2. See "O moei opere" [About my opera], in *Katerina Izmailova*, libretto (Moscow, 1934), pp. 11-13.

3. Underlined words followed by a word in brackets indicate a variant in the text between the 1934 libretto (1; see note 2) and the Russian/German text printed in the full orchestral score (2) published in 1979 by Edition Sikorski in Hamburg (no. 2313), which contains several errors in the hand-printed Russian, and in the libretto included with the Angel recording of the original version (SCLX-3866, 1979). Ditto for the bracketed complete lines. The English translation is the one by Joan Pemberton Smith in the Angel libretto.

4. The version consulted for this article has Russian and English texts, with the English-language translation done by L. Sudakova.

5. The Russian text and English translation are taken from the 1935 piano-vocal score, pp. 75-79.

6. See the two-volume orchestral score entitled *Katerina Izmailova*, Op. 29/114 (Moscow, 1965), I, p. 225.

16

At the Birth of Dmitri Shostakovich's Eighth Symphony

Grigory Shneerson (U.S.S.R.)

Summer of the war year 1943. The composers' retreat for creative work near the town of Ivanovo, situated northwest of Moscow. The Moscow and Leningrad composers Reinhold Glière, Sergei Prokofiev, Dmitri Shostakovich, Aram Khachaturian, Nikolai Miaskovsky, Dmitri Kabalevsky, Yuri Shaporin and Mikhail Gnesin, all recently returned from distant evacuation to cities in Siberia, the Urals, and Central Asia, had now settled here with their families in the administrative and agricultural buildings of a former poultry farm.

The Soviet Government had afforded the Union of Composers all the necessary amenities here for life and creative work. The natural beauty of Central Russia, the dense forests, bright green meadows, rural stillness—everything, it would seem, was disposed towards peaceful work and relaxation. However, the alarming daily radio dispatches from the fronts of the Great Patriotic War, the drone of airplanes protecting the night skies above Ivanovo, and the anti-aircraft guns hidden in the ravines and groves were a constant reminder of the military terror threatening our native land. Echoes of these battles, the heroic spirit of the struggle against enemy invasion, and the great national misfortune could not but find a reflection in the music being written by Soviet composers, including those living at the Ivanovo creative retreat. Prokofiev was completing work on *War and Peace,* based on Tolstoy. Page by page, Khachaturian was approaching the end of his Second Symphony, whose subject was entwined with the terrible events of the war. Shaporin was working on the cantata *A Tale of the Battle for the Russian Land.* Shostakovich inspired by the historic victory of the Red Army and its rout of Hitler's three-hundred thousand-strong army under the walls of Stalingrad, was hastening to finish his new, Eighth Symphony.

In the summer of 1943, I had managed more than once to visit Ivanovo, where my family was also living. On arrival at the retreat, I would become

immersed in the atmosphere of intensive creative labor by the eminent masters of Soviet music, united in a single patriotic impulse. This was a group of artists of various generations and diverse creative directions and individualities, ranging from the venerable Glière—student of Taneev and the first teacher of the young Seryozha Prokofiev—to the youthful Aram Khachaturian and Dmitri Shostakovich. All the inhabitants of the retreat were zealously working on new compositions. By a firmly established routine, the morning hours were set aside as "inviolable" for work, a time for solitude and compositional endeavors. Later there was time for meetings around the communal dinner table, for friendly conversations and the exchange of opinions about the events of the war or about current work, as well as for walks and mushroom hunts in the thick-spreading forest. Sergei Prokofiev especially loved to hike in the forest. I remember how once the two of us wandered for several hours searching for an exit from the woods, moving further and further from home. We were eventually brought out to the road by Prokofiev's faithful watchdog Zmeika.

In the evenings the composers frequently gathered in a large room of the main building, where there was a grand piano. They made music together, showed each other their freshly-composed pages, and occasionally played through finished pieces. In the course of these auditions, extremely interesting exchanges of candid and professionally astute opinion took place. How interesting it was to hear Prokofiev, Miaskovsky, Gnesin, Shostakovich, and Kabalevsky speak out, each "in his own key," about the music heard.

Not far off from the composers' retreat is the large village of Afanasovo. There, in several of the more spacious homes, the Composers' Union had grand pianos installed at which the composers could work. For his composing, however, Shostakovich preferred the more than modest accommodation of a former hen-house, situated on the territory of the poultry farm. A grand piano was squeezed into this hut, and a board nailed to one of the walls served as a writing desk. And on this slanting board in a former hen-house, Shostakovich wrote, in two-and-a-half months, the score of his Eighth Symphony, one of the crowning achievements of his creative genius.

In those years, I headed the Music Section of the All-Union Society for Cultural Relations with Foreign Countries (VOKS). Urgent requests from America and England came to us more and more frequently to send new compositions by Soviet composers, along with information about their creative activity and daily life. When I was in Ivanovo, therefore, I tried to photograph scenes from the life of the retreat's inhabitants. I was helped in this by Shostakovich's wife, Nina Vasilievna, an excellent photographer. *Life* magazine was particularly interested in these photos and printed a number of those taken by Nina Vasilevna in a November issue.[1] The American public was particularly interested at that time in the personality and work of Dmitri Shostakovich. This attention to Shostakovich had increased especially after

the première of the Soviet composer's Seventh ("Leningrad") Symphony, first performed in America on 19 July 1942, to the enthusiastic response of the Americans. At that time, the prominent conductors Leopold Stokowski, Sergei Koussevitzky, Artur Rodzinski, and Eugene Ormandy were in competition for the rights to the first U.S. performance of the Seventh Symphony. All these candidates fell by the wayside, however, when, with Shostakovich's consent, the rights for the première were given to the great Arturo Toscanini. On 19 July 1942, the symphony was broadcast by Toscanini and the NBC Orchestra from the large studio (8-H) of New York's Radio City. Heard by millions of radio listeners, the symphony achieved a social resonance unprecedented in the history of symphonic music. Perhaps unexpectedly even to themselves, the vast majority of the American listeners were able to comprehend and experience the musical content of the massive symphonic canvas, in which the stirring pages of the heroic struggle of the Soviet people against fascist barbarity were reflected with rare artistic conviction. The numerous comments in the American press, which unanimously praised the première, as well as the numerous subsequent performances of the Seventh Symphony in Boston, Philadelphia, Cleveland, and other American cities, all pay tribute to this.

The Eighth Symphony, like its predecessor, was also anticipated with great interest in the Soviet Union, America, and England. Once again a rivalry flared up among conductors and orchestras in the U.S.A. for the rights to the first performance of the new work. As *Life* informs us, in the end the rights were acquired by the Columbia Broadcasting System for ten thousand dollars and granted to the New York Philharmonic under the baton of Artur Rodzinski.[2]

The first performance of Shostakovich's Eighth Symphony in New York, on 2 April 1944, stimulated a new wave of comments in the press. I will cite a few lines from an article by Harriett Johnson:

> Trying to explain genius is a futile job. Just why the most significant music of Dmitri Shostakovich creates not only interesting sounds but synthesizes musical elements with a life-expression is impossible to analyse....A work like the Shostakovich Eighth Symphony...made me feel as if I were reliving with the composer, grim, tortuous and heroic experiences.[3]

Toscanini was also extremely interested in the Eighth Symphony. However, a projected performance by him did not take place because of Shostakovich's categorical refusal to sanction a change of tempo in one of the episodes of the first movement. An intensive exchange of telegrams between Toscanini and Shostakovich took place through the musical section of VOKS. Neither wanted to back down. Shostakovich insisted on the necessity of observing the tempo indicated by the metronome marking. In his last telegram, Toscanini advised that, with the marked tempo of the given passage, he would not be able to perform the symphony. The composer's answer followed with an expression of polite regret. Glimpses into the characters of both artists—their adherence to principle and their uncompromising attitude toward art—were fully revealed in this exchange of telegrams across the ocean.

Let us return, however, to the composer's retreat in Ivanovo. When I was there I could always see Shostakovich at work, hunched over his manuscript. The doors of his "hen-house" were always open. Outside noise, the hubbub of children playing around the retreat didn't bother him. I also saw him at the dinner table, on a walk, and at work in the fields; he sometimes took rake and pitchfork in hand and helped to rake the hay into stacks. In one of the pictures found in *Life,* we see him laughing gaily with a piglet in his arms.[4]

Meanwhile, work on the symphony approached its conclusion. Sometime in the middle of August, Dmitri Dmitrievich invited Aram Illich Khachaturian, Khachaturian's wife, the composer Nina Vladimirovna Makarova, and myself to hear the just-finished symphony. The hearing was conducted in one of the houses in Afanasovo where there was a good grand piano at which Khachaturian usually worked. Dmitri Dmitrievich seated himself at the piano and began to play without any preliminary remarks or explanations. Nina Vladimirovna helped turn pages. Aram Illich and I sat in a far corner of the room....

At this initial hearing performed by the composer, the substance of the symphony, a work that has now become a classic, struck me as enigmatic and difficult to understand. I am speaking about the enormously long first movement, *Adagio.* However, as the dramatic development of the majestic symphonic action unfolded, the profound ideological and formal content of the entire five-movement cycle became increasingly clear to me.

After the tragically bitter reflections and expressive outbursts in the slow first movement, two quick, sharply dynamic movements in march rhythm follow. This music depicts with utmost concreteness the sinister appearance of an insolently smug enemy, dreadful in his bestial power. The implacable, mechanically-steady ostinato motion (a type of *perpetuum mobile*) that permeates the orchestral fabric of the toccata-like third movement quickly engraves itself in our memory. The two final movements, the mournful *Largo* in the form of a passacaglia and the *Allegretto,* leave the strongest impressions. The music of the *Allegretto* is unexpectedly clear, tranquil, almost pastoral, and it ends with a radiant coda in the purest sonorities of a C major chord fading away....

After finishing his new work, Shostakovich stood up from the piano and silently gathered the pages of his score.

"Thank you, Dmitri Dmitrievich," exclaimed Khachaturian emotionally. And not another word. In rapt silence we went out onto the village roadway and sat down on a wooden bench in front of the little house where the Eighth Symphony had just been heard for the first time. I recorded the scene with my camera.

Performed for the first time anywhere on 4 November 1943 in Moscow by the State Orchestra of the U.S.S.R., conducted by Evgeny Mravinsky, the Eighth

Symphony was enthusiastically received by the audience. Shostakovich's new work received wide coverage in the Soviet press, though not without critical comments and polemical sallies that pointed out the difficulty of grasping the musical, as well as the esthetic and philosophical conception of the new composition. With the passage of years, Shostakovich's Eighth has received thorough ideological and aesthetic interpretation in the scholarly monographs and research of the outstanding Soviet musicologists and critics, such as Lev Mazel, Marina Sabinina, Lev Danilevich, Victor Tsukkerman, and Alexander Dolzhansky, who have unreservedly acknowledged it to be one of the most powerful creations of the great master. The most eminent musical scholar, Boris Asafiev has called the symphony "the greatest tragic epic of the terrifying period just endured by mankind."

Dmitri Shostakovich has not gone down in history as the leader of a school or as a trend-setter. Nevertheless, there are few composers who could have exerted such a strong influence on the development of contemporary composition. The artist and man are fused together in his uniquely original and powerful creative personality. Shostakovich's majestic cycle of fifteen symphonies will remain forever a living and stirring monument to our stormy epoch.

1 October 1981

Translated by Laurel E. Fay

Notes

1. "Shostakovich Sells Symphony for $10,000," *Life,* v. 15, no. 21 (22 November 1943), pp. 43-44, 46.

2. Ibid., p. 43.

3. Harriett Johnson, "The Shostakovich 8th Expresses Vital Ideas With Emotional Power," *New York Post,* 3 April 1944, p. 20.

4. "Shostakovich Sells Symphony," p. 44.

17

Shostakovich's Song Cycle *From Jewish Folk Poetry:* Aspects of Style and Meaning

Joachim Braun (Israel)

Dmitri Shostakovich's interest in Jewish matters—both musical and non-musical—is without precedent in the history of Russian or Soviet music. Elements of a Jewish musical idiom may be found in at least ten of his major works, beginning with the Trio, opus 67 (1944), and continuing up to the Symphony No. 13, opus 113 (1962). He also expressed his interest in ways other than by original composition: he completed Benjamin [Veniamin] Fleishman's opera *Rothschild's Violin* (1943) and served as well as editor-in-chief for the miscellaneous collection *New Jewish Songs* (1970).

Apart from its scope and persistence, Shostakovich's involvement with Jewish music and culture also differs from that of all earlier Russian composers in its very nature. The utilization of a pseudo-Jewish melodic idiom by nineteenth-century Russian composers reflected little more than a characteristically Russian "interest in everything Eastern,"[1] i.e., an interest in exotic coloration. But Shostakovich's appropriation of a Jewish idiom cannot be related either to the "folkloristic" concerns of a Musorgsky or a Rimsky-Korsakov or to the "philosophical" biases of a Rubinstein or a Serov. The uniqueness of his approach stems from the fact that Jewish culture in the U.S.S.R. exists on the borderline between the "permitted" *(de jure)* and the "anti-Soviet" *(de facto)*. Any Soviet composer's exploration of a Jewish idiom is consequently fraught with risk and potentially explosive. Shostakovich's fusion of East European Jewish *melos* with his own individual musical style (in particular, his use of modality, ostinato patterns, and the expressive interpolation of flatted scale degrees e.g., the second and fourth, sometimes the fifth, and even the octave) is such, that the works composed in this special style seem equivocal when subjected to theoretical analysis, depending on whether one emphasizes the ethnically Jewish connections encountered in particular style features or leaves such connections unremarked. This equivocality was probably what Shostakovich sought in his employment of the Jewish idiom. It

allowed him the flexibility of symbolizing both autobiographical and social concerns, while shielding himself, as composer, his performers, and his listeners from possible harassment from Soviet officialdom.

I have discussed the general problem of Shostakovich's "Jewish" compositions elsewhere.[2] In this essay I shall focus on the song cycle, *From Jewish Folk Poetry,* attempting to account for its genesis and, by analyzing its text and music, to approach an interpretation of its style and meaning. The cycle is one of Shostakovich's most beautiful and richly symbolic compositions, a masterpiece of the composer's "secret language" of dissent. From the very hour of its creation, it was embroiled in controversy.

From Jewish Folk Poetry, opus 79, belongs to the second "Jewish period" (1948-52) of Shostakovich's compositional career, together with the Violin Concerto No. 1 in A Major, opus 77, the String Quartet No. 4 in D Major, opus 83, the Twenty-Four Preludes and Fugues for Piano, opus 87, and the Four Monologues on Pushkin texts, opus 91.[3] The exact chronology of its composition, however, is not yet entirely certain. Unfortunately, it has not been possible to examine the manuscript owned by Shostakovich's widow Irina, but most secondary sources point to the year 1948.[4] Shostakovich's first biographer, David Rabinovich, locates the cycle in the year 1949,[5] but this could hardly be possible. The Soviet musicologist Vera Vasina-Grossman states that the source of Shostakovich's inspiration was "a small...book of translations from Jewish folk poetry, which came into his hands by accident."[6] This book was the collection *Jewish Folk Songs (Evreiskie narodnye pesni),* compiled by Y.M. Dobrushin and A.D. Yuditsky, and edited by Y.M. Sokolov. The colophon of the book shows that it was signed for publication on 19 March 1947.[7] It is known from the practices of Soviet book printing and distribution that the publication could not have reached private hands before the end of the year. This sets the *terminus a quò.*

Ludmila Poliakova[8] has argued convincingly that composition took place in the summer of 1948, while the testimony of Natalia Mikhoels, who was a close friend of the composer and the daughter of the great Jewish actor Salomon Mikhoels, seems to advance the date to the spring of 1948. According to Natalia Mikhoels, it was May 1948 when Shostakovich raised questions in her presence about the pronunciation of certain Yiddish words and about the rhythmic flow of the original folk texts, which Shostakovich knew only in Russian translation. Natalia was also present for the first home performance of the opus 79 on Shostakovich's birthday, 25 September 1948. (It was his habit to have new music performed at his birthday parties.) On this occasion Shostakovich, rubbing his hands nervously, introduced the recently finished cycle with the words: "I have here, you might say, some new songs."[9] This sets the *terminus ad quem.*

From Jewish Folk Poetry was thus created during the dark age of the *Zhdanovshchina,* a time which witnessed in the U.S.S.R. not only the greatest

assault ever upon Western and Soviet art, but also the virtual destruction of Soviet Jewish culture. The two occurrences were not unrelated, as Svetlana Alliluyeva, Stalin's daughter, has testified:

> It was in the dark days of the Party's campaign against the so-called "cosmopolitans" in art, when the party would pounce upon the slightest sign of Western influence. As had happened many times before, this was merely an excuse to settle accounts with undesirables. In this instance, however, the struggle bore an openly anti-Semitic character.[10]

The increase in official anti-Semitism in the months during and preceding the composition of opus 79 must be understood against the background of the establishment of the state of Israel by the United Nations, accomplished in the period between November 1947 and May 1948, and the consequent fear among the Soviet leadership of increasing self-consciousness on the part of Soviet Jews. The equation of "Jew" with "ideological undesirable" started to figure at this time in one political incident after another, which suggests what must have aroused Shostakovich's social consciousness and attracted him to the Jewish musical idiom.

One sequence of political events is particularly laden with significance. In mid-December 1947, Yevgenia and Anna Alliluyeva, relatives of Stalin's wife, were arrested and accused of espionage.[11] Several Jewish friends of the Alliluyevas, many of them scholars, were arrested on 27 December and accused also of espionage and of suspicious contacts with Salomon Mikhoels.[12] Then on 12 January 1948, Mikhoels was killed in Minsk on Stalin's orders.[13] Six months later, during June and July 1948, immediately after the proclamation of the state of Israel, the accusations against the Alliluyevas' friends were changed; now they were accused of Zionist sympathies and of the intention to leave the U.S.S.R. for Israel.[14]

On the day after the murder of Mikhoels, Shostakovich and other top Soviet musicians were attending the first day of a meeting convened by Andrei Zhdanov, Stalin's spokesman. Zhdanov gave his opening speech at 1:00 p.m. At 3:00 p.m., news of Mikhoel's death reached the assembled musicians.[15] At 5:00 p.m., Shostakovich spoke for the first time to the assembly. He accepted some of the criticisms leveled at him and publicly supported certain general goals for Soviet music: "Our art should advance, should be even better than it is now."[16] At 8:00 p.m. that evening, he joined Mikhoel's relatives and friends as they gathered at Mikhoel's home. (Also present was Shostakovich's biographer, David Rabinovich, who was to be arrested twelve days later and accused of suspicious contacts with foreigners.) Shostakovich spoke at the gathering about how "this" had started with the Jews but would end with the entire intelligentsia; then he added, "I wish I were in his [Mikhoel's] place."[17] On the third day of the meeting of musicians called by the Central Committee, Shostakovich spoke for the second time; now he fully acknowledged the

Party's criticisms: "I have made mistakes; I shall accept critical instructions...."[18]

Shostakovich had to endure an onslaught of denunciation in the months to follow. The Central Committee's Resolution of 10 February 1948 accused Shostakovich and other leading Soviet composers of "formalism" and "anti-people" tendencies in their music. Tikhon Khrennikov, the powerful First Secretary of the Soviet Composers' Union, further condemned the leading Western and Soviet composers, including Shostakovich, during the First All-Union Congress of Soviet Composers (19-25 April 1948). Then, the Soviet-dominated International Congress of Composers and Musicologists convened in Prague, 20-29 May 1948, and announced its support for the Central Committee's resolution condemning "cosmopolitanism" in music,[19] and in June and July, *Sovetskaia muzyka,* nos. 2 and 3,[20] carried a two-part article by the composer Marian Koval pronouncing Shostakovich's music "worthless," "fallacious," and "anti-people." Soon afterwards, nineteen leading musicologists, fourteen of them Jewish, were accused of "anti-patriotic activities" and "cosmopolitanism"; the latter designation became at this time a virtual synonym for "Jewish."[21] With the arrests of many of his Jewish friends, the mounting attracks in the press against the newly established Jewish state, and the official denunciations of Jewish intellectuals for their "cosmopolitanism," is it any wonder that Shostakovich should have adopted a Jewish idiom as a language of dissent?

The opus 79 was not released by the author for public performance until two years after the death of Stalin. These first public performances took place on 15 January 1955 in Leningrad, and five days later in Moscow. The performers were Nina Dorliak (soprano), Zara Dolukhanova (mezzo), Alexei Maslennikov (tenor), with the composer at the piano. In June of the same year, the cycle was published by the Musical Fund of the U.S.S.R. (Moscow) in an edition of 3000 copies.[22] On 19 February 1964, under the baton of Gennady Rozhdestvensky, the composer presented an orchestral version of the cycle in Gorki on the occasion of the Second Festival of Contemporary Music.

The distinguished subject of our *festschrift* explains the delay of the first performance in the following way:

> For the next few years [1947-52], Shostakovich planned his creative output in such a manner as to avoid political controversy. He wrote works that were ideologically unassailable— scores for patriotic films...., the oratorio *Song of the Forests....*, and so on. On the other hand, he composed several important works in a more complex idiom and laid them aside...; he obviously decided to postpone the premières until the artistic climate would be more relaxed.... Among the latter works are the Violin Concerto,...the String Quartet No. 4,...and the vocal cycle "From Jewish Folk Poetry."[23]

This account of Shostakovich's strategy during these years is not entirely plausible with regard to the song cycle. The Violin Concerto and the Quartet

may indeed be considered works of a "complex idiom." In fact, even after their first performances (in 1953 and 1955, respectively), they were still considered too involute by the conservative music critics.[24] *From Jewish Folk Poetry*, on the contrary, is an example of stylized urban folk art. The text is genuine folk poetry, and as such should have been regarded by Soviet aesthetic standards as raw material *par excellence* for musical setting. The music is written in complete accordance with the features of a popular genre: couplet form, a predominance of simple melody lines, and a folk-type accompaniment. This was the sort of music required by the Resolution of February 1948— "democratic," "melodious," and "understandable for the people"—as was pointed out by many Soviet musicologists, including one as mindful of political correctness as Israel Nestyev. Nestyev refers to the opus 79—together with the oratorio *Song of the Forests*, the cantata *The Sun Shines Over Our Motherland*, and some songs for films—as music written in response to the February Resolution.[25]

Why would a work written in complete accordance with the artistic requirements of the Party Resolution be withheld by the composer until a time when he thought the "artistic climate would be more relaxed"? There is, however, a possible explanation for this: At the time of the work's completion in summer-fall 1948, it had not been Shostakovich's intention to delay public performance. His having arranged a home performance in September was a risky move in itself, given the political climate during 1948. By way of contrast, he seems to have told no one about the existence of the Concerto or the Quartet, because he must have intended these works to be concealed from the beginning. By the autumn of 1948, the shock waves over the February arrests had subsided. Despite, or perhaps because of, the murder of Mikhoels and the imprisonment of other intellectuals, Shostakovich might now have thought of going ahead with a public performance. This interpretation would help to explain the choice of texts, the popular musical idiom, and the transparently propagandistic songs that end the cycle. Soviet Jewish culture, although endangered, had not yet been anathematized. For Shostakovich, an artist in despair and bowed-down under pressure from the state, the gloomy fate of Soviet Jews accorded with his own frame of mind and served as a vehicle for the expression of his feelings. But during November and December, only two months after the private home performance, the situation changed drastically: all things Jewish were now anathematized and equated with anti-Sovietism. The entire Jewish intellectual elite was either under suspicion or under arrest, including the compilers of *Jewish Folk Songs*, Dobrushin and Yuditsky.[26] There was now no chance for any public performances whatsoever of Jewish works, even those in a musical style completely in accordance with official requirements.[26a]

Conceived and composed as an expression of human desperation, *From Jewish Folk Poetry* had been turned overnight into an ideological protest of potentially nation-wide political significance—a remarkable case of sudden change in value and meaning of an artistic work due to circumstances independent of its creator. Shostakovich apparently had in mind the cycle's unexpectedly enhanced political clout when he turned in 1963, during a time of renewed anti-Semitism in the U.S.S.R., to arranging an orchestral version, having just completed his Thirteenth Symphony with the famous "Baby Yar."[27]

Of the eleven songs Shostakovich selected from Dobrushin and Yuditsky's Russian edition of *Jewish Folk Songs,* all but one were translations from the original Yiddish edition published by the same compilers in 1940.[28] The translations are literal for the most part, except for euphemistic "corrections" of Yiddish vulgarisms, the change of "engineers" to "doctors," and the substitution of "star" for "sun" as a symbol of happiness in the eleventh song (see table 3). The fifth song in the cycle was taken not from *Jewish Folk Songs,* but from a collection by Z. Skudinsky.[29] Shostakovich also adhered essentially to the order of the songs as they appeared in both the Russian and the Yiddish editions. This fact refutes the assertions of Soviet musicologists that Shostakovich designed the cycle to create a picture of human life from "birth" to "old age," and from "poverty" to "happiness."[30] The order of songs was predetermined by Dobrushin's collection, and Shostakovich just followed an approved folk song publication.[31] He did invent titles of his own for the individual songs.[32] In the orchestral version of the cycle, he replaced these titles with the first lines of the original songs (see table 1). It is difficult from this vantage point to speculate about Shostakovich's reasons for assigning new titles in the first place—state censorship? self-censorship?

In four cases Shostakovich altered the original folk song texts (see table 3). The change in the first song seems to be of purely artistic significance. Two of the changes, however, are of a political nature. In the third song, Shostakovich added the line "The Tsar holds him in prison" following the line "Your father is in Siberia" in the original—surely an attempt to avoid any possible misinterpretation. In the sixth song, the words "has converted" were replaced by "left with the police officer," thus substituting a secular, social issue for a religious one. The change in gender in the tenth song does not seem to be motivated by a clear-cut reason.[33]

Of greater implicit significance are the changes initiated in the orchestral version of the cycle, all of which, in fact, amount to restorations of the original texts from the Russian edition of *Jewish Folk Songs.* Shostakovich dropped his invented song titles, returned to the unaltered folk text of the first song, and removed the cautious reference to the Tsar in the third song. The restorations support the hypothesis about Shostakovich's reasons for altering the folk texts and my belief that he at first intended to go ahead with public performances in the early fall of 1948. They also indicate how strongly Shostakovich cared

Table 1. *From Jewish Folk Poetry*. Titles and Sources.

Title in opus 79	Title in opus 79 (orchestral)	Page no. in Dobrushin original	
		(Russian)	(Yiddish)
1. Lament about a dead baby	Sun and rain	43	18
2. The attentive mother and aunt	Hush-a-by	46	45
3. Lullaby	My son is the most beautiful	50	388
4. Before the parting	Oh, Abram!	71	84
5. The warning	Listen, Khasya	110	-
6. The abandoned father	Elye, the innkeeper	135	227
7. A song of privation	The roof is sleeping on the garret	171	327
8. Winter	My Shayndl is in bed	170	325
9. The good life	Oh, spacious fields	231	433
10. A girl's song	On the glade, near the forest	230	423
11. Happiness	I took my husband by the arm	234	461

Table 2. *From Jewish Folk Poetry.* Summaries

Song No.	Summary
1.	The song—a question and answer rhyme—tells of Moyshele, a baby who is born, rocked in a cradle, nurtured with bread and onion, and buried in a little grave.
2.	A lullaby: Daddy will go to the village and bring us an apple (or chicken, nuts, etc.) to make the head (or tummy, hand, etc.) strong.
3.	A cradle song about an exiled father: Sleep; your father is in Siberia, and my grief is great.... Hush-a-by.
4.	Parting with the beloved. The refrain "Oij, Abram, how can I stand being without you?!" alternates with reminiscences about the lovers' first dates.
5.	"Listen, Khasya! You mustn't go...with anyone! Else, you will weep...."
6.	Zirele, the daughter of an innkeeper has departed with a police officer *(pristav).* The desperate father offers her dresses, jewelry, etc., but she repels him and asks the police officer to "drive out the old Jew."
7.	A dance refrain, "Hop, hop, hop," alternates with the description of a baby in the cradle, hungry and "naked, without diapers."
8.	A song about abject poverty: My Shayndl is in bed with her sick child. There is no fire, and the wind blows. "Oij, children, weep; the winter is here again!"
9.	In the past I had only sad songs, and the fields did not blossom for me; now the kolkhoz is my home, and I am happy.
10.	Shepherdess's song: I play my little flute, and admire my country. Little flute, don't cry, do you hear; I am happy, and you have to play more gaily.
11.	The old shoemaker's wife goes to the theater with her husband. She recalls the blessings that surround her, and wishes to tell the whole country about her happiness: "The star shines above our heads...our sons have become doctors."

about the richly Aesopian language of the genuine folk texts, leaving little doubt in particular about his motivations in restoring the original text of the third song.[34]

Let us turn our attention to the division of the song cycle into tragic songs and songs that affirm happiness (nos. 1-8 and 9-11, respectively; see table 2). Soviet audiences are accustomed, indeed conditioned, to tolerate in works of Soviet art a certain degree of official propaganda and extraneous Marxist-Leninist rhetoric. While tacitly accepted by both artist and audience, this aspect of an art work may be disregarded or detached from the "intentional content" of the work itself.[35] In accordance with the "rules of the game," this extraneous content must nevertheless be present and in proper proportion to the other elements in the art work, as well as in proper setting and style.

"Tragic" songs and "happy" songs appear in the proportion 8:3 in Shostakovich's cycle, thus directly contradicting the explicit dictate of Socialist Realism that "the victorious,... heroic, bright, and beautiful" should be the focus of attention in a work of art.[36] The three "happy" songs, clumped together at the end of the cycle, obviously stand apart from the main body of the work. The subject matter changes abruptly from texts about poverty and misery to texts inflated with optimism, quite unlike the transition provided in

Table 3. *From Jewish Folk Poetry.* Comparison of Sources and Texts.

Song	Dobrushin (Yiddish) [DY]	Dobrushin (Russian) [DR]	Opus 79	Opur 79 (orchestral)
1.	The sun and the rain, The bride had a baby, The groom arrived, The bride floated away.	same as DY	The sun and the rain, The shine and the mist, The fog is low, The moon has darkened.	same as DR!
2.		same as DY	same as DR	same as DR
3.	Sleep, my child, my beautiful Sleep, my little son, Your father is a young Siberian, Sleep,....	My little son is the most beautiful in the world, I do not sleep, Your father is in chains in Siberia, Sleep, hush-a-by....	My little son is the most beautiful in the world. A light in the darkness, Your father is in chains in Siberia, The Tsar holds him in prison	same as DR!
4.	Oij, Rebecca, give me your pussy! ("Pussy" should be understood here in its bawdy sense, which accurately renders the Yiddish *piskenyu.* The Soviet editors' squeamishness in the face of the folk vulgarism is reflected in their substitution of the word "mouth.")	Oij, oij, Rebecca, give me your mouth, baby!	same as DR	same as DR
5.	—	(from Skudinsky)		
6.	Elye, the innkeeper Has put on his robe, So he was told, His daughter has converted.	same as DY	same as DR Elye, the junkman Has put on his robe; It is said, His daughter has left with the police officer.	same as DR same as opus 79
7.		same as DY	same as DR	same as DR
8.		same as DY	same as DR	same as DR
9.		same as DY	same as DR	same as DR
10.	I am happy in the kolkhoz.	I [masc.] am happy in my kolkhoz.	I [fem.] am happy in my kolkhoz.	same as opus 79
11.	My sons have become engineers— Only the sun shines above our heads.	My sons have become doctors— The star shines above our heads.	same as DR	same as DR

Jewish Folk Songs, where texts about work, fighting, and war form a bridge between the "tragic" and the "happy" songs. Distinct topical and formal features also divide the two song groups. The first (nos. 1-8) presents genre scenes, the second (nos. 9-11) presents pronouncements and slogans; the text of the first is based on folkloric elements and uses folk lexemes, that of the second exploits features of art song and uses the vocabulary of Soviet mass songs; the first uses the dialogue form typical of Jewish folk songs, the second eschews this structure; the first approximates stylized Jewish folk music, with ample use of "speech intonations," while the second reflects a mixture of the conventional *melos* of the Soviet mass song and the Russian art song. All of these differences create the sense that these two groups of songs are independent of, indeed alien to, one another.

Nearly every song of the cycle exploits the elliptical and connotative language characteristic of Jewish folk poetry in order to suggest certain half-hidden meanings. Dobroshin, the editor of *Jewish Folk Songs,* wrote in this connection:

> Here [in Jewish folk songs] maximal concreteness and exactness often turn into reticence. When two persons talk on things well know to them, they can speak in hints.... In Jewish folk poetry, phrases and verses of this kind, built on innuendo, are very often present.[37]

This innuendo possesses concrete meaning only for the initiated—in the case of Shostakovich's song cycle, for those acquainted with a particular social and artistic climate. Let me cite some examples. An implicit reference to the millions exiled to Siberia by the Soviet regime is obvious in the third song of the cycle, although the text itself refers to events during the 1905 Revolution.[38] The third song also relates to the fourth song, with its recurrent, desperate outcry, "Oij, Abram, how shall I live without you? / I, without you—you, without me / How shall we live apart?" The dramatic situation enacted here is clearly a consequence of the Siberian banishment depicted in the third song. The theme of religious conversion in the sixth song was widely construed by the Jewish audience—and afterwards by the non-Jewish audience, especially those belonging to ethnic minorities—as a warning about the possible loss of ethnic identity and the danger of assimilation.

The three "happiness" songs may well have been forcibly included in the original collection. The idiomatic wording of the Russian translation in the tenth song certainly suggests the presence of coercion:

Tol'ko, dukochka, ne plakat'!	Only, little flute, no weeping!
....	....
Slishish, zhizn' moia polna!	Don't you hear? My life is full!
Veselee, veselee,	More gaily, more gaily,
Dudochka, ty pet' dolzhna!	Little flute, you have to sing!

The "only no weeping," the "don't you hear," and the "more gaily," followed by the "have to" are more an *argumentum baculinum* than an overwhelming afflux of happiness. The concluding verse of the cycle, with its reference to "doctors" (implicitly Jewish ones at that!) and to a "star" on the head of the shoemaker's wife, was perceived by Soviet audiences as pure mockery. With the "Doctor's Plot" of Stalin's last days and the "yellow stars" of Nazi Germany still firmly in mind, these lines struck such a vein of accumulated grievance and fear that the effect could hardly be concealed. An eyewitness to the first performance relates: "a shivering, half-giggle, half-shudder swept through the audience."[39] Yet another detail of the first public performance confirms that already by 1955 wide circles were aware of the political implications of this work. The master of ceremonies who announced the program appended a significant word of explanation about the third song: "A mother sings a lullaby about her baby's father, who is in Siberia," he said. Then he added pointedly, "This takes place in Tsarist Russia." With these words, "the audience sat stunned," remembered the same eyewitness.

The Jewish musical idiom probably came to Shostakovich's direct attention in the late 1930s when the young Jewish composer Benjamin Fleishman (1913-41) studied with him at the Leningrad Conservatory. Fleishman had already begun work on *Rothschild's Violin,* a one-act opera based on Chekhov's novel of the same title, when, in September 1941, he was killed in the war. Shostakovich completed the work, editing and orchestrating what Fleishman had left incomplete. "His memory is sacred to me," Shostakovich would write many years later.[40]

In Fleishman's opera some of Shostakovich's Jewish style is foreshadowed. Three episodes—the orchestral opening with the first chorus, the second orchestral *tutti* (rehearsal numbers 30-42),[41] and Rothschild's flute solo (42-46)—establish all the musical material of the work. Most of the music is strictly modal, with the use of flatted scale degrees and bitonal effects. The latter originate to a certain extent in genuine *klezmer*[42] performance, which often sounds out of tune, although in reality it is based on untempered scales. The modal tunes are set against a pedal accompaniment, which produces a primitive type of bitonality.[43] Minor modes, extensively used in East European Jewish folk music, are dominant. The use of an "um-pa" accompaniment and the highly characteristic "iambic prima"[44] suggest the sound of a folk orchestra. Traits of Shostakovich's individual style are also present, as in the case of the transposed D-eS-C-H motif (bars 1-4).[45] The opera makes characteristic use of "musicalized speech," a type of recitative imitating speech intonations, which originated from two quite different sources—the Dargomyzhsky-Musorgsky approach to text setting in art music and the ancient practice of cantillation in rendering Jewish liturgical texts.

Songs 1, 3, 4, 5, 6, and 8 of Shostakovich's opus 79 all employ the device of "musicalized speech." Although the Musorgskian strains in Shostakovich's

music in general are well-known, his "Musorgsky-ism" [*musorgskianstvo*][46] is of special significance for his "Jewish style." Musorgsky wrote about his interest in "musical declamation" that he was "departing from the conviction that human speech is strictly controlled by musical laws," and that he considered "the mission of the art of music to be the reproduction in musical sounds of not only the nuances of the emotions but, even more important, the nuances of human speech."[47] Dobrushin, speaking about the East European Jewish folk song, wrote that what "vividly stands out [as] the one most characteristic folksong feature [is] the fundamental connection with spoken language, with the manner of speaking of the Jewish masses."[48] Thus, we witness in Shostakovich a case of overlap between principles cultivated in Russian art music and traditional features found in Jewish folk art. Shostakovich drew upon these two related approaches in order to create his own kind of "musicalized speech," which Soviet audiences perceived to be inspired by Jewish traditions, but which could also be interpreted as purely Russian in origin—a typical manifestation of Shostakovich's twofold style.

The genre-scene character and subject matter *(zhanrovost'; siuzhetnost')* of *From Jewish Folk Poetry* also reflect Shostakovich's conjuncture of Russian classical tradition and Jewish folk tradition. Musorgsky's "folk-scenes" *(narodnye kartiniki)* characteristically dealt with the fate of the "little man" or the "humble man," a familiar figure in Russian literature and art from the time of Gogol. The comic and the tragic converged in the "little man's" everyday life, with the tragic perhaps predominating. The Soviet musicologist Arnold Sokhor claims that *From Jewish Folk Poetry* "is in fact the first composition which [had] revived in our time . . . the tradition of vocal scenes, pictures, and portrait sketches that comes from Dargomyzhsky and Musorgsky."[49] Similarly, the miniature genre scene is also found in Jewish folk song where it stems to a great extent from the Jewish folk theater (*Purimshpil:* Purim-games), and particularly from the art of the *badkhan.*[50] "The Jewish folk song is always inclined towards a genre-scene character [siuzhetnost'], towards a story," wrote Dobrushin.[51] The Yiddish folk song "was born in the cellars of the poor man, in the cramped tailor-shop, in the shoemaker's closet, at the sewing-machine, and at the joiner's bench."[52] With a few changes in social setting, then, the hero of the Jewish folk-scenes, with his "laughter through tears," is very like the "little man" we encounter in Gogol's stories and Musorgsky's songs.

There is an important distinction, however, between these two cultural concepts of the "little man." The "little man" of Russian art song suffers from social inferiority and spiritual impoverishment. The Jewish "little man" is, first and foremost, economically impoverished; but, though oppressed by a dark social power and by rigid officialdom, as with any folk hero, his reason and his spirit remain strong and dominant. This distinction was ignored by Soviet musicologists, who felt constrained to interpret the cycle only in terms of 19th-

century Russian art music tradition; the intelligent Soviet listener, however, generally accepted the Jewish "little man" on his own terms.

Stylistic interpretation of *From Jewish Folk Poetry* can be complete only by taking into account all three of the cycle's aspects: the Jewish, the Russian, and the Shostakovichian. The latter two have been widely discussed, but the Jewish element has hardly ever been mentioned, and occasionally even concealed. Aside from short periodical reviews,[53] four musicological studies on the cycle have been written. The first, by Vera Vasina-Grossman, a leading Soviet expert on vocal chamber music, appeared five months after the cycle's first performance. In her nine-page article, she devotes all of *nine lines* to the subject of our interest here:

> The new vocal cycle is written on texts from Jewish folk poetry. The composer used only the poetry of the folk songs, which he viewed only as a poetical creation. By setting his music to texts of folk songs, Dmitri Shostakovich, naturally, could not avoid the folksong genres and the intonational and modal features of Jewish folklore.[54]

Eighteen years later, in *Istoriia muzyki narodov SSSR* (1973),[55] Vasina-Grossman added not a single word to her reconsideration of the piece.

The second study, after Vasina-Grossman's article, was by Ludmila Poliakova, who devoted twenty lines of her twenty-five-page booklet (1957) to the Jewish sources of opus 79; expanding on Vasina-Grossman's points, she declares that the music is "certainly Russian in its humanitarian content, is real Russian music about another people."[56]

An elaboration of this idea appears in two other studies from the late 1960s. Arnold Sokhor's article, "The Big Truth about the 'Little Man,'" typifies the best Soviet musicological writing, but even Sokhor denies the use of actual folk melodies and the pervasive connections with Jewish musical tradition.[57] The most significant point encountered in the article relates to Sokhor's brief reference—for the first time in Soviet musicology—to a Jewish "national character," thereby touching upon a controversial Marxian concept which at that period was finding its way back into Soviet aesthetics.[58] "Shostakovich achieved in his music deep psychological truthfulness, which was the main requirement for a faithful reproduction of the national character."[59]

The most recent study, Tatiana Kurisheva's doctoral thesis of 1968, contains an eighty-one-page chapter devoted to opus 79 that is an example of how Soviet formal analysis typically avoids considering the dangerous area of cultural context and meaning by hiding away in the purely structural aspects of the music. Although she is much more specific, Kurisheva basically concurs with Vasina-Grossman's interpretation of the Jewish element in opus 79 as exotic flavoring.[60] While recognizing that this tiny song cycle "belongs to the most important works of the composer," Kurisheva never actually discloses the reasons for its importance.[61]

In examining the musical message of *From Jewish Folk Poetry,* we must reject, first of all, the recurrent assertion that Shostakovich made no use of Jewish folk tunes. The second song is Shostakovich's version of the folk song "Are rushing, are flowing..." (S'loyfn, s'yogn...), which appears in Emil Seculetz's collection, and, in fragmentary form, in a collection of Moshe Beregovsky and Itzik Fefer.[62] It is of interest that the original text of the melody in the Seculetz collection reads: "Black clouds rush, and flow / Your father sends greetings from Siberia... / He digs deeper, and deeper / Digs the grave for the lie... / He is not the first, and not the last / Who dies in the field." Can this text have been unknown to Shostakovich; can his choice of a melody associated with a Siberian subject have been purely accidental? (see ex. 1)

Ex. 1

FP = Shostakovich: *From Jewish Folk Poetry*
ES = Emil Seculetz: *Yiddishe folks-lider*

Generally considered to be "bright" and "humorous," Song No. 2 has tragic strains which probably derive from the original text, a typical *Hobelbanklied.* Shostakovich stresses the tragic by inserting into the tune's $\frac{2}{4}$ flow, four $\frac{3}{4}$ bars, and this always on the flat sixth. This $c\flat$ is interpreted by Kurisheva as the "Russian 'romance' sixth."[63] From our perspective, however, a "Jewish" interpretation seems more accurate: the $c\flat$ is the sixth of the *freigish,* the altered Phrygian—a typical Jewish *shteiger* which, according to Beregovsky, bears equally with the "altered Dorian" the semantics of "lamentation, complaint, and grief."[64]

An interpretation of Song No. 2 as being in E Major is not the only one possible. The *g* natural may be considered the raised third of the *freigish* on $e\flat$, rather than the usual major third of E Major. The implied Phrygian $f\flat$ is just a bar away, and the accompaniment is careful not to overstep the "hollow" fifth ($e\flat$-$b\flat$). If a $d\flat$ appears, it is the $d\flat$ of the modal suffix (see explanation in n.64); and when the accompaniment adds something, it is the altered Dorian, using another Jewish mode together with the characteristic device of switching from one mode to another. With the addition of the neighbor-note motion on *d,* we have a compound Jewish mode with the characteristic modal suffix. In this

way, this "most Russian" song (as Kurisheva describes it)[65] can be interpreted just as easily as a Jewish song.

This is not the only case of a direct relationship between opus 79 and Jewish folk tunes. Song No. 5 is a version of a Jewish *freilekhs* (dance tune) transcribed in 1935 by Beregovsky from performers at the Moscow Jewish Theater.[66] A similar fragment appears in Mikhail Gnessin's symphonic piece, *The Jewish Orchestra at the Ball of the Town Bailiff* (1926), a classic of Soviet Jewish music, and widely known among musicians in Moscow (see ex. 2).

Ex. 2

B62 = Moshe Beregovsky: *Yevreiske narodnye pesni*
Gnessin = Mikhail Gnessin: *The Jewish Orchestra at the Ball of the Town Bailiff*, opus 41

Yet another example is provided by the melody of the folk song "Oij Abram,"[67] which can be regarded as a primitive prototype of Shostakovich's Song No. 4. The descending fourth *e'-b* (again, as in Song No. 5, at the same pitch) provides the skeleton of both melodies. The Hasidic tune from Idelsohn's *Melodienschatz* is also closely related to Shostakovich's song.[68]

Song No. 6 presents an interesting case of the "re-Westernization" of a Jewish tune. Written in $\frac{3}{4}$ meter, the song approaches its dramatic high point— "Drive out the old Jew!"—through a section wherein Zirele announces her decision to marry the police officer. Here the rhythm acquires the character of a waltz, with rests on the downbeat. Sharp dissonances appear in the waltz accompaniment, along with stylized scale passages *à la* Weber, endowing the music with a bitterly sarcastic quality typical of Shostakovich's method of suggesting "evil" by means of parody. The waltz itself is alien, of course, to Jewish folklore, so that the very sound of such a characteristically Western

genre underscores the unnatural character of Zirele's action. But there is more. Many tunes in the *klezmer* repertory, in particular the songs of the popular *badkhan* Elyokum Zunser (1840-1915), were "created" through modal and textural transformation of popular Western melodies. In the case of Song No. 6, Shostakovich started with a Zunser-derived melody (see ex. 3), restored its purely Western major-scale basis and texture, and thereby "re-Westernized" what had become a Jewish tune. What more effective way to stress for Jews the alien and tragic character of religious conversion![69]

Ex. 3

ID9:581 = Idelson: *Hebräisch-orientalischer Melodienschatz*, v. 9, song No. 581

Song No. 11, which caps the group of so-called "happiness" songs, often elicits discomfort or vexation from Soviet audiences. It was not really an appropriate choice as the final song for the cycle. The entire section referring to the "blessings" that now surround the Jewish shoemaker's wife seems somehow ridiculous. Moreover, the "humor" in this "good-natured" song lacks "good humor," contrary to what has often been asserted.[70] Much has been written about Shostakovich's "malicious humor," achieved by transformations of popular urban folk melodies or genres (as in the use of the valse in Song No. 8). Sarcasm and scorn are certainly present in this particular "happy" song. Its melody is strongly related to, if not directly derived from, familiar Hasidic tunes. In Shostakovich's version, however, the melody has acquired a blunt, rhythmical monotony, with its dull repetition of every tone.

The $c_\flat$ (lowered fifth) that appears at the climax of the song on the words "we got $(c_\flat)$ two tickets for the parterre" clearly distorts the pure Hasidic melody. Then again, the "darkening" effect occurs on the words "the star $(c_\flat)$ shines

Ex. 4

*The c♭ appears only in the last section of the tune

above our heads." An obtuse "um-pa" accompaniment dominates the entire song (44 bars out of 58). In the second stanza every line is accompanied by a Phrygian motif "Oij!" which Shostakovich has added to the text: "And I want to tell the entire country, Oij! / About my happy and bright fate, Oij! / My sons became doctors, doctors, Oij! / The star shines above our heads, Oij!" In this context the "Oij!"—a typical feature of Jewish folk songs—sounds parodistic. To complete the sense of parody, a sudden modulation takes place in the last bars of the song from F minor to F Major, with octave leaps *à la* Soviet mass song. The chromatic line *g-g♭-f-e* adds a mocking laugh. The entire song, a parody of a folk tune, thus reveals itself as a parody of the idea of happiness.

The Jewish sources of opus 79 do not suggest themselves purely through musical parallels. Most of the songs are written in genres typical of Jewish folk music: lamentation (nos. 1 and 8), lullaby (nos. 2 and 3), *freilekhs* (nos. 4 and 7), and genre scenes (nos. 5 and 6). The ethnically unmarked genres of lyrical song (nos. 9 and 10) and of parody (no. 11) appear in the last group of "happy" songs, thus underlining once again their alien nature.

Perhaps the most characteristic feature of East European Jewish folk music is its tendency to an "extrapolation of mood."[71] This peculiar trait is richly explored in opus 79: a single, gay dance-motif develops into ecstatic, self-obsessed automatism (nos. 4 and 7); a lyrical, melancholy subject turns into tragic music, bordering on a state of catharsis (nos. 1 and 8); a calm piece of everyday advice concludes in a deliriously whispered warning (no. 5). Only in the last three songs, where the mood is constant and unequivocal, do we miss this sort of development.

All the songs are basically composed in the two simplest song forms: the binary or couplet form (nos. 2, 4, 7, 8, 10, and 11) and the ternary form (nos. 1, 3, 5, 6, and 9). Song No. 8, the last of the "tragic" songs, represents with its developmental couplet form (ab a'b' a") a kind of culmination. This culmination, or sense of finality, is also evident in the distribution of the vocal parts:

1.	S + A	3.	A	9.	T
2.	S + A	4.	S + T	10.	S
		5.	S	11.	S + A + T
		6.	A + T		
		7.	T		
		8.	S + A + T		

(S - soprano; A - contralto; T- tenor)

Opening with an introduction (nos. 1 and 2) and moving through a progressive interchange between the singers (nos. 3-7), the cycle culminates in the vocal trio of no. 8. The last three songs of the cycle follow a more formal approach to the "appended" trio in no. 11. The accumulation of intensity that culminates in Song No. 8 is also supported by the expanded ambitus of both the solo parts and the piano score at that point: in no. 8, G♯-b' for the singers and CCC-b' for the piano; while in no. 11, only F-g' for the singers and FFF-g' for the piano.

Throughout the cycle, rhythmic patterns and formulas of articulation characteristic of Jewish folk music are used extensively. Subdivisions of the strong beat, syncopations, and the "iambic prima" occur in all eleven songs. Oftentimes, identical rhythmic structures can be found for the melodies in opus 79 and for folk melodies (e.g., Song No. 7 and the folk song "Good evening, Brayne").[72] In eight songs Shostakovich has used the "um-pa" accompaniment (mostly on a pedal bass) typical of *klezmer* bands. It is absent only in songs no. 5, which is based on a folk melody, no. 6, where its absence may stress the alien quality of the situation (i.e., the religious conversion), and no. 9, the first of the "happy" songs. (In the latter song, the entrance into an artificial, marionette world is marked by an accompaniment *à la* Schubert.)

Shostakovich's use of modality is probably the most complex feature of his music. The various investigations of his melodic-harmonic system suggest a multitude of possible interpretations, from a relatively conventional major-minor approach by the traditionalists (L. Danilevich, A. Dolzhansky, V. Bobrovsky) to those of more recent researchers who stress the Western and Eastern folk roots of his highly individual and modal style (E. Fedosova, S. Skrebkov, Y. Tyulin, V. Sereda). The very existence of such a wide spectrum of theoretical possibilities seems to substantiate the equivocality of Shostakovich's music. Skrebkov, for example, points out that the distinctive Shostakovichian lowered fourth degrees serves as a significant source of auditory deception, since it sounds as a major third.[73] From our perspective, the melodic-harmonic system on which opus 79 is based should not be construed as the major-minor system with instances of altered scale degrees, but as a distinctive modal system with a strong affinity for the Jewish *shteiger*. We have already mentioned this in connection with Song No. 2; it also has implications for the D-eS-C-H formula (see n. 64). Let us add some other examples.

Song No. 4 is referred to in all studies as being in A minor. The first twelve bars, over a pedal on *a,* consist of three modal nuclei. The first, with an oscillation between the lower and upper neighbor notes, *d♯* and *f,* focuses on *e;* the next, with a diminished fourth, *a - d♭,* sounds above a F-minor chord; the last one encompasses the oscillating *d♯* within a raised third, and through a Phrygian *c* resolves both unstable units into a *freigish* mode on *b.* This, as substantiated by the following main subject of the song *(meno mosso),* turns out to be the upper tetrachord of a mode centered on *e.* A Hasidic dance tune establishes a *freigish* on the same *e.* The tonal feel of the song is not A minor, despite the A-minor ending. The A minor here is only a kind of "deception," while the actual modal center is *e.* The scale basis of the song corresponds to an artificial symmetrical mode that leans towards the *freigish:*

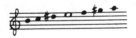

Further instance of auditory deception in opus 79 are: major third = raised third from the *freigish* (Song No. 2); lowered second = Phrygian natural (nos. 3, 6, 10); lowered fourth = raised third from the *freigish* (nos. 3, 5); lowered fifth = raised fourth from the altered Dorian (no. 11).

The middle part of Song No. 1, for example, is usually interpreted as Mixolydian on *e♭* with lowered second.[74] Our ears tell us, however, that this section is Phrygian with the raised third of the *freigish,* along with the typical modal suffix of *d♭* and *c.* Modal ambiguity is further secured by the instability of tonal focus throughout the song, where B minor, B♭ Major, and E♭ Major vacillate (ex. 5).

Ex. 5

FP
No. 1

The harmonic frame of Song No. 3 may be interpreted as C minor with a lowered second and a "split" fourth. Yet another interpretation might be to regard the entire song as in *freigish* on *c.* The *e* that occurs each time with an *e♭* can be explained as a splitting of the third to imitate the untempered augmented second which occurs naturally in Jewish folk performance. (A similar device—simultaneous use of the minor and major third—is found in the final bars of Gnessin's "Romance" from *The Jewish Orchestra.* [ex. 6])

Ex. 6

FP
No.3

The frequent occurrence of the "split" fourth (nos. 3, 4, and 5) can be explained as an "interaction of two modal tendencies"; that is to say, the raised fourth belongs to the Jewish altered Dorian, while the lowered fourth characterizes Shostakovich's personal style.[75] The "split" fourth may also involve the interaction of two Jewish modes: the raised third (lowered fourth) of the *freigish,* which becomes manifest because of the Phrygian second, and the abovementioned altered Dorian fourth. This sort of instability, which results from two modal collections on a single fundamental, is a typical feature of Jewish traditional music. Such an interpretation of the chromatic inflections in Shostakovich's music, i.e, their being derived from the *freigish* and the altered Dorian modes, opens up new possibilities for insight into *From Jewish Folk Poetry,* yet in no way limits more traditional analytical descriptions. Such a musical dualism, auditory and theoretical, symbolizes the delicate interplay between the established Soviet and the "semi-official" Jewish in Shostakovich's cycle.

A degree of tonal instability rare in the first eight songs may also be intended to underscore the ephemerality of the "happiness" represented in the

last three songs. Song No. 9 concludes on a first-inversion F♯-Major triad. No. 10 begins in *freigish* on *c* and ends in Mixolydian on *a*. And No. 11 concludes the entire cycle, or, perhaps, leaves it open in a tritone relationship with No. 1 (B:F).

One of the most striking structural devices utilized in opus 79 is the lietmotive. Its significance here is certainly not "pure[ly] musical," as maintained by Kurisheva,[76] if one takes into account its strong ethnic coloration. Although the basic structure of the motive remains constant enough, and it clearly dominates the entire cycle, it never appears twice in the same form and therefore may be defined as a leitmotive only with some reservation. Nonetheless, its integrity as a motive is secured by both modal and rhythmic-melodic features, namely, the augmented second, typical of the two Jewish modes (*freigish* and altered Dorian), and the descending, stepwise chain of "iambic primas."

Ex. 7

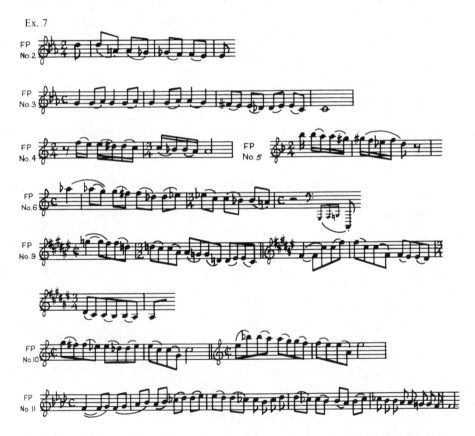

"Iambic primas" are certainly not the exclusive property of Jewish folk music. Western musicians from the time of the Baroque have also exploited the device. Its distinctive structure, with the double accentuation of each scale degree, inevitably highlights the individual melodic traits of whatever mode constitutes the scale basis. This quality is of decisive semantic significance in the case at hand: in East European Jewish folk music, the *freigish* and the altered Dorian impart to the "iambic prima" its specific Jewish flavor. The device is widely used in Jewish folk songs. In Beregovsky's collection, for example 33 of the 150 tunes make use of the "iambic prima," and some 60% of these are in *freigish* or altered Dorian.[77] In *From Jewish Folk Poetry*, the "iambic prima" of the leitmotive is linked to an altered *freigish*, an alloy of the pure *freigish* and the altered Dorian (½–1–1½–½–½).

In its most complete form the leitmotive appears in No. 3 (see ex. 7), the Siberian song, which seems to embody the idea of the cycle *à toute outrance*. Four times the entire motive appears, and the melodic subject of the song itself is a variation of the motive (or *vice versa*). In Songs Nos. 2, 4, and 5, only fragments appear, while the motive is absent from Songs Nos. 1, 7, and 8. In Song No. 6, the motive appears for the last time in the first and principal part of the cycle (nos. 1-8). Here, at the height of tragedy, the moment of ideological collapse, the motive sounds on the words "Come back, Zirele, my daughter!" after the converted daughter shouts, "Drive out the old Jew!" Although its basic structure is preserved, the motive is now expanded to a diminished octave extending downward from the flat sixth, moving through the tonic *c*, and ending on the natural sixth on the weak beat. In the process, it acquires a highly unstable character, emphasized by a *fortissimo* C-major *tirata* in the contra-octave, which concludes with a descending leap of a seventh to CCC just as the final two notes of the leitmotive (b♭-a) sound *pianissimo* in the vocal part on the whisper, "Zirele, my daughter." This radical transformation of the leitmotive and its dramatic confrontation with the alien-sounding *tirata* suggest the breakdown of a tradition, the confrontation with "evil" (in this case, religious conversion), and a final cry of despair at the loss of posterity.

Following the climax in Song No. 6, the leitmotive does not appear for two songs. No further spiritual devastation is possible; only physical well-being can deteriorate, and this indeed happens in Songs Nos. 7 and 8. With Song No. 9, the motive rapidly loses its ethnic character as well. It has assumed a pure Phrygian coloration by the end of Song No. 9, and in No. 10, it even loses its augmented second, coming to conclusion with an authentic cadence, which is entirely alien to the Jewish modes. In Song No. 11, the characteristic descending motion of the "iambic prima" disappears as well, replaced by movement both upward and downward. The Picardy third in the final F-minor chord concludes the metamorphosis, obliterating any sense of

ethnic intrinsicality. The transformation, indeed the destruction, of a spiritual world has been accomplished.

From Jewish Folk Poetry stands as striking evidence of the complexity and ambiguity characteristic of both the culture in which the composer lived and created, and his own life. It seems to me that the work's uniqueness, its special place in Soviet music, and perhaps in world music, is secured by its distinctive Aesopian language, its remarkable intermingling of the obvious and the latent, which constitutes its real meaning and its symbolism. The fate of Soviet peoples, the complications of Soviet life, and the ironies of an officially imposed doctrine of optimism and happiness have been expressed by Shostakovich through a Jewish musical idiom that, because of its special status in Soviet society, was able to serve at the time of its creation as an ideal vehicle, and simultaneously as a "screening device,"[78] for the composer's artistic and ethical self-expression.

Volumes 31 and 32 of Shostakovich's *Collected Works* (Moscow, 1982) became available to me only after this article was in final page proofs. According to the *Collected Works,* which states that both the piano and orchestra scores of *From Jewish Folk Poetry* are preserved at the Central State Archive of Literature and Art of the USSR, the first eight songs of the piano version are dated 1-29 August 1948 and the last three songs are dated 10-24 October of the same year. This unequivocally confirms that the last three songs were composed separately and in addition to the main body of the cycle, and after the at-home performance of the cycle on the composer's birthday. The date of the orchestra version is given as 1 October 1948. This is not only surprising, but it contradicts other sources which mention 1963 or 1964. Did Shostakovich finish the orchestra score before the last three songs of the piano version? How could it be that he was simultaneously using different versions of texts and song titles?

Notes

1.   V. Stassov, *Selected Essays on Music,* tr. Florence Jonas (New York, 1968), p. 72.

2.   J. Braun, *Jews and Jewish Elements in Soviet Music* (Tel-Aviv, 1978), pp. 146-66; J. Braun, "The Double-Meaning of Jewish Elements in the Music of Shostakovich,"a paper read at the XIII Congress of the International Musicological Society (Strasbourg, August 1982); a more general study of the subject is in preparation.

3.   The works of Shostakovich concerned with Jewish subjects or employing a Jewish idiom fall into three chronological periods. The first, 1943-44, saw the composition of the Trio, opus 67, and the completion of Fleishman's opera and occurred during a time when information on the real dimensions of the Nazi Holocaust first reached the Soviet people. The second occurred during the last years of Stalinism, when Soviet Jewish culture was conspicuously and virtually destroyed. All the "Jewish" compositions from this period, with the exception of the Twenty-Four Preludes and Fugues for Piano, opus 87, were first performed only after a delay of between five and seven years. The third, 1959-63, saw the composition of the Cello Concerto No. 1, opus 107, the Quartet No. 8, opus 110, and the Symphony No. 13, opus 113, and the orchestral version of opus 79. This period coincided with the advance of a new wave of anti-Semitism in the U.S.S.R.

Of the twenty-three vocal-instrumental chamber works in Shostakovich's *oeuvre*, three form a separate corpus together with the opus 79: *Eight English and American Folk Songs*, without opus (1944), *Spanish Songs*, opus 100 (1956), and an *a capella* work, *Two Russian Folk Song Arrangements*, opus 104 (1957). All four are set to authentic folk poetry; all represent a musical style which may be described as stylized folk music; all, as can be shown by textual and musical analysis, are loaded with significant national and ideological connotations; and all were composed in the period 1944-57. These compositions brought to life a new style in Soviet music that was to influence those Soviet Russian and, especially, Soviet minority composers who, in the 1960s and '70s, formed the New Folklore Wave—a movement notable for its overtones of anti-establishmentarianism and national self-determination. See the interview with Edison Denisov in *Musica*, no. 4 (1970), pp. 391-92, and the response to that interview in *Sovetskaia muzyka*, no. 10 (1970), pp. 44-46; also R. Lampsatis, "Dodekaphone Werke von Balsys, Juzelinnas, und der jüngeren Komponisten generation Litauens," Ph. D. thesis, Technische Universität, Berlin, 1977; M. Tarakanov, "Neue gestalten und neue Mittel in der Musik," *Beiträge zu der Musikwissenschaft*, issue 1-2 (1968), pp. 42-64; J. Braun, "Zur Hermeneutik der Sowjetischbaltischen Musik," *Zeitschrift für Ostforschung*, no. 1 (1982), pp. 76-93.

4.   *D. Shostakovich: Notografícheskii spravochnik* [Reference guide to the music] (Moscow, 1961), p. 39; *Dmitri Shostakovich: A Complete Catalogue*, comp. M. MacDonald (London, 1977), p. 25; L. Danilevich, *Nash sovremennik* [Our contemporary] (Moscow, 1965), p. 323.

5.   D. Rabinovich, *D. Shostakovich: Composer* (Moscow, 1959), p. 124.

6.   *Istoriia muzyki narodov SSSR* [Music history of the peoples of the U.S.S.R.], ed. Yu. Keldysh and M. Sabinina (Moscow, 1973), v. 4, p. 276.

7.   *Evreiskie narodnye pesni* [Jewish folk songs], comp. Y. Dobrushin and A. Yuditsky, ed. Y. Sokolov (Moscow, 1947), p. 2.

8.   L. Poliakova, *Vokal'nyi tsikl D. Shostakovich* [D. Shostakovich's vocal cycle] (Moscow, 1957), p. 3.

9.   N. Mikhoels, personal interview conducted by the author on 12 March 1981, Tel-Aviv.

10.   S. Alliluyeva, *Only One Year* (London, 1968), p. 148.

11.   Ibid., p. 56.

12.   L. Tumerman, *Moi put' v Izrail'* [My path to Israel] (Jerusalem, 1977), p. 72.

13.   Alliluyeva, op. cit., p. 149.

14.   Tumerman, p. 72.

15. N. Mikhoels, personal interview.

16. A. Werth, *Musical Uproar in Moscow* (reprint; London, 1968), p. 26.

17. N. Mikhoels, personal interview.

18. Werth, op. cit., p. 26.

19. *Sovetskaia muzyka,* no. 4 (1948), p. 97. The resolution of support was signed by H. Eisler, A. Bush, M. Flothuis, and A. Mendelssohn, among others.

20. The half-year delay in the February and March issues of *Sovetskaia muzyka* (nos. 2 and 3) was apparently the result of uncertainty about how to handle the new situation; or perhaps there was simply a lack of authors willing to deal with the subject.

21. See *Sovetskaia muzyka,* no. 2 (1949), p. 36. Increasing anti-Semitism moved hand in hand with increasing Zhdanovism in literature and the arts. Anti-Semitism based on musical esthetics and musical esthetics molded by anti-Semitism emerged as a particular characteristic of twentieth-century totalitarian systems.

22. Stanley Krebs errs in his statement that the work is unpublished; see his *Soviet Composers and the Development of Soviet Music* (London, 1970), p. 198. All of the later publications of opus 79, including that in Shostakovich's *Collected Works,* v. 32 (Moscow, 1982), are reprinted from the first edition.

23. B. Schwarz, *Music and Musical Life in Soviet Russia: Enlarged Edition, 1917-1981* (Bloomington, 1983), p. 244. A similar account is presented in K. Meyer, *Dmitri Shostakowitsch* (Leipzig, 1980), p. 152.

24. *Sovetskaia muzyka,* no. 7 (1956), pp. 6-7.

25. I. Nestyev, "Put' iskanii" [The Path of (creative) explorations], *Sovetskaia muzyka,* no. 11 (1956), pp. 12.13.

26. Some four hundred Jewish scholars, writers, artists, and musicians were arrested in the period November 1948-February 1949; most of them were shot in August 1952. See J. Cang, *The Silent Millions* (New york, 1969), pp. 93-116.

26a. When this manuscript was in print a new source came to my attention: Shostakovich's letter written on the 22nd January 1949 to a friend, the well-known composer Kara Karayev. Shostakovich wrote: "Dear Karik! Thank you for your letter. I am not very well. . . I have not yet presented my Jewish songs, I will do this in some ten days. As their fate is of interest for you, I will write you more about this presentation . . ." (Dmitri Schostakovitsch, *Erfahrungen,* ed. Christoph Hellmundt and Krysztof Meyer/ Leipzig: Reclame, 1983/, pp. 215-216). Shostakovich is probably speaking about a presentation at the Composer Union. Did this take place or not? In any case the letter confirms that the composer thought about going ahead with the performance of op. 79. The revision of this decision indeed came only in late January or February 1949, at the height of the anti-Semitic wave, perhaps in connection with the attack on musicologists in February.

27. The unpublished orchestral score of opus 79 was made available to me through the courtesy of Hans Sikorski Verlag in Hamburg, BRD, for which I express my sincere thanks.

28. *Yiddishe folks-lider,* comp. and ed. Y Dobrushin and A. Yuditsky (Moscow, 1940).

29. Skudinsky, *Folklor-lider,* v. 2 (Moscow, 1936), p. 161.

30. Poliakova, op. cit., p. 6; T. Kurisheva, "Kamernyi vokal'nyi tsikl v sovremennoi sovetskoi muzyke" [The vocal chamber cycle in contemporary Soviet music], candidate's thesis, Tchaikovsky State Conservatory of Music, Moscow, 1968, pp. 29-30.

31. It seems possible that Shostakovich's selection of texts for songs No. 9 and No. 10 was influenced by the example set by M. Vainberg. On 13 May 1948, Vainberg's *Sinfonietta* was praised at a meeting to the Composers' Union. The work carries the epigraph: "Jewish songs also begin to sound on the kolkhoz fields—not the songs of the past, full of sadness and misery, but new happy songs of productivity and labor" [see *Sovetskaia muzyka,* no. 4 (1948), p. 97]. Vainberg was the husband of Natalia Mikhoels and a close friend of Shostakovich.

32. The reference to "aunt" in the title of the second song of opus 79 is a mistranslation. The Yiddish "tatyunya" (the diminutive of "tate"—daddy) is mistakenly translated as the Russian "tyotia" (aunt).

33. The reason for the change in the tenth song from a male noun to a female noun is rather puzzling. Why should the kolkhoz shepherd be a girl? The argument that this change was engendered for artistic reasons, because songs No. 9 and No. 10 are "male" songs, is not compelling. No. 9 is a much more appropriately "female" song than No. 10, and Shostakovich himself changed the order of these two, deviating from that in the Russian edition of *Jewish Folk Songs.* A shepherd's work was not usually performed on the kolkhoz by a female. Could it be that the change was intended to point up the lack of reality in this depiction of "happiness"?

34. In consideration of this fact, an edition of the opus 79 with the original Yiddish text put to Shostakovich's music seems entirely justified. Such an edition is in preparation by the publisher Hans Sikorski in Hamburg, edition and text underlay by J. Braun.

35. I am using Roman Ingarden's term here.

36. B.S. Shteinpress and I.M. Iampol'sky, authors-compilers, *Entsiklopedicheskii muzykal'nyi slovar',* 2nd ed., rev. and enl. (Moscow, 1966), p. 486.

37. *Evreiskie narodnyi pesni,* p. 9.

38. The symbiotic semantics of "Jewish" and "Siberia" is not a singular occurrence in Shostakovich's vocal works. In his *Four Monologues on Pushkin Texts,* Shostakovich juxtaposed "The Candle in the Jewish hut" [V evreiskoi khizhine lampada] and "In Deep Siberian mines" [V glubine sibirskikh rud], thereby drawing an unavoidable analogy between the two tragic events of Soviet history in 1952.

39. N. Mikhoels, personal interview.

40. *Sovetskaia muzyka,* no. 3 (1980), p. 31.

41. V. Fleishman, *Skripka Rotshil'da* [Rothschild's Violin] (Moscow, 1965).

42. M. Gnessin, *Stat'i, Vospominaniia, Materialy* [Articles, Reminiscences, Materials] (Moscow, 1961), p. 205. *Klezmer* (Hebrew: kley + zemer = musical instrument) refers to Jewish folk musicians known from the late Middle Ages in Europe, but especially active and popular among both the Jewish and non-Jewish populations of the Ukraine and Byelorussia in the eighteenth and nineteenth centuries.

43. The classic example of this type of bitonality is found in Hans Neusiedler's *Juden Tanz* from 1544, probably the first piece of notated *klezmer* music.

44. The (a) "iambic prima" and (b) the "trochaic prima" are terms introduced by Alexander Dolzhansky in his *24 Preliudii i fugi D. Shostakovicha* [D. Shostakovich's 24 preludes and fugues] (Leningrad, 1963), pp. 42, 63, to describe two types of melodic-rhythmic figures with a unisonal repetition:

45. The D-eS-C-H (D-E♭-C-B) is a musical transcription of the composers' name in German: D. SCHostakowitsch.

46. M. Sabinina, *Shostakovich-simfonist* [Shostakovich the symphonist] (Moscow, 1976), p. 283.

47. Quoted from *Musorgsky: In Memoriam 1881-1981*, ed. Malcolm Hamrick Brown (Ann Arbor, 1982), p. 3.

48. *Evreiskie narodnye pesni*, p. 9.

49. A. Sokhor, "Bol'shaia pravda o 'malen'kom' chelovke" [The big truth about the "little" man], in *Dmitri Shostakovich*, ed. L. Danilevich (Moscow, 1967), p. 257.

50. *Badkhan* is a Jewish folk comedian or jester; also, a musician *(klezmer)* or actor, akin to the medieval jongleur.

51. *Evreiskie narodnye pesni*, pp. 11-12.

52. Ibid., p. 4.

53. *Sovetskaia muzyka*, no. 3 (1955), pp. 103-4; no. 12 (1956), p. 109.

54. V. Vasina-Grossman, "Novyi vokal'nyi tsikl D. Shostakovicha" [D. Shostakovich's new vocal cycle], *Sovetskaia muzyka*, no. 6 (1955), p. 10.

55. *Istoriia muzyki narodov SSSR*, v. 4, pp. 276-79.

56. Poliakova, op. cit., p. 9.

57. Sokhor, op. cit., p. 255.

58. M. Kagan, *Lektsii po marksistsko-leninskoi estetike* [Lectures on Marxist-Leninist aesthetics] (Leningrad, 1971), pp. 641-46.

59. Sokhor, op. cit., p. 258.

60. Kurisheva, op. cit., p. 77.

61. Ibid., p. 27.

62. E. Seculetz, *Yiddishe folks-lider* (Tel-Aviv, 1970), p. 147; *Yiddishe folks-lider*, comp. M. Beregovsky and I. Fefer (Kiev, 1938), p. 318.

63. Kurisheva, op. cit., p. 95.

64. M. Beregovsky, "Izmennyi doriiskii lad v evreiskom muzykal'nom fol'klore" [The altered Dorian mode in Jewish musical folklore], in *Problemy muzykal'nogo fol'klora narodov SSSR* [Issues in the musical folklore of the peoples of the U.S.S.R.] (Moscow, 1973), p. 388. Besides the natural minor, the two most characteristic East European Jewish folk music modes *(shteigers)* are the *freigish* (Phrygian with a raised third) and the "altered Dorian"

(Dorian with a raised fourth). The latter is related to the "Ukrainian" mode, and the fusion of the two is close to the "Hungarian" mode. In different sources a somewhat different rendering of the *shteigers* is given, but the modal "suffix" is a constant feature:

See. H. Avenary, "Music," *Encyclopedia Judaica,* ed. Cecil Roth and Geoffrey Wigoder (Jerusalem, 1972), v. 12, p. 621; M. Beregovsky, *Evreiskie narodnye pesni*[Jewish folk songs] (Moscow, 1962), pp. 16-18; A.Z. Idelsohn, *Jewish Music in its Historical Development* (reprinted., New York, 1975), pp. 25-26, 137-43, 184-92; Idelsohn, *Hebräisch-orientalischer Melodienschatz,* v. 9, (Leipzig, 1932), pp. x-xv.

The augmented second in these modes goes back to the traditional Jewish *ahava-raba* mode; it allows for distinctive modulational possibilities to other modes, as well as for shifts of the same mode to other scale degress (see Idelsohn, *Jewish Music,* p. 190). The positioning of the diminished fourth—the "D. SCHostakowitsch" interval—in these modes also suggests the possibility of relating the formula D-eS-C-H to them, in addition to the regular modal implications involving a *finalis* on *d* or *b♭*, as pointed out in E. Fedosova, *Diatonicheskie lady v tvorchestve D. Shostakovicha* [The diatonic modes in the works of D. Shostakovich] (Moscow, 1980). A good example, from among several possibilities, is the "study-*shteiger*" from Idelsohn's *Jewish Music:*

65.   Kurisheva, op. cit., p. 94.

66.   Beregovsky, *Evreiskie norodnye pesni,* songs nos. 111 and 113, p. 235.

67.   Seculetz, op. cit., song no. 37.

68.   Idelsohn, *Hebräisch-orientalischer Melodienschatz,* v. 9, songs nos. 153 and 560.

69.   Ibid., song no. 581.

70.   Poliakova, op. cit., p. 23.

71.   Gnessin, op. cit., p. 201.

72.   Beregovsky and Fefer, *Yiddishe folk-lider,* p. 284.

73.   S. Skrebkov, "Kak traktovat' tonal'nost'" [How to interpret tonality], *Sovetskaia muzyka,* no. 2 (1965), p. 92.

74.   Kurisheva, op. cit., p. 36.

75.   Ibid., p. 70.

76.   Ibid., p. 78.

77.   Beregovsky, *Evreiskie narodnye pesni.*

78.   I am using Edward Lowinsky's term, from his *Secret Chromatic Art in the Netherlands Motet* (New York, 1946), p. 169, which has inspired to a great extent my approach to the interpretation of Soviet music.

18

Notes on the Soviet Avant-Garde

Joel Sachs (U.S.A.)

The existence of a substantial circle of "modern" composers in the U.S.S.R. still comes as a surprise to most Western musicians. The brutal cultural repression of the Stalin period, which obliterated the avant-garde of the 1920s, is only too well known, thanks particularly to Professor Boris Schwarz's vivid recounting of it in his *Music and Musical Life in Soviet Russia, 1917-1981* (enlarged ed.; Bloomington, 1983). Furthermore, while we in America read that the Soviet government since the early 1960s has relaxed some aspects of its cultural policy and some of its guidance of style in the arts, we hear virtually no music by current Soviet composers. Taken altogether, this causes many people to assume that compositional life there is moribund. To be sure, ignorance is a time-honored basis for presumptions of non-existence. So, at least, it would seem to judge by the many students in introduction-to-music courses who have never heard a note of Brahms.

For the American musician who actually learns about Soviet modern music and wishes to perform it, a very real problem looms: where does one get it? Must one resort to secret couriers and persons well connected? How, in fact, does one even begin to determine what composers and which compositions are worth seeking out? Actually, the last question is not easily answered with respect to *any* country, especially vast ones. Even the attempt to develop an overview of contemporary music in America is a formidable task, given the fact that so much new music goes unpublished and unrecorded. How much more formidable a task in the case of the U.S.S.R., especially for a musician like me who does not speak or read Russian and has not had the opportunity to visit that country.

The curious fact remains, however, that by all accounts it is still easier to get a feeling for Soviet new music in the West than in the U.S.S.R. itself. Works in modern styles are not often performed there in publicized concerts, but instead at unadvertised "private" events in such places as the recital hall at the Composers' Union headquarters. The small amount of new music that has

been recorded barely begins to survey the repertory, especially of the younger composers. As a result, "modern music" remains unknown territory to any Soviet music lover not equipped to read scores. As discouraging as this may be for the Soviet modernist, the situation has improved dramatically in recent times. Until a few years ago, scores in styles other than the official "Socialist Realism" were generally kept in special libraries that were off limits to the non-privileged. (Whether any of this matters at all to the general concert-goer, whose taste is said to resemble that of his Western counterparts, is another question.)

Although the Soviet avant-gardist is no longer overtly repressed, he is given little encouragement. Perhaps the official attitude might be described as simple neglect—an unwillingness to devote any resources to music for a limited audience. It can be argued, of course, that market conditions in the West produce a similar effect, even in the absence of an official monopoly on distribution and performance. Moreover, in a centralized society, the power of an antagonistic individual can be magnified, so that those bureaucrats whose dislike of new music is intense to the point of active hostility may in fact be in a position to paralyze the objects of their hatred. There is also a continual concern about the possibility of a return to pre-liberal conditions.

The awkward situation faced by these Soviet composers can be illustrated by a personal story—the history of how Cheryl Seltzer and I, co-directors of the ensemble CONTINUUM, educated ourselves on the subject of Soviet new music. Our appetites had been whetted by our acquaintance with (and our two concerts of) the late works of Shostakovich, which are still not well known in the United States. In addition, we remembered hearing a fascinating program of music by Soviet avant-gardists of the 1920s and early 1960s, organized by Joel Spiegelman, which we heard some years ago at a meeting of the New York City chapter of the American Musicological Society. With this in mind, we decided to try to present a concert of Soviet modern music at Lincoln Center in January of 1981. We knew, however, that we were taking a step in the dark.

A logical way to start was by contacting Professor Boris Schwarz, who immediately indicated his desire to help us. Before we could meet, however, he telephoned with the astonishing news that, by an odd coincidence, he had just received a letter from an American, who has requested anonymity, in possession of a large collection of scores, records, and tapes that had been carried out of the Soviet Union. The American, about to leave the United States, wished in particular to find a repository for these scores, as well as ways to get the music performed—in a sense, to build a Noah's Ark, lest the old flood waters of cultural repression again rush in upon the composers. I left New York once to see the music. On examining the collection, I right away recognized that there was more than enough fine music for many programs. And as one might

expect, persons with an interest in this subject knew other, like-minded individuals, and we were soon introduced to more sources of compositions. Many had been recorded, but scores were available for only a handful.

One of the most striking recorded pieces was Alfred Schnittke's Concerto Grosso.[1] His name was, in fact, one of several already known to Mrs. Seltzer and me before the project began, but it was just a name. He was, for example, the first composer mentioned when I asked a leading East European musician for recommendations about new music. But how were we to get performance materials for this or any other ensemble composition that we knew only through a recording? This seemed like a major stumbling block. Even for music by so important a composer as Shostakovich, we had been warned that if orchestral parts were not already in the United States, it could take years to get them from the Soviet Union, and firm performance schedules could not be relied upon. How much more difficult it would probably be in the case of works by men and women who were officially disdained! It was July 1980; January 1981 was drawing disconcertingly near.

Shortly afterwards, I went to London, and in the course of another project unrelated to either the U.S.S.R. or to this century, delivered some documents to the B.B.C., for whom I was doing some consulting regarding their massive library of script materials for music broadcasts. Although this library had barely reached the letter "H," I wisely inquired about Soviet music. David Mather, the director, has a phenomenal memory and promptly produced a script and tape of a recent broadcast of Soviet music for clarinet, percussion, and piano/harpsichord. Suddenly, his memory again went into action, he excused himself, and shortly returned with a freshly printed miniature score of the Schnittke Concerto Grosso, which bore a Boosey & Hawkes cover (over a Wiener Philharmonischer Verlag imprint). I immediately realized that Boosey might have a set of orchestral parts, and, after dashing the two blocks to their rental library, knew that our performance would be possible. At the very least, the parts could be imported from London.

On my return to New York, I inquired at Boosey's New York office about the Schnittke, only to be steered to G. Schirmer, the American agency for the official Soviet exporter V.A.A.P. (the Soviet copyright and distribution office). Schirmer informed me that during the time since our difficulties over Shostakovich, V.A.A.P. had changed from a department of negligence and obstructionism into a businesslike operation that understood the foreign-currency earning potential even of new music. Although the wheels at V.A.A.P. might grind slowly, there should be relatively little difficulty obtaining the materials we needed. What was more astounding was the discovery that virtually every composition in the collection I had originally seen was obtainable through normal channels by G. Schirmer! Though comforting for us, this raised the question of why someone would have gone to

all the trouble of "spiriting" this music to the West. A possible explanation was his understandable concern that, should the political winds shift, the music might not be treated with such businesslike tolerance. An avant-garde had, after all, existed under Lenin, but was then obliterated. Alternatively, he might simply have thought that by bringing the collection to the West, he could stimulate interest in it. To many people, however, the most likely explanation was that it never occurred to him that the music could be obtained abroad, since it is so difficult to obtain in the USSR. He would not have been alone in his ignorance. Hardly a single person whom we have encountered is aware that one can merely place an order for new music of modernist tendencies. (Make no mistake: orders get lost; parcels arrive from Moscow addressed in Cyrillic to the past director of Schirmer's concert department, despite numerous requests to do otherwise, and disappear for months in the mail room.) It goes without saying, however, that to order music, one must know what music to order. If there were a Schnittke, or a Denisov, or others whose names appear in Professor Schwarz's book, if there were composers whose music had startled us at Joel Spiegelman's concert years before, then there had to be more, and younger composers as well. But who were they? What were they writing? Which ones really deserved attention?

Gradually we began to find answers to these questions. The original collection from the U.S.S.R., apparently selected by a knowledgeable person to represent diverse trends and talents, became a great resource. (It is now at the Library of Congress, with a copy at the New York Public Library.) We began to obtain brochures that the Hamburg publisher Sikorski had prepared for the composers it represents under agreement with V.A.A.P. A kind employee at the New York Public Library compiled a list of composers whose names he had seen repeatedly in Soviet periodicals. From these and other sources, we felt we were identifying a group of men and women who seemed to be respected exponents of up-to-date ideas and techniques. In the end, we decided for practical reasons to confine ourselves to the older generation. This would focus our efforts, give us a selection of mature composers, and allow our concert to honor the pioneers.

When forming the program, we had a few basic criteria. First, we wanted to have only music of the highest caliber, because we knew that listeners might tend to dismiss the music as mere novelties by culturally isolated, naïve composers. Second, we wanted to represent the immense variety of styles found among Soviet composers. Third, we hoped to avoid having only Moscow composers. Fourth, all the music had to be "legal"—i.e., published in the Soviet Union. (The performance of "illegal" music abroad might cause the composers very great problems at home.) The remarkable composer Arvo Pärt, who had recently moved to Vienna, caused us some debate, since we feared that having an emigré's music in the program could place the others in a delicate position. After asking the advice of numerous knowledgeable people, we concluded that

the quality of his music and the great influence he had exerted before emigrating would have made it almost immoral to exclude him.

While we were going through the lengthy process of selection—new works were continually arriving—we began to face the very sensitive question of publicity. Obviously, this concert could be an "event" even in New York, a city in which the creation of an "event" is no mean feat. By presenting the concert as a protest against political repression—the Afghanistan invasion was fresh in everyone's mind—we could draw great attention to ourselves, but simultaneouly place the composers, by implication, in a most awkward position. On the other hand, if we avoided the realities of the composers' situation entirely, we might run the risk of the concert seeming to be "official," thus inviting the attention of anti-Soviet protest groups. A political slant could also have other unwelcome repercussions. It would misstate our case, which was that the composers' works could speak for themselves; and it might excite unrealistic expectations which few new works could possibly satisfy. We felt obliged to find a path that would give the concert maximum exposure with a minimum of possible misunderstanding. The very title, "U.S.S.R.: Unveiling the Avant-Garde," was arrived at only after many discussions about words like "underground," "hidden," and the like. Even the term "avant-garde" bothered us; but because it suggested the pioneering role of these composers within Soviet society, it seemed to be the most appropriate designation to use.

As we had anticipated, the program was widely reported, both before and after the concert. The reporters for the most part understood the delicacy of the matter. Annalyn Swan of *Newsweek* and Professor Harlow Robinson, who writes for the *New York Times,* are to be particularly commended for describing the problems of these composers without being politically provocative. Perhaps the best summary of the potential impact of the concert came in a remark made by Schnittke to a reporter from *Newsweek's* Moscow office. He suggested that the increased interest among Western musicians was forcing Soviet authorities to take their modern composers seriously—to realize that they were cultural resources that deserved attention.

This is the program, of which probably all but the Silvestrov and Grabovsky pieces were U.S. premières:

Two piano pieces   Arvo Pärt (b. 1935)
    For Alina (1979)
    Variations for Arinushka's Recuperation (1980)

Triada, for piano solo (1962)   Valentin Silvestrov (b. 1937)

Ode to the Memory of
    Ernesto Che Guevara,   Edison Denisov (b. 1929)
    for clarinet, percussion and piano (1968)

From Japanese Haiku, for tenor, flute,   Leonid Grabovsky (b. 1935)
  bassoon, and xylophone (1964)

Introitus, concerto for piano and
  chamber orchestra (1978)   Sofia Gubaidulina (b. 1931)

Concerto Grosso, for two violins, amplified Alfred Schnittke (b. 1934)
  prepared piano, harpsichord, and 21 strings (1977)

We were pleased that this program could combine composers from several areas of the U.S.S.R. and could embrace the stylistic diversity for which we had aimed. Although we could not represent everything, the program left no doubt that after the trends of 1930-60 in the West had finally reached the Soviet Union during the post-Stalin thaw, Soviet composers very quickly assimilated them and became entirely up to date in their techniques. Serialism, electronics, mixed media, chance procedures, infusions of jazz and popular music, all have played their part in modern Soviet music.

Edison Denisov is the senior member of the new-music circle, by virtue of his age and length of involvement in modern styles. His *Ode to the Memory of Che Guevara* was composed during the heyday of the impact of post-Webern pointillism, serialism, and rhythmic complexity. Despite the familiar features—contrasts of dynamics and register, "atonality," the typically 1960s instrumental combination, and especially Denisov's love of extremely complex, overlapping rhythmic relationships—he nonetheless instills the idiom with a very personal lyricism that makes the composition immediately coherent to the ear. The climax of *Ode,* a brilliant and dramatic "explosion" (which is framed by a sustained, rather quiet introduction and coda) possessed for us a curious feature: it was virtually impossible for the performers to coordinate their parts because of the rhythmic complexity. We learned after the performance,[2] and with considerable amusement, that the section had originally been an improvisation, but that at the time of publication, Denisov was prevailed upon to write it out. Apparently he did so in a way that precluded a thoroughly settled (and potentially "stiff") realization (ex. 1).

The style of the *Ode* is very characteristic of Denisov and other Soviet composers of the 1960s. Since then, however, Denisov has turned to greater linearity that combines "modernity" with some fruits of his continuing study of folk song. Microtonal writing, long of interest to him, has become very prominent in recent works.

Silvestrov and Grabovsky are leaders of the Ukrainian new-music circle, another primary force in the Soviet avant-garde. Valentin Silvestrov's extended piano cycle, *Triada,* is probably one of the earliest works to use the serial method in its post-war form. Leonid Grabovsky, called by Joel

Ex. 1   E. Denisov, *Ode to the Memory of Ernesto Che Guevara*

c 3526 к

Spiegelman "the Henry Cowell of the Soviet Union,"[3] provides moments of great frivolity in his tiny song cycle, *From Japanese Haiku.* In this sparse, appropriately aphoristic set, written as if Webern had provided the accompaniment for fragments of folk melodies, the tenor is asked to sing at one point while pinching his nose shut, and at another, while beating gently on his chest with his fists. Both produce sounds which cannot quite be described, but can easily be duplicated by the reader.

Denisov, Silvestrov, and Grabovsky, for all the individuality of their musical personalities, were easily recognizable on this program as members of the avant-garde mainstream of the post-war period. Even apart from the matter of quality, their work, and that of numerous others, was a step of monumental importance for the previously isolated Soviet musicians. However, the question of quality was far from secondary in our planning. Well aware that some listeners in the West can be very patronizing, we knew that many of them would quickly recognize Western techniques in such music and dismiss it as derivative before even giving it a fair chance to speak for itself. It would be wrong, of course, to deny that Soviet composers of the 1960s took many techniques from the West. Cut off for decades from the world of new music, their discovery of what they had missed came as an enormous flood of new ideas. Should they have ignored the techniques? If we say yes, then we must say that Bach should have ignored the Italian concerto style. The Soviet composer of the 1960s had to assimilate the new—to digest it, as Mozart did in Paris—and to make it his own. Predictably, many Soviet compositions of that period have little to recommend them to the performer. But weak, derivative music is hardly a Soviet monopoly. Furthermore, the composers of this senior generation were, on average, only about thirty years old in the early 1960s. Their work at the time was the product of young, developing composers. Fully mature composers of a highly modernist tendency simply did not exist in the U.S.S.R. of that period. In planning our program, we could not ignore that formative decade, but we had to avoid carefully anything that did not seem fully convincing to us. That the three works selected are so striking and so individual, and so musically mature, is all the more impressive. The more recent music by these composers proves that the promise of their youth has been borne out.

Arvo Pärt, Sofia Gubaidulina, and Alfred Schnittke went through a similar process of absorbing Western techniques, but they were represented on our concert by their very recent work, that is to say, by compositions from their maturity. Pärt, a leader of the Estonian avant-garde, also had his post-Webern phase, after which a striking simplification of style took place. Many of his scores of the late 1960s and early 1970s superficially resemble those of Morton Feldman. (It is said that the Estonians have had easier access to Western trends, because scores could come in via Finland.) Then with increasing religious fervor preoccupying him, Pärt turned to a simple lyricism that reminds one,

perhaps, of the serious religious compositions of Satie. Pärt was in a way both a minimalist and an early convert to the "new lyricism"; this combination, along with the sheer force of his personality, prevents his music from sounding like a rehashing of an earlier century. If his consonant, melodious pieces sound so accessible that we fail to perceive how they are "avant-garde," then we should remember that, in writing works with liturgical texts using chant-like melodies or in casting overboard the fashionable bombast of Socialist Realism, Pärt was displaying singular courage, particularly as a native of a Soviet republic that has a record of anti-Soviet bias.

Sofia Gubaidulina is described by her acquaintances as a woman of fiercely independent spirit, an uncompromising adherent to moral principle, and something of a mystic, who has made every sacrifice for her work. A native of Chistopol in the Tatar Autonomous Soviet Socialist Republic, she was trained in Kazan and then in Moscow, where she has lived for some years. Like Pärt, she is said to be an enormous personal and musical inspiration to young composers. She directs a group of composer-performers who tour the U.S.S.R., playing in a combination of Western and traditional, especially Central Asian, styles. Her work embraces everything from the elaborately composed to the improvised, in conventional and electronic media; some of her compositions have employed traditional Central Asian intruments. *Introitus* makes an excellent introduction to her music. The title is, of course, liturgical, and is reflected in the extensive, sustained, chant-like solos for the piano, which alternate with and gradually make peace with an increasingly active, skittering mass of sound in the chamber orchestra (strings and a few winds). It is from beginning to end work of great lyricism, using no "method" such as serialism, but building upon pitch areas of diverse sorts—modal, tonal, pandiatonic, non-tonal, chromatic, and microtonal. By means of the contrast between microtonal and tonal passages, that quality of Eastern-Western fusion at the heart of her music is realized.

Of the six composers, Alfred Schnittke is the one who has gained the most celebrity at home and in the West. While this is due in great measure to the tireless efforts of his friend, the violin virtuoso Gidon Kremer, for whom Schnittke has composed numerous pieces and who has played and recorded them frequently, Schnittke's rewards are finally validated by the quality of his music and its startling compositional personality. He has evolved into one of the few composers of recent years who can combine compositional skill, integrity, and originality with a high level of accessibility to intelligent listeners from both inside and outside the usual circle of contemporary-music devotees. His successes have been so remarkable that a recent communication from the U.S.S.R. describes him as the lion of those intellectuals, who, half a decade ago, would pay him no attention. More telling, perhaps, is another communication reporting an article in the Soviet press that criticizes the "excessive praise" being heaped on him.

Ex. 2   A. Schnittke, *Second Sonata for Violin and Piano*

Ex. 3   A. Schnittke, *Second Sonata for Violin and Piano*

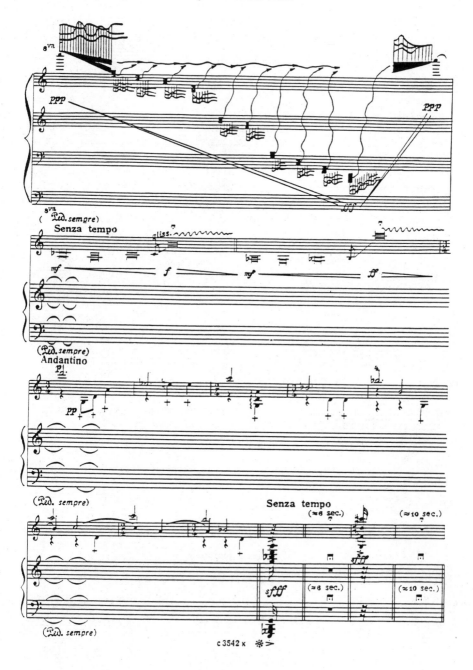

c 3542 к

Ex. 4   A. Schnittke, *Second Sonata for Violin and Piano*

c 3542 к

positive response that it has had. In some sense, the Concerto Grosso is pure, raw Schnittke; in another, it seems to be the product of a different mind, for by 1977, Schnittke's style had altered drastically.

The composer describes his Requiem (1974-75) as the turning point in his work. Written in a vastly simplified, very melodious and triadic style, this piece seems to parallel similar events in Western music, although it is possible that the model of Arvo Pärt, rather than some vague notion of "new oldness," was the important stimulus for Schnittke. The Requiem was, to my knowledge, Schnittke's first piece to enjoy a real success in the U.S.S.R., making him a significant figure in the intellectual world there.

Another work, in a related style, may be more accessible to Western musicians, thanks to its recent publication by Sikorski. This is the Quintet for piano and strings—half an hour of sparse, slow, extremely intense writing similar in character to some of the last works of Shostakovich. Here, Schnittke eschews the collage-like surface, preferring instead to deal exhaustively with a radically limited musical cosmos and to unfold a myriad of its related facets. The Quintet demands of its listeners virtually the opposite of the Second Sonata—the ability to sustain concentration while moving through very subtle variants of the same ideas, rather than an ability to shift from one mood to its opposite in an instant.

The Concerto Grosso combines both the earlier and the transformed Schnittke. Like the Second Violin Sonata, its shape revolves around a collage of superficially unrelated thoughts that are striking in their simplicity and energy. The difference, however, lies in the types of material, which might be called "post post-Webern"—every idea is "singable"!

Schnittke has described the Concerto Grosso as a play of three spheres—the modern, the baroque (specifically Vivaldi), and the popular, the last having a deliberately slight and somewhat trite character. The interaction of the three produces a profound drama in which the listener is never quite sure which force is winning or when the next bit of whimsy will interrupt the almost nightmarish energy. So startling is the sequence of events that, in my experience, some listeners are even more puzzled on first exposure to it than to the Second Sonata, despite the Concerto Grosso's singable tunes. (Happily, these listeners are often totally captivated on second hearing.) This drama of style has, once again, an almost Ivesian quality of mirroring and simultaneously revising life (and the history of music).

No analysis of the Concerto Grosso can begin to do it justice; much of its beauty lies in its surprises. Nonetheless, to whet the appetite, a few things must be said about its six movements (a four-movement baroque concerto with cadenza and coda). What strikes the ear is the unusual dissolution of baroque thematic ideas into swirling, rhythmically electrified tone clusters. What may not strike the ear at first is the relationship of the two. This example, from the second movement, will substitute for paragraphs of description (ex. 5):

Ex. 5   A. Schnittke, *Concerto Grosso*

Ex. 5 (continued)

The strikingly "diagonal" visual appearance of this passage, which is characteristic of most of the concerto, seems to carry over to the sphere of the audible. While I, as the concerto's conductor, naturally cannot vouch for the precise degree to which its inner compositional unity communicates itself to listeners who have not seen the score, many persons, on a single hearing, have confirmed my impression that the contours of the germinal ideas are so clear that the counterpoint can to some extent be heard within the clusters. This combination of the cluster principle and its polyphonic working-out gives the concerto as a whole a remarkable coherence.

Another arresting feature is the manner in which the "popular" components appear. The intrusiveness of the waltz in the second movement is heightened by its being twelve-tone; that of the tango in the fifth movement by its instrumentation (harpsichord, accompanied, in the eighteenth-century manner, by two violins, with interruptions by buzzing tone-cluster chords in the orchestra). And when the somber, folkish opening makes its final appearance as a coda, its prophet, the prepared piano, has been amplified to monstrous proportions, so as to overwhelm totally all that has come before— an eerie vision of the triumph of the popular.

That the divergent moods and styles can coexist is again a result of Schnittke's miraculous instinct for pacing. It also grows out of the totally interlocking thematic recurrences and transformations among the movements. So cleverly have the basic ideas been selected that, at the climax of the central slow movement—at the very peak of its monumental twenty-one voice, partly microtonal canon—when the soloists come forth with fragments from Tchaikovsky and Berg violin concertos, even these scraps of music have been logically prepared (ex. 6).

Like the Second Violin Sonata, the Concerto Grosso plays humor and seriousness off against each other with almost alarming skill. This dualism of the two moods seems constantly to stimulate Schnittke's imagination, provoking him to combine them in different "dramatic" contexts. This is, if anything, the unifying mark of his varied *oeuvre,* for each time he returns to the idea, he pursues it in a new way and with new means. Indeed, his treatments of that recurring "theme" do not seem to be characterized by any particular way of composing, or by any reliance upon any specific techniques; and the freshness of his reconsiderations of these antipodes saves his fascination with them from becoming a mannerism. No matter what the style of any individual composition, Schnittke manages to communicate, above all, that elusive quality of the master composer that we, at a loss for words, simply call a quality of intense commitment. This may explain why, as he himself has said to me, reactions to his music are almost always very strong, either positive or negative, but rarely lukewarm. Not many composers can boast of this, for extreme reactions seem to be a measure of real originality, of the creation of a truly distinctive musical language.

Ex. 6   A. Schnittke, *Concerto Grosso*
         Bracketing indicates Schnittke's quotations from the
         Tchaikovsky and Berg Violin Concertos.

Ex. 6 (continued)

Unlike Schnittke, the other five composers are more easily categorized. To claim this, however, is not intended to belittle them, any more than one would wish to deny the uniqueness of Mozart by pointing out that he was, in many ways, a typical product of his time. Can anything be said of these six Soviet composers, all of whom we feel possess distinctive musical personalities, that might characterize them as a group, other than the accident of their birth in the U.S.S.R.? Is their music simply good music, or is it distinctively "Soviet"? To attempt to answer such questions may be like trying to decide if Beethoven is more German than Cherubini, or simply Beethoven rather than Cherubini. Some of the compositions do indeed possess a distinctive coloring that suggests a kind of "U.S.S.R.-ness," like those of Gubaidulina with their seeming Central Asian inspiration. But to determine how Denisov differs from many Western composers in the post-Schoenberg and post-Webern epoch is still more elusive. With him, and other Soviet composers, one is dealing with the highly personal application of compositional tendencies shared by many composers of many nations in the 1960s. All six Soviet composers write with a special character that may possibly derive from the fact that they received the new Western techniques more or less in one burst, at a time when they, already experienced young composers, could pick and choose from them at will. They did not have strong preconceptions, because they did not participate in the agony associated with the evolution in the West of those techniques, and thus escaped the strongly partisan atmosphere so often transmitted in composition training. All six seem, therefore, to have bypassed the aggressive modernity that can be found in many Western composers of their generation. Furthermore, because of the point in history at which they "discovered" these new methods, they inevitably refined them within the context of their own Socialist-Realist formative years. The resulting music is international in message, yet may also be "Soviet" in its relative accessibility. If it is true that a new "Soviet school" or "Soviet style" has resulted, I must confess with embarrassment that while I would wish upon no one the cultural isolation of the Stalin years, I am thankful for the splendid and belated musical legacy that the world is finally receiving.

Notes

The research behind the events described in this essay was made possible in part by a grant from City University of New York PSC-BHE Research Award Program.

1. Thanks to the *New Grove,* the standard English spelling of Schnittke's name may become Shnitke. However, in letters to me, written in German (his father's language, thus the language of his surname), the composer has always spelled it "Schnittke."

2. Personal communication from Charles Neidich.

3. In the *New Grove,* "Grabovsky."

19

A Bibliography of the Writings of Boris Schwarz

Compiled by K. Robert Schwarz

Books

French Instrumental Music Between the Revolutions, 1789-1830. Ph.D. dissertation, Columbia University, 1950; 2nd ed. revised and enlarged, New York: Da Capo Press, 1984.

Great Masters of the Violin. Preface by Yehudi Menuhin. New York: Simon and Schuster, 1983.

Music and Musical Life in Soviet Russia, 1917-1970. London: Barrie and Jenkins, 1972 and New York: W.W. Norton, 1972; paperback ed., New York: W.W. Norton, 1973. A translation of the original edition was made into Chinese by Zhong Zi Lin, and published by the State Publishing House in Peking, 2 vols., 1979-81.

Music and Musical Life in Soviet Russia: Enlarged Edition, 1917-1981. Bloomington, IN.: Indiana University Press, 1983.

Musik und Musikleben in der Sowjetunion von 1917 bis zur Gegenwart. Trans. Jeannette Zehnder. Wilhelmshaven: Heinrichshofens Verlag, 1982.

Articles

"Amerikanische Interpreten und ihre Schulen." *Österreichische Musikzeitschrift* 31 (October 1976):520-25.
     The same article appeared in an English translation as "American Performers and American Music Schools" in the Special Bicentennial Issue of the *Österreichische Musikzeitschrift* (October 1976):54-58.

"Arnold Schoenberg in Soviet Russia." *Perspectives of New Music* 4 (Fall-Winter 1965):86-94. Reprinted in *Perspectives on Schoenberg and Stravinsky,* pp. 111-22. Edited by Benjamin Boretz and Edward T. Cone. Princeton, N.J.: Princeton University Press, 1968; reprint ed., New York: W.W. Norton, 1972. German translation as "Arnold Schönberg im russischen Kulturkreis." In *Bericht über den 1. Kongress der Internationalen Schönberg-Gesellschaft,* pp. 187-95. Edited by Rudolf Stephan. Vienna: Elisabeth Lafite, 1978.

"Beethoven and the French Violin School." *The Musical Quarterly* 44 (October 1958):431-47.

"Beethoveniana in Soviet Russia." *The Musical Quarterly* 47 (January 1961):4-21.

"Carl Flesch. Zu des Meisters 60. Geburtstag." *Allgemeine Musikzeitung* 60 (6 October 1933):477-78.

"Henri Wieniawski." *Central-Verein-Zeitung* [Berlin], 31 October 1935.

"Joseph Joachim and the Genesis of Brahms's Violin Concerto." *The Musical Quarterly* 69 (Fall 1983): 503-26.

"Karol Rathaus." *The Musical Quarterly* 41 (October 1955):481-95.

"A Little-Known Beethoven Sketch in Moscow." *The Musical Quarterly* 56 (October 1970):539-50. Reprinted in *The Creative World of Beethoven,* pp. 37-48. Ed. by Paul Henry Lang. New York: W.W. Norton, 1971.

"More Beethoveniana in Soviet Russia." *The Musical Quarterly* 49 (April 1963):143-49.

"A Musical Summer in Israel." *Tarbut* [magazine of the America-Israel Cultural Foundation], Fall 1973, pp. 24-26.

"Musical Thought in Soviet Russia." *The Listener,* 7 July 1960, pp. 16-17, 22.

"Recalling Carl Flesch as Teacher and Man." *Musical America,* October 1943, pp. 25, 34.

"A Revolutionary in Music" [Prokofiev]. *Phoenix* [newspaper of Queens College, C.U.N.Y.], 30 March 1965. Reprinted as "Prokofiev: A Personal Memoir." *Musical Heritage Review,* 12 February 1979, pp. 64-65.

"The Russian Violin School Transplanted to America." *Journal of the Violin Society of America,* Winter 1977, pp. 27-34.

"Shostakovich's Struggle for Creative Freedom." *Keynote* [WNCN-FM, N.Y. Program Guide], September 1981, pp. 6-13.

"Soviet Music Since Stalin." *Saturday Review,* 30 March 1963, pp. 55-56, 69.

"Soviet Music Since the Second World War." *The Musical Quarterly* 51 (January 1965):259-81. Reprinted in *Contemporary Music in Europe,* pp. 259-81. Ed. by Paul Henry Lang and Nathan Broder. New York: W.W. Norton, 1965.

"Soviet Scholars." *The New York Times,* 12 June 1960.

"Stravinsky in Soviet Russian Criticism." *The Musical Quarterly* 48 (July 1962):340-61. Reprinted in *Stravinsky: A New Appraisal of His Work,* pp. 74-96. Edited by Paul Henry Lang. New York: W.W. Norton, 1963.

"Tendenzen der amerikanischen Musikwissenschaft." *Neue Zürcher Zeitung,* 27 December 1973. Reprinted in *Österreichische Musikzeitschrift* 29 (March 1974):143-45.

"The Vicissitudes of Soviet Music." *Problems of Communism,* November-December 1965, pp. 67-82. Translated into Spanish in *Problemas del Comunismo,* November-December 1965, pp. 75-92; into Italian in *L'Est: Cultura e ideologia nell' URSS,* 30 December 1965, pp. 159-88.

Contributions to Collective Publications

"Arnold Schoenberg in Soviet Russia." In *Perspectives on Schoenberg and Stravinsky,* pp. 111-22. Edited by Benjamin Boretz and Edward T. Cone. Princeton, N.J.: Princeton University Press, 1968; reprint ed., New York: W.W. Norton, 1972. Reprinted from *Perspectives of New Music* 4 (Fall-Winter 1965):86-94. For German translation see citation under ARTICLES.

"Beethovens Opus 18 und Haydns Streichquartette." In Gesellschaft für Musikforschung, *Bericht über den Internationalen Musikwissenschaftlichen Kongress Bonn 1970,* pp. 75-79. Edited by Carl Dahlhaus, Hans Joachim Marx, Magda Marx-Weber, Günther Massenkeil. Kassel: Bärenreiter, 1971.

"Early Russian Violin Music: A Link Between Folk and Art Music." In International Musicological Society, *Report of the Twelfth Congress Berkeley 1977,* pp. 35-39. Kassel: Bärenreiter, 1981.

"The Evolution of Stravinsky's Violin Style." In *Stravinsky: Centennial Essays, San Diego 1982.* Berkeley: University of California Press, in preparation.

"Geiger um Mozart." *Mozart-Jahrbuch* (1978-79):228-35. Abbreviated version as "Geiger um Mozart: Eine Marginalie zum Köchel Gedenktag." *Neue Zürcher Zeitung,* 28/29 May 1977. Expanded and translated version as "Violinists Around Mozart." In *Music in the Classic Period: Essays in Honor of Barry Brook.* Edited by Allan Atlas. New York: Pendragon Press, 1984.

"Interaction Between Russian and Jewish Music and Musicians in the Nineteenth and Twentieth Centuries." In *Proceedings of the World Congress on Jewish Music, Jerusalem 1978.* Edited by Judith Cohen. Tel Aviv: The Institute for the Translation of Hebrew Literature, 1982.

"Khandoshkin's Earliest Printed Work Rediscovered." In *Slavonic and Western Music: Essays for Gerald Abraham.* Edited by Malcolm Hamrick Brown and Roland John Wiley. Ann Arbor: UMI Research Press, forthcoming.

"A Little-Known Beethoven Sketch in Moscow." In *The Creative World of Beethoven,* pp. 37-48. Edited by Paul Henry Lang. New York: W.W. Norton, 1971. Reprinted from *The Musical Quarterly* 56 (October 1970):539-50.

"Music." In *Russia and the Soviet Union: A Bibliographic Guide to Western Language Publications,* pp. 378-94. Edited by Paul L. Horecky. Chicago: University of Chicago Press, 1965.

"The Music World in Migration." In *The Muses Flee Hitler: Cultural Transfer and Adaptation,* pp. 135-50. Edited by Carla Borden and Jarrell C. Jackman. Washington: The Smithsonian Press, 1983.

"Musical and Personal Reminiscences of Albert Einstein. In *Albert Einstein: Historical and Cultural Perspectives—The Centennial Symposium in Jerusalem,* pp. 409-16. Edited by Gerald Holton and Yehuda Elkana. Princeton, N.J.: Princeton University Press, 1982.

"Musorgsky's Interest in Judaica." In *Musorgsky In Memoriam, 1881-1981,* pp. 85-94. Edited by Malcolm Hamrick Brown. Ann Arbor: UMI Research Press, 1982.

"New Trends in Soviet Music." In *Cultural Scene in the Soviet Union and Eastern Europe: Papers and Proceedings of the Sixth Annual Conference Organized by the Interdepartmental Committee on Communist and East European Affairs, McMaster University,* pp. 109-28. Edited by George Thomas. Hamilton, Ontario: McMaster University, 1973.

"Problems of Chronology in the Works of Viotti." In International Musicological Society, *Report of the Eleventh Congress Copenhagen 1972,* pp. 644-47. Edited by Henrik Glahn, Søren Sørensen, Peter Ryom. Copenhagen: Wilhelm Hansen, 1974.

"Shostakovich in Retrospect." In *Music in Civilization: Essays in Honor of Paul Henry Lang.* Edited by Maria Rika Maniates and Edward Strainchamps. New York: W.W. Norton, in preparation.

"Some Specific Problems in the First Movement" [of Haydn's Symphony No. 85 in B♭ Major]. In *Haydn Studies: Proceedings of the International Haydn Conference,* pp. 245-48. Edited by Jens Peter Larsen, Howard Serwer, and James Webster. New York: W.W. Norton, 1981.

"Soviet Music Since the Second World War." In *Contemporary Music in Europe,* pp. 259-81. Edited by Paul Henry Lang and Nathan Broder. New York: W.W. Norton, 1965. Reprinted from *The Musical Quarterly* 51 (January 1965): 259-81.

"Stravinsky in Soviet Russian Criticism." In *Stravinsky: A New Appraisal of His Work,* pp. 74-96. Edited by Paul Henry Lang. New York: W.W. Norton, 1963. Reprinted from *The Musical Quarterly* 48 (July 1962):340-61.

"Die Violinbehandlung bei Schubert." In *Zur Aufführungspraxis der Werke Franz Schuberts,* pp. 87-96. Edited by Roswitha Karpf. Beiträge zur Aufführungspraxis, 4. Munich: Emil Katzbichler, 1981.

"Violinmusik." In *Streichinstrumente,* pp. 46-94. Musikinstrumente in Einzeldarstellungen, 1. Kassel: Deutscher Taschenbuch Verlag/ Bärenreiter, 1981. Reprint, with corrections, of *MGG* article of same title.

"Viotti—eine Neubewertung seiner Werke." In *Violinspiel und Violinmusik in Geschichte und Gegenwart: Bericht über den internationalen Kongress am Institut für Auffürungspraxis der Hochschule für Musik und darstellende Kunst in Graz vom 25. Juni bis 2. Juli 1972,* pp. 41-46. Edited by Vera Schwarz. Beiträge zur Aufführungspraxis, 3. Vienna: Universal, 1975.

"Zur Uraufführung von Beethovens *Missa Solemnis* in St. Petersburg." In Gesellschaft für Musikforschung, *Bericht über den Internationalen Musikwissenschaftlichen Kongress Bonn 1970,* pp. 559-61. Edited by Carl Dahlhaus, Hans Joachim Marx, Magda Marx-Weber, Günther Massenkeil. Kassel: Bärenreiter, 1971.

Contributions to Encyclopedias

Encyclopédie de la musique [Fasquelle]. S.v. "Mestrino, Nicola"; "Molique, Bernhard"; "Rathaus, Karol."

International Musicological Society and the International Association of Music Libraries. *International Inventory of Musical Sources/ Répertoire International des Sources Musicales.* Munich: G. Henle and Kassel: Bärenreiter, 1960- . Series A/I, vol. 9: *Einzeldrucke vor 1800,* edited by Otto Albrecht and Karlheinz Schlager. S.v. "Viotti, Giovanni Battista."

Die Musik in Geschichte und Gegenwart. S.v.: Cartier, Jean-Baptiste; Elman, Mischa; Ernst, Heinrich Wilhelm; Lafont, Charles Philippe; Lees, Benjamin; Mason, Daniel Gregory; Menuhin, Yehudi; Mestrino, Nicola; Molique, Bernhard; Mondonville, Jean-Joseph Cassanéa de; Nardini, Pietro; Onslow, Georges; Polledro, Giovanni Battista; Porter, Quincy; Pugnani, Gaetano; Rathaus, Karol; Rieti, Vittorio; Rode, Pierre; Rovelli, Pietro; Schwarz, Boris; Senallié, Jean-Baptiste; Somis, Giovanni Battista; Somis, Lorenzo; Vieuxtemps, Henri; Violinmusik; Viotti, Giovanni Battista; Wieniawski, Henri; Wieniawski, Irene; Wieniawski, Joseph; Zimbalist, Efrem.

The New Grove Dictionary of Music and Musicians. S.v.: Alard, Delphin; Auer, Leopold; Bériot, Charles de; Boehm, Joseph; Bortkievich, Sergei; Cartier, Jean-Baptiste; Elman, Mischa; Ernst, Heinrich Wilhelm; Flesch, Carl; Fuchs, Joseph; Fuchs, Lillian; Galamian, Ivan; Garbuzova, Raya; Gimpel, Bronislaw; Gingold, Josef; Glazunov, Alexander; Goldberg, Szymon; Graudan, Nikolay; Harth, Sidney; Heifetz, Jascha; Huberman, Bronislaw; Khachaturian, Aram; Khrennikov, Tikhon; Kogan, Leonid; Kreisler, Fritz; Kroll, William; Lafont, Charles Philippe; Mason, Daniel Gregory; Mestrino, Nicola; Miaskovsky, Nikolai; Milstein, Nathan; Mischakoff, Mischa; Molique, Bernhard; Nardini, Pietro; Oistrakh, David; Oistrakh, Igor; Paganini, Nicolò; Persinger, Louis; Piatigorsky, Gregor; Polledro, Giovanni Battista; Pugnani, Gaetano; Rathaus, Karol; Rieti, Vittorio; Rode, Pierre; Sarasate, Pablo de; Sevčik, Otakar; Shebalin, Vissarion; Shostakovich, Dmitri; Shumsky, Oscar; Silverstein, Joseph; Somis, Giovanni Battista; Somis, Lorenzo; Stern, Issac; Szigeti, Joseph; Temianka, Henri; Vieuxtemps, Henri; Violin Literature; Weinberg, Moissei; Wieniawski, Henri; Wieniawski, Joseph; Yellin, Thelma; Ysaÿe, Eugène; Zimbalist, Efrem.

Sohlmans Musiklexicon. S.v. "Sovjetmusiken" [under "Sovjetunionen"].

Editor and/or Translator

Flesch, Carl. *Violin Fingering: Its Theory and Practice.* English adaptation by Boris Schwarz. Foreword by Yehudi Menuhin. London: Barrie and Rockliff, 1966. reprint ed., New York: Da Capo Press, 1979.

Glinka, Mikhail. *Complete Works.* Edited by Boris Schwarz. New York: University Music Editions, 1971. On microfiche. Newly edited version of original Russian edition (18 vols.; Moscow, 1955-69).

Herold, Ferdinand. *Two Symphonies: No. 1 in C and No. 2 in D.* Edited by Boris Schwarz with the assistance of K. Robert Schwarz. The Symphony 1720-1840, Series D Vol. IX. Edited by Barry S. Brook. New York: Garland Publishing, 1981. Published together with George Onslow (q.v.), *Two Symphonies: Opus 41 and Opus 42.*

Kreutzer, Rodolphe. *42 Etüden.* 2 vols. Analytical edition by Carl Flesch. Translated by Boris Schwarz. Zürich: Hug, 1953.

Onslow, George. *Two Symphonies: Opus 41 and Opus 42.* Edited by Boris Schwarz with the assistance of K. Robert Schwarz. The Symphony 1720-1840, Series D Vol. IX. Edited by Barry S. Brook. New York: Garland Publishing, 1981. Published together with Ferdinand Herold (q.v.), *Two Symphonies: No. 1 in C and No. 2 in D.*

Book Reviews

Bakst, James. *A History of Russian-Soviet Music. Journal of the American Musicological Society* 20 (Summer 1967):304-7.

_____. *A History of Russian-Soviet Music. Problems of Communism,* July-August 1967, pp. 69-70.

Boyden, David. *The History of Violin Playing From Its Origin to 1761. The Musical Quarterly* 53 (January 1967):109-22.

Brainard, Paul. *Giuseppe Tartini: La raccolta di sonate autografe per violino. Notes* 34 (March 1978):603-65.

_____. *Le sonate per violino di Giuseppe Tartini: Catalogo tematico. Notes* 32 (March 1976):552-53.

Brown, David. *Tchaikovsky—The Early Years: 1840-1874. Notes* 36 (March 1980):649-50.

Carse, Adam. *The Orchestra From Beethoven to Berlioz. Journal of the American Musicological Society* 3 (Fall 1950):267-70.

Deutsch, Otto Erich. *Franz Schubert: Thematisches Verzeichnis seiner Werke in chronologischer Folge.* New edition, edited by Neue Schubert-Ausgabe and Werner Aderhold. *Musica* 33 (January-February 1979):69-70.

Dunning, Albert. *Pietro Antonio Locatelli: Der Virtuose und seine Welt. Journal of the American Musicological Society* 36 (Spring 1983):157-61.

Farish, Margaret. *String Music in Print. Notes* 31 (September 1974):60-61.

Fishman, Nathan, ed. *Kniga Eskizov Beethovena za 1802-1803 gody [A sketchbook by Beethoven for the years 1802-1803]. The Musical Quarterly* 49 (October 1963):519-26.

Garden, Edward. *Balakirev: A Critical Study of His Life and Music. Notes* 25 (September 1968):31.

Ginsburg, Lev. *Giuseppe Tartini.* Translated by Albert Palm. *Notes* 34 (March 1978):603-5.

Hanson, Lawrence and Elisabeth. *Tchaikovsky: The Man Behind the Music. Slavic Review* 27 (March 1968):167-68.

Misch, Ludwig. *Neue Beethovenstudien und andere Themen. Notes* 25 (September 1968): 41-42.

Nestyev, Israel V. *Prokofiev.* Translated by Florence Jonas. *The Musical Quarterly* 47 (April 1961):263-70.

Österreichische Komponisten des XX. Jahrhunderts. Notes 31 (September 1974):61.

Prieberg, Fred K. *Musik in der Sowjetunion. Problems of Communism,* September-October 1966, pp. 74-75.

Prokofiev, Sergei. *Prokofiev by Prokofiev: A Composer's Memoirs.* Edited by David H. Appel. Translated by Guy Daniels. *High Fidelity/Musical America,* November 1979, pp. MA 18-20.

Schoenberg, Arnold. *Style and Idea.* Edited by Leonard Stein. *Notes* 32 (March 1976):524-26.

Schwarz, Vera, ed. *Der junge Haydn: Wandel von Musikauffasung und Musikaufführung in der Österreichischen Musik zwischen Barock und Klassik. Notes* 30 (September 1973):66-67.

_____. *Violinspiel und Violinmusik in Geschichte und Gegenwart. The Musical Times* 118 (September 1977):732.

Seaman, Gerald R. *History of Russian Music.* Vol. 1: *From Its Origins to Dargomyzhsky. Slavic Review* 29 (December 1970): 745-47.

Sollertinsky, Dmitri and Ludmilla. *Pages From the Life of Dmitri Shostakovich. High Fidelity/Musical America,* March 1981, pp. MA 18-19.

Stasov, Vladimir. *Selected Essays on Music.* Translated by Florence Jonas. *The Musical Quarterly* 55 (October 1969):580-83.

Stephan, Rudolf, ed. *Bericht über den 1. Kongress der Internationalen Schönberg-Gesellschaft, Wien 4 bis 9 Juni 1974. Notes* 35 (June 1979):882-83.

Taruskin, Richard. *Opera and Drama in Russia As Preached and Practiced in the 1860s*. *Notes* 39 (June 1983):849-50.

Tschaikowsky Institut International. *Systematisches Verzeichnis der Werke von Pjotr Iljitsch Tschaikowsky*. *Notes* 31 (September 1974):61.

Music Reviews

Berwald, Franz. *Violinkonzert in Cis*. Edited by Folke Lindberg. *Notes* 32 (March 1976):620-21.

Borghi, Luigi. *Six Violin Concertos and Sixty-Four Cadenzas*. Edited by Gabriel Banat. Introduction by Frederick Neumann. Masters of the Violin, 1. *Notes* 38 (June 1982):932.

Copland, Aaron. *Duo for Violin and Piano*. *Notes* 38 (December 1981):419-20.

Delius, Frederick. *Sonata in B for Violin and Piano (op. posth.)*. *Notes* 35 (March 1979):714-16.

Mozart, Wolfgang Amadeus. *Klaviertrios* [complete]. Edited by Wolfgang Plath and Wolfgang Rehm. *Notes* 38 (December 1981):419-20.

Paganini, Niccolo. *Concerto in mi minore per violino (op. posth.)*. *Notes* 32 (September 1975):129-30.

———. *Nel cor più non mi sento, per violino principale con accompagnato di violino e violoncello o di pianoforte; Sei preludi e caprice d'adieu, per violino solo*. Edited by Paul Bulatoff. *Notes* 37 (December 1980): 410-11.

———. *Quartetto primo per violino, viola, violoncello e chitarra; Quattro sonatine per violino e chitarra; Serenata für 2 Violinen und Gitarre*. *Notes* 34 (June 1978):966-67.

———. *12 Duette für Violine und Gitarre; Moto Perpetuo für Violine und Gitarre*. Edited by Paul Bulatoff. *Notes* 35 (December 1978):420.

Tartini, Giuseppe. *Sei sonate op. II Le Cène, per violino e basso continuo*. Edited by Edoardo Farina. *Notes* 37 (December 1980):405.

Viotti, Giovanni Battista. *Four Violin Concertos* [Nos. 7, 13, 18, 27]. Edited by Chappell White. *Notes* 35 (December 1978):407-9.

Record Reviews

"Baroque for Bow and Strings." *Saturday Review*, 26 October 1963, pp. 65-67. Review of Pietro Locatelli, *L'Arte del violino, Op. 3*. Performed by Suzanne Lautenbacher and the Mainz Chamber Orchestra conducted by Günther Kehr. Vox SVBX 540/1, 1962. Antonio Vivaldi, *L'Estro armonico, Op. 3*. Performed by various soloists and the Paris Chamber Orchestra conducted by Paul Kuentz. Decca 110070/1/2, 1963. *Il cimento dell'armonia e dell'invenzione, Op. 8*. Performed by Reinhold Barchet and the Pro Musica String Orchestra conducted by Rolf Reinhardt. Vox VBX-32, 1962.

"The Brahms of Francescatti and Heifetz." *Saturday Review*, 28 December 1963, p. 57. Review of Johannes Brahms, *Concerto for Violin and Orchestra*. Performed by Zino Francescatti and the New York Philharmonic conducted by Leonard Bernstein (Columbia MS 6471, 1963); by Jascha Heifetz and the Chicago Symphony Orchestra conducted by Fritz Reiner (RCA LSC-1903, 1963).

"The Complete Handel for the Violin." *Saturday Review*, 28 February 1970, pp. 84-85. Review of Georg Friedrich Händel, *Violin Sonatas* [complete]. Performed by Edward Melkus and others. Archiv 198-474/5, 1969.

"Corelli, Torelli, Locatelli." *Saturday Review*, 27 June 1964, p. 66. Review of Arcangelo Corelli, *Concerti Grossi Op. 6*. Performed by the Virtuosi di Roma conducted by Renato Fasano. Angel S-36130, 1963. Arcangelo Corelli, Francesco Manfredini, Pietro Locatelli, Giuseppe Torelli, *Weihnachtskonzerte*. Performed by the Mainz Chamber Orchestra conducted by Günter Kehr. Archiv 198-147, 1963.

"Heifetz's Beethoven Again." *Saturday Review,* 27 July 1963, p. 43. Review of Ludwig van Beethoven, *Sonatas for Violin and Piano* [complete]. Performed by Jascha Heifetz, Emanuel Bay, Brooks Smith. RCA Victor LM-6707, 1963.

"Italian Baroque." *Saturday Review,* 24 April 1965, pp. 63, 71. Review of Tomaso Albinoni, *Twelve Concerti a Cinque, Op. 9.* Performed by the Italian Baroque Ensemble conducted by Vittorio Negri Bryks. Dover HCR 5225/6/7, 1964. Francesco Geminiani, *Four Concerti Grossi from Op. 2 and Op. 4.* Performed by Gli Accademici di Milano conducted by Dean Eckerstein. Dover HCR 5232, 1964. Pietro Locatelli, *Twelve Concerti Grossi Op. 1.* Performed by I Musici Virtuosi di Milano conducted by Dean Eckerstein. Dover HCR 5233/4/5, 1964.

"The Mis-tuned Violin." *Saturday Review,* 31 August 1963, p. 39. Review of Heinrich Franz Biber, *15 Sonatas for Scordatura Violin....* Performed by Sonya Monosoff and others. Cambridge CRS-811, 1962.

"Mussorgsky—Sorochintsy Fair." *The Musical Quarterly* 43 (April 1957):274-77. Review of Modest Mussorgsky, *Sorochintsy Fair.* Performed by soloists, chorus and orchestra of the Slovenian National Opera conducted by Samo Hubad. Epic SC-6017, n.d.

"A New *Boris* by Christoff." *Saturday Review,* 11 May 1963, pp. 68-69. Review of Modest Mussorgsky, *Boris Godounov.* Performed by Boris Christoff, other soloists, and the Paris Conservatoire Orchestra conducted by André Cluytens. Angel SDL-3633, 1963.

"Shaporin and Shebalin." *Saturday Review,* 27 February 1965, pp. 54-55. Review of Yuri Shaporin, *The Decembrists.* Performed by soloists, chorus and orchestra of the Bolshoi Theatre conducted by Alexander Melik-Pashaiev. Vissarion Shebalin, *The Taming of the Shrew.* Above performers conducted by Zdenek Chalabala. Ultraphone ULP-123-6, 1964.

"Szeryng, Ricci, and Bach." *Saturday Review,* 31 May 1969, pp. 53-55. Review of Johann Sebastian Bach, *Sonatas and Partitas.* Performed by Henryk Szeryng (Deutsche Grammophon 139-270/1/2, 1968); by Ruggiero Ricci (Decca DL 71042-71051-71052, 1967).

"Two Tchaikovsky Masterpieces." *Saturday Review,* 6 March 1976, pp. 38-39. Review of Pyotr Illych Tchaikovsky, *Eugene Onegin.* Performed by soloists and orchestra of the Royal Opera House- Covent Garden conducted by Georg Solti. London OSA 13112, 1976. *Pique Dame.* Performed by soloists, chorus and orchestra of the Bolshoi Theatre conducted by Mark Ermler. Columbia M3-33828, 1975.

"Virtue and Virtuosity in Bach." *Saturday Review,* 31 October 1970, p. 55. Review of Johann Sebastian Bach, *Six Sonatas for Violin and Harpsichord.* Performed by James Buswell and Fernando Valenti (Vanguard VCS 10080/1, 1970); by Sonya Monosoff, James Weaver, and Judith Davidoff (Cambridge CRS B-2822, 1970).

Reports on Congresses, Meetings, and Concerts

"Charles Castleman, violin." *High Fidelity/Musical America,* March 1982, pp. MA 27-28.

"Continuum: All- Schnittke Program." *High Fidelity/ Musical America,* June 1982, pp. MA 26-27.

"Continuum: Soviet Avant-Garde Music." *High Fidelity/ Musical America,* June 1981, pp. MA 29-30.

"Erfolg der *Scala* in Washington: Vier italienische Opern im Kennedy-Center." *Neue Zürcher Zeitung,* 23 September 1976.

"Haydn-Erstaufführung in New York." *Neue Zürcher Zeitung,* 13/14 December 1980.

"A Haydn-Stravinsky Celebration." *High Fidelity/ Musical America,* February 1982, pp. MA 32-33. Review of Chamber Music Society of Lincoln Center series of September 1981.

"The International Musicological Congress: The Accent is Global." *High Fidelity/ Musical America,* December 1977, pp. MA 27-29. Report on International Musicological Congress, Berkeley, 1977.

"Internationale Musikwissenschaft: Uebersicht eines thematisch revolutionären Kongresses." *Neue Zürcher Zeitung*, 17/18 September 1977. Report on International Musicological Congress, Berkeley 1977.

"Israel." *The Musical Times* 114 (October 1973):1043. Report on Israel Festival, Summer 1973.

"Israel-Festival: Neue Werke von Darius Milhaud und Josef Tal." *Neue Zürcher Zeitung*, 31 July 1973.

"Joseph Haydn in Washington." *Neue Zürcher Zeitung*, 10 November 1975.

"Lucerne Festival is International." *Musical Courier*, 15 October 1952, p. 9.

"Mozart-Festspiele in Washington." *Neue Zürcher Zeitung*, 5 June 1974.

"Musicologists at Salzburg." *The New York Times*, 27 September 1964. Report on 1964 International Musicological Congress.

"Musikalischer Austausch: Nord- und südamerikanische Musik am Interamerikanischen Musikfest." *Neue Zürcher Zeitung*, 1 July 1976.

"Musik und Wissenschaft: Gelungene Verbindung am Schubert-Fest in Detroit." *Neue Zürcher Zeitung*, 5 December 1978.

"Musikwissenschaftlicher Kongress in Berkeley." *Österreichische Musikzeitschrift* 32 (November 1977):506-8.

"Neuere Musik aus Sowjetrussland: Sechs Komponisten in einem New Yorker Konzert." *Neue Zürcher Zeitung*, 4 February 1981.

"Paris: die Romantische Epoche— Festveranaltungen des Kennedy-Centers in Washington." *Neue Zürcher Zeitung*, 31 May 1979.

"Salzburg Premieres Strauss' *Love of Danae*." *Musical Courier*, 1 October 1952, p. 5.

"San Francisco Symphony Orchestra in eigenen Haus." *Neue Zürcher Zeitung*, 30 September 1980.

"Schoenberg und Ives: Zwei Tagungen in Washington und New Haven." *Neue Zürcher Zeitung*, 3 December 1974. Reprinted as "Schoenberg- und Ives-Tagungen in den USA" in *Österreichische Musikzeitschrift* 30 (January- February 1975):67-68.

"Schubert-Symposium in Wien." *Neue Zürcher Zeitung*, 26 February 1974.

"Shlomo Mintz, violin." *High Fidelity/ Musical America*, August 1982, p. MA 28.

"Vienna." *The Musical Times* 115 (October 1974):872-74. Report on the Bruckner and Schoenberg Festival, Summer 1974.

"Washington als Musikstadt: Wettbewerbe als Anregungen." *Neue Zürcher Zeitung*, 30 September/1 October 1978. Report on Friedheim and Rockefeller awards at Kennedy Center.

"Wiederentdeckte Stücke von Maurice Ravel." *Neue Zürcher Zeitung*, 7 March 1975.

Record Annotations

Adolf Busch and Rudolf Serkin. Works by Beethoven, Bach, and Schumann. Performed by Adolf Busch, Rudolf Serkin, Frances Magnes, and the Busch Chamber Players. Odyssey Y3 34639, 1977.

Bach, Johann Sebastian. *Sonaten und Partiten.* Performed by Nathan Milstein. Deutsche Grammophon 2709-047, 1975.

Beethoven, Ludwig van. *Violinkonzert.* Performed by David Oistrakh and the Bolshoi Symphony Orchestra conducted by Alexander Gauk. Musical Masterpiece Society MMS 2017, n.d.

Borodin, Alexander. *String Quartet No. 1 in A Major.* Performed by the Borodin Quartet. Odyssey/Melodiya Y 33827, 1975.

Brahms, Johannes. *Violinkonzert.* Performed by Ricardo Odnoposoff and the Frankfurter Opernorchester conducted by Carl Bamberger. Musical Masterpiece Society MMS-145, n.d.

Dvorak, Antonin. *Violinkonzert in a-moll, Op. 53;* Glazunov, Alexander. *Violinkonzert in a-moll, Op. 82.* Performed by Riccardo Odnoposoff and the Orchestre Concerts de Paris conducted by Walter Goehr. Musical Masterpiece Society MMS- 2100, n.d.

The Heifetz-Piatigorsky Concerts. Performed by Jascha Heifetz, Gregor Piatigorsky, and Leonard Pennario. Columbia M 33447, 1976.

Jascha Heifetz in Concert at the Dorothy Chandler Pavillion. Performed by Jascha Heifetz and Brooks Smith. Columbia M2 33444, 1975.

Kabalevsky, Dmitri. *Colas Breugnon.* Performed by soloists, chorus, and orchestra of the Moscow Musical Theatre Stanislavsky and Nemirovich-Danchenko conducted by Georgi Zhemchuzhin. Columbia/Melodiya M3 33588, 1976.

Khachaturian, Aram. *Spartacus* [complete ballet]. Performed by the Bolshoi Theatre Orchestra conducted by Algis Zhuraitis. Columbia/Melodiya D4M 33493, 1975.

Mozart, Wolfgang Amadeus. *Klavierquartett in g-moll (K. 478), Klavierquartett in Es-Dur (K. 493).* Performed by Pina Pozzi and the Pascal String Quartet. Musical Masterpiece Society MMS-2118, n.d.

_____. *Streichquartette* [complete]. Performed by the Pascal String Quartet. Musical Masterpiece Society MMS-2111-17, n.d.

Ochi Chornya: Twenty Russian Folk Songs. Performed by the Soviet Army Chorus, the Osipof Folk Orchestra, the State Academy Chorus of the USSR, and the Piatnitsky Chorus under various conductors. Columbia/Melodiya M 33822, 1976.

Prokofiev, Sergei. *The Gambler.* Performed by soloists, chorus, and orchestra of the All-Union Radio conducted by Gennady Rozhdestvensky. Columbia/Melodiya M3 34579, 1977.

Rachmaninoff, Sergei. *Francesca da Rimini.* Performed by soloists, chorus, and orchestra of the Bolshoi theatre conducted by Mark Ermler. Columbia/Melodiya M2 34577, 1977.

Ruggiero Ricci: Virtuoso Music for Solo Violin. Performed by Ruggiero Ricci. Columbia M 35159, 1979.

Schubert, Franz. *Trio in B-Dur, Op. 99.* Performed by Serge Blanc (violin), Leo Rostal (cello), and Leo Nadelman (piano). Musical Masterpiece Society MMS-119, n.d.

Shostakovich, Dmitri. *The Nose, Op. 15.* Performed by soloists, chorus, and orchestra of the Moscow Chamber Opera conducted by Gennady Rozhdestvensky. Columbia/Melodiya M2 34582, 1978.

_____. *Symphony No. 2 ("To October") ; Symphony No. 3 ("May Day").* Performed by the Royal Philharmonic Orchestra and Chorus conducted by Morton Gould. RCA LSC-3044, 1968.

_____. *Violin Sonata Op. 134; Viola Sonata Op. 147.* Performed by Gidon Kremer and André Gavrilov (violin sonata); Fedor Druzhinin and Mikhail Muntyan (viola sonata). Columbia/Melodiya M 35109, 1979.

Sviridov, Georgi. *Choral Music [Spring Cantata, Choruses from Incidental Music to Tolstoi's 'Tsar Fedor Ivanovich,' Concert in Memory of Alexander Yurlov, Three Miniatures].* Performed by the Yurlov Choir and the Large Symphony Orchestra of Moscow Radio and Television conducted by Alexander Yurlov, Vladimir Fedoseyev, and Yuri Ukhov. Columbia/Melodiya M 34525, 1975.

Tchaikovsky, Pyotr Illyich. *The Enchantress.* Performed by various soloists and the Moscow Radio Symphony Orchestra and Chorus conducted by Gennady Provatorov. Columbia/Melodiya M4X 35182, 1980.

_____. *Iolanta.* Performed by soloists, chorus and orchestra of the Bolshoi Theatre conducted by Mark Ermler. Columbia/Melodiya M2 34595, 1978.

_____. *Pique Dame.* Performed by Vladimir Atlantov, Tamara Milashkina, Valentina Levko, etc. and the chorus and orchestra of the Bolshoi Theatre conducted by Mark Ermler. Columbia/Melodiya M3 33828, 1975.

_____. *Violin Concerto; Meditation Op. 42 No. 1.* Performed by Isaac Stern and the National Symphony Orchestra conducted by Mstislav Rostropovich. Columbia M 35126, 1978.

Viotti, Giovanni Battista. *Konzerte für Violine und Orchester: Nr. 16 e-moll, Nr. 24 h-moll.* Performed by Andreas Röhn and the English Chamber Orchestra conducted by Charles Mackerras. Archiv 2533-122, 1972.

Miscellany

Introduction to *Concertino Op. 132 for Violoncello and Orchestra* (reduction for violoncello and piano) by Sergei Prokofieff. Edited by Mstislav Rostropovich and Dmitri Kabalevsky. New York: Leeds Music/Music Corporation of America, 1965.

Introduction to *Quintet for Two Violins, Viola, Violoncello, and Piano, Op. 57* by Dmitri Shostakovich. New York: Leeds Music/Music Corporation of America, 1964.

"Rimsky's Boris Must Go." *The New York Times*, 9 June 1968. Letter to *The New York Times* concerning Rimsky-Korsakov's version of *Boris Godounov*.

Index

TEXTBOOK RENTAL POLICY

1. Check your e-mail for specific deadlines, penalties, hours, etc.
2. Last day to return textbooks with no penalties is the 1st business day following the final exams.
3. A fine will be assessed on books returned from the 2nd business day through the 5th business day following final exams.
4. Books not returned by the fifth business day following the last day of finals will be assessed a purchase fee which is due and payable by the early fee payment deadline of the following semester.

   Failure to pay this debt will result in this account being turned over to an outside collection agency. Student is responsible for all related cost (collection/attorney fees in the amount of 33 1/3% of the principal, interest, late fees, and related court cost).
5. Books are issued by barcode number. Books with incorrect barcode will be confiscated and returned to the rightful renter.
6. Books are available for purchase at anytime. See store for details.

This book is the property of
Textbook Rental @ SLU

HIST 493/ 593
Price 65.25
MBI:3160 Adpt:2033

31600048